NICARAGUA:
THE FIRST FIVE YEARS

NICARAGUA:
THE FIRST FIVE YEARS

edited by
THOMAS W. WALKER

PRAEGER

New York
Westport, Connecticut
London

Library of Congress Cataloging in Publication Data

Nicaragua: the first five years.

Includes index.
1. Nicaragua—Politics and government—
1979- . Addresses, essays, lectures.
2. Nicaragua—Economic policy—Addresses, essays,
lectures. 3. Nicaragua—Social policy—Addresses,
essays, lectures. 4. Nicaragua—Foreign relations—
1979- .—Addresses, essays, lectures.
I. Walker, Thomas W.
F1528.N5176 1985   972.85′053   83-3467
ISBN 0-275-90177-7 (alk. paper)
ISBN 0-275-91660-X (pbk.: alk. paper)

Library of Congress Catalog Card Number: 85-3467
ISBN: 0-275-90177-7
ISBN: 0-275-91660-X

First published in 1985

Praeger Publishers, One Madison Avenue, New York, NY 10010
A division of Greenwood Press, Inc.

Printed in the United States of America

The paper used in this book complies with the
Permanent Paper Standard issued by the National
Information Standards Organization (Z39.48-1984).

10 9 8 7 6 5 4 3 2

Contents

NICARAGUA:
THE FIRST FIVE YEARS

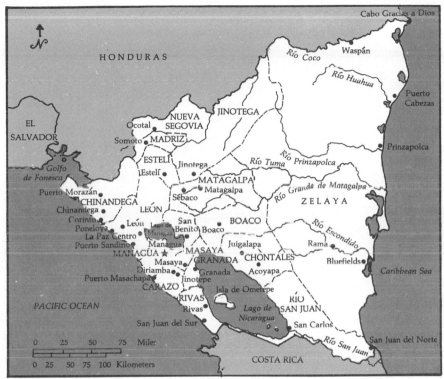

Nicaragua

Map from Thomas W. Walker, *Nicaragua:The Land of Sandino* (1981)

By permission of Westview Press

PART I

INTRODUCTION: REVOLUTION IN GENERAL, NICARAGUA TO 1984

THOMAS W. WALKER

Books on revolution have often left something to be desired. The subject evokes intense emotion and the literature, as a result, is often distorted. On the one hand, some authors are simply unwilling to attribute even the smallest error or human flaw to the revolutionaries. On the other hand, there soon appears a competing "literature" of deliberate "disinformation" and "black propaganda" (frequently underwritten by economically powerful counterrevolutionary interests) that is designed exclusively to discredit the revolutionary process.[1] In addition, since revolution is a highly marketable topic, there are the inevitable hastily thrown-together journalistic efforts. Lacking depth, historical perspective, and real concern for fact, these further contaminate the historical record.

Added to this, one finds that even the well-trained scholar honestly attempting to produce an objective overview of a given revolutionary experience inevitably faces an unusually difficult task. Revolutions, by definition, are rapidly changing processes. To stay "on top" of all important aspects of a given revolutionary experience and produce a solid, comprehensive study is an awesome challenge for any one individual. Moreover, this task is made even more difficult if, as is often the case, a covert effort is being made to distort and discredit virtually every aspect of the revolutionary experience. At such times, the scholar is faced with the task of determining, one by one, which alleged flaws of the revolution are real and which, on the other hand, are carefully planted distortions or straight-out fabrications.

These are some of the considerations that motivated the editor of this volume to organize a collective approach to documenting the Nicaraguan revolution. It appeared that if one could put together a team of scholars— each having a discrete, individual assignment—it might be possible to produce a comprehensive study without sacrificing accuracy.

The Nicaraguan Revolution was of interest to the editor for two reasons. First, having done an M.A. thesis (subsequently published by the University of Arizona Press in 1970) on the *Christian Democratic Movement in Nicaragua*, he was one of the few North American social scientists with the then dubious distinction of having studied politics in that hitherto seemingly unimportant country. Second, from 1972 onward, he had regularly taught a course on Revolution in Latin America.

Thus the idea of organizing a collaborative approach to the study of the Nicaraguan Revolution took shape almost immediately after the Sandinist victory in 1979. The first fruition of this idea was an edited work entitled *Nicaragua in Revolution* (New York: Praeger, 1982). A product of the effort of two dozen scholars, this study examined the insurrection, power and interests, and programs and policy through the first year and a half of Sandinist rule.

Nicaragua: The First Five Years follows in this tradition. It is designed to give a comprehensive examination of the Nicaraguan Revolution through its fifth anniversary in July 1984. It is not, however, an updated "second" edition. Well over half of the authors were not involved in the first effort and, although many of the old topics were retained (particularly those related to public policy and power and interests), some were dropped (those related to the insurrection) and a number of new ones added. The text of all but two chapters[2] is completely new.

The authors of this volume come from a variety of backgrounds and disciplines. Though the majority are North Americans, there are three Europeans and five Latin Americans, including three Nicaraguans. Their disciplines range from the social sciences and history to city planning, law, and business administration. They have in common, however, the fact that virtually all are scholars (Ph.D. candidates or academicians) with field experience *in Nicaragua*. This, then, is *not* the work of the functional equivalent of "Kremlinologists." To have studied Nicaragua from afar, as social scientists often do with more closed societies, would have been absurd. Throughout the entire period under examination, Nicaragua was an amazingly open and easy place in which to do research[3]—regardless of one's political orientation.

In order to allow maximum space for the findings of the authors, this introduction will be short. Its objective is simply to set the Revolution in perspective (1) by discussing the concept and historical experience of "revolution" in Latin America, and (2) by tracing the social, economic, and political history out of which the Nicaraguan Revolution flowed.

REVOLUTION

As the term is commonly used by social scientists, "revolution" implies a process of rapid social, economic, and political change that normally entails physical violence and results in a restructuring of the relationship between classes. The old privileged class, or classes, is displaced by a formerly subservient class. A common symptom of real revolution is a massive outflow of emigrés composed largely of individuals from the former privileged class.

If one employs this definition in examining the history of Latin America, one quickly arrives at the conclusion that, contrary to popular belief, "revolution" is a very rare phenomenon indeed in that part of the world. Though many Latin American countries have undergone frequent extralegal changes in government via successful revolts, coups d'etat, golpes de estado, and the like, few have subsequently experienced any serious attempt at the reordering of social and economic structures. Even if one accepts incomplete or abortive efforts, it is clear that real revolution has never even been tried in most of the Latin American countries. Even in the supposedly turbulent twentieth century, only a handful of countries have witnessed the coming to power of avowedly revolutionary groups that subsequently embarked on programs of real revolutionary change. Generously, one might include seven in this category: Mexico, 1911–40; Guatemala, 1945–54; Bolivia, 1952–64; Cuba, 1959 to date; Peru, 1968–75; Chile, 1970–73; and Nicaragua, 1979 to date. Of these would-be revolutions, five eventually died, were crushed, or were transformed into nonrevolutionary systems before significant social and economic restructuring could be completed.

Why, one might ask, given the record to date, did Latin American revolutionaries persist? Part of the answer is that for many Latin Americans who were sincerely concerned about the terrible social condition of the bulk of the peoples of the region, a violent approach to structural change seemed to be the only viable solution. By the late twentieth century, it was fairly obvious, to those who cared to see, that very basic structural impasses stood in the way of human development for the vast majority of the people of Latin America. Furthermore, these blockages did not appear amenable to gradualist, nonviolent reforms such as those advocated by the United States from the time of the ill-fated Alliance for Progress in the early 1960s through the equally ineffective "human rights campaign" of Jimmy Carter late in the next decade. Quite simply, as gross national product (GNP) grew in most countries and a tiny privileged middle sector and upper class became increasingly affluent, the human condition of the vast majority of the people of Latin America either improved hardly at all, stagnated, or actually declined. And, this pattern seemed stubbornly to persist whether the political form of the movement was liberal "democracy" (a la Colombia from the late 1950s onward), one-man dictatorship (Paraguay under Alfredo Stroessner or Haiti under the Duvaliers), or military rule (Brazil from 1964 onward and Chile after 1973).

The roots of the problem seemed to lie in a complex of social, economic, and political factors that many Latin American scholars and, later, an increasing number of North Americans and Europeans, came to refer to as "dependency."[4] Though the *dependistas* (as the writers who examined this subject were called) often disagreed with each other on specifics, a general consensus began to emerge to the effect that the social stagnation of Latin America was due in large part to the combination of an income-concentrating, externally oriented and conditioned form of capitalism with political systems controlled by the same minority classes that were receiving the bulk of the benefits from the distorted economic growth taking place.

Under these conditions, capitalist "development" in Latin America clearly was not following the pattern set by the industrialized countries. In the so-called developed world, the common man had attained a crucial economic (and therefore political) role as a consumer. Therefore, even if there was such a thing as a "ruling class," it was not in that group's interest to use its political power to exploit the common citizen to the extent that he or she could no longer consume. However, this was not true of Latin America, where capitalist economics were heavily externally oriented. There the tiny middle and upper classes that controlled the political systems derived most of their income directly or indirectly from export or from the local manufacturer of products dominated by multinational corporations that they, not the masses, consumed. Under these conditions, the common citizen was important not as a consumer but rather as an easily exploitable source of cheap labor. Therefore, there was little or no economic incentive for the elite-dominated governments of Latin America to call upon their own class or classes to make the very real sacrifices necessary to improve the lot of the vast majority of the people.

Nor was there much apparent political incentive for such reforms. One of the most basic principles of politics is that benefits flow to groups in society more or less in direct proportion to their ability to exert pressure or to exercise power. Although the United States at the beginning of the Alliance for Progress solemnly admonished the ruling classes of Latin America to implement reform or suffer the consequences of Castro-like revolution, Washington quickly made such reforms appear to be politically unnecessary by providing Latin America's military establishments with so much "counterinsurgency" military aid that the privileged elites actually came to feel quite immune from the coercive power of the mass of the people. As a result, paradoxically, social injustice and exploitation were allowed to mount to the point where violent revolution would eventually be the only hope or option for most Latin Americans.

Another reason that Latin American revolutionaries did not give up is that they were increasingly convinced that history was on their side. They drew confidence from the fact that each previous revolutionary attempt— successful or not—had added to the "technology" of revolution. Though the U.S. Department of State and the popular press were fond of depicting

Latin American revolutionaries as sinister "terrorists" and thugs bent on delivering their countries into the hands of the Soviet Union, that picture was far from accurate. If we can generalize from the Nicaraguan experience and from scattered information from other countries, these people tended to be highly motivated and patriotic young men and women drawn disproportionately from the ranks of high school and university teachers and students. As such, they were intellectually active people with a much better than average awareness of national and regional history. Clearly, they felt that the history of revolution in Latin America held valuable lessons.

One of the insights that history seemed to offer was that there are no peaceful shortcuts to "revolution." Of the seven revolutionary experiments mentioned above, the three that came to power without violent struggle, and therefore without either mass mobilization or the dissolution of the conventional military establishment, were eventually overthrown with little difficulty by the military. Here we refer not only to the democratically elected revolutionary governments of Guatemala (1954) and Chile (1973), but also the Peruvian revolution, which was strangled in 1975 by the same military institution that had given it birth in the first place.

On the other hand, the Latin Americans had also learned that guerrilla warfare could not succeed without mass support. Such backing had been a major key to the success of the guerrillas in Cuba in 1959. Fidel Castro and his comrades had purposely cultivated a mass following not only through the clandestine broadcasts of "Radio Rebelde," but also by treating peasants with respect and by implementing social reforms in liberated areas. Yet, by the same token, guerrilla movements in the 1960s and early 1970s had met with a series of defeats due largely to their relative isolation from the people. For some reason, Ché Guevara in Bolivia, the Tupamaros of Uruguay, Carlos Marighela in Brazil, the Colombian Revolutionary Armed Forces (FARC), and so on—highly motivated though they may have been—had failed to win the "hearts and minds" of the local populaces. Undoubtedly, some of their lack of success could be attributed to the façade of legitimacy of the elite regimes they were opposing. But much of it could be credited to their failure to communicate effectively with the masses.

Latin American revolutionaries had also learned much about what to do once in power. There was a growing awareness that the challenge of running a revolutionary system is as great as, or greater than, that of seizing power in the first place in that it requires sweeping and effective innovation on a number of fronts simultaneously. For many observers, the failure of the Mexican, Guatemalan, Bolivian, Chilean, and Peruvian revolutionary experiments was attributable, at least in part, to a relative lack of bold, unified, and decisive actions. In some cases, the revolutionary leaders were stymied by obstacles beyond their control (unreconstructed military institutions, constitutional constraints, and so on), but in others, they appear to have been unnecessarily timid.

It was clear that if a "revolution" is, indeed, to be "revolutionary," it must immediately embark on a number of social programs designed to improve the human condition of the previously exploited majority. These would include some variant of agrarian reform; projects and legislation designed to advance public health, education, and housing; increased emphasis on the rights of rural and urban workers; and an effort to resurrect and nourish popular, "native" culture.

Each of the revolutionary experiments mentioned earlier featured most, if not all, of these types of reform. From these experiences, much had been learned about what "worked" and what did not. This was especially true in the areas of agrarian reform and education. In the former, some revolutionary governments had simply redistributed land without much technical follow-up (Bolivia being an excellent example), while others (such as Cuba) had opted for collectivized utilization and extensive state control. There were advantages and disadvantages to both approaches.

In education, the problem to be tackled first in most countries was mass illiteracy. In the elite-oriented systems of prerevolutionary Latin America, an aware and well-educated citizenry, if not seen as downright dysfunctional, was certainly never a high-priority goal. Quite the reverse is true in a real revolution, where a literate and involved populace is viewed as the focal point and motor of development as well as the principal guardian of the revolutionary system. From the Mexican Revolution through its Cuban successor, literacy campaigns were often the centerpieces of revolutionary social policy. In Mexico in the 1920s, José Vasconcelos, the country's first Minister of Education, embarked on a sweeping program of revolutionary public education, including a literacy campaign. Through this program, poor Mexicans not only learned to read and write, but also developed a renewed pride in Mexican culture and a sense of the basic goals of their revolution. While the Mexican campaign was relatively primitive— informally organized, it suffered from a very unfavorable student-teacher ratio—it *did* contain a very important idea: that literacy training should involve not only the teaching of reading and writing, but also a deliberate program of political and social consciousness-raising. This idea applied in the more ambitious and better organized literacy campaigns of Cuba (1961) and Nicaragua (1980) would bear remarkable fruit.

Another lesson of history was that mass mobilization is extremely important to the survival and success of any revolution. Each of Latin America's revolutionary experiments involved some emphasis on the development of mass organizations. In the more primitive cases, this amounted to little more than formal constitutional protection for the worker's right to organize and some governmental support for unions in their claims against private businesses, particularly foreign businesses. The Cuban Revolution, however, added a new dimension to the concept of mass mobilization. In addition to mobilization through specific organizations for rural and urban labor, students, women, and so on, the Cubans also created a vast network of grass-roots neighborhood groupings called the Committees for the Defense of the Revolution (CDRs). Organized late in 1960 with the initial purpose of mobilizing the Cuban people to guard against mounting counterrevolutionary activity, the CDRs eventually took on a variety of additional important functions. By mobilizing volunteer labor at the local level, they helped cut the cost of government programs. They served as two-way conduits of communication between the government and the people. And they were important devices for political socialization in that they gave the Cuban people an opportunity to become involved in, and therefore more aware of, and committed to their revolution. For a short while, the Cuban example appeared to have been transplanted to Peru, where the leaders of that country's military revolution created an agency entitled The National System to Support Social Mobilization (SINAMOS) for the explicit purpose of building a mass base for that otherwise elite-run "revolution." Eventually, however, when the popular pressures created by SINAMOS came to threaten the military's sense of order, the whole idea was modified and then scrapped. Though it had failed in Peru, the Cuban concept of mass mobilization would eventually come to play an even more important and innovative role in the Nicaraguan Revolution.

History also demonstrated that another important ingredient in successful revolution is political socialization. Of course, every society engages in political socialization—the transmission from one generation to the next of values and patterns of behavior supportive of its political system. In the United States, children are taught in the schools and in voluntary organizations to salute the flag, to recite the Pledge of Allegiance, to venerate national heroes and traditions, and generally to be good U.S. citizens. In a revolutionary society, political socialization is even more important since, in such a setting, there is an immediate need both to dismantle elitist, dysfunctional, prerevolutionary values and to build a new sense of nationhood and citizenship consonant with a more egalitarian system. An early example in revolutionary political socialization was set by Mexico's José Vasconcelos. His programs in public education (the literacy campaign, for instance) and popular art and culture (the famous revolutionary muralists)—heavily laced, as they were, with a nationalist and revolutionary message—served as an example for similar or more sophisticated programs adopted elsewhere. In addition, from Cuba onward, the much-expanded concept and practice of mass mobilization provided new vehicles for the massification of revolutionary values. Finally, the technological revolution in the mass media made it possible for revolutionary leaders to speak directly and frequently to their people.

Over the decades, Latin Americans had also learned much about regional economics. Frustrated in the late 1950s and 1960s by the total inadequacy of "gringo" theories of development in explaining the continuing and, in some cases, deepening misery of most of the people in most Latin American countries, they generated their own theories of "dependency" that seemed to them, and later to many U.S. scholars, to relate more closely to reality. Armed with these perceptions, they then felt better able to cope with the designing and running of a revolutionary economy. Though, for small states, economic *dependence* on external commerce and technology would continue to be a fact of life, the socially regressive variant, *dependency*, might be eliminated if the state would take over the "commanding heights" of the economy and reorient productive capacity and excess profit in a socially responsible direction. This might not even involve total socialization of the economy. Indeed, Fidel Castro, apparently regretting his nationalization of most of the Cuban economy, is said to have advised the Nicaraguans to try to preserve "responsible" private enterprise. "Responsible" businesses presumably would maintain full production, not export capital, refrain from exploiting workers, and pay their fair share in taxes.

In addition, revolutionary economic planners would have to take into consideration the U.S. "track record" in using economic destabilization as a way of destroying populist or revolutionary governments (Brazil, 1964; Chile, 1973; Jamaica, 1980). Accordingly, any revolutionary government would naturally seek to diversify its external commercial ties so as not to be excessively vulnerable to the very real possibility of destabilization orchestrated from Washington. This does not mean that a revolutionary regime would necessarily want completely to sever its ties with the United States. Much of Cuba's economic difficulties can be attributed to its isolation from U.S. markets and technology. However, given past experience, it would simply be prudent to avoid overdependence on any one country—especially one that had a tendency to interpret national revolution rather consistently from a myopic cold-war perspective.

Finally, some revolutionary experiences, notably those of Bolivia and Cuba, underscored for many Latin Americans the need to avoid excessive indebtedness. In Bolivia, it could be argued that the United States had co-opted and eventually derailed the revolution through its role as creditor. Perhaps sensing that the revolution could be destroyed from within, Washington was quite willing in the late 1950s and early 1960s to underwrite the Bolivian government with large loans. Having done so, it then was in a position to offer advice on how to run the economy. When following this advice led to labor unrest, the United States helped retrain and equip the "revolutionary" armed forces to deal with these "threats to stability." Eventually, in 1964, the by-then quite reactionary military overthrew what was left of the "revolution." In Cuba, on the other hand, the U.S. move to isolate the revolutionary government from Western markets and financial sources drove it into an increasing economic and therefore political dependence on the Soviet Union. This dependence was then augmented by the low productivity of a heavily socialized economy and the high cost of maintaining an armed force adequate to defend Cuba's sovereignty against the proven aggressiveness of its neighbor to the north while at the same time carrying out badly needed social programs. The obvious lesson from both of these cases was that future revolutionary governments should mobilize the material and human productive capacity of the nation more efficiently so as to make high foreign debts less necessary. A state-controlled, but not totally nationalized, economy might be one answer. A greater reliance on self-help and voluntary labor might be another. Both of these were to be tried in Nicaragua.

Yet another major lesson of history was that any revolution should be prepared to defend itself from inevitable counterrevolution—domestic, international, or both. In the first place, it had long been obvious that any genuinely progressive or revolutionary government would be foolish to *assume* friendly behavior on the part of the U.S. government. The United States had made incursions into Mexico during the early years of its populist revolution. It had recruited and prepared surrogate exile invasion forces for Guatemala (1954) and Cuba (1961). It had trained the local military establishment that quashed the revolutionary experiment in Bolivia (1964). It had sent U.S. Marines into the Dominican Republic in 1965 to block the return to power of social democratic forces that it had mistaken for "communist." And it had used economic destabilization and CIA covert action to prepare the "ambient" for the Chilean military coup of 1973.[5] And, if externally generated counterrevolutionary activity was to be expected, so too was its domestic counterpart. An authentic revolution involves the reallocation of scarce resources in behalf of the hitherto exploited majority. Luxury for the few is sacrificed in the name of social justice for the many. This, of course, represents a real threat to the middle-sector and upper-class minorities. For this reason, it is fully predictable that these elite minorities will eventually regroup their forces—political, economic, intellectual, and military—and channel them into counter-revolutionary activities.

But Latin American revolutionaries had also learned a great deal about tactics of defense against counterrevolution. A first obvious lesson was that no revolution can survive the counterrevolution as long as the traditional military establishment remains intact. The cases of Guatemala, Chile, and

Peru had demonstrated that such military organizations would inevitably turn to counterrevolution in behalf of the privileged sectors.[6] Furthermore, it was also obvious that U.S. influence within a supposedly "revolutionary" armed force could have the same disastrous result (Bolivia, 1964). What was needed, instead, was the creation of a loyal and politically and socially conscious revolutionary armed institution. This would require an emphasis on literacy for the troops as well as political and social education at all levels. It would also necessitate a firm rejection of all military aid from nonrevolutionary countries when such aid was tied to the acceptance of officer and (or) troop training programs. The Cuban Revolution followed these tactics: the Peruvian one did not.

There were other measures that a revolutionary government could take to prepare itself for the inevitable counterrevolution. The Cuban experience, for instance, had demonstrated that it was useful to augment the strength of the regular armed forces by creating a mass volunteer militia. While the latter cost relatively little, it provided a margin of preparedness that proved useful in times of danger such as during the Bay of Pigs Invasion in 1961. In addition, nonmilitary mobilization through grass-roots organizations such as the neighborhood defense committees could help a revolution defend itself, especially against domestic counterrevolution. The CDRs in Cuba played a crucial role in preventing domestic collaboration with the Bay of Pigs invaders. But, in the long run, the best defense against counterrevolution had been, and always would be, the quick and effective implementation of a revolutionary social program designed to uplift the condition of the masses. In positively affecting the lives of the poor, the revolution could build a bulwark of popular support that could withstand the attacks of the former privileged minority and its traditional international protector.

Latin Americans also had learned much about the concept and practice of "democracy." Over the years, it had become quite clear that liberal democracy in any society tends to protect and preserve the social status quo. In those few "developed" countries where *relatively* high levels of social justice exist—England, Sweden, the United States, and so on—this type of democracy serves to reinforce *relative* equality. By the same token, however, in the very inegalitarian societies of Latin America, it was clear that the tiny privileged elites rarely had much difficulty in manipulating ostensibly "democratic" systems to produce governments and public policy that actually reinforced and perpetuated inequality. This was not surprising given the fact that such elites enjoyed tremendous economic resources, a vast advantage in education, and control of most of the mass media. In prerevolutionary Latin America, liberal democracy, then, was an empty ritual and a real obstacle to social change.

However, even in a revolutionary setting, liberal democracy had proven to have its drawbacks. In Bolivia and Mexico it had helped cause the revolutionary systems to degenerate into a sort of directionless populism in which politicians, while promising benefits for everyone, were afraid to call for needed sacrifices. In addition, it was clear that the holding of national elections could increase a revolutionary's system's vulnerability to international political manipulation via the tactic of economic destabilization.

These perceptions of democracy posed a real dilemma. While most were deeply committed to democracy in theory, Latin American revolutionaries had become highly skeptical of the narrow *liberal* definition and practice. Many Latin Americans felt that "democracy" ought, first of all, to include social and economic dimensions. It was predictable, therefore, that social revolutionaries in the late twentieth century would be wary of implementing political democracy of a type that either would block major social restructuring or could be manipulated from abroad in a counter-revolutionary direction via the tactic of economic destabilization. The building of democracy from below by means of mass mobilization through grass-roots functional and neighborhood organizations would be stressed instead. The revolutionaries would argue that whereas liberal democracy had allowed the people only a ritualistic and ineffective role every few years, "popular democracy" gives the common citizen political participation on a continuous and meaningful basis.

Of course, there were many other lessons that revolutionaries could, and did, draw from the history of twentieth-century Latin America. No short introduction can adequately describe the various facets of this growing awareness. Suffice it to say that many Latin Americans were fortified in their revolutionary purpose both by their command of history and by the growing conviction that there was no nonviolent way out of the structural impasse that held the vast majority of their fellow countrymen in misery.

NICARAGUA: A BASIC DESCRIPTION

Nicaragua is, and always has been, a land of considerable potential.[7] She resembles the state of Iowa in extension (57,143 square miles as opposed to 56,290), population (2.5 and 2.9 million, respectively), and the unusually high quality of much of her land. She also has considerable potential for geothermal and hydroelectric energy, significant lumber and mineral resources, and rivers and lakes positioned in such a manner as to make her an ideal site for an interoceanic waterway. In addition, her people are relatively homogeneous and culturally integrated. Practically all Nicaraguans are mestizo—a mixture of Caucasian and Indian—and share an Hispanic culture. Little racial prejudice exists. Finally, Nicaraguans are a friendly, outgoing people with ample cause to be proud of things *Nica* such as their distinctive cookery, music, dialect, literary heritage, and sense of humor.

Ironically, however, when the popular forces finally achieved power in 1979, most Nicaraguans were still living in abject poverty. Though the annual GNP had reached a little over $800 U.S. per capita, it was very poorly distributed. Until the Sandinist Revolution, over half of all Nicaragua's citizens had been expected to make do on between $200 and $300 per person per year in a country where the cost of food, clothing, and so on, was almost as high as in the United States. Not surprisingly, most Nicaraguans lived in inadequate housing, dressed and ate poorly, and had little or no access to education, health care, and other public services. The average life expectancy at birth in 1979 was 53 years, ten years shorter than that for Middle America as a whole and a full eighteen years short of the equivalent statistic for Cuba, at the time Latin America's leader in that respect.[8]

This ironic condition of mass misery in a land of natural riches is best understood in terms of the concept of dependency discussed earlier. Quite simply, since the arrival of the Spaniards in the sixteenth century, Nicaragua's human and material resources had been used consistently for the benefit of a small, privileged, export-oriented minority. Frequently, the domestic system of exploitation had been reinforced by the country's relationship with foreign powers. Throughout this sad history, however, there also ran a long and inspiring tradition of popular resistance that was to culminate in 1979 in the triumph of the Sandinist Revolution.

THE COLONIAL PERIOD

When Spaniards under the command of Gil González first arrived in western Nicaragua[9] in 1522, they encountered a fairly advanced agrarian society. The approximately 1 million native inhabitants of the region—descendants of immigrants and refugees from the Maya and Aztec civilizations to the north—lived in numerous cities and villages ranging in population from a few hundred to tens of thousands. Though society was organized along feudal lines, land was held communally, with each family having access to a designated plot. On these parcels, the people grew corn, cassava, chili, beans, tobacco, and vegetables. While some of what they produced went in tribute to the local chiefs, the rest could be consumed by the family or sold in local markets. Though the people undoubtedly suffered occasional hardships as a result of intertribal warfare and periodic crop failure, this was a relatively self-contained system that appears generally to have functioned adequately in satisfying the basic human needs of even the common citizen.

The Spanish conquest appears to have had an immediate and devastating impact on the Indian civilization of the area. After some initial resistance led by Chiefs Diriangén and Nicarao, the *Conquistadores* were eventually able to consolidate Spanish control over the region. Superimposing themselves on the preexisting feudal structure, they demanded tribute in gold and, when that was depleted, Indian slaves. Both "commodities" were exported: the gold to Spain and the slaves to other colonies where they normally perished within a few months or years. By the 1540s, the lucrative export of slaves and widespread death through contact with common European diseases, against which local natives had no natural immunity, caused the Indian population of the region to plummet to a few tens of thousands.[10] This holocaust also had an equally striking impact on the economy in that it all but destroyed the region's labor-intensive agricultural system. Though some traditional farming persisted here and there, most of the rich lands of Nicaragua soon reverted to jungle or were exploited less intensively for the raising of cattle to produce hides, tallow, and salted meat for sale to other colonies. The process of dependent underdevelopment had begun.

After the gold and slave "booms" of the early colonial period had subsided, Nicaragua became a sleepy backwater of Spain's colonial empire. Monopolizing the colony's human and material resources, the tiny Spanish elite accrued wealth through ship-building, intermittent gold-mining, and the export of agricultural and cattle products. A state of mutual suspicion and rivalry developed and festered between the cattle-based, self-styled "aristocrats" of the city of Granada on Lake Nicaragua and the more commercially oriented elites of the administrative capital, León, to the northwest. To make matters worse, from the middle of the seventeenth century onward, the underpopulation of the colony and the ostentatious concentration of wealth in the hands of a privileged minority also made Nicaragua a prime target for attacks from pirates from Northern Europe, especially England.

THE FIRST CENTURY OF "INDEPENDENCE"

In the early nineteenth century, Nicaragua achieved her independence in three stages, first as part of the Mexican Empire of Agustín de Iturbide in 1821, then as a member of the Central American Federation in 1824, and finally as a technically sovereign state in 1838. During most of the next nearly 100 years, the country was to be buffeted by foreign intrigue and intervention and torn by intra-elite conflict.

Both of these themes came into play during the first two decades after "independence." During this time, the privileged classes of León and Granada (who eventually came to call themselves "Liberals" and "Conservatives," respectively) sent rag-tag armies into battle with each other to determine which city and elite was to enjoy the spoils of running the country. Meanwhile, the discovery of gold in California in 1848 and therefore renewed interest in Nicaragua's potential as a site for a trans-oceanic waterway drew Britain and the United States into intermittent competitive meddling in the area.

Eventually, the whole process came to a climax in 1855, when the Liberals invited an American soldier-of-fortune, William Walker, to help them defeat the Conservatives. Not long after bringing them to power, however, Walker pushed his Liberal allies aside and declared himself president. Slavery was legalized and English became the official language. This bizarre turn of events not only catalyzed both parties and all of the other Central American republics into a virtual holy war against the Yankee interloper, but also so discredited the Liberals that the Conservatives were able to rule Nicaragua with little opposition for the next third of the century.

From then until the last decade of the century, Nicaragua enjoyed relative political calm under a series of regularly "elected" Conservative presidents. A new constitution was adopted in 1858, a coffee "boom" began, and Managua, which had become the compromise capital in 1851, grew and prospered.

Under this superficial calm, however, economic changes were taking place that were to have a profoundly adverse effect on Nicaragua's common citizens. In the turmoil and confusion of the first half of the nineteenth century, Nicaragua's international dependency relationship had been temporarily disrupted. During this period, a small independent peasantry began to flourish again and the rudiments of an internal marketing system began to develop. The sudden world demand for coffee in the second half of the century, however, provided a powerful incentive for the traditional elites to seek new land and cheap exploitable labor. The Conservative governments, therefore, passed a series of laws—notably the Pedro Joaquín Chamorro Law of 1877—that effectively drove peasants and Indian communal land holders off their land and turned them into an impoverished and dependent rural proletariat. Though the rural poor rose up against their oppressors in the "War of the *Comuneros*" in 1881, the government enforced the new "order" at a cost of about 5,000 dead.[11]

In 1893, conservative hegemony finally came to an end in a successful uprising that eventually elevated a Liberal, José Santos Zelaya, to the presidency. Zelaya, who held power as dictator-president for the next 17 years, was certainly no great champion of social justice. He continued to open up "new" lands to the coffee growers. However, he was a modernizer and nationalist. He reorganized the military and the government, fostered public education, separated church and state, and so on. As a nationalist, he defied the British by reasserting full sovereignty over Nicaragua's Atlantic Coast, championed Central American integration, and firmly rejected a canal treaty proposal by the United States that he viewed as potentially injurious to Nicaraguan sovereignty.

Zelaya's nationalism, however, eventually got him into trouble. The United States, which had become a colonial power as a result of the Spanish American War of 1898, resented the independent spirit of this Central American leader. Decisionmakers in Washington felt that they knew best what was good for these "backward" countries. Therefore, late in the first decade of the twentieth century, when Zelaya began negotiating with other foreign powers for the building of a Nicaraguan canal, which would have competed with the U.S. waterway at Panama, the United States encouraged the Conservatives to rebel. When they did so in 1909, Washington sent a military force to Bluefields on Nicaragua's Atlantic coast to see to it that the rebellion not be put down. Zelaya himself resigned in 1909 and the Conservatives took power in 1910.

One last spark of Liberal nationalism flared up in 1912, when Liberals and dissident Conservatives led by Benjamín Zeledón attempted to overthrow the palpably corrupt and inept Conservative government. Just as Zeledón's forces were on the verge of victory, U.S. marines were sent in to restore "order." Ordered by U.S. officials to cease his rebellion, Zeledón fought on, warning the U.S. commander that he and his country would bear the "tremendous responsibility and eternal infamy that history would attribute to you for having employed your arms against the weak who have been struggling for the reconquest of the sacred rights of [their] fatherland."[12] The young Liberal patriot was soon defeated and, with apparent U.S. acquiescence, executed by the Conservatives.

For most of the period from 1912 to 1933, Nicaragua was physically occupied by U.S. troops in an apparent effort to achieve some sort of pro-U.S. stability. During the first occupation, from 1912 to 1925, the United States ran Nicaraguan affairs through a series of Conservative presidents. It was a symbiotic relationship. The Conservatives could not have held power without U.S. help and Washington could now ask for certain favors from their clients. The most important of these was the signing in 1914 and ratification in 1916 of the Bryan-Chamorro Treaty, which gave the United States the same sort of canal-building rights that Zelaya had withheld years earlier. It was not that the United States actually intended to build a Nicaraguan canal. Rather, this was simply a way of preventing any other country from doing so.

By the mid-1920s, U.S. decisionmakers had convinced themselves that the Conservatives were now ready to carry on without the presence of U.S. troops. They were wrong. Within a few months of the first U.S. withdrawal in 1925, fighting broke out between Liberals and Conservatives and, late in 1926, Marines landed in Nicaragua again.

This time Washington arranged a peace settlement between the leaders of the traditional parties that allowed the Liberal elite a place at the table. Indeed, as a result of the U.S.-supervised elections of 1928 and 1932, Liberals were elected president. The Americans, however, were the *real* rulers of Nicaragua. As one U.S. scholar commented in reference to the powers of the first elected Liberal, the United States "controlled his regime from a number of points: The American Embassy, the Marines . . . ; the Guardia National, with its United States Army officers; the High Commissioner of Customs; the Director of the Railway; and the National Bank."[13] It was in this period that Nicaragua signed with Colombia the very concessionary Barcenas Meneses Esguerra Treaty of 1928. As a result of this treaty, she gave up her claim to the Providencia and San Andrés Islands directly off her Atlantic coast. Though clearly not in Nicaragua's interest, this treaty helped assuage Colombian anger over the U.S.-engineered loss of her province of Panama in 1903 while it voided additional Colombian claims that tended to cloud the validity of some U.S. rights under the Bryan-Chamorro Treaty.

Probably the two most important features of the second occupation, however, were (1) a prolonged and rather successful guerrilla war that Augusto César Sandino waged against the American occupiers, and (2) the creation of the U.S.-trained and -equipped Nicaraguan National Guard. A poor mestizo, who had been embued with the ideas of the Mexican Revolution while working for a U.S. oil firm in Tampico in the early 1920s, Sandino was the one Liberal officer who refused to sign the U.S.-sponsored peace treaty of 1927, choosing instead to fight on against the Yankee occupiers. "The sovereignty and liberty of a people," he proclaimed, "are not to be discussed but rather to be defended with weapons in hand." He and his small army of peasants and workers quickly learned the tactics of guerrilla warfare and, in spite of such U.S. tactics as the aerial bombardment of "enemy" population centers and the forced relocation of peasants, the guerrillas were able to harrass the Americans with relative impunity until the foreign troops finally left in 1933.[14]

The creation of a national constabulary to maintain pro-American stability in Nicaragua had long been a dream of U.S. officials.[15] During the second occupation, the "threat" posed by the "bandit" Sandino gave the project additional urgency. The development of a powerful and professional National Guard would, it was hoped, "Nicaraguanize" (if you will) a war that had become so unpopular in the United States that Congress eventually voted to cut off all funding for it. From the vantage point of history, however, what was really important about the Guard was that it created a new, powerful, and uncontrollable factor in Nicaraguan politics. Its first Nicaraguan commander, Anastasio Somoza García, appointed as the Americans prepared to leave the country, was to use the Guard as the central factor in fashioning and maintaining a dynastic dictatorship that would oppress and abuse the Nicaraguan people for well over four decades.

THE SOMOZA PERIOD

Although, in all fairness, such an outcome was probably not foreseen at the time by most U.S. policymakers, the transition from Yankee occupation to Somoza dictatorship took place fairly rapidly. The son of a medium-scale coffee farmer, Anastasio Somoza García had worked his way into the top position in the Guard largely through his ability to ingratiate himself with the Americans. A graduate of the Pierce School of Business Administration in Philadelphia, he spoke fluent English and knew how to make himself "one of the boys" when around Americans. After the U.S. troops left, he worked quickly to consolidate his power by purging all Guard officers who might have stood in his way; by ordering the capture and murder of Sandino in 1934 (even though Sandino had formally signed a peace agreement in which his safety and that of his men had been explicitly guaranteed); and by cultivating the loyalty of the Guard by allowing officers and men alike to engage in various corrupt activities. In a short while, he began openly defying the elected president and, in 1936, he dropped all pretenses, staged a *coup*, and had himself "elected" president. He was inaugurated on New Year's Day, 1937.

The Somozas were to run Nicaragua virtually as a private estate until the Sandinistas drove them from power in 1979. Anastasio Somoza García ruled directly as president or indirectly through puppet presidents from 1937 until 1956, when a young poet-patriot, Rigoberto López Pérez, carried out a suicidal but successful assassination attempt. After the *ajusticiamiento*, or "bringing to justice" as Nicaraguans call it, Somoza's sons, Luis Somoza Debayle and Anastasio Somoza Debayle took over. Luis was president from 1956 to 1963. The family then ruled through puppet presidents until 1967, when Anastasio Jr. had himself "elected" president for a term that was to have lasted until 1971. Once in office, however, he amended the constitution to allow himself another year in the presidency, and then stepped down for two years while a puppet Triumvirate oversaw the writing of another constitution that allowed him to be reelected in 1974 for another term scheduled to have lasted until 1981.

There were differences in style among the Somozas. Luis, for instance, stood out from the other two in that he *seemed* to be less personally greedy and more concerned with improving the dynasty's "democratic" and developmentalist image. Of course, this style fit nicely with the proclaimed goals of the Alliance for Progress, begun during Luis's presidency. But, in reality, all three Somozas were dictators who ran the affairs of their country to their personal benefit and against the interests of the vast majority of their countrymen.[16]

The Somoza formula for rule was simple and effective: (1) appease and co-opt "important" domestic power contenders, and (2) cultivate the "friendship" of the United States. In the very unequal society of prerevolutionary Nicaragua, the major domestic power contenders were the church; the agricultural, industrial, and commercial elites; the leadership of the traditional parties; and the military. Though originally identified with the Conservatives, the church hierarchy switched its allegiance to the Somozas during the presidency of the first Somoza and continued to support the dynasty until the late 1960s. The monied elite benefited from the family's *laissez-faire*, income-concentrating economic philosophy and from the nearly total absence of governmental interest in protecting the rights of urban and rural workers. The majority segment of the Liberal Party supported the dynasty simply because the Somozas were, after all, "Liberals." And, in order to maintain a facade of democracy, the Somozas even saw fit frequently to buy Conservative "opposition" participation in electoral campaigns by offering the leaders of that party various benefits ranging from bribes to minority participation in government.

The most important domestic power factor, however, was the military. The Somoza family employed two tactics in maintaining its loyalty. First, they made sure that the top command of the Guard remained at all times in the hands of a family member. Equally important, they consciously worked to isolate the military psychologically from the Nicaraguan people by allowing it to become a sort of Mafia in uniform that controlled the rackets and took kickbacks and bribes for a variety of activities—legal and illegal. Since Nicaraguans of all classes hated the Guard, the Somozas could always remind them that if the family were ever overthrown, the Guard would be in grave trouble.

The second major tactic of the Somozas was the careful cultivation of the United States. This was accomplished through personal as well as political means. On the personal plane, all of the Somozas were educated in the United States, spoke fluent English, could turn on U.S. mannerisms at will, and were skilled at manipulating Americans. At the same time, in the realm of international politics, the Somozas were always obsequiously "pro-American." The enemies of the United States were automatically their enemies, be they the Axis Powers during World War II or the Communists thereafter. Accordingly, Nicaraguan territory was used by the United States for military bases during World War II and for the training of CIA (Central Intelligence Agency) surrogate invasion forces for Guatemala (1954) and Cuba (1961). Nicaraguan troops joined U.S. forces in the occupation of the Dominican Republic in 1965 and were offered, but politely refused, during the Korean and Vietnam "conflicts." In return, the United States sent ambassadors to Managua who were usually enthusiastically friendly to the Somozas. In addition, especially in the 1960s and 1970s, U.S. foreign aid—economic, "social," and military—poured into Nicaragua, and more members of Somoza's National Guard received training in the United States or at U.S. bases in Panama than was true of any other Latin American military establishment.[17]

The social impact of Somoza rule was profound and generally negative. Though a large and entangled social-service bureaucracy was created in the early 1960s in order to take advantage of opportunities provided by the Alliance for Progress, few benefits "trickled down" to the mass of the people. The new programs served largely as a way of providing employment and opportunities for the personal enrichment of the Somoza elite and its middle-class allies. Meanwhile, the developmentalist economic policies of the regime were causing very real hardship for the common citizen. As the international demand for additional products such as cotton grew, "new" lands were opened to the monied elite. As in the days of the coffee "boom" almost a century before, individual peasants once again were driven from the land—this time primarily from the Pacific lowlands. This process of rural dislocation contributed in turn to an accelerated rate of urbanization, especially in the late 1960s and 1970s. Unfortunately, by this time the social-service bureaucracy, which might have helped ease the suffering of the rural-urban migrants, was so hopelessly corrupt and inept that the problems of the poor were, in fact, largely neglected.

The disintegration and collapse of the Somoza system began in the early 1970s under Anastasio Somoza Debayle. During this period, Nicaraguans of all classes became increasingly alienated by the intemperate dictator's growing greed and brutality. Two major events accelerated the process of popular disaffection. The first was the "Christmas" earthquake of 1972, which destroyed most of the capital city, Managua. In the wake of this disaster, Somoza and his accomplices used their control of the government to funnel international relief funds into their own pockets. Very little was done for the disaster victims and, until the Sandinist victory, most of Managua remained an unreconstructed moonscape. Two years after the quake, when the Sandinist Front of National Liberation (FSLN) pulled off a very successful hostage-ransom operation, Somoza again reacted with intemperance. Humiliated and enraged by the FSLN's success, the dictator declared a state of siege, instituted full censorship of the press, and launched the Guard on a campaign of terror in rural areas where FSLN guerrillas were believed to be operating. Hundreds of peasants were raped, tortured, and (or) murdered outright; many others were taken away never to be heard from again.[18]

By the mid-1970s, Somoza was in serious trouble. His excesses had generated opposition from such widely diverse groups as labor, the church hierarchy, and a large segment of the commercial and industrial elite. Furthermore, the dictator's flagrant disregard for human rights won him considerable international notoriety. In 1977, with the inauguration of human rights advocate Jimmy Carter, even the "friendship" of the Somozas' long-term protector, the United States, became less certain.

Though there was a tendency in the United States following the Sandinist victory to either blame or praise the Carter Administration for consciously promoting the downfall of the Somoza system, such assertions are quite unwarranted. It is highly doubtful that the Carter Administration ever desired the overthrow of the Somoza system, much less the coming-to-power of the popularly-based FSLN. The decision to push "human rights" in Nicaragua seems to have been based on profound misperceptions of Nicaraguan reality. Apparently it was felt that Nicaragua would be a good, low-risk testing ground for the human rights policy. Not only was Somoza sure to follow orders, but also the administration had received assurance from U.S. military attachés working with Somoza's Guard that the guerrilla "threat" had been wiped out during the rural "counter-insurgency" operations of the previous two years. In fact, almost immediately after Somoza, under heavy pressure from Washington, lifted the state of siege and reinstated limited freedom of the press in September 1977, popular opposition to the tyrant and the system he headed began to mount. The leading opposition daily, La Prensa, was filled with reports of the corruption and brutality of the Somoza regime. In October, the FSLN demonstrated that it was alive and well by attacking National Guard outposts in several provincial capitals. Simultaneously, "The Twelve," a group of prominent business, religious, and professional leaders, denounced the regime and called for a solution that would include the FSLN. In sum, the United States had failed to perceive that an artificial injection of civil and political liberties into a system built on the denial of basic social and economic justice can have a highly destabilizing effect.

Within a couple of months, the struggle that many Nicaraguans refer to as the "War of Liberation" had begun. The United States now worked with greater urgency to arrange a political compromise between Somoza and his traditional opposition in order to preserve the Guard and Somoza's Liberal Party and, at the same time, exclude the popularly-based FSLN. But most Nicaraguans rejected these schemes for what they contemptuously called "Somocismo without Somoza"—and the revolutionary process moved inexorably toward its final outcome.

The catalyst that triggered the War of Liberation was the murder on January 10, 1978, of beloved La Prensa editor, Pedro Joaquín Chamorro. This and the very clumsy government cover-up that followed led that month to riots and a nationwide general strike. Though these failed to topple the dictatorship, popular discontent boiled over once again in February, when the inhabitants of an Indian barrio called Monimbó in the city of Masaya rose up against the National Guard and held government troops at bay with an assortment of pathetic hand weapons and home-made contact bombs for almost a week. Though this prototype insurrection was bloodily suppressed, student strikes and other acts of defiance continued into the summer.

In August 1978, Nicaraguans were stunned by the disclosure of a "secret" letter from Carter to Somoza congratulating the latter for his promise to improve the human rights situation in Nicaragua. Exasperated by this news and wanting to recapture the initiative, the FSLN later that month carried out their famous "Operation Pigpen," in which a small group of commandos seized the national legislative palace and held over 1,500 hostages until the dictator once again agreed to meet a series of stinging demands. Next came another prolonged businessmen's strike and the famous "September Uprisings" in which young people ("Los Muchachos") in most of the cities of Nicaragua, assisted by FSLN regulars, rose up—Monimbó style—against the dictator. Poorly armed, the insurgents were eventually forced to withdraw from one city after another, leaving Somoza's troops free to carry out a bloody and indiscriminate "mop-up" operation against the civilian population, bringing the death toll to over 5,000.[19]

From October to the following June, both sides prepared for the future. Somoza bought the time he needed to finish liquidating his immense assets and to transfer capital abroad by craftily negotiating with the traditional opposition and the Americans who were still pursuing the phantom of a peaceful elite-based "solution." Meanwhile, with the financial help of various groups, including the Social Democratic parties of Western Europe, and the logistical support of such widely disparate governments as those of Costa Rica, Panama, Venezuela, and Cuba, the FSLN rearmed itself with light weapons purchased on the international arms market. The regular FSLN army was expanded from a few hundred to several thousand and, throughout the country, neighborhood Civil Defense Committees worked feverishly to prepare for the next insurgency.

The "Final Offensive" was announced early in June 1979. Barricades were erected in working-class neighborhoods throughout the country and, one by one, Somoza's garrisons were overcome. Alarmed by the near certainty, now, of a popular victory, the United States asked the Organization of American States (OAS) to send a "peacekeeping force" to Managua, a transparent attempt to preserve the old system. This proposal was unanimously rejected by the OAS. On July 17, Somoza fled the country and, two days later, the FSLN entered Managua and accepted the surrender of what was left of the Guard.

The War of Liberation had cost Nicaragua around 50,000 lives, or approximately 2 percent of her population. In the United States, that would be the equivalent of a loss of around 4.5 million people, or over 75 times the U.S. death toll in the entire Vietnam conflict. But as Nicaraguans reminded the author on his trip there a few days later, freedom, justice, and national dignity are sometimes worth such a price.

THE REVOLUTIONARY SYSTEM

With the victory of the FSLN, the social configuration of political power in Nicaragua, and the philosophy behind it, changed abruptly. Unlike the Somozas, who had based their power in a corrupt, foreign-trained military establishment and in a small internationalized elite, the Sandinistas drew their strength—and their revolutionary mandate—from the mass of the people. The system of government that emerged in the first half decade of Sandinist rule reflected this reality. On the one hand, the formal structures of government—the Governing Junta of National Reconstruction, the Council of State, and the various ministries—reflected a genuine and pragmatic desire on the part of the revolutionary leadership to maintain a pluralistic, multiclass approach to revolution. Yet on the other hand, it was clear from the start that these formal organs were ultimately responsible to the National Directorate of the FSLN, which had created them in the first place. The nine-man Directorate, in turn, drew its political strength from its direct control of the armed forces (the Sandinist People's Army, the Sandinist Police, and the Sandinist Popular Militias) and from the people themselves. Constrained by harsh financial limitations and motivated by a long-standing belief in grass-roots participation, the Sandinistas had built on the legacy of voluntarism begun during the insurrection to the point that by mid-1984, around half of the adult (16 years old and above) population had been enlisted in various pro-Sandinista popular organizations. These, in turn, were providing the margin for success in national defense and virtually all government-promoted social programs.

Given these political realities, the personnel who composed the formal apparatus of government, while enjoying wide freedom in designing and implementing revolutionary reforms, had no option whatsoever to betray the humanistic goals for which so many people had given their lives. Accordingly, as will be shown in the chapters on revolutionary social policy, the government worked effectively, imaginatively, and with great dedication to implement a wide variety of changes designed to uplift the human condition of the mass of the people.

The philosophical or ideological foundation of the new system was a matter of considerable controversy. Practically from the start, the former privileged minority and their allies in the conservative hierarchy of the Catholic Church and the pro-business daily, La Prensa, saw the Sandinistas as harbingers of a future Communist state in which religion, private enterprise, and most civil and political liberties would be abolished. The fact that this specter failed to take on flesh during the first half decade did not assuage their hysteria. Added to these domestic tensions were increasingly strident and alarmist accusations coming from conservative forces in the United States. The 1980 National Platform of the Republican Party "abhor[red] the Marxist-Sandinist takeover" in Nicaragua and, in 1981, the new Reagan Administration immediately mounted a massive propaganda campaign designed to convince the U.S. public and the world that Sandinist Nicaragua was little more than the first ugly Communist domino in a Soviet conspiracy to enslave Central America. Distortions and fabrications were turned out in rapid succession[20] with the effect that, by 1984, the popular image of Nicaragua in the United States was extremely negative and the mass media, including the network news programs, had even begun to refer quite casually to the "Communist" regime in Managua.

The reality of the situation, however, was quite different. True, most of the leaders of the Sandinist Revolution were Marxists or Marxist-Leninists. They had never tried to deny that fact. However, this simply meant that they—like an increasing number of Third World intellectuals—saw economics as the major determinant of social and political matters, believed in the reality of class struggle, identified Imperialism as a major problem for the Third World, saw military and educational establishments as inherently political, and so on. However, their acceptance of these ideas did not mean that they believed in the possibility of creating Marx's Communist utopia in Nicaragua or that they were, or had any intention of becoming, obedient puppets of what Reagan was fond of calling the "empire of evil," the Soviet Union. In fact, another component of their ideology—nationalism—was as strong as, or stronger than, their Marxism. Accordingly, the overriding concern of the young revolutionaries who governed Nicaragua during this period was to reconstruct the country, defend its hard-won sovereignty and dignity, and uplift the human condition of its popular masses. Where the efficient and practical pursuit of these concerns conflicted with ideology, the latter almost always gave way.

Finally, in addition to being Marxists, many of the Sandinistas were also devout Catholics. They had been inspired by the 1968 Conference of Latin American Bishops at Medellín, Colombia, which had denounced the oppressive nature of Latin American social, economic, and political structures and had urged the faithful to make "a preferential option for the poor." Many had been involved in the early 1970s in the massive effort carried out by progressive Catholics to mobilize and raise the social and political awareness of the poor. Most of the Sandinista leadership—religious or not—felt that religion should be respected and, if possible, the church should be encouraged to remain involved in the revolutionary process. On several occasions, high FSLN leaders explicitly rejected Marx's famous contention that religion is "the opiate of the people." And, while sectors of the conservative church hierarchy often seemed determined to confront the Sandinist state, the FSLN leadership seemed equally intent on preserving the Catholic humanist component that distinguished their revolution from others that had come before.[21]

In sum, the Sandinist Revolution was something new and innovative—a blend of nationalism, pragmatic Marxism, and Catholic humanism. In all likelihood, that is precisely why it was so threatening to conservative ideologues in the United States. Small wonder they were working so tenaciously to try to discredit and destroy this unusual experiment.

NOTES

1. "Disinformation" is one of the major tools that "great powers" use to destabilize or discredit their enemies. The Western press is fond of pointing to cases of distortion in the state-controlled media of the USSR. And, of course, few can forget the tactic of the "big lie" as practiced by Adolf Hitler. However, we should also remember that during World War I, British government propagandists deliberately fabricated stories about the "horrible Hun" in order to solidify support for the war effort at home and to nudge U.S. public opinion—and, hence, the U.S. government—away from a position of neutrality. The U.S. government has also frequently used disinformation against its chosen enemies—particularly Latin American revolutionaries or "leftists" in the years after World War II. Disinformation was one of the tools used by the CIA in its successful push to overthrow the elected revolutionary government of Guatemala in 1954. It was also used in creating the conditions that led to the overthrow of Chile's elected Marxist president, Salvador Allende, in 1973. A decade later, even the U.S. popular press was discussing its use by the United States in Central America. *Newsweek*, for instance, reported in 1983 that "several lower-ranking State Department officers with experience in that country" had confirmed that disinformation was being

employed in El Salvador to "convince the civilian population that the guerrillas, not the Army were the real bad guys. . . . " The same journal also observed (to the surprise of very few specialists on Nicaragua) that the CIA had been "masterminding a variety of propaganda activities to destabilize the Sandinistas." "America's Secret Warriors," *Newsweek*, October 10, 1983, p. 39. On Guatemala, see Stephen Schlesinger and Stephen Kinzer, *Bitter Fruit: The Untold Story of the American Coup in Guatemala* (New York: Doubleday, 1982). For CIA efforts in Chile, see U.S. Congress, Senate, Staff Report of the Select Committee to Study Governmental Operations with Respect to United States Intelligence, *Covert Action in Chile* (Washington, D.C.: U.S. Government Printing Office, December 18, 1975).

2. Much of the background information in the rest of this introduction is from the introduction to *Nicaragua in Revolution*. Parts of the chapter on the military that the editor coauthors in this volume with the late Stephen M. Gorman are from Gorman's fine contribution to that earlier volume.

3. In this regard, the editor would like to thank the hundreds of Nicaraguans of various political points of view who assisted the chapter authors in their research. In particular, the editor is very grateful to Saul Arana and Sofía Clark of the North American Section of the Nicaraguan Foreign Ministry for helping some of the authors by setting up appointments and providing letters of introduction. However, it is indicative of the openness of Nicaragua during this period that a number of the authors never saw fit to call upon the Foreign Ministry for the assistance it had so generously offered each of them.

4. For useful discussion of "dependency," see the series of articles devoted to that subject in *The Latin American Research Review* in the 1970s and early 1980s.

5. For ample documentation of the successful U.S. destabilization of Chile, see U.S. Congress, *Covert Action in Chile*.

6. This, by the way, is the reason many observers were so deeply skeptical about the U.S.-sponsored experiment in "moderate" civilian-military "revolution" that came to power in El Salvador on October 15, 1979.

7. For a more adequate introduction to Nicaragua than can be provided in the space allowed for this chapter, see Thomas W. Walker, *Nicaragua: The Land of Sandino* (Boulder, Colo.: Westview Press, 1981, 1985).

8. 1979 World Population Data Sheet (Washington, D.C.: The Population Reference Bureau, 1979).

9. The inhabitants of the sparsely populated eastern half of Nicaragua tended to be hunters or gatherers of South American origin.

10. This amazing process of depopulation is quite well documented. For a sound and scholarly examination of the subject, see David Richard Radell, "Native Depopulation and the Slave Trade: 1527–1578," in his *An Historical Geography of Western Nicaragua: The Spheres of Influence of León, Granada, and Managua, 1519–1965* (Berkeley: University of California, Ph.D. dissertation, 1969), pp. 66–80.

11. For a good account of the process of social dislocation caused by the coffee "boom," See Jaime Wheelock Román, *Imperialismo y Dictadura: Crisis de una Formación Social* (México: Siglo Veintiuno Editores, 1975).

12. From a handwritten letter from Zeledón to Col. J. H. Pendleton, Masaya, Nicaragua, October 3, 1912. Facsimile copy courtesy of Zeledón's grandson, Sergio Zeledón.

13. Ralph Lee Woodward, Jr., *Central America: A Nation Divided* (New York: Oxford University Press, 1976), p. 200.

14. Two of the better books on Sandino are Neil Macaulay, *The Sandino Affair* (Chicago: Quadrangle Books, 1967), and Gregorio Selser, *Sandino* (New York: Monthly Review Press, 1981).

15. For an excellent study of the relationship between the United States, the Nicaraguan National Guard, and the Somoza dynasty, see Richard Millett, *Guardians of the Dynasty: A*

History of the U.S.-Created Guardia Nacional de Nicaragua and the Somoza Family (Maryknoll, N.Y.: Orbis Books, 1977).

16. During their long domination of Nicaragua, the Somozas accrued massive holdings in virtually every sector of the economy. By 1956, when Anastasio Somoza García was killed, the family was worth around $50 million. By the time Anastasio Jr. was "elected" a decade later, this fortune had tripled to around $150 million. At the time of the 1972 earthquake, it was commonly estimated at $300 million. When Somoza was overthrown, he was believed to have been worth well in excess of a half a billion dollars—no one knows for sure.

17. Millett, *Guardians*, p. 252.

18. Amnesty International, *The Republic of Nicaragua: An Amnesty Report* (London: Amnesty International, 1977).

19. For a remarkably frank discussion of this grisly operation, see Inter-American Commission on Human Rights, Organization of American States, *Report on the Situation of Human Rights in Nicaragua* (Washington, D.C.: General Secretariat of the OAS, 1978).

20. Practically every aspect of Nicaraguan reality was distorted in Reagan Administration pronouncements. For a discussion of some of these distortions, see Thomas W. Walker, "The Nicaraguan-U.S. Friction: The First Four Years," in Kenneth M. Coleman and George C. Herring, *The Central American Crisis: Sources of Conflict and Failure in U.S. Policy* (Wilmington, Del.: Scholarly Resources, 1985), pp. 181–186.

21. See Chapter 5 on religion in this volume and Laura N. O'Shaughnessy and Luis H. Serra, *Church and Revolution in Nicaragua* (Athens: Papers in International Studies, Ohio University Press, 1985).

PART II
POWER AND INTERESTS

Authentic revolution implies a significant restructuring of the social configuration of power. A government responding to the organized demands and interests of the formerly dispossessed majority replaces one based in the support of a privileged and influential minority. By these criteria, what took place in Nicaragua in the five years following the Sandinista victory was clearly revolutionary. Interestingly, however, the process by which power was reallocated was remarkably nonviolent.

The chapters in this section address themselves to various aspects of power and interest in the new Nicaragua. The first two examine the formal structures of government, national and regional. In John Booth's chapter, we look at an interim system of national government that—though created and guided by the FSLN Directorate—contained significant mechanisms for non-Sandinista input and pluralism. This system was superseded by a government elected on November 4, 1984, and inaugurated on January 10, 1985. The latter was to write a new constitution. The chapter by Charles Downs describes the unusual experiment in governmental decentralization and regionalization begun in 1982.

The other chapters in this section delve into the role of interest groups in the new Nicaragua. Here we see a dramatic shift in power and influence away from traditional privileged groups toward organizations representing the impoverished majority. The main pillars of the new system were the Sandinista grass-roots organizations and the Sandinista armed forces. As of 1984, the grass-roots organizations had come to provide around half of the adult population (aged 16 and older) with a locus for political participation; and the Sandinista military had efficiently contained an unprecedently large, CIA-directed, counterrevolutionary effort.

But there were problems. Counterrevolutionary forces had exploited ethnic fears and mistakes by Spanish-speaking Sandinistas to create problems for the new government among the ethnic minorities of the Atlantic Coast. A large segment of the Catholic hierarchy, apparently fearing a loss in power and influence, had come to play an increasingly strident and counterrevolutionary role. All attempts by the Sandinistas aimed at reconciliation had failed to reverse the conservative hierarchy's drift toward confrontation. There were problems, too, with the bourgeoisie and the opposition press that expressed its interests.

For a new revolutionary system attempting to preserve pluralism and a mixed economy, the noncooperative and often confrontational behavior of these dissatisfied minorities was a major obstacle. Furthermore, the tendency among the opposition to confront and obstruct, rather than to negotiate and accommodate, was reinforced and perpetuated by the belief in some circles that U.S. Marines, if not the armed counterrevolution, would ultimately come to their rescue.

Chapter 1
The National Governmental System

JOHN A. BOOTH

Nicaragua's revolutionary political regime originated in the widespread popular insurrection of 1977–79 that overthrew Anastasio Somoza Debayle, the third president of a dynasty that had ruled since 1936. Within five years the Sandinist National Liberation Front, the principal military opponent and leader of a broad political coalition against the Somoza regime, established an institutional framework for continued revolutionary transformation of Nicaraguan society. In comparison to other twentieth-century revolutions, Nicaragua's Sandinist government remained remarkably pragmatic in its programs and unusually tolerant of its domestic critics.

The transitional nature of the revolutionary government complicates its study as a harbinger of Nicaragua's political future. As this went to press, the national elections of November 1984 had just chosen Daniel Ortega Saavedra, Coordinator of the Junta from 1979 to 1984, as president to replace the revolutionary Junta, and a National Assembly to replace the Council of State and to write a new constitution. Although this chapter focuses mainly upon the structure and operation of the revolutionary system from 1979 to 1984, some possible characteristics of the new regime will also be considered.

POLITICAL PARTIES AND INFORMAL GOVERNMENT

The Sandinist National Liberation Front's nine-member Joint National Directorate (DN) acted as a de facto board of directors of the Nicaraguan revolution from 1979 through 1984. The authority of the FSLN and DN was not primarily formal, but informal. The FSLN's mandate to rule was partly moral, stemming from its 18 years of anti-Somoza struggle and from its military victory over the National Guard. Its authority was also partly practical, as National Directorate members dominated the revolutionary security forces after coming to power.

The DN's formal authority was embodied in the revolutionary constitution, the Fundamental Statute of the Government of National Reconstruction, in only brief references. The Junta was to be "designated by the Revolutionary Movement,"[1] which after the fall of the old regime in effect meant the DN, probably in consultation with other anti-Somoza political groups. The Fundamental Statute also "substitute[d] for the National Guard of Nicaragua a new National Army . . . to be formed by the combatants of the Sandinista National Liberation Front [and other appropriate citizens and] provisionally commanded by the military chiefs and leaders of the armed movement that put an end to the dictatorship,"[2] an obvious reference to the FSLN.

Despite persistent ideological shadings among members of the three tendencies (Proletarian, Prolonged People's War, and Insurrectionist), the DN's collegial decisionmaking and firmly held policy against personality cults moderated internal differences and gave revolutionary policy a markedly pragmatic cast. Decisions on issues that evoked sharp internal debate within the DN were reportedly taken only with a six-vote majority. Continual speculation about a schism within the DN or of a radicalization of the revolution under the lead of one faction or another failed to prove valid.

National Directorate members held key government positions in order to shape revolutionary policy. Daniel Ortega Saavedra was Coordinator of the Junta; Tomás Borge Martínez headed the Interior Ministry; Humberto Ortega Saavedra, Defense; Jaime Wheelock Román, Agriculture and Agrarian Reform; Henry Ruiz, Planning; and first Bayardo Arce Castaño and later Carlos Núñez Téllez served as President of the Council of State. The FSLN also established an extensive political organization including neighborhood Sandinist Defense Committees (CDSs), the Nicaraguan Women's Association, the July 19th Sandinist Youth, the Rural Workers' Association (ATC), the National Farmer's and Cattleman's Union (UNAG), and the Sandinist Workers' Central. The national headquarters of the FSLN provided organization, planning, programs, literature, training, and propaganda materials.

Escalating external threats to the Revolution after 1981 effectively strengthened the FSLN and its mass base by promoting the rapid growth of the popular militia and the establishment of the CDSs' nationwide "revolutionary vigilance" program. The external threats, in contrast, undermined the organizational and communication capacity of several other legal political parties. The 1982–84 state of emergency restricted public meetings and established press censorship, disabilities felt more by other parties than by the FLSN.

The revolutionary government's Fundamental Statute legitimized party diversity by including "distinct political sectors" on the Junta and by granting Council of State representation to seven parties other than the FSLN.[3] These parties (see Table 1.1, later in this chapter, for a list) held posts in the Junta, cabinet, bureaucracy, and Council of State. Even after several parties and other organizations coalesced into a formal opposition coalition, they continued to participate in national political life. Although the opposition never dominated public policymaking after 1979, it did influence administration and policymaking. Even under censorship (1982–84) opposition parties' critiques of proposed policy were regularly presented and discussed in the Nicaraguan press. Prior to the 1984 election the Junta eased censorship and meeting restrictions to facilitate party contact with the public.

In sum, five years of revolutionary government clearly enhanced the FSLN's control of the polity, but it also institutionalized a role for opposition. Legal partisan opposition to the FSLN developed, operated openly, and even participated in government throughout the period. The state of emergency weakened some opposition parties, but they received some relief during the 1984 election campaign. Modern revolutionary movements have rarely tolerated any open opposition, much less institutionalized it. This fact makes the FSLN's opposition's continued existence, not to mention its participation in national political life, an extraordinary political occurrence and one of the most distinctive features of the Nicaraguan Revolution.

FORMAL GOVERNMENT

The formal government of revolutionary Nicaragua was established by decree of the Governing Junta of National Reconstruction in the Fundamental Statute of the Republic of Nicaragua on August 22, 1979. This revolutionary charter abolished the previous Constitution and constitutional laws, and dissolved the former Congress, Supreme Court of Justice, Courts of Appeals, Labor Courts, and "remaining structures of Somocista power."[4] Other laws remained in effect until the new government could review and revise them. The Fundamental Statute established three governing branches: the Junta and bureaucracy, the Council of State (the Junta's authority considerably overlapped that of the Council of State), and the Courts of Justice.

The Executive Branch

The Governing Junta of National Reconstruction (JGRN or Junta) was established in exile in Costa Rica in early 1979 to replace the presidency of the old regime and to carry out the program of the rebel movement.

Following Somoza's July 1979 fall the Junta exercised formal executive authority in Nicaragua. The JGRN was guided in its decisions and actions by the policy line of the National Directorate of the FSLN as transmitted through liaison Daniel Ortega, a member of both bodies. The revolutionary constitution, the Fundamental Statute, provided for the Junta to be designated "by the Revolutionary Movement from among the distinct political and socioeconomic sectors of Nicaragua."[5] In effect, this meant designation by the FSLN's DN.

The first five-member Junta included Ortega, Sergio Ramírez Mercado, Moisés Hassán Morales (all from the FSLN), Violeta Barrios de Chamorro, widow of former *La Prensa* editor Pedro Joaquín Chamorro, and businessman Alfonso Robelo Callejas of the Nicaraguan Democratic Movement (MDN). Junta decisions were to be made by majority vote but despite the political diversity of its first members, its decisionmaking was normally by consensus. Violeta Barrios resigned from the Junta in early 1980 for personal reasons. Alfonso Robelo broke with the FSLN over the changed membership of the Council of State and resigned from the Junta soon after Mrs. Chamorro. Arturo Cruz Porras, an international banker, served briefly on the Junta in 1980–81 but left to become Nicaragua's envoy to the United States. Moisés Hassán left the Junta for a cabinet post in 1981. From 1981 through 1984 the Junta's members were Ortega, Ramírez, and Rafael Córdoba Rivas of the Democratic Conservative Party.

The Junta legislated by decree from July 1979 until May 4, 1980, when the Council of State began operation. During its first ten months the JGRN emitted over 700 decrees that established the basic structures, personnel, laws, and procedures of the revolutionary regime. This extraordinary volume of legislation reflected both the war's devastation and the new government's determination to effect a profound transformation of Nicaraguan society.

After May 1980, the Junta shared legislative authority with the Council of State. Junta-passed decrees submitted to the Council for approval took effect within ten days if not acted upon. If the Council made its nonbinding recommendations for revisions to a Junta decree within ten days, it returned to the JGRN, which could accept or reject the Council's proposals. The Junta accommodated many of the Council's suggested amendments. In 1980–81 the Junta introduced far more legislation in the Council than did the Council itself, but the two bodies were at rough parity by 1981–82, and the Council more than doubled the Junta's initiatives in the 1982–83 legislature.

The revolutionary bureaucracy consisted of various agencies and functional ministries headed by ministers from various political parties among the anti-Somoza coalition. Non-Sandinistas held technical and less political portfolios, but FSLN DN members occupied key ministerial posts in order to assure control of defense, internal security, agrarian reform, and planning. Reorganization of the national bureaucracy was extensive. Moreover, the great expansion of the public sector (nationalization of Somocistas' properties, foreign commerce, insurance, and banking) required considerable public institution-building. The Junta's own staff, including public administration experts and social scientists in the State Information and Promotion Directorate (DIGE), Ministry of Planning officials, and planners from the affected agencies played key roles in government reorganization.[6] Press reports and documents published by Nicaraguan bureaucracies indicated ongoing evaluation, "self-criticism," and reform in many agencies and policy areas.[7]

The vastness of this administrative reorganization was revealed by the new government's decrees. Of some 200 emitted by the Junta in the last five months of 1979, 44 created or modified public agencies and 4 others established norms for civil servants; 8 more established taxes or regulated the handling of public funds. In 1980 the Junta emitted almost 400 decrees, of which some 127—almost one-third—affected bureaucratic entities or set norms for public employees.[8] Many old autonomous agencies were folded into the central cabinet ministries, reducing their policy independence and utility as sources of graft. The JGRN also established several new decentralized agencies for various purposes (for example, to promote tourism and film production, operate water and sewer service, produce electricity).

Not only were new institutions and new norms for public servants established, but administrative adjustments were continual. Between 1979 and 1982 many agencies underwent repeated modifications of their organic laws and administrative procedures. Such changes affected not just the central government, but municipalities as well, whose governing statutes were altered three times in 1979–80. Moreover, in 1982 a program of administrative decentralization went into effect, partly in an effort to improve the state's capacity to operate in the event of an invasion. These reforms profoundly altered Nicaraguan local government personnel and performance.[9]

Planning played an important role in the revolutionary government almost from its inception. The Ministry of Planning coordinated the development of public sector plans with technicians and planners from other ministries. Planning produced the annual national plans of 1980 and 1981, which projected revenues and expenditures and outlined goals and policies. Although extensive planning continued, the publication of national plans was suspended for security reasons in 1982.

One goal of the Revolution was to involve Nicaraguans in national decisionmaking, but at first popular input was less than hoped. After 1979, however, several major programs developed extensive citizen participation, especially at the level of implementation. The first great effort to include the public as active collaborators with the state was the successful 1980 Literacy Crusade, which eventually involved hundreds of thousands of volunteer teachers and students. Also in 1979–80 the FSLN organized the CDSs in neighborhoods throughout the country. In addition to their partisan function, the CDSs "transformed themselves into little neighborhood governments"[10] that carried out various administrative functions from vigilance to food distribution to health care program administration. In 1981 the Ministry of Education's advisory Popular Education Collectives conducted a "national consultation on education" to set national education goals. Also begun in 1981 were Popular Health Days, in which CDSs, local health committees, and other groups conducted cleanups, education programs, and vaccinations.

Citizen input and participation were influential in certain policy areas, sometimes in unexpected and—from the government's perspective—unfortunate ways. For example, the government's policy of wage austerity met considerable opposition from labor unions and their members. Pressure for higher wages was intensified by the rapid organization of the work force in 1979–80 and remained a persistent problem.[11] Similarly, agricultural policy shifted several times between 1979 and 1983, due in part to the increasingly important input of peasants organized into the Rural Workers' Association and small farmers in the National Farmer's and Cattlemen's Union. Health policy planning also changed due to pressure from different constituencies. For instance, the 1979–80 emphasis on building centralized institutional health infrastructure (hospital construction, curative medicine programs) ceded to pressure from nonmedical ministerial employees and communities for preventive, community-based, and participatory medical programs.[12]

After the fall of Somoza, policy execution remained in substantially the same hands as before. The new regime, aided by a few Sandinistas and other anti-Somoza coalition cadres, invited most former lower- and middle-rank bureaucrats back to their old posts. With revolutionaries and their allies in most important supervisory and policymaking jobs, ministries and agencies continued their operations as before until new goals and procedures could be elaborated. Despite efforts to avoid excessive bureaucratization, the new government grew so rapidly that the Junta soon had to reduce the number of public employees for the sake of economy.

One intriguing phenomenon of the bureaucratic transition was the establishment of a new administrative culture characterized by productivity, honesty, and a strong public service orientation. Revolutionaries in the bureaucracy stressed such changes, and the Junta emitted several decrees establishing standards of behavior for public employees, including

Decree No. 39 (September 3, 1979), a "Law Concerning the Moral Integrity of Public Functionaries and Employees." To the pleased astonishment of most Nicaraguans, corruption and the traditional hostility and disdain with which public employees treated their clients diminished markedly.

Tensions inevitably developed between old and new public employees, despite determined efforts to foster cooperation and harmony. Furthermore, as the extent of the revolutionary transformation of the Nicaraguan bureaucracy became clear, further tensions arose within many agencies between activist public employees politically "aligned (*alineados*) with the revolutionary process" and others less interested in politics, who complained of politicization of technical processes and bias in which the alineados received preference for promotions over the merely technically competent.[13]

The Council of State

Legislative authority was shared between the Junta and the Council of State after the latter's inauguration in May 1980. The Council had the following powers: to approve or propose reforms to laws submitted to it by the JGRN, to initiate its own legislation, to reform administrative subdivisions (at the initiative of the JGRN), to authorize the functioning of civic and religious entities (that is, concede juridical personality), to write an electoral law and a draft constitution (at the initiative of the JGRN),[14] to ratify treaties and conventions concerning boundaries and maritime limits, to regulate all questions of citizenship and patriotic symbols, and to require information from cabinet ministers and agency heads.[15]

The Council of State was not a strong legislature, since legislative authority over many administrative matters and budgets resided exclusively with the Junta, as did the extensive emergency powers put into effect in 1981. The JGRN had an absolute veto over Council-initiated legislation, while the Council, in contrast, lacked a corresponding veto over Junta-initiated bills. Council-proposed reforms or objections had to be considered by the Junta but could be overridden. The Council was not, however, a mere rubber stamp—it frequently influenced Junta-initiated legislation, and more than 100 of its own bills became law by 1983. Two indexes of the Council's policymaking importance were the length of its sessions—from May through December of each year, plus special extended sessions as in early 1984—and the extent and intensity of delegates' debate and participation over policy matters.

The Council's leadership resided in a President and Executive Committee,[16] elected by simple majority from among the membership. The President exercised several important powers, including presiding over plenary sessions, naming the members of working commissions, and directing the Council's staff. FSLN National Directorate member Bayardo Arce Castaño occupied the Council's presidency in 1980–81 but was rumored to be too conflict-prone for the give and take of legislative debate. The FSLN replaced Arce with Carlos Núñez Téllez, also of the DN, who presided over the Council of State from 1981 to 1984.

Representation in the Council of State was not geographic but corporate. Council members had to be Nicaraguan citizens over 18 years of age, and they were designated by the organizations they represented (see Table 1.1). According to the previctory Puntarenas agreement among the rebel coalition groups, the Council was to have 33 members, but the FSLN National Directorate and the Junta expanded its membership to 47 in April 1980. Because most of the new members were from groups allied with the Sandinistas, non-Sandinista groups attacked the move as a power grab. The incident precipitated Alfonso Robelo's resignation from the Junta, although the MDN retained its seat in the Council of State until Robelo and other top MDN figures went into exile in 1982. This expansion of the membership of the Junta helped coalesce the emergent opposition faction within the Council of State.

Membership in the Council expanded to 51 seats in the second session (1981–82) (see Table 1.1). Two of the new seats went to a new pro-Sandinista small farmers group, UNAG, split off from the ATC. (The ATC lost one of its three Council seats with the formation of UNAG.) One new seat each went to the Ecumenical Axis (MEC-CELADEC), a Protestant organization, and to the Liberal Constitutionalist Movement (MLC); and one additional seat went to the Center for Union Action and Unity (CAUS). In protest over aspects of revolutionary policy, three organizations boycotted their Council of State seats in 1982–83: The Democratic Conservative Party (PCDN), the Association of Miskitus, Sumos, and Ramas (MISURASATA), and the Union of Nicaraguan Agricultural Producers (UPANIC).

By its fourth session (1983–84) the Council of State had developed considerably. On July 13, 1982, the Council inaugurated its new seat in the renovated former Central Bank building adjacent to the Junta's House of Government in Managua. The Council had established a review, *Monexico*, named for a consultative assembly of indigenous leaders discovered by the first Spanish to arrive in Nicaragua.[17] The Council had also established a developing legal library, a small professional consulting staff to assist in legal and technical research, and other documentary resources.

The Council was organized into nine standing working commissions: Defense and Interior, Justice, External Affairs, Labor and Social Security, Health and Welfare, Education and Culture, Production and Agrarian Reform, Finance and Popular Consumption, and Community Services, Urban Reform, and Human Settlements. Of the 60 proposed bills studied

TABLE 1.1

MEMBERSHIP AND VOTING STRENGTH IN THE COUNCIL OF
STATE, 1982–1983

Organization	Number of seats
Political parties	
Sandinist National Liberation Front (FSLN)	6
Independent Liberal Party (PLI)	1
Nicaraguan Socialist Party (PSN)	1
Nicaraguan Popular Social Christian Party (PPSC)	1
Nicaraguan Democratic Movement (MDN)	1
Democratic Conservative Party (PCDN)	1
Social Christian Party (PSC)	1
Liberal Constitutionalist Movement (MLC)	1[a]
Popular organizations	
Sandinista Defense Committees (CDSs)	9
July 19th Sandinista Youth (JS 19)	1
Nicaraguan Women's Association (AMNLAE)	1
Labor organizations	
Sandinista Workers Central (CST)	3
Rural Workers Association (ACT)	2
Independent General Workers Confederation (CGTI)	2
Nicaraguan Workers Central (CTN)	1
Union Unity Confederation (CUS)	1
Central for Union Unity and Action (CAUS)	2[a]
Federation of Health Workers (FETSALUD)	1
Guilds and other social organizations	
Armed Forces (FF.AA.SS.)	1
National Association of Clergy (ACLEN)	1
National Council of Higher Education (CNES)	1
National Association of Educators (ANDEN)	1
Nicaraguan Journalists Union (UPN)	1
Association of Miskitus, Sumos, and Ramas (MISURASATA)	1
National Confederation of Professional Associations	1
National Union of Farmers and Cattlemen (UNAG)	2[b]
Ecumenical Axis MEC-CELADEC	1[a]
Private sector organizations	
Nicaraguan Development Institute (INDE)	1
Nicaraguan Chamber of Industries (CADIN)	1
Confederation of Chambers of Commerce (CCCN)	1
Nicaraguan Chamber of Construction (CNC)	1
Union of Nicaraguan Agriculatural Producers (UPANIC)	1
Total representation	51

[a]One seat added in 1981

[b]New as of 1981; one of its seats formerly belonged to the ATC. *Sources:* Consejo de Estado, República de Nicaragua, *Instauración tercera legislatura* (Managua, May 4, 1982), pp. 8–15; and John A. Booth, *The End and Beginning: The Nicaraguan Revolution* (Boulder, Colo.: Westview Press, 1982), Table 9-1, p. 188.

by the Council of State in 1982–83, 16 were introduced by the Junta (see Table 1.2a). Fifteen Junta-initiated bills were approved, the other was returned to the Junta for further study. Of the 44 bills introduced by members of the Council itself, five were rejected, two postponed or suspended, and the remainder were approved. Two of the rejected and suspended bills were introduced by the Nicaraguan Socialist (communist) Party (PSN) and involved urban and rural land tenure matters. Two labor unions (CUS, CST) each introduced a bill to reinstate suspended Easter holidays, but neither was approved.[18]

Overall, the volume of legislation in the Council of State declined in both the second and third sessions. Meanwhile the share of the bills introduced at the initiative of the Junta declined from about 60 percent in the first legislature to about 25 percent in the third (Table 1.2a). The subject matter of legislation also evolved in the early years; the second legislature's heavy emphasis on administrative matters (similar to the JGRN's extensive preoccupation with administrative reorganization from 1979 to 1981) shifted more toward political matters in the third legislature — (Table 1.2b). The fourth (1983–84) session also heavily emphasized political matters; it wrote a military draft law, a political parties law, and an election law specifying the nature of and conditions for the November 1984 elections. Taken together, the declining volume of legislation and the shift away from administrative subject matter indicate that the principal base of the Sandinista revolutionary program had been established by 1984. Moreover, the rising share of Council of State legislative initiatives suggests increasing independence and maturity for this body vis-a-vis the executive.

One key aspect of the Council of State was the participation of several political parties and the emergence by the end of the first legislative session of two opposing coalitions. The National Patriotic Front (FP), a coalition of parties that supported revolutionary programs, included the FSLN, the Popular Social Christians (PPSC), the Independent Liberals (PLI), and the Socialist Party (PSN). The opposition Democratic Coordinating Committee (CD) included the Social Christians (PSCN), Nicaraguan Democratic Movement (MDN), Liberal Constitutionalists (PLC), Social Democrats (PSD), the five private sector groups, and two unions, the CTN and CUS.

Council debate over many issues, especially the Parties Law, Electoral Law, and Draft Law, was often sharp and protracted. Since the CD opposition coalition was consistently in a minority, it rarely prevailed on all its points when it directly confronted the Patriotic Front or the FSLN and its affiliates. The proregime coalition, however, did not entirely disregard the minority opposition's concerns. When Council debate revealed intense

TABLE 1.2
ACTIVITY OF THE COUNCIL OF STATE, 1980–83

2a. Origin and Disposition of Bills, 1980–83.

	I	II	III
Session	1980–81	1981–82	1982–83
Bills introduced (total)	95	77	60
by Junta	56	40	16
by Council	39	37	44
Bills passed	73	73	54
Bills rejected, postponed, or suspended	22	4	6

2b. Subject Matter of Bills Approved[a], 1981–83.

Subject Matter of Bill	1981–82		1982–83	
	Percent	Number	Percent	Number
Administrative	29	(21)	16	(8)
Political	21	(15)	50	(27)
Social	22	(16)	10	(5)
Economic	12	(9)	4	(2)
Cultural	16	(12)	18	(9)
Other	—		2	(1)
Total	100	(73)	100	(52)

[a]Classification of subject matter by Council staff. *Sources:* Consejo de Estado, República de Nicaragua, *Segunda legislatura* (Managua, 1981), p. 11; *Monexico*, No. 2, April 1983, pp. 223–276.

CD opposition on a bill's particulars, the FSLN and the FP often conceded important points to the CD. For instance, 30 percent of the Parties Law approved in 1983 reportedly had been altered at opposition initiative by the Council from the FSLN's draft proposal.[19]

Neither the Council of State's opposition nor proregime coalition was monolithic. The discussion of the Electoral Law in early 1984, for example, opened fissures in the ranks of both the FP and the CD over specifics of the bill. The effect of the November 1984 election upon the Council of State's two coalitions may well have been still more corrosive. In addition to acrimony within both coalitions over the date of the elections (late 1984 versus 1985), there was disagreement within the CD over whether to participate in the elections at all. The PLI, moreover, withdrew from the Patriotic Front to pursue its 1984 campaign independently of the FSLN.[20]

The Judiciary

The Fundamental Statute vacated the benches of the old regime's courts. The JGRN then appointed new justices and judges, chosen for expected competence and honesty and not necessarily associated with the FSLN. The Junta emitted no fewer than eight decrees related to judicial matters in 1979 alone. Major concerns of the early court reorganization were the elimination of corruption and improving the quality of jurisprudence. By 1982 the major problems cited with the courts involved technical problems and severely overcrowded criminal dockets. For example, in 1982 "10,500 persons were processed by the criminal courts but 65 percent of them were not sentenced, only 8.7 percent were tried in a timely manner; more than 5,000 of those detained persons remained in prison."[21]

In 1979 and again in 1983 the nation's Jury Courts were reformed, ultimately reducing their jurisdiction to only the most severe felony crimes in order to unclog crowded jury-trial dockets. Also in 1983 most other crimes were assigned to the jurisdiction of the regular Courts of Justice. In 1980 the Junta established the Superior Labor Court, and in 1981 it created Agrarian Courts. In 1983 exclusive criminal jurisdiction (except in crimes requiring accusations by the victim) was given to the Attorney General and new, more modern criteria of proof were adopted in criminal proceedings. Numerous revisions of legal codes in criminal matters were decreed between 1979 and 1984, with the general goal of modernizing and improving judicial practice.[22]

Revolutionary systems have often used courts as policy tools, but Nicaragua apparently did so while simultaneously improving judicial independence and decisionmaking. Judges regularly ruled against the government, which generally complied with court orders. In 1980 a national law of *amparo* empowered the courts to order redress of administrative excess or error. This law greatly expanded the judicial review power of the courts, but was temporarily suspended by the state of emergency that went into effect in early 1982 and was subsequently extended for several periods well into 1984. Despite the limitation on redress of grievances caused by the suspension of amparo, the Ministries of Justice and Interior manifested continued concern about citizens' rights by seeking (and receiving in 1983) laws expressly outlawing and increasing the penalty for abuse of authority by persons in uniform.[23] A Zelaya judge who sentenced several hundred Miskitu to jail on faulty grounds was removed from office and the victims were released.

Nicaraguan courts collaborated most closely with the Sandinist regime in the trial and punishment of Somoza henchmen and National Guard troops captured during the triumph over the Somoza regime. In December 1979 the JGRN established highly political Special Tribunals to try several thousand prisoners accused of crimes on behalf of the previous government, and to educate the Nicaraguan public about the old regime's vices. Their three-judge panels included as members two ordinary citizens, typically victims of crimes by the Somoza regime, and had several defects from a civil libertarian's point of view.[24] The Special Tribunals, however, were not star-chamber proceedings because all accused had legal representation, the media had access to the trials, and the law applied was not written ex post facto but was the previously extant penal code. Moreover, of some 4,550 defendants, 267 were acquitted and charges against 30 were dropped for lack of evidence. Some 38 percent of those convicted were sentenced to five or fewer years, and 29 percent from 20 to 30 years, the maximum permitted under Nicaraguan law.[25]

The Electoral System

Under intense discussion during the third and fourth Council of State sessions, the election system took shape in late 1984. Although popular organizations and communities elected members of municipal reconstruction juntas, no formal national elections were held until November 4, 1984. The Fundamental Statute had provided for the Junta to convoke elections for a National Assembly "whenever the conditions of national reconstruction might permit."[26] The Electoral Law of 1984 provided for the simultaneous election of a President, Vice-President, and 90-member National Assembly, all for six-year terms. The Assembly was to have both legislative and constituent powers and would thus draft a new constitution to replace the Fundamental Statute. The Assembly's constituency was to be multimember geographical districts with proportional representation of parties according to their share of the votes. Municipal elections were to take place at a later date.

The elections were overseen by a fourth branch of government, the Supreme Electoral Council (CSE), which established the voter registry and conducted the balloting and vote count. Voter registration was supported by all parties and the Church; 1,560,580 persons registered, an estimated 94 percent of the eligible population of persons sixteen years or older. Marred initially by some disturbances, the three-month campaign was generally conducted openly; all parties had a public subsidy and equal, ample, and uncensored access to public television and radio time. The voting system, designed with the assistance of representatives of the Swedish Electoral Commission, provided for complete secrecy of the vote and opposition scrutiny of polling and voting. The election was flawed by the refusal of the CD coalition to take part, and by the last-minute withdrawal of the PLI presidential candidate. The election itself was conducted with virtually no irregularities; turnout was 75 percent. Daniel Ortega and Sergio Ramirez of the FSLN won the presidency and vice-presidency with 67 percent of the valid votes. The FSLN won 63 percent of the National Assembly (61 seats), with the remainder distributed as follows: PLI 10 percent of the vote, 9 seats; PCD 14 percent, 14 seats; PPSC 6 percent, 6 seats; PSN 1 percent, 2 seats; Communist Party 2 percent, 2 seats; Marxist-Leninist Popular Action Movement 1 percent, 2 seats.[27]

PROSPECTS

As of late 1984, five years of revolutionary government had established certain patterns and trends likely to persist for the middle run—barring, of course, a national catastrophe like the widely feared possibility of a U.S. invasion or a dramatic deepening of war with counterrevolutionary forces.

The party system began to define itself much more clearly after the elections. The FSLN had greatly legitimized its rule and would remain the dominant national political movement, controlling the presidency and the National Assembly. The FSLN National Directorate would continue to guide public policy and strongly shape the new constitution. Six other parties won enough votes to survive in the Assembly and among them had 37 percent of its votes—enough to deny the FSLN the two-thirds majority that would be a key to complete Sandinist control of the constitution drafting. The conservative opposition (PPSC, PLI, PCD) would likely form a working coalition to oppose the FSLN in the Assembly. The parties in the abstaining CD (especially the Social Christians and Social Democrats) appeared likely to face decline and even legal dissolution, but a dialogue between the FSLN and the opposition—including CD and church elements—held some promise for their political survival.

Daniel Ortega's presidency promised considerable continuity in executive operations. International pressures for the maintenance of political pluralism would probably lead the FSLN to tap other parties for a few cabinet posts. The National Assembly was likely to build upon the traditions and institutions established during the five sessions of the revolutionary Council of State. The fusion between the FSLN and the armed forces and police—a key guarantor of the security and integrity of the Revolution—was likely to persist in the short run. Indeed, it appeared that FSLN involvement in the national bureaucracy overall would continue at existing levels for many years. Eventual formal separation of the party from the state—especially from the security apparatus—would come only after a cooling of revolutionary ardor and winning of greater security for the Revolution itself, and might yet be decades away.

NOTES

1. Article 11, in *Leyes relacionadas con el Consejo de Estado* (Managua: Consejo de Estado, República de Nicaragua, 1981), p. 8.

2. Articles 24, 26, in ibid., p. 11.

3. Articles 11 and 16, respectively, in ibid., pp. 10–11.

4. Cited from ibid., p. 7.

5. Ibid., p. 8.

6. This material is drawn mainly from interviews with Paul Oquist, Manuel Cordero, and Ariel Granero, of DIGE; and Juán Javané and Róger Vásquez of the Ministry of Planning, Managua, 1980.

7. See, for example, Carlos Tünnerman Bernheim, *Hacia una nueva educación en Nicaragua* (Managua: Ediciones Distribuidora Cultural, 1983), pp. 269–290; *Barricada*, August 12, 1983, p. 1; *Barricada Internacional*, March 5, 1984, p. 9.

8. *Leyes relacionadas*, pp. 87–103.

9. See Charles Downs' chapter on local and regional government in this volume and *Envío Monográfico* (Instituto Histórico Centroamericano, Managua), No. 9 (June 1983), p. 25.

10. *Envío Monográfico*, June 1983, p. 24.

11. *Barricada*, August 12, 1983, p. 1; *Barricada Internacional*, March 5, 1984, p. 3.

12. Carmen D. Deere, Peter Marchetti, S. J., and Nola Reinhardt, "The Evolution of Agrarian Reform Policy in Nicaragua: 1979–1983," *Latin American Research Review* (1985 forthcoming).

13. John M. Donahue, "The Politics of Health Care in Nicaragua before and after the Revolution of 1979," *Human Organization*, 42 (Fall 1983): 264–272.

14. Information from conversations with internationalists working in Nicaraguan bureaucracies.

15. Decree No. 338, Estatuto General del Consejo de Estado," as published in *Leyes relacionadas*, pp. 25–29.

16. The Junta also included three Vice-Presidents and three Secretaries.

17. Francisco Pérez Estrada, "Estado aborigen nicaragüense," *Monexico* 1 (November 1982): 7–11.

18. Data from *Monexico* 2 (April 3, 1983): 223–276.

19. Luis Rivas Leiva, President of the Social Democratic Party, interviewed in *La Nación Internacional*, March 8–14, 1984, p. 8.

20. *Barricada Internacional*, March 5, 1984, p. 3, and February 27, 1984, p. 3–7; *La Nación Internacional*, March 1–7, 1984, p. 7.

21. Quote from Tomás Borge (p. 52) in discussions by Tomás Borge, Minister of Interior, and Carlos Argüello Gómez, Minister of Justice, *Monexico* 1 (November 1982): 51–67.

22. *Monexico* 2 (April 1983): 36–41; *Leyes relacionadas*, p. 83.

23. *Monexico* 1 (November 1982): 67–70.

24. Americas Watch, *On Human Rights in Nicaragua* (New York, May 1982), pp. 27–29.

25. Ibid., p. 30.

26. Article 28, in *Leyes relacionadas*, p. 11.

27. Election material from author's observations, and the "Report of the Latin American Studies Association Delegation to Observe the Nicaraguan General Election of November 4, 1984," *LASA Forum*, Winter 1985, pp. 9–43.

Chapter 2
Local and Regional Government

CHARLES DOWNS

The Sandinista victory of July 1979 brought about an immediate complete transformation of three key institutions: (1) the political leadership of the old state (head of state, ministers, and so on) fled or was removed, the national assembly was dissolved, and a Government Junta of National Reconstruction (JGRN, Junta de Gobierno de Reconstrucción Nacional) was named to run the government; (2) the forces of repression (Guardia Nacional, police) were dissolved, most of their members imprisoned or expelled from the country, and they were replaced by the forces of the FSLN; and (3) the heads of local governments fled, resigned, or were removed and replaced by Municipal Juntas for Reconstruction (JMR, Juntas Municipales de Reconstrucción). Most other institutions underwent some changes, but none to the degree of these three. While initial changes in the national government and armed forces were commonly recognized in international press reports, later alterations in local government and the development of a regional government system received scant attention outside of Nicaragua.

Two years after the violent end of the Somoza dynasty, local governments were under the authority of three- or five-person JMRs. Viewed as a group, a majority of their members were either agricultural

I would like to express my appreciation for the assistance and openness of many dedicated local, regional, and national government representatives. The research summarized herein would not have been possible without their cooperation, although I, of course, am solely responsible for the opinions and conclusions expressed.

The first half of this chapter is a revised and updated version of an article written with Fernando Kusnetzoff: "The Changing Role of Local Government in the Nicaraguan Revolution," *International Journal of Urban and Regional Research* 6, (1982). Portions reprinted with permission. For a more detailed study of the first two years of local government, see the monograph coauthored with Fernando Kusnetzoff: *Decentralization from Above and Below: The Base of Local Government in Nicaragua* (Berkeley: Institute of International Studies, 1981). All translations are by the author.

workers, peasants, or urban workers until they entered public office, and most had never completed their primary school education. The geographic areas they governed remained the same as those of the time of Somoza (despite much debate about their "rationality"): 136 *municipios*, composed much like U.S. counties, with an urban center surrounded by a rural area, with the majority of the population typically residing in the latter. These 136 municipios were historically grouped into 16 *departamentos* without a governmental structure of their own, but beginning in 1982 they were organized in nine administrative regions, each with a government *delegado* at its head.

While the geographic subdivisions did not change, the personnel, operations, and role of government did. Originally, they were virtually always the province of the landed or urban elite, often the personal fief of an individual wealthy local landowner or businessman. While carrying out their main social functions of collecting taxes and registering births and deaths, they were an intermediate step of patronage, providing access to a moderate amount of power, income, and opportunities for corruption for local supporters of the regime. With the defeat of Somoza, many local officials fled, in some cases replicating on a smaller scale the final acts of pillage of the dictator, as they looted the local treasury, destroyed existing records of property and population, and carried what equipment they could across the border. While certainly not all local officials were dishonest or chose to flee, both they and their employees were soon replaced, and the turnover was virtually complete. In fact, the only clear requirements specified for being a member of the new JMRs were to "be over twenty-one years of age, a citizen in the full exercise of ones rights, of known honesty and moral character, be a resident of the locality, and not have had any relation with the corruption of the previous regime."[1] As of 1984, the JMRs were composed of people who had no previous experience of working in local government, and only about 5 percent of their employees had worked for the old regime.

Following the initial transformations produced on the heels of the popular Triumph, there were further developments and changes with regard to the JMR, its personnel, and its relation to other local governmental and nongovernmental institutions, and later the development of regional government structures. These changes can be considered in four periods defined by the primary objective problem to be faced at the national and local levels. These are: recovery from the emergency caused by the final period of the war of liberation (second semester 1979); reconstruction of that which was destroyed during the war (1979 to mid-1981); preliminary institutional consolidation of the JMRs and local political relations (mid-1981 to mid-1982); and regionalization and decentralization of the central government (mid-1982 through 1984).

Needless to say, there were overlaps and not all local governments were equally representative of the type or timing of changes. While tasks and activities of all phases continued simultaneously, only one was dominant at any given time. Thus these periods characterize changes in the system of subnational government as a whole and are crucial for understanding its crises and development.

RECOVERY FROM THE WAR EMERGENCY

The first phase of the JMRs corresponds to the period of initial recovery from the war. In this period the JMRs were created to directly embody the broad national unity created in the struggle to overthrow Somoza, to reestablish the state by representing the authority of the central government as well as the views of the local population, and to act through emergency measures when necessary to resolve critical problems with relatively little central assistance.

At the time of the victory, the FSLN and the broad political alliance that had supported it found themselves in charge of a war-ravaged country without a central government to direct it. It is conservatively estimated that 35,000 people (1.5 percent of the national population) died in the final eight-month effort to overthrow Somoza, 80 percent of whom were civilians killed by government bombardment. An additional 100,000 were wounded and another 40,000 children orphaned.[2] Some $500 million of property damage was done, a large number of factories were partially or totally destroyed, planting had been interrupted, and fleeing government and military leaders had looted the national treasury, illegally transferring out several hundred million dollars, and leaving only about $3 million in reserves—worth approximately 1.5 days of imports. In addition, the flow of food, water, medical supplies, and so on, had been interrupted in many parts of the country.

The new government's attempt to respond to the emergency of sheltering, feeding, and caring for the population while setting the society functioning again was complicated by a further problem: While a national government had been formed representing the unity of the social forces that had opposed Somoza, at the local level in most places there was neither a representation of that unity nor a government to direct practical activities.

Three responses were tried in the first days: (1) the regional FSLN military commander was often called upon to act as the highest authority in the area; (2) the Comités de Defensa Civil (CDCs, Civilian Defense Committees; later, CDS Sandinista Defense Committees), which previously organized noncombatants and provided logistic support to the anti-

Somoza struggle, coordinated neighborhood cleanup campaigns, saw that the homeless were housed, food was distributed to all, and so on; and (3) in the major urban areas liberated during the final two weeks of the war, local juntas were established to represent the unity of the national government (still in exile) and direct local affairs. These juntas, composed of respected and charismatic individuals known for their opposition to Somoza and commitment to democracy, were ratified in public assemblies. In the first weeks and months after victory this became the basic procedure followed to establish the JMRs throughout the country.

RECONSTRUCTION

The second period, which can be dated from about October 1979, focused on reconstruction from the war, once the worst period of emergency was past. Factories and machinery began to be rebuilt or replaced and put back into operation, while planting resumed on farms. Significant amounts of soft loans and other foreign aid were received and applied to the systematic reconstruction of Chinandega, Estelí, Managua, León, Matagalpa, and Rivas—the six cities that had suffered the most severe damage in the war. Lesser grants and loans were provided to the JMRs of small and medium sized municipios to carry out important repairs and fill long-standing needs, especially in the public health area (slaughterhouses and markets). In one year, the JGRN's Secretariat for Municipal Affairs (SAMU, Secretaría de Asuntos Municipales) provided financing to local governments for 25 times more local improvement projects than Somoza's municipal development agency had financed during its entire two-year existence.

In many respects this was a period that focused on "catching up," with goals that seemed clear and reasonable. On the physical side this meant reconstruction to replace what existed before the war in the main cities, plus the provision of facilities accepted as normal in most countries: for example, paved streets, running water, rain and waste water drainage, markets, and so on. On the social side this involved resolving the worst problems of backwardness—the very high illiteracy, infant mortality, and endemic disease rates—by means of the literacy and public health campaigns.

During this period the problems tackled were relatively evident; the issues were technical ones of how to go about it and what should be the priorities given limited resources. At the beginning of this period the office that had overseen the naming of JMRs around the country was expanded and reorganized into SAMU in order to respond to the flood of requests for assistance in personnel training, operations, financial and technical aid, and so· on. This change characterized the JMRs as well. The shift from the principal need for charismatic leadership and unity during the postwar emergency to dealing with the problems of major reconstruction with financial and technical assistance, together with carrying out the normal tasks of local administration (vital statistics and tax collections) placed new and different demands on local officials. Some did not adapt well to the greater weight of administrative tasks, and some turnover in personnel resulted.

While the reconstruction period was characterized most strongly by the problems of extensive physical rebuilding as well as ongoing administration, there were other important social and political changes that affected local government. The activities of government were carried out by people representing the popular unity embodied in the Revolution, individually without previous experience in government and as a group from classes that had not previously shared in power. It was not to be a simple change in personnel; these people believed in the importance of maintaining and developing the popular participation that had made the Revolution possible and should, it was felt, define the priority of problems to be solved in the future. Thus, while the concept of reconstruction was fairly straightforward, it was carried out under the control of new political forces, seeking a greater involvement of the mass of the population, resulting in changes in both operations and priorities (for example, the decision in one city to pave the streets connecting the city center to outlying poor neighborhoods before repairing central streets).

In the same way that some JMRs did not adapt well to the administrative demands of this period, others had difficulties with the demands of the necessarily more open and sometimes conflictual forms that mass participation involves. The consensus among JMR *coordinadores* (heads) was that the population held the JMRs responsible for all that occurred in their territory, and thus it was the JMRs that felt the pressure whenever a problem arose, regardless of which government agency was really at fault. Some members resigned as a result, and in some other cases the grass roots organizations exercised their right to demand their recall. The JMR of one large city illustrates both of the preceding pressures:

> The first Junta was nominated during the war, and had a very important role during a certain time. It was nominated by popular consensus, in an open public meeting, which the *Somocistas* took advantage of to send a helicopter with a 500 pound bomb—but everyone escaped unharmed. Its work centered mainly on the creation of a broad political front, the solution of problems of supplying food, water, electricity, etc., and the initiation of plans for reconstruction. These were immediate problems, not medium term ones like paving streets, building schools, etc. Once the war was over and the euphoric period following it had passed, the JMR

no longer corresponded well to the new situation. It did not succeed in carrying out the necessary political work: the *coordinador* had little contact with the base, and the JMR became distant from the grass-roots organizations. At the same time, neither did it carry out the necessary renovation of the internal structures of the local administration. It produced neither clear direction nor planning, and left the administrative part in great disorder. There was a need for greater charisma and ability than that of the JMR.[3]

Whether turnover resulted from administrative or political demands, replacements were chosen through a process of consultation by local FSLN leaders with the grass-roots organizations of the area who selected the new JMR members. For example, one five-person JMR included two members selected by the CDS:

They were elected through a process that began with block-level elections, which presented candidates at the *barrio* (neighborhood) level, leaving eight final candidates out of which two were elected by the city-wide executive of the CDS. The CST and the ATC each elected their representatives internally as well.

This process commonly gave a strong representation to the CDSs, which were organized to focus on neighborhood and local affairs; but it also included representatives of whichever other organizations were locally important, be they CST (urban unions), AMNLAE (women), ATC (rural unions), UNAG (small farmers), teachers, and occasionally even political parties.

Thus while JMRs in the first phase were composed of individuals selected as charismatic and trusted local citizens, after turnover in the second phase they consisted of representatives chosen by the principal mass organizations. Nevertheless, the administrative tasks came to predominate over the political ones during this period, in part because the very limited budgets (more than 50 percent of JMRs operated on budgets of less than $10,000 annually—not enough to pay their staff minimum wage, let alone make local improvements) led the JMR members to take on many of the local administrative responsibilities, but also because many of the priority tasks of the reconstruction period were largely administrative.

This period involved much experimentation with mass participation in local decisionmaking and implementation. Many communities gained improvements (water supplies, street paving, clinics, and school buildings) that were possible only through the multiplication of government resources by the organization and labor of the community applied to local priority projects. Community input took many forms, including personal contacts, large public meetings, demonstrations, and in some cases organized advisory councils representing local organizations (community organizations, chambers of commerce, local progressive notables, and so on).[4] Thus, while carrying out reconstruction tasks, the JMRs were in the midst of experimentation with new forms of organizations, decisionmaking, and implementation.

As noted earlier, the JMRs had very limited resources with which to respond to local problems and priorities. While resources were generally scarce, most of the material resources were in the hands of one or another central government agency. The local or regional offices of these agencies generally had their own directives from a central office to which they were accountable, and convincing them to adapt their plans to locally determined priorities often required a certain amount of sometimes conflictual pressure.

Partly in response to this problem, but largely to facilitate planning and complementarity while reducing redundancy between agencies, sectorial coordinating committees at the regional or departmental level (CPCR, Comités Programáticos de Coordinación Regional [Regional Program Coordinating Committees]) were established for the agencies involved in each of five areas: agriculture, industry, trade, infrastructure, and social services. The CPCRs also included representatives of the Ministry of Planning, local government, and of the grass-roots organizations relevant to the sector. A Departmental Planning Council was also established, composed of the heads of each CPCR, the delegate of the Ministry of Planning, the local government of the main city, and representatives of the departmental committees of each of the grass-roots organizations as well as of the FSLN. While without binding authority, these bodies increased cooperation in decisionmaking and reduced the frictions resulting from its attempts to exercise that influence. The main limitations encountered in their operation involved the lack of importance attributed to them by some ministerial delegates to the CPCR, the lack of information some of these delegates had about their own ministry's plans, and the excessive centralization of much ministerial decisionmaking that did not leave leeway for local delegates to adjust their plans.

Coordinating councils for the JMRs of each departamento (Intermunicipales) were also created during the reconstruction period to help resolve these problems. The Intermunicipales, composed of the JMR coordinators, sought to provide a mutually supportive forum to share resources and experiences, to analyze problems of the JMRs and municipios, and to propose corrections for inappropriate government actions as well as to request needed training or investments. The JMR coordinators were unanimous in their enthusiasm for this body, saying: "The Intermunicipal is a very positive development—one of the most positive things that has been tried. Spirit is very high there as we face our problems together, gathering the experiences of different municipios and juntas that may be applicable elsewhere." Again, although without binding authority, they proved very useful for the exchange of practical information, coordination of demands and pressure, and served as a possible nucleus for a future departmental government.

PRELIMINARY INSTITUTIONAL CONSOLIDATION

The period of reconstruction drew to a close in about mid-1981. Not all that had existed previously had been reconstructed, but a large share of it had and other steps had been taken toward removing the worst scars of backwardness. Political discussion focused on possible lines of future political, economic, and social development and the institutional changes they might entail. In the meantime efforts were made to spread and consolidate the most useful experiments in dealing with the three major problem areas already identified: internal functioning of local government itself, relations to grass-roots organizations, and relations to central government agencies.

Local Government

The effective functioning of the basic local government unit—the JMR and its administrative staff—encountered three basic problems by the end of the second year of the Revolution. First, there was disruption resulting from unpredictable turnover of JMR members. As of June 1981, roughly 40 percent of Junta members had entered as the result of change in the local JMR. The second problem was the lack of clarity in the local governments' political and administrative tasks, causing one or both to suffer. The importance of this problem and the disruptive impact of JMR turnover were increased by the fact that some 90 percent of JMR members had administrative responsibilities. These overlapping responsibilities in turn resulted partially from the third problem: the fact that local government typically did not have sufficient funds for staff nor for local improvement projects.

A number of partial solutions were considered. The issue of simultaneous political and administrative demands on the same people underlay many of the other problems. Thus a policy was implemented to specify and separate these functions as clearly as possible. To make this policy more feasible, by reducing the economic pressures that contributed to the problem, SAMU began subsidizing the salary expense of maintaining a minimum staff of four for the administrative tasks, permitting the JMR to concern themselves more with the political ones. Finally, while local governments will never have enough resources for all necessary local projects, they in fact had enough for almost none. Recognizing that effective local decisionmaking requires that some resources be under the discretionary control of local government, efforts were made to provide such funds.

Generally, experience showed that the principal resources for local development were those in the hands of the sectoral ministries, and those resulting from the contribution of the organized population. In addition to bettering the internal functioning of local government, its improved overall functioning depended upon the development of communication and influence mechanisms linking the JMRs, the grass-roots organizations, and the central government agencies.

Local Population and Grass-Roots Organizations

As suggested by the common saying that "the JMRs are the face of the Revolution," improvements in local conditions and in the relations between the local government and the populations were often the most visible changes brought about by the Revolution. Throughout the country people at all levels insisted on the importance of close relations between JMRs and the organized population, while noting some of the complexities of such relations. A CDS departmental representative said: "They should always work closely together: CDS, Junta, state agencies. In that way both the grass-roots organizations and the Juntas will be strengthened, but only to the degree the central government responds." And the coordinator of a populous urban municipio insisted:

> The JMRs must work in close relation with the grass-roots organizations. There is a tendency to use the CDSs as a support for the JMRs and other state agencies, when they actually need our support. Many forget that the grass-roots organizations are not there simply to consolidate the JMRs, but rather they can consolidate each other by taking care to reinforce the appropriate role of the grass-roots organizations. They should be put at the front of the masses, supported, and always taken into consideration. In the final analysis, it is the JMRs and the state agencies that, within their limits, can respond to local problems, not the CDSs. But it is important that they be felt in all decisions and public administration. They can be consolidated by channeling the JMRs' work through the grass-roots organizations, which in turn will help con- solidate the JMRs.

JMR and CDS representatives insisted that such close relations were important to strengthen both the grass-roots organizations and the JMRs; to guarantee the representativity of local government and orient its decisions; to provide support for the JMRs in negotiations with other governmental and private agents; and to contribute resources and labor directly to solving some problems. In addition to these concrete local reasons, the political project of the Sandinista Revolution, with its nationalist, democratic, and popular orientation, emphasized the importance of the participation of the organized population in the management and direction of the state, and it focused on the relation beween the JMRs and the grass-roots organizations as one of the primary bases for the development and expression of popular power.

Such relations took place in many ways, but especially through the direct representation of grass-roots organizations on the JMRs, open meetings to inform and seek information from the population, consultation with the community as to specific and general local problems and priorities, and, finally, working together to remedy them. However, the relations of informing and consulting with the local population frequently depended upon informal and personal contacts, which were very effective in some cases but necessarily subject to wide variations. In particular, they sometimes proved inadequate to maintain a balance between local urban and rural interests as well as to include business interests.

Based on the success of local consultative councils in a few areas, Popular Municipal Development Councils were formed around the country. Some three-fourths of JMRs had such advisory councils by the second quarter of 1982. These councils demonstrated the extent to which some problems were the result of lack of information and poor communication, and thus the importance of continuing efforts to develop sufficient channels of two-way communication between JMRs and the population. Another mechanism generally adopted was to hold periodic "Face the People" public assemblies to discuss local administration and municipal problems.

As with all other activities of the JMRs, if a strong involvement of the grass-roots organizations and population was to be sustained, there was a need for some discretionary resources available to use according to their criteria and some possibility of influencing the use of central government resources.

Relations with Central Government Agencies

As suggested earlier, various agencies of the central government had the resources and direct responsibility for most of the maintenance and investments necessary for local improvements, and their action or inaction produced many of the conflicts between local government and others. In discussion with JMR members and central government delegates this situation was often described in terms of the "unresponsiveness" of one or the "interference" of the other. But it was actually a product of the particular structure of unbalanced interdependence in which they were bound.

This was a conflict over who was to decide on the use of public resources, and more generally what were the respective roles of local territorial governments and central sectoral agencies. Underlying this conflict was the strong centralization of ministerial decisionmaking in Managua, such that many regional delegates were not empowered to adapt their programs—and often were not even fully informed as to their own ministry's plans for work in the area. A CDS departmental representative accurately summed up the situation:

> By necessity the Junta has taken on the role of the central government agencies. The JMR members are representatives of the grass-roots organizations and have understood the role of a departmental government. Due to the lack of decentralization the state agencies do not have the autonomy to decide on their own work programs. As a result, the Junta is presented with many problems that do not belong to it, and is expected to resolve them.

The experiments with voluntary coordination mentioned earlier improved the situation significantly but had apparently reached the limits possible given the extreme centralization of decisionmaking, information, and resources. In the second quarter of 1982 the problem of centralization became a direct concern of the leadership of the government and of the FSLN. The resulting policy of decentralization had far-reaching implications not only for local government but for government, politics, and development as a whole.

REGIONALIZATION AND DECENTRALIZATION

In 1982 the main public events commemorating the anniversary of the Revolution were held in Masaya, a symbolic shift of concentration away from Managua. Anniversary speeches are typically occasions to announce major new policies, and this was no exception. The only new policy presented on July 19, 1982, was the establishment of nine regions with their respective authorities, responsible to resolve problems as they arose, adapt central policies to local conditions, and generally improve the operations of government. Regionalization, as a first step in a thorough-going decentralization, was to be a major reform of the state apparatus. In the following pages I will consider the main rationales for this policy, the measures actually adopted and projected, and a preliminary evaluation of the situation after two years, noting in particular the impact on local government.

Decentralization was the radical institutional approach adopted in response to two types of problems—regional inequalities and government inefficiency—as well as to build on successful limited experiences with regional or departmental coordination and decisionmaking.

Regional inequalities were approached from several perspectives. Any measure of economic or industrial development, or public or private sector investment, or of public health conditions (infant mortality, and so on) will show the predominance of the Pacific—and especially of Managua—over the rest of the country. Differences also stand out between the cities and the rest of the country, as well as between regions, with the Atlantic Coast area at the bottom of most comparisons and a special case in terms of lack of integration with the rest of the country. Regionalization signified an immediate partial response to these inequalities by providing increased human and technical resources to most regions, along with a direct allocation of investment funds to the regional governments and an insistence on considering regional distribution in the evaluation of proposed public sector investments. While decentralization would not resolve all existing problems, it would facilitate greater attention to the specific problems and potential of each region, permitting development planning according to the economic potential of each region.

The main goal of decentralization was to improve the efficiency of government operations and the effectiveness of the use of public resources. "The central pillar of revolutionary expression, the way the content of the Revolution is materialized, is the action of the government" argued one FSLN commander.[5] But centralization of decisionmaking in Managua and the lack of coordination between ministries rendered that action much less effective than it should have been. The centralization of decisionmaking at the upper levels of all ministries brought about large and unnecessary delays on both small and large issues and it often produced inappropriate decisions. Furthermore it congested the central ministries with details while stifling local initiative. While centralization already existed during the Somoza regime, it was now a much greater problem precisely because of the quantum increase in government programs and initiatives brought about by the Revolution. The solution: bring decisionmaking power closer to the problems, build on local initiatives, and use them to stimulate the central ministries to improve their own programs.

Decentralizing decisionmaking would not be sufficient to deal with the fact that responding to most problems required the joint action of several agencies. As one FSLN leader put it, "all state services are mutually dependent . . . and therefore require coordination."[6] For this to be effective requires that the agencies being coordinated have similar competences in terms of both hierarchical and geographic authority.

Given the ineffectiveness of the formal decisionmaking structure, a sort of regime of exception continued to exist, and necessary decisions were often made by people without the formal authority to do so. This commonly immersed FSLN militants in the details of government operations, to the detriment of their political work. Arguing that "the role of FSLN militants should not be to execute government policy, but rather to carry out political organizational work and support and watch over all activities involved in transforming the country,"[7] the FSLN leadership saw regionalization as an important step in the institutionalization of the government so that each body could fulfill its own responsibilities.

Finally, the decision to regionalize was also based on a certain accumulation of experience, starting with the development of separate but coordinate fronts during the insurrection, continuing through the experiments of department-level coordination described earlier, and culminating in a number of emergency situations in 1982 (armed invasion, flooding, drought) that were dealt with through specially created regional authorities. Viewed as quite positive, this experience served as the basis for the regionalization and decentralization begun in the second half of 1982.

Decree No. 1081, of July 26, 1982, established nine administrative regions for all government functions: six Regions (each composed of two to four departments) and three Special Zones (all on the Atlantic Coast, two corresponding to northern and southern Zelaya and one to the department of Río San Juan) as shown in Figure 2.1. The law also named a delegate of the coordinator of the JGRN as the highest decisionmaking authority in each region, charged with ensuring coordination of government activities, within the guidelines of the National Plan, and mandated the naming of regional delegates for each of seven priority ministries. Thus began the first phase, "regionalization and coordination," to be followed by a second phase of "decentralization and dual subordination," followed in turn by a third phase of "full regional government and economic administration." The government set no time limits for the phases and recognized that they were likely to overlap somewhat.

The first phase would involve the creation of more effective institutional structures and authority at the regional level together with the preparation of a regional development plan and the practice of coordination. The second phase would encompass the implementation of the approved plan, with the regional authority providing operational direction and the respective ministries providing normative direction. The third phase was understood as the full functioning of the relations developed in the previous two periods, augmented by greater budgetary resources and authority over public sector enterprises of regional or local significance. The following pages consider the development of the first phase in the period up to spring 1984.

First, the Regionalization Law established the regions and named the

FIGURE 2.1 REGIONS AND SPECIAL ZONES

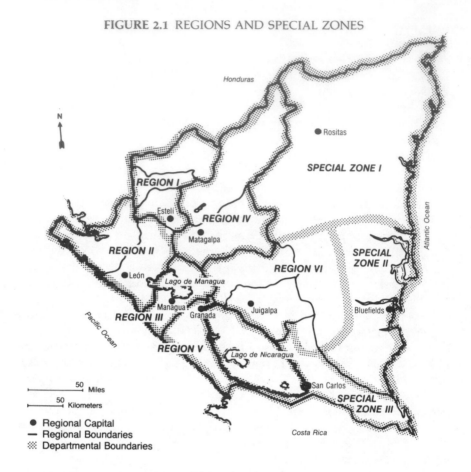

delegates of the JGRN who were to head each region. During the ensuing six weeks their budgets were approved, they took office and began hiring staff. At the same time the FSLN was reorganized under Regional Committees, and the mass organizations began similar restructuring processes.

Second, two secretariats supporting the Regional Government Delegate began taking shape. The Secretariat of Municipal Affairs was to oversee and develop the JMRs and local participation. The Technical Secretariat, composed of a Secretary and staff from the Planning Ministry, the Census Institute, and the national Budget Office, was to oversee government operations and develop a regional plan.

Third, the following priority ministries received expanded budgets and began naming their regional delegates: Agrarian Reform and Development (MIDINRA), Public Works (MICONS), Internal Commerce

(MICOIN), Education (MED), Health (MINSA), Industry (MIND), and the Banking System (SFN).

Fourth, sectoral commissions were established to coordinate the ministries grouped into productive, social, or infrastructure development. In addition an Institutional Council was established, composed of all government agencies, where broader regional policy was to be discussed.

Finally, a Regional Revolutionary Council was established, composed of the region's government agencies, JMRs, mass organizations, and other political and military structures. It was defined as a consultative body to analyze regional issues, receive periodic reports of government actions, and help find solutions to problems encountered.

Together these measures were intended to create a regional level of authority able to respond to some immediate problems, to develop its own plans for future development, to direct the various ministries and government as a whole in the search for the best way to use all available resources, to develop the institutional capacity of the government and each ministry to fulfill its responsibilities, while institutionalizing a channel of regional popular participation.

Overall the regionalization phase of the decentralization centered on important institutional reforms to further administrative efficiency and economic development. It largely achieved its goals and provided a significant improvement in the speed and effectiveness of government action. Government programs were now seen as less bureaucratic and more appropriate to local conditions. This could be seen not only in routine administration and decisionmaking, but also in the increased number and variety of regional development programs, whose growth reduced Managua's share of public sector investment from 75 to 40 percent. But it did not all take place smoothly.

Problems immediately arose with the naming of the vice-ministerial-level regional delegates for each of the priority ministries. Many ministries had difficulty finding sufficient people competent both technically and politically to head and staff their regional delegations. Some ministries created tensions by not respecting the spirit of the reforms and not consulting with the new head of the region regarding their own delegations. Most of the regional capitals did not have sufficient housing, office space, and so on, to cope with the resulting influx, contributing to the difficulty of finding personnel. While these problems existed throughout the country, they were much more severe in the Atlantic Coast Special Zones. Initial proposals spoke of massive transfers of personnel from Managua, thus avoiding further increases in state employment and budgets. However, the actual transfer proved to be less and the net increases greater than expected. Still, nearly all the delegations of priority ministries were functioning by the end of 1982. Once they began functioning many practical questions arose regarding the degree of authority, autonomy, and resources of these delegations together with the legitimate degree of intervention of the regional governments. These problems, reflecting the difference between voluntary coordination and dual subordination, were likely to continue for some time.

It soon became clear that significant bottlenecks were resulting from the nonpriorization of certain ministries. It was generally recognized that regionalization could not progress very far without regional planning. While advances had been made in planning, the Planning Ministry—the core of the regional governments' Technical Secretariat—was not regionalized. Its regional offices remained directly dependent only on the national office of regional planning. Similarly the Census Institute was criticized for collecting largely irrelevant data that were sent to Managua and returned only after many months. Other ministries whose lack of regionalization was identified as an obstacle included Transportation (MITRANS), Fishing (INPESCA), and Housing (MINVAH).

Coordination improved, but not through the structures designed for that purpose. The sectoral coordinating commissions began functioning in late 1982, with the appropriate regional delegates or heads of departmental offices in their absence. Most of the commissions had ceased functioning by mid-1983. There were a number of causes. Immediate difficulties arose because of the continuing lack of information, authority, and resources in the hands of the various regional delegates and officials. Many of the problems brought to the commissions focused on relations between an office and its central ministry, or other specific situations for which the agency wanted the support of the head of the region. These problems could be more productively dealt with in bilateral meetings rather than taking up the time of the full commission. Furthermore, once certain major problems were resolved, the regional governments sought to avoid substituting themselves for the ministries, insisting that the latter carry out their own functions properly. In general, the infrastructure commission failed because its member ministries were not decentralized and lacked the ability to commit their own resources; the social commission for lack of any clear project of its own; and the economic commission duplicated and generally merged into the existing agrarian reform commissions.

While the proximate source of the breakdown of the commissions was the existing insufficient level of decentralization, a more basic cause was the fact that most necessary coordination was between rather than within sectors and involved some or all of the productive sector ministries. Starting in early 1984, coordination was being established around particular programs or issues that required a high interdependence between ministries. Depending on the region this might be the agricultural cycles of coffee, cotton, grains, and so on, resettlement programs, public health, or others. This had not resolved the question of the respective authority of the ministry, regional delegation, or regional government, but was contributing to smoother implementation of government programs while establishing clear areas and mechanisms of coordination. Furthermore, the definition of necessary mutual responsibilities facilitated government and popular participation in oversight.

A further step to increase oversight of the implementation of regional decisions, coordination, and effective rapid response at the local level can be seen in the development of a zonal level of administration, generally grouping together one to three municipios. The head of the region appointed a zonal delegate to oversee the actions of the ministries in that zone. The regionalized ministries in turn reorganized their structures to include a zonal level of authority and sought to define their own programs to this level. This structure developed from the highly successful experience of responding in this way to the problems of defense, production, and relocation of refugees during the counterrevolutionary assault on the area of Jalapa in the spring of 1983. One year later it was still an evolving structure, with a wide range of relations between zonal delegates and JMRs. But it was clear that it provided an essential element to more effective governance by the JMRs and greater popular participation.

The Nicaraguan regionalization was a set of thoroughgoing institutional reforms intended to improve state administration. While oriented toward improving government responsiveness to local needs, the reforms did not concern themselves particularly with institutions of democratic participation. They were administrative reforms and did not try to integrate the experience of the JMRs regarding participation. The one such institution contemplated by the reforms—the Regional Revolutionary Council—did not function as hoped. Instead the regional governments encouraged participation through "Face the People" sessions, annual public progress reports of government programs and goals, and individual meetings with interested organizations. In addition, some Popular Municipal Development Councils continued to function, and beginning in early 1984 some councils were broadened with representatives from rural communities and new settlements that arose with the development of cooperatives and massive relocations occasioned by the counterrevolutionary aggression.

CONCLUSION

Local government was one of the institutions most thoroughly transformed in the early period of the Revolution. Leadership was transferred to the previously dispossessed, especially to farmers, agricultural laborers, and workers. As the body responsible for governing its territory, it became the focus of participation and demands unleashed by the Revolution, and it tried to move the greatly expanded gamut of public sector activities in the direction it felt best corresponded to local needs and national priorities.

During the first two and one half years of the Revolution major progress was made in developing this national experiment in local popular government and democracy. Unlike the situation in many other countries, in the Nicaraguan Revolution local government demonstrated the important political, economic, and social roles it can fulfill, particularly in terms of directing popular mobilization, encouraging democratic participation, and transforming institutional relations both within the state and between the state and population. Of the three broad problems encountered, two were being resolved. Local officials were learning to fulfill their administrative responsibilities and forms of local democratic participation were being developed and institutionalized. The essential remaining problem was to direct and coordinate central government programs in directions most appropriate to local needs and development, given that their local offices were powerless to direct their own activities, the JMRs had no legal authority over them, and all their decisions had to be made in the central offices in Managua.

Regionalization was the first step in responding to the problem of centralization. It involved a set of institutional reforms and, while not all regions or ministries developed at the same rate, it was largely successful in meeting its goals. Government activities now responded much better to local conditions, and major steps were taken toward institutionalizing the government: ministries were assuming more of their responsibilities, and the JMRs came to resolve higher level problems through recourse to the regional government rather than to the FSLN.

However, the regional government did not always act locally through the JMRs. In the short term, the development of the regional governments was partially at the cost of the JMRs. In part, this was because they lost the de facto power some exercised at the departmental level; but more importantly, it was because to a certain extent they were abandoned while attention was focused elsewhere.

It was certainly necessary to strengthen the state, in the sense that the regionalization had, before the JMRs could be developed further. An institutional infrastructure now existed that could allow both to develop further. Some ministries felt the regionalization and influence of regional governments had already gone too far. They pointed to the increased demands they received from the local population and government, and compared that to their very limited resources. But the increase in popular demands and supervision was a necessary product of increased government development activities and the general conviction of the people that it was *their* government. As the Secretary for Municipal Affairs for one region said,

> popular participation can be conflictual, but that is what has always given life to the JMRs, and has made them best able to interpret local needs and government programs. It might be more comfortable for the ministries and bureaucrats if there were not wider participation, but that is not popular power—that is not revolution.

NOTES

1. Ley Creadora de las Juntas Municipales de Reconstrucción, Article 5 (Managua, January 28, 1980).

2. United Nations Economic Commission on Latin America, *Notas sobre la economía y el desarrollo de América Latina*, No. 301–302 (Santiago, Chile, 1979).

3. Unless otherwise specified, all quotations are from interviews carried out by the author.

4. See Charles Downs, "Building Democracy from the Ruins," *Nicaraguan Perspectives*, No. 6 (Summer 1983), for a discussion of one of the first such advisory councils. Formed as a direct response to local business opposition to a new local tax schedule, it successfully provided a channel of input for all sectors of the population, even resulting in higher tax revenues due to increased business cooperation.

5. Commander Bayardo Arce, interviewed in *Barricada*, August 14, 1982.

6. Ibid.

7. Ibid.

Chapter 3

The Grass-Roots Organizations

LUIS HÉCTOR SERRA

The objective of this chapter is to analyze the role of the major grass-roots organizations (*organizaciones populares*, OPs) and the problems and contradictions they confronted in the first stage of the Sandinista Revolution. Before the overthrow of Somoza, the Revolution promoted a broad-based process of organization and popular participation in various aspects of social life. Through the grass-roots organizations an original type of democratic political system then developed in revolutionary Nicaragua. The revitalization of the political parties in preparation for the November 1984 elections did not change the fundamental characteristics of this political system, which rested on the OPs, which, in turn, recognized the leadership of the FSLN.

THE SPECIFIC GRASS-ROOTS ORGANIZATIONS

Large, broad-based organizations first developed during the insurrectional period (1978–79) and then grew very rapidly after the overthrow of Somoza. The repression exercised during 44 years of dictatorship had restricted the development of grass-roots organizations that might have questioned the power of Somoza. After the Triumph, virtually all OPs declared their support for the revolutionary process and recognized the leading role of the FSLN. Thus, one can interchangeably refer to "mass organizations," "popular organizations," "Sandinista organizations," grass-roots organizations," or "revolutionary organizations." As of mid-1984, the six principal OPs were the Sandinista Defense Committees, the Sandinista Workers Federation, the Rural Workers Association, the National Union of Farmers and Ranchers, the Luisa Amada Espinosa Nicaraguan Women's Association, and the Sandinista Youth.

The editor would like to thank Charles Roberts of the Central American Historical Institute at Georgetown University for the skillful translation of this chapter and Chapter 17.

The largest OP in both membership and geographic coverage were the Sandinista Defense Committees, which were created on a territorial basis. The CDSs were initiated during the insurrection, as Civil Defense Committees, carrying out such tasks as organizing the supply of basic goods to the population, keeping track of Somocistas and common delinquents, providing safe houses and arms deposits for combatants, and generally supporting the struggle against the dictatorship. The important role played by neighborhood organizations in the insurrection was one of the original characteristics of the Sandinista Revolution.

The CDSs were the most heterogeneous OP, as they took in the most diverse social sectors. Membership was open to all persons 14 years of age or older, without regard to sex, religious beliefs, or membership in any other social or political organization. In this first stage of the Revolution the CDSs were oriented to the integral defense of the nation and to community development. By 1984 there were 15,000 CDS Base Committees organized by block or housing nuclei throughout the country (with the exception of Northern Zelaya). Approximately 520,000 to 600,000 members participated.[1] There were also OPs for urban and rural labor.

Before the overthrow of Somoza, grass-roots organizations were mostly developed among the trade union sector, though such unions reached only 6 percent of the urban working class.[2] The proletariat was small as a result of the country's industrial underdevelopment, in which small productive units prevailed. The trade union movement was weak as a result of repression, high structural unemployment, and the variety of existing trade union federations.

In July 1979 there were 133 trade unions, with 27,020 affiliates. By December 1983, however, there were 1,103 unions registered with the Ministry of Labor, with a total of 207,391 members. The unions supportive of the Revolution constituted 93 percent of the total, with 88 percent of the membership.[3] The most important were the Sandinista Workers Federation (Central Sandinista de Trabajadores, CST) with 504 unions and 111,498 members of the urban proletariat, and the Rural Workers Association (Asociación de Trabajadores del Campo, ATC), with 480 unions and 40,000 affiliates based in the rural work force.

The CST expanded rapidly after the Triumph, with an average of 32 new unions per month in its first year. During its first period it experienced serious friction with other trade union federations, including both rightist and ultraleftist federations, which promoted strikes and work stoppages for economic demands that did not take into account either the limitations of the national economy or the character of the new state. By 1984, many unions that had belonged to those federations voluntarily joined the CST.

The ATC arose in March 1978 out of the Rural Workers Committees that first formed in 1976 to protest the miserable working conditions of the peasantry and the repression suffered at the hands of the National Guard. Another initial source of members for the ATC was the movement of the Delegates of the Word formed by progressive Catholics. In its first stage, the ATC organized both agricultural workers and private producers with small- and medium-sized landholdings. In 1981 the private producers formed their own organization. The ATC then developed for the most part on the state farms.

The ATC and CST were the main forces behind the process of trade union unification that led, in 1981, to the creation of the Trade Union Coordinating Committee of Nicaragua (Coordinadora Sindical de Nicaragua, CSN). The CSN also included the General Federation of Independent Workers (Central General de Trabajadores Independiente, CGTI), linked to the Nicaraguan Socialist Party; the Center for Trade Union Action and Unity (Central de Acción y Unidad Sindical, CAUS), linked to the Nicaraguan Communist Party; and the Workers Front, linked to the Popular Action Movement. Other participants in the CSN included the Nicaraguan Journalists Union, the Association of Nicaraguan Educators, and the Public Employees Union (all supportive of the FSLN). The CSN agreed that it was necessary to unify the revolutionary workers' movement around the tasks of improving working conditions, being on the lookout for decapitalization and administrative inefficiency, ensuring compliance with labor regulations, drawing up new labor laws, reorganizing categories and wages, raising worker productivity, and defending the Sandinista Revolution.

The National Union of Farmers and Ranchers (Unión Nacional de Agricultores y Ganaderos, UNAG) broke off from the ATC in 1981, taking with it the small- and medium-scale private agricultural producers. It represented a numerous and important productive sector that supplied 78 percent of basic agricultural products and 41 percent of the export crops.[4] UNAG's Plan of Struggle, principles, and the election of the organization's leadership in 1981 all came about as the result of discussions and meetings throughout the country at the village, municipal, and regional levels. Three years later, UNAG included 75,000 individual producers and cooperative members with a range of religious and political beliefs from every region of the country. UNAG's efforts were aimed at strengthening the peasantry's capacity to participate economically and socially in order to raise agricultural production and the standard of living of the producers.

The Luisa Amanda Espinosa Nicaraguan Women's Association (AMNLAE) was begun in 1977 as the Association of Women Confronting the National Problem (AMPRONAC), which was designed to defend human rights and to promote the participation of women in the resolution of the nation's problems. After the Triumph, AMNLAE incorporated women of all sectors, through neighborhoods and workplaces. Its work was oriented to the defense of the Revolution and to overcoming sexual inequalities and problems that Nicaraguan women confronted in various aspects of social life.

The Sandinista Youth Organization (Juventud Sandinista, JS) had a rich series of antecedents in the university and high school student movements that served as a source of Sandinista leaders in the 1960s and 1970s. After the fall of Somoza, the National Literacy Crusade, based on the mobilization of tens of thousands of young people, contributed enormously to the strengthening and growth of the JS. In 1984 the JS brought together approximately 30,000 youth organized in 880 local committees (células de base) in schools and workplaces throughout the country.[5] The principal tasks of the JS were the defense of the Revolution, mobilization for the volunteer work brigades, and promoting culture, learning, and sports among the youth. The JS also promoted the Sandinista Children's Association (ANS) for Nicaraguan children ages 7 to 14. Their activities included cultural, artistic, and sports festivals; camping vacations, exchanges of children from other regions and countries; and visits to workplaces, army and militia training centers, and tourist sites. The ANS tried to develop values of fraternity, cooperation, and patriotic and antiimperialist consciousness.[6]

THE FUNCTIONS OF THE GRASS-ROOTS ORGANIZATIONS

We can summarize the many tasks carried out by the different grass-roots organizations in these five years as falling into three basic areas: socioeconomic development, overall defense, and the development of a democratic political system.

The Socioeconomic Development Projects

The victory over the Somoza dictatorship served as an indelible lesson for the people; it gave the poor confidence in themselves and a certainty that no task was impossible to carry out. The enormous expansion of the grass-roots organizations after the Triumph allowed for the unification of the forces and capacities of the population in carrying out the arduous tasks of rebuilding a country destroyed in the war of liberation, revitalizing a weak economy, and defending the homeland.

The various projects undertaken by the Government of National Reconstruction and the FSLN would not have been possible without the active participation of the grass-roots organizations. Their role was key in the areas of education, health, production, and supply of basic goods to the population. The organized participation of the people in these projects was consistent with both the Sandinista principle of developing a democratic system and the economic need to reduce the costs of such projects through the voluntary work of its beneficiaries. The following are some of the socioeconomic development projects in which the OPs played a key role.

Promoting Production. All of the grass-roots organizations were involved in this task, though it was the principal responsibility of the UNAG. This organization, through its Zone Councils and Production Committees (the latter organized by crop), channeled the agricultural producers' demands to the relevant state organs. These concerned inputs, seeds, machinery, roads, and silos, among others. UNAG was not limited to simply passing along information regarding the producers' problems; rather, it promoted the capacity of the grass-roots and intermediate-level committees of the organization to resolve their own problems. It also maintained a critical and watchful eye on the government institutions responsible for agriculture, so as to assure that its members' needs were efficiently attended to.

UNAG played a key role in carrying out several of the tasks planned by the Agrarian Reform program, such as the selection and distribution of lands and property titles, the formation of cooperatives, technical assistance and the extension of credit, the construction of rural collection and storage centers, marketing, and determining prices to be paid to agricultural producers. It even promoted the handing out of titles guaranteeing individual producers that their lands would not be subject to expropriation for those producers who feared their lands would be affected by the agrarian reform and had been confused by counterrevolutionary propaganda. UNAG also promoted voluntary cooperation among producers, forming work brigades as well as sharing equipment and work animals.[7]

The main objective of the trade union organizations was the economic reconstruction of the country and the raising of productivity. Worker participation was promoted on a limited scale in handling information and overseeing management in public, private, and mixed capital businesses, for the purposes of discovering decapitalization or managerial inefficiency. The unions played an important role in checking managerial ineptitude and corruption in private, state, and mixed enterprises.

The union OPs also promoted voluntary work days, conservation of resources, and the innovators' movement to solve the problem of the lack of spare parts and material caused by the lack of foreign exchange and the partial economic blockade imposed by the U.S. government. The revolutionary unions tried to solve labor-management conflicts through negotiations, avoiding work stoppages, which would have had a negative impact on production. In addition, they supported the government's wage policy, which tried to link wage incentives to worker productivity and sought to define uniform wage categories for different skills and trades.[8]

The JS played a key role in organizing Student Production Battalions, which during school vacations helped make up for the labor shortages in the coffee and cotton harvests. This voluntary work was carried out annually from December to March. Besides helping to raise production, this activity helped young people appreciate manual labor and brought them closer to the peasantry. The JS mobilized 22,066 young people throughout the country in the 1983–84 harvests. Another 16,000 volunteers were organized by the CDSs, UNAG, Public Employees Union, Ministry of Interior, and Militias. Finally, 1,742 volunteers from solidarity movements in other countries rounded out the volunteer pool for the harvest.[9]

In speaking of production one must also mention the Production Collectives organized by AMNLAE and the CDSs in the areas of sewing, ceramics, and handicrafts. The OPs also promoted the functional equivalent of "victory gardens" for the production of fruit, vegetables, and basic grains in neighborhoods and workplaces. These tasks fulfilled the triple objective of lowering unemployment, raising production, and improving the standard of living for the poor majority.

Supplying Basic Consumer Goods to the Population. The grassroots organizations played an important role in supplying basic consumer goods to the population at official prices. The CDSs bore the brunt of this work, as they carried out a census of all inhabitants by neighborhood and were in charge of the distribution of such products through government stores or People's Stores. These People's Stores were run by private merchants whom the CDSs supported because of their honesty and efficiency, and who therefore obtained a state concession to sell such basic goods at official prices. The work of the CDSs in this field expanded once the Consumer Protection Law was passed in June 1984. This measure confined the sale of eight basic products to authorized channels in an effort to bring an end to the hoarding and speculation of some private merchants. People's Inspectors (members of the CDS trained by the Ministry of Domestic Commerce) oversaw the supply of basic goods.

The union organizations also promoted the creation of supply outlets in workplaces, to provide basic consumer goods to workers. This service was criticized, for as there was no coordination with the CDSs, those who worked where there were supply outlets were able to purchase twice as much at official prices.[10]

In rural areas, UNAG organized Rural Supply Centers in even the most isolated areas in order to attend to the needs of the peasantry. Nonetheless, it was not easy to overcome the problems of deficient roads in the countryside, the high degree of dispersion of the peasantry, and the lack of transportation. For example, in Region 5 (Boaco and Chontales, and part of Southern Zelaya) there were some 485 rural supply posts by mid-1984, but these covered only 45 percent of the villages in the region, obliging many peasants to travel several hours in order to get to the nearest post.[11] UNAG also organized the sale of agricultural producers' products to the government channels, in order to bypass from the start the private distribution channels that had inflated the price or hoarded goods only to sell them at higher prices in times of scarcity.

Educational and Cultural Development. The grass-roots organizations carried out most of the work involved in the National Literacy Crusade. They mobilized thousands of people for tasks such as the census of all illiterate people, the training of the literacy teachers (*brigadistas*), distributing and producing the teaching materials, and providing transportation, communication, and medical attention for all of the young literacy volunteers. The Crusade was the first great challenge faced by the OPs after the overthrow of Somoza. The experience helped the organizations develop leadership and organizational networks, extend their presence among their respective constituencies, and in general strengthen their organizational capacity. The JS contributed 52,180 young people, the CST and ATC mobilized 16,630 workers, and the CDSs, AMNLAE, and ANDEN (National Association of Nicaraguan Educators) also contributed 16,630.[12]

After the literacy campaign the grass-roots organizations, with the support of the Ministry of Education, also carried out the adult education program. This program, which extended and followed up on the literacy campaign, involved 160,000 students organized in 19,100 Popular Education Collectives meeting every day throughout the country. It also had a positive impact on the OPs by improving the reading and writing skills of the poor and raising their political awareness through a collective and critical model of self-education. The teachers in the adult education program, many of whom had just become literate in the Literacy Crusade and most of whom were peasants, tended to become the most outstanding local leaders of the OPs.[13]

The National Consultation was another important educational project of the grass-roots organizations. Its purpose was to define the principles and objectives of Nicaragua's new educational system. In early 1981 some 50,000 people within the OPs discussed a questionnaire that was then processed by the Ministry of Education in order to draft the strategic objectives of educational policy. The final document was later approved by the government Junta.

At the same time, the grass-roots organizations developed their own training programs for their affiliates and leaders, which emphasized themes related to the principles and character of the organization, work methods, the principles of the Sandinista Revolution, and the analysis of Nicaraguan society. Members of the OPs participated in special programs promoted by the Ministry of Education, such as accelerated primary and secondary education courses, and some received scholarships to study abroad.

The grass-roots organizations promoted construction and repair work in schools throughout the country through an agreement in which the Ministry of Education or an international agency would provide the materials and the OPs, the labor. They also participated in the creation of Child Development Centers and preschools in order to attend to the educational development of children in neighborhoods and workplaces and to free mothers for gainful employment.

The JS promoted various activities to improve academic output in schools and universities. These included the Science and Production Days in the high schools and University Days for Scientific Development. These annual programs promoted research and student creativity geared to national development needs. By 1983, 3,147 research projects involving 17,476 students had been stimulated. The JS also played a key role in cultural work through the "Leonel Rugama" Artistic Movement, which in 1983 included 4,000 amateur artists. The "Bosco Monge" Sports Movement also mobilized 60,000 youth for 1983 competitions. The other OPs promoted cultural creativity through festivals, religious festivities dedicated to patron saints, public mobilizations, and other activities in which the cultural abilities of the Nicaraguan people were demonstrated. The organizations, in coordination with the Ministry of Culture, participated in the Popular Culture Centers, which sponsored workshops in poetry, theater, painting, and music. Similarly, they promoted sports in neighborhoods, rural villages, and workplaces through the Volunteer Sports Committees and the Sports Leagues, in coordination with the Nicaraguan Institute of Sports.

In sum, the educational work of the grass-roots organizations contributed decisively to overcoming historic levels of illiteracy and cultural backwardness. The OPs also helped foster a scientific understanding of reality and the inculcation of the values of solidarity and cooperation among the population.

Promoting Public Health.   The grass-roots organizations also engaged in Popular Health Days (Jornadas Populares de Salud), massive preventive medicine campaigns coordinated by the Ministry of Health (Ministerio de Salud, MINSA). In addition to sitting on the national and regional committees created in coordination with MINSA to plan the campaigns, the OPs provided trainers who gave workshops to "multiplier" trainers, who in turn trained the health brigadistas in charge of carrying out the campaigns at the local and neighborhood levels. In 1981, 1982, and 1983, 12 campaigns were waged to combat poliomyelitis, malaria, dengue fever, diarrhea in children; to improve hygiene and sanitation; and to give first-aid training. In 1983 alone, the grass-roots organizations provided 36,000 brigadistas, who worked in every village and neighborhood in the country, greatly controlling and limiting illnesses.[14] The CDSs played a key role in sanitation in the neighborhoods. Residents would frequently mobilize on weekends to get rid of accumulated garbage, to clean storm sewers, build latrines, dry up stagnant waters, and explain to people the minimal hygienic measures to be taken to prevent contagious disease. The trade union organizations in coordination with the Ministry of Labor assured that occupational health standards were being met so as to diminish the risk of work-related illnesses and accidents.

Community Development. Another task of the grass-roots organizations was the overall improvement of the squatter settlements and housing in general. After Typhoon Aleta (May 1982), thousands of Nicaraguans were moved from flooded areas to new settlements, thanks to the joint effort of the government and the OPs. Though the typhoon's material damage was much greater in Nicaragua than in neighboring Honduras, Nicaragua's dramatically lower death toll—13 as opposed to over 200— clearly reflected the effectiveness of the grass-roots organizations, which immediately mobilized to aid the flood victims. The typhoon aid efforts gave rise to new "sites and services" neighborhoods known as *urbanizaciones progresivas* (progressive neighborhoods) on well-located urban lands, in which the government planned the lots and streets, leveled the land, and provided services such as drinking water. The grass-roots organizations, especially the CDSs, had to organize the relocation and distribution of the population.

The OPs also played a role in the relocation of people living in war zones. Volunteer brigades from the grass-roots organizations helped resettle these peasants on new lands, provided free of charge by the government, and helped to build housing and organize agricultural production.

In the few "build-your-own" housing programs sponsored by the Ministry of Housing or international organizations, the task of the grass-roots organizations was to organize and motivate the population to participate in the collective work. In the new housing complexes built by the state the role of the grass-roots organizations was to help ensure that the new units would be distributed to the neediest families, in accordance with criteria jointly set by the organizations and the Ministry of Housing.

The CDSs also played a key role in promoting volunteer work days to carry out tasks such as building a community center or a neighborhood park, installing water facilities, repairing streets, planting trees, putting in playgrounds for children, and reinforcing and cleaning storm sewers during the rainy season. The CDSs were also in charge of ensuring that the rent laws were followed to protect tenants from the frequent abuses by landlords.

The Sandinista Youth organized housing construction brigades in rural areas, one example being housing for the workers on the banana plantations at Tonala, Chinandega. The Public Employees Union of the Telecommunications Corporation organized brigades to put up the telephone lines between the Atlantic and Pacific coasts, as well as in other parts of the country.

National Defense by the Entire Population

The second basic function of the OPs was to help organize national defense in every part of the country. Immediately after Ronald Reagan's inauguration in 1981, the activity of the counterrevolution grew and the grass-roots organizations were forced to dedicate more and more of their efforts to defense. In 1983 and 1984 the *contra* offensive grew to the point that defense became the fundamental task of the grass-roots organizations. The government's scarce economic resources—inadequate to maintain a large professional army—and the participatory concept of Sandinista military doctrine made it inevitable that the grass-roots organizations would bear the brunt of the nation's defense.

The most widespread form of participation promoted by the organizations was Civil Defense. The purpose of this effort was to diminish the risks of a catastrophe, whether this be caused by a war or by natural phenomena. Civil Defense was organized on every block and in every village and hamlet, in workplaces and in schools. Responsibilities were broken down into first-aid brigades, fire-fighting brigades, and brigades to clean up ruins, to care for children, the elderly, and pregnant women, and to guarantee the supply of provisions. Civil Defense was also in charge of building bomb shelters and instructing the population what to do in case of air raids and natural catastrophes.

Another form of massive participation was the revolutionary Night Watch, which was promoted above all by the CDSs. Night Watch, organized in neighborhoods, schools, and workplaces, mobilized 250,000 nightly in the neighborhoods alone and was successful in reducing crime and preventing sabotage and other counterrevolutionary activities.

The Militia (Milicias Populares Sandinistas, MPS) were another facet of the OPs. These units, organized according to geographical area, received military training on evenings and weekends and were responsible for defending their zone. Most impressive were the Militia organized in the rural areas of northern Nicaragua, the Self-Defense Cooperatives organized by UNAG. In these cooperatives the peasants took turns around the clock standing watch and working with their rifles slung over their shoulders in response to the continuous attacks from the contra forces based in Honduras. By the end of 1983 there were approximately 300,000 members of the MPS. The distribution of arms to this huge sector of the population was a clear refutation to the misinformation of the U.S. government, which sought to portray the FSLN as a tiny group that had imposed an iron dictatorship without popular participation.

The grass-roots organizations were also responsible for forming Reserve Infantry Battalions (Batallones de Infantería de Reserva, BIR). The BIR were given intensive training and were then mobilized for six to eight months to the battle fronts. Beginning in mid-1983 the grass-roots organizations also had the task of promoting draft registration among young men ages 16 to 21 as part of the Patriotic Military Service law. The OPs explained the nature of the draft law, promoted registration, and organized communication between the relatives and the young people who had been mobilized. At the same time they organized voluntary donations of blood, provisions, clothing, and money for battalions that were on the front line.

The Voluntary Police project was also taken on by the grass-roots organizations as a way of collaborating with the Sandinista Police in detecting and controlling delinquency in those areas that the Sandinista Police were unable to cover because of a lack of resources.

The OP effort to offset counterrevolutionary propaganda was also considered part of the overall defense program. The grass-roots organizations constantly worked to provide information and interpretation of national and international events. This work was carried out through talks, small meetings, newspapers, murals, flyers, and radio programs. A major effort was made to explain that economic problems affecting the population were in large part a result of the U.S. aggression against Nicaragua, which had caused losses of some 2 billion cordobas ($200 million) between 1981 and the first quarter of 1984, not counting the expenses involved in mobilizing, obtaining arms, and unrealized profits.[15]

Building a Democratic Political System

The third function of the grass-roots organizations was to develop a new system of popular participation in public affairs. An evaluation of accomplishments in this area should focus on two factors: the capacity of the grass-roots organizations to promote the interests of the poor majority within the state and the FSLN; and the mechanisms of participation and representation of the general population in the grass-roots organizations. In regard to the first, it should be noted that the Sandinista Revolution never proposed establishing a definitive and clear-cut separation between the FSLN, the state, and the mass organizations; but rather it advocated relative autonomy and a certain division of functions since it was understood that all three grew out of a single project of national liberation and social justice.

The main vehicle of grass-roots participation in the government was the Council of State, the colegislative body of the new state until the end of 1984. All of the country's political parties and social organizations, a total of 32 institutions with 51 members, were represented in the Council of State. The OPs had 44 percent of all the members. Those with more members had more seats. Thus the CDSs had nine seats, the CST had three, the ATC had two, UNAG had two, and the rest of the grass-roots organizations had one representative each. In these five years the organizations expressed the interests of their constituencies through bills, requests for reports, motions, and declarations. Of the bills introduced by the grass-roots organizations, 83 percent became law, albeit with some changes.[16]

In some cases the grass-roots organizations promoted an extensive process of discussions at the local level of bills brought before the Council of State in order to get input from the general population as well as to make people aware of the government's laws. Some of the more prominent of such laws were those concerning father, mother, and child relations, protection for the revolutionary Night Watch volunteers, and a law to regulate housing sponsored by the CDSs (which did not pass).

Another key mode of participation of the grass-roots organizations in governmental decisionmaking were the specific commissions established to coordinate with different ministries and state institutions. For example, the National Council of the Agrarian Reform was set up to organize the agrarian reform and to advise the leadership of the Ministry of Agricultural Development and Agrarian Reform (MIDINRA). UNAG and ATC participated in this Council on behalf of the OPs, while the leadership of MIDINRA, the Agrarian Reform Research Center, and the Ministry of Planning participated on behalf of the state. Similar councils were established in each region and zone throughout the country. National, regional, and local Production Commissions were also set up for each major agricultural product: cotton, coffee, beef, milk, sugar, and rice. This process took place in all other areas of the state apparatus as well. Thus the OPs participated in the National Educational Advisory Council and the National Adult Education Council together with representatives from the Ministry of Education; the National Commission for the Health Campaigns with representatives from the Ministry of Health; the National Supply Commission with representatives from the Ministry of Internal Trade; the Regional Committees for Housing Affairs with representatives from the Ministry of Housing; the Credit Committees with the Ministry of Finance. The grass-roots organizations also participated on the advisory councils of the regional and municipal government boards across the country.

The OPs had the opportunity to express the concerns of the social sectors they represented in these commissions. Decisionmaking was generally by consensus or by a simple majority, after extensive discussions. Nonetheless, the main role of the organizations was to advise the government.

The grass-roots organizations also influenced government through a number of direct channels such as the "Face the People" weekly TV show. On this show members of the government Junta would face the population of a neighborhood or municipality, to respond to people's questions or complaints. Similarly, town meetings were held with local and regional officials to discuss problems affecting a particular area or in which the grass-roots organizations would demand accountability for government administration. On the other hand, the OPs enjoyed direct access to officials of any government office or entity in special cases or when no formal mechanisms for coordination had been set up. There were several cases in which government officials failed to respond to the demands of the grass-roots organizations and were later dismissed from their posts after the organizations held demonstrations against them.

The grass-roots organizations and the FSLN had an even closer relationship, since the OPs recognized the FSLN as their legitimate vanguard, that is, as the party that should lead the Revolution and thus the grass-roots organizations as well. This recognition was based on the historic role of the FSLN in its unwavering struggle against the dictatorship, its ties to the masses, its ability to provide leadership as demonstrated in the overthrow of the dictatorship, and its work promoting the consolidation of the grass-roots organizations.

It is an error to view the OPs as simple instruments of the FSLN, as the guidelines they received from the FSLN were based on feedback from the local level and, to a significant degree, from the grass-roots organizations themselves. As was pointed out by then-Secretary General of the CDS, Iván García: "Following the leadership of the FSLN doesn't mean that the FSLN imposes its criteria over the workers in an authoritarian fashion. To the contrary, the FSLN enriches its political concepts and strengthens its position as vanguard by understanding the concerns of the workers."[17]

Of course the question of the relationship beween the grass-roots organizations and the FSLN is closely related to the question of the internal functioning of the popular participation within the FSLN itself, which is beyond the scope of this chapter. Nonetheless, one must understand that the FSLN was extremely careful in choosing its members. Only those who had demonstrated a prolonged commitment to struggle for popular interests could aspire to its ranks. Thus the best leaders of the OPs tended also to be members of the FSLN. Their positions as leaders of the grass-roots organizations were not the result of vertical imposition by the FSLN, but rather of a delegation of responsibility from the grass-roots level, with the party agreeing. As a result of their political commitment, their capacity for hard work, and also their party discipline, members of the FSLN who were in the grass-roots organizations helped strengthen their organizational structures and the promotion of popular interests. The FSLN also ensured the effective participation of the OPs in the state and worked to ensure that the state respect the role of the grass-roots organizations. As Sandinista leader Carlos Núñez indicated,

> with the leadership of the FSLN the mass organizations are guided by two important courses of action: in the first place, our mass organizations should watch over and work to strengthen the political project of the revolution; and secondly, they should effectively express, channel, and receive the most pressing needs of the masses.[18]

The relative autonomy of the grass-roots organizations was publicly observed on several occasions when the FSLN and the OPs assumed different positions—such as in early 1980 when the ATC opposed the FLSN's position regarding returning lands to landowners who had been associated with the dictatorship—and was able to modify the FSLN position.[19] Another well-known case was AMNLAE's position supporting applying the Military Service Law to women, which the FSLN delegates in the Council of State opposed. The result was to allow for the voluntary participation of women in the military service.

The FSLN, as the maximum leadership body of the whole revolutionary process, took into account the concerns of each OP and balanced them with the needs of the other social sectors, within the strategic guidelines of the revolution and within the current context of events. As a result of this process of overall coordination of the revolutionary process, the FSLN gave direction to each grass-roots organization as to the objective possibilities of their specific proposals, and as to the general guidelines for work that could be developed by each OP in order to strengthen itself and promote the strategic project of the revolution.

The OPs without a doubt demonstrated a growing capacity over the first five years to participate in the formulation and implementation of state policies, and in this way they involved the majority of the people in governmental decisionmaking. The close relationship between the OPs and their leadership, the FSLN, did not obstruct their capacity to express the concerns of their members at the local level. The leadership of the FSLN made it possible to channel the interests of each grass-roots organization within the totality of the country's interests, in accordance with each specific moment.

The second aspect to be considered in evaluating the role of the OPs in building a democratic system were the mechanisms of membership organization and participation. We have already mentioned that the grass-roots organizations were open to all persons corresponding to the social sector of each grass-roots organization, irrespective of one's religion, sex, or political affiliation, with the exception of those who were opposed to the Revolution. The leaders of the OPs were periodically chosen and ratified by the membership and were accountable to it. This mechanism gradually spread to every level and every region, and to all the grass-roots organizations. In the first stage the leaders of the OPs were those persons who had played an important role against the dictatorship, and were backed by their constituency. Nonetheless, it became apparent that having played an important role in the insurrection was not a sufficient condition for being able to assume a leadership position in a grass-roots organization. There were even abuses by leaders who, in the first period after the overthrow of Somoza, adopted a *caudillo* or traditional boss style of rule. Thus the OPs set out to remove opportunists and incompetent personnel from leadership positions and to establish stable and democratic procedures to choose and evaluate the leadership at every level. For example, after an energetic letter from Sandinista leader Bayardo Arce to the CDSs regarding the continued abuses, a process of critical evaluation of leaders and election by the grass-roots membership at every level of the organization was launched.

A mechanism of direct democracy often used by the grass-roots organizations was the assemblies, in which concerns of local members were raised; possible solutions were collectively discussed; and leaders of grass-roots organizations, the state, and the FSLN reported on their work and were held accountable. UNAG, in particular, became known for its periodic assemblies of agricultural producers. In early 1984, for example, they began in Region VI (Matagalpa and Jinotega), with assemblies in different zones that mobilized over 5,000 producers, and ended with a Regional Assembly in which the results of the earlier assemblies were summarized in a "Plan of Struggle" containing the small farmers' various demands of the state and their commitments in terms of developing the economy and improving the rural standard of living. In that same assembly each member of the Regional Board of Directors of UNAG was ratified by applause. This same process was carried out in other regions, culminating on July 9 in a National Assembly that drafted a "National Plan of Struggle" and chose the National Board of Directors of UNAG.

The organizational structure of the OPs had to conform to the division of the country into regions and zones that had been carried out by the government. Thus there were four basic organizational levels of the grass-roots organizations:

1. Local/Grass-roots Level: for example, a CDS on a city block, an UNAG cooperative, or the Sandinista Youth organization at a particular school.

2. Zonal Level: for example, the Zonal Committee of the CDSs, and the Zonal Council of UNAG.

3. Regional Level: for example, the Regional Committee of the CDSs, or the regional Board of Directors of UNAG.

4. National Level: for example, the National Committee of the CDSs, or the National Board of Directors of UNAG.

Two-way communication took place between each level. Although the fulfillment of instructions emanating from the higher level was obligatory, there was a broad margin of flexibility in adapting general directions to the specific conditions of each region and zone. There was a division of labor at each level in order to attend to the different needs of the grass-roots organizations. For example, there was a Secretary of Economic Defense in each CDS in charge of food supplies; a Secretary of Community Development to attend to matters of housing, health, and education; a Secretary of Organization and Finances in charge of internal organizational operations and the budget; a Secretary of Training and Education in charge of educating the members and providing information; and a Secretary of Social Defense in charge of revolutionary vigilance and the militia. The important decisions at each level were made in meetings of the whole committee or the steering committee, by collective agreement, although the responsibility for implementing decisions might lie in the hands of a specific secretary. That is, to a greater or lesser degree, the OPs practiced collective leadership, trying in this way to avoid concentrating power in the hands of a single individual and to enrich decisions through the con-tributions of everyone. Similarly, critical and constructive evaluation was a practice that the OPs periodically used as a mechanism to overcome mistakes and improve work methods.

Without a doubt the application of these principles and methods of organization was uneven and gradual; but one could note a significant improvement in these five years. The participation of grass-roots member-ship grew through the election and removal of representatives and the promotion of felt needs. The practice of collective discussion and problem-solving turned the grass-roots organizations into true schools of political socialization and democratic consciousness-raising. The coming together of people on a daily basis in the Popular Education Collectives, CDSs, cooperatives, union committees, local JS branches, or women's committees to freely express their concerns and carry out a variety of social activities was a real advancement of the people as a protagonist in building a new society.

That daily exercise of popular participation was accompanied by a growing awareness of one's own capacity and right to choose one's destiny. According to Domingo Páramo, a peasant and member of the Milton Dinarte Cooperative, "For us democracy means that we can all be leaders. Thus the Assembly of all members of the cooperative is our highest authority and we want all the members to work on the Board of Directors of the Cooperative, so we rotate each year."[20]

CONTRADICTIONS AND LIMITATIONS OF THE GRASS-ROOTS ORGANIZATIONS

The achievements discussed thus far should not cause us to overlook the problems that confronted the grass-roots organizations and the weaknesses they continued to suffer five years after the Triumph. The organizations themselves scrutinized with self-critical maturity their own problems and errors; within a revolutionary perspective this type of honest evaluation is necessary in order to overcome problems. For didactical purposes we break this issue down into the following five subcategories, all of which are tightly interwoven.

The Opposition and the Counterrevolution

The principal problem for the OPs was the military, economic, political, and ideological aggression carried out by those forces allied to the imperialist project of destroying the Revolution. The leaders of the grass-roots organizations were a prime target for the mercenary bands that invaded the country. The cooperatives, schools, community centers, and supply centers built by the population organized in OPs were systematically destroyed by these bands.

On the other hand, the grass-roots organizations were the target of an adverse propaganda campaign by the small bourgeois parties and certain religious sectors. These groups, which had shared power with the Somoza family, perceived the growing process of organization and participation of the OPs as an inadmissible insubordination on the part of the "inferior classes." Ecclesiastical figures such as some Catholic bishops prohibited the clergy and their parishioners from participating in the grass-roots organizations, to which they referred in their sermons as "communist mobs."

The trade union organizations continually had to confront their bosses' refusal to comply with the labor laws. After five years of revolution there were still businessmen like Bolaños Geyer, President of the Superior Council of Private Enterprise (COSEP), who were so bold as to fire their workers simply for trying to organize a union. In another area, the CDSs struggled hard to control speculators who would hoard basic consumption goods and resell them at exorbitant prices.

In that context of growing military aggression and an economy in crisis—by 1984, defined as a "war economy"—the grass-roots organizations centered their efforts on defense tasks, weakening their efforts in other areas. In many cases the sector-specific demands of the OPs were subordinated to the policy of national unity in the face of external aggression, which included the "patriotic" bourgeoisie as well as merchants, white-collar employees, workers, peasants, and professionals. For the sake of national unity the popular sectors had to limit demands that might have adversely affected the interests of other sectors. Of course those limits were difficult to establish a priori; but without a doubt the priority of national unity served as a comfortable excuse for reformist sectors, bureaucrats, and reactionaries to delay revolutionary transformations and avoid criticism by the general population. The priority of defense and economic development placed the leaders of the grassroots organizations in a difficult position vis-a-vis the demands of their constitutents. This was the case, for example, with the union organizations regarding wage demands, or AMNLAE and the demands of combatting discrimination against women in a more decided fashion.

In that context of ever-greater aggressions in 1983 and 1984, the dividing line between opposition and counterrevolution, between those sectors that dissented with some aspects of the revolutionary process and those identified with the intervention forces, became increasingly difficult to perceive. This polarization led some leaders of the OPs to develop Manichean attitudes that identified any criticism or dissidence as "counterrevolutionary." The belligerent climate, characterized by the constant death of young people and innocent women and children, led certain OPs to use force to stop the publicity activities of the opposition, such as those carried out by church leaders. These attitudes were justified in the eyes of the conscientious revolutionary sectors but were incomprehensible to, or condemned by, confused and politically backward sectors. Accordingly, they had a negative effect on the image of the grass-roots organizations, on the incorporation of these same people into the OPs, and on frank and open criticism within the grass-roots organizations.

Economic Problems

Certain characteristics of the Nicaraguan economy—such as seasonal employment of the work force during the harvest seasion, the large tertiary or "informal" sector of the economy, and the closing of sources of employment due to the shortage of imported materials and spare parts— affected the stability of members of the OPs and thus their organizational capacity as well. For example, the ATC was unable to organize effectively agricultural workers who spent only three months a year in the coffee, cotton, and sugar harvests. On the other hand, other grass-roots organizations lost that part of the membership that went off to the harvest for those three months. The high degree of dispersion of the rural population, which included an estimated 50 percent of the nation's total population, also made the organizational work of the OPs difficult.

The large productive weight of the capitalist sector in the economic structure meant the perpetuation of individualistic and consumerist ideas, traditions, and patterns of behavior that were in contradiction to the efforts of the OPs to foment voluntary cooperation to solve collective problems.

The economic crisis, aggravated by a deterioration in terms of trade, the commercial and financial boycott imposed by the Reagan Administration, and by military aggression, meant a fall in income levels and supply of basic goods. The OPs, as the channels for the expression and solution of the people's problems, gradually received more and more complaints and demands, which the organizations by themselves were unable to resolve. The state, which suffered the same economic crisis and which was making defense the priority for its scarce resources, was also unable to resolve such problems. The only possible response the grassroots organizations could give was to explain the causes of the economic crisis and to promote austerity, organization, and creativity in the use of the scarce resources that were available. The OPs even had to put a halt to popular demands that exceeded what was economically possible. At the same time these organizations had to request that people increase their hours of voluntary work and their participation in the national defense effort. In the June 1984 National Assembly of the trade union mass organizations, Sandinista leader Víctor Tirado López asked that the workers cover the jobs that had been carried out by those workers mobilized in the defense effort. The work of the OPs in defense and the economic crisis was of great concern, for the experiences of other revolutionary processes had indicated that production and popular mobilization cannot be maintained for a long time on the basis of moral incentives alone. Thus, the difficult economic situation might lead the grass-roots organizations gradually to lose their legitimacy in the eyes of their constituencies.

The economic crisis also affected the availability of material and human resources to the OPs. The possibility of having full-time paid personnel diminished, as did their capacity to possess the material resources their work required. At the same time, this problem was also linked to the lack of political will to give the OPs the budget necessary for them to function efficiently.

Problems in State-OP Relations

The contradictory relationship between the grass-roots organizations and the state in this initial stage of the Sandinista Revolution was due in part to a lack of definition as to their respective functions and quotas of power, and in part to their both having the character of institutions involved in a single process of social transformation.

Both the state and the OPs faced the challenge of transforming themselves into revolutionary institutions capable of carrying forth the revolutionary process throughout society. In this regard the grass-roots organizations had the advantages of having a direct tie to the population and control by their grass-roots bases, besides being institutions that basically formed after the Triumph and that mainly represent workers. The state apparatus, on the other hand, represented a broad alliance of classes, inherited many personnel and work styles from the Somocista state, and had an indirect tie to the population, which was mediated by the OPs.

Thus there was a contradictory relationship between the grass-roots organizations and the state, which flowed from the following facts:

- The grass-roots organizations participated in government decision-making, and carried out various socioeconomic development projects.
- The grass-roots organizations defended the state vis-a-vis the opposition and the counterrevolution.
- But the grass-roots organizations also critically controlled the state in order to assure that effective attention was given to the needs of the population.

In this relationship, the main problems faced by the OPs were the bureaucratism of certain state entities and functionaries; the implementation of social development projects by the state with no previous communication with the appropriate OPs; or the reduction of the grass-roots organizations to the simple role of implementers of projects planned and decided upon by the state.

One response of state officials to criticisms leveled by the OPs was that these organizations possessed neither the technical capacity to offer counterproposals nor the material or human resources needed to carry them out. The underlying questions were: "Who should have those technical and material resources?" or "What proportion of resources should go to the state and what to the grass-roots organizations?"

Certainly the number of tasks that the grass-roots organizations were expected to carry out was disproportionately large given the scarce financial and human resources they possessed. From this point of view, the achievements of the OPs in the first five years take on greater significance, as they were accomplished "with one's fingernails," as is popularly said in Nicaragua. In contrast, any state entity had greater material and technical resources than all the grass-roots organizations together. There were few members of grass-roots organizations who worked full time for their organization for a minimal wage. The worst aspect of this situation was that many of these full-time workers were soon drawn to state positions that offered better salaries, further weakening the grass-roots organizations that had trained them.

Problems in FSLN-OP Relations

While we have indicated the character of this relationship between the FSLN and the OPs as well as the benefits that it brought both parties, it is important to analyze problems that also arose. In practice, a lack of definition and confusion of functions between the OPs and the FSLN were the predominant problems of FSLN militants working in the grass-roots organizations, even though the definition of functions may have been clear theoretically to the top Sandinista leadership. For many of these Sandinista militants working in the OPs it was difficult to separate the authority and political orientations that corresponded to their party structures from those of their organizations. This confusion served to undercut the broad and pluralistic character that prevailed among most of the grass-roots organizations, especially when those militants adopted radical positions within the OPs. Although theoretically party activities should have reinforced the work of the grass-roots organizations, in practice there were often conflicting activities and instructions, with the party receiving first priority. A rigid application of the principle of democratic centralism as conceived within the FSLN, establishing, among other points, that "the decisions of higher bodies are absolutely obligatory for lower bodies," placed those FSLN militants that worked in the OPs at the disposition of the party authorities. Especially in cases where there was no previous consultation within the grass-roots organization as to the viability of a given decision, this came to weaken the work of the organization and to establish a vertical pattern in the relationship between the organization and the FSLN. A frequent example was the reassignment of grass-roots organization leaders who were also members of the FSLN to party jobs without regard to the subsequent weakening of the OPs.[21]

Another problem in the relationship between the FSLN and the organizations was that at times the party's role as the guiding force of the grass-roots organizations was confused with its broader role of leadership and direct action, which meant substituting the party for the OPs, thereby impeding the formation and development of their organizational capacity and their ability to promote popular interests. Some FSLN base committees within the OPs took on the functions of discussion, criticism and self-criticism, and decisionmaking concerning the work of the grass-roots organizations that should have been conducted within the OPs by both FSLN and non-FSLN members so as to strengthen the organizations.

In 1984 it appeared that the relation between the FSLN and the grass-roots organizations was likely to grow closer. In the National Assembly to be elected that November, the OPs would not participate directly as they had in the Council of State, but rather through their party representatives. This was one more reason to try to overcome the weaknesses that had existed in the relationship between the FSLN and the grass-roots organizations, so as to fulfill the objective posed by the National Directorate of the FSLN of having a dialectical relationship between the vanguard and the masses.

Internal Weaknesses of the Grass-Roots Organizations

We have already mentioned the small number of full-time leaders in the grass-roots organizations. The local-level leaders were generally people who worked or studied full time, and who had little time and energy to dedicate to the many tasks of the OPs. This problem was aggravated by a low educational and technical level and limited experience and organizational training, especially among local- and intermediate-level leaders, many of whom had trouble reading and writing.

This weakness was due to the legacy of educational backwardness, but it also resulted from the failure of the OPs to take a strong interest in training their members. The agitational and momentary tasks, the daily activism to "resolve problems," was the prevalent practice in the grass-roots organizations. The prolonged and systematic work involved in training its leaders and members was neglected, with the exception of the training offered by the FSLN to its members who worked in the OPs. In general the grass-roots organizations neglected the strategic tasks that in the long run would strengthen their organizations and promote the work of the Revolution, emphasizing instead more immediate goals and projects.

The frequency of rotation of leadership personnel positions was another factor related to the low level of the capacities of leaders, as it made it difficult to accumulate experience in a particular area and to specialize. Transfers within the same organization, to other organizations, the state, or the FSLN were common. Other noteworthy areas of difficulty in the grass-roots organizations were weaknesses in investigating the reality of their sector, in planning of work, and in evaluating their activities. The lack of information systems within the grass-roots organizations obliged them to depend on the state's information, and therefore undermined their autonomy vis-a-vis the state. The lack of coordination with other OPs, or with the state, was another frequent problem. For example, there was confusion between the CST and the ATC as to which organization had responsibility for organizing agroindustrial workers; and between the CDSs and AMNLAE as to responsibility for certain aspects of community development; and between UNAG, the CDSs, and ATC regarding responsibility for the rural population.

Further, popular participation within the grass-roots organizations fluctuated, with high involvement during critical periods, for example, during U.S. military maneuvers along the border, during health campaigns, or patriotic activities such as July 19 each year. These variations in the degree of mobilization of the population corresponded not only to the problems discussed above but also to the historic tradition of disorganization and individualism and could not be transformed in just five years of revolution. For many, participating in sports, watching TV, or drinking rum were still more appealing than spending free time participating in the voluntary work projects organized by the OPs. Nonetheless, in the war zones the grass-roots organizations became much more consolidated than in the Pacific Coast Region. Similarly, the mobilization of the population was massive and rapid when there was a perceived imminent danger of invasion by U.S. troops, as happened in November 1983 and March 1984.

The problems and contradictions of the grass-roots organizations after five years of the Revolution should be seen in the context of the achievements discussed earlier. It is most important to see the Revolution, and its grass-roots organization, as a dynamic process. The predominant characteristics in the OPs in this initial stage were a growing ability to overcome initial errors, a massively expanded membership, and an increasing capacity to consolidate their role as vehicles of participation in and democratization of Nicaraguan society. These tendencies were reinforced in the political determination of the top-level Sandinista leadership to consolidate the capacity of the grass-roots organizations to express the popular interests.

CONCLUSIONS

By 1984 the OPs had become the main channels of organization and participation for the population. Through them the collective interests of the poor majority were expressed. They promoted popular participation in workplaces, schools, neighborhoods, universities, the militia, cooperatives, and rural communities across the country. In just five years the grass-roots organizations, led by the FSLN, had made it possible for the majority of Nicaragua's adult population to participate in the decisions that affected their social life. In this way the organizations became practical, permanent schools of political socialization and democratic consciousness-raising.

This social and political system created by the Sandinista Revolution was profoundly democratic, even though general elections with political parties were not held until the end of 1984. In poor countries where the majority of people are undereducated, democracy cannot be reduced to a model, such as that which exists in developed capitalist countries, where participation of the people is confined to casting one's vote every few years. Each sovereign people has the right to develop its *own* political model in accordance with its *own* specific conditions. In its short life, the Sandinista Revolution had, without a doubt, developed a system of popular participation that was unique in Central America. This achievement was not free of errors and contradictions, but it was all the more significant for having taken place in the context of an acute economic crisis and an unjust war directed by the most powerful country on earth.

NOTES

1. Agrarian Reform Research Center (CIERA), *La democracia participativa en Nicaragua* (Managua: CIERA, 1984), p. 56.

2. Gabriel García Marquez et al., "El Movimiento Obrero," in *Los Sandinistas* (Bogotá: La Oveja Negra, 1979), pp. 266–269; and "Aparición de los sindicatos en Nicaragua," *El Trabajador*, January 19, 1980 (Managua: CST), p. 5.

3. "Nicaragua's Labor Unions in the Face of Aggression," *Envío*, No. 35 (1984), p. 4c. The trade union federations, besides the CST and ATC, were as follows: General Labor Confederation-Independent (CGTI), founded in 1963, of Marxist orientation, and linked to the Nicaraguan Socialist Party, with 17,177 affiliates and 19 unions; Nicaraguan Workers' Confederation, founded in 1972, of Christian Democratic orientation, linked to the Social Christian Party, which is opposed to the Revolution, with 2,734 affiliates and 21 unions; the Center for Trade Union Action and Unity (CAUS), founded in 1973, of Marxist orientation, linked to the Communist Party, which critically supported the Revolution, with 1,939 affiliates and 15 unions; the Confederation for Labor Union Unity (CUS), of Social-Democratic orientation, linked to the Social Democratic Party, which is opposed to the Revolution, with 1,670 affiliates and 17 unions. Also see "Lunes Socio-Económico 48," *Barricada*, April 23, 1984, p. 3.

4. UNAG, "Los pequeños y medianos productores agropecuarios" (Managua: UNAG, 1982).

5. In its first year there was debate as to whether the Sandinista Youth organization should be selective and have the character of a youth branch of the party, or if it should be a mass (grass-roots) organization. The decision was to have both features—that is, that the organization should work in a broad fashion among the youth, and at the same time it should be demanding and selective so that young people who joined might later become FSLN members. It was also decided that the Sandinista Youth could not be just a rigid and exclusively political organization, but that it should be flexible, positive in spirit, and in touch with the broad concerns of Nicaraguan youth. Similarly, the organization began to expand beyond the schools to factories, the armed forces, and the peasantry, in order to incorporate youth from all sectors of society. See the magazine Muchachos (Managua: Juventud Sandinista, monthly since 1982).

6. "La ANS, desarrolla las mejores cualidades en los niños," Barricada, July 13, 1983.

7. An important achievement of UNAG was the cancellation of the producers' debts to the financial system, which resulted from crops lost due to bad weather and to the producers' location on marginal lands during the Somoza period. The cancellation was not indiscriminate; rather, the producers organized in UNAG evaluated the deserving cases in each village.

8. Marvin Ortega, "La participación en la questión de las empresas agropecuarias del estado," paper presented at the fifteenth Latin American Sociology Conference, Managua, October 1983. "Lunes Socio-Económico No. 47 and No. 53," Barricada [date missing].

9. La democracia, pp. 63–68.

10. The letters-to-the-editor section of Barricada newspaper was the vehicle of expression for these and other criticisms from the general population to the government entities and the grass-roots organizations themselves.

11. "Lunes Socio-Económico No. 55," Barricada, June 18, 1984.

12. Hugo Assmann, Nicaragua triunfa en la alfabetización (Costa Rica. DEI, 1981). Ministry of Education, La educación en tres años de Revolución (Managua: Ministry of Education, 1982).

13. Rosa María Torres, "La Post-Alfabetización en Nicaragua," Cuadernos de Pensamiento Propio (Managua: INIES, 1983).

14. DECOPS, Ministry of Health, Managua, 1984.

15. Daniel Ortega Saavedra, "Informe de la junta de gobierno en la apertura de la quinta legislatura de consejo de estado," Managua, May 4, 1984.

16. Council of State, "Primera Legislatura," "Segunda Legislatura," Monexico, Nos. 3 and 4 (1981, 1982, 1983, 1984).

17. Iván García, "Papel de los trabajadores en el Plan 1980," mimeographed speech (Managua: CST, 1980), p. 20.

18. Carlos Núñez Téllez, "El papel de las organizaciones de masas en el proceso revolucionario" (Managua: DEPEP, 1980), pp. 20–21.

19. Joseph Collins, What Difference Could a Revolution Make? (San Francisco: Institute for Food and Development Policy, 1982), pp. 81–82.

20. Taped interview, May 1984.

21. Gary Ruchwarger, "Las organizaciones de masas Sandinistas y el proceso revolucionario" (Managua, 1984), p. 16 (unpublished manuscript).

Chapter 4
The Armed Forces

STEPHEN M. GORMAN
THOMAS W. WALKER

One of the major accomplishments of Nicaragua's revolutionary government was the creation of an entirely new military establishment completely dedicated to the political-economic programs of the Sandinista Front. The revolutionary armed forces that were organized into a regular army immediately after the fall of Somoza succeeded in quickly consolidating the hegemony of the Sandinista Front as the vanguard of the revolutionary process. Later, during the Reagan Administration, they proved effective in containing unprecedentedly large CIA-sponsored counterrevolutionary incursions from across both borders. In this chapter we will examine the evolution, organization, and revolutionary roles of the Sandinista Popular Army (EPS) and, to a lesser extent, the Sandinista Police (PS) and Sandinista Popular Militias (MPSs).

EVOLUTION OF THE SANDINISTA ARMED FORCES

The Sandinista Front was formed in 1961 from a number of smaller resistance movements and remained extremely limited in its activities during its early years. Two insurrectionary models guided the FSLN during the formative years between 1961–67: the rebellion of Augusto César Sandino (1927–33), and the more recent Cuban Revolution.

Sandino had created a fairly large, highly mobile army drawn overwhelmingly from the peasantry and rural proletariat; it operated over a large expanse of backland. After early attempts to take and hold fortified towns, Sandino restricted his activities to hit-and-run tactics and to

Stephen M. Gorman, who originally agreed to write this chapter, died suddenly in July 1983. With the kind permission of Steve's wife, Carol Ann, Thomas Walker edited and updated Steve's contribution to *Nicaragua in Revolution* (Praeger, 1982) to produce this chapter, which is dedicated to his memory. Walker, of course, assumes full responsibility for the content and opinions expressed in the last part of the chapter beginning with the title "The Defensive Phase: 1981–84."

establishing a loose "control" over remote areas of the countryside. These areas were protected by an elastic defense that permitted attacking forces to penetrate rebel districts but prevented the enemy from destroying rebel forces or holding territory. The Front had intended to repeat Sandino's rebellion to achieve the objectives outlined in the *foco* (rural "focus") theory that grew out of the Cuban experience. Specifically, the FSLN intended to (1) drain the central government's strength through a protracted war of attrition, (2) achieve national recognition as the political-military vanguard of the antiimperialist, anti-Somocista struggle, and (3) precipitate the internal decomposition of the dictatorship.

Two events in 1967 taught the Sandinistas that, in view of the increasing efficiency of counterinsurgency forces in isolating and destroying incipient guerrilla uprisings in the countryside, neither the example of Sandino nor the Cuban Revolution would be easily reproducible. These were the defeat of Ernesto "Che" Guevara's guerrilla band in Bolivia at the hands of U.S.-trained counterinsurgency forces, and the battle of Pancasán in Nicaragua itself. In the latter, Somoza's U.S.-trained Guardia surrounded, isolated, and killed some of the FSLN's best cadres in a rural foco.

The essential weakness of both the Cuban model and that of Sandino, as demonstrated by these events in 1967, was the predilection to concentrate military operations exclusively in the countryside, where the central government could contain and destroy rebel forces with minimal impact on the rest of the country. The FSLN responded by adjusting its strategy to the concrete realities of Nicaragua after 1967. This included increasing attention to urban organization, which could complement and support continued guerrilla operations in the countryside. (The FSLN had actually begun urban organizational activities as early as 1963, but only on a limited scale.) By the early 1970s, the FSLN had created an extensive network of clandestine organizations in the leading cities, increased its recruitment from universities and unions, and established training centers close to urban areas where students and workers received basic military instruction.[1] From that point forward, the Sandinista Front (working through different factions at times) followed a dual strategy of guerrilla warfare in the countryside aimed at the gradual accumulation of revolutionary forces, and the preparation of the urban masses for an eventual popular insurrection. As James Petras observed immediately after the Sandinista victory in 1979, this proved to be one of the keys to the overthrow of Somoza, since "both the guerrilla movement and the mass urban insurrectionary organizations were necessary for the maintenance of each other's struggle."[2] Significantly, however, control and direction of the armed resistance to the dictatorship remained with the guerrilla leaders in the countryside.

Between 1970 and 1974, the FSLN conducted numerous commando operations alongside its organizational activities in the cities, culminating in the December 1974 raid on a party given in honor of the U.S. Ambassador to Nicaragua, Turner Shelton. The objectives of these operations were threefold: increase the FSLN's political visibility, demonstrate to the masses the vulnerability of the dictatorship, and obtain ransoms and the release of political prisoners. The December raid was especially successful in all three respects, but it also provoked a major counteroffensive by the National Guard (Guardia Nacional, GN) over the next three years that severely damaged the armed resistance in the country. Urban cells were infiltrated and destroyed, and large areas of the provinces were turned into free-fire zones.[3]

From January 1975 through September 1977, the FSLN was thrown completely on the defensive. The apparent success of the Guardia in repressing the resistance led to a factionalization of the FSLN over political-military strategy and three rival "tendencies" arose within the Sandinista Front stressing different revolutionary lines.[4] The tendency that followed the original FSLN strategy most closely was the Prolonged Popular War (GPP) faction. The GPP remained committed to rural guerrilla warfare patterned after the Cuban Revolution designed to involve the enemy in a war of attrition. Its leaders perceived the Revolution as a struggle for the accumulation of forces (for example, experience, organization, weapons, numbers, and so on) in which guerrilla activities were preferable to premature mass insurrectionary tactics. A popular insurrection was considered appropriate only when the correct "insurrectionary moment" had been achieved through guerrilla warfare.

A second faction, the Proletarian tendency (TP), proposed to concentrate on the organization of the urban working class as the most direct and effective strategy for preparing the ground for a future mass-based insurrection. The TP argued that the capitalist development of Nicaragua had turned the proletariat into the most revolutionary class. As Jaime Wheelock explained, the Proletarian tendency was concerned that the Sandinista Front become "more than simply a guerrilla force or an organization of more or less radicalized university students, but the vanguard organization of the working class. . . ."[5] Like the prolonged popular war tendency, however, the TP understood the revolutionary process as a prolonged struggle in which the masses (in this case the urban proletariat) would have to be carefully prepared both politically and militarily for the final offensive at the correct "insurrectionary moment."

In contrast to the GPP and TP factions, the Terceristas (Third Force) called for the immediate initiation of urban insurrectionary activity in cooperation with all opposition parties (including the progressive bourgeoisie). This revolutionary line was bitterly attacked by the other two tendencies because, in their view, it threatened to draw the armed resistance into a premature frontal assault on the dictatorship. This opposition with the Sandinista Front notwithstanding, the Terceristas, with the spontaneous support of some local citizens, carried out spectacular attacks on GN garrisons in several major cities in October 1977. These effectively exploded the myth that the dictatorship had successfully contained and destroyed the armed resistance. Spontaneous civilian participation in these operations illustrated the growing revolutionary potential of the country and allowed the FSLN to retake the initiative against the Guardia. It also demonstrated that the three FSLN tendencies were, in effect, complementary and therefore opened the way to the reunification of the Front.

The next major FSLN offensive came in August 1978 with the seizure of the National Palace, which succeeded in gaining release of prisoners, payment of a ransom, and broadcasting of political communiqués. The following month, the action also helped detonate a popular insurrection that was joined by Sandinista guerrillas who felt obliged to defend the population against the military reprisals of the GN. Thereafter, the Sandinista Front was confronted with the dilemma that, while it was still not strong enough to engage the GN in a frontal assault, its limited armed actions in built-up areas increasingly sparked popular resistance to the dictatorship with the result that FSLN guerrillas were then forced to defend such areas.[6] This tended to draw guerrillas into fixed-location warfare at times and in places other than of their own choosing. But it also permitted the FSLN leadership to appreciate that the correct insurrectionary moment was near. The most important prerequisite to initiating the final offensive then became the reunification of the FSLN.

The three tendencies agreed in principle to reunification in June 1978. Negotiations took place during late 1978 and early 1979, and complete reunification was achieved by March 1979 (although it had been announced as early as December 1978 by Tomás Borge). By this time, the Sandinista armed forces had acquired, if only superficially, many of the attributes of a regular army. In subsequent operations, some ground forces received air cover from the fledgling Sandinista air force, and attacking guerrilla columns began to employ artillery against fortified GN locations. Finally, a unified central command coordinated actions on six fronts (Northern, Southern, Eastern, Western, Central, and Internal [Managua]), while each front, in turn, contained its own general staff.

The final offensive began on May 20, 1979. Up to this point, the strength of the Sandinista Front had been estimated at no more than 1,200 guerrillas, and the largest military operation had involved a column of only 200 guerrillas (the April 7–14 occupation of Estelí). But in May the FSLN launched three simultaneous actions: attacking Jinotega in the north with a column of 350 guerrillas, entering important districts of Managua with a column of 200 guerrillas, and invading Nicaragua from Costa Rica with a column of 300 guerrillas. On June 4 the FSLN called a general strike as fighting in the north shifted to Chinandega, León, and Matagalpa. On June 8 the Battle for Managua began in earnest as 300 popular militias were joined by Sandinista guerrillas. These actions led to an upward revision of estimated FSLN strength to 5,000.[7] But in effect the number of veteran Sandinista guerrillas probably never exceeded 2,000, the remainder being composed of popular militias more or less under Sandinista control, a detachment of foreign volunteers drawn from throughout Latin America, and partially trained Sandinista reserves called into action from the universities and factories. Finally, there were numerous individuals who spontaneously took up arms against the Guardia.

By late June the FSLN had captured León, Masaya, and at least 15 other important cities. Somoza's indiscriminate bombing finally forced the FSLN and popular militias to retreat on June 27 from Managua to Masaya, which had been turned into a Sandinista training camp for recruits. But on July 5 the Sandinista southern front captured Jinotepe, setting the stage for a three-pronged assault on Managua from the north, southwest, and east. Unable to obtain foreign military intervention to rescue his regime, Somoza abandoned the country on July 17. On July 19 Sandinista forces entered the city.[8]

The tenacity with which the GN defended the Somoza regime, the scale of the conflict, and the sophistication of the FSLN military organization all combined to produce a revolutionary army that easily succeeded in filling the power vacuum left by the collapse of the Guardia. This was important because it allowed the FSLN leadership to consolidate political power quickly and impose national order. This latter point was extremely significant, since an inability to maintain order after the fall of Somoza could easily have been used by the United States to conjure up an image of social disintegration in Nicaragua in order to justify military intervention. Moreover, the size, discipline, and fighting experience of the Sandinista armed forces, together with their obvious popularity with the people, served as persuasive deterrents to external intervention.

THE CONSOLIDATION PHASE: 1979–1980

From their earliest days, the Sandinistas had never accepted the myth that military establishments were, could be, or even should be politically neutral. Instead, they viewed armed forces as an inevitable instrument of class control. In most Latin American countries such control was exercised in behalf of the privileged minority. In Nicaragua, however, the FSLN was determined that the military would now serve the interest of the impoverished majority. Therefore, in the first year and a half after their victory, they worked to turn the small FSLN army and other loosely affiliated troops into a class-conscious Sandinista armed force capable of defending their mass-based revolution against probable internal and external counterrevolutionary efforts.

Organization and Composition of the Armed Forces

Figure 4.1 illustrates the institutional relationships that were established between the army, police, and militias after July 1979. At the top of the command structure was the Sandinista National Directorate (Dirección Nacional Conjunta, DNC), which had come into existence with the reunification of the FSLN. The DNC was composed of the three ranking members from each of the three tendencies, all of whom held the rank of Commander of the Revolution. The DNC exercised ultimate authority over the military and police forces. That authority went unchallenged by either the five-member Government of National Reconstruction or the 47-member Council of State (which did not come into existence until May 1980) during the first year of the new government.

The actual organization of the new armed forces was worked out by three members of the Sandinista National Directorate who formed a subcommittee on the military immediately after the fall of Somoza. These three individuals subsequently assumed the most important positions within the armed forces. Tomás Borge became Minister of Interior with control over the Sandinista Police and the State Security Forces. Under Somoza, police activities were performed by the National Guard, meaning that the Ministry of the Interior created after the Revolution represented a new power structure in Nicaraguan politics. Humberto Ortega Saavedra became Commander-in-Chief of the EPS and, in January 1980, also Minister of Defense. The third member of the DNC subcommittee on military organization, Luis Carrión, became Vice-Minister of Defense and second-in-command of the Sandinista Popular Army.

Although Figure 4.1 depicts an institutional separation of police and military responsibilities, in practice the ministries of Interior and Defense were closely interrelated. The head of each ministry sat on the DNC, which allowed for a constant exchange of information and coordination of activities. In addition, at the base of the organizational structure police and soldiers frequently participated in joint operations in efforts to control counterrevolutionary activities. Even at the level of the EPS General Staff, there existed a direct linkage with the Ministry of Interior. For example, the 11-member General Staff appointed in July 1979 included two ranking Sandinista officials from the Ministry of Interior: Edén Pastora, Vice-

FIGURE 4.1 INSTITUTIONAL RELATIONSHIPS

Minister of Interior; and Hugo Torres, Chief of State Security. The linkages between the ministries of Defense and Interior and the concentration of key offices among a handful of Sandinista veterans served to consolidate the DNC's authority over the armed forces.

The precise responsibilities of the General Staff, whose size was subsequently increased to include two women commandantes, were not entirely clear during this period. The EPS copied the Cuban example of establishing regional general staffs capable of directing military operations in different areas of the country in the event that an enemy cut communications with the central command or destroyed the national General Staff. Had a national emergency required a central command to coordinate an overall military response during the first year, that responsibility would likely have been performed by the DNC as much as by the official General Staff itself. The primary responsibilities of the General Staff were concerned with organizational and operational questions, especially the standardization of weapons, the elaboration of a formal system of military ranks, and the imposition of a level of discipline consistent with the requirements of a regular army.

The standardization of weapons was a central concern for both the EPS and the police. When questioned on plans to standardize weapons in the EPS in November 1979, Luis Carrión responded that the arms market is a difficult one. We are seeking favorable conditions in Europe, the Arab countries, and in the United States. Without doubt, the diversity of arms which we are using at this moment is going to create problems; further on we will have to think about standardizing them which will mean discarding some. But our principal problem at this point in time is to acquire weapons of whatever type and from whatever source.[9]

Within the Sandinista Police, the use of strictly combat weapons was not discontinued until May 1980 when police were limited to weapons more consistent with law enforcement activities.[10] The diversity of weapons used by the armed forces created obvious problems in formalizing training programs and setting up an efficient supply system, but the overall amount of armaments and munitions in the possession of EPS appears to have been quite adequate during the first year and a half.

The absence of a formal system of ranks also caused complications for the professionalization of the EPS during the period. Below the three highest ranks recognized by the EPS (Comandante de la Revolución, Comandante Guerrilla, and Comandante), all that existed were the semiofficial "ranks" of primero responsable, segundo responsable, and so on (first in charge, second in charge, and so on). These ranks were routinely applied to anyone in position of responsibility regardless of the size or function of the detachment commanded or the permanency of the command in question. By early 1980, however, the EPS announced a system of ranks (modeled somewhat after the Cuban army) to go into effect on the first anniverary of the Revolution.

Obviously the most fundamental factor affecting the professionalization of the army was discipline, which in turn was conditioned by the composition of the troops. The Program of Government issued by the FSLN just before the fall of Somoza specified that the new army would be

formed from the combatants of the FSLN; soldiers and officers [of the GN] that have demonstrated honest and patriotic conduct in the face of the corruption, repression and treason of the Dictatorship and those that fought for the overthrow of the Somocista regime; from all sectors of the Nation that engaged in combat for liberation and desire to join the new Army; and from able citizens who offer themselves for military service.[11]

The army that took shape after July closely resembled the one outlined in this document, but its heterogeneity made the imposition of a uniform standard of discipline difficult.

For example, although the DNC outlawed capital punishment after assuming power, some Sandinista units in the countryside (composed of peasants or under the command of radicals) carried out summary executions and unlawful confiscations that were then concealed from the central authorities. When these abuses were discovered, a thorough purge was carried out within the EPS.[12] Other groups that had fought for the overthrow of the dictatorship, such as the Milpas (Anti-Somoza Popular Militas, under the control of the Trotskyist Workers Front), proved too extremist to be incorporated into the EPS and were therefore pressured (not always successfully) to disband. But by far the most serious obstacles to the professionalization of the new army were a high rate of illiteracy and a low level of political consciousness among non-FSLN troops.

A census within the EPS in late 1979 showed an illiteracy rate of approximately 45 percent. To correct this problem, literate troops were assigned to provide ongoing instruction in educational basics to illiterate troops. To contend with the lack of adequate political orientation among some of the recruits, on the other hand, political-cultural sections were established at all levels and in all regional commands to provide continuing political indoctrination, as well as instruction in basic personal hygiene, which was found to be deficient among recruits from the lowest social classes.[13] Political training was considered to be on a par with military training. As one officer connected with the General Staff explained, troops needed to fully understand whose interests they were protecting and who the enemies of those interests were. Otherwise, EPS members would eventually fall into the same elitist, antipopular practices as the former National Guard.[14]

The content of political-cultural training in the military stressed the evolution of the Sandinista struggle, the legitimacy of the Sandinista Front's role as the vanguard in the revolutionary process, and the preeminently popular character of the new regime. While Marxist-Leninist principles were not directly interjected into the indoctrination process, the ideological thrust was essentially socialistic (although private property was not categorically rejected). The responsibility of soldiers to set moral examples for the population, to take advantage of every opportunity to work with members of the popular classes, and to avoid developing particularistic interests that might weaken their identification with the disadvantaged were especially significant elements of political-cultural training. The ideal soldier, according to the model projected by the Sandinista leadership, was one willing to oppose any and all threats to the material and spiritual well-being of the masses. A particularly interesting facet of the training was the attention given to working with children. Accordingly, the military sponsored a variety of recreational and cultural programs aimed at bringing soldiers and children together, which had a predictable socializing impact on both groups.

The decision to indoctrinate EPS members in Sandinista ideology brought some criticisms from the bourgeoisie that called for a depoliticization of the armed forces. In response, Tomás Borge pointed out that

> there is no apolitical army in the world. This is a sophism. . . . There are no apolitical armies: every one serves some determinant political purpose. In the case of Nicaragua, the EPS is a Popular and Sandinista Army. It is not by accident that we call it such.[15]

The attention to political instruction clearly strengthened DNC control of the armed forces, and also helped overcome the threat of factionalism within the army posed by its heterogeneity. Political instruction was reinforced by volunteer work projects in which EPS detachments harvested coffee, helped clean up barrios, or engaged in other activities together with civilian labor brigades.

The actual size of the EPS remained a military secret after the victory, but by mid-1980 it probably numbered between 13,000 and 18,000. The core of the army was the FSLN guerrilla veterans, of which possibly no more than 1,300 remained in the military after the fall of Somoza. Two other components were ex-National Guard troops (especially those who had defected before the final defeat of Somoza), and members of the Sandinista-led popular militias who saw action during the final offensive (between 2,500 and 3,500). The remainder of the EPS was recruited mainly from among those who could prove some form of participation in the struggle against Somoza. The percentage of women in the EPS by the end of its first year was between 8 and 10 percent (women had represented 25 percent of FSLN combatants during the Revolution).[16]

The inclusion of a small percentage of former GN members in the EPS requires some clarification as does the small percentage of women incorporated into the new army. Most (although certainly not all) of the brutality associated with the GN was committed by the 3,000 elite troops under the command of Anastasio Somoza's son. Those who were apprehended were tried before special tribunals. Other GN elements who were drawn overwhelmingly from poor social backgrounds and who merely followed orders and committed no crimes against the people were considered capable of resocialization by the FSLN. Nevertheless, by early 1980 leaders of the EPS claimed that no ex-Guardia remained in the Sandinista Popular Army (which may have meant that their former identification with the GN had been completely overcome, since troops openly conceded the continued presence of former GN elements in the EPS.).[17]

The reduction in the percentage of women in the new army resulted both from the diluting effect of heavy male enlistment after July 1979 and from the active encouragement of the EPS command for women to assume nonmilitary duties in the reconstruction of the country. In the event of foreign invasion, women were still considered suitable for combat duty, but during peacetime they were considered to be better suited for administrative and technical positions. Those women that remained in the military were not fully integrated into male units, but instead were provided with separate quarters or, more frequently, an allowance for off-base housing (usually with their families).[18]

The length of military service remained "indeterminant" during this period, although plans existed to fix minimum terms of enlistment at between two and three years. In practice, the EPS was interested in recruiting career soldiers. Basic training for recruits ranged from three to six months depending on the educational level and military experience of the individual. The Cuban government supplied an unspecified number (approximately 200–300) of military personnel to assist the Sandinista Popular Army in basic training, setting up advanced training programs, and as military advisors for regional commands. Veteran troops were used immediately after July to begin training Sandinista Popular Militias in areas of the country where the danger of counterrevolutionary activities seemed greatest. It was projected that by the end of the first year there would be over 100,000 fully trained individuals organized into MPSs throughout the country capable of rapid mobilization and integration into the EPS.

The MPSs were organized at the level of neighborhoods (usually in conjunction with the Sandinista Defense Committees) or by workplace and served not only as a reserve for the army but also as extensions of the Sandinista Police. Although the MPSs proved an effective and economical way of augmenting the strength of the EPS, plans were already in the making by late 1979 to replace the militias at some future point with mandatory military service.[19]

According to Luis Carrión, once the size of the EPS had been stabilized and its members fully trained, a draft would be instituted that would provide 30,000 to 40,000 recruits a year with military training, following which they would serve for a set number of years in the reserves. To provide training for such a large number of draftees each year would require a low turnover within the regular army itself, which explains why the EPS sought career enlistees almost from the outset. To minimize the financial burden of maintaining such a large military establishment the military (and especially the reserves) would increasingly assume civic responsibilities that could directly increase national productivity. The regular army itself was intended to level off at roughly the size of Somoza's National Guard, but the national defense would be made significantly stronger through the system of reserves.[20]

Another issue connected with efforts to professionalize the EPS was remuneration for officers and enlistees. A general policy established for the government as a whole set a maximum salary for any public employee of approximately 10,000 cordobas per month (or about $12,000 a year) in addition to housing and food allowances for certain categories of enlistees. It was recognized that the professionalization and stabilization of the composition of the EPS would require higher pay in the future, but, in this period, the General Staff was forced to rely almost exclusively on moral incentives to attract, motivate, and retain quality enlistees in the EPS.[21]

Finally, it is necessary to comment on the efforts of the Sandinista leadership to prevent even the slightest U.S. influence in the new Nicaraguan armed forces. Although the Sandinista Front called on the United States to supply the new regime with weapons immediately after the overthrow of Somoza, this probably indicated a desire to disarm the interventionist lobby in Washington more than it signaled a willingness to continue Nicaragua's traditional reliance on American military assistance. The request was rejected by Washington, but the United States did offer to (1) provide training programs for Nicaraguan military personnel in the United States, (2) send U.S. military advisors and instructors in noncombat military areas to Nicaragua, and (3) provide over $2 million in noncombat military assistance to the new government. (This third offer involved money that had been originally allocated to the Somoza government but that had been held up after the United States applied an arms embargo to the country late in the war.)

Not only did the Sandinista leadership reject all three offers, but it moved to restrict access by members of the U.S. military mission (attached to the U.S. Embassy in Managua) to Nicaraguan military personnel. After early 1980, embassy personnel were required to obtain the prior permission of the Nicaraguan Defense Minister before either visiting Nicaraguan military installations or talking with EPS officers. The intention of such restrictions and precautions appears to have been to lessen the (albeit remote) possibility of U.S. political influence in the new Nicaraguan armed forces. The behavior of the Sandinista leadership in setting up the new military apparatus exhibited an awareness of the potential political ramifications of an armed forces less than enthusiastically committed to revolutionary reform. Thus the measures to prevent virtually any form of U.S. influence in the armed forces were consistent with other policies in this field.

The Role of the Armed Forces in the Revolution

The Program of Government issued by the FSLN just before the fall of Somoza clearly envisioned a major role for the new army in the reconstruction of Nicaragua society:

The national Army will maintain a permanent association with the civil population and participate actively in the tasks of reconstruction and development. To accomplish this its members will be organized into different technical specialties and professions.[22]

Although the armed forces forged close ties with the general population, and participated whenever possible in the effort to rebuild the country, little progress was made during this period either to develop technical capabilities within the military directly related to national reconstruction or to involve the EPS in a major role in public-works projects. Two explanations can be offered for this. First, the serious educational deficiencies within the EPS required that basic instruction precede any large-scale program of technical training. Second, the urgent need after the overthrow of the dictatorship to organize a national defense against internal and external threats to the Revolution forced the armed forces to concentrate primarily upon their military role. Nevertheless, whenever possible the armed forces either participated in, or lent direct support to, a wide range of socioeconomic projects during the first year and a half after the Sandinista victory. We will review the separate primary roles performed by the EPS, PS, and MPSs in the following discussion, but it should be kept in mind that all three worked in close cooperation in a variety of activities.

The Sandinista Popular Army performed three major roles during this period. It defended the Revolution from internal and external armed threats, provided logistical and other forms of support for socioeconomic projects, and supplied emergency labor in critical areas of the economy.

The major sources of armed aggression against the Sandinista regime were ex-Guardias, the ultraleftist Milpas, and right-wing guerrillas. After the fall of Somoza, as many as 2,000 members of the defeated National Guard escaped to Honduras, where they concentrated near the Nicaraguan frontier. The EPS was forced to station a large proportion of its best-trained soldiers in the northern provinces to defend against periodic incursions by ex-Guardian elements. The Sandinista Popular Army also attempted to strengthen the defenses along the northern frontier by giving priority to the organization and training of the Sandinista Popular Militias in the northern provinces, especially Estelí. Although the EPS generally succeeded in deterring any large-scale counterrevolutionary actions by ex-Guardia units, isolated attacks by groups of Somocista soldiers crossing into Nicaragua continued throughout the period.[23]

The ability of the revolutionary government to protect participants in important projects like the Literacy Campaign from attacks by counter-revolutionary groups was viewed as a crucial test of Sandinista strength. The EPS responded by establishing closer ties with mass-based popular organizations such as the Sandinista Defense Committees, the Association of Rural Workers, and, of course, the MPSs. While countering the threat of remaining GN elements in the north, however, the EPS also had to contain the paramilitary activities of the Milpas in the leading urban centers.

The Milpas engaged in a number of counterrevolutionary acts, ranging from keeping workers out on strike through armed intimidation to attacks on banks to finance ultraleftist activities. But the overall intention of the Milpas was to push the government further to the left by forcing it to quicken the tempo of reform and not to involve the EPS in a protracted armed struggle. Accordingly, it was possible for the FSLN to pursue a dual strategy of attempting to strike a political bargain with the Workers Front that controlled the Milpas, while at the same time the EPS contained and limited the activities of the Milpas.[24]

A more serious threat was posed by the Democratic Armed Forces (Fuerzas Armadas Democráticas, FAD), which began operating in the central provinces in early 1980. The FAD was a right-wing guerrilla organization financed in large part by some members of the livestock component of the agroexport bourgeoisie. Its largest armed action was the capture of San José de los Remates in the province of Boaco in May 1980. Twenty heavily armed FAD members were able to attack the EPS command in Los Remates and hold the town of 2,000 for over five hours. Within a week of the attack, however, State Security Forces had rounded up 42 individuals suspected of involvement, including important members of the Livestock Federation of Nicaragua accused of financing FAD activities and providing their *fincas* as training centers.[25]

Defending the revolutionary government against these sources of armed opposition forced the EPS to concentrate most of its attention on purely military functions. According to the information officer of the EPS, the central responsibility of the army during the period remained military preparation. But to the extent that time and resources permitted, the EPS filled other roles as well. In particular, the army remained available for the transportation of supplies and workers involved in government programs or reconstruction projects. When it was discovered that many of the volunteers in the Literacy Campaign sent into remote areas could not be adequately fed by the families they were sent to teach, it became largely the responsibility of the EPS and PS to undertake a crash program to deliver provisions to these areas. Another form of participation by the EPS in the recovery of the country after the insurrection was the use of soldiers to help harvest the first coffee crop. However, because of the pressing need to concentrate on military training in the regular army, the MPSs were used more often than the EPS in civic work projects and agricultural labor.[26]

The Sandinista police frequently found themselves participating closely with the EPS in controlling counterrevolutionary groups and lending material and physical assistance to national reconstruction programs. The PS also received sufficient military training to participate in national defense since in the event of a foreign threat, as Tomás Borge explained, "the police and soldiers of the Sandinista Popular Army are going to go to the same trenches and shed the same blood."[27] But under normal conditions it was intended that the functions of the police and army would be quite distinct. According to Borge,

> the members of the State Security Forces, the Sandinista Police and the Sandinista Popular Army form part of the same family and regardless of where they go they must be coordinated. United in the same force, the only thing that has to be understood is that their functions are distinct. The police are responsible for maintaining order, protecting the people— especially children and the weak—from delinquents and from antisocial enemies. . . . The army should concentrate on constant military training in order to be ready as a vanguard force in the hour of combat to confront the armed enemies of our Revolution. . . . [28]

In practice, the PS actually did concentrate on law enforcement during the first year and a half. Three important objectives of the PS Central Command were reducing street crime, controlling vice, and enforcing what might be termed morality and public welfare laws.

During the last stages of the civil war, a large quantity of weapons fell into the hands of the general population, reaching some elements that had not participated in the struggle against the GN. The breakdown of the old order, coupled with a sharp rise in the number of weapons held by private citizens, helped give rise to an increase in violent crimes after the Sandinista victory. The problem was compounded by the appearance of numerous youth gangs involved in drug traffic and armed robberies and related activities. To contend with the problem, the police began to conduct well-coordinated raids in early 1980, arresting "known delinquents" for "illicit association" (when more serious charges could not be pressed). By late May 1980, the Sandinista Police Central Command was able to announce a decline in crime rates in certain categories.[29]

In the area of vice and public welfare, the police were charged with enforcing a wide variety of laws intended to moralize society and eradicate the social legacies of the decadent Somoza dynasty. Two targets of this campaign were prostitution and alcoholism. But efforts to control prostitution and drunkenness were complicated by a number of interrelated factors. First, there was a shortage of resources with which to set up rehabilitation programs and thus enforcement of laws against prostitution, for example, could only be punative (and prostitutes were not considered criminals). Second, the enforcement of laws like those prohibiting the consumption of alcohol in the marketplaces or the sale of intoxicants before certain hours often brought the police into conflict with members of the lowest social classes and therefore detracted somewhat from efforts to increase solidarity between the police and the people. In essence, the FSLN was forced to recognize that governments cannot legislate morality. Thus, police turned a blind eye to prostitution until June 1980, when some limited efforts were finally made to enforce laws against prostitution, but laws controlling alcohol continued to be only sporadically and unevenly enforced. For instance, laws restricting the sale of beer before afternoon were universally disregarded by the public, and the police relied mostly on warnings against lower-class proprietors caught violating the law rather than arrests or citations.

While the EPS concentrated primarily on military functions, and the PS on law enforcement, the Sandinista Popular Militias filled a number of roles in the revolution. The MPSs served as a reserve for the army, and also as an extension of the police. Members of the MPSs were frequently employed to guard public installations or aid police in major operations. Those militias organized in factories were used to protect the installations and equipment from destruction by ultraleftist elements (such as the Milpas) during labor disturbances, or from owners who might attempt to decapitalize their facilities in anticipation of expropriation. In some neighborhoods the MPSs took over a large share of the responsibility of the Sandinista Police, while in the countryside they were assigned to protect volunteers in the Literacy Campaign from right-wing terrorist activities.

In practice, it was the MPSs during the first year and a half that provided much of the voluntary labor for harvesting crops, building public facilities, and cleaning up the barrios. Manpower constraints and the need to concentrate on intensive military training severely limited the ability of the EPS to participate in the reconstruction of the economy. Indeed, given the high rate of unemployment among the general population, there was no real demand for the army to supply manpower that could be easily mobilized through the CDSs, MPSs, and other mass-based organizations. Rather, the actual purpose of occasionally providing troops from the regular army to participate in voluntary labor projects was to forge closer ties with the people.

A final role performed by the armed forces as a whole that must be touched on involved the suppression of political opposition. The FSLN promised a pluralist revolution, and, to a surprising extent for a group that held a decisive power advantage, it observed that pledge. There was considerable, if not complete, freedom of the press during this period and the bourgeois opposition was permitted to organize and criticize the government after it became alarmed with the perceived direction of revolutionary reform in early 1980. But the Sandinista Front, nevertheless, showed itself willing to carry out selective repressions against specific groups it considered potentially dangerous. Accordingly, the police and State Security forces were used on a number of occasions to capture political opponents of the regime who sometimes were then held secretly in violation of the new Statute of Rights by the FSLN, or were convicted on vague and often unsubstantiated charges.[30] However, it should be stressed that the government did not use the armed forces in a systematic program of repression, that those who were detained were not mistreated as had been the practice under Somoza, and that the prison terms of these few actually convicted of political crimes tended to be relatively short. Therefore, the fact that the EPS, PS, and even the MPSs were employed to limit some forms of political opposition should not overshadow the reality that the Sandinista government actually exhibited considerable restraint in view of its complete and undivided control of the military institutions of the state. Indeed, its behavior in the area of civil and political rights compared very favorably with that of the majority of Latin American governments and, notably, with the three Central American regimes to the north.

The Significance of the Consolidation Phase

The Sandinista Front succeeded in consolidating and institutionalizing its control over the new armed forces during its first year and a half in power, which in turn contributed significantly to the FSLN's control over the direction of governmental policies. Therefore, the creation and rapid development of the Sandinista Popular Army, the Sandinista Police, and the Sandinista Popular Militias stands out as one of the major political achievements of the immediate postwar period. Several factors facilitated the FSLN's efforts to build a new and effective military apparatus in Nicaragua. First, the length of the Sandinista Front's struggle against the Somoza dictatorship forged an experienced and politically oriented cadre of guerrillas that was able to serve as the core of the new army. It was not necessary for the new revolutionary leaders in Nicaragua to rely, even in part, on the prerevolutionary military establishment. Equally important, the Sandinista leaders who assumed the command positions within the armed forces demonstrated early their intentions of imposing discipline and centralized authority over the military and their willingness to purge dissident elements even from among their own ranks. This emphasis on discipline and centralized authority was complemented by a vigorous program of political-cultural training of recruits. This created a noticeably different institutional mentality within the Nicaraguan armed forces from that found in other so-called revolutionary Latin American countries.

Finally, the precautions against the establishment of even a modicum of U.S. influence in the new armed forces helped protect the revolutionary orientation of the army and its loyalty to the Sandinista Front.

THE DEFENSIVE PHASE: 1981–84

The beginning of 1981 was a watershed for Nicaragua, marking the start of a period in which national defense would become an overriding priority for the new revolutionary system. Whereas 1980 had been officially dubbed "The Year of Literacy," 1981, 1982, and 1983, respectively, bore the titles, "The Year of Defense and Production," "The Year of Unity in the Face of Aggression," and "The Year of Struggle for Peace and Sovereignty." This increased concern with defense was by no means a matter of irrational paranoia as U.S. officials were fond of portraying it. It coincided with the administration of a U.S. president, Ronald Reagan, who was unambiguously and menacingly hostile to the Nicaraguan Revolution. In mid-1980 the Republican National Platform had "abhor[red] the Marxist Sandinist takeover" in Nicaragua. Advisors to candidate Reagan had advocated various tactics to destroy the Revolution. And, immediately after Reagan's victory, a representative of the president-elect, while on a fact-finding mission to Central America, asked at least one prominent Nicaraguan businessman what the U.S. could do to help overthrow the Sandinistas.[31]

From the Reagan inauguration onward, U.S. aggressiveness toward Nicaragua escalated steadily.[32] By March the U.S. media were reporting that Nicaraguan and Cuban exiles were openly (and in clear violation of international law) training in paramilitary camps in Florida and elsewhere with the objective of "liberating" their homelands.[33] Secretary of State Alexander Haig spoke of "going to the source" to stop arms shipments he alleged were being sent to the Salvadoran insurgents from the Socialist bloc via Cuba and Nicaragua. In December, President Reagan signed the "finding" authorizing CIA-sponsored covert action in Nicaragua. In 1982 and 1983 these plans were put into action as the economic infrastructure was sabotaged and thousands of CIA-supported counterrevolutionary troops (President Reagan called them "Freedom Fighters") began attacking Nicaragua from bases in Honduras and Costa Rica. By 1984 the two CIA-sponsored contra armies (The Nicaraguan Democratic Forces [FDN] in the North and the Democratic Revolutionary Alliance [ARDE] in the South) were reported by U.S. government sources and the Sandinistas as having grown to a combined strength of between 10,000 and 15,000 men. (A proportionately equivalent invasion of the United States would number between 850,000 and 1,280,000 troops.) In addition, there was a massive U.S. military buildup in Honduras and a series of ever larger joint U.S.-Central American military exercises near Nicaragua's borders.

The contra activities alone inflicted hundreds of millions of dollars of infrastructural damage and resulted in thousands of deaths and much suffering. In words sadly familiar to those of us who had traveled through Nicaragua and talked with survivors of the contra war, an American priest recounted the human impact of the activities of one contra "task force" in his parish, Bocana de Paiwas, in August and September of 1983:

In the township of Anito, they killed 6 people, robbed 50,000 córdobas, burned 8 houses and an outboard motorboat used by the cooperative for river transportation, blew up part of the chapel with a mortar shell, and, to say farewell, shot another mortar shell into a group of people who had come together for the burial of one of the victims.

In Ocaguas, the FDN "freedom fighters" murdered two campesinos. One was stabbed and had his eyes dug out before being killed. The other was hung from a beam of his own home. On the same day (September 1), in Las Minitas, they burned 6 houses and all the clothes that the cooperative had on sale. Before leaving, they killed the wife of the militia chief with a gunshot to the head. They killed a campesino from El Guayabo, who happened to be passing through Las Minitas, because he was carrying his UNAG membership card.

The task force arrived in El Guayabo the next day and killed 9 people. One of the victims was a 14-year-old girl who was raped by several men and later decapitated. They threw her body into a brook and placed her head in the road at the entrance to the village. They did the same with the head of another campesino. Three women were forced to roll in the mud like pigs for the amusement of the contras. At gunpoint, they were made to lie face down in the mud for a considerable length of time, after which the contras fired on them. One was killed, another was wounded, and the third was not injured. Later, they raped another woman and entered a house where they proceeded to murder a couple in the presence of their 3 children. The contras then burned 4 houses without allowing their occupants enough time to save their clothing or tools, just as they had done elsewhere.

The task forces abducted 15 campesinos from the different townships. As were the 150 who had arrived with the contras, the newly kidnapped campesinos were forced to carry packs of provisions and ammunition weighing between 80 and 100 pounds. Campesinos abducted by the contras are given one meal a day and live as prisoners with the constant threat of being shot if they attempt to escape.

However, Arcadio Pérez Mendoza, a delegate of the Word in Las Minitas and the father of several militia members, did escape. He revealed what his abductors talked about in his presence. "We're going to cut off your head so that we can drink your blood," said one of them. Another said, "No, let's hang him until his tongue sticks out to punish him for not telling us where his sons are."

Two women from Anito whose houses were burnt told of how the counterrevolutionaries showed them their new weapons (FALs) while talking about President Reagan's support for the FDN. They also showed large sums of money. One campesino was told that he would be paid 40,000 córdobas if he joined the contras. They stole a Bible from Valentín Velázquez, a delegate of the Word in Anito. "This way, the people around here will see that we are Christians," the FDN members said.[34]

In addition, there were major "leaks" from various U.S. government agencies about contingency plans being readied by the Pentagon for a direct U.S. military invasion of Nicaragua. The first, which emerged late in 1983 and was code-named "Operation Pegasus," called for a U.S. invasion early in 1984 to follow on the heals of an attempt by the armed forces of Northern Central America to militarily "pacify" Nicaragua. The second, about a year later, forsaw an incursion by Honduran forces followed by a U.S. air attack and ground invasion in February 1985. Both Pegasus and its sequel were to be triggered by some sort of essentially fabricated incident either on the Honduran border or in Nicaragua.[35] While the Sandinistas were aware that these "leaks" could have been a deliberate attempt to frighten and pressure them, it would have been foolish of Managua to completely discount them.

Not surprisingly, the Sandinist armed forces changed significantly during the first three and a half years of the Reagan Administration. Better and more standardized weaponry was acquired, principally from the Socialist bloc. The army, militia, police, and security forces grew in number, received more professional training, and became more diversified in function. And a military draft, first envisioned right after the victory, was finally implemented.

Throughout, the Reagan Administration portrayed these changes as evidence that Nicaragua was being built into a platform for "communist" expansionism in the region. Carefully staged televised "briefings" by military and intelligence experts conveyed the impression of Nicaragua as a regional superpower preparing to spring on its defenseless neighbors.[36] In fact, however, not long after one of these TV spectaculars, a subcommittee of the House of Representatives' Committees on Intelligence issued a staff report in which it noted, among other things, that, while U.S. intelligence services were publicly trumpeting Nicaragua's supposed offensive capabilities and intentions, there had been "classified briefings, whose analytic judgments about Nicaragua's intentions were quite distinct from those that appeared implicit in the [public] briefing on the build-up."[37] A little over a week later before another congressional committee a well-informed authority on the military establishments of the Central American countries reconfirmed that Nicaragua's military establishment was clearly defensive in nature and that it would be "ludicrous" for Nicaragua, with almost no air force and other major military inadequacies, to attempt an invasion of Honduras,[38] the country that Washington was billing as the most likely target.

The real purpose of the buildup was defensive. It is unlikely that the Sandinista leadership nurtured any illusion that a small country such as theirs could ever withstand a full-scale, direct U.S. invasion. However, the arms buildup did serve two realistic purposes: (1) to contain the contras and to prepare to withstand any attack by Central American armies acting as U.S. surrogates, and (2) to insure that the costs of a direct U.S. invasion would be so high to the invader that the United States would not see the reconquest of Nicaragua as worthwhile. Nicaragua, they frequently warned, would not be "another Grenada."

Armaments

The arms buildup during this period *was* significant but at no point did Nicaragua attempt to acquire the type of hardware that would have given it an overall offensive potential. Early on, there was an effort to standardize the light arms carried by the EPS and the militia. For the former, Eastern block AK-47 automatic rifles soon replaced the Belgian FALs, U.S. M-16s, and Israeli Galils and Uzis that had been used in the War of Liberation. In addition, some militiapersons soon received 1950s-vintage Czech BZ-52 ten-shot rifles. Eventually, since the "BZs" were obsolete in comparison with the weaponry carried by the contras, the militia—or at least those in war zones—were also issued "AKs." The older weapons, of course, were not discarded: One often saw them in the hands of militiapersons or guards in areas away from the front.

From mid-1981 onward, Nicaragua also began accelerating its acquisition of various pieces of heavy military hardware. Included were dozens of Soviet-made T-54 and T-55 tanks that were immediately identified by Washington as a threat to neighboring Honduras. Yet, as one expert pointed out, these tanks were hardly potential instruments of aggression against that country, since (1) under optimal conditions, it would take them ten hours, lumbering along the Pan American Highway (the only road that would accommodate them), to get to the Honduran capital of Tegucigalpa; (2) all this time, they would be facing the most powerful air force in Central American (that of Honduras) with virtually no air protection from Nicaragua; and (3) the "specs" for these tanks indicate that they might not even be able to negotiate the steep grade in some parts of that mountain highway.[39] The much more probable intended use was to destroy armored and transport vehicles in the event of a full-scale invasion from the north. Throughout the period the tanks saw little or no action against the contras.

Other armaments included about a dozen French- and Soviet-built patrol boats (the contras frequently attacked by sea as did CIA commandos in their destruction of diesel storage facilities at Corinto late in 1983 and their mining of Nicaraguan harbors in 1984); several Soviet-built helicopters (originally used in the Literacy Crusade but also essential in fighting the contras); a wide variety of antiaircraft guns and ground-to-air missile launchers (which subsequently downed a number of U.S.-supplied contra aircraft including several light civilian-type planes, helicopters, and at least two C-47 cargo planes); a number of large-caliber rocket launchers, howitzers, and mortars (which proved very effective in dealing with pockets of invading contras); eight Soviet-built light transport aircraft; and an assortment of Socialist bloc trucks. Again, this hardware was largely defensive in nature and most of it was acquired after 1981.[40]

In most respects these armaments were adequate in dealing with the contras and roughly balanced the military hardware of Honduras. However, in air power, Nicaragua was at an alarming disadvantage. With a fleet of over 70 U.S.-, Israeli-, and French-made warplanes—most of them modern jets[41]—Honduras had the biggest air force in Central America and one that dangerously dwarfed the half dozen or so Korean War-vintage planes the Sandinistas had inherited from Somoza and the eight more recently acquired light Soviet-built cargo planes.[42] For several years Nicaraguan leaders talked of purchasing fighter jets from the USSR or France; but the United States torpedoed a French sale in 1982 and threatened Nicaragua into not importing Soviet MIGs. Pilots for the MIGs did receive training in Bulgaria and it was frequently rumored that the planes themselves were ready in Cuba, but, as of late-1984, none had arrived in Nicaragua. Nicaragua faced a harsh dilemma: While the MIGs would be crucially important in the event of a full-scale invasion, their importation might well trigger just such an attack.

The Nature of the Armed Forces

The nature of the armed forces also changed during this period. Total military manpower grew in response to the external threat. The army was expanded from 13,000-18,000 in 1980 to around 24,000 in the period from 1981 to 1983, to probably over 40,000 in 1984. The first jump came soon after the inauguration of Ronald Reagan. The second followed the large-scale contra incursions of 1983. In the latter case the regular army was increased by regrouping some of the best militia troops into reserve army battalions (Batallones de Reserva) and by instituting a general draft (the Patriotic Military Service). Within the army, special ranger units (the Irregular Combat Battalions [BLI]) were created to search out and destroy the contras in remote areas.

It is impossible to estimate accurately how many militiapersons there were at a given point in time. A rough guess would be that they numbered between 60,000 and 100,000 in 1984. But it is clear that their fighting capacity had increased noticeably as the contra war deepened and the threat of U.S. invasion grew. Little more than patriotic marching groups in 1980 and 1981, the *milicianos* had come to shoulder a major role in the war by 1984. Armed, by then, with AK-47s, these civilian soldiers were often the first line of defense.

The nature of militia organization also changed. Territorial militia—organized by geographical location—replaced the amateur militias set up by mass organizations or according to workplace several years before. In addition, a cordon of Kibbutz-like Self-Defense Agricultural Committees had been created in or near battle zones. Their members were given land to farm and the weapons (AK-47s) with which to defend it. They were both milicianos and private or cooperative farmers at the same time. And, like milicianos throughout the conflictive zones in general, they were often fierce and motivated fighters.

The third branch of the armed forces—the police and the state security units—had changed, but not as much. The few thousand police persons (many were women) were concerned mainly with public safety functions in the urban areas. Unarmed or lightly armed, they were often assisted by volunteer police and by volunteers of the Vigilancia Revolucionaria, a sort of neighborhood crime watch that patrolled many neighborhoods through-out the night to respond to minor emergencies and control petty crime and delinquency. On the other hand, the state security forces had grown in function and probably also in manpower. The rough equivalent of the FBI in the United States, they had become very adept in uncovering and dismantling attempts to set up counterrevolutionary networks in the interior of the country. From 1980 to 1984 several alleged counter-revolutionary groups were uncovered and impressive evidence about them—videotaped confessions, weaponry, and so on—was presented to the public on television. The state security even had a special crack contingent called the Pablo Ubeda ranger unit. As of mid-1984, all efforts to set up a fifth column in the interior of the country had failed dismally.

The Human Rights Performance of the Armed Forces

Overall, the behavior of the Sandinist armed forces in the area of human rights was quite good. The major human rights monitoring organizations—Amnesty International, Americas Watch, and the Human Rights Commission of the Organization of American States—were invited by the revolutionary government to visit Nicaragua on various occasions. While their reports expressed concern over some matters such as the occasional arbitrary short-term imprisonment of political opponents and suspected subversives, they did not corroborate the Reagan Administration portrayal of Nicaragua as one of Latin America's most flagrant human rights offenders. These groups could find little evidence of the extreme types of human rights violations so common under such U.S.-backed regimes as Guatemala and El Salvador. There were apparently no government-sponsored death squads, no officially sanctioned use of physical torture, and few extralegal executions or "disappearances."[43] While, as in any society, there were occasional excesses by individual armed personnel—including rape, murder, and other forms of brutality—the usual response by the government was to investigate and discipline those responsible.

Socialist Bloc Influence and Support

Socialist bloc assistance to the Nicaraguan armed forces, while important, did not warrant the inflated alarmism with which it was treated by the Reagan Administration. It is true that Nicaragua did purchase or obtain most of its weaponry from the Socialist bloc. But, in fairness, it is hard to imagine what else it could have done once the United States not only refused to sell it arms but also actively pressured other non-Communist countries to follow suit.

There was also the charge that the Sandinist armed forces were essentially run by an alleged 2,000 Socialist bloc advisors—mainly Cubans. However, judging from the Reagan Administration's flawed record for veracity in matters of this sort, it is likely that the real figure was closer to the 200 cited by both Cuba and Nicaragua. It should be remembered that immediately following the U.S. invasion of Grenada, the United States claimed that there were well over 1,100 Cubans on the island and that all were "well trained professional soldiers" who had been "impersonating" civilians. The Cuban government insisted that there were only 784 and that most were civilians. Eventually, the U.S. government divulged figures and information that showed that the Cubans had been correct on *both* counts.[44]

Finally, it was clear that, in the long run, Nicaragua's defense was largely Nicaragua's responsibility. On various occasions the Soviets had publicly stated that they would *not* defend Nicaragua militarily in the event of a U.S. invasion. Cuba might be defended but not Nicaragua. This, coupled with the fact that the Soviets stubbornly refused to respond favorably to Nicaragua's requests for hard-currency assistance, meant that Nicaragua had good reason to try to seek accommodation, rather than confrontation, with the United States.

CONCLUSION

The Sandinist armed forces were clearly one of the major support pillars of the new revolutionary system. Forged in the 18-month War of Liberation, they had grown and developed into institutions that, while normally moderate and restrained in their treatment of law-abiding civilians, had proven capable of containing subversion from within and an unprecedentedly large CIA-sponsored counterrevolutionary invasion from across both borders. In spite of massive material and financial support from the United States, the contras had failed miserably even in their most minimal objective of seizing and holding at least one population center to serve as a base for their alternative government. In addition, hundreds of thousands of Nicaraguans, in one way or another, had participated in the defense of their fatherland. This involvement had raised their political awareness and commitment to the Revolution. Any attempt to reconquer their country would come at a high cost to the invader. Nevertheless, there was near-universal hope that a more generalized war could be avoided and that Nicaragua's scarce financial resources could be redirected toward alleviating the pressing human problems of the impoverished majority.

NOTES

1. Eduardo Crawley, *Dictators Never Die: A Portrait of Nicaragua and the Somoza Dynasty* (New York: St. Martin's Press, 1979), pp. 148–154; and James Petras, "Whither the Nicaraguan Revolution?" *Monthly Review* 31 (October 1979):7–9.

2. Petras, "Nicaraguan Revolution," p. 11.

3. The political objectives of the December action are discussed in Jaime Wheelock, *Diciembre victorioso* (Managua: Secretaria Nacional de Propaganda y Educación Política, 1979). The repression that followed is discussed in an interview with Humberto Ortega Saavedra in "La estrategia del triunfo," *La Prensa*, January 4, 1980.

4. The positions of all three tendencies are presented in "Sandinista Perspectives: Three Differing Views," *Latin American Perspectives* 6 (Winter 1979):114–127.

5. Ibid., p. 122.

6. See Gabriel García Márquez, "Sandinistas Seize the National Palace," *New Left Review*, September 1978, pp. 79–88, and part two of "La estrategia del triunfo," *La Prensa*, January 4, 1980, p. 1.

7. *Latin America Political Report* 13 (June 1, 1979), pp. 161–62; and *Latin American Political Report* 13 (June 8, 1979), pp. 169–170.

8. The Battle for Managua is described in detail in Roger Mendienta Alfaro, *El último marine* (Managua: Editorial Unión, 1980). A useful source on the final offensive in general is Carlos Núñez Téllez, *Un Pueblo en Armas* (Managua: Secretaria Nacional de Propaganda y Educación Política del FSLN, 1980).

9. Interview with Luis Carrión, "La guerrilla se transforma en ejercito regular, "*Cuadernos de Marcha* 1 (January–February 1980):99–100.

10. *Barricada*, June 4, 1980, p. 7.

11. *Programa de gobierno* (Managua: Junta de Gobierno de Reconstrucción Nacional, 1979), p. 4.

12. See interview with Tomás Borge, "El poder lo tienen las classes tradicionalmente explotadas," *Cuadernos de Marcha* 1 (January–February 1980):86.

13. See *Barricada*, January 29, 1980, p. 1.

14. Interview by Stephen Gorman with Roberto Sánchez, Director of Press and Information for the EPS, Managua, June 2, 1980.

15. Borge, "El poder lo tienen las classes," p. 87.

16. Estimates are based on discussions Gorman held with the staff of the U.S. Military Attaché at the U.S. Embassy, Managua, May 27, 1980; interviews by Gorman with reports from *La Prensa* in January and June 1980; and the interview by Gorman with Roberto Sánchez, June 2, 1980.

17. Roberto Sánchez stated in June 1980 that no ex-Guardias remained in the EPS. This was contradicted in conversations with platoon leaders from El Chipote, the EPS Central Command, and by individuals connected with the U.S. Embassy.

18. Interview by Gorman with Roberto Sánchez.

19. See Luis Carrión, "La guerrilla se transforma," on the role of the militias. For an example of segregation of men, women, and children in the militias, see *Barricada*, June 4, 1980, p. 7. Other information on the militias was obtained from interviews conducted by Gorman in Pochocuape, Managua, during January, May, and June 1980, and in Estelí during May 1980.

20. Luis Carrión, "La guerrilla se transforma," pp. 98, 99.

21. See interview with Adolfo Chamorro Téfel, ex-*responsable* in charge of personnel and housing for the EPS in *Barricada*, December 29, 1979, p. 7.

22. *Programa de gobierno*, p. 4.

23. At least seven individuals involved with the Literacy Campaign had been killed by the first anniversary of the Revolution. The most politically disturbing act was the murder of Georgino Andrade, an area coordinator for the Literacy Campaign in a rural village. See *El Nuevo Diario*, May 23, 1980, p. 1.

24. *La Prensa*, June 5, 1980, p. 1.

25. See *El Nuevo Diario*, May 28, 1980, p. 1; and *La Prensa*, June 5, 1980, pp. 1 and 4.

26. Interview by Gorman with Roberto Sánchez.

27. *Discurso del Comandante Tomás Borge durante la promoción policial de la escuela Carlos Agüero E.* (Managua: Oficina de Divulgación y Prensa, Ministerio del Interior, December 16, 1979), p. 1.

28. Ibid.

29. *El Nuevo Diario*, May 28, 1980, p. 9.

30. The Statute is reproduced in Pedro Camejo and Fred Murphy, eds., *The Nicaraguan Revolution* (New York: Pathfinder, 1979), pp. 43–55.

31. From a conversation between Walker and a prominent agroindustrial magnate (and trusted friend) in the summer of 1980. The businessman, who will remain anonymous, had been trying to explain the new system to the Reagan envoy and was shocked by the question.

32. See Chapter 21 in this volume by William M. LeoGrande. Also see Thomas W. Walker, "The Nicaraguan-U.S. Friction: The First Four Years," in Kenneth M. Coleman and George C. Herring, eds., *The Central American Crisis: Sources of Conflict and the Failure of U.S. Policy* (Wilmington, Del.: Scholarly Resources, 1985), pp. 157–189.

33. Eddie Adams, "Exiles Rehearse for the Day They Hope Will Come," *Parade Magazine*, March 15, 1981, pp. 4–6.

34. Father James Feltz as quoted in "The Counterrevolutionaries: What Kind of Freedom Fighters Are They?" *Envío* 3, No. 29 (November 1983):4b, 5b.

35. Council on Hemispheric Affairs, "Reagan Administration Taking Two Track Approach to Nicaragua: Talk Peace, Prepare for War," press release, August 30, 1984.

36. See Chapter 21 in this volume by William M. LeoGrande.

37. U.S. House of Representatives, Staff Report, Subcommittee on Oversight and Evaluation, Permanent Select Committee on Intelligence, "U.S. Intelligence Performance on Central America: Achievements and Selected Instances of Concern," September 12, 1982, Mimeographed, p. 43.

38. Lt. Col. John H. Buchanan, USMC (Ret.), Prepared Statement Before the Sub-committee on Interamerican Affairs, Committee on Foreign Affairs, U.S. House of Repre-sentatives, "U.S. Military Aid to Honduras" (Washington, D.C., September 21, 1982), mimeographed, p. 4.

39. Ibid.

40. Most of this information on arms is drawn either from personal observation or from Jozef Goldblat and Victor Millán, *The Honduras-Nicaragua Conflict and Prospectives for Arms Control in Central America* (Solna, Sweden: Stockholm International Peace Research Institute, 1984); and U.S. Department of Defense, *Soviet Military Power, 1984* (Washington, D.C.: U.S. Government Printing Office, 1984).

41. Goldblat and Millán, *The Honduras-Nicaragua Conflict*, p. 526.

42. Ibid., p. 532; and U.S. Department of Defense, *Soviet Military Power*, p. 122.

43. For detailed and balanced examination of human rights in Sandinist Nicaragua, see Amnesty International, *Report of the Amnesty International Missions to the Republic of Nicaragua, August 1979, January 1980 and August 1980* (London: Amnesty International, 1982); Amnesty International, "Nicaragua Background Briefing: The Persistence of Public Order Law Detentions and Trials" (London: Amnesty International, December 30, 1982), mimeographed; Amnesty International, *Prepared Statement of Amnesty International, USA on The Human Rights Situation in Nicaragua Before the Subcommittee on Human Rights and International Organization, U.S. House of Representatives, September 15, 1983* (Washington, D.C.: Amnesty International, 1983); Americas Watch, *Human Rights in Nicaragua* (New York: Americas Watch, May 1982); Americas Watch, *Human Rights in Nicaragua: November, 1982 Update* (New York: Americas Watch, 1982); Americas Watch, *Human Rights in Nicaragua* (New York: Americas Watch, April 1984); and Organization of American States, Inter-American Commission on Human Rights, *Report on the Situation of Human Rights of a Segment of the Nicaraguan Population of Miskito Origin* (Washington, D.C.: General Secretariat of the OAS, 1984).

44. See Stuart Taylor, Jr., "In Wake of Invasion, Much Official Misinformation by U.S. Comes to Light," *New York Times*, November 6, 1983.

Chapter 5
Religion and Politics

MICHAEL DODSON
LAURA NUZZI O'SHAUGHNESSY

The Sandinista Revolution reached its fifth anniversary steeped in controversy over the fate of organized religion within the revolutionary process. This controversy was rooted in several causes, including the Sandinista leadership's clear embrace of some aspects of Marxism, their propensity to use a rhetoric of class conflict, and their pursuit of public policies intended to favor the poor, sometimes at the expense of the privileged. Some observers interpreted these signs as indicating that an underlying Sandinista intention was to foster and deepen class struggle in Nicaragua. In their view, since orthodox Marxism is hostile to religion, Sandinista policy was aimed also at provoking class struggle in the churches, with a long-range goal of undercutting the importance of organized religion in society.[1] Was this concern over religion in revolutionary Nicaragua warranted or misplaced? Was religion in jeopardy or could it prosper and play a significant role in the new society? Was the FSLN particularly hostile to the Catholic Church and intent upon its destruction? These are important questions that we will address. We will argue that concern for religion in Nicaragua was justified, but not primarily for the reasons cited by the Revolution's critics. The view that religion was necessarily imperiled in a society whose leaders were under the influence of Marxism ignored a number of factors in the unique experience of Nicaragua that ought to have been taken into account.

First, the churches, both Catholic and Protestant, played an unprecedented role in the popular insurrection that overthrew Somoza. They contributed both ideas and concrete actions to the revolutionary movement that coalesced during the 1970s. Many Christians joined the political struggle for religious reasons and embraced the victory of the FSLN-led insurrection as the fulfillment of both a spiritual and historic political process. For them the practice of religion within the Revolution was a positive expectation.

Second, the increased pluralism and decentralization in the Catholic Church that resulted from the innovations of Medellín meant that Christians participated in the anti-Somoza struggle on different levels,

119

under the sway of diverse "theologies," and hence with different expectations. Broadly speaking there were two Nicaraguan churches at the time of the insurrection. On one side were those Catholics, led by the hierarchy, who opposed Somoza and desired a new politics for Nicaragua. For the most part, these Catholics did not collaborate with the FSLN and did not seek a social revolution. In the other church were those Christians who supported the insurrection actively and acknowledged the leadership of the FSLN. Conflict between what might be called "the two churches of the insurrection" became a major element of post-Triumph Nicaraguan politics.

A third reference point is the wider setting of changing values and perspectives among the Latin American churches. The decisions taken by the bishops at Medellín put Latin Catholicism on a new footing by identifying the church with the poor. The bishops urged study and denunciation of "structural" injustice and called for changes in economic and political arrangements that had become "mechanisms of oppression." This revolutionary language was retained at Puebla, Mexico, in 1979 where the bishops endorsed the development of Christian Base Communities (CEBs) as the most appropriate vehicle for promoting the church's presence and liberating action among the poor. Protestants adopted similar positions in their own meeting at Oaxtepec, Mexico, in 1978.

Medellín, Puebla, and Oaxtepec placed the churches in the midst of social and political struggle and on the side of the poor in Latin America. Yet many of these church leaders sought to confront injustice, poverty, and oppression without entering the realm of partisan politics. In their minds a prophetic church could work on behalf of the poor without becoming "political." This distinction was severely tested in the experience of the churches in the Nicaraguan Revolution where the FSLN and the churches both claimed to be working in behalf of the poor. The Nicaraguan Revolution was their first opportunity to test this new religious commitment in a society where revolution was actually taking place.

The final reference point is the revolutionary process itself. Two aspects stand out. First, the insurrectionary phase was highly participatory and very broadly based within Nicaraguan society. To repeat, many of the participants were Christians inspired by their religious faith. The insurrection released vast energies of pent-up frustration and hope, and institutionalized channels had to be created to give direction to these energies. In the second phase there was the legitimation of the revolutionary movement, led by the FSLN, and the creation of a broad range of popular organizations to respond to now-acknowledged demands for a better life, for greater security, and for a voice in one's destiny. The Revolution opened up the political arena to popular participation on a scale unprecedented in Central America. The churches, having declared themselves to be identified with the poor majority, now were confronted with a government that also identified with the poor majority and declared its intention to transform society in their interest.

IDENTIFICATION WITH THE POOR AND DEMOCRATIZATION

The conversion of the Latin American Catholic Church to serious involvement in social issues has been the subject of a large and growing literature.[2] Many writers have remarked how deeply this venerable institution seemed to change in a very few years, sometimes portraying the change as a religious "revolution" in the area of theology and pastoral activity among the poor. Theologians developed a "theology of liberation," priests and religious moved into working-class neighborhoods and peasant communities, and bishops condemned unjust social structures and political systems. Meeting in Medellín, Colombia, in 1968, the bishops of Latin America pledged to put the weight of the church on the side of the poor in their struggle for liberation.[3]

In a theological sense, this reorientation came in response to the appeal of the Second Vatican Council to open the church more fully to the world and its temporal problems. From the standpoint of the institutional church in Latin America, it responded to a perception of the declining importance of religion and the church in people's lives. Though self-interested in this sense, the change brought about by the work of many thousands of church people was profoundly renewing and spiritually energizing for the faithful. Over time it had a regenerative impact within the church. As we will see, progressive Christians in Nicaragua were inspired by the spirit and guidelines of Medellín to develop new ecclesiastical structures and carry out pastoral plans that mobilized the poor at the grass roots. Such mobilization encouraged the poor to demand a better life and to insist on the democratization of social and political structures. This commitment to the poor resulted in direct repression of the church in response to the emergence of revolutionary movements in the mid-1970s and Christian involvement in them.[4]

The norms by which the church was to be guided in the 1980s were set out by the Latin American bishops at Puebla. It is helpful to establish a "Puebla viewpoint," since that meeting provided a baseline to which Nicaraguan Christians often turned in trying to define the church's role in the new revolutionary society. Puebla took place as the Nicaraguans were preparing their final assault on the Somoza dictatorship, but the final documents were issued before the popular Triumph. Therefore, with the exception of Cuba, there was no revolutionary regime in Central or South America with which the church had to contend. For this reason the political frame of reference for the bishops was primarily the authoritarian regimes of the right that prevailed in much of the region. The Cuban experience was not treated directly, leaving Marxist regimes to be treated in the abstract, in light of what were presumed to be the logical consequences of their doctrines or ideologies.

A first premise of the Puebla documents was that the church should continue the initiative of Medellín to declare its "preferential option for the poor." This meant being of service to the poor not only by promoting their interests but by "drawing closer to them."[5] The poor challenged the church constantly "to be an agent of justice and to take up their cause as a matter of right, not of charity."[6] From this starting point the bishops went on to stress the structure and activity of the CEB. The CEBs occupied a special place in the post-Medellín church that was to continue with renewed emphasis after Puebla. Indeed, the CEB's were "one of the causes for joy and hope in the Church," for "they had become centers of evangelization and moving forces of liberation and development."[7] Putting the matter this way the bishops acknowledged that giving increased status to base-level Christian communities was valuable both spiritually and materially. In fact, it became difficult to separate the two dimensions, for by integrating them each was enchanced. This benefited the individual and vitalized the church. It was also clear that grass-roots participation was the key to this success. The CEBs "accentuate committed involvement in the family, one's work, the neighborhood, and the local community."[8] Not only did the common people find their religious experience "expressed, valued and purified," but "they were given a concrete opportunity to share in the tasks of the church and to work committedly for the transformation of the world."[9]

In sum, the bishops reconfirmed the church's decision at Medellín to shift the focus of pastoral action to a lower level of the institutional church. This shift of focus accorded a new measure of autonomy to the local level and invited more active participation by the laity. In structural terms this shift led to a process of decentralization, bringing about a diffusion of decisionmaking and authority, which, in turn, fostered the cultivation of a new ethos of shared responsibility and authority. That is, it stimulated development of a more democratic ethos as the people themselves took charge of Bible study, worship, and community development.

Not that Puebla turned the faithful loose to worship and engage in social action without the assistance and supervision of the priesthood. On the contrary, the CEBs were expected to function in "authentic communion with their bishops."[10] In fact, the Puebla documents insisted that "in each local church the bishop is the principle and foundation of its unity." Nevertheless, the documents also made clear that the bishops were expected to "promote, guide and accompany the CEBs in the spirit of the

Medellín Conference."[11] This new model of the church, then, seemed to presuppose close contact and identification between the priests and bishops and the members of the base-level Christian communities. It also presupposed a spirit of dialogue and mutual respect in which the real-life conditions and choices of the laity at the grass roots were to be given preferential treatment. It was, in short, a remarkably democratized model of the church, perhaps much more so than the bishops realized. The effort to enact this model in revolutionary Nicaragua led to much conflict within the Catholic Church and heightened tensions between church and government. To appreciate the nature of this conflict it will be useful to review briefly some models of democratic participation to see how alternative democratic possibilities bear on the political struggles arising from the Revolution.

MODELS OF DEMOCRATIC PARTICIPATION

The modern concept of democracy owes much to a religious revolution. The Protestant Reformation gave rise to such Puritan sects as the Levellers, who argued that "man had no obligation to any government that sought to control him for anything but his own benefit. . . . "[12] This doctrine derived from Luther's notion of the "priesthood of all believers." When translated into secular terms by such writers as Locke, Rousseau, and Jefferson, this became the doctrine that only the consent of the governed makes government legitimate. The question was, how would this consent be expressed? Would all citizens share equally in the expression of consent?

It has been suggested that there are really two democratic traditions in the modern era: one characteristically Anglo-American, the other more typically French, or continental.[13] The first tradition follows the ideas of Locke and Madison while the second follows Rousseau and Bosanquet. The Anglo-American tradition rests on Locke's restricted version of consent, which sees legitimate political authority as the product of a contract between the people and the government wherein the people agree to obey in return for the government's pledge to protect their rights, especially their property rights. Such a system was entirely compatible with sharp social class differences in which only the propertied minority actually participated in government. The poor majority was left only with the right to rebel if government authority became oppressive. Madison added to this scheme an explicit attack on pure democracy as the "tyranny of the majority"[14] and urged a republican form of government that has come to be called representative democracy. It is also called constitutional democracy due to the "separation of powers and checks and balances" that limit power and thwart the participatory excesses of "majorities." In short, the Lockean, Madisonian approach to democracy places greater emphasis on liberty and the protection of individual rights, and on contractual or constitutional stability than on the equality of all citizens and the active expression of their consent through participation in the exercise of political authority. Their political theory, like that of the English and American Revolutions with which they are associated, "was never detached from a theory of society which accepted status as a matter of course and as not only compatible with political freedom but even as a condition of it." The democratic tradition that they represent, then, grew out of "a political rather than a social revolution."[15]

The second democratic tradition is epitomized in the historical setting and goals of the French Revolution, which attacked the privilege and status of the old social order. The revolution sought to incorporate the lower classes into political life by abolishing the status and privilege of the aristocracy and of such corporate bodies as the church, and by encouraging mass participation. Rousseau thought that such participation fostered individual dignity and facilitated moral education. This approach to democracy implies both a social and a political revolution and values political equality and participation more highly than the Anglo-American tradition.[16]

Both of these democratic traditions were at play in revolutionary Nicaragua. They were not mutually exclusive since they shared values and institutions in common, but they were in tension with one another, particularly concerning such issues as political equality, participation, and privilege. In the period of the Popular Insurrection everyone in Nicaragua spoke the language of democracy as they united in opposition to the corrupt system of privilege and oppression represented in Somocismo. But some envisioned a transition to a new democratic system constructed in the image of the Anglo-American model, which will be referred to here as the "liberal model" or simply as "liberalism." Others had in mind a "popular model" designed to accommodate what Central Americans call "the logic of the majorities." Its focus was succinctly captured by Comandante Daniel Ortega: "For us, democracy is organization of the people. For us, democracy is agrarian reform. For us, democracy is rights for the workers. For us, democracy is sovereignty and self-determination."[17] As the Revolution unfolded, proponents of the two democratic models came into conflict and the Catholic Church, itself undergoing a process of democratization, was fully caught up in this conflict.

THE CHURCH AT THE GRASS ROOTS

At the time of Medellín, the Nicaraguan church at the parish level, where it had direct contact with the people, was almost completely lacking in the vitality that came to characterize it after 1979. With only a few isolated exceptions, there were no pastoral programs or Christian communities that encouraged the people to participate in the life of the church. There was little intrachurch dialogue and diocesan priests, who were predominantly Nicaraguan, were poorly trained, generally pre-Vatican II in orientation, and had little contact with the largely foreign-born priests of the religious orders. In this setting little work of a socially relevant nature was done by the church.

"The spirit of Medellín was introduced to Nicaragua by a movement of young priests, whom the Somocista daily *Novedades* called 'the seven priests of Marx.' . . . "[18] Energized by the ideas of Medellín these priests began to push for change and experimentation at the grass-roots level. Their guiding initiatives led to the establishment of the earliest CEBs in Managua, on the Atlantic Coast, in rural areas north of Estelí, and on the Islands of Solentiname. The "Mother Church" of the CEBs in Nicaragua, the community of Saint Paul the Apostle in Managua's Fourteenth of September neighborhood, became a "pilot parish" under this initiative. It spurred base-level organization and set up programs to train lay leaders. Members of St. Paul organized retreats attended by priests and laity from other poor neighborhoods of Managua. As one woman, who joined the CEB in 1970, pointed out in an interview after the Triumph, these pastoral activities within the church helped greatly to strengthen family life in the parish. It brought husband and wife closer together, and helped individual parishioners to integrate the various aspects of their lives. Within the neighborhood it led to a much stronger sense of community solidarity.[19]

Another current that fed the renovation of the church was the Catholic student movement. In 1970 students at the Jesuit Central American University attempted to challenge the "developmentalist" orientation of the curriculum and its tacit support of the Somoza dictatorship. When university officials refused to discuss grievances with the students, the latter turned to a new tactic of seizing churches. Over the next year there were various seizures, one leading to the release from jail of some students and members of the FSLN. Finally, more than 100 students were arrested by the government and expelled from the university. Out of this group emerged the Revolutionary Christian Movement that, in the late 1970s, contributed much tactical support and even leadership cadres to the Sandinista Front.[20]

The Revolutionary Christian Movement itself became rooted in the emerging CEBs in Managua's eastern zones. Leaders of the movement settled in Barrio Riguero where they engaged in serious Bible study and reflection on the social situation under the tutelage of the parish priest (one of the original "seven priests"). After 1973 Christian youth groups were formed in other CEBs, such as San Antonio Parish, and in a number of Catholic high schools. In these religious settings at the grass roots young

Christian activists deepened their religious faith, established contact with the FSLN, and formed a commitment to the popular struggle to rid Nicaragua of the dictatorship.

In the countryside, church innovation included the creation of two important religious programs called the Delegates of the Word and the Agrarian Education and Promotion Center (CEPA). CEPA was created in 1969 by the Jesuits to provide training for peasant leaders. Originally based in the Western zone of the country around Carazo and Masaya, CEPA eventually expanded northward to León and Estelí. Over a period of several years, as it became clear that peasants could not improve their economic situation without organizing, the CEPA program came to center more and more on creating peasant organizations that could engage in political action. For Christians working in CEPA this was a radicalizing process, theologically and politically. It led some into active sympathy with the FSLN long before the first insurrection broke out in September 1978. Some joined the armed struggle, while others took leadership roles in the FSLN-sponsored Association of Rural Workers, which was set up in 1977. As with the CEBs, this grass-roots activity of priests and lay Catholics working with peasants flourished outside direct supervision and control of the bishops. When the bishops perceived that they could not contain CEPA to activities they regarded as appropriately religious and nonpolitical, they attempted to pressure the organization and restrict its activities. By the time of the insurrection, CEPA had cut its formal ties with the church and regarded itself as an independent Christian organization. At the Triumph it was closely allied with the FSLN.[21]

The Delegates of the Word was a program intended to make lay religious leadership possible in rural areas not regularly served by a priest. The Delegates were peasants trained to lead Bible study and worship among their own people as well as to provide rudimentary literacy training and health services. As with the Christian communities in the urban areas, religious services led by Delegates generally consisted of dialogues, keyed to Biblical texts, that dealt with the immediate economic and social problems of the community. Not surprisingly, the Delegates tended to become leaders of CEBs in the rural areas. Such leadership made them targets of National Guard repression, which provoked the institutional church to voice some opposition to Somoza; it drove many Delegates and the CEBs they represented to support the FSLN.

Thus, during the decade from Medellín to the outbreak of insurrection in Nicaragua, significant new grass-roots religious consciousness had been achieved, facilitated by the creation of base-level Christian communities and such church programs as CEPA and the Delegates of the Word. This new consciousness, however, was not uniform across the country. In the Diocese of Granada and the Prelature of Juigalpa, for example, it scarcely existed. Nor did one find it in the middle- and upper-class parishes of Managua. But in Managua's poorest neighborhoods, in Estelí, Matagalpa, León, Chinandega, and Masaya, Christians at the grass roots had a measure of organization and had attained a significant level of religious self-awareness and political understanding. Religious awareness and political commitment became integrated and mutually reinforcing, thereby facilitating the entry of these communities into the popular insurrection. The situation in Estelí illustrates the change wrought by this work at the base level. There Christians began consciously preparing for the insurrection in the spring of 1978 and by September an entire parish, composed of 56 CEBs, was organized to support the popular struggle.[22]

While these profound changes were occuring in the Catholic Church, Nicaragua's Protestants did not remain unaffected. Protestant ministers and laity, like their Catholic counterparts, experienced the same challenge to their faith in light of the unfolding insurrection. As a result of their faith many of them participated in the Revolution and subsequently in the reconstruction process.

The dominant organization of Nicaragua's Protestants, the Protestant Development Committee (CEPAD), was formed as a result of the 1972 earthquake that destroyed much of Managua. In the midst of gross misuse of relief funds by the Somoza regime, Nicaragua's Protestant community coalesced to deal with the emergency situation. Starting from a membership of three regional committees in 1972, CEPAD came, by 1984, to have a network of 12 regional committees and 90 percent of Nicaragua's Protestant churches were affiliated with it.[23] Thus, CEPAD gave Protestants an established organization through which they could participate in the revolutionary process. This meant that across ecumenical lines there were many Christians who saw the Triumph as an unprecedented opportunity for the churches to support a popular revolution.

Immediately after the Triumph, in August 1979, an ecumenical center of theological reflection was established in Managua by clergy who had been closely identified with the popular struggle. Named the Antonio Valdivieso Center (CAV), in honor of a Nicaraguan bishop who was martyred in the colonial era for his defense of indigenous peoples, its purpose was to promote dialogue and cooperation with the government and to encourage active Christian participation in the Revolution. The CAV began immediately to establish or deepen links with progressive Christian organizations in other countries. It entered into copublishing arrangements with the Departmento Ecuménico de Investigaciones (DEI) of San José, Costa Rica, with MIEC-JECI, a Church documentation center in Lima, Peru, and with the Comisión Evangélica Latino Americana de Educación Cristiana (CELADEC), also based in Lima.[24] In five years these publishing activities grew extensively and by 1984 the CAV operated a well-stocked bookstore to diffuse its pastoral and educational materials.

The CAV also sponsored seminars and conferences, bringing together theologians, pastors, members of CEBs, government leaders, and persons from abroad who were supportive of the Revolution. As the CAV grew so did the scope and depth of these activities. By 1984 its publications department was producing regular columns in *El Nuevo Diario*, an independent newspaper sympathetic to the Revolution. In addition, it was forming an ecumenical theology school and had departments devoted to leadership training and the development of pastoral and social projects at the grass roots.[25]

The work of the CAV was complemented by that of the Instituto Histórico Centroamericano (IHCA), which published a monthly review of important events and trends in revolutionary Nicaragua and often touched upon religious issues. Working in concert, IHCA and the CAV brought together a potent intellectual leadership and the mass-based Christian organizations. They not only provided a forum wherein people who support the Revolution could meet, they also worked in a variety of ways to promote church involvement in the projects of the Revolution. Moreover, their leaders were a living link between the pre- and post-Triumph phases of the revolutionary process. As such they provided a formidable source of Christian support for the Sandinista Revolution.

In the five years following the Triumph two key problems confronted this grass-roots Church that sought so optimistically to develop a meaningful role in the work of the Revolution. On the one hand the bishops resisted this effort, striving to reassert control over the activities of the CEBs. In the case of the CAV, IHCA, and CEPA, where it had less direct control, the hierarchy sought to disassociate these from the church, thereby raising a question about their religious authenticity. In the case of the CEBs themselves a major tactic was to remove priests and religious from parishes that included CEBs closely associated with the Revolution. This led to numerous conflicts within the church. The complement to this practice was the effort to create new pastoral programs (or restructure old ones) controlled and directed by the hierarchy and priests loyal to them. The Latin American Bishops' Conference (CELAM) made significant funds available to the Nicaraguan bishops in support of this policy.

On the other hand, the sheer magnitude of the demands made upon these grass-roots Christians by the Revolution placed them under severe stress. The tasks of the Revolution were enormous. Some Christians who sought initially to maintain active roles of leadership in their CEBs while taking on the political and organizational tasks of reconstruction found the political tasks eclipsing their work in the church. Even though they might see political work to be a part of the work of the church, they were sometimes forced to neglect their spiritual and pastoral tasks. Often, those affected were the most qualified lay persons in the CEB. Since the majority of the FSLN supporters at the parish level were members of the CEBs, this created a difficult problem for Christians who wished to support the Revolution but remain active in the church.[26]

THE CATHOLIC HIERARCHY

Much of the tension that developed in the Nicaraguan church after the Triumph can be traced to the different understandings that the base of the church and the hierarchy had of "democracy" and of the church's role in society. Members of the CEBs came to realize that political activity and religious commitment were inseparable. Nicaragua's bishops, however, did not fully accept the mandate of social change implicit in the Medellín and Puebla documents. They preferred to maintain a traditional European distinction between the proper "nonpartisan" role of the institutional church and the individual's personal social and political activism arising from the teachings of the church. When faced with the reality of a revolutionary society, they could not accept the political advocacy implied in the Medellín documents because these implications did not belong within the context of traditional European teachings. As a result, the bishops faced a dilemma. Their commitment to separation of church and state, a key element of the liberal European tradition, seemed to imply that the church as institution could not participate in the political programs of the Revolution. At the same time, the social teachings of post-Medellín Catholic doctrine called on the church to participate in the political tasks of building a more just society. The positions taken by the bishops toward the FSLN and its political program, and toward initiatives coming from within the church, must be explained in the context of this dilemma. To compound the problem, the bishops never endorsed a world view that included direct democratization, either for the church or the polity. So, a division between the hierarchy and Christians who were organizing CEBs was already evident at the Triumph. What united different levels of the church in this period was only a shared opposition to Somoza.

Prominent themes in the letters the bishops wrote in the years immediately preceding the Sandinista victory illustrated the integration of their view of democracy and traditional Christianity. They placed greater emphasis on reform of institutions as a political solution than on structural transformation, and they hesitated to condone violence as a political option. For example, in a letter of August 1978 criticizing the Somoza regime, the bishops called for better public administration (an end to the pervasive corruption and incompetence of public employees), more prudent control of the federal budget, and improved health services. This letter cites the 1971 Synod of Bishops rather than Medellín and recalls a classic Thomistic view of the church in the world. On the eve of the September uprising the bishops wrote: "To fight for justice, peace, the development and defense of the rights of man is not making partisan politics, but instead working for that which is fundamental for the common good."[27] Such a view derives more from European theology than from the prophetic Latin American theology of Medellín.

Because their main contention was that a truly Christian solution to social problems should be above partisan politics, the bishops were ambivalent about directing the faithful concerning the resolution of political conflicts. At times they appeared obliquely to endorse the need for the structural transformation called for at Medellín; yet their endorsement was cautious, lacking the causal analysis that made the Medellín documents so powerful. The bishops wrote, for example, that "the originality of the Christian message doesn't directly consist in the affirmation of the necessity for structural changes (but) instead in the insistence on the conversion of man. . . . "[28] Examining specific issues rather than treating generalized statements of the "common good" suggests that in a subsequent letter the bishops favored a reformist liberalism and assumed that such views were representative of what the "people" wanted:

- the authentic exercise of the rights of political association, unionization, and the free election of officials
- the guarantees of a judiciary, independent of political power, which gives just recourse to its citizens
- the suppression of laws that violate the freedom of expression of individuals and institutions.[29]

The bishops' attitude toward the National Guard and their absence of any show of support for the FSLN at the time of the Triumph also demonstrated their propensity for reform and accentuated the differences between the hierarchy and the base of the church. Whereas many young Christians took up arms in the popular insurrection against the National Guard, the bishops did not criticize the Guard as an institution. They warned Guardsmen that they would have to "account for their warlike actions," but called only for the reorganization of the National Guard "on the basis of the national interest." They proposed restructuring the Guard to prevent nepotism and giving it a smaller allocation from the national budget. This suggestion was unacceptable to the FSLN and to Christian combatants. Again, although in June 1979 the Episcopal Conference defended the "legitimate rights of popular insurrection under certain circumstances," on July 7, just 12 days before the Triumph, they issued an

appeal for national nonpartisan unity based upon the Christian commitment to peace. They took this position even though they acknowledged
that "reason had collapsed and the established system had not responded to
the incessant demands of its citizens."[30] In short, the bishops aspired to
reform the Somoza system, initiating moderate change that would increase
pluralism but avoid revolution. In this posture they did not support the
fusion of religious and political action that was actually endorsing the
Revolution in Nicaragua.

To summarize, by the time of the Triumph the Catholic hierarchy and
the FSLN viewed each other with caution. The bishops distrusted the
revolutionary program, its ideology, and its base of support.[31] On the one
hand they worried that the government would take over religious customs
traditionally controlled by the church. On the other hand, they were
concerned about the participation of Catholics in the mass organizations
and the CEBs. In Catholic tradition, lay activity is supervised by priests
who are loyal to the bishops. Therefore, the CEBs were a problem for the
institutional church, as was Catholic participation in the mass organizations, because it was difficult to control the spontaneity and autonomy of
Catholics in these organizations. The bishops were fearful that if these
revolutionary Christians continued to unite grass-roots religious commitment to the poor with loyalty to the Revolution the government's
authority would supersede that of the Church.

These embryonic fears of the institutional church were sharpened
during the celebration of the Jornada Navideña (Christmas Festivities) in
1980. Such typical and venerated religious customs as La Purísima were
seen as preempted by the government and the mass organizations when the
Ministry of Social Welfare announced that it would take part in the
celebration of Christmas. According to Father Edgard Parrales, then
Minister of Social Welfare, each child, rich or poor, should enjoy the
Christmas season and receive at least one gift. These would be distributed
through the Social Welfare Ministry by volunteers from the Sandinista
Defense Committees. The response of the episcopate to this departure from
tradition was to issue a call for a week-long Catholic celebration of La
Purísima in Masaya, which would include a series of processions in honor
of Mary, recitations of the rosary, and a public celebration of first
communion. Presumably these would shift attention away from the
government's Christmas activities. Nevertheless, government participation
in the Christmas festivities grew each year. In 1983, for instance, workers
in six government ministries erected shrines to the Virgin near their offices
in Managua. On the night of La Purísima these shrines became the site of a
huge celebration which drew over 100,000 Nicaraguans. The faithful sang
and prayed while the leaders of the revolution honored the centuries-old
tradition by distributing over 20,000 handicraft gifts to the children.[32]

THE CONTROVERSY OF THE PRIESTS IN GOVERNMENT

While a generalized sentiment of mistrust predates the Triumph, the fears of the Catholic bishops became focused as the work of national reconstruction took shape. A turning point was the creation of the Council of State in 1980. At that time it became clear that groups supporting the Sandinistas would have a majority in the Council of State and that the government was not likely to pursue reformist policies based in liberalism. The expansion of the Council prompted the resignation of Junta members Violeta de Chamorro and Alfonso Robelo, an influential businessman who criticized the government for its "totalitarianism." In May 1980 the Council of State was formally inaugurated and the Catholic hierarchy issued its first call for the resignation of the priests who held cabinet positions: Miguel D'Escoto, Minister of Foreign Relations; Ernesto Cardenal, Minister of Culture; Fernando Cardenal, Director of Sandinista Youth; and Father Parrales, Minister of Social Welfare.

The presence of these priests in government was symbolically and substantively important, for it highlighted the differing views of authority and participation among five key actors, including: Archbishop Obando y Bravo and the conservative faction within the hierarchy; the priests themselves, who were in effect asked to choose sides; the Nicaraguan government, which needed their expertise and requested their services; the laity who, through the CEBs, strongly supported the presence of the priests in government; and the Vatican, whose role was important but ambiguous.

In their call for the priests' resignation the bishops argued: "the exceptional circumstances have passed and Christian laity can occupy the political offices with no less effeciency than the priests who are presently occupying them." When the priests refused to resign, arguing that the exceptional circumstances still prevailed, the bishops responded with a confrontational communiqué that insisted on their resignation.[33] To the conservatives in the hierarchy the presence of the priests in government was a sign that the church was not maintaining a "nonpartisan" identity. Perhaps if these men had been lay Catholics their participation would have been more palatable to the hierarchy and more consistent with the teachings of Puebla and the 1971 Synod of Bishops, but as priests they carried greater religious responsibility than the laity. From the dualistic viewpoint of the bishops, the religious role precluded the political one. The priests' presence also gave evidence of the existence of religious toleration that the government had proclaimed in its Official Communiqué Concerning Religion.

Despite the bishops' insistence the priests again refused to sign. This seemed to confirm the hierarchy's suspicions as to their loss of authority in a changing church. Not only did the priests agree publicly with the government that the exceptional circumstances were not over, they also challenged the underlying premise of the bishops' view of the proper role of the church in saying: "We declare our unbreakable commitment to the Popular Sandinista Revolution, in loyalty to our people, which is the same as saying, in loyalty to the will of God."[34]

Sensing that they had reached an impasse, both the government and the hierarchy sent delegations to Rome to seek support for their respective positions, but the Vatican refused to settle the issue. Instead, the bishops were told to resolve the situation themselves, "taking into consideration each particular case."[35] In July 1981 the bishops reached an agreement with the priests that permitted them to remain in the government on the condition that they not administer the sacraments in public or private. Following this temporary resolution of the crisis, the government set up a regular channel of communication called the Permanent Commission for Dialogue with the bishops. The dialogue was suspended in February 1982 following the release of a bishops' letter that severely criticized the government for its handling of the Miskitu Indians. Contacts between the church and the government were revived subsequently and continued throughout the first five years of the Revolution despite frequent strain. Bilateral relationships existed in every diocese in Nicaragua. The relationship between the church and the government was consistently at its most tense in the Managua archdiocese.

Sandinista relations with the Miskitus were problematic, especially since the 1982 relocation of over 8,000 Miskitus away from the Honduran border. While the government justified this relocation on several grounds, including the danger of raids from Honduras into Miskitu settlements and the defense of the national territory, much international criticism was directed at the policy. In the midst of the controversy the bishops released a communiqué that harshly criticized the Nicaraguan government for violating the inalienable rights of individuals, families, and entire villages. The tone of this "Miskitu letter" was strikingly similar to criticisms made by opponents of the FSLN and the letter lacked the underpinning of religious principles found in earlier hierarchical statements criticizing government policy. The government, in short, saw the letter as openly political and it led to a sharp deterioration in church-state relations at that time.

DIVISIONS AMONG THE BISHOPS

While the divisions within the Catholic Church and between the Catholic hierarchy and the government were impossible to conceal, divisions within the bishops' conference itself were less apparent. In the years following the Triumph, despite a high degree of public unity, doctrinal and political differences underlay the bishops' letters and public statements as the following two letters illustrate. The bishops' response to the FSLN Communiqué Concerning Religion was defensive in tone and served better to express fears of the Revolution than to address the issues raised in the communiqué. Dated October 17, 1980, it warned of "ideological control of the revolution" and of a tendency to adopt the "dogmatic rigidity of other previously known models." It implied that the government encouraged atheism and intentionally provoked divisions within the church.[36] The following week the bishops released another document entitled "Jesus Christ and the Unity of his Church in Nicaragua," which in part reiterated some of the traditional criticisms mentioned in their reply to the FSLN communiqué. However, within this statement one also finds a measure of self-exploration and an attempt to analyze the unique role of Christ in Nicaragua. "We are aware of the novelty of the historical experience that we are living, we find ourselves at the beginning of a new era in the life of Nicaragua. We believe that this movement gives us the possibility and responsibility to remake our nation from its foundations."[37]

It is difficult to assume common authorship of letters that are as contradictory in their perceptions of the revolutionary process and in their tone as were those two letters. Indeed, it is unreasonable to infer complete agreement among the bishops on these contentious matters. In fact, on several controversial issues the bishops took different positions publicly. The ultimatum demanding the resignation of the priest-ministers in June 1981 was signed in the name of the Episcopal Conference, yet Bishop López Ardón was not aware of the letter before it was released.[38] Several other bishops, while agreeing in spirit with the directive, were more willing than the archbishop to work for compromise. Before he was named Bishop of León, Monseñor Barni spoke with the priests and offered his services to obtain an extension from the Pope. Bishop Schlaefer of Bluefields also said that the Pope could grant an extension of the exceptional circumstances in accordance with the Puebla documents.[39]

Another way to look at the matter is to note that most of the direct conflict within the church between hierarchy and base occurred in the Managua archdiocese. In the name of church unity, numerous actions were taken by Monseñor Obando against priests and religious whose pastoral work he considered divisive. Often such actions were taken without prior consultations with those affected and tended to be highly conflictual. In the parish of San Judas, a poor Managua neighborhood, Father Rafael Aragón Lucio was removed in this way, as were Sister Pilar Castellanos of Ciudad Sandino and Jesuit priests Luis Medrano and Otilio Miranda who worked in other poor areas of the city. The Sisters of the Assumption in San Judas were ordered by the Curia to move out of the parish house, and Father Pedro Belzunegui, who worked in Tipitapa, a poor Managua suburb, was replaced while he was out of the country.[40] In August 1981 a bitter controversy raged for weeks over Monseñor Obando's removal of Father Manuel Batalla from the Parish of the Sacred Heart in the Monseñor Lezcano neighborhood. The Superior of the Dominican Order traveled to Nicaragua to urge dialogue in the matter while parishioners occupied the parish church, demanding the priest's reinstatement. At the same time other spokesmen insisted on the bishop's right and duty to remove him for the sake of parish unity.[41] At the end of August it was decided that the priest would remain in the parish for the time being.

In July 1982 Archbishop Obando transferred from the poor neighborhood of Santa Rosa Monseñor José Arias Caldera who had been parish priest there since 1974. Father Arias was known for his frequent protection of young combatants during the popular insurrection and was identified as a "Sandinista" priest. Notice of his removal caused a strong reaction within the parish and its members gathered to hold a prayer vigil. While the parishioners were assembled, Auxiliary Bishop Bosco Vivas arrived, announcing that he had come not to initiate the dialogue that the parishioners had requested but to remove the ciborium. This provocative action led to a scuffle in which the bishop was pushed and fell. Subsequently, Monseñor Arias in an emotional farewell mass accepted the archbishop's decision and prayed for him. His parishioners responded less obediently, insisting that the hierarchy take them into account in its decisions. But the archbishop's answer was to excommunicate all those involved in the incident with Monseñor Vivas and place the parish church under interdict so that no religious services could be celebrated there.[42]

This intention to promote unity by removing discordant voices, or by separating priests and religious from the faithful in parishes that were deemed too closely allied to the FSLN or to the revolutionary process, was supported in a more structural way through the creation of the Comisión Diocesana de Laicos (Diocesan Lay Commission). This organ linked each parish to the Curia and to the archbishop, and served as an instrument with which to implement diocesan plans at the parish level. From the point of view of parish priests or CEBs attempting to work in concert with the Revolution, it appeared to be an instrument of control designed to forestall local pastoral initiatives and impose the pastoral strategy of the hierarchy. In general, this strategy entailed the avoidance of any direct collaboration with FSLN programs and projects.[43] The degree of conflict between hierarchy and base that prevailed in the Managua Archdiocese was exceptional. However, due to its dominant size and significance within the Nicaraguan church, severe conflict in the Archdiocese affected the mood and expectations of Christians throughout the country. Thus, a nervous atmosphere of mistrust and disunity afflicted the church when it was announced that Pope John Paul II would visit Central America in early 1983.

THE PAPAL VISIT AND ITS AFTERMATH

In the midst of these deep theological and political divisions within the church, Pope John Paul II visited Nicaragua as part of his pilgrimage for peace in Central America. Apparently the Pope was hesitant to visit Nicaragua and his trip was in doubt several times. John Paul was anxious about the Marxist leanings of the Nicaraguan government, having been informed about Nicaragua by forces in CELAM and the Pontifical Commission for Latin America that were decidedly hostile to the Nicaraguan Revolution. The Pope's misgivings about Nicaragua seemed to be confirmed at the outdoor mass that he celebrated in the July 19 Plaza on March 4th. Toward the end of his homily as he condemned the "popular church" and called for unquestioning loyalty to the bishops he was repeatedly interrupted by Sandinista supporters who shouted "popular power" and "we want peace."

The Pope's remarks did not contribute to restoring unity within the church or between the church and the government. By exhorting the faithful to obey their bishops, most noticeably Archbishop Obando, the Pope displayed little sensitivity to the divisions among the bishops themselves and little understanding of the recent religious experience of the Christians at the grass roots. It is probable that the Pope only exacerbated the strains in the institutional church in Nicaragua. Those Christians who participated in the CEBs and were labeled by others as a "people's church" found no solace in the Pope's criticism of the "people's church" as "absurd and dangerous." Although they rejected the notion of a "parallel church" and maintained that they too were Catholics who followed God's laws and received the sacraments of the church, they were nevertheless put on the defensive by the Pope's speech.[44] In addition, many Christians were deeply upset by the Pope's unwillingness to pray for the souls of more than 700 Nicaraguans, many of them Delegates of the Word, who had given their lives defending the Revolution from Honduran-based contra attacks. By 1984 it appeared that Pope John Paul's attempt to unify the Nicaraguan church by asserting papal authority probably would not succeed in the long run. In the short run, however, the authority of the archbishop and the Episcopal Conference was strengthened while the democratizing tendencies of Catholic doctrine were undercut. Bishops sympathetic to such tendencies were hesitant to challenge the archbishop and his supporters in public. This public display of unity was short-lived but temporarily served to heighten the tension between grass-roots Christians and the hierarchy.

One major source of friction between the base of the Church and the hierarchy occurred because of the refusal of the bishops' conference to condemn the contra attacks from Honduras. It was no secret that these attacks were mounted by former National Guardsmen who have received "covert aid" from the Reagan Administration at least since November 1981. Yet when an Italian reporter asked Obando, "Is it true that there are Somocista guards fighting on the frontier?" the Monseñor replied: "Yes I believe there are Somoza guards, but not only former guardsmen, there are other people. . . . We do not have knowledge of planned aggression of the United States in Nicaragua since we are under a state of emergency which has ended freedom of expression. We only have one version of the truth." *El Nuevo Diario* spoke for many Nicaraguans when it responded: "The dead are also on one side."[45]

It was these attacks by contra forces that led at least one Nicaraguan bishop to break the public display of unity in the hierarchy. This was Bishop López Ardón of Estelí. In his diocese Christian-base communities had flourished and many Christians from Estelí had traveled to other regions of Nicaragua to help establish similar communities. Felipe and María Barreda were members of one such base community and were also lay members of the Pastoral Council of the diocese. As part of their commitment to the Revolution this couple volunteered to pick coffee near the Honduran border. In December 1982 they, along with four other workers from the CEB, were captured by a counterrevolutionary band. After lengthy negotiations with Honduras and appeals by the Barreda children to the Episcopal Conference to intervene on behalf of their parents, the Nicaraguan government was informed in July 1983 that the Barredas had been killed.[46]

In August a mass in honor of the Barredas (and what they symbolized for the new Nicaragua) was concelebrated by more than 30 priests. While Bishop López did not attend, he released a letter in which he publicly condemned the kidnappings and assassinations of many Delegates of the Word and members of the CEBs at the hands of the Somoza bands. He praised the Barredas for their example of Christian love and condemned the military and economic campaign undertaken against Nicaragua. He expressed his fears of an imminent war and concluded by asking for the solidarity of other dioceses in the search for peace.[47] Thus, the authoritative demand for unity that the Pope issued in March was overtaken by events in a matter of months. In May 1983, when Archbishop Obando denied knowledge of American support for contra attacks on Nicaragua, no other Nicaraguan bishop had disagreed with him publicly. However, by August the external situation had deteriorated so profoundly that one bishop was moved to make a public statement that clearly broke the public unity of the bishops' conference.

THE CHURCHES AND THE MILITARY SERVICE LAW

The strain in church-state relations became most apparent in the controversy surrounding the law of Patriotic Military Service, which the government proposed in the summer of 1983. Beginning in October all males between the ages of 17 and 25 were to register for the draft and be required to serve two years of military service. Before this law was even discussed in the Council of State the Episcopal Conference issued a strongly worded communiqué entitled "General Considerations on Military Service." This communiqué proclaimed and encouraged the right of conscientious objection because the law was, in the hierarchy's view, designed to draft and indoctrinate young men into service, not of the nation, but of the Sandinista party, which they considered to be illegitimate, totalitarian, and nonessential to Nicaragua's sovereignty.[48] Again, however, there is evidence that not all the bishops were present when this communiqué was discussed initially and that subsequently not all agreed with the contents. Bishop Santi argued that it was the duty of Christians to defend their nation and that he was not informed of the communiqué. Bishop Schlaefer stated that Christians have the right to participate in their own national development.[49]

Christians in the CEBs came to the defense of the government, arguing that it was indeed legitimate and that obligatory military service is a legitimate power of the state. Others suggested that Vatican II did validate conscientious objection even in the event of a nation's legitimate defense. However, they argued that such conscientious objection does not question the legitimacy of the state. Besides the CEBs, such lay Catholic organizations as the Institute for Social Education in Estelí, formed to teach Nicaraguan history from the perspective of Christian faith, sponsored a three-hour meeting, attended by over 700 people, to explain the law. At this meeting Christians spoke in support of the proposed law.[50]

In the Protestant community one could also sense uncertainty about the military service law and its implications. To clarify some of these issues the leadership of CEPAD organized a well-attended nationwide meeting for its membership. This began with a moving homily by Dr. Gustavo Parajón, director of CEPAD, and was followed by a short talk by René Núñez, Secretary General of the National Directorate of the FSLN. Mr. Núñez then patiently answered questions for over two hours. This meeting concluded with some fears having been allayed and the channel of communication between these Protestant ministers and the government still open.

In fact, since the Triumph, a constant in the process of reconstruction was the sense of cordiality and dialogue between the government and CEPAD. CEPAD participated in many government-sponsored programs in flood relief, housing construction, and health care. At the same time, its related health care program, Provadenic, conducted its own programs, independent of the government. In general, Nicaragua's Protestants were satisfied with the thrust of the government's program of reconstruction and felt they had a vital contribution to make. Their willingness to work in the Nicaraguan Revolution may be explained by the distinction CEPAD's leaders make between the Nicaraguan and Cuban revolutions. In their view, Christians did not play an initial, important role in the Cuban Revolution because as soon as the revolutionaries attained power much of the community fled. CEPAD's leadership argued that as Christians they had to stay and influence the Revolution. Thus there was clear support for the reconstruction process in word and in deed within the Protestant community but not a loss of Protestant identity.[51]

CEPAD's flexibility allowed Nicaragua's Protestants to offer support to the government while maintaining the right, if necessary, to offer criticism and advice. CEPAD was the host organization for the "Witness for Peace" program, which gave North American Christian witnesses the opportunity to live in communities near the Honduran-Nicaraguan border. At the same time CEPAD was opposed to the short-lived "taking of the churches" in the summer of 1982. At that time, approximately 30 Protestant churches that were alleged to have been engaged in counterrevolutionary activity were taken over by members of the mass organizations. Several of these churches in the rural areas were at least nominal members of CEPAD. CEPAD's leaders took the position in discussion with the government that all of the churches should be returned to their pastors. CEPAD's member churches, as well as the independent churches, were given back to their pastors as a result of negotiations carried out at the neighborhood level. The peaceful resolution of what could have become an ugly crisis was notable because it again demonstrated at the grass-roots level the strength and flexibility of popular Christian participation in the Revolution as well as the continuity in the relationship between CEPAD and the Sandinista government. During the insurrection CEPAD had supported the FSLN and in the 1980s it declared that in the event of an invasion its churches would be placed at the service of the government to be used as refugee or first aid centers.

Unfortunately relations between the institutional Catholic Church and the Sandinista government did not show the same degree of flexibility and cordiality. In fact, tense relations, which were apparent since the insurrection, almost reached the breaking point during Easter week in 1984 when the Episcopal Conference released a "Pastoral Letter on Reconciliation." The bishops argued, as they had since July 1979, that society itself had become subject to a materialistic ideology that repudiated the church "founded by the apostles and their successors, the legitimate bishops." While this section of the Easter message simply reiterated ideas stated before by the bishops (and the Pope in March 1983), what apparently angered many Nicaraguans was the bishops' view that the violence and destruction in Nicaragua was the result of internal causes, the solution to which was to be found in personal reconciliation and a dialogue that included even those who had taken up arms against the government. In fact, in December 1983 the government issued a fairly generous amnesty that excluded only those who participated in the leadership of the counterrevolutionary movements. Subsequently, the Bishops' Conference, which consistently refused to acknowledge the involvement of the United States in the "civil" war, maintained complete silence concerning the U.S.-backed mining of Nicaragua's harbors in March-April 1984. The bishops' call for reconciliation did not strike a sympathetic chord among a broad cross-section of Nicaraguan people and it placed further stress on the Catholic Church's relationship with the government. Ironically, and perhaps ominously for the future of the institutional church, this partisan call for political reconciliation was issued at a moment when the mood of reconciliation was most strikingly absent within the church itself.

CONCLUSION

Religion was one of the most dynamic, sensitive, and controversial arenas of the revolutionary process in Nicaragua. While both religious leaders and Christians generally welcomed the fall of Somoza, the seeds of division among Christians over how to adapt to the Revolution had already been sown prior to the Triumph. However, the tension between those in the church who welcomed a social revolution led by the FSLN and those who were skeptical or opposed did not become evident until after the Triumph.

Post-Triumph Nicaragua was the scene of revolutionary, democratizing trends within the churches and the broader society. Democratizing initiatives within the Roman Catholic Church ran parallel with, and were complementary to, the efforts of the FSLN to organize the popular sectors. Even though such initiatives seem to fall within the guidelines adopted by the Latin American bishops at Puebla, initiatives that acknowledged the pluralistic nature of the church and strongly endorsed the Christian-base communities, they were viewed with alarm by the Nicaraguan hierarchy. In the unique situation of Nicaragua, encouragement of the CEBs and commitment to the poor majority at the base by Latin American church leaders fostered grass-roots participation and threw open the door to development of a popular democratic model. During the first five years of the Revolution, this development proceeded apace, encouraged by the FSLN but at the initiative of Christians themselves.

Threatened by this development and mistrustful of the intentions of the FSLN, the Catholic hierarchy sought to impede the cultivation of ties between the religious base and the revolutionary political movement. This led to conflict between base and hierarchy and between church and state. In general, and in contrast to what hostile critics have said, the conflict within the church was more threatening to its religious and institutional integrity than conflict between the church and the government.

Conservative Catholics, including some bishops, feared the Revolution because they feared the way it mobilized the masses and organized the grass roots. The resultant participation threatened their concept of church unity based on unquestioning obedience to hierarchical authority. These Catholics sought repeatedly to enlist the support of church authorities outside the country, including the Pope. In an ironic way this response mirrored the broader fate of the Revolution itself. Outside actors were frequently called upon by participants in the revolutionary process or sought to intervene on their own initiative. The Vatican and CELAM saw vital interests at stake for the church in Nicaragua in the same way that the Reagan Administration saw vital interests at stake for the U.S. position in the world. Yet in the long run only the Nicaraguans would define the proper nature of their revolution and proper role of the churches within it.

NOTES

1. The FSLN expressed itself publicly on the subject of religion in the fall of 1980. See the "Comunicado Oficial de la Dirección Nacional de FSLN Sobre la Religión" in *Barricada*, October 7, 1980, p. 3. President Reagan spoke of government persecution of the church in Nicaragua in his speech to the Joint Session of Congress, April 27, 1983, and reiterated the charge in a nationally televised speech of May 9, 1984. Particularly forceful statements of how the Sandinista Revolution threatens the churches are: Humberto Belli, *Nicaragua: Christians Under Fire* (Garden City, Mich.: The Puebla Institute, 1984); and Michael Novak, "The WCC in Nicaragua," *National Review*, March 9, 1984, p. 46.

2. See Thomas Bruneau, *The Political Transformation of the Brazilian Catholic Church* (Cambridge: Cambridge University Press, 1974); and Daniel Levine, *Religion and Politics in Latin America* (Princeton, N.J.: Princeton University Press, 1981).

3. See "The Church in the Present Day Transformation of Latin America in Light of the Council" Section II in *The Gospel of Peace and Justice*, edited by Joseph Gremillion (Maryknoll, N.Y.: Orbis, 1976).

4. See Daniel Levine, *Churches and Politics in Latin America* (Beverly Hills, Calif.: Sage Publications, 1979), especially the article by Brian Smith; and Penny Lernoux, *Cry of the*

People (New York: Penguin Books, 1982).

5. John Eagleson and Philip Scharper, eds., *Puebla and Beyond* (Maryknoll, N.Y.: Orbis, 1979), p. 222.

6. Ibid., p. 265.

7. Ibid., p. 136.

8. Ibid., p. 211.

9. Ibid., p. 213.

10. Ibid., p. 135.

11. Ibid., p. 213.

12. Richard Wollheim, "Democracy," *Journal of the History of Ideas* 19, no. 1 (January 1958):228–229; and Christopher Hill, *The World Turned Upside Down: Radical Ideas During the English Revolution* (New York: Viking Press, 1972).

13. Wollheim, "Democracy"; and George H. Sabine, "The Two Democratic Traditions" in *Philosophy Review* 61, no. 4 (October, 1952):451–474.

14. James Madison, *Federalist*, No. 10.

15. Sabine, "Two Democratic Traditions," p. 459.

16. Carole Pateman, *Participation and Democratic Theory* (Cambridge: Cambridge University Press, 1970), pp. 22–27.

17. Fort Worth *Star-Telegram*, February 29, 1984.

18. Pablo Richard and Guillermo Meléndez, ed., *La Iglesia de los Pobres en América Central* (San José: DEI, 1982), p. 149.

19. Interview by T. S. Montgomery, Managua, February 27, 1980.

20. Richard and Meléndez, *La Iglesia*, pp. 156, 165.

21. Philip Wheaton and Yvonne Dilling, *Nicaragua: A People's Revolution* (Washington, D.C.: EPICA), pp. 23–24.

22. Interview by T. S. Montgomery, Estelí, February 12, 1980.

23. For a more extensive discussion of the origins of CEPAD, see Michael Dodson and T. S. Montgomery, "The Churches in the Nicaraguan Revolution," in *Nicaragua in Revolution*, edited by Thomas W. Walker (New York: Praeger, 1982), p. 167.

24. See Penny Lernoux, "The Latin American Church" in *Latin American Research Review* 15, no. 2 (Spring 1980):201–211.

25. Interview by Michael Dodson with James Goff, Managua, April 13, 1983.

26. "Nicaragua: Un Vistazo Sobre las CEBs," *Centro Regional de Informaciones Ecuménicas* (México, D. F., Vol. 7, Nos. 133–134, October 1983), pp. 14–15.

27. Conferencia Episcopal de Nicaragua, "A Los Hombres de Buena Voluntad," August 3, 1978.

28. Ibid.

29. Conferencia Episcopal de Nicaragua, "En Los Dias de Guerra," July 7, 1979 (n.p.).

30. Ibid.

31. See, for example, their letter of July 31, 1979, which harshly criticized a reconstruction process that had not yet begun.

32. This information was supplied by Thomas W. Walker, who was in Nicaragua for the 1983 Christmas season.

33. "Comunicado de la Conferencia Episcopal de Nicaragua," *Sacerdotes en el Gobierno Nicaragünse: Poder o Servicio?* (San José, Costa Rica: DEI, n.d.), p. 9.

34. "Primera Respuesta de Sacerdotes," June 8, 1981 in ibid., p. 12.

35. Declaration of the Special Mission that went to the Vatican, October 20, 1980.

36. "Documento de la Conferencia Episcopal de Nicaragua," October 17, 1980, *Nicaragua: La Hora de los Desafíos* (Lima: Centro de Estudios y Publicaciones, 1981), p. 121.

37. *Jesus Christ and the Unity of His Church in Nicaragua* (Managua: Editorial Unión, 1980), p. 3.

38. See the testimony of Bishop López Ardon in *Pax Christi International Human Rights Reports of the Mission: Nicaragua* (Antwerp, Belgium: Omega Books, 1981), p. 98.

39. *El Nuevo Diario*, May 20, 1980.

40. "Problems with the Church in Nicaragua," *Envío*, No. 4 (September 1981), p. 2.

41. See articles in *El Nuevo Diario*, August 19, 20, 24, and 27; in *La Prensa*, August 24, 25, and 27; and in *Barricada*, August 20 and 26, 1981.

42. *Amanecer*, No. 12 (September 1982), pp. 4–5.

43. Interview of Father Antonio Castro by Michael Dodson, Managua, June 2, 1983.

44. In our conversations with revolutionary Christians their reaction to being labeled a "parallel church" ranged from confusion, to insult, to resentment.

45. *El Nuevo Diario*, May 25, 1983.

46. "Mártires de la Iglesia y de la Revolución" in *Amanecer*, July-August 1983, pp. 14–15. See also *El Tayacan*, August, 1983. Interviews by Laura Nuzzi O'Shaughnessy were also conducted with several priests from Managua and Estelí (August 1983).

47. "Mártires de la Iglesia y de la Revolución."

48. *La Prensa*, September 1, 1983.

49. *El Nuevo Diario*, September 6, 1983.

50. "Noticias del Pueblo," *Amanecer*, October, 1983, pp. 16–17.

51. This analysis of CEPAD is based upon interviews by Laura N. O'Shaughnessy with Gilberto Aguirre, Gustavo Parajón, and Sixto Ulloa, as well as attendance and informal conversations with CEPAD members at several CEPAD-sponsored meetings during the summers of 1981, 1982, and 1983.

Chapter 6
Women

MAXINE MOLYNEUX

The course of the Nicaraguan Revolution in its first five years posed the question of the relationship between social upheaval and its effects on women in a particularly acute form. On the positive side, the Revolution had a major mobilizing impact upon Nicaraguan women, and they played a significant part in it, both in the overthrow of the Somoza dictatorship and in the consolidation of the postinsurrectionary regime. In the insurrection itself, women fought in the guerrilla army, comprising 30 percent of the FSLN's combat forces and providing some of its leading commanders. The political support organization for women, the Association of Women Confronting the National Problem (AMPRONAC), had up to 8,000 members at the time of the Sandinista victory—a significant response from the adult female population.[1] After 1979, women were involved in a series of programs designed to strengthen the revolutionary state and broaden its impact: in the party and mass organizations, in the social and economic reforms, and in the auxiliary security forces, the militia, and Revolutionary Guard Duty. The Sandinistas both before and after the seizure of power made the emancipation of women a major, and sustained, goal.

This process of mobilizing women, and of Sandinista commitment to their emancipation, was severely constrained, however, by a number of factors. These limited the degree to which the overthrow of the political dictatorship, and the accompanying social change, simultaneously challenged the prevailing forms of gender inequality. In the first place, Nicaragua remained an extremely poor country and, with effective U.S. pressure, loans were reduced to a trickle by 1984. The material resources available for realizing a program of radical social change—to provide education, welfare, jobs, housing, and child care facilities—were therefore scarce. At the household level, the shortages of goods in the market, a factor that particularly affects women, had become acute by 1983. Second, the pressures of the counterrevolutionary war took their toll on programs to emancipate women. Time and effort as well as resources were diverted to other priorities. Third, the decisiveness of the political revolution that ousted Somoza was not matched by a comparable change in attitudes and social structures. The increasingly oppositional conservative wing of the Catholic Church, with its institutional weight and ideological hold, was a powerful obstacle to a program to emancipate women. A complementary dimension was the pervasive *machismo* of Nicaraguan life, a value system in part underpinned by widespread internal migration under which men had relations with several women and left them to bring up the children. The social situation of the majority of Nicaraguan women at the moment of the Revolution also allowed no easy solutions: illiteracy of well over 50 percent, concentrated in the rural areas, employment in the least remunerative and stable jobs, together with widespread legal discrimination combined to render the double oppression of women, on class and gender grounds, particularly acute.

Yet the difficulties faced by a program of women's emancipation were not confined to these objective obstacles of the history and circumstances of Nicaragua. For the ambiguity of women's roles in the Nicaraguan Revolution was inscribed within the very momentum of the Revolution itself and of the organization of the FSLN. The Front's victory came about in a two-phase process: guerrilla war by a revolutionary vanguard in the period up to 1978, mass and often spontaneous uprisings in the final months. The success of this process could not automatically overcome the problem it encapsulated—of an alliance of Front and population that was preliminary: One that needed consolidation by substantial political work in the postinsurrectionary period. This general question was equally pertinent to women: Many had supported the Revolution with their blood and their courage and had rallied in the insurrections. But whether the Revolution would continue to command their loyalty and support remained to be seen. If, to this preliminary nature of support for the Sandinistas, one adds the fact that women of different classes and capacities would respond to the Revolution in different ways, then the question of their support for and benefits from the Revolution becomes even more complex.[2] As with all social groups, the link between women and the revolutionary process, the Front and the state, was something that had to be reproduced and developed at each stage of the Revolution.

This political question of the relationship *between* the Front and women was compounded by a question internal to the Front itself, namely its conception of the program of women's emancipation. The commitment to this principle in the 1969 FSLN Program was repeated in the Statute of Rights and Guarantees of Nicaraguans of September 1979, which proclaimed the full equality of men and women with respect to citizen's rights and duties, juridical personality, work, wages, and family relations, and pledged the state to "removing all obstacles" to achieving that equality.

But this commitment was a conditional one; in FSLN terms it located the goal of women's emancipation within "the context of Nicaraguan reality" and within the broader strategy of the FSLN. This meant that policies for advancing the cause of women's emancipation would be pursued so long as they contributed to, or did not detract from, the realization of other, broader goals. Nora Astorga, a founding member of AMPRONAC and Deputy Foreign Minister put it like this:

> In Nicaragua we cannot conduct a struggle of a Western feminist kind. This is alien to our reality. It doesn't make sense to separate the women's struggle from that of overcoming poverty, exploitation and reaction. We want to promote women's interests within the context of that wider struggle.[3]

Although this necessarily narrowed the scope of the campaigns for improving women's position, the FSLN was careful to acknowledge the irreducibility of women's oppression and the need, in particular, to confront the issue of ideology. In his important speech on the occasion of AMNLAE's third anniversary, Tomás Borge made this position clear:

> Economic development on its own is not enough to achieve the liberation of women, and neither is the mere fact of women organizing. There must be a struggle against the habits, traditions and prejudices of men and women. We must launch a difficult and prolonged ideological struggle, a struggle equally undertaken by men and women.[4]

The FSLN, like comparable revolutionary governments elsewhere, was therefore concerned both to improve the position of women and to encourage their participation in the three main areas of revolutionary consolidation and reconstruction: economic development, political activity, and national defense. It was in order to accomplish these tasks while advancing the cause of women's emancipation that AMPRONAC was transformed in September 1979 into the new mass organization for women, AMNLAE (the Luisa Amanda Espinosa Association of Nicaraguan Women).[5] The restructuring of women's social position, envisaged in the FSLN program, was therefore one that was clearly defined: politically, in that the women's organization was to work in close collaboration with, and under the general direction of, the FSLN, and theoretically, in terms of the way in which this restructuring was to be achieved. At its Constitutive Assembly, at the end of 1981, AMNLAE defined its role as "giving women an organic instrument which would permit them to integrate themselves as a decisive force in the program of the revolution; and moreover, express in an organized manner, both their concerns and their social, economic and cultural aspirations." The Assembly also defined six main areas of activity in which AMNLAE would seek to promote the full participation and improve the position of Nicaraguan women:[6]

1. Defense of the Sandinista Revolution.
2. Promoting women's political and ideological consciousness, and advancing their social, political, and economic participation in the revolution.
3. Combating legal and other institutionalized gender inequalities.
4. Promoting women's cultural and technical advancement, and entry into areas of employment traditionally reserved for men, combined with opposition to discrimination in employment.
5. Promoting respect for domestic labor, and creating child care services for working women.
6. Creating and sustaining links of international solidarity.

These goals did not represent the full extent of AMNLAE's involvement in programs to improve the participation and situation of women, nor did they represent the full range of Sandinista activities that had positive implications for women. Other initiatives in the areas of public welfare, health, housing, and education provided the wider context within which these specific goals were advanced. These are discussed elsewhere in this volume, but it is important to note that in many cases the impact of the welfare programs affected women from the poorer classes more profoundly, at least in the short term, than some of AMNLAE's specific goals.

Nonetheless, the first five of these goals were the main focus of Sandinista activity with regard to women per se and embodied certain important principles that informed other areas of policy. The discussion that follows therefore considers the efforts that AMNLAE made under each of the five main headings during the first five years of the Revolution.

DEFENSE OF THE REVOLUTION

Security was the priority of the FSLN from the moment of Triumph; and it became an even more absorbing activity with the intensification of the counterrevolutionary war in the period after 1982. It was a priority for AMNLAE, too, because the safeguarding of the Revolution was, as the resolution stated, "the political guarantee for the achievement of women's emancipation." The fact that women participated so actively in the insurrection meant that there was a fund of experience and commitment upon which the Front could draw in the new military confrontations it faced. Yet the manner in which women participated in the defense of the Revolution differed from that in which they contributed to making it.

The central instrument for defending the Revolution was the Sandinist Popular Army, the EPS. At the time of the victory women made up almost 40 percent of its forces and 6 percent of its officers. Six women (as well as some 30 men) were awarded the rank of Comandante Guerrillero in recognition of their combat role in the Revolution, and some of these women continued to train army and militia recruits. But the postrevolutionary period saw a gradual transfer of women from combat roles to backup positions. Of the women who fought in the FSLN forces up to 1979, only one-quarter were still in combat units by 1981. Subsequently, more women were moved into administrative positions, while others were reallocated to civilian government positions and to the police force.[7]

This redeployment of women away from combat roles was met with a mixed response. In Estelí, on the war front, it was vigorously resisted by women soldiers who complained of not being taken seriously by their male comrades, and of being expected to combine their combat duties with traditional female tasks such as cooking for the troops. AMNLAE's General Secretary in the region, Martha Mungia, expressed the sense of injustice felt by many women: "We can't limit our participation in defense to secondary roles because we would be leaving empty the place in the front line which was filled by the women who died for their country [in the war against Somoza]."[8] But other women in the Front saw the move as inevitable. In the words of Gladys Baez, the first woman to join the guerrilla forces and to fight in the mountains: "Women have proven themselves to be heroic, combative, courageous and able. But we are less tough, we march slower and above all we have children. You can't have a regular army poised for instant mobilization based on a floating population."[9]

AMNLAE nonetheless put up a spirited defense of women's right to be treated as equals even in the army. In the event, a compromise was reached and in January 1981 the first all-woman reserve unit was established in Estelí on the orders of Edén Pastora, at that time in charge of the Militia. By 1982 there were seven all-women reserve battalions, but over the next two years these were gradually dissolved into mixed battalions.

The exclusion from active service remained an issue. When the decree concerning conscription was debated in the Council of State in 1983, AMNLAE delegates opposed it because, again, it exempted women. Magda Enríques, an AMNLAE delegate to the Council, recounted what happened:

> We raised one and a half problems for them. The mandate from our grass roots was to struggle to the end to get equal status so we called two general assemblies in Managua to discuss the whole issue. We demanded scientific, not emotional, explanations for the exclusion of women.

There was a national debate in the media. In the end they agreed to accept women volunteers into active service, which was something of a victory. Of course we AMNLAE delegates were the only ones to vote against this resolution because it still did not settle the issue of principle.[10]

However, other efforts to incorporate women into security activity were pursued with a considerable degree of success. The militia was open to all aged between 16 and 60. Not all members were trained for combat, but they were deployed on guard duty and were prepared for the possibility of having to take over and run factories, installations, and offices in the event of war. In 1984 the militia's membership was believed to total around 50,000, 45 percent of whom were estimated to be women.

Civil defense provided a separate, and increasingly important, area of security, one in which women also played a vital part. Two associated efforts were organized in this field: the Sandinista Defense Committees (CDS), organized on a neighborhood basis to oversee the running, and resolve the problems, of particular locations, and Revolutionary Guard Duty, a system of local guard duty operating by day and night. About 50 percent of the membership of the CDSs were women, as were up to 80 percent of those in the guards. In July 1983 there were reported to be more than 50,000 women guards in the country, 20,000 of them in Managua alone.[11] The demands of the increasingly tense security situation obviously contributed to this mobilization of women, and considerable efforts went into preparation for what the future would hold, in terms of air attacks, sabotage, and invasion. But these civil defense organizations were also involved in reducing crime and in coping with natural disasters. During the floods of 1982, the emergency committees set up to deal with the effects of the disaster worked under the slogan "AMNLAE in the front line of civil defense." Women were therefore present, and increasingly mobilized, throughout the organizations of revolutionary defense in Nicaragua—in the EPS, militia, CDS, Revolutionary Guard Duty, and in the Voluntary Police. Many of those most active in these bodies were also AMNLAE members, and AMNLAE had a role in organizing some of this activity.

AMNLAE was also involved in defense of the Revolution in a less direct manner, through its political role in support of the FSLN and through local organizations such as the Association of Mothers of Heroes and Martyrs, an active support organization of the FSLN. This association sought to invest motherhood with a positive political and combative connotation, as well as to provide personal support for the bereaved and those anxious about relatives posted to the war front. But this mobilization of woman for national defense was double-edged. Insofar as women were placed in a predominantly supportive role in the Sandinista military system, they lost an element of the equality they had won in the Revolution itself; and the relentless strains of national defense, although leading to an increase in women's participation, inevitably distracted the efforts of the Front and AMNLAE, as well as of Nicaraguan women as a whole, away from the tasks of transforming, along more egalitarian lines, women's position in society itself. Yet in the midst of the contra war, although support among some groups declined, the participation of women in the Revolution was greater than at any time since 1979.

PROMOTING POLITICAL AND IDEOLOGICAL AWARENESS AND GREATER PARTICIPATION

The central organization for promoting political mobilization and education was the FSLN, within which women made up a sizable minority. In 1984 women were said to comprise 22 percent of the total, and it was officially claimed that they made up over one-third, or 37 percent, of the leadership cadre.[12] Although there were no women in the nine-member Junta that comprised the FSLN leadership, the Vice-President of the Council of State was a woman, and women assumed positions of responsibility in the party at the regional level. On three occasions after 1979, women filled ministerial posts.[13]

Beyond the Front itself there were the mass organizations, some of whose members were also in the Front, but the majority of whom were not. These organizations acted as two-way transmission systems between the FSLN leadership and the population, and through which the wishes and complaints of the membership were relayed to the top. Mass organizations or movements were responsible both for politicizing their constituencies and representing their interests. Among other functions, they publicized the aims, policies, and achievements of the Revolution and encouraged participation in its campaigns. Apart from the CDSs, women were also well represented in the Sandinista Youth, where they made up around 50 percent of the membership. But they remained a small minority in the trade unions, and until a campaign to redress the situation during 1983–84, they were virtually absent from the associations of agricultural workers. However, as a result of this campaign, by mid-1984 women made up over 40 percent of the membership of the Rural Workers' Association.[14]

AMNLAE's own organizational capacity grew substantially over the first five years. At its Constituent Assembly in 1981 a seven-woman National Directorate was elected, headed by a General Secretary, with other

Secretaries responsible for Organization, Health, International Relations, Information and Education, Defense, and as a liaison with the Council of State.[15] A similar structure was duplicated at departmental and municipal levels. Total card-carrying AMNLAE membership by 1984 was given by an AMNLAE spokeswoman as 85,000, although its mobilizing capacity was said to be considerably greater. From 1981 onward, AMNLAE encouraged the establishment of Work Committees, comprised of three to five members, which were set up in factories, plantations, places of learning, state and private institutions, markets, and hospitals. They were charged with "promoting fuller participation of women, political and ideological clarification, co-ordinating with other organizations to promote the tasks of the Revolution." These Work Committees were also designed to ensure that the trade unions and employers observed the laws against discrimination against women, and they tried to promote women's interests as they were defined at the sectoral level. By 1983 in Managua alone there were 211 Work Committees with more than 8,000 affiliates.[16]

A major focus of AMNLAE's activities was initially the specific campaigns launched around social issues. Women participated in large numbers in the mass Literacy Campaign of 1980, and in the health campaign of the following year. The former mobilized a large number of women teachers—60 percent of the total—and some 12 percent of those teaching in it were AMNLAE members. Another 20 percent of AMNLAE's members entered the literacy classes. Nearly 200 Committees of Mothers for Literacy were formed to undertake housekeeping and other tasks for the crusade participants. Many women benefited substantially from the campaign—196,000 became literate as against a total of 210,000 men. This was proportionally less than the percentage of illiterates (60 percent) that women accounted for, but it nevertheless represented a considerable opportunity for educationally deprived women.[17]

A similar picture of female mobilization and benefit could be seen in the health campaign of 1980–81, and in the continuing program of health initiatives, such as Health [Teach-in] Days (Jornadas Populares de Salud). Over 77,000 people joined the health brigades organized by AMNLAE and other mass organizations to carry out basic preventive health and education, and women made up the great majority of those involved in such campaigns: 80 percent of the health brigade activists and 75 percent of the "health multipliers" or practical teachers.[18] Overall women's participation in activity of this kind and related forms of voluntary work was high. In the immediate postrevolutionary period it was women who cleaned up neighborhoods and helped reorganize community life—a commitment to local political involvement that was reflected in their active participation in the CDSs.

COMBATING INSTITUTIONAL INEQUALITIES AND DISCRIMINATION AGAINST WOMEN

Within a few weeks of coming to power the FSLN initiated measures to alter the legal position of women. In response to one of the demands of AMPRONAC, Article 30 of Decree No. 48 banned the media's exploitation of women as sex objects. This swift action highlighted the fact that the FSLN considered the law to be an instrument for equalizing relations between the sexes, as well as being a site of conflict between revolutionary and prerevolutionary values. Whereas other reform measures led to an improvement in the political and material conditions of women, along with other subjected groups, legal reform confronted traditional relations between the sexes directly, by removing certain male privileges and challenging some of the others that remained. As an instrument of struggle, legal reform was an effective means of achieving three aims; the popularization of government policies and objectives, the democratization of judicial procedures to allow a measure of popular participation in the formulation of the law, and the utilization of the proposed reforms as a means of increasing awareness of those social problems that the government sought a popular mandate to change.

AMNLAE spearheaded the campaign to reform the legal status of women. Its permanent representative on the main legislative body, the Council of State, was responsible for drafting, circulating, and presenting new legislation for ratification. Following the passing of the law against media exploitation of women, several other laws relating to women and the family were approved by the Council. In some cases, old laws, already on the statute books but not implemented, were revived and reaffirmed. One such law embodied the principle of equal pay for men and women performing the same work. This was implemented in many state enterprises and cooperatives, sometimes against the wishes of male workers. Other measures allowed for the reduction of the working day where this was particularly long, as in the case of rural workers and domestic servants. Health and safety provisions of industrial workers were also improved, and steps were taken to ensure that women in some enterprises received their entitlement of four weeks of maternity leave on full pay before childbirth and eight weeks afterward.

The position of women workers in the rural sector was radically improved in 1982 by a decree based on a provision in the 1979 Statute of Rights under which wages were no longer paid only to the male head of family but to all workers over age 14 on an individual basis. This enabled the contribution of women workers to receive greater social recognition and provided them with their own income. Two other new laws, which addressed male-female relations directly, aroused considerable controversy. The first, the Law of Relations between Mothers, Fathers, and Children of 1981, aimed "to regulate equality of rights and duties between men and women with respect to [their] common children." The law sought to remove men's special privileges over custody in divorce settlments (known as *patria potestad*) and recognized the legal rights of illegitimate children.

Even more controversial was the Provision Law drafted in 1982. This attempted to redefine family responsibilities more broadly than the existing legislation, which only stipulated a parental obligation to provide children with the basic necessities of life. This law was important not only for the reaction it aroused but also for what it revealed about Sandinista thinking concerning the emancipation of women. For it was designed to fulfill two goals that were seen as complementary: on the one hand, to promote greater family cohesion, and on the other to redress some of the injustices from which women suffered. Policies on the family were formulated within a perspective that defined it as a "basic institution of society," entitled to the support and protection of the state. AMNLAE saw its role as helping to strengthen the Nicaraguan family, and this was considered necessary for two reasons. First, as an institution the family had suffered from the erosion of kin ties and from the historical prevalence of male out-migration. Second, given the lack of resources available for public welfare, the family, and in particular the extended household, could be encouraged to meet some of these needs. In this spirit the Provision Law therefore aimed to promote "greater family reciprocity and responsibility" by making all adult members legally liable for maintaining the family unit. This meant that all income earners should contribute financially and share in the household tasks.

The second aim of the Provision Law was to improve the position of both women and children by giving them a more secure financial base within the family. This was intended to offset the effects of the high rate of male desertion, migrancy, and serial polygamy, which left women as the sole providers for their children: With a total fertility rate of 6.3, Nicaraguan women bore large numbers of children and this, coupled with the fact that 34 percent of Nicaraguan households were female headed (60 percent in Managua), was a major constituent of female poverty.[19] The new law sanctioned a practice already established at INSSBI (the Welfare Ministry), which made it possible for women to claim aid from the father of their children provided he acknowledged paternity. It thus gave the state increased powers to ensure that such aid was provided and specified that this could be in cash, kind, or even in the form of housework, a novel feature of the Provision Law. When this law came up for public discussion in 1982 it generated considerable controversy. AMNLAE convened over 100 Popular Assemblies to discuss its provisions and these were attended by trade unionists, market women, CDS members, and public sector employees. Fewer men than women attended, as they were said to feel threatened by AMNLAE and its campaigns of law reform. There was also a lively debate in the national press about the place of women's emancipation in the process of revolutionary consolidation.

The amended law was eventually presented to the Council of State in October 1982, and here, too, it generated a heated debate. In defense of the law, AMNLAE argued that its principal aim was to strengthen the family and thus provide better conditions for the nation's children by giving them a more secure environment. The law was criticized on the grounds that it was not realistic, in calling for changes in the difficult area of male-female relations, particularly at that time. Some critics were more straightforward in expressing the fear that it could polarize relations between the sexes and so weaken the struggle against the main enemy, the counterrevolution. The law was referred back to AMNLAE for redrafting to meet some of these objections. It was approved by the Council of State in November 1982, but as of mid-1984 it had still not been ratified by the Junta.[20]

Beyond the conjunctural question of the relation between women's emancipation and defense of the Revolution there lay a deeper problem: namely, whether the law adequately identified the causes of the weakness of the family. These lay in the marked gender inequalities that prevailed and that privileged men in certain ways. It was therefore doubtful whether the family could be strengthened without tackling the roots of these privileges, and confronting the issue of machismo, and thereby questioning the basis of male-female solidarity. Merely making men legally responsible in the financial realm was not adequate to the task of what Tomás Borge called "humanizing social relations."[21] Yet even such mild proposals as these opened AMNLAE to the charge of waging a "sex war," a charge it vigorously denied. Magda Enríques, a member of AMNLAE's national directorate, maintained: "These were issues of common concern to men and women. By improving the position of women we also helped to remove from men the burden of their own oppression."[22] Yet issues that threatened to divide the sexes were treated with caution. In a situation where priority was given to national defense, and the Revolution's survival was seen as the guarantee for any process of women's emancipation, progress in this area was to remain piecemeal.

IMPROVING AND EXTENDING WOMEN'S ECONOMIC AND SOCIAL POSITION

Women's entry into productive activity was considered by AMNLAE to be both an important precondition for women's emancipation and a contribution to the national development effort. It consequently sought to increase women's training and employment opportunities, although this proved particularly difficult in the prevailing conditions of capital scarcity. After the victory, women played an increasingly important part in the Nicaraguan economy. In 1971 they formed only 17 percent of the economically active population but this had risen, according to government estimates, to 41 percent by 1982.[23] This made female participation rates in Nicaragua almost double the average for Latin America as a whole, and even if some allowance is made for different accounting methods, a substantial increase nonetheless appears to have taken place. However, most women workers were still concentrated in areas where incomes were low. Approximately 20 percent of economically active women worked in agriculture, with similar percentages for personal service and petty marketing activities.[24] In the urban centers many women worked in the large informal sector; two-thirds of the urban labor force remained outside permanent wage employment and women comprised 70 percent of this category.[25] Work conditions were better in formal sector urban employment, but women accounted for only 15 percent of the work force here and were chiefly concentrated in the conventional areas of female employment: textiles, chemicals, and foodstuffs.

AMNLAE focused its efforts on alleviating the situation of the most deprived women, and to this end it took three main initiatives. In the first place, both jobs and training in semiskilled occupations were provided through the establishment of production collectives. This program began in 1980, and small enterprises were established at the same time, to produce low-cost utilities such as clothing and pottery. By 1983 there were over 50 collectives in which AMNLAE participated, 18 of them entirely run by the women's organization. Some of these functioned as rehabilitation centers that trained exprostitutes in skills such as sewing and tailoring.[26]

The second component of this program began in August 1982 and involved a campaign to promote the cultivation of family plots. The official aim was, once again, "to integrate women into production." AMNLAE undertook to provide seeds of basic staple vegetables and helped in planning cultivation. The campaign was considered to be a great success: only a year after it began over 400 individual plots and 23 communal ones had been established. In the following year, the number of plots worked under this scheme more than trebled.[27]

The third campaign initiative was directed specifically at the rural areas, where from 1983 AMNLAE made its priority the amelioration of the situation of rural women, a particularly deprived group. The redistribution of land under the provisions of the Agrarian Reform—to private, cooperative, and state cultivation—brought a substantial number of women into production for the first time, and the 1981 Law of Agricultural

Cooperatives included as one of its stated objectives the greater involvement of women in both production and related administrative activities.
The pattern of increased female productive activity varied, however,
according to region. One reason for this was the different degrees of effort
devoted to mobilizing and integrating women, and the other was that
recruitment of men for the defense of the Revolution was uneven. In some
cases the demands of the war on the male labor force produced changes in
the traditional division of labor, with women taking over jobs previously
performed by men and becoming the principal agrarian producers. Perhaps
the most affected regions were those of Matagalapa and Jinotega, where by
February 1984 women made up as much as 40 percent of the rural work
force.[28]

Finally, AMNLAE encouraged women to acquire technical and
vocational training in areas from which they were traditionally excluded.
This was assisted to some degree by a general rise in female enrollment at
school and the complementary rise in the number of women in higher
education. Five years after the Revolution, women accounted for over 40
percent of university students, an increase of almost 100 percent on 1979
figures. However, there was also a need to redirect young women into more
challenging and socially necessary roles.[29] In 1984 high school students
were given a series of seminars in vocational training and a special effort
was made to encourage girls to enter areas such as agricultural engineering
and technology. With support from AMNLAE and the FSLN, some
women began to enter areas previously closed to them. The most striking
advance in this respect was the graduation of five women pilots by 1984.
The first of these, Saida Gonzalez, became a fighter pilot and was killed in
1984 while on duty near the war front.

PROMOTING RESPECT FOR DOMESTIC LABOR AND
CREATING CHILD CARE SERVICES

From its inception AMNLAE devoted considerable efforts to improving
and changing women's position in the home. Its papers, first *La Voz de la
Mujer* (Woman's Voice) and later *Somos AMNLAE* (We Are AMNLAE),
founded in 1982, published both political and theoretical articles on the
need to free women from the burden of domestic responsibilities, as well as
proffering advice on how to lighten the chores of keeping house, sewing
clothes, and cooking.[30]

AMNLAE's view was that domestic labor should be shared as well as
given greater social recognition. Moreover, child care should not devolve
solely upon women but should be equalized with the state providing
appropriate support systems that would also help to improve the care of

children. However it was only in 1982 that these issues came to the forefront of public discussion when the Provision Law was debated. Article 1.2 of the law stated: "Domestic labor is one of the pillars on which the family rests, and to which all members who are able and have the opportunity to do so must contribute, regardless of sex." At the Popular Assemblies held in 1982 to discuss the law in draft, this clause received considerable attention from AMNLAE officials and substantial support from the women present.[31] Despite some opposition to it as "impractical," the clause remained in the final version of the law; yet it was noticeable that public discussion, and hence stimulation of awareness on the issue had significantly declined by 1983. AMNLAE's legal office established on March 8, 1983, assumed responsibility for explaining the provisions of the law to individuals wishing to invoke it. In the absence of a popular and sustained campaign around this issue, however, it was difficult to see how the law could really promote greater equality between men and women in the domestic sphere.

If progress in equalizing domestic labor was therefore limited, more public attention focused on the social and economic dimensions of the household, especially as a result of prevailing shortages that the counter-revolutionary war had exacerbated by late 1983. AMNLAE conducted a number of campaigns designed to increase women's awareness of the implications of their housekeeping practices for the economy as a whole, and to point out how women, through their own individual efforts, could help to stretch the family income and thus reduce the pressure on wages, as well as help conserve scarce or expensive resources. In 1982, named the Year of Austerity and Frugality in the Family, AMNLAE called on women to be better housewives in order to preserve national resources and help the rationed basic foodstuffs go further. AMNLAE's argument was that domestic labor had a different significance under socialism to that under capitalism: If in the latter it benefitted the capitalist, in the former it protected the resources of the Revolution. A publicity campaign called on women to save imported glass bottles for recycling in order to reduce the foreign exchange bill. Such campaigns were designed to serve a dual function: a strictly economic one, whereby changes in housekeeping practices alleviated the burden on the national economy, and a broader political one, of mobilizing women and increasing their consciousness of the Revolution through their participation in such campaigns.[32] The Family Plot campaign (reminiscent of the program to promote family "victory gardens" in the United States during World War II) was also conceived with similar ends in view.

Positive as they were in some respects, such mobilizations of women around domestic issues reflected a deeper ambiguity in the FSLN's policies toward women; while these were concerned with challenging traditional female stereotypes in the public arena, less attention was given to the private, domestic sphere. The most resilient and indeed powerful of female representations, that of motherhood, remained unassailed by the changes that had taken place in other areas. This was to be expected in a society where motherhood received religious confirmation, but it also acquired official support in the public emphasis on Mothers' Circles, Mothers' Demonstrations for Peace, and Mothers of Martyrs masses. These more heroic aspects of revolutionary motherhood, however, went along with a traditional conception of women's reproductive duties. The conservative Catholic Church's opposition to contraception and celebration of motherhood as women's primary role provided the ideological underpinning to Nicaragua's high birth rate. The Sandinistas were unable, as a result, to legalize abortion or make contraception widely available. Large numbers of abortions continued to be carried out in conditions that endangered the health and lives of many women.[33] Lea Guido, Minister of Health, summed up the FSLN's position: "While we don't have a problem of overpopulation, far from it, abortion and contraception are a human right. We want to make these available but since there is opposition to it, we must be careful how we proceed."[34]

More progress was registered in the field of child care, although the limited resources available and the reluctance of men to play their part meant that this remained an obstacle to women's greater participation in extradomestic activities, in both rural and urban areas. While the state's provision of child care facilities continued to fall short of demand, their numbers steadily increased over the years following the Triumph. By mid-1984, 22 Child Development Centers, catering to approximately 2,500 children, were established in the urban areas, while in the countryside, 21 Rural Infant Services absorbed 1,631 children. But by 1984 these comprehensive systems, which combined child care with educational, health, and nutrition needs, could not be expanded because of financial constraints. Instead, more attention was focused on increasing the number of Children's Lunchrooms designed to provide working children and those from the poorest families with a main meal each day while encouraging them to attend school. About twenty of these, involving some 5,000 children, were in existence by 1984.[35]

CONCLUSION

The evidence suggests that, in the period after 1979, women continued to participate in large numbers in the revolutionary process, as combatants against counterrevolution, organizers of welfare programs, and workers in the various branches of the economy. Most women, and especially those from the more disadvantaged groups, also benefitted practically from the welfare policies implemented by the Sandinista state as well as from AMNLAE's specific programs. They gained more access to health, education, training, and housing; their basic provisions, although rationed, were until 1984 heavily subsidized. These benefits, a direct product of the priorities and policies of the state, had a particular significance for women, who, by virtue of their place within the sexual division of labor, were disproportionately responsible for the provision of basic needs.

Some progress was also made in equalizing gender relations, especially through women's greater participation and prominence in social life, but also through legal reform. For many women the Revolution raised their expectations and fundamentally changed their lives. Judged by their own goals the Sandinistas had achieved a substantial amount by 1984. Yet they were not complacent about the results, nor could they be.[36] The limits of the process were also clear. Most women were still located in the least rewarding jobs and in areas where they had traditionally predominated; the legal measures designed to equalize the burden of domestic labor remained largely ineffective in the absence of a sustained campaign to combat entrenched attitudes; legal procedures such as in the case of divorce still favored men, and women had not gained reproductive freedom. Magda Enríques expressed the feeling in 1984:

> When we look back and see how much we have achieved we are very proud. But when we see how much there is still left to be done, that's when we feel angry because there is so much more we could be doing that we are not able to do because of the War. But women are defending the gains of the revolution; they know it offers the only opportunity and the only guarantee for improving their lives.[37]

There can be little doubt that, whatever the shortcomings of the process and however "conditional" the support of the Sandinistas was for women's emancipation, the Revolution had nevertheless introduced major, positive reforms in the position of women, and that the survival of the regime was indeed a precondition for the maintenance and continuation of these changes. The example of Grenada—where the U.S. military intervention of October 1983 was immediately followed by the public reemergence of prostitution, the ending of welfare programs, disbandment of the National Women's Organization, and mass unemployment— demonstrated this link all too clearly.

The fate of women in Nicaragua in the first five years and beyond was conditioned to a greater degree than was usual by external forces. These limited the capacity of the government and organizations like AMNLAE to implement a far-reaching reform program. Yet the paradox of the war was that while it certainly divided many women, not only along class lines, it also created the conditions in which women were increasingly mobilized in support of the Revolution's gains. The spontaneous mobilizations of women in the prerevolutionary period were therefore to a considerable extent transformed in the first five years into an organized and institutionalized defense of the regime they had helped to bring to power.

NOTES

1. For accounts of women's role in the anti-Somoza struggle, see Margaret Randall, *Sandino's Daughters* (London: Zed Press, 1981); Susan Ramírez-Horton, "The Role of Women in the Revolution" in *Nicaragua in Revolution* edited by Thomas W. Walker (New York: Praeger, 1982); and Elizabeth Maier, *Nicaragua, la Mujer en la Revolución* (Mexico: Ediciones de Cultura Popular, 1980). Neither the present text nor other accounts deal with the specific situation of ethnic minority women.

2. This question of the heterogeneous nature of "women's interests" and of their support for and benefits from the Revolution is critically evaluated in my article "Mobilization without Emancipation? Women's Interests, State and Revolution in Nicaragua," in *Critical Social Policy*, No. 10 (Summer 1984), and also published in *Desarrollo y Sociedad*, No. 13, January 1984, and *Feminist Studies* (forthcoming).

3. Author's interview, Managua. This and some of the other interviews cited here were carried out during a research trip to Nicaragua in August and September 1982, sponsored by the Nuffield Foundation. (Nora Astorga was awarded the title of Comandante Guerrillero for her role in the guerrilla struggle. She was appointed ambassador to the United States in 1984 but the U.S. government refused to allow her to take up the post. The reason given was her part in the assassination of Reinaldo Perez Vega, a well-known torturer and one of Somoza's close advisors.)

4. Speech by Tomás Borge, published in *Barricada* on October 4, 1982.

5. The name commemorates the first woman combatant (a seamstress) to be killed by Somoza forces.

6. AMNLAE, *Documentos de la Asamblea Nacional* (Managua 1982).

7. J. Deighton et al., *Sweet Ramparts* (London: War on Want and the Nicaraguan Solidarity Campaign, 1983).

8. AMNLAE, *Mujer, Revolución*, July 19, 1981.

9. Author's interview, London, March 1984. Magda Enríques is the member of the AMNLAE Secretariat responsible for Education and Information.

10. Author's interview, London, March 1984.

11. *Somos AMNLAE*, July 1983.

12. Oficina de la Mujer, the bureau that coordinates FSLN and AMNLAE policy, provided these figures.

13. These were Lea Guido, Minister of Health; Daisy Zamora, Deputy Minister of Culture; and Nora Astorga, Deputy Foreign Minister. Ctde Dora María Téllez was the Vice President of the Council of State.

14. Author's interview with Magda Enríques, 1984.

15. In 1982 Glenda Monterrey assumed the role of General Secretary from Gloria Carrión, a move that was seen to coincide with efforts to make AMNLAE "more responsive to the needs of working class women." New elections for the Secretariat were scheduled for June 1984.

16. *Barricada*, September 29, 1983.

17. *Una Mujer Donde Esté Debe Hacer la Revolución*, AMNLAE pamphlet (Managua, 1982).

18. *Somos AMNLAE*, No. 1, May 1982.

19. According to Ministry of Planning statistics, in the poorest income-earning sector in Managua there are 354 women for each 100 men.

20. The situation remains legally ambiguous since the law did have some force through the invocations at tribunals of "common law."

21. Tomás Borge's speech.

22. *Una Mujer Donde Esté.*

23. AMNLAE, *La Mujer Trabajadora*, April 1984.

24. Deighton et al., *Sweet Ramparts.*

25. Women worked out of necessity; 85 percent of female heads of households went out to work.

26. Prostitution was made illegal after the victory, although it remained an important survival strategy for poor women. The Sandinistas tried with comparatively little success to provide alternative income-generating projects for exprostitutes. See Deighton et al., *Sweet Ramparts*, for an account of these prostitution rehabilitation centers.

27. Interview with Magda Enríques, March 1984.

28. A CIERA (Centro de Investigación y Estudios de la Reforma Agraria) survey of 1981 found that women represented 36 percent of the cotton harvest workers and at least 28 percent of the coffee harvest workers. See Carmen Diana Deere, "Co-Operative Development and Women's Participation in the Nicaragua Agrarian Reform," *American Journal of Agrarian Economics*, December 1983.

29. Despite the increase in participation, the female dropout rate remained high. In order to counter one of the reasons for this, AMNLAE organized seminars in sex education for final-year high school students.

30. *Somos AMNLAE* also ran a series designated to teach readers about reproduction and family health.

31. This was evident in the seven assemblies I attended.

32. Author's interview with Glenda Monterrey, General Secretary of AMNLAE, September 1982.

33. In 1981 a Managua hospital was admitting an average of 12 women a day as a result of illegal abortions. The main maternity hospital there recorded four to five admissions weekly resulting from similar circumstances. See Deighton et al., *Sweet Ramparts.*

34. Author's interview, Autumn 1982.

35. Figures provided by the Oficina de la Mujer.

36. Tomás Borge alludes to this in his speech.

37. Author's interview, March 1984.

Chapter 7
The Bourgeoisie

DENNIS GILBERT

The Nicaraguan bourgeoisie played a pivotal role in the struggle against Anastasio Somoza. As part of the triumphant revolutionary coalition led by the FSLN, the bourgeoisie claimed positions of power in the new government and secured guarantees to protect capitalist class interests. But within a year of Somoza's fall, the Sandinistas had shoved representatives of the bourgeoisie to the margins of political power and assumed control of the "commanding heights" of the economy. Bitter confrontations between the government and the private sector became a central feature of the Nicaraguan Revolution. Yet, after nearly five years of Sandinista rule, most production remained in private hands, an ironic state of affairs that was unlikely to change in the near future.

ORIGINS AND STRUCTURE OF THE MODERN BOURGEOISIE

The decades following World War II were a period of rapid growth and differentiation for the Nicaraguan bourgeoisie. Diversification of the traditional agro-export sector and industrial development, encouraged by the Central American Common Market, powered rapid GNP growth. It is probable that more Nicaraguans were victims than beneficiaries of this expansion. For example, in the 1960s and 1970s, while GNP nearly tripled, the rate of childhood malnutrition doubled.[1] Nonetheless, postwar expansion, particularly in cotton cultivation and light industry, produced new affluence for a fortunate minority and introduced new names into the national bourgeoisie. The result was a restructuring of social and economic relationships at the top of Nicaraguan society.

On the eve of the Nicaraguan Revolution, the private sector of the economy was composed of four entrepreneurial strata: the Somoza group,

I am grateful to Mary Erikson, William LeoGrande, Tommie Sue Montgomery, Lawrence Pezzullo, Rose Spalding, and John Weeks for comments on various drafts of this chapter. Their assistance in no way commits them to my conclusions.

the Banco de Nicaragua and Banco de America groups, the middle
bourgeoisie, and small producers and merchants. A large part of the
national economy was controlled by the major economic groups in the first
two strata.[2] The Somoza family and its close associates ran an extensive
economic empire of agricultural, commercial, industrial, and financial
enterprises, built through liberal use of state power and resources during
four decades of Somoza rule. The family's private fortune was independently estimated at $400 to 900 million.[3] The Banco de Nicaragua
(BANIC) and Banco de America (BANAMERICA) groups emerged in the
1950s and 1960s, in part as defensive responses to the Somozas relentless
aggrandizement. Each was a coalition of businessmen and families that
controlled diverse enterprises crystallized around a bank. Together the
BANAMERICA and BANIC groups controlled an estimated 20 percent of
the GNP.[4]

The "middle bourgeoisie" included all modern producers and major
retailers not tied to the big economic groups. This category contained many
enterprises that were relatively small—for example, a 100-acre farm
growing coffee for export or a factory with a few dozen workers producing
cosmetics—but they could be distinguished from the multitude of peasant
farms, artisan shops, neighborhood stores, and street peddlers in the
bottom stratum by their application of modern technology and administrative methods. This chapter will be especially concerned with the
middle bourgeoisie, the most dynamic of the four strata through the period
under review. However, the term "bourgeoisie" will be used to refer to the
two middle strata.

THE BOURGEOISIE AND SOMOZA

The attitude of the bourgeoisie toward the Somozas in the postwar decades
has been described as "ambivalent."[5] The broad social and economic
policies of the regime in areas such as labor, taxation, infrastructure
development, and industrial promotion were clearly tilted toward the
bourgeoisie. At the same time, the expanding economic power of the
Somozas, their arbitrary seizures of property, and their use of government
resources and regulatory mechanisms to gain private advantage alienated
broad sectors of the bourgeoisie.

Responses varied. Some members of the bourgeoisie looked after their
own interests by cutting cynical political deals with the Somozas; one result
of this tendency was the factionalization of the parties traditionally
dominated by the upper class. Between 1948 and 1967 there were a series of
coup attempts against the Somozas involving some members of the
bourgeoisie, though none gained broad bourgeoisie support. The most

significant opposition to the regime came from the emergent middle bourgeoisie, whose members were by and large not well represented by the traditional parties, not individually powerful enough to make attractive deals with the regime, and generally more progressive than the established rich.

The organ that best represented the middle bourgeoisie was not a party but the Superior Council of Private Enterprise (COSEP),[6] an umbrella organization formed by private sector associations, including the chambers of industry, commerce, and agriculture. In the 1960s, COSEP periodically clashed with the regime over specific matters of economic policy and regulatory corruption. But gradually COSEP turned its attention toward broader social and political concerns. The organization shared the reformist outlook that motivated the Alliance for Progress—the sense that moderate change was the best prophylactic barrier to radical revolution.[7]

Somoza's tenuous relations with the bourgeoisie degenerated sharply in the aftermath of the earthquake that leveled central Managua in 1972. Somoza and his allies looted the relief funds that poured in from abroad. Construction firms, real estate companies, banks, and other enterprises tied to the Somozas monopolized the lucrative reconstruction business. The bourgeoisie resented the Somoza's aggressive extension of their economic empire and was alarmed by evidence of increasing popular discontent in the wake of the disaster.[8]

In the years following the quake, the middle bourgeoisie became increasingly determined in its opposition to the regime. Its members backed and led two broad opposition coalitions that sought Somoza's removal: the Democratic Liberation Union (UDEL) and its successor, the Broad Liberation Front (FAO). (COSEP was one of the member organizations of FAO.) In contrast, the more conservative BANIC and BANAMERICA groups held themselves aloof from efforts to depose the dictator.

The leadership of the FSLN took careful note of the evolution of the middle bourgeoisie. In the period 1975–77, the FSLN was a relatively small, sharply divided movement, forced into a defensive posture by the government's massive counterinsurgency campaign. One FSLN faction, the "Terceristas" (Third Way) argued for a new strategy emphasizing more daring military operations and the formation of broad alliances with other groups opposed to the dictatorship, in particular the "progressive bourgeoisie." In mid-1977 the Terceristas took a key step toward implementing this strategy when they formed the "Group of Twelve," a committee of economic, cultural, and religious notables who publicly endorsed the FSLN. Among them were well-known businessmen and several professionals closely linked to the bourgeoisie.

The Group of Twelve conferred a new element of legitimacy to the FSLN and provided a convenient front for dealing with the bourgeois political opposition. For a time, the Group was part of FAO. However, a deep ideological chasm remained between the FSLN and the middle bourgeoisie. While the middle bourgeoisie was open to a program of social reform, its principle concern was the removal of Somoza, whom it increasingly regarded as a threat to its own interests and to social stability. "The problem," commented a COSEP spokesman, "is the man . . . just get rid of him." The FSLN, on the other hand, contemplated a radical transformation of national institutions that would begin only with Somoza's departure. "The question," the FSLN's founder Carlos Fonseca wrote in the 1960s, "is not only to bring about a change of the man in power, but to overthrow the exploiting classes and achieve the victory of the exploited."[9]

The dramatic events of 1978 produced a decisive shift in the direction of national political events and the political role of the bourgeoisie. The year opened with the assassination of Pedro Joaquín Chamorro, leader of UDEL and editor of *La Prensa*, Managua's most prestigious daily paper and principal organ of the bourgeois opposition. Few doubted that the Somozas were responsible for his death.[10] The event galvanized public opinion in general and bourgeois opinion in particular. Chamorro was a member of one of Nicaragua's best known upper-class families. His murder violated the implicit code of conduct that has traditionally regulated behavior among gentlemen in Latin American politics. "One does not," explained a Nicaraguan banker some years later, "kill people of a certain 'social condition.' " A government might, on occasion, shoot peasants. Members of the bourgeoisie are subject to deportation, perhaps prison, but murder was beyond the pale.

In the aftermath of Chamorro's assassination and an enormous popular demonstration at his funeral, COSEP called for a national work stoppage to support demands for prosecution of the assassins and the resignation of the dictator. The strike, which was widely observed, lasted three weeks and produced frequent demonstrations and violent confrontations between authorities and the strikers. It did not, however, attain either of its objectives.

In the course of 1978, the organized middle bourgeoisie lost the political initiative to the FSLN. The Terceristas captured popular imagination with dramatic strokes such as the seizure of the National Palace in August. While the efforts of the bourgeois opposition failed to budge Somoza, they contributed to the rapidly expanding popular mobilization that fed the ranks of FSLN supporters. That tendency was clearly demonstrated when a national strike called by FAO in late August turned into the massive September insurrection, led by the FSLN. The insurrection was ruthlessly suppressed by Somoza's National Guard at a cost of 5,000 lives and extensive damage to provincial cities,[11] but the defeat only redoubled the following of the FSLN, which immediately began planning a new offensive.

As the Sandinistas gained the political initiative, bourgeois attitudes toward the FSLN were shifting. Many sons and daughters of bourgeois families joined the Sandinista Front, typically associating themselves with the Terceristas. These links and the relatively moderate political rhetoric of the Terceristas drew an expanding sector of the bourgeoisie to the FLSN. But it was the mindless brutality of the regime's response to the September insurrection that crystallized the change in bourgeois thinking. In the wake of that disaster, even the conservatives of BANIC and BANAMERICA (now fearful of an FSLN victory) supported talks between FAO and the government designed, once again, to induce Somoza's voluntary departure. Much of the middle bourgeoisie went even further and began actively supporting the insurgents with money, arms, refuge, and other forms of assistance. Reservations about the FSLN were set aside. All attention was focused on a single goal: toppling Somoza. As one anti-Somoza activist recalls the period, the prevailing attitude in middle bourgeois circles was, "There is no alternative. Come what may—it can't be worse than this."

THE BOURGEOISIE AND THE CONSOLIDATION OF SANDINISTA POWER

In planning the government that would assume power on July 19, 1979, the FSLN chose to ease its own transition to power by emphasizing the same broad alliance strategy that had characterized its approach to the last phase of the military struggle. Well before Somoza fled Managua, the middle bourgeoisie was offered significant participation in the new government and important legal guarantees for its political and economic interests. Alfonso Robelo, a COSEP activist who headed his own political party (the reformist Nicaraguan Democratic Movement, MDN), and Violeta de Chamorro, widow of the assassinated publisher, were named to a five-member Junta on which the FSLN had only one official representative. The key economic policy posts in the cabinet—Planning, Finance, and the Central Bank—all went to men whose solid business and banking backgrounds were reassuring to both the local private sector and international financial interests.

The general program announced by the new Junta in June foresaw a "mixed economy" of private, state, and joint enterprises. The state would "recover" the properties "usurped" by the Somozas and their allies. There would be an agrarian reform and substantial reorganization of the financial sector and of foreign and domestic commerce. However, the Junta promised that the state sector would be of "precise extent and clearly delimited characteristics" and that the "properties and activities of the private sector" would be "fully guaranteed and respected."[12]

What was being proposed sounded like a social democratic experiment, potentially acceptable to the middle bourgeoisie. Members of that class would hardly object to the expropriation of the Somocistas. Reorganization of the financial sector and foreign commerce were most likely to affect the major economic groups and might actually benefit the middle bourgeoisie. Much of the private sector, including many of COSEP's best known leaders, were quite ready to adapt to the mixed economy delineated by the Junta. Moreover, the program continued reassuring guarantees of formal democratic rights—an important opening for the press, parties, and political money controlled by the bourgeoisie. COSEP and the bourgeois parties would receive a substantial block of seats in the Council of State, a national assembly sharing legislative powers with the Junta.

By the time Nicaraguans celebrated the first anniversary of the victory over Somoza, however, events had undermined much of the optimism the initial program had inspired in the bourgeoisie. The Sandinistas had moved systematically to consolidate their own political hegemony.[13] It soon became apparent that the balance of forces on the five-member Junta was less fluid than had been assumed. Robelo and Chamorro found themselves powerless and both resigned in April 1980. Several months earlier the cabinet had also been reshaped, eliminating conservatives and asserting Sandinista control. In laying the groundwork for the Council of State, the Sandinistas diluted the representation of the bourgeois parties and private sector organizations that had been agreed to in the June program by increasing the representation of the mass organizations tied to the FSLN.

It gradually became apparent that all significant lines of power were converging on the nine comandantes of the National Directorate of the FSLN. They dominated the Junta and the Council of State, controlled the military, and personally held the most important cabinet portfolios, including Defense, Interior (police), Planning, and Agriculture-Agrarian Reform.

Political control enabled the FSLN to strengthen the state's capacity to direct the economy. Two critical steps taken in the first year were the nationalization of the entire financial sector and of the commercialization of major exports. These measures assured the Sandinistas control over the disposition of investment credits and use of precious foreign exchange. By monopolizing the major sources of hard-currency income, the state limited the ability of the bourgeoisie to pressure the government and protect its own interests by moving capital abroad.

The bank takeovers, together with the nationalization of Somocista properties, shattered the major economic groups. A few large firms that had been associated with the BANAMERICA and BANIC groups remained. But the private sector had been radically restructured. The medium-sized enterprises of the middle bourgeoisie now predominated.

1980: THE BOURGEOIS POLITICAL CHALLENGE

In the wake of the FSLN's political consolidation, the first in a series of bourgeois-Sandinista political crises began to develop. By early 1980 a confluence of economic and political developments was feeding bourgeois fears about the direction of the Revolution. Freed from the restraints imposed by the Somoza regime, labor unions were becoming increasingly aggressive. One result was a series of worker seizures of urban and rural enterprises, some of which were subsequently expropriated by the government. Anxieties about the security of private property were further exacerbated by the promulgation of a "decapitalization" law at the beginning of March. Decapitalization refers to disinvestment through such devices as allowing plant and machinery to run down while profits are pocketed or paying high salaries to family members who have no active participation in the firm. The law presupposed worker participation in detecting disinvestment and economic sabotage—an implicit attack on traditional management prerogatives. In light of these developments, COSEP and other private sector voices began to demand that the government clarify its attitude toward private enterprise.

Businessmen were also unsettled by political developments, which did not appear to be leading toward the Western democratic institutions to which the middle bourgeoisie, at least, was committed. According to a diplomatic observer with extensive private sector contacts, the bourgeoisie believed "that the only way to protect themselves economically was to have political rights."

The strain developing between the Sandinista Front and the bourgeoisie was reflected in a struggle for editorial control of *La Prensa*. In April the paper was shut down by a strike that pitted publisher Xavier Chamorro, who had taken over the paper after his brother's murder, against family members holding the majority of the outstanding stock. Xavier had remained an enthusiastic supporter of the Revolution, while other family members were growing skeptical of the FSLN. When the family majority faction attempted to remove Xavier, most of the staff walked out in support of the publisher. In bourgeois circles, suspicion grew that the conflict reflected an attempt by the FSLN to seize control of the country's most important editorial voice.

The political crisis was brought to a head by Robelo's resignation from the Junta over bourgeois representation on the Council of State, on April 23—days before the Council was to be inaugurated. Robelo had not, in fact, functioned as a private sector representative on the Junta, either by actively championing bourgeois interests or by serving as an intermediary between the government and the bourgeoisie, which had come to regard him as a renegade. But coupled with the quieter departure a few days earlier of his colleague Violeta de Chamorro and the unannounced resignation of Central Bank president Arturo Cruz, Robelo's resignation in protest challenged the legitimacy of the Sandinista political system. The bourgeoisie seized the moment to press its demands on the government. COSEP entered into direct negotiations with the National Directorate, mediated by U.S. Ambassador Lawrence Pezzullo.

The settlement they reached provided government reassurances of respect for the private sector, most concretely embodied in a new *ley de amparo*, a law providing court protection in the event of arbitrary administrative action against persons or property. The National Directorate also agreed to announce dates for elections and to protect democratic rights generally. A parallel settlement at *La Prensa* returned the paper to the stockholding majority and provided Xavier and his supporters with the resources to start *El Nuevo Diario*, a new pro-Sandinista daily.[14] (*La Prensa* became the principal organ of the bourgeois opposition as it had been under Somoza.) With these concessions, COSEP representatives took their seats in the Council of State when it was inaugurated on May 4, in an atmosphere of reconciliation and harmony. Later that month Robelo and Chamorro were replaced on the Junta by men of suitably bourgeois backgrounds.

The settlement of the April crisis appeared to promise a renewal of the bourgeois-Sandinista partnership. Instead, it proved to be a momentary truce in a developing political war. The conflict broke into the open again in November. The month began with the election of a new, reactionary American president (a development the Sandinistas later argued encouraged bourgeois intransigence). In Nicaragua there were sharp exchanges between the government and Robelo's MDN, over the government's denial of permission to hold an outdoor rally in the town of Nandaime and the sacking of MDN headquarters in Managua by Sandinista militants. On the tail of these events, COSEP issued an elaborate analysis of government policies, bitterly critical of the FSLN, and withdrew its representatives from the Council of State.

The COSEP analysis censured the treatment of MDN, the FSLN's continuing vagueness about elections, and the expanding power of the state sector, but the document's most striking passages dealt with its authors' perception of the national political atmosphere being created by the FSLN and the media and mass organizations tied to it. They found "a state of political uncertainty in which the spectre of Marxist-Leninist socialism looms in the panorama of national life . . ." and concluded with the charge that "the most radical sectors of the FSLN Party, with open Marxist-Leninist tendencies," were working to implant a "Communist" system in Nicaragua.[15]

These accusations seemed to move the conflict to a new plane, but whatever attention they might have attracted was immediately undercut by news that Jorge Salazar, Vice-President of COSEP and head of UPANIC (Union of Nicaraguan Farmers), had been killed in a shoot-out with state security agents. The authorities reported that Salazar and several less-known private sector figures had been involved in a conspiracy to overthrow the government, that Salazar had been transporting arms when he was stopped, and that he had died resisting arrest. The government conceded that Salazar himself was unarmed at the time of the incident.

Salazar's death further hardened attitudes on both sides. Sandinista suspicions about the loyalty of the bourgeoisie were confirmed (although only Salazar among the top leaders of the private sector was involved). In bourgeois circles the government's claim of a conspiracy was not generally denied, but many believed that Salazar had been the victim of entrapment drawn into the plot by government agents. Whatever the case, his death reinforced the message that had been delivered publicly to the bourgeoisie a few days earlier by a member of the National Directorate. Avoid "adventures," warned Comandante Carlos Núñez. "[The FSLN] took power by arms and created the instruments to defend power. We will do everything within our reach to defend this revolution."[16]

Thus, by the end of 1980, the FSLN had demonstrated its determination to meet any political or military resistance from the bourgeoisie. By then also, the shape of a loose coalition opposed to Sandinista rule—here labeled the Bourgeois Coalition—was apparent. At the center of the coalition was the middle bourgeoisie, represented as before by COSEP. Other key members were the editors of La Prensa, most of the hierarchy of the Catholic Church, and several bourgeois political parties. These elements were united by a sense that the Sandinistas were opposed to political democracy and capitalism and, more vaguely, represented a threat to the bourgeoisie's way of life. The coalition was committed to the West and was supported, in varying ways, by several Western democracies.

The Bourgeois Coalition unquestionably constituted the most significant internal opposition to the FSLN, though its members were not the Revolution's only domestic opponents. Others included two small, non-Sandinista labor confederations, which frequently associated themselves with initiatives of the bourgeois political parties, and certain ultra-left political and labor groups.

1981: THE JULY DECREES AND THEIR AFTERMATH

On July 19, 1981, the second anniversary of the Triumph over Somoza, the government unveiled a stunning package of economic measures, including a stringent new decapitalization law, a broad agrarian reform law, a decree expropriating 13 major private firms, and a law providing for the expropriation of properties belonging to individuals absent from the country for more than six months. All of these measures reflected the FSLN's growing frustrations with the economic performance of the private sector. In announcing them, Junta leader Daniel Ortega denounced "unpatriotic investors and producers who have decapitalized factories and farms, who in 1978 under Somoza invested 1,260 million córdobas and now hardly manage to invest 589 million córdobas." Comandante Ortega went on to accuse the bourgeoisie of limiting investment in order to force its will on the country. "This is a private sector that is consciously playing with fire, that wants to destroy popular power to impose the power to rob and oppress the workers."[17]

On visits to Nicaragua in early 1981, Joseph Collins, a food and agriculture advisor to the Nicaraguan government, found intense concern with decapitalization among leaders and supporters of the Revolution. In the streets he heard the rallying cry, "Against decapitalization— confiscation!" A government economist complained that the problem was endemic. "It's not as if there are just four or five of the big guys," he told Collins. "If there were, you could round up one or two and make an example of them." The bourgeoisie was subjecting the country to "death by a million cuts."[18]

On one level, the July measures could be read as a benign restatement of the official attitude toward private enterprise: operate efficiently, maintain your investment, obey the laws concerning labor, health, and so on, and you can keep your business forever. The agrarian reform law, for example, placed no limit on the size of private holdings as long as they were farmed fully and efficiently. In announcing the new legislation, Ortega responded to bourgeois concerns by pledging the government to fight "lockouts, strikes, seizures, all of the ways which the rank and file can deplete capital."

The bourgeoisie, however, interpreted the decrees as new evidence of government hostility. They viewed the expropriation decrees as arbitrary and regarded the decapitalization and agrarian reform law as a threat to the future of private enterprise. While willing to concede that some of the firms that were nationalized had indeed been subject to decapitalization, they argued that others had not and that even the decapitalized firms were taken without regard to proper legal procedures—for example, enterprises that were expropriated after they had been occupied by their workers. When they saw the land-reform legislation, bourgeois leaders were more impressed with the prohibition of court appeals than with the liberal attitude toward large landholdings. Business leaders concurred with government assertions that private investment had fallen to anemic levels, but they blamed the situation on the investment climate created by the policies of the Sandinista government.

The bourgeois counterpoint to charges of decapitalization was the demand for clarification of the "rules of the game." Private enterprise, according to COSEP's November 1980 analysis, operated "under a permanent threat of expropriation or illegal seizure." Bourgeois spokesmen asserted that business confidence could not be restored unless the government established stable rules that clearly defined the limits of the state sector within the mixed economy and put an end to arbitrary confiscations.

In the initial years of the Revolution, bourgeois economic misbehavior and Sandinista response set up a dynamic of their own. To cite concrete examples, the industrialist who ran down his plant while paying generous dividends, the farmer who left land idle in the sight of land-hungry peasants, and the cattleman who took out a government herd-expansion loan that he quickly converted to dollars to be banked abroad—all were contributing to the country's economic problems and stimulating popular political pressures on the government for corrective action. But anti-decapitalization legislation and antibourgeois rhetoric intensified the behavior they sought to control by undermining private sector confidence in the future of the mixed economy.

In this atmosphere, what Sandinista leaders said was at least as important to the bourgeoisie as what the Sandinista government did. Thus the bourgeois reaction to the new measures was shaped by the accompanying rhetoric, which suggested a shift in the attitudes of the National Directorate. A key member, Agricultural Minister Jaime Wheelock, had gone on record in June questioning the mixed economy: "If we are going to have an economy here that robs and decapitalizes, we prefer to close that type of economy down completely."[19] At the July 19 celebration and in the months that followed, the top leaders of the Revolution placed renewed emphasis on class and class conflict.

On July 19 the class theme was present in the passage from Ortega's speech quoted above and in subsequent remarks by Tomás Borge, a powerful colleague on the National Directorate. Borge picked up Ortega's discussion of the "unpatriotic bourgeoisie." After making it clear that he regarded them as constituting a vast majority of their class, Borge asked the Sandinista crowd: "Who decapitalized the country? Who assassinated Sandino and celebrated in an orgy of champagne and blood? Who made contributions under the table to Somoza's election campaign? Who grabbed up the peasants' land and has kept the workers under the yoke of oppression?" To each question the audience responded, "The Bourgeoisie!"[20] The most explicit public reference to this theme by a member of the Directorate came a month later in a speech by Humberto Ortega, Minister of Defense. His remarks, which subsequently became controversial for explicit references to Marxism-Leninism, defined the Sandinista revolution as "profoundly classist" and the bourgeoisie as "our internal class enemies."[21]

While Ortega's characterization of the bourgeoisie as the Sandinista Revolution's internal class enemy was a perfectly accurate observation, such language was hardly reassuring to the leaders of the bourgeoisie. While some speeches by members of the National Directorate were more conciliatory than the ones quoted above, they did not alter the effect of these blunter statements.[22]

The bourgeoisie presented its response to the FSLN in a sharply worded letter to Daniel Ortega, as chairman of the Junta, from the officers of COSEP. Written October 19, the letter appeared in La Prensa the next day and was disseminated internationally. Its character is revealed in an early passage: "Upon reflecting on the conduct of domestic policy and foreign policy . . . we identify an unmistakable ideological line, Marxist-Leninist in pattern, which is confirmed in the discourses of the members of the National Directorate." The letter seldom addresses specific policies. It focuses almost entirely on the rhetoric of the Sandinista leaders and the undisclosed political agenda regarded as implicit in their language. The Sandinistas are accused of advancing "a Marxist-Leninist project behind the backs of the people," of preparing a "new genocide" (this in response to an extravagantly phrased speech by H. Ortega), and of leading the nation to "the doors of destruction."

The COSEP letter was published at a time when the Sandinista Revolution was under intense attack in the international press and by spokesmen of the Reagan Administration. It was interpreted by the FSLN leadership as part of a coordinated international effort to destroy the Revolution—in the words of an official statement, "a frank and open destabilizing effort complementing plans which international reaction and the defeated Somocistas are attempting to unleash from abroad."[23] Almost immediately, the government ordered the arrest of the authors, simultaneous with that of the leaders of CAUS (Center for Trade Union Action and Unity), an ultraleftist labor organization, which had been harassing the government with aggressive labor actions and radical criticisms of

Sandinista policies. The two groups were tried together under public security legislation on charges couched in terms of a destabilization campaign. Within ten days of the publication of the COSEP letter, sentences were handed down: 7 months for the COSEP leaders, 29 for the CAUS officials.

Under intense international pressure, the Nicaraguan authorities released the COSEP prisoners in February, halfway through their sentences. (The CAUS prisoners were left to languish in jail.) The Sandinistas had reacted sharply to the letter because of COSEP's international weight. Now, facing a severe balance-of-payments problem and increasingly explicit threats from the Reagan Administration, the government felt compelled to release the prisoners for the same reason. Upon their release, the COSEP leaders stressed their appreciation to foreign governments and business organizations that had worked on their behalf.[24] Their supporters had included President José López Portillo of Mexico, a key international backer of the Revolution, who would soon arrive in Managua to accept a medal from the Nicaraguan government. López Portillo was reportedly under considerable pressure from his own organized private sector in the COSEP matter.

1982-84: PRODUCERS WITHOUT POWER

The events that shaped bourgeois-Sandinista relations from the death of Salazar in November 1980, through the July decrees, to the COSEP jailings in October 1981 appeared to be driving toward a definitive denouement. But as the fifth anniversary of the Revolution approached in 1984, the future of the bourgeoisie in the Sandinista state was no clearer than it had been at the end of 1981. Neither side had taken decisive action in the interim, and the Revolution was unfolding in ways that deflected attention from the bourgeoisie. The conservative hierarchy of the Catholic Church replaced the bourgeoisie as the focus of domestic opposition; the country's severe foreign-exchange shortfall, aggravated by the American-orchestrated financial blockade, overshadowed concerns with decapitalization; and the U.S.-supported contra forces became the overriding preoccupation of the National Directorate.

After the release of the COSEP prisoners, Sandinista policies aimed at restoring a working relationship with the bourgeoisie in economic matters without conceding bourgeois political rights. The objective, as described by Comandante Jaime Wheelock, was a "bourgeoisie that just produces, without power, that limits itself to exploiting its means of production and that utilizes these means of production to live, not as instruments of power, of imposition."[25]

In early 1982 the Second Sandinista Assembly, a periodic congress of

Sandinista notables, called for the establishment of "guarantees" for "principled entrepreneurs" who contribute to the national economy and for the negotiation of "patriotic production agreements between the state, the private sector and the working classes."[26] If by "guarantees" the assembly meant property guarantees, little was accomplished in the two years that followed. However, a series of production agreements was negotiated between the state and the private sector, dealing with such matters as price, production levels, credit, and access to foreign exchange. In manufacturing there were accords with individual firms and some industrial sectors, but the most significant agreements were the crop-by-crop understandings that covered most of the agricultural bourgeoisie.

The agreements in agriculture varied substantially, reflecting the relative economic and organizational strength of the producers. At one extreme were the rice growers, technically sophisticated, few in number, represented by a strong national organization, and facing robust demand for an annual crop, vital to the national diet. Each of these factors contributed to the growers' bargaining power and enabled them to obtain a generous price and other economic concessions. The coffee planters presented a sharp contrast to the rice producers on virtually every count. In particular, they were saddled with a perennial crop, which reduced their capacity to withhold production in the face of low prices. Unlike rice farmers, coffee growers claimed to be losing money during most of this period.

Neither the rice growers nor the coffee producers saw any kind of long-term guarantee to the private sector in the production agreements. Like other members of the bourgeoisie, they regarded the accords as an effort by the Sandinistas to prop up the economy with short-term incentives to entrepreneurs. "They gave us lines of credit," reflected an industrialist in August 1983, "but they didn't give us security for the future."

In late 1983, government and private economists informally estimated private participation in the economy at 55 to 60 percent of the GNP. However, businessmen insisted that such figures overestimated the position of private enterprise in the mixed economy since their power to administer their own firms had been sharply reduced by government regulation. The government had, in fact, restricted managerial freedom to set prices, lower or raise wages, fire workers, buy raw materials, redeploy capital, obtain credit, or buy foreign exchange. Moreover, private participation in the economy was gradually declining because of continuing expropriations and the limited private contribution to new investment (most new investment was being made by the government).

The Sandinistas had managed to rein in the militants who had been responsible for factory and farm seizures in the initial years of the

Revolution. Nonetheless, new expropriations did not consistently conform to the rule of immunity for producers who operate efficiently and maintain their capital, which was implicit in the July 1981 legislation. Sometimes the government used eminent domain as a basis for nationalization, a legal rationale that did not require the authorities to demonstrate that a firm was violating the law. Moreover, the bourgeoisie was convinced that confiscation had become a political weapon. Officials of COSEP and its member organizations did seem to be favored government targets. The current or past presidents of COSEP (the Chamber of Industries), and UPANIC (the Agriculturalists Union) were all expropriated. In the case of UPANIC President Ramiro Gurdían, the reason was explicit. After Gurdían publicly recognized "the right" of the United States to cut off Nicaragua's sugar quota, Junta member Sergio Ramírez announced that Gurdían's banana plantation was being taken; Gurdían, explained Ramírez, could not "be a member of the revolutionary state because we need owners who are clear regarding the danger represented by this measure taken by the United States."[27] It made little difference how frequent eminent domain or political expropriations were; they appeared unpredictable to the bourgeoisie and reinforced the notion that there were no secure rules for the entrepreneur under the Sandinistas.

The capacity of the bourgeois leaders to respond publicly to Sandinista policies they disliked was severely limited after the government imposed a "state of emergency" in March 1982. The decree, issued in the wake of a series of CIA-inspired contra attacks on civilian targets in Nicaragua, suspended most constitutional guarantees, including the freedom of the press, the right of assembly, and the right to strike. The state of emergency assured firm control of labor but also brought prior censorship of La Prensa and tight restrictions of the activities of bourgeois political parties.

COMANDATES AND CAPITALISTS FACE THE FUTURE

Interviews with businessmen and private sector leaders conducted periodically from 1982 to 1984 consistently revealed deep, often passionate, bourgeois disaffection with the FSLN. Throughout that period, no significant sector of the bourgeoisie supported the Revolution. Even businessmen whose firms had positive relations with the government harbored negative attitudes toward the Sandinistas. An industrialist who was receiving attractive investment loans and cheap foreign exchange to import machinery contended that the government was wrecking the economy, had created a perilous political situation, and wanted to convert Nicaragua into another Cuba ("They think it's beautiful," he added sarcastically). Another industrialist, operating profitably in a sector he described as strongly supported by the government, said of the Sandinista leadership: "They have no capacity to govern. They want to do away with us. All their speeches contain an open or implicit threat. It's them or us." A major entrepreneur, who ran a profitable mixed enterprise and reported that that he was treated well by his Sandinista partners, said he supported COSEP, which "represents the feelings of the majority of the private sector."

A rare member of the bourgeoisie who maintained friendly relations with the FSLN (in part, because of family ties) and had worked to bridge the gap between the private sector and the government was almost apologetic about his position: Some aspects of the Revolution frightened him. The mass organizations were too powerful, they were "dangerous." Certain of the comandantes were "extremists" and had done enormous damage with their rhetoric. He admitted that he had been criticized by others of his class for his contacts with the government but he argued that the only way to influence events was to participate in them. He would, he said, rather be in the ring contending with the bull than up in the stands watching.

As some of these remarks suggest, the bourgeoisie suspected that the Sandinistas' ultimate intention was the total elimination of the private sector. A rice grower with an American agronomy degree commented: "We believe that when all the technocrats they are training in Cuba and the USSR return, they will confiscate us." Asked what the government wanted from the private sector, a major cotton planter responded, " 'Obey! Produce as long as I want you to. I'll cut your throat when I want. Be my servant. Do as I say until I'm ready to dispose of you'. . . . If they don't fall, the private sector is condemned."

Bourgeois attitudes toward the FSLN were reflected in their assessments of American foreign policy. Publicly, bourgeois representatives were noncommittal about the American-supported contras. But by 1984 they were supportive in private. Asked about U.S. policy, a top business leader responded flatly, "I love it." A leading industrialist contrasted Carter and Reagan approaches. He preferred the latter: "A demonstration of force . . . it's the only thing the Sandinistas understand." Such appraisals represent a shift from earlier attitudes. Interviews with private sector leaders conducted in January 1982, when the contra operation was only getting under way, had revealed patriotic resentment of the rhetorical threats then emanating from Washington.

In 1984 there was a division of bourgeois opinion on one key matter: the prospect of an American invasion. While some clearly favored such a move, others (including the two men quoted above) were leery of its consequences for an already war-battered nation and hopeful that the existing military and economic "pressures" could force some sort of compromise between the Sandinistas and their domestic opponents.

In the face of the bourgeoisie's clear hostility and undynamic economic performance, the FSLN continued to regard the mixed economy as part of its official line. "We want to create a country where social classes can co-exist," National Directorate member Bayardo Arce told the Miami *Herald* in 1983.

> The bourgeoisie has its future guaranteed in this country as never before. Let them have their businesses, their money, their schools, their servants, their trips to Miami. We have never wanted to get rid of the bourgeoisie. We do not want to do it now. We are not going to do it.[28]

Arce's words might be discounted because of their petulant tone and intended American audience. But in a concurrent interview published in Spanish and obviously aimed at an international leftist audience, his colleague Jaime Wheelock emphasized the importance of profit incentives; spoke of "long-term security" for producers "and their children"; and contended that as long as "revolutionary power" was in place, a "social transformation" might be based on selective expropriation of the means of production.[29]

In Wheelock's conception of the Sandinista economy, the powerlessness of the bourgeois producers is a prerequisite to social transformation. This notion was pervasive in Sandinista thinking about the future of the mixed economy. A second-tier Sandinista party official interviewed in mid-1984 said of the bourgeoisie: "As long as they produce, they can continue. We need to take advantage of the experience of the private sector. . . . [But] politically in this country they have no future. They will have to fit into the economic plans of the state." A few months earlier, a vice-minister concerned with economic policy voiced the same idea: "As long as they don't question the authority of the Revolution, they will continue. There is no political project to do away with the private sector. It depends entirely on their willingness to participate."

There were clearly some unstated problems in this position. In particular, are the owners of the means of production ever powerless? The example of the rice growers might make us wonder. Could a powerless bourgeoisie be productive, or does the investor confidence that appears to be a prerequisite to capitalist dynamism depend on bourgeois power over the state? The performance of the Nicaraguan bourgeoisie under Sandinista rule suggests the latter.

It is likely that many Sandinista leaders harbored unstated reservations about the mixed economy. Wheelock and lower-ranking Sandinistas who echoed him were stating the official line. However, their position received little overt support from the other members of the National

Directorate. Bourgeois leaders and others who dealt with the comandantes were aware of a split among them over treatment of the private sector and related issues. As generally depicted, the division was between "pragmatists" such as Wheelock and Daniel Ortega and "ideologues," including Tomás Borge and Planning Minister Henry Ruiz, who were regarded as committed to a fully socialized economy and centralized planning.

The silence of most of the comandantes regarding these issues only bolstered the bourgeoisie's conviction that the FSLN was merely tolerating the mixed economy as a temporary expedient. In a 1982 May Day speech, Borge appeared to endorse such a strategy. He presented an overview of the stages of human historical development that was clearly drawn from Marx and Lenin. Turning to Nicaraguan history, he described the current stage (la nueva etapa) of revolutionary development as one in which collaboration with the bourgeoisie had to be maintained in order to defeat "imperialism."[30] The implication, in the light of an emphasis on proletarian revolution earlier in the speech, was that a future stage would dispense with the bourgeoisie. In earlier speeches two other Sandinista leaders had made similar suggestions.[31]

In sum, by the fifth anniversary of the Revolution, the bourgeoisie and much of the FSLN had one thing in common: a sense that existing arrangements were transitory. In the words of a well-known industrialist, "Nicaragua has been converted into a roulette game. Other places they bet on horses. Here everything is on the line." What each group most wanted from the future was to be rid of the other. But for a variety of reasons neither was likely to have its wish fulfilled soon.

The bourgeoisie, having been stripped of its most potent weapons, was in no position to challenge the FSLN. It no longer controlled the financial system, and most foreign-exchange earnings were beyond its reach. Thus it could not strangle the Sandinista economy, however much its undynamic performance might cause the economy to languish. Its press was under tight control. It could not appeal to the military, since the military was unambigously Sandinista.

However, as the release of the COSEP prisoners and the negotiating strength of the rice growers suggest, the bourgeoisie was not defenseless. It had powerful allies: in particular, the hierarchy of the Catholic Church, whose influence over sectors of the population important to the FSLN was substantial; and certain governments in the West, whose attitude was critical to a regime facing external aggression and contending with grave economic problems. Unless the Soviet Union were to commit its own power to Nicaragua's defense and assume the burden of Nicaragua's enormous foreign exchange gap—it did not appear anxious to do either—the Sandinistas would have to remain sensitive to the reactions of West European and Latin American governments. At the same time the FSLN, as its leaders repeatedly acknowledged, was in no position to dispense with the services of the bourgeoisie, on whose managerial and technical talents the national economy still depended.

The war also contributed to the domestic stalemate. If there was any chance of a negotiated settlement of bourgeois-Sandinista differences, it could never be realized so long as the fighting continued. Under external attack, the Sandinistas were resistant to accommodating a class whose loyalty was suspect, while the bourgeoisie was unlikely to come to terms with the Sandinistas as long as its members sustained the hope that the revolutionary regime might be eliminated or radically restructured by force.

Thus, on the eve of the fifth anniversary of the Triumph over Somoza, a resolution of the conflict between the Sandinista Revolution and the Nicaraguan bourgeoisie was nowhere on the horizon.

NOTES

1. Inter-American Development Fund, *Social and Economic Progress in Latin America* (Washington, D.C., 1978), pp. 141 and 333.

2. This conceptualization of the private sector ignores foreign holdings that were, in fact, relatively insignificant in the Nicaraguan economy. On American holdings, see Jorge Castañeda, *Contradicciones en la Revolución* (México: Extra, 1980), p. 20–24.

3. Jaime Wheelock, *Nicaragua: Imperialismo y Dictadura* (Havana: Editorial de Ciencias Sociales, 1979), pp. 163–176; and George Black, *The Triumph of the People* (London: Zed, 1981), p. 34.

4. Harry Strachen, *Family and Other Business Groups in Economic Development* (New York: Praeger, 1976), pp. 48–50.

5. John Booth, *The End and the Beginning: The Nicaraguan Revolution* (Boulder: Westview, 1982), p. 98.

6. COSEP was originally "COSIP," but reorganized and renamed itself during the period under discussion here. To avoid confusion, I have used "COSEP" throughout.

7. Booth, *The Nicaraguan Revolution*, pp. 101–3.

8. Black, *Triumph*, pp. 58–62.

9. Ibid., p. 90.

10. Chamorro's death was later attributed to Somoza's son, Anastasio Somoza Portocarrero, and his business partner, who had been subjects of a *La Prensa* exposé.

11. Black, *Triumph*, pp. 126–132.

12. Junta de Gobierno de Reconstrucción Nacional, "Programa de la Junta de Gobierno de Reconstrucción Nacional," *Comercio Exterior* (México) 29 (1979):893–901.

13. Stephen Gorman, "Power and Consolidation in the Nicaraguan Revolution," *Journal of Latin American Studies* 13 (1981) pp. 133–149.

14. John Nichols, "The News Media in the Sandinista Revolution" in *Nicaragua in Revolution*, edited by Thomas W. Walker (New York: Praeger, 1982); Black, *Triumph*, p. 343–5.

15. COSEP, *Análisis Sobre la Ejecución del Programa de Gobierno de Reconstrucción Nacional* (Managua, 1980).

16. *Nuevo Diario*, November 13, 1980.

17. *Barricada*, July 30, 1981.

18. Joseph Collins, *What Difference Could a Revolution Make?* (San Francisco: Institute for Food and Development Policy, 1984), p. 44.

19. *Nuevo Diario*, June 13, 1981; see also Collins, *What Difference*, p. 42.

20. Tomás Borge et al., *Sandinistas Speak* (New York: Pathfinder, 1982), p. 134.

21. Humberto Ortega, *Discurso del Ministro de Defensa . . . en la Clausura de la Reunión de Especialistas* (Managua: Ejército Popular Sandinista, 1981).

22. See, for example, "FSLN Confirma Diálogo," *La Prensa*, October 17, 1981.

23. *Barricada*, October 22, 1981.

24. *La Prensa*, February 15, 1982.

25. Jaime Wheelock, *El Gran Desafío* (Managua: Editorial Neuva Nicaragua, 1983), p. 35.

26. *Barricada*, February 1, 1982.

27. New York *Times*, June 19, 1983; on political use of expropriation, see Wheelock, *El Gran Desafío*, p. 35.

28. Miami *Herald*, August 14, 1983.

29. Wheelock, *El Gran Desafío*, pp. 37–41.

30. *Nuevo Diario*, May 14, 1983.

31. Ortega, *Discurso*, p. 12; Henri Weber, *Nicaragua: The Sandinista Revolution* (London: Verso, 1981), p. 70.

Chapter 8
The Media

JOHN SPICER NICHOLS

All societies limit the range of public discussion during times of conflict,[1] and revolutionary Nicaragua has been no exception. The Sandinista government, which was under attack from domestic and foreign opponents since 1979, steadily assumed control over the public communication system in Nicaragua and limited debate on a variety of sensitive political, religious, and economic matters. Therefore, the important questions in studying the Nicaraguan media are not whether the media were controlled or should be controlled. Rather the issue is whether the conditions existed (or might eventually exist) under which a wide range of information and opinion could be exchanged among a wide range of people if and when the level of conflict in Nicaragua is eventually reduced.

BACKGROUND

Understanding the important role of the newspaper *La Prensa* in the Nicaraguan Revolution is essential to answering this question. The newspaper's long-time editor Pedro Joaquín Chamorro Cardenal was first and foremost a political activist. As the descendant of one of Nicaragua's most prominent political families, which included four Conservative presidents, Chamorro dedicated his entire life to the overthrow of the Liberal Party regime of the Somoza family. In his early years, Chamorro was arrested, jailed, or exiled on a variety of charges, including organizing violent political demonstrations, running guns, leading an invasion force to overthrow the government, and participating in the assassination of Anastasio Somoza García, the first of the Somoza family dynasty. In his later years, Chamorro reverted to less overt opposition to the Somoza

The research for this chapter was funded in part by the School of Journalism of The Pennsylvania State University (R. Dean Mills, Director) and conducted with the cooperation of Francisco Campbell and Sofia Clark of the Nicaraguan Foreign Ministry and Anthony C. E. Quainton, U.S. Ambassador to Nicaragua.

dictatorship through the family-owned newspaper *La Prensa* and conventional party politics.[2]

Chamorro's venomous editorial attacks enraged Somoza, who responded by repeatedly censoring or otherwise repressing *La Prensa*. The censorship of *La Prensa* earned this previously obscure political combatant a reputation among regional press organizations and human rights groups, which placed pressure on the regime to end the repression. When Somoza periodically succumbed to international pressure and ended the censorship, Chamorro renewed his harsh attacks, provoking a new round of censorship. Somoza was never able to escape from this downward cycle, which contributed to his demise.

Of particular importance was Chamorro's relationship with the Inter American Press Association (IAPA), a Miami-based organization of publishers of privately owned newspapers in the hemisphere. The major function of the conservative publishers' association has been to classify the countries of the hemisphere according to its narrow definition of press freedom and to censure those not practicing Western libertarianism.[3] Chamorro served as an IAPA director, member of the executive commitee, and vice-president of its powerful Freedom of the Press Committee. In the 1960s and early 1970s, a time when most North Americans thought references to Central America meant Iowa, Chamorro was winning regional media awards, was a popular speaker to U.S. media groups, and was well known among U.S. media opinion leaders. It is important to note that Chamorro's awards and popularity were not for anything he wrote (or, for that matter, anything he was prevented from publishing). His influence was based largely on the simple fact that he was the object of repression by one of the hemisphere's more repugnant dictators.

In short, the Somoza regime could not have picked a better target for assassination if it had a masochistic desire to earn the enmity of the foreign press. The January 1978 killing of Chamorro by assassins believed to be sympathetic to Somoza (if not under the direction of Somoza or his lieutenants) not only rallied the North American press against the regime and helped to bring Nicaragua to the top of the U.S. foreign policy agenda, but it also enlarged the domestic opposition. Probably more than any other single event, this assassination solidified the opposition of the moderate business community, the church, and the urban middle class, which were already disgruntled by Somoza's gross corruption, and led the group into an uneasy alliance with the dissimilar opposition forces of the FSLN. That coalition was instrumental in the overthrow of Somoza.[4]

After the assassination, *La Prensa*, under the direction of the Chamorro family, removed its mask as a news medium and engaged in overt sedition. The newspaper's offices were used to coordinate much of the urban opposition, and a sizable number of the staff, including the slain editor's youngest son, Carlos Fernando Chamorro, were Sandinista fighters or supporters. The Somoza national guard responded by destroying the newspaper plant in the final days of the insurrection.

Although the Chamorro family was united in its opposition to the Somoza regime, it was badly divided over what it supported. When *La Prensa* resumed publication in August 1979 after the fall of Somoza, the family split into two factions. Xavier Chamorro, who replaced his slain brother as editor, argued that *La Prensa* should support the new Sandinista government as long as it represented the needs of the Nicaraguan people. The other faction of the family, led by Pedro Joaquín Chamorro Barrios, Jaime Chamorro Cardenal, and Pablo Antonio Cuadra (respectively, the oldest son, another brother, and a long-time associate of the murdered editor), favored a closer alliance with business and church leaders, who were emerging as opposition to the Sandinistas. The intense family squabble was resolved when Xavier Chamorro was given 25 percent of the newspaper's assets to start a competing daily, *El Nuevo Diario*, in May 1980. While the vast majority of the technical and editorial staff joined *El Nuevo Diario*, *La Prensa* retained its facilities, a small minority of the staff, and, most important, its name. Compounding the family division, Carlos Chamorro had become editor of *Barricada*, the official voice of the FSLN and the only other daily newspaper in the country.

Purged of its progressive faction, the unified leadership of *La Prensa* resumed its traditional stance as arch-critic of the government. The newspaper attacked the increasingly Marxist orientation of the Sandinista-dominated ruling junta and editorialized in support of church and business leaders, who struggled with the Sandinistas for power. As foreign and domestic opposition to the Sandinistas escalated and Nicaragua's economic problems worsened, the government became increasingly sensitive to *La Prensa's* criticism and correspondingly promulgated stringent regulations for the nation's media. In September 1980 the Junta issued decrees 511, 512, and 513 to supplement the 1979 General Provisional Law on the Media of Communication. The decrees provided for temporary suspension of a news medium for wrongful publication of information that compromised national security or the fragile national economy. The Directorate of Communication Media, a division of the Ministry of Interior, was designated to interpret and enforce the decrees. Next, in September 1981, the Junta issued the Laws of Maintenance of Public Order and Security and Economic and Social Emergency, which provided for jail terms of up to three years for those found guilty of disseminating false economic information or other forms of "economic sabotage."[5] Finally, on March 15, 1982, after a series of skirmishes with counterrevolutionary forces and sabotage acts, the Sandinista government, citing the threat of a U.S.-backed invasion, declared a State of Emergency. Under the decree, all radio newscasts were suspended, all radio stations were required periodically to join a government network, and all radio and print media were subject to prior censorship.[6] Other rights guaranteed by the Statute on the Rights of Nicaraguans, issued by the new government in August 1979, were not affected by the State of Emergency.

La Prensa was closed by the Directorate of Communication Media for the first time on July 10, 1981. In the first five years of the Revolution, the newspaper was closed a total of seven times and failed to publish nearly two dozen times because of heavy censorship, delays caused by censorship, or in protest against government restrictions.[7] The official censorship of La Prensa was accompanied by violent demonstrations in front of the newspaper's offices, alleged harassment of some staff members, vandalism of the homes of Chamorro family members, and increasingly ugly exchanges between La Prensa and the Sandinista leadership. The few privately owned radio stations that broadcast news or opinion critical of the government suffered similar and in some cases worse fates, but foreign and domestic attention was focused on La Prensa, the only opposition print medium in Nicaragua. Except for a brief thaw in late 1983 when the government greatly reduced (but did not eliminate) censorship of La Prensa and made a special allocation of scarce foreign exchange so that La Prensa could purchase the newsprint necessary to continue publication, strict Sandinista control of the media continued at this writing. The control was closely correlated to the deterioration of relations with the domestic opposition, primarily sectors of the church and the business community, and to intensified foreign pressure by counterrevolutionaries sponsored by the United States.

CENSORSHIP OF LA PRENSA IN CONTEXT

"So long as there continues to exist a vast plan for military aggression and economic, political and ideological destabilization originating in the United States government, the Nicaraguan state has a legitimate right to establish censorship . . . " said Carlos Chamorro, editor of the Sandinista newspaper Barricada. "Personally, as a journalist, I am not in agreement with censorship," he added, "but I do agree that necessary measures must be taken to prevent the news media from being used to destabilize the country. . . . "[8]

During its entire existence, La Prensa primarily had been a political weapon intended to overthrow the existing government. In the tradition of the newspaper's slain editor, many of La Prensa staff engaged in overt revolutionary or counterrevolutionary activity. For example, two top Sandinista commanders, Bayardo Arce and William Ramírez, worked as La

Prensa reporters while attempting to overthrow the Somoza reigme. Similarly, two reporters working for the postrevolutionary *La Prensa* were tried and convicted of counterrevolutionary activity, and a few members of the Chamorro extended family were active counterrevolutionaries.[9]

"We know *La Prensa* is conspiring against us," said Commander Ramírez. "I used to be a conspiring journalist myself. What they are trying to do at *La Prensa* we have already done. We know all the tricks."[10]

Aside from overt political activities, the editorial function of *La Prensa* was decidedly different than that of U.S. media. The United States theoretically prizes political criticism in the media, but that criticism is hardly (if ever) intended to overthrow the existing system. Rather, criticism in the U.S. media is seen as a means of maintaining the existing political system in functional balance. For example, the reporting of Watergate by the U.S. media protected the political system from manipulation and thereby perpetuated the governmental status quo. While the U.S. media may express a preference for one political party over another, most people would be hard pressed to think of a daily newspaper in the United States that openly advocates a change in the country's form of government. In contrast, the traditional goal of *La Prensa* always was to overthrow the existing political order.

Just as the ends of *La Prensa* were different from those of the U.S. media, so too were the means. The U.S. media derive their power from their ability to disseminate information and opinion to mass audiences. However, *La Prensa*'s power was not rooted in its content or audience. By any reasonable journalistic standard, *La Prensa* was a newspaper of unusually low quality. Before and after the Revolution, it was consistently irresponsible, sensational, poorly written and edited, and frequently inaccurate.[11] For example, during early 1982, *La Prensa* gave extensive coverage to the so-called Sweating Virgin, a religious statue in a Managua barrio that supposedly exuded drops of water. *La Prensa*'s articles, written by codirector Pedro Joaquín Chamorro himself, implied that the "apparition" was sweating for Nicaragua.[12] Not exactly the stuff that wins Pulitzer prizes.

Further, most of the material censored from *La Prensa* was readily available from other sources. Stories banned from *La Prensa* frequently appeared in *Barricada* and *El Nuevo Diario*,[13] and most important information or opinion that did not appear in the dailies was heard from the church pulpit or foreign radio, including Voice of America and clandestine broadcasts from the contras.

Even if *La Prensa*'s content were of higher journalistic quality and unavailable elsewhere, its influence still would have been limited. In a country where the majority of the population was newly and/or marginally literate, no newspaper was particularly influential beyond the urban upper and middle classes. Even though *La Prensa* had the largest circulation, it printed only about 55,000 copies daily for a nation of nearly 3 million people. Even with a significant pass-along relationship, La Prensa reached only a small elite. The vast majority of the Nicaraguan people rarely (if ever) came in contact with a copy of La Prensa. But paradoxically, almost everybody in the country and every foreign observer with a passing knowledge of Nicaragua knew of the existence of the newspaper and its plight. In short, La Prensa's power was not derived from bringing news and opinion to mass audiences. Rather, its sizable international and domestic reputation was based almost entirely on the fact that it was censored by the government.

Therefore, it was in the best interests of La Prensa to provoke continued censorship. Without censorship, it would be judged on its dubious editorial quality by a very limited audience. Consequently, a cat-and-mouse game between La Prensa and the government emerged. The editors almost gleefully baited the government in print and, in turn, the censors, made paranoid by wartime pressures and La Prensa's seditious tradition, searched for hidden meanings in every line of copy. As a result, innocuous and sometimes silly content was censored from the paper. "La Prensa now . . . has increased its level of provocation," said Nelba Blandón, head of the Directorate of Communication Media and the chief government censor. "Its objectives are very simple: to force us to censor as much of the information as possible for their later appearance in front of the world as victims of the totalitarians."[14] The Sandinistas seemed to be caught in the same dilemma regarding La Prensa as was the Somoza regime.

ALLEGATION OF CIA DISINFORMATION

While La Prensa's active opposition to the Sandinista government was obvious and admitted, accusations that the newspaper engaged in a covert "disinformation" campaign directed by the U.S. Central Intelligence Agency were denied by Pedro Chamorro and were not clearly documented. Many top Nicaraguan officials, including several of the FSLN National Directorate, implied or directly charged that La Prensa was in cahoots with the CIA. The implication was that if the newspaper was a stooge of a hostile foreign power instead of a legitimate voice of domestic opposition, then censorship was justified.[15] But when pressed for proof, they all conceded their allegations were based on the following questionable evidence:

1. *Subliminal Propaganda.* In a series of papers and articles, Frederick S. Landis charged that La Prensa was engaged in subliminal propaganda, a psychological warfare technique in which a propagandist

can supposedly achieve a significant political effect by reaching the audience at a subconscious level.[16] According to the subliminal seduction theory, media messages laced with hidden cues by psychological warfare specialists can change attitudes and political behaviors without the audience being aware of the source of their conversion. Landis argued that *La Prensa* was using subliminal techniques similar to those used by the Chilean newspaper *El Mercurio* during the period that it was supported by the CIA in its attempt to destabilize the Allende regime. Landis concluded that this was "prima facie evidence of a psychological operation run by a hostile intelligence agency."[17]

Although the subliminal persuasion thesis was popular during the Cold War and has some resilience today in public mythology, it has been widely discredited in the academic literature. According to *Human Behavior: An Inventory of Scientific Findings*,

> There is *no scientific evidence* that subliminal stimulation can initiate subsequent action, to say nothing of commercially or politically significant action. And there is nothing to suggest that such action can be produced "against the subject's will," or more effectively than through normal, recognized messages."[18] (Emphasis added.)

2. *Association with IAPA.* Like his father, Pedro Joaquín Chamorro Barrios won awards from and held leadership positions in the InterAmerican Press Association. In addition, the association gave technical and financial assistance to help *La Prensa* resume publication after the insurrection, sent a high-level delegation of publishers to Managua to confront the Sandinista government over its pressure on *La Prensa*, and conducted a vigorous publicity campaign in support of the newspaper throughout the hemisphere.[19] While many of the most prestigious newspapers in the hemisphere, including the New York *Times*, and the Washington *Post*, are similarly associated with IAPA, the publishers' organization also briefly cooperated with the CIA, according to the New York *Times*. An investigation of media-CIA links by the *Times* listed the IAPA as one of the agency's "covert action resources" because it apparently assisted in the CIA in the anti-Allende propaganda campaign.[20] IAPA's history with the CIA was widely cited by critics of *La Prensa*, but there was no evidence of a current CIA-IAPA link.

3. *Covert Funds to Central America.* Numerous press reports indicate that a portion of U.S. covert aid was earmarked for domestic opponents of the government in Nicaragua and some was being used for "propaganda activities to destabilize the Sandinistas."[21] However, these reports have never specifically mentioned *La Prensa*.

The concept of "disinformation" was popularized by Arnaud de Borchgrave and Robert Moss in their best-selling novel *The Spike* (New

York: Crown, 1980) and carried to its ridiculous extreme by right-wing polemicists, such as James L. Tyson, author of *Target America: The Influence of Communist Propaganda on U.S. Media*. Tyson claimed that Soviet KGB agents had infiltrated or manipulated the major U.S. media and, thereby, were destroying the country from within. For proof, he simply examined published works of prominent journalists, and if their reportage was "in harmony with the Communist line," Tyson labelled them Communist agents or dupes.[22] Similarly, Tyson examined the coverage of major U.S. media on important conservative issues and concluded that the New York *Times*, the Washington *Post*, all three television networks, and even *Reader's Digest* were manipulated by Soviet disinformation. In short, any U.S. journalist whose reporting was to the left of Darth Vader was a Communist agent or sympathizer.

The disinformation thesis was built on the dubious premise that media messages, particularly those crafted by psychological warfare speciaists with a secret bag of tricks, can easily manipulate the attitudes and behaviors of the audience. In contrast, sociological and psychological research have strongly indicated that communication effects result from a complex interaction of variables (the most important of which is the motivation of the audience) and that direct, mainline effects of the media on the political process are rare.[23]

The fatal flaw in the disinformation argument is that one who can recognize disinformation, by extension, can also recognize the pure, unvarnished truth. In this author's opinion, truth is a scarce commodity and those who claim to have a corner on the truth, particularly in a politically polarized atmosphere, such as that in Nicaragua, should be regarded with suspicion.

The evidence of *La Prensa* involvement with the CIA, therefore, was highly circumstantial. In the absence of solid proof to the contrary, it should be assumed that *La Prensa* was a legitimate voice of domestic opposition. The allegations of CIA disinformation were unfortunate not only because they were unproven and supplied easy justification for censorship, but also because they diverted attention from the major source of *La Prensa*'s power, which was, according to this chapter, the simple fact that it was being censored and not *what* it published or was prevented from publishing.

RANGE OF DEBATE IN NICARAGUA COMPARED TO UNITED STATES

The various press associations, human rights groups, and other organizations that evaluate freedom of expression around the world have a tendency to compare the conditions in a given country with a nonexistent media utopia in the United States. When compared to the libertarian *theory* of the U.S., the *reality* of any media system comes up short. But when realities are matched, it becomes evident that all nations severely curtail dissent during times of national crisis. During every U.S. war, most of them fought to protect the world from dictators or totalitarians, the government tightly controlled the range of public discussion. Take for example World War I.[24] The declaration of war in April 1917 quickly led to an anti-German hysteria in the United States. Federal, state, and local governments passed numerous laws restricting dissent, and the courts, as a rule, interpreted them as broadly as possible. Thousands—perhaps tens of thousands—of U.S. citizens were prosecuted under these laws for uttering "anti-war" remarks.[25] The most notorious of those laws was the federal Espionage Act of 1917. One of the many provisions of the law made interference with military or recruiting activities a crime punishable by up to 20 years in prison, and another made it illegal to mail printed material that violated any other section of the act. By conservative estimates, at least 2,000 people were indicted under the law and at least 877 of them were convicted, almost all for what they said or wrote. In addition, more than 100 publications were banned from the mails.[26]

None of the laws was found unconstitutional, and the use of the Espionage Act to limit dissent was specifically upheld by the U.S. Supreme Court in *Schenck* vs. *United States*. Schenck had been convicted of distributing a circular that opposed the conscription law and called on the public to resist the law in an unspecified way. In that landmark decision, Justice Oliver Wendell Holmes wrote for the court:

> We admit that in many places and in ordinary times the defendants in saying all that was said in the circular would have been within their constitutional rights. But the character of every act depends upon the circumstances in which it is done. The most stringent protection of free speech would not protect a man in falsely shouting fire in a theatre and causing a panic. It does not even protect a man from an injunction against uttering words that may have all the effect of force. The question in every case is whether the words used are used in such circumstances and are of such a nature as to create a clear and present danger that they will bring about the substantive evils that Congress has a right to prevent. It is a question of proximity and degree. When a nation is at war many things that might be said in times of peace are such a hindrance to its effort that their utterance will not be endured so long as men fight and that no Court could regard them as protected by any constitutional right.[27]

Given that the United States was a relatively mature and homogeneous political system during World War I and was not particularly threatened by the fighting, the range of public discussion tolerated in Nicaragua during the first five years of the Revolution was remarkable.

Despite assertions by President Reagan, IAPA, and others[28] that the control of the Nicaraguan media was virtually totalitarian, the diversity of ownership and opinion was unusual for a Third World country, particularly one at war. In the summer of 1984, two of the three daily newspapers were privately owned. *El Nuevo Diario*, while supportive of the Revolution, criticized specific programs and operations of the government, and censors permitted *La Prensa* to publish, for example, manifestos of opposition political groups and a pastoral letter critical of the regime.[29] The official FSLN paper *Barricada* also engaged in tactical criticism of the government and established several features designed to encourage feedback from a broader range of Nicaraguans.[30] Also books, periodicals, and other publications were printed by political parties, university groups, and other nongovernment organizations. Billboards with messages from opposition political parties were commonplace around the country.

Radio was without question the most important medium of entertainment and information in Nicaragua. In 1984, the majority of the approximately fifty stations on the air were privately owned. Two of the private stations produced their own news programs, and four other independent producers supplied news programs to other private and government radio stations. None of them was subject to prior censorship.[31] The People's Radio Broadcasting Corporation, an entity of the government, owned fifteen radio stations, most of them expropriated from the Somoza family and its supporters, and owned shares of several other privately owned stations.[32]

Radio Sandino, the official station of the FSLN, and the Voice of Nicaragua, the official station of the Junta, subscribed to the Leninist principle of constructive criticism and regularly aired programs, such as "Direct Line," which were intended to facilitate a dialogue between the listeners and public officials or other guests on the program. Similarly the country's only two television channels, both operated by the FSLN, regularly aired public feedback programs, such as "Face the People." However, only about 10 percent of the TV programming was locally produced. The largest portion of the programming came from the United States and Mexico.[33]

The New Nicaraguan Agency, a national and international news service, operated under the mixed ownership and management of *El Nuevo Diario*, the People's Radio Broadcasting Corporation, and the Junta and was not subject to prior censorship.[34] In addition, the Nicaraguan news media subscribed to a wide variety of other international news services, ranging from the Associated Press of the United States to Tass of the Soviet Union.

PROGNOSIS FOR WIDER RANGE OF DEBATE

Would a wider range of public discussion emerge in Nicaragua if and when the level of conflict was reduced? According to censor Nelba Blandón, the answer was yes. "When the danger to Nicaragua from armed attacks by ex-Somoza guardsmen disappears, La Prensa would again be allowed to commit the sin of publishing lies," she said.[35] However, the issue was far more complex than a simple administrative decision. Three interrelated ideological, economic, and social factors were sure to influence to a large extent the evolution of the mass communication system in Nicaragua and the degree and nature of controls exercised over public debate:

1. *Ideology.* Much of the Sandinista rhetoric was classic Third World socialism, but the actual media policy that was emerging during the fifth year of the Revolution was uniquely Nicaraguan. Various speeches, interviews, and writings of the FSLN leadership and other media policy-makers emphasized: (a) the rights of society to receive important and useful information instead of the rights of the individual or a social class to send information, (b) the definition of news as a social good rather than an economic commodity, and (c) the use of the media for the mobilization of society toward common goals, such as national defense, literacy, or economic development.[36] "Revolutionary journalism should be the machete, the rifle, the grenade and the cannon in the firm and calloused hands of our workers and peasants, for we are at war . . . ," Commander Luis Carrión Cruz, member of the FSLN National Directorate and Deputy Interior Minister, told the Union of Nicaraguan Journalists. "We cannot waste energy in this war on anything that does not contribute to the rapid and effective material, political and ideological destruction of the people's enemies."[37]

However, to the extent that ideology is manifest in a nation's laws, the new Nicaraguan media policy was not consistent with Marxist doctrine and was a clear concession not only to Nicaragua's history and culture but also to the special role of La Prensa. In its fifth and final session, the Council of State debated the draft Mass Media Law, "which proposes regulations to guarantee freedom of expression, as well as to defend the interests of the country and its people, who could be affected by an irresponsible use of this freedom."[38] The media law was intended to replace the hodgepodge of laws and decrees affecting the media before the 1984 elections, but the Council of State was unable to reach agreement on provisions, such as registration of journalists, state ownership of television, post hoc sanctions for wrongful publication, and a variety of other media controls. Although the legislation was not finalized, the FSLN proposal was highly significant because it would have institutionalized the continuation of *nongovern-*

ment, albeit closely regulated, channels of public communication and criticism. In contrast, all media in a totalitarian Marxist system are owned and operated by the party and state and such complex regulations are unnecessary.[39]

2. *Economy*. International communication researchers consistently have found close correlations between a nation's level of economic development and the degree of controls on the media. Poor countries have a much more narrow range of public debate and criticism than rich countries.[40] Attempting to recover from a devastating revolutionary war and series of natural disasters and facing a counterrevolutionary war aimed in large part at the country's productive capacity, Nicaragua did not have the economic conditions that historically have fostered a wider range of public debate. In fact, the range of debate that existed during the first five years of the Revolution exceeded what would be expected in a country at its level of economic development.

3. *Social Differentiation*. The media are integral threads woven into the fabric of society and reciprocally affect and are affected by social conditions. The media are not autonomous actors but rather reflect the relevant power groupings in society. Consequently, complex social systems in which social power is highly differentiated tend to have media that serve a critical function. In these societies, mostly large, modern industrial states, the media initiate social action and maintain discourse among the diverse power bases that would not be able to solve their conflicts without the channels of mass communication. On the other hand, less complex systems in which social power is monolithic tend to have media that avoid conflict and attempt to build a consensus. Because the relatively few powerholders in these primarily Third World societies can easily resolve their differences through interpersonal communication, conflict-oriented mass media are not necessary for maintaining the social system.[41]

While Nicaragua in 1984 was far less complex than a modern industrial state such as the United States and political power was concentrated in the hands of the Sandinistas, the Nicaraguan power structure was far from monolithic. The Church, the private business sector, and active political opposition groups were also important power-holders. To the extent that these and other groups retained power, Nicaraguan channels of public communication were likely to carry a commensurate degree of criticism of the government. "If we have a mixed economy, we must have a political system that corresponds to that," said Carlos Chamorro, director of the FSLN's *Barricada*. "We want to institutionalize dissent and opposition."[42] In preparation for the 1984 elections, the Nicaraguan Council of State passed two laws accomplishing just that. The Political Parties Law guaranteed the right to establish political parties and to disseminate one's political ideology, and the Electoral Law guaranteed the political parties access to the media during the election campaign period.[43]

Of particular importance was the relationship between La Prensa and the Church, a major powerholder in Nicaragua. Following the purge of progressive elements from La Prensa, the newspaper markedly increased its coverage of religious matters and consistently advocated the position of the Church in the escalating confrontation between the curia and the government. In turn, Archbishop Miguel Obando y Bravo repeatedly expressed solidarity with La Prensa and, in his homilies and pastoral letters, called for an end to censorship of the newspaper. In August 1981, while La Prensa was suspended by the government, the archbishop even held a mass in La Prensa's offices to pray for the future publication of the newspaper. La Prensa had been suspended for erroneously reporting that a high government official had accused Obando y Bravo of instigating counter-revolution. This symbiosis was crucial to the continued power of both the church hierarchy and La Prensa and presented formidable opposition to the government.[44]

CONCLUSIONS

Given the prevailing ideology, the level of conflict, and the socioeconomic conditions, the limits of media criticism that existed during the first five years of the Nicaraguan Revolution seemed likely to continue for the next five years. A major impediment to a wider debate was La Prensa. For decades, the newspaper derived its power from being censored. La Prensa's rhetoric about press freedom notwithstanding, an end to censorship was not in its best interests. Although the Sandinistas might replace censorship with other forms of media control, any overall reduction of control was likely to result in a new round of provocations by La Prensa and repression by the government.

All members of the Chamorro family and the Sandinista leadership agreed that censorship had done great harm to the Nicaraguan Revolution. The only disagreement was whether the benefits outweighed the debits. Commanders Tomás Borge and Carlos Núñez, the members of the FSLN Directorate primarily responsible for media issues, took the position that censorship was a necessary evil.[45] Perhaps in time they would come to realize that their censorship of La Prensa was ultimately a greater threat to the regime than the uncensored content of the newspaper.

The perspective of Carlos Chamorro, both a prominent member of the newspaper family and an avid Sandinista, was a hopeful sign that such an evolution was possible.

The Revolution was not born with a preconceived communication policy, nor does it have for the moment something that we are able to call a model. We are in a process of learning, experimenting and searching, and we believe that our most valuable school has been this permanent confrontation with the bourgeois press inside the framework of Nicaraguan political pluralism.[46]

NOTES

1. John D. Stevens, "Freedom of Expression: New Dimensions" in Mass Media and the National Experience: Essays in Communications History, edited by Ronald T. Farrar and John D. Stevens (New York: Harper & Row, 1971), pp. 15–17. Frederick S. Siebert, Freedom of the Press in England 1476–1776 (Urbana: University of Illinois Press, 1965), pp. 9–10; Paul L. Murphy, The Constitution in Crisis Times 1918–1969 (New York: Harper & Row, 1972); John Spicer Nichols, "The Mass Media: Their Functions in Social Conflict," in Cuba: Internal and International Affairs, edited by Jorge I. Domínguez (Beverly Hills, Calif.: Sage Publications, 1982).

2. For more detailed discussion of the history and development of the Nicaraguan media, see John Spicer Nichols, "The News Media in the Revolution," in Nicaragua in Revolution, edited by Thomas W. Walker (New York: Praeger, 1982), pp. 181–199; and Nichols, "The Nicaraguan Media: Revolution and Beyond," in The Nicaraguan Reader: Documents of Revolution Under Fire, edited by Peter Rosset and John Vandermeer (New York: Grove Press, 1983), pp. 72–79.

3. Jerry W. Knudson, "The Inter American Press Association as Champion of Press Freedom: Reality or Rhetoric?" Unpublished paper presented to the meeting of the International Communication Division, Association for Education in Journalism, Fort Collins, Colorado, August 21, 1973.

4. John A. Booth, The End and the Beginning: The Nicaraguan Revolution (Boulder, Colo.: Westview Press, 1982), pp. 157–158; Walker, Nicaragua in Revolution, passim.

5. Jonathan Evan Maslow, "Letter from Nicaragua: The Junta and the Press—A Family Affair," Columbia Journalism Review, March/April 1981, pp. 46–52 (also see "Footnote to Nicaragua," Columbia Journalism Review, November 1981, p. 82); Instituto Histórico Centroamericano, "The State of Emergency: Background, Causes and Implementation," in Rosset and Vandermeer, The Nicaraguan Reader, pp. 65–71; Lars Schoultz, "Human Rights in Nicaragua," LASA (Latin American Studies Association) Newsletter 13 (Fall 1982), pp. 9–13.

6. "Government Establishes Control of Media," Managua Domestic Service, translated and transcribed in Foreign Broadcast Information Service (hereafter FBIS), March 17, 1982, p. 9.

7. M. L. Stein, "A Lone Free Voice in Nicaragua," Editor & Publisher, May 19, 1984, p. 16.

8. "Chamorro Brothers Discuss Freedom of Press," O Estado de São Paulo (Brazil), translated and transcribed in FBIS, April 17, 1983, p. 74.

9. Nichols, "News Media in the Revolution," p. 188; "La Prensa Journalist Sentenced to 3 Years," Radio Sandino, translated and transcribed in FBIS, June 19, 1981, p. 13; Stephen Kinzer, "Nicaraguan Rebels Ask Peace Talks," New York Times, December 2, 1983, p. A3; Karl E. Meyer, "The Editorial Notebook: Sticks, Stones and Somocistas," New York Times, June 28, 1983, p. A26.

10. Lawrence Wright, "War of Words: Nicaragua's Newspaper Family Tears Itself Apart Over Its Revolutionary Legacy," Mother Jones, June 1983, p. 40.

11. Hodding Carter, "Nicaragua: Campaign '84," *Inside Story*, Public Broadcasting Service, April 13, 1984; Charles Burke, "Ideological Bias in Nicaraguan Newspapers." Paper presented to the Association for Education in Journalism, Corvallis, Oregon, August 1983; Nigel Cross, "Revolution and the Press in Nicaragua," *Index on Censorship* 2 (1982), pp. 38–40; David Kunzle, "Nicaragua's *Prensa*—Capitalist Thorn in Socialist Flesh," typewritten manuscript.

12. Katherine Ellison, "The Censor and the Censored: Nicaragua's High-Stakes Cat-and-Mouse Game," *The Quill* (Society of Professional Journalists), November 1982, p. 29.

13. "Chamorro on Censorship, Economy, Military," Radio Cadena YSKL (San Salvador), translated and transcribed in *FBIS*, December 1, 1983, p. 18.

14. Hodding Carter, "Nicaragua: House Divided," *Inside Story*, Public Broadcasting Service, October 13, 1983.

15. "Interior Minister Borge Attacks La Prensa," Radio Sandino, translated and transcribed in *FBIS*, February 4, 1982, pp. 5–15; Carter, "House Divided."

16. For example, see Frederick S. Landis, "Virgins and Demons: CIA Media Operations in Nicaragua." Paper presented to Latin American Studies Association, Washington, D.C., March 1982.

17. Fred Landis, "CIA Mass Media Operations," *Granma* (Havana), November 28, 1982, p. 9.

18. Bernard Berelson and Gary A. Steiner, *Human Behavior: An Inventory of Scientific Findings* (New York: Harcourt, Brace & World, 1964), p. 95.

19. "La Prensa Reappears: Aid Rushed to Stricken Plant," *IAPA Updates*, No. 19 (September 17, 1979), p. 1; "Ramírez Discusses Press Freedom with IAPA," Radio Sandino, translated and transcribed in *FBIS*, November 17, 1981, pp. 10–14; Wilber G. Landrey, "Newspaper's Fight for Survival," *IAPA News*, December 1981, pp. 9–10.

20. John M. Crewdson and Joseph B. Treaster, "Worldwide Propaganda Network Built and Controlled by the C.I.A.," New York *Times*, December 26, 1977, p. 37.

21. "America's Secret Warrior," *Newsweek*, October 10, 1983, p. 39; "C.I.A.'s Nicaragua Role: A Proposal or a Reality," New York *Times*, March 17, 1982, p. A10; United Press International, "$5.1 Million Is Sought for Sandinista Foes," New York *Times*, June 24, 1982, p. A5, Raymond Bonner, "President Approved Policy of Preventing 'Cuba-Model States,'" New York *Times*, April 7, 1983, pp. 1 & 16.

22. James L. Tyson, *Target America: The Influence of Communist Propaganda on U.S. Media* (Chicago: Regnery Gateway, 1981), p. 229.

23. See Maxwell E. McCombs, "Mass Communication in Political Campaigns: Information, Gratifications and Persuasion," in *Current Perspectives in Mass Communication Research*, edited by F. Gerald Kline and Phillip J. Tichenor (Beverly Hills, Calif.: Sage Publications, 1972), p. 170; Sidney Kraus and Dennis Davis, *The Effects of Mass Communication on Political Behavior* (University Park: The Pennsylvania State University Press, 1976).

24. The following discussion of U.S. media during World War I is a synthesis of John D. Stevens, *Shaping the First Amendment: The Development of Free Expression* (Beverly Hills, Calif.: Sage Publications, 1982), pp. 44–54.

25. Ibid., p. 48.

26. Ibid., p. 47.

27. Ibid., p. 51–52.

28. "Prepared Text of Reagan Speech on Central American Policy," New York *Times*, May 10, 1984, p. A16; *Central America: Defending Our Vital Interests* (Address by President Reagan before a joint session of Congress, April 27, 1983), Current Policy No. 482, (Washington: U.S. Department of State, Bureau of Public Affairs, April 1, 1983); "Sandinista Law Ends Freedom of the Press," *IAPA News*, July 1982, pp. 12 & 13.

29. Interview with Xavier Chamorro, director of *El Nuevo Diario*, Managua, October 4, 1982; Hedrick Smith, "Nicaragua Elections Likely in '85 Despite New Snag, Diplomats

Say," New York *Times*, February 6, 1984, pp. A1 & 8; Richard J. Meislin, "Nicaraguan Assails Bishops in Renewed Conflict," New York *Times*, April 26, 1984, p. A10.

30. Interview with Carlos Fernando Chamorro Barrios, director of *Barricada*, Managua, October 4, 1983; Carlos F. Chamorro, "Experiences of the Revolutionary Communication in Nicaragua." Speech to the International Forum of Social Communication on the XX Anniversary of *El Día*, Mexico City, June 25, 1982 (mimeograph in Spanish).

31. Interview with Lieutenant Nelba Blandón, director of Directorate of Communication Media, Ministry of Interior, Managua, October 6, 1983.

32. Interview with Leonel Espinoza, head of communication media, Department of Political Education and Propaganda, Managua, October 5, 1983; Carlos Chamorro, "Experiences of Revolutionary Communication"; "Junta Creates Radio Broadcasting Corporation," Radio Sandino, translated and transcribed in *FBIS*, May 14, 1981, p. 14; "Advances in National Broadcasting Reported," Radio Sandino, translated and transcribed in *FBIS*, July 22, 1982, p. 13.

33. U.S. Information Agency, "Country Data: Nicaragua," January 1, 1983 (mimeograph).

34. Interview with Carlos García Castillo, general director of the New Nicaraguan Agency, Managua, October 5, 1982; and interview with Blandón.

35. Clarence W. Moore, "Censors Mightier Than Pen?" *The Times of the Americas*, September 14, 1983, p. 8.

36. "Commander Borge Speaks at *El Nuevo Diario*," Managua Domestic Service, translated and transcribed in *FBIS*, May 24, 1982, pp. 16–18; "Ramírez Discusses Press Freedom," Radio Sandino in *FBIS*; Carlos Núñez Téllez, untitled speech given on the IV anniversay of *Barricada*, Managua, August 29, 1983 (mimeograph).

37. "Luis Carrión Views on Revolutionary Journalism," Radio Sandino, translated and transcribed in *FBIS*, May 17, 1983, p. 17.

38. "The Mass Media Law," *Weekly Bulletin*, New Nicaraguan Agency, May 19, 1984, pp. 4–5.

39. "Parliament Suspends Media Law Debate," *Weekly Bulletin*, New Nicaraguan Agency, June 16, 1984, pp. 1–2; interview with Manuel Eugarrios, delegate of the Union of Nicaraguan Journalists to the Council of State, Managua, October 5, 1983; interviews with Espinoza and Carlos Chamorro.

40. Stevens in Farrar and Stevens, *Mass Media*; John C. Merrill and Ralph L. Lowenstein, *Media, Messages, and Men: New Perspectives in Communication* (New York: David McKay Co., 1971); Francisco J. Vásquez, "Media Economics in the Third World," in *Comparative Mass Media Systems*, edited by L. John Martin and Anju Grover Chaudhary (New York: Longman, 1983), pp. 265–280.

41. Phillip J. Tichenor, George A. Donohue, and Clarice N. Olien, *Community Conflict and Press* (Beverly Hills, Calif.: Sage Publications, 1980); Nichols, "Mass Media in Social Conflict," in Domínguez, *Cuba*; Vásquez, "Media Economics," in Martin and Chaudhary, *Comparative Mass Media Systems*; Stevens, "Freedom of Expression," in Stevens and Farrar, *Mass Media*.

42. Smith, "Nicaragua Elections," p. 8.

43. "Law of Political Parties: Decree No. 1312," *La Gaceta* (Official Daily of Nicaraguan Government), September 13, 1983, p. 2 (in Spanish); "Nicaragua," *Mesoamerica*, April 1984, pp. 6–7; "Electoral Law Takes Effect," *Weekly Bulletin*, New Nicaragua Agency, March 31, 1984, pp. 4–6.

44. "Archbishop Expresses Solidarity with La Prensa," Radio Corporación translated and transcribed in *FBIS*, August 24, 1981, p. 13; Raymond Bonner, "Humiliation of Priest Fires Nicaragua," New York *Times*, August 21, 1982, p. 2; Meislin, "Nicaraguan Assails Bishops."

45. "Núñez Stresses Importance of Press Censorship," Central American News Agency translated and transcribed in *FBIS*, July 14, 1982, p. 12; "Chamorro Brothers Discuss Freedom of Press"; "Commander Borge Speaks"; Carter, "House Divided."

46. Carlos Chamorro, "Experiences of Revolutionary Communication," p. 16.

Chapter 9
Ethnic Minorities

PHILIPPE BOURGOIS

By the end of the fifth year, tensions with ethnic minorities had become an Achilles heel of the Nicaraguan Revolution: militarily, the Atlantic Coast region where the minorities lived had exploded into an arena of bitter fighting; politically, accusations of human rights violations against the indigenous population had damaged the Revolution's international image; and morally, the inability to incorporate minorities—the most marginal sector of Nicaraguan society—into a full participation in the revolutionary process had contradicted Sandinista political principles. Although the Nicaraguan government committed errors in its policies toward the Coastal—*Costeño*—population, the crisis can best be understood from a historical perspective, as the outcome of several hundred years of tension between ethnic minorities and the Mestizo national majority. In the final analysis, the responsibility for the conversion of these historic tensions into a fratricidal war lies with the United States, which armed, trained, and provided international legitimation for the counterrevolutionary—contra—forces, thereby preventing a peaceful solution based on dialogue and compromise from emerging.

This chapter could not have been written without the assistance of the Center for Investigation and Documentation of the Atlantic Coast (CIDCA), especially that of its director, Galio Gurdián, who made the documentation at CIDCA available to me and included me in several theoretical discussions on the Coast organized by the Center. Edmundo Gordon, the CIDCA director in Bluefields, prepared the outline for this chapter and much of the analysis is his. Marc Edelman, Judy Butler, and Charles Hale provided comments on earlier drafts; theoretical discussions on ethnicity with Eric Wolf were helpful as well. Finally I would also like to thank Commander Lumberto Campbell and the Regional Government for Special Zone II for having facilitated my brief period of fieldwork in South Zelaya in 1983. I take full responsibility, however, for any errors in interpretation and analysis presented in this chapter.

CHRONOLOGY OF EVENTS FOLLOWING THE OVERTHROW OF SOMOZA

Ethnic minorities at the time of the revolutionary Triumph represented less than 5 percent of the national population and were all located in the Atlantic Coast Province of Zelaya, the poorest, most isolated region in the nation.[1] The Miskitu Amerindians, numbering 67,000, were the largest minority group and lived, along with some 5,000 Sumu Amerindians, in the northeast—the Moskitia—near the Honduran border. Together they comprised 25 percent of their province's total population. The Creoles were the second largest minority group, an English-speaking, Afro-Caribbean population of just under 26,000, concentrated mostly in the southern coastal port of Bluefields. Also in South Zelaya were 1,500 Garifuna, a people of Afro-Amerindian descent, and some 600 Rama Amerindians. Finally, Mestizos, the product of European, Amerindian, and some African admixture were the dominant ethnic group, both at the regional and national levels, constituting over 180,000, or 65 percent, of the Atlantic Coast population.

From the outset, the Revolution encountered problems in the Coast. Prior to the Triumph there had been almost no fighting or clandestine organizing in Zelaya. Consequently, especially in the Miskitu-dominated North, there was no indigenous revolutionary leadership forged in struggle. The first major Sandinista/Amerindian tension arose when the Miskitu demanded the recognition of an ethnic-based mass organization. Although the Sandinistas initially thought the fundamental interests of minorities could be represented in the class-based mass organizations that operated at the national level, out of revolutionary principle, they acceded.

MISURASATA[2], the new indigenous mass organization, was given political legitimacy, logistical support, and a seat on the National Council of State by the new government.

MISURASATA seized the democratic opening provided by the Revolution in order to mobilize militantly throughout the Moskitia on a platform of indigenous rights devoid of class content. Although the organization lobbied for concrete economic gains, its central thrust was to stress the dignity—and, indeed, it turned out later, the superiority—of the Amerindian identity. Furthermore, the Amerindian nationalist tone of the organization struck a responsive chord in most of the over 300 impoverished Miskitu agricultural communities. A full-fledged indigenous revitalization movement caught hold and MISURASATA emerged as a powerful force in Northern Zelaya to the point of challenging Sandinista political influence.[3]

Relations between MISURASATA and the FSLN were confrontational from the outset. MISURASATA leaders lacked a class consciousness and FSLN cadre, most of whom were from the Pacific provinces, were ill-prepared to deal with the historical patterns of interethnic domination and tension that they encountered in the Atlantic. In practice, however, in response to minority demands during the first year and a half, the Nicaraguan government passed more legislation favorable to the indigenous population than had any previous government in the history of Central America. Most notably, a bilingual education law was passed in the Council of State and a literacy campaign was launched in Miskitu, Sumu, and English. The government also commissioned MISURASATA to prepare a study on indigenous land rights, stating its willingness to grant communal land titles to the indigenous communities.

In South Zelaya, on the other hand, the ethnic organization purporting to represent the Afro-Caribbean population, known as the Southern Indigenous Creole Community (SICC), was not recognized by the FSLN as a mass organization since it was openly against the government from its inception, and it never emerged as a powerful movement. Tensions, however, exploded in the South in late September and early October of 1980 with street demonstrations and the paralyzation of economic activity in Bluefields. The crowd, which was multiethnic but largely Creole, was protesting the presence of "communist" Cuban primary school teachers and doctors in the town. Through a process of dialogue, compromise, and flexibility the FSLN sensitized itself to local concerns, and tensions in Bluefields were slowly dissipated. Nonetheless, although few Creoles subsequently took up arms and joined the contras, they tended to remain apathetic toward the revolutionary process.

In the Miskitu-dominated territory in the Northeast, however, the process of confrontation, negotiation, and compromise did not defuse Sandinista/Amerindian tensions. February 1981, when the leadership of MISURASATA was detained (33 individuals) and accused of fomenting "separatism," marked the turning point.[4] All those arrested were released within two weeks, with the exception of the main leader, Steadman Fagoth. The Ministry of Interior made public documents found in the Somoza government's abandoned files demonstrating that Fagoth had been an informer in Somoza's Secret Service.[5]

During the arrests in the community of Prinzapolka, eight people, including four Sandinista soldiers, were killed when a MISURASATA leader was being detained for questioning. News of the arrests and the deaths, enhanced by grossly inaccurate rumors of mass assassinations, swept the isolated communities of the Coco River, and up to 3,000 young Miskitu men crossed the river into Honduras, declaring themselves to be refugees. Blood had been spilled and the Miskitu movement assumed a millenarian mystique; rumors abounded that the young Miskitu men were arming to return, and that the United States was going to recognize "secret" nineteenth-century treaties between the Miskitu king and the British Crown guaranteeing nationhood for the Moskitia.

The Costeños had not suffered repression from Somoza's National Guard, and consequently, to the surprise of the Sandinistas, the Miskitu were indifferent to the evidence of Fagoth's Somozist attachments. The Nicaraguan government was unprepared for the militance of the continued support for Fagoth, who had by this time become, in the eyes of many Miskitu, a revered leader ordained to bring them redemption. In response to Miskitu popular pressure, the government, evidently hoping that dialogue and compromise were still possible, granted Fagoth conditional release one month later. Fagoth, however, promptly crossed into Honduras to join with former National Guardsmen and Somoza supporters and began emitting tirades in Miskitu against the "sandino-communists" on the Somozist clandestine radio station "September 15."[6]

By August 1982, most of MISURASATA's leaders had joined Fagoth in Honduras, including Brooklyn Rivera, who had been second in command. MISURASATA was renamed MISURA and integrated into the National Democratic Force (FDN) with economic, military, and logistical aid, as well as political legitimation and international media support, from the Central Intelligence Agency. Rivera later broke with Fagoth in 1982 to form a rival contra organization affiliated with the Revolutionary Democratic Alliance (ARDE) based in Costa Rica. In a January 11, 1984, interview, Rivera accused Fagoth of having allied himself with " the dirtiest, most assassinating right wing elements of the Honduran army . . . [choosing] the dirtiest Somozists expelled from the FDN for thievery and murder, as his protective godfathers."[7]

MISURA's first major military offensive, "Red Christmas," began in November 1981 with attacks on the Miskitu border communities along the Coco River.[8] Within less than two months 60 civilians and Sandinista military were killed. Faced with this military crisis in January 1982 the Nicaraguan government ordered the evacuation of the civilian population from the war zone to an uninhabited region approximately 50 miles inland, christened Tasba Pri. At this point the Sandinistas were responding essentially to military exigencies: to defend the civilian population supportive of the Revolution from contra reprisals; to prevent the Somozist-MISURA alliance from establishing a civilian base of support along the Coco River; and to prevent civilians from being caught in government-contra crossfire.

Less than half of the Coco River population, some 8,500 Miskitu and Sumu, were relocated to Tasba Pri; another 10,000 chose instead to cross into Honduras where they became refugees. The emergency evacuation under war conditions of such a large number of people on short notice was a profoundly traumatic experience for all involved. Human rights organizations, however, while critical of aspects of Sandinista policy toward the Miskitu, stated that there was no evidence of systematic abuse on the part of the FSLN.[9]

Beginning in July 1982, simultaneous with the joint U.S. and Honduran military maneuvers underway in the Atlantic region only a few miles from the Nicaraguan border, there was a sharp intensification of Miskitu contra activity. Large numbers of government troops, most of whom were Mestizos from the Pacific, were sent to defend the zone. According to a report by the Center for Investigation and Documentation of the Atlantic Coast (CIDCA), an autonomous research institution in Nicaragua affiliated with the National Council on Higher Education (CNES), there was insufficient control over the military commanders in Zelaya from July through September 1982 and there were cases of "reprehensible" behavior by government troops ranging from "cultural disrespect—a function of historic racism" to actual "physical abuse" and "bodily harm."[10] CIDCA noted that this resulted in cases of civilian loss of life.[11]

The FSLN publicly condemned these excesses and over 44 soldiers, including officers, were prosecuted and given prison sentences.[12] By 1984, 70 percent of local security forces were Costeños, and Pacific Coast recruits received seminars before being assigned to Zelaya.[13] In an attempt to restore lost trust, the Sandinistas granted a general amnesty to virtually all the Miskitu arrested for counterrevolutionary activity, releasing 307.[14] Indeed in the introduction to an April 1984 report on Nicaragua, the Americas Watch, a U.S.-based human rights organization, noted:

> The most important improvement has taken place in relations with the Miskito Indians.
> We have previously said that human rights violations in Nicaragua most severely vicitimized the Miskito population. Accordingly, the Americas Watch is very pleased by the positive developments affecting them.[15]

Just as the human rights record of the Sandinistas improved from late 1982 through 1984, that of the Miskitu contra deteriorated. All "collaborators" of the "sandino-communist dictatorship" were considered fair military targets by the anti-Sandinista guerrillas. The result was the assassination of school teachers, literacy trainers, and even peasants trained as volunteer health workers in the government's new "barefoot doctor" program. It was against their fellow Amerindians, however, that the Miskitu contra were cruelest. For example, Myrna Cunningham, a Miskitu doctor (the only one who existed) and Regina Lewis, a Miskitu nurse, were kidnapped during Red Christmas in 1981 and gang raped by a squad of Fagoth's men who were singing religious hymns.[16]

Rivera, who described himself as having been "very intimate" with Fagoth—"closer than a brother"—claims that by 1982 Fagoth had become "psychopathic," with a "persecution trauma" and was "totally blinded and sick with power and personal ambition." He states that Fagoth tortured and killed young Miskitu men in the refugee camps when they refused to join MISURA.[17] Indeed, by 1983, press reports began surfacing that MISURA was using force to conscript Miskitu refugees.[18] Similarly, officials at the United Nations High Commission for Refugees in Honduras made private declarations that MISURA was the greatest security problem faced by refugees in Honduras.

Although somewhat more careful with their public image, Rivera's troops—like Fagoth's—also engaged in human rights abuses against the civilian population in 1983–84. The most dramatic of these documented cases was the kidnapping of Thomas Hunter, a Creole who headed an artesanal fishing cooperative in the coastal community of Tasbapaunie in southern Zelaya. Rivera's troops took Hunter to their camp in nearby Punta Fusil and after protracted torture finally killed him, but not before cutting off his ears and forcing him to eat them.[19]

From 1982 through 1984 the heartland of Miskitu territory had become a war zone. The goal of the contras was to declare a provisional government in the Moskitia and, presumably, subsequently to "invite" a U.S. "peace-keeping force." Even though local FSLN cadre were showing greater sensibility to the complicated issues of racism and indigenous rights, there were no short-term perspectives for definitive reconcilation. As long as the United States continued funding and training the contras the situation would remain fundamentally a military problem. Indeed the continuous deepening of the war had reduced the area within which civilians could live safely in North and Central Zelaya, resulting in further small-scale population relocations out of the war zones inside Nicaragua and an increase in the number of Amerindian refugees in Honduras. The exigencies of defense and the violent instability caused by guerrilla warfare hindered the emergence of a working relationship between the Amerindians and the Sandinistas based on dialogue, peaceful confrontation, and compromise. The question remains, however, why it was so easy for the CIA to find thousands of young Miskitu men willing to engage in violent armed struggle? To grapple with this question, the profound historical roots of the conflict must first be examined.

HISTORIC ROOTS OF THE CONFLICT

There are historical reasons why militarist Amerindian nationalism would strike a responsive chord among so many Miskitu. By trading with the European buccaneers preying on Spanish shipping in the Caribbean during the sixteenth and seventeenth centuries, the Miskitu became the first Amerindian people on the Central American littoral to obtain firearms. With their superior fire power, they not only resisted Spanish conquest but also "conquered" almost 700 miles of the Atlantic seaboard from Trujillo, Honduras, through Chiriqui Lagoon in Panama.[20]

The Miskitu military expansion became so crucial to the British strategy for wresting control of the Caribbean mainland from the Spanish that the Governor of Jamaica formalized the British/Miskitu "alliance" in 1687 by crowning one of the many Miskitu leaders "King of the Mosquitia." Indeed the British systematically promoted the concepts of Miskitu militarism and national sovereignty in order to legitimize their own colonial expansion into the region: "We . . . mounted . . . [the fort] with cannon, hoisted the Royal flag and kept garrison to show that this independent country of the Mosquito Shore was under the direct sovereignty and protection of Great Britain."[21]

Ironically the Miskitu had long been at the center of international power struggles. In the 1700s it was Spain versus Great Britain; in 1984 it was the United States versus Nicaragua. The manipulation of the Miskitu contras by the United States, therefore, was analogous to the Miskitu/ Great Britain relationship noted by a historian in 1774:

> [the Miskitu] . . . have always been, and still are, in the place of a standing army; which without receiving any pay, or being in any shape burthensome to Great Britain, maintains the English in firm and secure possession, protects their trade, and forms an impenetrable barrier against the Spanish, whom they keep in constant awe.[22]

Modern-day Miskitu mystified the former existence of an Amerindian king into a symbol of nationalist aspirations. For example, in the 1970s under Somoza there were repeated rumors that the Miskitu king had returned and was circulating throughout the lower Coco River preparing his people for secession. Similarly, when MISURASATA was in its early formative stage in 1980, elderly Miskitu sometimes talked of "working for the return of the king."[23] On a more neutral level, the Miskitu could still point out descendants of the "royal family"; they used to argue over the true location of the cache holding the defunct Monarch's scepter and crown jewels. In this context, debates over whether or not the Miskitu were a national minority became academic. The Miskitu did not fulfill the objective requisites necessary to constitute a sovereign nation-state. At the same time, however, Amerindian nationalist ideology was a part of their ethnic identity and the contras, especially Fagoth, succeeded in distorting these nationalist aspirations in order to provoke confrontation with the new Nicaraguan government.[24]

The tensions between ethnic minorities and the Nicaraguan Revolution were not limited to being merely a "Miskitu problem" and a "black problem," or even strictly an ethnic problem. Even the Mestizos from the Coast were less enthusiastic about the Revolution than those living in the Pacific provinces. Nicaragua, like almost all Central American nations, faced an Atlantic Coast region that had been integrated historically into a different social formation from that of the national mainstream. The entire Atlantic seaboard of Central America was penetrated by U.S. multinational corporations beginning in the late 1800s. Because of the physical isolation of these zones, the foreign companies established an unparalleled level of control. The classic example, of course are the banana companies that established mini nation-states on the Atlantic Coast of every single nation in Central America (except for El Salvador, which has only a Pacific Coast).[25]

In Nicaragua the most important North American companies extracted minerals, lumber, and bananas strictly for export to the United States. The coastal economy had no linkage with that of the rest of the country. There was more regular transport and commerce from Bluefields to the United States than to the interior of the country. Indeed, it was easier to get to the Moskitia from New Orleans than from Managua.

This economic domination was reflected culturally and politically in the consciousness of the local population and even affected the actual ethnic composition of the region. For example, most of the Afro-Caribbean people in Central America arrived as migrants at the turn of the century, seeking wagework in the burgeoning North American companies. The extensive U.S. investments also repeatedly attracted U.S. Marines to protect them, and from 1912 through 1933 North American troops occupied the country with but a brief respite in 1925–26. The Marines spent a disproportional amount of their time on the Coast.[26]

Out of this protracted period of economic and military domination by the United States there developed a profoundly anti-Communist, pro-North American political ideology among the Creole, Miskitu, and, to a lesser extent, the Mestizo Costeños. This was exacerbated by the conservative and the likewise fervently anti-Communist and pro-North American tenor of the Moravian Church, the strongest ideological influence on the Miskitu and Creole peoples. The rigidity of the ideological template of the local population—especially the older generation—resulted, for example, in complaints by elderly folk in Bluefields over the "spread of communism" when they mistook a group of visiting North American tourists for Soviet military advisers.

The FSLN was largely unaware of this stark contrast in political identity between the Pacific and Atlantic populations. In the first years the FSLN, for example, mechanically introduced to the Coast the same political symbolism (slogans, songs, heroes, chants, and so on) that had been effective in the Pacific. In contrast, the Voice of America and the contra radio stations were skillfully responsive to local ideological prejudices. This was exacerbated by the war emergency, which focused revolutionary slogans more on nationalistic, patriotic themes such as defense of the homeland, rendering them less flexible or adaptable to local ways of thinking.

Another legacy of the North American enclave on the Atlantic Coast was a history of internal colonialism. The previous regimes had not bothered to administer or develop the region. There had been a minimal local presence of petty bureaucrats who contented themselves with minor taxes and kickbacks from the foreign corporations that were busily extracting the region's natural resources. North American corporations and aid agencies had provided the few social services available, further confirming to the local populace the "superiority" of North America. Five years after the Revolution, many Costeños insisted that the Atlantic Coast still contributed more to the national economy than it received in government services and investments, despite the fact that the reverse was actually the case. Furthermore, with the massive expansion in government welfare services following the Revolution, the local population was sensitive to overrepresentation of Pacific Coast functionaries in these new coveted jobs.

The ethnic compostion of the FSLN prior to the revolutionary Triumph reflected the marginality of the Atlantic Coast to national politics. There were no FSLN members of Sumu, Rama, or Garifuna descent, just a handful of Miskitu descent, only a slightly larger number of Creole revolutionaries, and not many Mestizo Costeño cadre. The Sandinistas, therefore, lacked representatives who spoke the same language as the ethnic minorities or who were familiar with the problems of the region. Once again South Zelaya had an advantage over the North since the commander and "Delegate Minister"—roughly equivalent to governor— of the zone was an English-speaking Creole, and the majority of the FSLN's limited number of Costeño cadre were from the Bluefields area. Significantly, in June 1984 a Miskitu woman was appointed "governor" for North Zelaya. Consequently, by the fifth year of the Revolution, the two highest political administrative posts in the regions of ethnic minority concentration were held by minorities themselves.

Another legacy confronting the FSLN was the historically entrenched pattern of ethnic and class domination. Nicaragua's ethnic minorities, unlike the majority of workers and peasants in the rest of the country, suffered a dual form of domination: class exploitation *and* ethnic oppression. The Miskitu, Sumu, and Rama were at the bottom of this local class-ethnic hierarchy, performing the least desirable, most poorly paid jobs.[27] In the gold mines in Bonanza, for example, the Miskitu and Sumu were usually relegated to the most dangerous, strenuous tasks in the pits, where they suffered from the highest rates of silicosis, a permanently debilitating lung disease.[28]

Above the Amerindians but below the Creoles came the Mestizo population, many of whom were landless laborers recently migrated from the Pacific provinces. Like the Miskitu, they engaged in poorly remunerated agricultural wage labor and had a high level of illiteracy and alcoholism.

The Creoles dominated the skilled jobs. Because of their superior education they tended to obtain white-collar employment in disproportionate numbers. Since the decline in activity of the foreign corporations in the region over the previous half century, many Creoles had withdrawn from the local labor market, relying instead on income earned as seamen on foreign vessels or on cash remittances from family members in the United States. Above the Creoles there was a stratum of upper-class Pacific-born Mestizos (usually of lighter complexion than the poorer Mestizos) who held administrative and political appointee positions. Finally, until the Triumph this ethnic-class hierarchy was capped by a minuscule layer of North American and European whites who owned or ran the few companies still operating in the Coast, such as the gold mines or the lumber export firms.[29]

This class hierarchy was accompanied by acute racial prejudice. Mestizos and Creoles presented the "inferiority" of the Miskitu and other Amerindians as a matter of common sense. In turn, the working class and peasant Mestizos looked down upon the Creoles for their dark complexion but the Creoles—whether dark or light complexioned[30]—insisted upon their superiority over the Pañias (Spaniards).

It would be ahistorical to expect it to have been possible to eradicate quickly these patterns of interethnic domination, so solidly rooted in local class inequalities. Indeed these patterns of ethnic-class hierarchy existed with local variations throughout all the nations of the Central American Atlantic littoral. Racism was an integral part of the social formations spawned by the multinational enclaves.[31]

By the end of the fifth year of the Revolution, theoreticians within the revolutionary process were beginning to publish analyses of the dual nature of ethnic/class domination in Zelaya. For example, a CIDCA document noted that there was an inherent tendency for class-conscious movements composed of the dominant ethnic group of a country to subordinate the struggle against ethnic oppression to that of economic exploitation. The document concludes that in the case of Nicaragua, "class exploitation and ethnic oppression are inextricably interconnected both in history and in the present. Therefore, one form of domination cannot be successfully eradicated without a conscious, simultaneous struggle to eliminate the other."[32] Ironically the contras, for all their indigenous rights rhetoric, had evidently not learned this lesson. In fact in mid-1984 a prominent member of ARDE resigned from the organization, citing racism against the Miskitu as one of his primary motives.[33]

Perhaps the most explosive psychological legacy of this history of dual domination was the neurosis of internalized racism on the part of the Amerindians at the bottom of the hierarchy. This explains why so many Miskitu could be mobilized into a virtually suicidal war. The Miskitu contras appealed to these deeply ingrained sentiments of heartfelt injustice and humiliation. Through MISURASATA and later MISURA, Fagoth offered the Miskitu people, who had always been ridiculed and exploited by the surrounding ethnic groups, an illusion of racial superiority. For example, he advocated the expulsion of the Mestizo population from the Moskitia and the relegation of second-class citizenship status to the Creoles.

Such radical, ethnic-nationalist revival movements, often combined with a messianic and millenarian mystique, are a sociological phenomenon common to ethnic minorities suffering from social and economic discrimination throughout the world. Comparable examples of mass mobilization include the Ghost Dance movement among North American Indians in the 1870s and 1890s, the numerous cargo cults of the Melanesian islands, and the Mamachi religion of the Guaymi Amerindians in Panama during the 1960s.[34] These movements unleash energies that have been distorted by decades or even centuries of oppression and alienation.

By detailing the historical and anthropological origin of the dichotomy between the Pacific and Atlantic Coast populations in Nicaragua we have seen that the problems existed well before the Sandinistas. Let us look now at how the underlying ethnic tensions were catalyzed by the revolutionary process.

THE POSTREVOLUTION FACTORS

Ironically it was the Revolution itself that initially mobilized the Miskitu. The Sandinistas not only introduced a genuine democratic opening into Nicaraguan political and social life, but also an infectious sense of hope and omnipotence. Daily the radio urged everyone, including the Miskitu, to organize, to be proud of being poor, and, above all, to demand their just rights. Rivera, a Miskitu contra leader who detested the Sandinistas, recognized his debt to them: "Of course the Revolution made this whole movement possible. The fervor of the revolutionary triumph injected into the soul, heart and atmosphere that everybody could express themselves and participate. Before there was no incentive . . . we were just asleep."[35]

The original strategy of the Revolution was to integrate the ethnic minorities into the revolutionary process by providing concrete solutions to their material needs.[36] Subsidies were established for farm implements and inputs; technical aid was dispensed free of charge; crops were purchased at guaranteed prices; credit was made accessible and cheap; electricity was brought to the countryside; and schools and health clinics were built in even the most remote communities. An all-weather road from the Pacific was completed (1982) and telephone and television connections were extended. This campaign to reactivate the economy and build infrastructure, however, was offset by the initial disruption caused by the revolutionary transition and later, more dramatically, by the contras' campaign of economic sabotage. Economic infrastructure worth millions of dollars was destroyed. Constant ambush of transport routes resulted in food shortages in the isolated rural communities and prevented the delivery of social services since even nurses and agricultural extension agents were killed by the contras. Furthermore, the de facto economic embargo on the country by the United States further exacerbated the already tenuous economic situation as precious fishing and transport craft, as well as other productive machinery, were paralyzed for lack of spare parts and foreign exchange.

Significantly in the South where the military situation was somewhat less critical, the rural communities received more of the benefits of the Revolution: schools, health clinics, artesanal fishing cooperatives, subsidized river transport, and so on. These communities, many of which were largely Garifuna and Creole, were noticeably more appreciative of the revolutionary process.

This economic dynamic, however, did not affect the urban-based Creole population to the same extent. The principal economic problems faced by Creoles in Bluefields were not poverty and unemployment. The Creoles represented, to a certain extent, a miniature consumer economy, receiving much of their income from cash remittances or savings from previous out-migrations. The Revolution's emphasis on meeting the needs of the poorest sectors, therefore, actually lowered their standard of living. The Central Bank was channeling scarce foreign currency to build schools in the countryside rather than to assure adequate supplies of toothpaste and toilet paper in urban centers.

While many Creoles were disaffected by their inability to purchase consumer goods, a significant sector of Creole intelligentsia accepted jobs in the expanded local government ministries, and some became revolutionaries. This was not the case for the Miskitu equivalent of the Creole intellectuals, that is, the dozen university-educated Miskitu or the more numerous community-level Miskitu Moravian ministers. The generally lower literacy level of the Amerindians, their limited skills in interethnic interaction, and the more antagonistic status of Amerindian/Mestizo ethnic relations resulted in relatively few Miskitu being selected for employment in white-collar government jobs. In contrast to the Creoles, therefore, most of the educated Miskitu "elite" were not incorporated into the public service sector and instead became the backbone of the Miskitu contra movement. Although not wealthy by any standard, this Miskitu intelligentsia did not share the impoverished semiproletarian class position of the majority of the people. Consequently, they failed to appreciate the progressive economic changes being promoted by the Revolution. Instead they reacted most strongly to the continued manifestations of ethnic oppression, since that is what affected *them* most directly on the personal level.[37]

Ultimately, the factor that most obstructed reconciliation between the Sandinistas and alienated Costeños was the war itself. The war disrupted more than just the economy. It reduced the space for politically acceptable dialogue. The Sandinista leadership repeatedly recognized the Revolution's errors in the Atlantic Coast, and specifically cited heavy-handedness and cultural insensitivity on the part of FSLN cadre.[38] The war, however, forced military defense rather than flexibility and self-criticism into the foreground.

U.S. INTERVENTION

This takes us full circle to the core of the problem: U.S. intervention. If Fagoth and the MISURASATA leaders had not been provided with sophisticated military hardware, intensive military training, and millions of dollars of spending money, they could not have engaged in protracted armed struggle. There would have been serious conflicts between the ethnic minorities and the Sandinistas, but it would not have escalated into a bloody war; it could have been resolved through a nonviolent—albeit tensely charged—process of negotiation and accommodation.

Minorities suffering from ethnic oppression feel their injustice deeply and have a tremendous potential for militant mobilization. The FSLN leadership had not been aware of the complexity of the situation in the Atlantic Coast. Few Sandinistas had ever been to the region; no systematic analysis of the indigenous minority question existed. Tragically, this was not the case for the United States. The Defense Department and the CIA have spent millions of dollars analyzing ethnic minorities throughout the Third World.[39] The manipulation of indigenous peoples with historical grievances has become a recurrent pattern in North American interventions. The most spectacular example of this strategy was the military mobilization of the Hmoung in Southeast Asia (along the Thailand/Laos border) behind U.S. objectives.[40]

In the particular case of Nicaragua, the real fear of the Central Intelligence Agency and the U.S. State Department, therefore, was not that the Sandinistas might mistreat their ethnic minorities, but rather the reverse. The Sandinista attempt to dismantle, in a democratic—although sometimes clumsy and insensitive—fashion, the historical patterns of interethnic domination and class exploitation on the Atlantic Coast threatened to set a "subversive" precedent for other multiethnic nations. Therefore, by promoting armed struggle and prolonging an agonized blood bath, the United States hoped to prevent or perhaps at least to retard, the emergence of that liberating example.

NOTES

1. Because of the isolation of the Atlantic Coast no definitive census of the Amerindian populations exists. For the most accurate population estimates, as well as an excellent demographic history of the Coast, see Centro de Investigaciones y Documentación de la Costa Atlantica (CIDCA), *Demografía Costeña: Notas Sobre la Historia Demográfica y Población Actual de los Grupos Etnicos de la Costa Atlántica Nicaragüense* (Managua: CIDCA, 1982). CIDCA arrived at its population figures by counting the number of houses appearing in aerial photographs of the Atlantic Coast.

2. MISURASATA stood for "the Unity of the Miskitu, Sumu, Rama, and Sandinistas," but the Miskitu dominated the organization. Prior to the Revolution there had been an indigenous organization named ALPROMISU (Alliance for Progress of the Miskitu and Sumu), but its leadership had largely been coopted by Somoza. In June 1984 the first meetings were held in North Zelaya to found a new Miskitu mass organization (MISATAN).

3. See Philippe Bourgois, "The Problematic of Nicaragua's Indigenous Minorities," in *Nicaragua in Revolution*, edited by Thomas W. Walker (New York: Praeger, 1982), pp. 303–318.

4. CIDCA, *Trabil Nani: Historical Background and Current Situation of the Atlantic Coast of Nicaragua* (New York: Occasional Paper of the Riverside Church Disarmament Project, 1984), p. 23; and Roxanne Dunbar Ortiz, "Miskitus in Nicaragua: Who is Violating Human Rights?" in *Revolution in Central America* edited by Stanford Central America Action Network (Boulder, Colo.: Westview, 1983), pp. 466–470.

5. *Barricada*, February 25, 1981; and *El Nuevo Diario*, February 25, 1981.

6. *Foreign Broadcast Information Service*, 1981, Vol. VI, No. 099, p. 25; *Diario las Américas* (Miami), July 11, 1981.

7. In this same January 11, 1984, tape-recorded interview in Tibás, Costa Rica, Rivera accused Fagoth of forcing the Miskitu "into a fratricidal war . . . [converting them] into cannon fodder in the hands of the Somozists, the CIA and all those kinds of people." He also admitted that "it might be true that I'm playing Imperialism's game"; nevertheless, his troops, were coordinating their military actions with those of Fagoth. See CIDCA, *Trabil Nani*, p. 40; and Americas Watch, *Human Rights in Nicaragua* (New York: Americas Watch, April 1984), p. 43.

8. See CIDCA, *Trabil Nami*, pp. 24–26; and Americas Watch, *On Human Rights in Nicaragua* (New York: Americas Watch, May 1982), pp. 56–59.

9. Americas Watch, *On Human Rights*, pp. 58–71; Americas Watch, *Human Rights in Nicaragua*, pp. 9–11; and San Francisco *Examiner*, March 1, 1982, citing a U.S. Ecumenical Rights Commission Report.

10. CIDCA, *Trabil Nani*, p. 52.

11. CIDCA, "The Atlantic Coast: A Policy of Genocide?" *Envío* 3, no. 35 (June 1984):8b. See also Americas Watch, *Human Rights in Central America: A Report on El Salvador, Guatemala, Honduras and Nicaragua* (New York: Americas Watch, June 1984), p. 18.

12. For example, a sublieutenant in Lapán, Zelaya, was sentenced to eighteen years for rape. See Americas Watch, *Human Rights in Central America*, p. 23; CIDCA, *Trabil Nani*, p. 54; and "Condena a Sub-Teniente del EPS que Abusó en Lapán," *Avances* (Zona Especial 1, Zelaya Norte, Nicaragua) 2, no. 15 (May 1984):3.

13. Charles Hale, "Ethnopolitics, Regional War, and a Revolution's Quest for Survival: An Assessment of the Miskitu Question in Nicaragua," *Alternative Newsletter* (Committee on Native American Struggles of the National Lawyer's Guild), June 1984, p. 19; in *Nicaraguan Perspectives*, Summer 1984, p. 34.

14. Americas Watch, *Human Rights in Nicaragua*, p. 12.

15. Ibid., p. 3.

16. Philadelphia *News*, December 10, 1982. For further details of contra atrocities against civilians, see "A Public Forum: Human Rights Violations and Violence in Nicaragua and El Salvador," chaired by Senator Edward Kennedy (Washington, D.C.: Transcript of Proceedings, Miller Reporting Company, May 25, 1984), pp. 25–63, and New York *Times*, March 7, 1985.

17. Tape-recorded interview with Brooklyn Rivera, January 11, 1984, Tibás, Costa Rica. Journalists who interviewed Fagoth in 1983 and 1984 likewise stated that Fagoth appeared "genuinely, certifiably, clinically insane."

18. "Evening News," Cable News Network Television, June 1, 1984; *El Tiempo* (Tegucigalpa), May 21, 1984; and *El Nuevo Diario*, February 2, 1984.

19. Information based on interviews with officials in charge of the artesanal fishing projects in Bluefields, October 1983. Also documented in Americas Watch, *Human Rights in Nicaragua*, p. 47, and CIDCA, *Trabil Nani*, p. 39.

20. For the best historical account of the Miskitu, see John Holm, *The Creole English of Nicaragua's Miskito Coast: Its Socio-Linguistic History and a Comparative Study of its Lexicon and Syntax* (London: University of London, Ph.D. dissertation, 1978).

21. Robert White, "The Case of the Agent to the Settlers on the Coast of Yucatán; and the Late Settlers on the Mosquito Shore . . ." (London: T. Cadwell, 1789), p. 45.

22. Troy Floyd, *The Anglo-Spanish Struggle for the Mosquitia* (Albuquerque: University of New Mexico Press, 1967), p. 67 citing Edward Long, *The History of Jamaica*, Vol. 3 (London, 1774), p. 320. In fact the Miskitu became so trusted by the British that on several occasions in the late 1600s and early 1700s they were brought to Jamaica to quash slave revolts.

23. Tape-recorded interview with Brooklyn Rivera, January 11, 1984, Tibás, Costa Rica.

24. Fagoth, for example, climaxed a speech in early 1981 with visions of a not too distant future when Mestizo Nicaraguans would have to show passports in order to enter Miskitu territory. See CIDCA, *Trabil Nani*, p. 23.

25. For example, a French Consul in Costa Rica complained to his superiors in 1904:

With elements of penetration such as the United Fruit Company and the Panama Canal Company, the United States have thereby as of now become the masters of the entire Atlantic Coast of Central America. The complete absorption of this part of the world is just a question of days barring a European intervention.

Taken from: Foreign Affairs Archives of the Quai d'Orsay (FAA), Paris, France, Nouvelle Série Tome 1, "Depêche de M. Emile Joré, Consul de France à San Jose," March 27, 1904:15. (Courtesy of research notes of Dr. Isabel Wing-Ching, University of Costa Rica).

26. For an account of military interventions in Bluefields at the turn of the century, see Lester Langley, *The Banana Wars: An Inner History of American Empire 1900-1924* (Lexington; University Press of Kentucky, 1983), pp. 53–72.

27. In fact, the Sumu and Rama are below the Miskitu in the ethnic/class hierarchy.

28. Tani Marilena Adams, *Life Giving Life Threatening: Gold Mining in Atlantic Nicaragua. Mine Work in Siuna and the Response to Nationalization by the Sandinista Regime* (Chicago: University of Chicago, Master's thesis, 1981), pp. 69–71.

29. In fact, right up to July 19, 1979, there was outright apartheid in the gold mines of Central Zelaya. Nonwhites—indeed even upper-class Mestizos—were forbidden from frequenting the housing compound reserved for management.

30. There was considerable variation in phenotype within the Creole population. Although they conceived of themselves as a unified ethnic group, it was considered "better" to have caucasian physical features and straight hair.

31. For an examination of the historic role racism and ethnic group differentiation played in the United Fruit Company on the Atlantic Coast of Costa Rica and Panama, see Philippe Bourgois, "Racismo, División y Violencia," *Diálogo Social* (Panama) 17, no. 164 (February 1984):18–25; for a slightly modified English translation, see Working Group on Multinational Corporations in Central America, "Racism and the Multinational Corporation: The Ethnicity of the Labor Force on a Subsidiary of the United Fruit Company in Limón, Costa Rica and Bocas del Toro, Panama," *Indigenous World/El Mundo Indígena* 3, no. 2 (1984): 7–10..

32. Edmundo Gordon Gitt (CIDCA), "La Labor del CIDCA y Aproximación Teórica a la Problemática de la Costa Atlántica de Nicaragua," in *Memoria del Seminario Costa Atlántica de Centroamérica*, edited by Carmen Murillo and David Smith (San José, Costa Rica: Confederación Universitaria Centroamericana, 1983), pp. 148 and 151.

33. Hugo Spadafora, "Errores de Edén Pastora," *La Nación Internacional*, June 7–13, 1984, p. 11.

34. See Bernard Barber, "Acculturation and Messianic Movements," in *Reader in Comparative Religion*, edited by William A. Lessa and Evon Z. Vogt (New York: Harper and Row, 1958), pp. 512–515; Peter Worsley, *The Trumpet Shall Sound: A Study of 'Cargo' Cults in Melanesia* (New York: Schocken Books, 1968); and Philip Young, *Ngawbe: Tradition and Change Among the Western Guaymi of Panama* (Chicago: University of Illinois Press, 1971).

35. Tape-recorded interview with Brooklyn Rivera, January 11, 1984, Tibás, Costa Rica.

36. See Bourgois "The Problematic of Nicaragua's Indigenous Minorities" p. 314.

37. With the case of Nicaragua in mind, Gordon Gitt in "La Labor del CIDCA," p. 150, discusses the tendency of intellectuals with upwardly mobile aspirations to dominate ethnic movements, thereby distorting their class orientations.

38. Hale, "Ethnopolitics," p. 17.

39. Eric Wolf and Joseph Jorgensen, "Anthropology on the Warpath in Thailand," *New York Review of Books* 15, no. 9 (December 17, 1970):26–35. A good example of a study "designed to be useful to military and other personnel . . . " is, Kensington Office of the American Institutes for Research, *Ethnographic Study Series: Minority Groups in North Vietnam* (Washington, D.C.: U.S. Government Printing Office, April 1972).

40. Roxanne Dunbar Ortiz, *Indians of the Americas: Human Rights and Self Determination* (New York and London: Zed and Praeger, 1984), pp. 229–239.

PART III
ECONOMIC POLICY

All political systems—revolutionary or not—rest on an economic foundation. When the economy does well, the political system is normally secure. When it begins to falter, the government may find itself in danger. The chapters in this section examine the economic policy and problems of revolutionary Nicaragua.

We begin with a chapter by Michael Conroy that attempts to classify and evaluate the performance of the economic model employed by the Sandinistas in the first five years. Here we find that, contrary to the impression one would gather from the Kissinger Commission Report on Central America, the revolutionary government had employed an economic model thoroughly consistent with prevailing non-Marxist "structuralist" approaches favored by most Latin American governments. Further, and again contradicting the intended impression of the Kissinger Report, Nicaragua's economic performance—as measured by growth in gross domestic product (GDP) for 1980, 1981, 1982, and 1983—had actually been among the best in Latin America.

Nevertheless, Nicaragua also faced a number of very serious economic problems. Sylvia Maxfield and Richard Stahler-Sholk examine the external factors constraining economic growth—not the least of which were a sharp drop in export commodity prices soon after the Sandinista victory and an elaborate program of economic destabilization orchestrated by the Reagan Administration. Laura Enriquez discusses the several dilemmas inherent to agroexport planning in revolutionary Nicaragua. Finally, John Weeks delves into the difficulties involved in stimulating productivity in an industrial sector that had probably already reached its limits of growth prior to insurrectionary war and that, after the Triumph, remained largely in the hands of a stubbornly non-cooperative private sector.

Chapter 10
Economic Legacy and Policies: Performance and Critique

MICHAEL E. CONROY

It may be a legitimate indicator of the historical significance of the first five years of the Nicaraguan Revolution that the controversy over the nature, origins, and success of its economic model went well beyond the selective use of statistics and the ritualistic invocation of ideological creed. The very basis for measuring absolute and relative performance in the economic arena are challenged by the complexity and profundity of social and economic changes that occurred in Nicaragua during the first five years.

The report of the Kissinger Commission issued in January 1984 claimed that the Nicaraguan economy was suffering from the worst economic performance of any of the Central American nations. The data that the report chose to use would appear to support that claim, even though the conclusion was developed using a technique that was strongly biased against the Nicaraguan experience.

The Kissinger Commission's sleight of hand involved comparisons across a different period of time for each of the five Central American countries. With respect to Nicaragua, for example, the Commission included the two and a half years of prerevolutionary economic decline from early 1977 through July 1979 in the period for which it held the Sandinista regime responsible. The Nicaraguan data covered a total of seven years. For El Salvador only six years were summed; for Costa Rica only four; and for Honduras and Guatemala, only three.

The Commission found: "By 1983 the real per capita income in Nicaragua was 38 percent below the peak level reached in 1977." The contraction of income per capita in all the rest of Central America, measured from an arbitrary "peak year" through 1983, was less. El Salvador had experienced a 35 percent decline, Costa Rica 23 percent, Guatemala 14 percent, and Honduras 12 percent. The conclusion that the report reached was highly critical of the fundamental model for economic

This is a revised and abbreviated version of a paper that first appeared in *Third World Quarterly*, October 1984, under the title: "False Polarisation? Differing Perspectives on the Economics of Post-Revolutionary Nicaragua."

development undertaken by the Sandinista Revolution. Economic performance had been poor, it asserted, "in part because of the disruptions caused by the revolution, in part because of the world recession, and in part because of the mismanagement invariably associated with regimes espousing Marxist-Leninist ideology."[1]

During the very same month that the Kissinger Commission Report was released, *Barricada*, the official newspaper of the FSLN, touted that in 1983 "Nicaragua obtained the highest rate of growth in all of Latin America, despite the commercial blockade, the financial pressures, and the Reagan administration's policy of military aggression."[2] Data from the United Nation's Economic Commission for Latin America (ECLA) support the claim. In fact, ECLA data discussed below indicate that economic growth during the first four full calendar years after the July 1979 Triumph of the Sandinista Revolution exceeded 22 percent in aggregate terms and surpassed 7 percent in per capita terms. These are the only years for which comparable data were available at the moment of the fifth anniversary. During those same four years, average economic growth in Central America as a whole was −5.7 percent overall and −14.7 percent in per capita terms.

We shall confine ourselves here to a critical review of the aggregate performance of the Nicaraguan economy, considered within the context of the broadly economic legacy inherited by the Sandinista government from Anastasio Somoza's regime. We shall review the major characteristics of the economic policies introduced by the Government of National Reconstruction during the first five years and discuss the criticisms of the policies that have come from a wide range of sources. Whether the economic policies of the first five years, whatever their results, should be called "Marxist-Leninist" will be an important corollary focus.

The exploration of these themes will lead us to several conclusions. Foremost among them is the recognition that the economic policies of postrevolutionary Nicaragua have been derived much more closely from the "structuralist" views of many non-Marxist theoreticians than from either the *laissez-faire* preferences of the Somoza era or from the examples of Soviet and Cuban communism to which Nicaragua was compared by the Kissinger Commission and by other critics at the end of the first five years. They also show historically important innovations in the application of many of the non-Marxist "structuralist" reforms that have been advocated not only by ECLA but also by the U.S. government in a variety of its aid programs in Latin America since the onset of the Alliance for Progress. The fact that Nicaraguan economic policies do not correspond to previous Marxist-Leninist models should not be taken to mean that Marxist analysis had been rejected by the Sandinistas. Rather, the evolution of policy in

Nicaragua was fundamentally pragmatic, borrowing from differing theoretical approaches in the struggle to create a viable set of policies appropriate to Nicaragua's needs. The mixed economy that resulted offered a basis for both efficient and equitable development in a more independent mode, using both markets and planning.

ECONOMIC PROBLEMS AT THE END OF THE FIRST FIVE YEARS

If we view Nicaragua superficially and in isolation, it might appear to many observers that the Nicaraguan economy performed very poorly over the first five years. Table 10.1 presents some indicators of the global economic picture through the end of 1983. Nicaragua's relatively strong growth in 1983 was, in fact, a recovery from an apparently very poor performance in 1982. From 1979 to 1983 the Nicaraguan economy generated cumulative growth of 22.5 percent, a dramatic increase, especially in view of the precipitous decline in the economy during the 1978–79 years of insurrection and civil war. But real growth per capita was only 7.7 percent over that time, less than 2 percent per year.

There were serious problems in the Nicaraguan economy, some of which are evident in Table 10.1. The widespread insurrection that brought an end to the Somoza dictatorship had dramatic consequences for the Nicaraguan economy in 1978, 1979, and 1980. Total output, exports, imports, and capital movements were all seriously affected; and the destruction, discussed below in greater detail, was far greater than that reflected in the table. Nicaragua generated extraordinary increases in production during the first two years of recovery from the civil war, but output fell again, by 1.4 percent, in 1982. The trend in growth rates was generally downward after 1980. The level of GDP per capita fell in 1982 by 3.9 percent, illustrating the fragility of current economic progress. Consumer prices increased by more than 20 percent per year for each year from 1980 to 1983, reaching a total four-year increase of more than 101 percent. And Nicaragua had historically been a country with low rates of inflation!

The nation's external imbalance was also clear and was not improving. Imports exceeded exports by an average of nearly $300 million in each of the last three years before the fifth anniversary, a very large trade imbalance for a nation that exported an average of only $450 million per year in those same years. These trade deficits were covered by net capital inflows that peaked in 1981 at $677 million, fell to $270 million in 1982, and rose again to more than $500 million in 1983. The consequences of

TABLE 10.1
NICARAGUA: EVOLUTION OF PRINCIPAL GLOBAL ECONOMIC INDICATORS

	1976	1977	1978	1979	1980	1981	1982	1983	1979–83
Real GDP (mil. of 1970 $)	1,168	1,241	1,152	863	944	1,024	1,004	1,057	
Percent change	5.1	6.3	-7.2	-25.9	10.7	8.7	-1.4	5.3	22.5
Real GDP/capita (1970 $)	487	501	450	326	341	359	342	351	
Percent change	1.6	2.8	-10.2	-27.5	6.7	5.3	-4.6	2.6	7.7
Consumer price changes (percent)	6.2	10.2	4.3	70.3	24.8	23.2	22.2	30.9	101.1
Total exports of goods									
Millions of current $	542	637	646	567	449	500	408	411	
Percent change	44.5	17.5	1.5	-12.2	-20.8	10.9	-14.2	0.7	-24.1
Total imports of goods									
Millions of current $	485	704	553	326	794	922	681	658	
Percent change	.6	45.2	-21.4	-41.1	143.6	11.7	-26.1	-3.4	101.8
Trade balance on goods	57	-67	93	241	-345	-422	-273	-247	
Net movement of capital	95	128	-70	-90	275	677	270	510	
Foreign public debt	653	867	964	1,101	1,290	2,163	2,789	3,400	
Percent change	9.7	32.8	11.2	14.2	17.2	67.8	28.9	21.9	208.8
Ratio of interest payments to exports of goods & services	6.5	7.1	9.3	9.7	15.7	15.5	31.7	36.1	

Sources: U.N. Economic Commission for Latin America, "Preliminary Overview of the Latin American Economy During 1983," E/CEPAL/G.1279, December 29, 1983; Economic Survey of Latin America, various issues; and Centroamérica: Evolución de Sus Economías en 1983 (Versión Preliminar), April 1984.

those capital flows were an increase in the external debt from $1.6 billion in 1979 to $3.4 billion in 1983 and an increase in the cost of servicing the debt (interest payments alone) from 16 percent of export earnings to 36 percent.

From the outset Nicaragua suffered an acute shortage of foreign exchange that required careful exchange rationing and caused a sharp reduction in the availability of most imported products. By the end of the period, the government was rationing as many as ten basic commodities, including sugar, cooking oil, and gasoline. There were reports of shortages of medicines in the hospitals, shortages of paper for books and school supplies, and many other shortages that were not nearly so obvious during prerevolutionary days. There was little or no investment in the private commerical sphere, and industrial production continued to fall. By the end of 1983 one international agency characterized the situation as follows: "an important expansion of production and employment alongside deep financial disequilibria, both internally and externally, and a decrease in the levels of private consumption per capita."[3]

A REGIONAL COMPARISON

However, Nicaragua's economic progress during those years takes on a very distinct image when it is compared with the historical record for Central America as a whole or for Latin America as a region during those same years. Table 10.2 places key dimensions of the Nicaraguan economy in such a context. The cumulative Nicaraguan economic growth of 22.5 percent from 1979 to 1983 must be compared with the Central American *average* growth experience over the same interval, a *decline* of 5.7 percent. It could also be compared with that of Latin America as a whole, a cumulative growth of only 2.7 percent over four years, less than 0.7 percent per year.

The real standard of living in Nicaragua, as measured however imperfectly by GDP per capita, improved by more than 7 percent from 1979 to 1983, without taking into consideration the significant redistribution of income, expansion of social services, and subsidies to the pricing of basic commodities that also occurred. This improvement for the Nicaraguan people took place at the same time that the standard of living was *falling* by a cumulative average of 14.7 percent in the Central American region and by 9.2 percent for Latin America as a whole.

It would be facile, and fundamentally incorrect, to argue that the relative Nicaraguan performance simply meant a "rebound" from the disasters that accompanied the insurrection in 1978 and 1979. One could only argue that there was a simple "rebound" if the damages incurred

TABLE 10.2
EVOLUTION OF COMPARABLE ECONOMIC INDICATORS FOR NICARAGUA, CENTRAL AMERICA, AND LATIN AMERICA (IN PERCENTAGES)

	1976	1977	1978	1979	1980	1981	1982	1983[a]	1979–83
Real GDP growth									
Nicaragua	5.1	6.3	-7.2	-25.9	10.7	8.7	-1.2	5.3	22.50
Central America[b]	6.1	7.5	3.1	-2.6	1.6	-1.7	-4.7	-0.4	-5.70
Latin America	5.5	5.1	4.7	6.6	5.9	1.5	-1.1	-3.3	2.76
Real GDP/capita growth									
Nicaragua	1.6	2.8	-10.2	-27.5	6.7	5.3	-3.9	2.6	7.67
Central America	2.9	4.3	0.04	-5.4	-1.4	-3.8	-7.1	-2.5	-14.71
Latin America	1.1	2.4	2.2	4.1	3.4	-0.9	-3.3	-5.6	-9.16
Consumer price changes									
Nicaragua	6.2	10.2	4.3	70.3	24.8	23.2	22.2	37.3	101.10
Central America	8.1	9.1	8.3	26.0	16.9	23.6	25.0	13.3	78.80
Latin America	61.5	40.1	39.1	54.1	52.8	60.8	85.6	130.4	329.60
Export growth									
Nicaragua	44.5	17.5	1.5	-12.2	-20.8	10.9	-14.2	0.3	-24.10
Central America	32.0	31.8	1.1	12.1	1.4	-7.2	-11.2	-2.4	-19.44

Latin America^c	15.1	18.9	7.5	22.1	18.2	2.0	-8.5	-1.3	27.40
Import growth									
Nicaragua	0.6	45.2	-21.4	-41.1	143.6	11.7	-28.0	5.0	101.80
Central America	15.3	31.3	7.9	1.6	35.6	-2.0	-21.2	2.7	15.08
Latin America^c	13.6	14.8	13.8	25.9	32.3	7.6	-19.9	-28.7	-8.70
Growth of foreign debt									
Nicaragua	9.7	32.8	11.2	14.2	17.2	67.8	29.3	21.0	199.3
Central America	25.8	27.1	24.3	27.1	25.1	51.1	11.9	22.4	151.6
Latin America^c	29.7	25.3	30.2	27.7	17.2	21.8	12.2	7.3	76.2
Ratio of interest payment to exports of goods & services									
Nicaragua	—	7.1	9.3	9.7	15.7	15.5	31.7	36.1	
Central America	—	5.3	7.2	7.9	11.2	14.1	21.3	22.7	
Latin America^c	—	11.9	15.1	18.8	23.3	31.3	46.2	39.1	

Sources: U.N. Economic Commission for Latin America, "Preliminary Overview of the Latin American Economy During 1983," E/CEPAL/G.1279, December 29, 1983; Economic Survey of Latin America, various issues; and Centroamérica: Evolución de Sus Economías en 1983 (Versión Preliminar), April 1984.

[a] Preliminary figures based on early 1984 estimates.
[b] Unweighted averages of the five traditional Central American nations: Costa Rica, El Salvador, Guatemala, Honduras, and Nicaragua.
[c] Non-oil-exporting countries only.

during the Revolution were not severe and if there had been no changes in the external markets faced by Nicaragua after the Revolution. But the losses and destruction during that period, as discussed in greater detail below, were profound and permanent. Furthermore, Nicaragua faced, over the period from 1980 to 1983, world market conditions for its exports and world financial conditions for its financing that were certainly no better than those faced by other Central American nations or by Latin America as a whole.

Table 10.2 also places other dimensions of Nicaraguan economic performance in a context that permits clearer evaluation. The rates of inflation experienced in Nicaragua were, in fact, comparable to those encountered in all of Central America. The four-year total of 101.1 percent for Nicaragua is only 23 percent above the regional average; and it is less than 33 percent of the average inflationary experience of Latin America as a whole during the same years. What the table fails to convey is the fact that the Nicaraguan program for rationing basic commodities kept the absolute cost of basic commodities at one-half the cost found in the rest of Central America and kept inflation in the prices of those basic commodities to less than one-quarter of the rate of inflation in the rest of the region.[4]

The decline in the value of Nicaraguan exports from 1980 to 1983, a total of 24.1 percent, was only slightly above the regionwide average decline of 17.9 percent. But Nicaragua managed to increase its imports (and, hence, total supply) far more than the region as a whole, adding increases in imports in all years but 1982 that were considerably above the average increases for the region as a whole, especially in 1982 and 1983 when Latin American import capacity fell by an average of more than 20 percent per year.

The fact that Nicaraguan debt grew by a factor of 1.9 since 1979 is less startling when viewed in the overall Central American context in which debt grew by 151.6 percent over the same period. The surge in the ratio of interest payments to exports of goods and services left Nicaragua at the end of 1983 with a ratio that is higher than the Central American regional average but below the Latin America average of 39.1.

These data on the first five years of economic results in "Nicaragua Libre" clearly reduce the opportunity to suggest that Nicaraguan economic policy can be dismissed as a simple failure. Using only the most aggregative measures, those favored by relatively conservative evaluators, one can see that the Nicaraguan economy produced results over four years that were distinctly better than either the Central American averages or the Latin American averages on most terms. Even if we ignore the widely documented internal social changes, advances in literacy, public health, and education, and the external military aggression to which Nicaragua has had to respond, the Nicaraguan economic record was impressive.

THE SOMOZA LEGACY

An evaluation of the magnitude of the achievement requires, nonetheless, a comprehensive understanding of the nature of the Somoza legacy, in terms of both the nature of the prerevolutionary economy and the economic devastation suffered during the insurrection. It is useful to reconstruct that legacy by reviewing, in turn, the analyses of the prerevolutionary economy offered by conservative observers of Nicaraguan development, critics from the United Nations, and more radical commentators.

One finds perhaps the best applications of the conservative perspective in the writings of World Bank and Inter-American Development Bank analysts. If one looks, for example, at the prerevolutionary reports they published on Nicaragua, the outlook and perspectives were quite sanguine.

The first World Bank mission to Nicaragua, from July 1951 to May 1952, reported that the principal weaknesses in the Nicaraguan economy were basically administrative: an "archaic fiscal system," an inadequate transportation system, an ineffective credit system, and the absence of "long range planning and . . . a concrete investment program within the government."[5] The mission's report called for programs to improve sanitation, education, and public health because, in its own words, "without exception, the mission found that in every sector of the economy high disease rates, low standards of nutrition, and low educational and training standards are the major factors inhibiting the growth of productivity."[6]

The role of the private sector, viewed as crucial from this perspective, was explicit. "Up to the present time," the report noted, "domestic private investment has, with few exceptions, done relatively little to develop the country's productive capacity." But, it noted,

> in view of the extraordinary opportunities for private investment, which should increase further with the rising rate of public investment and the moderate tax rates, private capital has a favourable economic environment
> It should play a major role in promoting the country's rapid development. It is particularly desirable that it do so."[7]

The mission concluded that the "progressive measures" undertaken by the Somoza government at that time, including reducing inflation by balancing the budget, beginning the formulation of a five-year plan, calling for fiscal reform and creating a National Economic Council composed of business leaders, represent "the achievement of a government alive to the needs of the country and with the will and desire to progress."[8]

If one reviews prerevolutionary issues of the Inter-American Development Bank's annual report on "Social and Economic Progress in Latin America," the problems that Nicaragua faced were antiseptically technical. Prices would tend to rise in some years because credit expanded too much, the government would begin one new program or another, and the only alarm that might be raised concerned "imbalances": occasionally excessive deficits, credit expansion that created inflation, balance-of-payments problems, and so on. "Economic progress" was defined, implicitly, as avoidance of crises, primarily crises in terms of major aggregate "imbalances." The problems of each year—whether unexpected declines in the prices of export products or increases in the costs of imports, capital inflows for new foreign investment projects or outflows in pursuit of better opportunities—were treated as the normal vicissitudes to which a nation must be prepared to adapt in order to progress.

Nicaragua was, from this conservative perspective, a country without significant and tangible obstacles to economic growth during the 1960s and 1970s. It was a country that participated in the Central American Common Market, grew relatively strongly through the 1960s, and suffered from the common problems of the entire region in the 1970s. It enjoyed the second highest average rate of GDP growth in the region from 1950 to 1960, 6.1 percent per year, well above the 4 to 5 percent experienced in Guatemala, El Salvador, and Honduras, and topped only by the 7.3 percent annual growth in Costa Rica. From 1961 to 1968, Nicaraguan aggregate growth was the strongest in the region; it averaged 9.8 percent per year, falling to an average of 6.7 percent per year from 1969 to 1977.[9] There was some attention drawn to a thirtyfold increase in foreign debt from 1960 to 1976 (from $21.7 million to $702.3 million), but since agricultural exports were also increasing, the debt servicing was not seen as a serious problem.

The Nicaraguan Revolution was a severe blow to the prospects for continued evaluation using such a conservative developmentalist perspective. The Kissinger Commission, although heavily weighted toward conservative business-based members, was forced to step well outside of the orthodox paradigm to explain the crisis. It turned, in fact, to ECLA for an historical overview of the crises in Central America. "In ECLA's judgment," the Commission reported, "and the other experts consulted on this point were in virtually unanimous agreement—'the fruits of the long period of economic expansion were distributed in a flagrantly inequitable manner.'"[10] The Commission was even less kind to the prerevolutionary Nicaraguan leaders in its postrevolutionary evaluation. The Somoza regime, it suggested, "was characterized by greed and corruption so far beyond even the levels of the past that it might be called a kleptocracy; it included a brazen reaping of immense private profits from international relief efforts following the devastating earthquake of 1972. . . . [and] repression became systematic and increasingly pervasive."

The World Bank's first postrevolutionary reassessment of Nicaragua also forced it to look at dimensions that it most often omits from its analyses. The Bank's 1981 report "discovered" vast inequality in the distribution of land: "fewer than 1,500 estates with over 350 hectares each controlled 38 percent of the land in farms and ranches. . . . In the most densely settled Pacific region . . . fewer than 750 farms had more than two-thirds of the farm land."[11] It found landless, desperate rural families: "about 50,000 before the revolution, equivalent to about one-fourth of the total number of rural families."[12] But to this day the World Bank avoids involvement in programs that expropriate and redistribute land (even with complete compensation) in response to these inequities.

The Structuralist View of ECLA

The structuralist interpretation of the Somoza legacy, to which the Kissinger Commission was forced to turn, has gained considerable increased credibility in view of the problems that the economies of the region have been facing for the past ten years. ECLA has emphasized three dimensions of the background for the Central American crisis that were specifically relevant to Nicaragua. The ECLA perspective, in looking at prerevolutionary Nicaragua, emphasizes the fundamental instability of the external orientation of the economy, the fact that "development" occurred for only a minority, and that it was "superimposed" on a strong prevailing existing minority structure of economic power leaving basically untouched the majority of the population of the nation.[13]

ECLA analyses of Nicaraguan underdevelopment note first that the limited growth that was achieved in the 1960s and 1970s was brought about by expansion of production for export into raw materials markets where prices were notoriously competitive, unstable, and depressed. They note, further, that Nicaragua is inevitably a small, fragile participant in the global economy, producing less than 0.5 percent of Latin America's total GDP with 0.8 percent of the region's population. That fragility and instability would be further emphasized by noting that 40 percent of the nation's internal financing during the 1970s came from foreign banks.

ECLA estimated (and the Kissinger Commission also echoed) that 63.7 percent of the population of Central America and 62.5 percent of the prerevolutionary Nicaraguan population were in a state of critical poverty, in the sense that their incomes did not cover their most basic needs. Nearly 35 percent of the Nicaraguan population was characterized as being in "extreme poverty." This meant that they "did not even have sufficient income to cover the value of the minimum shopping basket of food considered necessary in order to meet their biological nutritional needs."[14]

The concentration of wealth and its inherently antidemocratic consequences represent the third strain of structuralist approach to Nicaragua's past. The wealthiest 20 percent of the Nicaraguan population prior to the Revolution received 58 percent of all the income generated in the nation— the highest proportion in the region with the single exception of El Salvador, where the richest 20 percent receive 66 percent of all income. The poorest 50 percent of the population of Nicaragua received only 16 percent of all income, providing them with an average annual income of about one-tenth the average income of the wealthiest 20 percent.

A More Radical Evaluation

From the point of view of more radical Latin American and North American analysts, the structuralist analysis is inadequate; for the structuralists tend to avoid going beyond the identification of the elements of injustice and inefficiency to an analysis of the basic underpinnings of the society that created them. Marxist analyses of the prerevolutionary period of Nicaragua are more distinctly historical and more concretely global than the descriptions provided by the structuralist approach.

From the more radical viewpoint Nicaraguan underdevelopment is a direct and inevitable product of the role that it has been assigned or allowed to play in the development of the global capitalist system. Those periods of economic boom that it has known have been almost uniformly linked to direct foreign investment or foreign lending for the development of export products. The persistence of abysmal social and economic conditions represented a conscious attempt to keep the costs of reproducing the labor force to a minimum. Control of the nation by elites whose fortunes were amassed through participation in this international exploitation of the Nicaraguan working class was maintained as needed by the use of military force, foreign economic assistance, and an evolving regional and international network of defense agreements, economic pacts, and information exchange. Capitalist development at the global level was the source of Nicaragua's problem, not its solution.

Marxist interpretations of the prerevolutionary history delve more deeply into the nature of the growth spurt that Nicaragua enjoyed from 1950 to 1977 and into the class-based contradictions that were created. The export-led growth, especially the rapid expansion of commercial cotton production and import-substituting industrialization, created a new composition and differentiation of classes, according to Herrera Zúñiga.[15] The processes of cotton expansion provoked widespread displacement and proletarianization of the peasantry and clearly traceable concentration in land tenure. Central Bank data from the period indicated that the average rural wage worker in 1976 worked only 78 days a year and at an average salary of $2.50 per day.[16] Import-substitution under the Central American Common Market displaced additional thousands of artesanry workers.

The transformation of the state into a developmental protagonist, following the advice of the World Bank mission in 1953, led to consolidation of Somoza's control over virtually every aspect of the nation's developmental processes, converting the state into the proponent of the infrastructure projects needed by Somoza's private investment group and generating "an intense gamut of social and economic contradictions."[17] Somoza was able to co-opt much of his opposition through his control of state employment, projects, and subsidies to finance. But the same policies radicalized the opposition in the powerful economic groups that competed with his. The use of the state to subsidize private profits created the highest profits in the region but shifted the costs to consumers and nonbenefited producers. The use of the state's repressive powers left Nicaragua with no vent for worker protest; for Nicaragua had fewer than 11,000 unionized workers in 1975, less than one-fifth of the regionwide average.[18]

The high profitability of cotton production led to further expansion of many new firms and the duplication of investments and activities without the needed expansion of the domestic markets. The resulting reduction in levels of profits led businesses, with the open assistance of the state, to reinforce the levels of exploitation of workers during the early 1970s. The internal split in the bourgeoisie coincided with new forms of organization among the workers to resist the heavier hand of state intervention and repression, and the now-famed broad-based Sandinista Revolution resulted.

A Marxist interpretation of the last years of the Somoza regime would also note the "disciplinary role" played by international capital markets in keeping governments and, hence, nations "in line." The economic collapse of the Somoza regime began in 1978 when the September insurrection demonstrated to the world that the workers of Nicaragua had far greater possibility of resisting their roles than anyone had previously realized. It is an irony that can be read from even the statistical tables of the World Bank that the flight of domestic capital and a dramatic reduction in public and private foreign lending to Nicaragua in 1978, prior to the Revolution, undermined Somoza at precisely the moment when he needed more international assistance to resist the insurrection.

THE COSTS OF THE INSURRECTION

There is rather striking agreement among all sources on the costs of the Nicaraguan Revolution. Virtually the same estimates appear in Nicaraguan government documents, World Bank studies, and ECLA reports; and there is little difference in interpretation of the profundity of the long-term costs.

The toll was enormous. The lowest estimate of the human toll suggests that 30,000 people were killed in political violence during the last two years of the insurrection alone. This is ten times the number of persons killed in the Cuban Revolution, and the Cuban population was three times larger than that of Nicaragua. The more commonly cited statistic suggests 50,000 persons died from political violence over the five years prior to July 1979, including many thousands who disappeared without a trace.[19] The vast majority died at the hands of the Somoza government; and the greatest physical damage was attributed to the bombing and strafing of cities by the National Guard and to looting during the days of their waning control.

According to the World Bank, private investment shrank to virtually nothing during early 1979, construction was almost at a standstill, real GDP dropped by 25 percent, and nearly all production ceased during June and July. The income foregone from late 1978 to early 1980 because of the insurrection and its direct damages exceeded $2 billion, the value of a full year of GDP.[20] (That would be the equivalent of a $1.3 trillion loss to the U.S. economy at the same time.)

Direct damages to factories and stores and the looting of inventories of both raw materials and finished products affected nearly every business in the nation, whether bombed by Somoza's air force, caught in crossfire, or broken into during the disorders. The total direct damages estimated by a special ECLA mission during the months immediately following the end of the insurrection exceeded $480 million.

The World Bank mission a year later in October 1980 also estimated that the flight of capital prior to and during the conflict "exceeded half a billion dollars."[21] ECLA reported that the banking system, when nationalized, was found to have been "completely decapitalized," virtually insolvent because of many transactions during the last phases of the conflict, which were "of doubtful legality and completely illegal."[22]

Both organizations noted that the foreign debt inherited from the Somoza regime, approximately $1.6 billion, was a particularly acute problem. There had been extensive short-term borrowing from commercial lenders during the last two years of the Somoza era.

The crucial and immediate need for external financial assistance was emphasized by both reports. The very viability of the financial and monetary system and, as a result, economic stabilization in general depended upon obtaining ample new foreign resources to rehabilitate the nation's productive capacity, according to ECLA. "If it does not receive these resources, the country will face a cruel dilemma: a monetary disequilibrium and the unleashing of further inflation or an even greater contraction of economic activity under conditions when an elevated proportion of the population is now unemployed."[23]

The World Bank mission's assessment was identical. In the first place, it noted that "the negative consequences of the war are far from over. Per capita income levels of 1977 will not be attained, in the best of circumstances, until the late 1980s."[24] "The next two to three years will be difficult and the probabilities of debt-servicing and financing problems are high. However, if Nicaragua can obtain substantial financing in the near term, a considerable improvement in its creditworthiness three to four years hence can be foreseen. . . ."[25]

The Bank's assessment, however, seems to have been converted into a blueprint for subsequent anti-Nicaraguan policies, for it noted also that "any untoward event could lead to a financial trauma, since the country would not be able to obtain commercial financing as a buffer. Moreover, it would be very difficult indeed to restrain consumption for such a long period."[26] The mission's report concluded that "it would be highly desirable for the country to receive external assistance at concessional terms and in excess of the foreign exchange component."[27] Later, under U.S. pressure, that recommendation was superseded by a subsequent Bank study, discussed below, that became the basis for cutting assistance to Nicaragua from the Bank, converting Nicaragua into one of the few clients of the Bank worldwide who was then paying more back than they received.

THE ECONOMIC POLICIES OF THE POSTREVOLUTIONARY GOVERNMENT

The Government of National Reconstruction, which took office in July 1979, included representatives of the full spectrum of political perspectives that supported the Revolution. The Junta included business people, ranchers, guerrilla commanders, and representatives of the working class. The economic model that was adopted by that Junta, and that remained largely in effect through the first five years, reflected an early commitment to broad participation and economic pluralism. There were few major characteristics of Nicaraguan economic policy five years after the Revolution that were not originally implemented by that first, most broadly based, Junta.

The new Nicaraguan government officially characterized its goals as the pursuit of "development and the mixed economy." That mixed economy consisted, in the government's vision, of four principal sectors: traditional businesses in the private sector, the state sector, production cooperatives in the city and the countryside, and the peasant and artesanal sector.[28] The state sector consisted of traditional government production and services (postal services, telecommunications, defense, and so on) and the public sector that was created, with virtually universal support throughout the country, from the expropriated properties of Somoza and his closest personal, political, and business associates.

Somoza's control over the economy was so pervasive that the state found virtually 25 percent of all production in its hands immediately after the end of the insurrection, simply on the basis of the universally approved expropriation of the property of Somoza and his closest associates. By late 1980 the expansion of government services and the consolidation of state control over partially expropriated firms (by buying out minority partners) left 41 percent of production under direct state control.[29] The proportion remained roughly the same through the fifth anniversary, although there was some debate about whether the cooperatives should be classified as private or public. The distribution of titles to thousands of members of agricultural cooperatives for full private ownership of previously expropriated land increased the share of agricultural production in the private sector. But increases in productivity in state sector farms and industries expanded public sector production proportionately.

The "satisfaction of basic needs" was listed by the government as "the underlying principle of the overall development strategy."[30] It attempted, formally, to fulfill this goal by expanding popular participation in the provision of health and educational services, through agrarian reform, and by rechanneling credit to the small farmers, small private producers, cooperatives, and the state sector.

The consensus among many observers of the Nicaraguan economy suggests that the following were the other salient components of the economic strategies through the end of the fifth year after the Revolution:

Market pricing and allocation determined the vast majority of all economic decisions within the country. Although minimum wages were established (and enforced) for all areas and all types of work, there was no attempt to plan, allocate, or otherwise organize labor markets in the form that characterizes most of the actually existing Socialist countries.

Government control was created over all imports and exports through a new Ministry of Foreign Trade that was designed to eliminate the possibility of adverse foreign exchange movements through overinvoicing and underinvoicing in private import-export transactions, a chronic problem in much of Latin America. (This problem was, coincidentally, the reason why the United States encouraged the Salvadoran reform junta of 1980 to pursue the same nationalization of coffee exports.)

Two distinct waves of agrarian reform affected approximately 30 percent of all arable land, converting about one-third into privately held cooperative farms and the remainder into higher technology state farms. Unlike any other agrarian reform in Latin America, moreover, the Nicaraguan government issued a decree in December 1983 that provided for a "guarantee of inexpropriability" for any land in production, regardless of the size of the holding.

Nationalization of the banking system, similar in form and function to the nationalization of banking in Mexico, El Salvador, Costa Rica, and numerous other Third World nations, permitted the state to redirect credit toward small farmers, cooperatives, and high-priority foreign-exchange-earning private and public investment projects. Much of the rapid expansion in agricultural production that fueled the growth in overall production was directly attributable to these measures in coordination with the agrarian reform programs.

There was a government-encouraged increase in worker participation at all levels of production, including reinforced union organizations in commercial and industrial establishments, a national farm-workers association, and associations for all professional workers, including direct representation of these groups on the legislative Council of State. These groups were encouraged to monitor the application of the reinforced occupational safety and health legislation and to watch for "decapitalization" of firms and farms by private owners in opposition.

Private production in agriculture was stimulated, at times, by direct government production contracts signed in advance of planting that stipulated the purchase price of seed, the cost and frequency of chemical applications, and the guaranteed purchase price for the harvest. No farmer was forced to produce according to these contracts; there remained open markets for the sale of all agricultural products throughout the country.

Prices and wages were kept from rising by selective government price and wage controls. And there was a deliberate effort to keep nominal money wages at relatively low levels; the increases in the provision of social services, although somewhat intangible for many workers, were offered by the government as an alternative to higher money wages.

Rationing of several basic goods, primarily in Managua, was instituted to regularize and guarantee the provision of basic commodities, at subsidized prices to all families. Supplies of all rationed commodities (except gasoline) were traded freely in the marketplace at prices considerably above the subsidized basic ration price.

The consensus within the government on the continuation of these economic policies was reinforced in a public declaration of future economic policy, the "Economic Policy Guidelines, 1983–88," issued by the National Reconstruction Government in late 1983. This rather amazing document not only reviewed, from the perspective of the government itself, the first three years of postrevolutionary experience, it also outlined candidly the difficulties faced in the external sector, the problems of large and growing government budget deficits, and the difficult consequences for continued high unemployment of restraining the growth of the economy in order to lessen the deficits. Although the "Guidelines" made frequent reference to the distortions created by the need to divert large quantities of domestic resources toward national defense needs, it nevertheless proposed clear outlines for a national five-year investment program that would encompass both the private sector and the state. For a nation then at war against an estimated total of more than 15,000 contras financed, trained, and supplied by the CIA, it constituted a surprisingly calm public exercise in confidence in the future of Nicaragua.

DIFFERING ASSESSMENTS OF THE ECONOMIC STRATEGIES

The Nicaraguan government did not consider itself or call itself a "Marxist" government during the first five years, and there was no indication at the fifth anniversary that it intended to so do. There was, in fact, no nation in the world that called itself "Marxist" and that still depended on so many characteristics of the free-enterprise system. But that did not mean that those who had benefited under the *laissez faire* policies of the Somoza era could have been expected to accept the "changes in the rules of the game" that were embodied in the design of the new Nicaraguan society. The changes embodied in the new society were, in fact, "totalitarian" for them. They had lost significant elements of their opportunity to produce and trade without government intervention. They had also lost much of the political influence that they enjoyed when power was closely associated with personal wealth. It is not surprisingly, then, that representatives of the U.S. business press could find, whenever they wished, individuals who were willing to speak against the policies of the government.

From a conservative probusiness point of view, there were many problems with the strategies that had been followed and the nature of the "new Nicaraguan economy" that was being created. These attitudes are especially apparent in the publications of COSEP, the Private Enterprise Council, which continued to function and to comment publicly and vociferously on government policies. From the COSEP perspective, the new economic strategies concentrated excessive and inappropriate control in the public sector. This was then accompanied by excessive deficit spending that undermined the private economy and that was not sustainable. The profit incentives provided in production contracts were considered insufficient, and government encouragment of worker organizations meant that worker discipline broke down. Private investors argued that it was no longer attractive to invest in Nicaragua, even by comparison with the low comparable returns then available on investment in other parts of Latin America.[31]

COSEP also argued that the expansion of government production and the imposition of government controls over finance and exports represented an unstable balance of government and private sector that must tilt either one way or the other. Either there had to be movement toward much greater private sector domination of the economy or there would have to be a move toward full state socialism (which they simply called "communism").

The World Bank's assessment of economic conditions in Nicaragua reflected many of these positions.[32] The Bank's 1982 report, the last major report on Nicaragua that it issued prior to the fifth anniversary, reflected the internal political changes in the Bank as much as changes in conditions in Nicaragua. Between the first Bank visit and the second, Robert McNamara was replaced by William Claussen as president of the Bank and the Reagan Administration began to question the "political advisability" of continuing U.S. support for the Bank's programs.

The new leaders of Nicaragua had created, the report admitted, a "mixed economy [that] has left most productive and commercial enterprises in private hands, albeit under highly expanded government influence. . . ."[33] The Bank admitted that it had negotiated for the private sector in its dealings with the government, insisting on new "clear and consistent rules of the game for the private sector," acceptable to the Bank, as a precondition for any further Bank lending.[34] Although there was brief mention of the fact that Nicaraguan exports faced declining prices, the principal focus of the Bank's critique rested with the alienation of the private sector and the consequences that would have on future exports, especially in view of the "unknown but probable poor efficiency of the state industries."[35]

That the country was only "marginally creditworthy" by 1982 was blamed primarily on problems in the growth rate of exports, leaving Nicaragua with foreign-exchange shortages as the "overwhelming medium-term problem." Solution of the problem—the expansion of exports—was said to be contingent on private sector participation. And that private sector cooperation, the Bank concluded, "will not be achieved in the near future."[36]

The Alternative Structuralist View

ECLA has long led the hemisphere's campaign to increase awareness of the extent to which Latin American development problems are presently hindered by the deterioration in prices for products exported from the region and increases in prices of those that are imported. The campaign was particularly relevant to the first five years of the Nicaraguan Revolution. Table 10.3, for example, shows that Nicaragua generated strong increases in the *quantity* of exports in two out of three of the years for which the new government was responsible for plantings. Export production was up 13

TABLE 10.3
EVOLUTION OF EXTERNAL TRADE RELATIONS: NICARAGUA, CENTRAL AMERICA, AND NON-OIL-EXPORTING LATIN AMERICA

	1975	1976	1977	1978	1979	1980	1981	1982	1983[a]	1981–83
Exports: Percent growth of quantities										
Nicaragua	6.3	6.1	-2.7	6.7	-8.1	-30.7	13.0	-9.7	7.9	11.2
Central America[b]	2.3	5.8	1.2	5.0	11.5	-6.7	-2.1	-12.1	-4.7	-18.9
Latin America[c]	0.0	9.7	8.3	10.0	10.2	5.3	13.2	-3.3	9.1	19.0
Exports: Percent growth of unit values										
Nicaragua	-7.1	36.3	24.3	-4.9	-4.5	14.2	-1.9	-5.0	-5.0	-11.9
Central America	5.6	24.8	30.8	-3.8	0.5	8.9	-6.7	-1.4	-0.8	-8.8
Latin America	-0.7	8.9	13.8	-2.5	10.7	12.2	-7.1	-6.7	-5.1	-18.9
Imports: Percent growth of quantities										
Nicaragua	-22.4	-0.2	23.7	-28.8	-48.6	95.1	7.5	-31.4	6.8	-31.4
Central America	-12.3	10.3	16.8	1.7	-10.4	11.4	-6.5	-24.7	2.4	0
Latin America	-5.7	-3.8	4.8	5.3	9.1	2.2	-6.9	-17.7	-13.2	-24.6
Imports: Percent growth in unit value										
Nicaragua	15.0	3.4	6.3	10.3	14.6	23.1	3.9	5.0	3.0	3.9
Central America	12.9	5.1	10.1	6.4	13.8	19.6	4.8	4.6	0.4	0
Latin America	9.4	4.3	5.7	6.3	21.7	26.9	6.8	-3.2	-4.2	6.8
Terms of trade: Percent change										
Nicaragua	-16.1	17.7	27.4	-11.3	-11.9	-1.4	-5.8	-9.5	-7.8	-17.3
Central America	—	16.7	28.8	-9.9	-11.5	-3.8	-11.3	-5.7	-2.2	0
Latin America	-9.4	4.2	6.7	-7.6	-2.4	-7.2	-13.1	-7.6	-1.6	-22.3

Sources: U.N. Economic Commission for Latin America, "Preliminary Overview of the Latin American Economy During 1983," E/CEPAL/G.1279, December 29, 1983; and Economic Survey of Latin America, various annual issues.
[a] Preliminary data based on mid-year estimates.
[b] Unweighted averages for the five traditional Central American nations: Costa Rica, El Salvador, Guatemala, Honduras, and Nicaragua.
[c] Non-oil-exporting countries, that is, excluding Mexico, Peru, Venezuela, and Trinidad & Tobago.

percent in 1980 and 7.9 percent in 1983. The damages of the insurrection in 1979 that disrupted plantings of the crops to be exported in 1980 led to the 30 percent reduction in export production that year. The decline in 1982 has been directly attributed in a separate ECLA document to the severe floods of May 1982 that left 70,000 persons homeless and destroyed nearly 45 percent of the cotton plantings.[37] The net increase of 11.2 percent from 1981 to 1983 contrasts markedly with the *decrease* of 18.9 percent for the Central American region as a whole, including four nations that presumably had no similar "difficulties" with private sector production!

The prices that Nicaragua received for its export products, on the other hand, fell by 11.9 percent from 1981 to 1983, considerably more than the average for Central America (8.8 percent). At the same time, the international prices of the products Nicaragua imported increased by 11.9 percent in those same three years and by 35 percent from 1980 to 1983. Once again, that was a greater increase than either the Central American average (9.8 percent from 1981 to 1983, 29.5 percent from 1980 to 1983) or the non-oil-exporting Latin American average. The net weighted result of the two price trends is reflected in the "terms-of-trade" data also shown in Table 10.3. Nicaraguan terms-of-trade deteriorated by 24.5 percent from 1980 to 1983, and by 23.1 percent in the last three of those four years. The Central American regionwide average also showed considerable decline in terms of trade, but not equivalent to that faced by Nicaragua. ECLA's reports each year on Nicaragua noted, without comment or evaluation, the improvements in the economy that occurred. Improvements in the distribution of income and social programs that benefited broad sectors of the population, financed by expansion of the government deficit and covered by foreign borrowing, were juxtaposed by ECLA against the deterioration of the terms of trade and, for 1982, the severe "climatological" difficulties of the year. Those reports also noted, among the factors that Nicaragua had to face, "tensions provoked by groups opposed to the government that led to frequent situations of violence," "extraeconomic" factors such as the increase in allocations to national defense in response to that violence, "the obstruction of foreign capital markets," "capital flight," and "the resistance of some entrepreneurs to accept the economic policies of the government."[38]

ECLA noted in particular that the decrease in output in 1982 was closely associated with the government's difficulty that year in obtaining the external finance needed to cover the shortfall in exports.[39] "These adverse conditions alone," it noted, "would have been sufficient to slow the expansionary trend in the economy and the execution of a variety of social programs that were to have been initiated that year."[40] The year 1982 was also the first in which the deliberate policies of reducing financial assistance to Nicaragua were initiated by the World Bank. A rebound in external financial assistance in 1983 was accomplished despite the fact that the World Bank and the Inter-American Development Bank had acceded to strong and public pressure from the U.S. government to reduce lending to Nicaragua.

More-Radical Critiques

Some of the most coherent criticism from the Left of the Nicaraguan economic strategies came from within Nicaragua itself. Much of the Left outside of Nicaragua tended to hold in abeyance its critique of the Nicaraguan model because the external aggression that Nicaragua faced required that solidarity be considered first.

At risk of creating a caricature, one can extrapolate from private conversations and indicate the critique that might have been forthcoming. There are three dimensions of the Nicaraguan model that could be seen as inconsistent from a Marxist-Leninist perspective. First, the Sandinistas were creating a mass of internal contradictions and inconsistencies for the transition to a truly socialist state by offering or promising the private sector a continued and significant role in the economy. Second, the decision to continue to participate in the capitalist-dominated system of growth led by primary-product exports limited the possibilities for future growth as much as it limited the historical development of the nation and continued to subject the nation as a whole to the opportunities for U.S. economic boycotts and to the vagaries of international commodity price fluctuations. Third, the severity of the financial attack upon Nicaragua should have been anticipated at the time that Nicaragua agreed to honor the foreign debts of Somoza; with more than 35 percent of exports required by 1983 simply to serve the foreign debt, default and separation from the international financial markets would have enhanced the prospects for full and rapid transition to socialism.

One can find some of these theoretical criticisms even among the writings of those who support the new Nicaragua. Henri Weber, for example, noted that during the first year "the FSLN's 'generosity' towards its real enemies and false allies (the bourgeoisie) aroused some fears, both in Nicaragua and elsewhere, that the Sandinistas were giving in to the disastrous Stalinist line of 'revolution by stages' with the risk of losing control to the counter-revolution."[41] He also expressed concern that the FSLN's "productivist" austerity policy was roughly implemented and that it was "not winning them only friends."[42]

A good example of the internal critique from the left can be found in Vargas.[43] Writing in Nicaragua, he criticized the Sandinistas for their "consumerist" and "productivist" orientation, especially during the first years. They failed to take advantage, he suggested, of the ' 'passivity of the greater bourgeoisie and the relative neutrality of the middle and petty bourgeoisie" when they did not press for greater and more radical economic transformations in the first years.[44] He would have expanded the state sector much more rapidly.[45] Price freezes in the growing state sector effectively nullified savings in that sector, he suggests, and served to subsidize the profit levels of the private sector. Monetary expansion without essentially "squeezing" the private sector further created multiple opportunities for the private sector to maximize profits by channeling them into nonproductive, speculative ventures.[46] He criticized the government for insufficient *golpes* against the "privileged classes."[47] And, providing further irony, he suggested the same conclusion proposed by the World Bank at about the same time. It was, he suggested, "impossible to contemplate a 'harmonic,' equilibrated and parallel development of the private sector and the state sector."[48]

These comments are in no sense "representative" of all thinking about Nicaragua by adherents of the more radical analyses of underdevelopment. They do indicate, however, the extent to which much of Nicaraguan policy since the Revolution represented new and quite different approaches to the organization of a mixed economy. The Nicaraguan example created new waves of debate, opened new discussions of the possibilities for public and private interaction in the economy, and led to richer analysis by both structuralist and Marxist analysts of Latin American phenomena. The response from the conservative perspective, however, was reflected in a series of policies from the U.S. government that imply a fear of the Nicaraguan model (see Chapter 11 of this volume). The strength of the apparent fear raises further the significance of the model.

SUMMARY AND CONCLUSION

It is clear, first, that the set of economic policies implemented in Nicaragua represent, in almost every case, policies not only consistent with a long tradition of Latin American non-Marxist structuralist interpretations but also policies that have been advocated, supported, and even financed at one time or another by previous U.S. administrations. To brand them Marxist-Leninist, as if that might somehow justify economic and military aggression, is a disservice to all understanding of both Marxist and structuralist traditions. The Nicaraguan model, as developed during the Revolution's first five years, may be a threat to those who view the world solely from a conservative, orthodox, *laissez faire* perspective, for it was a real threat to those interests for which that perspective may provide a set of theoretical apologetics.

If Nicaragua were capable of demonstrating that a fundamentally "mixed" economy, with significant continued private sector production amid clear state regulation oriented first and foremost to the fulfillment of basic needs of the poor majority, could sustain growth and redistribution toward that majority, the Nicaraguan model would become exceedingly attractive to the impoverished majority of much of the rest of the world. If it remains the policy of the governments that identify with the orthodox *laissez faire* perspective to attempt to prevent the implementation of reforms like those of Nicaragua wherever they may appear, the impoverished majority of the Third World population will have further incentive to look at the Nicaraguan model of revolutionary insurrection to achieve those reforms.

The Nicaraguan economic model may be seen as an attempt to implement the "structuralist" policies of the Economic Commission for Latin America more fully and more systematically than ever before. The severity of the counterrevolutionary backlash may do more to discourage attempts at similar "mixed-economy" reforms in other countries than the marked failures of partial, half-hearted implementations of these approaches that have been seen widely throughout Latin America prior to the Nicaraguan Revolution.

There was little question at the fifth anniversary celebration that the Nicaraguan Revolution would survive beyond its five years. The nature of the economic system it would have at its tenth anniversary, however, remained unclear at the end of the first five years. The economic system that would characterize Nicaragua in the second five years was being melded in the crucible of open aggression. Every day of external economic and military tension lessened the likelihood that the existing private sector in Nicaragua would be left a major role in the economy of the future. It would be an important historical irony, and a major setback to the creation of new modes of economic organization, if the Nicaraguan experiment with a new form of mixed economy were forestalled by those who claimed to support the private sector role that was so strongly a part of that experiment.

NOTES

1. Kissinger Commission, *Report of the National Bipartisan Commission on Central America* (Washington, D.C.: U.S. Government Printing Office, 1984), p. 30.

2. "Nicaragua goza la tasa más alta de crecimiento en las Américas," *Barricada*, January 23, 1984, p. 1.

3. Economic Commission for Latin America (ECLA), *Notas Para el Estudio de América Latina, 1983: Nicaragua*, E/CEPAL/Mexico/1984/L.8.

4. Inforpress Centroamericana, "Nicaragua, Centroamérica 1983: Análisis Económicos y Políticos Sobre la Región (Guatemala City; Inforpress Centroamericana, December 1983), p. 27.

5. International Bank for Reconstruction and Development (IBRD), *The Economic Development of Nicaragua* (Baltimore: Johns Hopkins University Press, 1953), p. 4.

6. Ibid., p. 22.

7. Ibid., pp. 97–98.

8. Ibid., p. 6.

9. William Cline and Enrique Delgado, *Economic Integration in Central America* (Washington, D.C.: The Brookings Institution, 1978), p. 61; and Inter-American Development Bank, *Social and Economic Progress in Latin America* (Washington, D.C.: IDB, 1978), p. 8.

10. Kissinger Commission, p. 23.

11. World Bank, *Nicaragua: The Challenge of Reconstruction*, Report No. 3524-NI (Washington, D.C., October 9, 1981), p. 8.

12. Ibid.

13. ECLA, *The Crisis in Central America: Its Origins, Scope and Consequences*, E/CEPAL/G.1261 (Santiago, Chile, September 15, 1983), p. 1.

14. Ibid., p. 13.

15. René Herrera Zúñiga, "Los antecedentes de la victoria," *Nexos*, November 1979, p. 23.

16. Ibid., p. 24.

17. Ibid., p. 27.

18. Cline and Delgado, *Economic Integration*, p. 188.

19. ECLA, *Estudio Económico de América Latina, 1980: Nicaragua*, E/CEPAL/L.777 (Santiago, Chile: United Nations, May 1981).

20. World Bank, *Nicaragua*.

21. Ibid., p. 2.

22. Ibid., p. 24.

23. ECLA, *Nicaragua: Repercusiones Económicas de los Acontecimientos Políticos Recientes* E/CEPAL/G.1091 (Santiago, Chile: United Nations, August 1979).

24. World Bank, *Nicaragua*, p. ii.

25. Ibid., p. 57.

26. Ibid.

27. Ibid.

28. The Junta for National Reconstruction, "The Philosophy and Politics of the Government of Nicaragua," in *The Nicaragua Reader: Documents of a Revolution Under Fire*, edited by Peter Rosset and John Vandermeer (New York: Grove Press, 1983), pp. 254–268.

29. Ibid.

30. Ibid

31. Consejo Superior de la Empresa Privada (COSEP), *Análisis del Programa de Reconstrucción Nacional* (Managua, 1981).

32. World Bank, *Country Program Paper: Nicaragua* (Washington, D.C., February 16, 1982).

33. Ibid., p. 1.

34. Ibid., p. 12.

35. Ibid., p. 10.

36. Ibid.

37. ECLA, *Nicaragua: Las Inundaciones de Mayo de 1982 y sus Repercusiones Sobre el Desarrollo Económico y Social del País* (Versión Provisional), E/CEPAL/MEX/1982/R.2 (Mexico City: United Nations Economic and Security Council, June 22, 1982).

38. ECLA, *Estudios Económicos de América Latina, 1982: Nicaragua*, E/CEPAL/L.286/ADD.4 (Santiago, Chile: United Nations, 1983).

244 MICHAEL E. CONROY

39. Ibid., p. 1.

40. Ibid.

41. Henri Weber, "Nicaragua: The Sandinist Revolution," Chapter 5 in *Crisis in the Caribbean*, edited by Fitzroy Ambursley and Robin Cohen (New York: Monthly Review Press, 1983), p. 106.

42. Ibid., p. 111.

43. Oscar René Vargas, "Nicaragua: Economía y Revolución II," *Coyocoacan*, April-June 1981.

44. Ibid., p. 67.

45. Ibid., p. 83.

46. Ibid., p. 87.

47. Ibid.

48. Ibid., p. 88.

Chapter 11

External Constraints

SYLVIA MAXFIELD
RICHARD STAHLER-SHOLK

For Nicaragua, with a small economy extremely vulnerable to the vicissitudes of the international capitalist economy, dependency is a fact of life. Historically, the Nicaraguan economy depended on the revenue of two or three agricultural exports sold to two or three countries. It also depended on foreign loans to meet the shortfall between income earned on these exports and expenditure on imports. Almost all of Nicaragua's productive investment had to be financed by foreign loans because the country's capacity to generate domestic savings was so limited.

The overthrow of the Somoza regime raised hope for a new model of economic development that would mitigate the ill effects of dependency. As stated in the Sandinistas' first Economic Plan, "the Sandinista Reactivation Program has as additional objectives, besides the traditional model of reactivation: to progressively reduce the external dependence of the people of Sandino."[1]

The road Nicaragua had to follow after 1979 was not easy. The entire developing world faced an economic crisis marked by high interest rates and declining terms of trade for agricultural products; the Nicaraguan and other Central American economies were on a wartime footing; and the U.S. government was masterminding an international economic blockade of Nicaragua. Despite these difficulties, Nicaragua in the first five years after the Triumph over Somoza struggled toward managing its dependence with creativity, optimism, and a surprising degree of success.

DIVERSIFYING TRADE PARTNERS

A major goal of the new Sandinista government was to diversify the country's international economic relations. Exports accounted for about 30

Richard Stahler-Sholk is grateful for travel grants from the Graduate Division and the Center for Latin American Studies at the University of California/Berkeley, and the Tinker Foundation.

percent of GNP in the 1970s, and 60–70 percent of export earnings came from four primary products: cotton, coffee, beef, and sugar. Half a century of Somoza family rule had established a model of agroexport production that sustained the economic and political power of a narrow elite and an economic structure of exaggerated dependency on the United States for imports and finance. Instead of relying primarily on one country or region for aid and trade, the Sandinistas wanted to "walk on four legs"—that is, they hoped to develop balanced relations with four groups of countries: the United States, other developed capitalist countries, developing countries, and socialist countries.

Since early in this century, the United States had been Nicaragua's main trade partner. However, beginning in the 1950s, Nicaraguan dependence on the United States for export markets declined. Between 1950 and 1978, trade with the United States dropped from 75 percent of Nicaragua's total trade to 25 percent.[2] The rising importance of exports to Western Europe and the Central American Common Market (CACM) largely explains this change. However, dependence on the United States did not fall as much as these numbers seem to indicate. Much of the apparent diversification actually represented trade with U.S. multinational corporations that had moved to Central America and Europe during the 1950s and 1960s.

After the Sandinistas came to power, trade reliance on the United States declined further. While exports to the United States in 1980 accounted for 36 percent of total export value, by 1983 they were under 20 percent.[3] This shift was partly a reflection of conscious government policy to reduce reliance on U.S. markets, but in part it was also forced on Nicaragua by U.S. efforts to disrupt commerical relations.

For example, in May 1983 the United States suddenly cut the quota for sugar imports from Nicaragua by 90 percent, reallocating Nicaragua's portion to Honduras, Costa Rica, and El Salvador. Sugar was Nicaragua's third largest export, accounting for 9 percent of export earnings in 1982, with 57 percent of sugar exports going to the United States and major new investments in sugar production under way.[4] The U.S. move was condemned by the General Agreement on Tariffs and Trade (GATT) as a violation of GATT rules on quantitative import restrictions.

The U.S. action had several ironic twists. First, it is reminiscent of the sequence of events that led to Cuba's economic dependence on the Soviet Union. The Nicaraguan economy, however, was less dependent on sugar, and a huge Soviet subsidy was not an option. A second irony in the sugar quota action lies in the fact that over 50 percent of Nicaraguan finished sugar was produced by the private sector, and over 60 percent of the cane was planted by private farmers. Any loss of sugar export earnings would hurt the private sector, which the United States had seemed so anxious to protect. New markets were found for the 1983 sugar crop, primarily Iran and Algeria; but the new buyers would pay only 7 cents a pound, much nearer the world price than the highly subsidized 17 cents that the United States paid under its sugar import program.[5]

Nicaragua remained dependent on the U.S. market and vulnerable to disruption of commerce for several other exports. Meat and fish accounted for 14 percent of total 1982 exports, and the United States took 80 percent and 89 percent of those exports, respectively. Meat sales to the United States were temporarily interrupted by changes in U.S. Department of Agriculture standards; and in 1982 the United States threatened to cut off beef imports if Nicaragua went ahead with plans to purchase a certain breed of cattle from Cuba, ostensibly due to the risk of spreading hoof-and-mouth disease.[6] Bananas, making up 2 3 percent of exports in 1981, were marketed entirely in the United States; this created problems in October 1982 when Standard Fruit Company, a subsidiary of Castle & Cooke, suddenly pulled all its banana operations out of Nicaragua. The pullout violated a contract signed by Standard and the Sandinistas in January 1981, under which Nicaragua was to buy out the Standard operation for $13 million and the company was to provide technical assistance and marketing over a five-year period. In a coordinated action reminiscent of the copper transnationals' actions against Allende's Chile, the three big banana transnationals attempted to torpedo Nicaragua's efforts to market its own bananas without Standard. However, through quick action, Nicaraguan government representatives were able to arrange sales in California and sign a one-year shipping contract with a U.S. firm, in order to resume banana exports.

A number of other factors disrupted Nicaraguan trade with the United States. The U.S. blockade of Cuba affected Nicaragua when the Nicaraguan chemical company Policasa, which imported inputs from the United States, tried to export polyvinyl chloride to Cuba in 1982. The U.S. Commerce Department also used technology-export restrictions and other technicalities to delay licenses for U.S. exports to Nicaragua.[7] The U.S. closing of all Nicaraguan consulates in June 1983 also made it difficult for Nicaragua to carry on normal commercial relations with the United States. Moreover, Nicaragua's external financing crunch necessitated a reorientation of trade toward countries that offered export credits.

U.S. disruption of trade with Nicaragua still did not approach the level of the full-scale commercial blockade directed against Cuba since 1960. However, the precipitous character of the disruptions required an accelerated (and therefore more costly) diversification.

The Nicaraguans fared well in their effort to diversify by increasing trade with the other three groups targeted in 1979. Exports to developing countries grew from 19 percent of total Nicaraguan exports in 1980 to 25 percent in 1982. China, Taiwan, and Mexico became important new markets, accounting for much of this growth. Trade with developed countries (excluding the United States), already relatively large in 1979, continued to account for over 40 percent of total exports, with no single country accounting for more than 10 percent.[8] As Table 11.1 shows, sales to Japan and the socialist countries increased significantly.

On the import side, Nicaragua made several improvements in the first five years as well. The most important source of imports throughout the period was the developing country group, accounting for close to half of all imports. One dramatic change in this category came in imports from Mexico, which increased tenfold between 1980 and 1983, due primarily to oil imports. Imports from the socialist bloc grew from next to nothing to a sizable share of total imports.

Although trade with the socialist bloc grew in the first five years, Nicaragua remained overwhelmingly dependent on trade with the capitalist world, and the United States continued to be the country's single largest trading partner. The increase in trade with the socialist countries reflected a move away from exclusive commercial relations with capitalist countries rather than a policy of alignment with the Soviet bloc.

While the overall value of imports from the United States declined, Nicaragua remained dependent on her northern neighbor in several strategic product categories. In 1982 the United States supplied 42 percent of imported chemicals (used largely in agricultural production), 64 percent of imported raw materials used in all production, and 44 percent of imported spare parts.[9] Spare parts were critical in keeping the Nicaraguan economy running, particularly because much of the country's machinery—in sugar production, for instance—dated back to the early decades of this century. Because of this strategic reliance, the Nicaraguans were particularly concerned with reducing dependence on the United States in these areas. The Ministry of Industry (for its chemical, instant coffee, cereal, beer, and tanning plants) and the state-owned oil company both relied on the United States for over 80 percent of the spare parts needed in their daily operations.[10] In some cases spare parts could have been bought in other Latin American countries, but the prices would have been higher because these countries produce under U.S. patents. This form of dependence seemed likely to persist for some time, because the alternative of converting the entire industrial plant to machinery and technology provided by other industrialized countries was costly.

Imports of petroleum and petroleum products, clearly crucial to the economy, constituted an area of particular vulnerability for the Nicaraguans. A large percentage of petroleum derivatives were imported by Esso, which bought exclusively from the United States. Until 1983, Esso had allowed six months for payment on these imports; thereafter, in a

TABLE 11.1
NICARAGUA: DIVERSIFICATION OF TRADING PARTNERS (PERCENT OF TOTAL TRADE)

Economic Regions	1977		1980		1981		1982		1983	
	Exports	Imports	Exports	Imports	Exports	Imports	Exports	Imports	Exports	Imports
Central American Common Market	21.0	21.6	16.7	33.9	13.9	21.1	12.9	15.1	7.8	15.3
Latin American Integration Association	2.6	14.7	0.1	20.2	2.2	26.0	3.6	27.2	2.1	23.5
Mexico	(1.2)	(2.0)	(—)	(2.2)	(1.8)	(12.0)	(3.5)	(20.0)	(2.1)	(19.8)
Venezuela	(1.4)	(11.4)	(—)	(16.8)	(0.1)	(8.7)	(0.03)	(5.2)	(—)	(0.6)
European Economic Community	28.4	12.6	28.8	7.8	19.4	11.5	23.5	14.1	25.7	9.7
United States	22.8	28.8	36.0	27.5	25.8	26.3	22.0	19.0	18.1	19.4
Japan	11.0	10.1	2.8	3.2	11.2	2.8	11.1	2.4	15.3	2.4
Canada	0.4	0.7	6.3	1.2	5.2	2.4	4.5	1.6	1.5	2.5
COMECON (Council of Mutual Economic Assistance)	1.0	0.3	2.7	0.2	7.3	3.3	7.4	11.5	12.7	16.6
Others	12.8	11.2	6.6	6.0	15.0	6.6	15.0	9.1	16.8	10.6
Total	100.0	100.0	100.0	100.0	100.0	100.0	100.0	100.0	100.0	100.0

Source: Office of Planning, Ministry of Foreign Trade.

series of antagonistic moves, including refusing to continue renting Nicaragua the tankers used to import oil from Mexico, Esso demanded cash on receipt.[11] This change in credit policy was characteristic of changes in the policies of many U.S. firms doing business with Nicaragua in this period.

Until 1982, Nicaragua received most of its oil supply from Venezuela and Mexico on concessionary terms under the San José accords. Venezuela ceased sale in 1982 as a result of Nicaragua's failure to make contracted payments. This left Nicaragua entirely dependent on Mexican supply at a time when Mexico was reportedly under pressure from the International Monetary Fund (IMF) to cease its oil shipments to Nicaragua.[12] Mexico announced reduction of concessionary oil supplies to Nicaragua at the end of 1983. The Soviet Union subsequently began oil shipments, reportedly supplying 25 percent of Nicaragua's oil imports in early 1984.[13] Nicaragua's dependence on oil imports was underscored by the CIA's sabotage attacks on oil storage and pipeline facilities at Corinto and Puerto Sandino in September/October 1983, which destroyed over 3 million gallons of fuel. The CIA-directed mining of Corinto harbor, which began in January 1984, posed new obstacles to Nicaraguan commerce, since most of Nicaragua's foreign trade passed through Corinto.

GENERATING FOREIGN EXCHANGE BY PROMOTING EXPORTS

In addition to dependency on a limited number of trade partners, the Sandinista government faced the related problem of relying on export of a limited number of commodities. Since World War II the Nicaraguan economy had depended on four main exports: cotton, coffee, sugar, and beef, which together accounted for 60–70 percent of exports by the 1970s. Actually this made Nicaragua more crop-diversified than many other small developing countries; Cuba, for instance, depended since World War II on one crop—sugar—for well over 50 percent of the country's export earnings. Nevertheless, sudden variation in the world price of one of Nicaragua's main export crops or an unusually low crop yield would send the whole modernized portion of the economy into depression.

Nicaragua's historical model of development (that is, dependence on a few agricultural exports, coupled with extreme concentration of power and wealth at the disposal of the exporting elite) fostered division of the economy into a dynamic sector impelled by production for export and a stagnant sector of subsistence farmers producing basic grains. Because of this dualism, economic booms in the export-oriented sector historically did not help to develop the Nicaraguan economy as a whole. This model of development also led to neglect of the nonexport-oriented sector, decline in production of basic subsistence crops, and increasing need to import basic foods.

Ideally, to overcome this dependence, Nicaragua needed to diversify its exports and promote those exports that, through linkages with production of other goods and services, would help stimulate the entire domestic economy. However, the economy could not be transformed overnight, and the Nicaraguans were caught between the desire to diversify their exports and the need to promote those exports that were proven foreign exchange earners. Reactivating traditional exports implied a problematic reliance on the national bourgeoisie. Yet the need to earn foreign exchange to pay debts and to buy vital imports was more urgent than the need to diversify.

In the first five years after Somoza's overthrow, Nicaragua was unable to generate a trade surplus, although the gap was narrowed. The first step in trade policy after the Sandinista victory was to nationalize foreign trade and create a series of separate state enterprises, each responsible for marketing one of Nicaragua's main exports, including cotton, coffee, sugar, and meat and fish. Between 1980 (the first full year of Sandinista economic management) and 1983, Nicaragua's trade deficit fell 20 percent, from nearly $450 million to $350 million.[14] However, this primarily reflected a large reduction in imports rather than a great rise in export income.

Agricultural export promotion was an immediate necessity for reactivating the economy. In the case of two of the country's three main export crops, Nicaragua met the production challenge with relative success in the first three post-1979 production cycles. This was due in part to an export incentive law passed in early 1982. This law allowed agricultural export producers to claim a percentage (varying for each product) of their earnings in "Certificates of Foreign Exchange Availability," which could be used for dollar-based import at the favorable "parallel" exchange rate. The volume of cotton exported grew almost fourfold between 1980 and 1983, while that of sugar almost doubled.[15]

Despite growth in agroexport *volume*, the total *value* of exports actually declined in the first five years of the revolutionary reconstruction process because of a worldwide downswing in agricultural prices (see Table 11.2). As shown in Table 11.2, declining terms of trade for agricultural products meant that Nicaragua had to export more and more just to be able to maintain constant foreign exchange income. The cost of manufactured imports rose relative to agricultural prices. For example, in 1977 it took 4.4 tons of Nicaraguan coffee to buy a tractor; by 1981 it cost 11.2 tons of coffee.[16]

While Nicaragua's major agricultural exports suffered declining terms of trade, industrial exports were crippled by the country's worsening

TABLE 11.2
NICARAGUA'S TERMS OF TRADE INDEXES (1970 = 100)

	1977	1978	1979	1980	1981	1982
Terms of trade for goods	112.3	96.5	91.9	89.5	83.0	72.9
Buying power of exports of goods*	177.4	164.4	141.2	84.5	89.5	69.6

*Quantity of exports, adjusted by the index of terms of trade.
Source: CEPAL [Economic Commission for Latin America], "Notas para el estudio de América Latina, 1982: Nicaragua," E/CEPAL/MEX/1983/L.13 (United Nations, March 1, 1983).

foreign exchange shortage and by regional economic stagnation. The foreign exchange shortage limited importation of productive inputs for industrial products such as plastics, pharmaceuticals, insecticides, and other chemicals. Consequently, industrial production declined 3 percent in 1982, and industrial exports fell from close to 20 percent of total exports in 1980 to 15 percent in 1982.[17] Since Nicaragua was only a competitive exporter of industrial products within Central America, the decline of Central American trade due to regional warfare accentuated the drop in Nicaraguan industrial exports.

Given the external constraints on traditional agricultural and industrial export possibilities, Nicaragua launched a program to promote nontraditional agricultural exports. Under this program, every product Nicaragua had ever exported was reviewed for its net foreign-exchange-generating potential, existing domestic production capacity, marketability, and the domestic economic linkages it could promote. From over 170 products reviewed, 14 were selected for promotion. These included sesame seeds, melons, peanuts, mangos, ginger, castorseed, garlic, and onions. The program was quite successful: The value of nontraditional exports rose from $14 million in 1979 (2 to 3 percent of total exports) to $39 million in 1983 (10 percent of total).[18]

IMPORT SUBSTITUTION

Through promotion of exports and reduction of imports, the Sandinistas projected that they would achieve a trade balance by 1990.[19] However, based on their record during the first five years, and unless the declining trend in Nicaragua's terms of trade were reversed, that goal would have to be achieved primarily by substituting domestic products for imported ones.

In 1980 Nicaragua's largest import categories were consumer nondurables (24.2 percent of total imports), oil (19.6 percent), and raw materials for industry (28.0 percent). Expenditure on consumer nondurables was reduced 48 percent by 1982, primarily by restricting imports of luxury goods and goods such as soap, which are produced domestically at somewhat lower quality than imports.[20] Two projects were launched to further reduce food imports. One was an African palm project. African palm yields an oil that, refined, is a perfectly acceptable if nontraditional cooking oil. Although Nicaragua had the capacity to refine oil, the country was importing all oil used in cooking. A project was also launched to grow cocoa, which was also imported.

Fuel oil remained one of Nicaragua's largest import expenditures. A large geothermal plant, Momotombo, tapping volcanic heat to generate electricity, became operational in 1983. The plant reduced oil import expenditures 10–15 percent, saving the country between $20 and $30 million out of an average oil import bill for 1980–82 of $156 million annually (roughly 20 percent of import expenditure).[21]

In an effort to reduce import of raw materials and capital goods used in industrial production, the government launched an "innovators program" under which workers were rewarded for designing methods to substitute domestically produced goods for imported ones. Among numerous examples of worker creativity is the case of several railroad maintenance workers who designed and constructed a crane for lifting heavy cargo that would have cost $70,000 to import, for the equivalent of $26,000 in córdobas.[22]

The private sector's response to lack of foreign exchange has been mixed. One positive example is the case of the country's major rum company. Privately owned and operated, the company reduced its imports from $5 million a year to $1.3 million in 1983 through a series of innovations in the production process. These included recovering bottles (92 percent of all bottles were recycled); building a workshop for repairing the cardboard packaging boxes; inventing a formula for the labeling glue that used domestically available ingredients; and substituting domestic products for imported chemical inputs.[23]

HARNESSING FOREIGN EXCHANGE TO IMPROVE SOCIAL WELFARE

Another aspect of international economic dependency is that due to inequalities inherent in the organization of the international economy;

developing countries have a tendency to run balance-of-payments deficits, build up "addictions" to foreign loans, and face recurring foreign exchange crises. Nicaragua was no exception. Of the various mechanisms that developing countries have adopted to alleviate these crises—including the traditional IMF formula of currency devaluation and domestic deflation, the new orthodox economic liberalization pioneered in Chile and Argentina in the 1970s, and capital controls combined with multiple exchange rates— the Sandinistas chose a combination of exchange controls and domestic austerity designed to burden the wealthy more than the poor.

The Nicaraguan banking system was reorganized under state control in 1980, and acquisition of foreign exchange for import or travel abroad was, by 1983, completely controlled by the Central Bank. The Bank subsidized or taxed imports and exports of goods and services by varying the price charged or paid for foreign exchange. In response to a foreign exchange crunch that had become desperate by mid-1981, the Sandinistas adopted a multiple exchange rate system that held back excessive demand for imports by regulating the distribution and cost of foreign exchange. The official exchange rate remained 10 córdobas to 1 dollar, but the Central Bank added a "parallel" rate of 28 to 1. This amounted to a targeted devaluation, to subsidize certain exports and to tax nonessential imports.

Despite national control of banking and this multiple exchange rate system, capital flight and black market sale and purchase of dollars continued to be a problem. In 1982, capital flight was estimated at $113 million, or 5 percent of GNP.[24] In addition, the black market exchange rate went from 40 to 1 in January 1983 to 90 to 1 in January 1984. In an attempt to control these problems, a series of new exchange control policies were announced in January and May 1983. To reduce the incentive for foreigners to exchange dollars on the black market, as of January 1983 foreign visitors were required to pay for lodging and international phone calls in dollars, and to change a minimum of $60 at 10 to 1 (later, 28 to 1) upon entering the country. Foreign travel by nationals was discouraged by changing the calculation of airfares from 10 to 1 to 28 to 1. In addition, government-licensed foreign exchange houses, found to be closely linked to the black market, were closed so that all foreign exchange dealings had to be carried out directly through the banking system. Possession of more than $500 on one's person or in one's home was made illegal. Unlimited dollar deposits could be made with the banks, but a ceiling of $10,000 was placed on the amount that could be withdrawn annually.

In addition to foreign exchange controls aimed at stemming capital flight and curbing the black market, the Sandinistas established criteria for allocation of foreign exchange that were intended to shift import consumption patterns in favor of the poor and to distribute the burden of import restrictions.

Allocating scarce foreign exchange required mechansisms for coordination with the private sector. In late 1981 and early 1982, the Nicaraguan government began to set up commissions for each productive sector, with representatives of both the relevant government ministries and business organizations, to draw up lists of priority categories of imports. The Nicaraguan Import Company (ENIMPORT) was set up to centralize review of public sector imports. Despite initial private sector suspicions, the allocation of foreign exchange did not discriminate against private producers in favor of state enterprises.[25] By mid-1982, each productive sector had set up technical commissions that met on a weekly basis to draw up priority lists for specific products to be imported.

A complementary Nicaraguan government structure evolved for reviewing the sectorial recommendations in light of available foreign exchange and making allocative decisions. The Technical Commission on Importation and Exportation (CTIE) received import requests, reviewed them with the appropriate agency/sector, and then forwarded them to the Commission for the Assignment of Foreign Exchange (CAD). The latter body, which met every two weeks and was presided over by Junta member Sergio Ramírez, included the Minister of Foreign Trade and the President of the Central Bank of Nicaragua. The CAD gave final authorization to the Central Bank to release foreign exchange. Top-priority items for the CAD in 1983 were foodstuffs, medicines, and certain basic goods considered to be essential inputs for production; importers of these items could purchase foreign exchange at 10 córdobas to the dollar. Goods falling under the category of "necessary" imports could be imported at 15 to 1.

The change in the types of goods and services imported during the first five years of the revolutionary process reflected the effort to give priority to the needs of the poor. In housing, for instance, there was a decline in imports of construction materials such as glass, wood, and special cement, and of furnishings such as rugs, electrical appliances, and kitchen utensils for the houses of the urban middle class; and a simultaneous increase in imports of prefabricated housing for the lower classes. In the case of transport, by 1982 imports of individual cars were down to 38 percent of the 1978 import level, while imports of buses and trucks had grown 113 percent, and of bicycles 222 percent. The change was also dramatic in food imports. Expenditure on basic food imports rose from $18 million in 1978 to $66 million in 1982, while expenditure on luxury food imports fell from $13 million in 1978 to $7 million in 1982.[26] With demand for basic foodstuffs soaring and production hampered by lack of foreign exchange to import necessary inputs, the Sandinista government instituted a system of price subsidies and rationing to insure food supplies for the poor.

In addition to changing short-run consumption patterns in favor of

the poor, another goal of the Sandinistas' international economic policy was to allocate foreign exchange in such a way as to promote domestic savings and investment and to reduce long-run reliance on foreign exchange. Although emphasis was placed on immediate mass consumption, long-term investment needs were not neglected. Between 1980 and 1982, expenditure on imports of construction and capital goods for agricultural and industrial production more than doubled, rising from 13 percent of total import expenditure to 24 percent of the total.

However, efforts to deepen Nicaragua's domestic economy and to promote domestic savings and investment could not be expected to bear fruit for many years. In the meantime, the Sandinistas had to continue to supplement domestic savings with foreign loans in order to satisfy the high capital formation expenditure necessary to reconstruct and transform the Nicaraguan economy. The minimum investment program for 1983–87 called for $2 billion.[27] Incomes from former Somoza properties and state control of export earnings were the primary domestic sources of investment funds, but these were not enough. The nature of the Sandinista mixed economy and political ideology precluded the use of other potential sources, such as nationalizing productive private capital or squeezing the poor. Historically, foreign direct investment in Nicaragua has not been large, and despite the Sandinistas' very lenient foreign investment law, it showed no signs of growing in the 1980s. Given these constraints, combined with rising debt service payments, the imperative to find foreign financing was great.

THE SEARCH FOR FOREIGN AID, LOANS, AND CREDITS

When the Government of National Reconstruction took stock of Nicaragua's international financial accounts in July 1979, red loomed everywhere. Somoza and his cohorts had siphoned over $500 million out of Nicaragua in the two years before they left. In the final days of the old regime, government ministries were ransacked, state bank accounts were drained, and Somoza's son went from bank to bank with a squad of National Guardsmen taking every cent of foreign exchange they could find. They left foreign exchange reserves amounting to only $3.5 million, and a $1.6 billion foreign debt (the highest per capita debt in Latin America at the time). The fighting and aerial bombing by the National Guard during the final eight-week Sandinista offensive left much of the country's economic infrastructure in ruins. Reconstruction was further hindered by floods and drought in 1982, which cost the country $447 million in crop loss and destruction—as much again as the cost of the war damage.[28] To rebuild the country, to survive as a nation, the Sandinistas had to seek large international loans, donations, and credits.

The Sandinistas chose to honor the foreign debt inherited from Somoza, which added to their burden, because they hoped it would give them a good credit rating internationally and bring in new loans. The decision, which surprised many observers who had expected Nicaragua to repudiate the debt, also reflected the multiclass base of the Revolution.

Although the Sandinistas ultimately won hegemony over the bourgeoisie in the class alliance against Somoza, they could not exclude them from the revolutionary government.[29] The private sector still represented some 60 percent of national production, and the Sandinistas were committed to a mixed economy. Bourgeois participation in the government helped limit immediate U.S. hostility and initially encouraged capitalist economic assistance to Nicaragua Libre. As George Black puts it,

> to stave off economic disaster, the Sandinistas . . . required a large injection of foreign aid with no strings attached, and a renegotiation of the . . . foreign debt on favorable terms. This in turn imposed constraints. Any . . . moves against the preserves of the bourgeoisie . . . would be guaranteed to invoke the wrath of the U.S., endangering the Sandinistas' indispensable friendships abroad and their requests for aid from foreign governments.[30]

The FSLN also deemed the entrepreneurial, managerial, and technical skills of the bourgeoisie vital to the reconstruction process. For their part, the representatives of the private sector remained in the government because they believed that with the economic and political assistance of their international friends, they could channel Nicaraguan development within a capitalist framework unfettered by Somoza's personal greed.

Private sector support and international credit came as a package deal. The private sector had much to gain directly from good relations with international financiers. International loans would help it economically, as well as strengthen it politically vis-a-vis the Sandinistas. The Carter Administration continued its strategy of trying to bolster the private sector by channeling aid to it directly. Of the $75 million Carter aid package, $60 million was earmarked for the private sector. In addition, House approval of the aid was predicated on the Sandinistas' appointment of "moderates" to the ruling Junta. The FSLN-dominated government needed the international funding that the private sector could attract, but it was wary of the political leverage this conferred on the capitalist members of the government.

Nicaragua could not have circumvented the problems created by the interplay of FSLN/private sector/international interests, short of going the Cuban route of relying on the Soviet Union for foreign aid. From the Soviet standpoint this was impossible, for economic reasons. The Soviets were unable and unwilling to bear the cost of supporting Nicaragua the way they had supported Cuba.[31] From the Nicaraguan point of view, there was no desire to exchange dependence on the United States for dependence on the Soviet Union. In addition, the Cubans themselves advised against the Soviet option, supporting instead the Sandinista decision to try to preserve a mixed economy.

Given the country's serious need for external finance, the complex role of the private sector and its international allies in the Nicaraguan Revolution, and the limits of Soviet assistance, debt repudiation was not among the choices open to the Sandinistas. This combination of international and domestic constraints is reflected in the reason for repayment given by a Sandinista member of the ruling Junta: "We are not going to give any argument against us . . . to the counter-revolutionaries . . . who are looking for any excuse to get at us."[32]

So, in 1980 Nicaragua renegotiated its $580 million debt to commercial banks, which yielded an unusually lenient settlement that provided for a five-year grace period on principal repayments.[33] Between 1980 and 1982, Nicaragua made every interest payment on its foreign debt, a record almost unparalleled anywhere in Latin America in those crisis-ridden years. (This record helped countries friendly to Nicaragua to continue their bilateral assistance to Nicaragua in the face of U.S. pressure to halt it.) However, despite Nicaragua's efforts to be a good "citizen" of the international financial community, the Reagan Administration began almost immediately to organize an international financial blockade.

Bilateral U.S. aid was cut beginning in February 1981 when $15 million of the $75 million loan approved under Carter was blocked by the Reagan Administration. One month later, a $10 million PL-480 wheat credit was suspended, and in April 1981 an $11 million loan for rural education and health care was cut. At the end of April 1981, the United States announced indefinite suspension of all aid to Nicaragua, including an end to Export-Import Bank guarantees to finance U.S. exports to Nicaragua.[34] Nicaragua was pointedly excluded from the Caribbean Basin Initiative, Reagan's emergency 1982 aid supplement to bolster Central American and Caribbean countries against the supposed revolutionary threat to the region. Of the $495 million in U.S. aid programmed for Central America in 1982, Nicaragua was allotted 1.2 percent.[35]

In mid-1981 Nicaragua was placed on a financial "hit list" by the Reagan Administration. In an official memo, U.S. representatives to the international lending institutions were instructed to prepare technical excuses to veto any loans proposed for Nicaragua.[36] With 19 percent of the votes in the IMF, 11 percent in the World Bank, and 35 percent in the Inter-American Development Bank (IDB), the Reagan Administration waged a battle to blockade aid to Nicaragua while increasing aid to U.S.

allies in Central America. This was similar to the strategy used by the United States against Chile during Allende's tenure. "Make the economy scream," Nixon had ordered after Allende's election. "Not a nut or bolt shall reach Chile."[37]

In October 1981 a World Bank report on Nicaragua essentially endorsed Nicaraguan reconstruction plans. But by February 1982 the report had been revised, and the U.S. hand was clearly visible. The new report criticized Nicaraguan development on highly political grounds and recommended drastic cutbacks in Bank lending: "The Sandinista movement has always been . . . anti-American," the report stated as part of its rationale, and "the Reagan administration is unhappy about the Marxist-Leninist bent. . . . " Nicaragua received no aid from the World Bank after 1981, and aid from the IDB fell from $113 million in 1979 to $1 million in 1983.[38]

The June 1983 U.S. veto of a small, usually routine loan extension in the IDB provoked severe criticism from U.S. allies. A statement released by 500 West European parliamentarians and politicians in July 1983 said they were "appalled" that financial support for Nicaragua had been "curtailed by an act of deliberate policy by the Reagan Administration," adding that it "is unacceptable that attempts are being made to strangle the people of Nicaragua by economic isolation."[39]

U.S. pressure also extended to commercial loans. In the last three years of the Somoza dictatorship, when Nicaragua was often in de facto default on its debt payments, the private banks authorized credit lines of more than $100 million annually.[40] Between 1979 and 1983, by contrast, Nicaragua paid over $575 million in debt service and received only $12 million in private bank credits.[41] Plans for a $130 million loan arranged by an international banking syndicate fell through in early 1982 amidst charges that the Reagan Adminstration was "putting pressure on leading banks against providing financial support" to Nicaragua. Then-Assistant Secretary of State for Inter-American Affairs Thomas Enders said at the time that Nicaragua would not be readmitted to the "aid community" until the Sandinistas complied with U.S. demands to guarantee political pluralism in Nicaragua and halt supposed arms shipments to the FMLN (Farabundo Martí National Liberation Front) in El Salvador.[42] The State Department also put pressure on U.S. banks not to participate in a $30 million credit line being organized by Bank of America in early 1983.[43] The U.S. government's Inter-Agency Country Exposure Review Committee, whose risk assessments strongly influence private bank lending, downgraded Nicaragua's classification from "substandard" to "doubtful" in early 1983, despite Nicaragua's regular payments on its debt.[44]

As a consequence of this blockade and the declining terms of trade for

TABLE 11.3
NICARAGUA: PRINCIPAL MEANS OF FINANCING IMPORTS (MILLIONS OF U.S. $)

Sources	1980		1981		1982		1983	
	Amount	Percent	Amount	Percent	Amount	Percent	Amount	Percent
Donations	81.0	9.1	56.8	5.7	23.5	3.0	56.9	7.1
Lines of credit	86.3	9.7	102.7	10.3	117.3	15.1	154.5	19.1
Treaties	—	—	—	—	141.3	18.2	159.7*	19.8
Liquid foreign exchange	719.9	81.2	759.9	76.0	307.0	39.6	268.2	33.2
Barter	—	—	—	—	9.4	1.2	15.1	1.9
Other	—	—	80.0	8.0	177.0	22.9	152.5	18.9
Total	887.2	100.0	999.4	100.0	775.5	100.0	806.9	100.0

Source: Office of Planning, Ministry of Foreign Trade.
*According to Ministry of Planning.

Nicaragua's exports, there was a marked change in the sources of Nicaragua's foreign exchange. Export earnings, multilateral loans, and commercial loans all declined sharply as a percentage of total foreign exchange inflow, while bilateral credits rose. The result was a decrease in liquid foreign exchange and an increase in tied loans and credit lines for specific projects, as Table 11.3 illustrates. This limited Nicaragua's freedom to choose its imports and trade partners and made debt service payments more difficult to meet.

As multilateral and U.S. loans dried up, financing from socialist countries (mostly export credits) came to represent a larger share of total external resources (see Table 11.4).

As the foreign debt grew from $1.6 billion in 1979 to $3.3 billion in 1983, debt-service payments ate up an increasingly large percentage of export earnings, rising from 20 percent of export earnings in 1980 to nearly 50 percent in 1983.[45] When the debt service burden became unmanageable in 1983, the Sandinistas decided to prioritize payment. Since no new assistance was forthcoming from the private banks, it was deemed most important to maintain good relations with official multilateral and bilateral lenders. Debts to these creditors were paid, while $140 million in accumulated interest payments due private banks between March 1983 and March 1984 were renegotiated in an agreement signed in February 1984. The Sandinistas expected to continue having to prioritize debt payments.[46]

The Sandinistas' continued success in acquiring bilateral assistance from a wide variety of countries helped the country survive declining terms of trade, U.S. economic aggression, and regional economic stagnation. In

TABLE 11.4
SOURCES OF EXTERNAL FINANCING CONTRACTED, 1979–82
(IN PERCENTAGES)

	1979	1980	1981	1982	1979–82
Multilateral	78	33	13	17	31
Bilateral	22	67	87	83	69
Western countries	22	48	72	36	48
Western Europe	6	12	9	7	9
United States	—	14	—	—	4
Latin America	16	22	48	28	30
Africa/Asia	—	—	15	1	5
Socialist countries	—	19	15	47	21
	100	100	100	100	100

Source: Nicaragua, International Reconstruction Fund (FIR), July 1983.

1983, for instance, Nicaragua announced receiving aid and/or credits from West Germany, Argentina, Austria, Yugoslavia, Peru, Sweden, North Korea, Mexico, the USSR, Canada, and Denmark. In addition the Sandinistas hoped the financial taps, especially in Europe, would open wider after the 1984 elections. Despite the wide diversity of countries offering assistance, annual levels of external financing fell from a high of $617 million in 1981 to $253 million in 1983, while the country's needs kept growing.[47]

With the politicization of lending in the international financial institutions and the escalation of CIA-directed sabotage against economic targets, Nicaragua's external economic constraints were increasingly complicated by the multifaceted U.S. destabilization campaign. For example, damage to the economy in 1983 from U.S.-backed guerrilla attacks was estimated at $130 million, or one-third of export earnings.[48] Under such pressures, the Sandinista government managed its foreign economic relations with resilience and resourcefulness.

NOTES

1. Ministerio de Planificación, *Plan de reactivación económica en beneficio del pueblo, 1980* (Managua, 1980), p. 114.

2. "Nicaragua's Trading Partners," *Update* (Washington, D.C.: Central America Historical Institute, January 1984).

3. Ministerio de Comercio Exterior, *Boletín Estadístico, Comercio Exterior 1980–1982*, No. 3 (Managua, 1983) (hereafter cited as *Foreign Trade Bulletin*). See also Robert Henriques Girling, "Nicaragua's Commercial Policy: Building a Socially Responsive Foreign Trade," *Latin American Perspectives* 10, no. 1 (Winter 1983).

4. Junta de Gobierno de Reconstrucción Nacional, *Informe 4 de mayo 1983* (Managua, 1983); Ministerio de Planificación, "Comercio exterior de Nicaragua con E.U.A." (Managua, May 1983); and "U.S. Wields Sugar Sword," *Central America Report*, April 15, 1983.

5. Interviews, Ministry of Foreign Trade, August 1983. See also John Cavanagh and Joy Hackel, "U.S. Economic War Against Nicaragua," *Counterspy* 8, no. 3 (March-May 1984).

6. *Informe 4 de mayo 1983*; and *Latin America Regional Reports/Mexico & Central America* (London), January 13, 1984.

7. Interviews, Central Bank of Nicaragua and Ministry of Planning, December 1982; and Ministry of Foreign Trade, August 1983.

8. *Foreign Trade Bulletin*.

9. "Nicaragua's Trading Partners."

10. "Comercio exterior de Nicaragua."

11. Washington *Post*, October 15, 1983.

12. *Uno Más Uno* (Mexico), October 3, 1983.

13. "Soviet Help to Sandinistas: No Blank Check," New York *Times*, March 28, 1984.

14. *Foreign Trade Bulletin*.

15. Ibid.

16. *Barricada*, Lunes Socio-Económico No. 17, September 5, 1983.

17. *Foreign Trade Bulletin*.

18. This figure includes sesame seeds, which in 1983 were reported in a category separate

from that of nontraditional exports. *Foreign Trade Bulletin*; and interviews, Ministry of Foreign Trade, August 1983.

19. Interview, Ministry of Foreign Trade, January 1984.

20. *Foreign Trade Bulletin*.

21. Ibid.

22. *Barricada*, March 8, 1983.

23. Interview with Luis Enrique Chamorro, Director of Compañía Licorera de Nicaragua S.A., January 1984.

24. *Latin America Weekly Report* (London), June 10, 1983.

25. Data from interviews, Central Bank of Nicaragua, January 1983.

26. *Barricada*, Lunes Socio-Económico No. 20, September 26, 1983.

27. Fondo Internacional para la Reconstrucción, "Efectos económicos de la agresión contra Nicaragua" (Managua, July 1983). The full program calls for investments of $3.3 billion; see Inter-American Development Bank, *Nicaragua*, Report prepared for Brussels meeting on financial and technical assistance to Central America (Washington, D.C., 1983), pp. 25–27.

28. CEPAL, "Nicaragua: Las inundaciones de mayo de 1982 y sus repercusiones sobre el desarrollo económico y social del país," E/CEPAL/MEX/1982/R.2/Rev. 1 (Mexico, July 2, 1982); and E. V. K. FitzGerald, "The Economics of the Revolution," in *Nicaragua in Revolution*, edited by Thomas W. Walker (New York: Praeger, 1982).

29. On the role of the private sector, see Richard Sholk, "The National Bourgeoisie in Post-Revolutionary Nicaragua," *Comparative Politics* 16, no. 3 (April 1984); and Henri Weber, *Nicaragua: The Sandinist Revolution* (London: Verso, 1981), pp. 61–85. On the consolidation of the FSLN position in the government, see Stephen M. Gorman, "Power and Consolidation in the Nicaraguan Revolution," *Journal of Latin American Studies* 13, no. 1 (May 1981).

30. George Black, *Triumph of the People: The Sandinistas Revolution in Nicaragua* (London: Zed Press, 1981), p. 187.

31. See *Latin America Weekly Report*, December 3, 1982; and Dev Murarka, "Five Fetters on Soviet Policy in Central America," *South*, May 1982.

32. Quoted in Nicholas Asheshov, "Endgame in Managua," *Institutional Investor*, September 1979, p. 189.

33. See: Sylvia Maxfield, "Revisitando la trampa de deuda: El caso de Nicaragua," *Gaceta Internacional* 1, no. 3 (October–December 1984); and Richard S. Weinert, "Nicaragua's Debt Renegotiation," *Cambridge Journal of Economics* 5, No. 2 (June 1981).

34. Interviews at U.S. Embassy, Managua, August 1981; and International Reconstruction Fund (FIR), July-August 1983; *Central America Report*, July 16, and August 20, 1982.

35. 'Efectos económicos." Nicaragua ended up refusing a $5.1 million grant from USAID in August 1982 that was to be given exclusively to the private sector opposition group, COSEP. See "Thumbs Down on Tied Aid," *Central America Report*, August 20, 1982.

36. "U.S. Charged With Bias in IMF Votes," *Wall Street Journal*, May 18, 1983.

37. Jim Morrell and William Jesse Biddle, "Central America: The Financial War," *International Policy Report* (Washington, D.C.: Center for International Policy, March 1983); and "How the U.S. Uses Its Lending Vote," *Latin America Regional Reports/Mexico & Central America* (London), January 13, 1984.

38. See World Bank, *Country Program Paper: Nicaragua* (Washington, D.C., February 16, 1982); "Bank Shock for the Sandinistas: Political Factors Prompt a Secret Call for Slashed Aid," *South*, No. 25 (November 1982); and "U.S. Will Oppose Loans to Nicaragua," *Washington Post*, July 1, 1983.

39. Diana Johnston, "Leftists Fight World Bank Blockade," *In These Times*, August 10–23, 1983, p. 8.

40. Central American Historical Institute, *Update*, No. 8 (Washington, D.C., November 1982).

41. Calculated from *Cable Centroamericano*, July 5, 1982, p. 96; and Instituto Histórico Centroamericano, *Envío*, No. 24 (June 1983), p. 9c.

42. "Nicaragua Loan Talks Reported," *New York Times*, March 10, 1982; and "Nicaragua Taps U.S. Banks to Help Fill Payments Gap," *Journal of Commerce*, March 9, 1982.

43. Richard Karp, "The Nicaraguan Gambit," *Institutional Investor*, March 1983.

44. Mark E. Hansen, "U.S. Banks in the Caribbean Basin: Towards a Strategy for Facilitating Lending to Nations Pursuing Alternative Models of Development." Paper prepared for Policy Alternatives in the Caribbean and Central America Conference (Washington, D.C., October 1983), Part IIA, pp. 7–8.

45. *Cable Centroamericano*, July 5, 1982, p. 105; and "Efectos económicos."

46. Interview, Ministry of Foreign Trade, January 1984; and Tim Coone, "No Miracles to be Expected," *Financial Times*, March 20, 1984.

47. Fondo Internacional para la Reconstrucción, "Resumen de la cooperación externa recibida por Nicaragua" (Managua, July 1983).

48. Coone, "No Miracles." See also Michael E. Conroy, "External Dependence, External Assistance, and 'Economic Aggression' Against Nicaragua," Kellogg Institute, University of Notre Dame, June 1, 1984.

Chapter 12
The Dilemmas of Agroexport Planning

LAURA J. ENRIQUEZ

Since the end of World War II, a number of countries have tried to carry out a fundamental transformation of their social structure. Marx had argued that revolutions would take place in those countries where capitalism was most developed. Consequently he looked to England and the industrializing countries to lead the world in progressive social change. Instead, it has been in the Third World—in Vietnam, Mozambique, Angola, Cuba, and Nicaragua—where popular forces have set in motion the process of social change. Ironically, these Third World revolutions have had to contend with hostility and intervention from the very industrialized countries for which Marx held out such great hope. In addition, these revolutions have been faced with an array of obstacles that are the product of their historical development within an international economy. These obstacles have posed formidable internal barriers to social transformation beyond the constraints imposed by the advanced capitalist countries.

In its attempts to create a more equitable society, Nicaragua experienced the constraints of both external opposition and internal impediments. Nicaragua's limited resources were increasingly consumed in defending the country's borders against external aggression from counterrevolutionary forces trained and financed by the U.S. government. Yet equally important for the future of the Nicaraguan Revolution were the internal barriers limiting flexibility in domestic policymaking. This chapter will examine one example of the manner in which these internal barriers conditioned the revolutionary policies of the new government: the tension between the country's need for expanding agroexport production and the implementation of a series of agrarian reform policies designed to alter radically the historical social structure of Nicaraguan society.

The Agrarian Reform Program was one of the central features of the social transformation carried out by the Nicaraguan Revolution. As in most Third World countries, agriculture was the basis of the Nicaraguan economy. Thus the changes that the agrarian reform attempted to bring

The author wishes to thank the Centro de Investigación y Asesoría Socio-Económica (CINASE) for its institutional support and Richard R. Fagen, Paul Lubeck, and Douglas Murray for their assistance in the research for this chapter and for their helpful comments on various drafts.

about had a serious impact on the national economy. Agroexport production had dominated the agrarian sector since capitalism was introduced in the region. By 1977 cotton and coffee production alone were responsible for bringing in over 50 percent of Nicaragua's foreign exchange earnings.[1] The need to maintain this agroexport production while carrying out agrarian reform generated serious strains on the policies of the Sandinista government.

The issue of labor supply in the agroexport sector is a striking example of .the tensions that confronted agrarian reform.[2] Many of the policies aimed at improving the lives of the rural poor disturbed the delicate balance that had developed to meet labor demands in the agrarian sector. This effect was particularly felt during the critical months of the harvest. Thus surfaced the contradiction between the harvest labor demands required to maintain agroexport production and the basic structural changes in the agrarian sector that grew out of the demands for a more equitable distribution of the nation's resources.

THE DEVELOPMENT OF THE AGRARIAN SECTOR

The dependency of agroexport production upon a large seasonal labor supply was rooted in the historical development of the agrarian sector. This development had taken place over the course of several hundred years, moving in stages as the production of each new agroexport crop evolved.

Nicaragua's first major agroexport crop was cacao, which was initially produced around 1560, and Mexico was the primary market for export. With a boom and bust pattern characterizing its development, cacao continued to be grown throughout the colonial period. At the beginning of the seventeenth century, Nicaragua began producing indigo, which soon replaced cacao in terms of its importance in agroexport production. In addition to reinforcing the emerging agroexport model of development, indigo production initiated the dramatic seasonal variation in labor demands that have characterized the agrarian sector ever since.

Indigo production differed from that of cacao because it involved

> relatively little field work and for most of the year the plantations and the *obrajes* [dyeworks] were deserted, while the local indigenous population tended its own crops or cattle. However, indigo processing required a considerable amount of labor and seasonal labor requirements for two to three months were very high.[3]

This pattern of labor demands, being strongly seasonal in nature, increased in importance with each new crop added to Nicaragua's historical repertoire.

Coffee production, which took off at the end of the nineteenth century, absorbed more land into the agroexport sector and seasonal labor became even more widespread. The introduction in the 1950s of cotton to the agroexport production picture brought this pattern into the second half of the twentieth century. Cotton production placed greater emphasis on seasonal labor. However, it broke with the historical pattern in the agroexport sector by largely abandoning subsistence production as a complementary feature to seasonal labor. Cotton production thus symbolized the complete penetration of capitalism into the agrarian economy, particularly through the proletarianization of its work force.[4]

In order to understand the depth of this transformation we turn now to the distribution of the labor force involved in each type of production. It is important to bear in mind that as of 1980 Nicaragua had a population of approximately 2.8 million people and that more than 45 percent of the economically active population (EAP) worked in the agrarian sector.[5] Thus

> coffee, cotton and sugar cane occupied a permanent work force of 35,000 people, while during the harvest ... up to 300,000 men, women and children were mobilized. Then, with the arrival of "dead time" they returned to their own or rented parcels of land or suffered the scourge of unemployment.[6]

In sum, "more than 60 percent of the work force is concentrated in the dry summer months, for the harvests."[7] In cotton production this figure reached 90 percent of the total number of workers.[8]

The other side of this enormous demand for labor was the subsistence production that took place during the rest of the year. During the dead time many of these harvest workers returned to small plots (minifundios) where they produced basic grains for subsistence. Mayorga stated that "poor rural workers or semiproletarians who cultivate small parcels of land and sell their labor during the harvests, make up approximately 53 percent of the agricultural EAP."[9]

This complementary relationship between harvest labor and minifundio production had two sides to it. On the one hand, the small plots on which these laborers grow basic grains during most of the year did not provide enough to allow for the subsistence of the campesino families.[10] They were forced to supplement their income by working in the harvests, thus meeting the harvest labor needs for the agroexporters.[11] "On the other hand, the logic of this type of agrarian capitalism requires extremely cheap labor since its backward and dependent character forces it to function in the form of superexploitation."[12] This need for cheap labor had been easily accommodated by the fact that these harvest wages were "only" supplemental income. That is, these wages were not expected to sustain the worker and his family.

Another important source of harvest labor was the urban informal sector.[13] The expansion of cotton production was responsible for the displacement of large numbers of campesinos. This displaced group had two options: to move to the agricultural hinterland where they worked tiny plots, every year being pushed further into the frontier as agroexport production expanded; or to move into urban areas. Those who migrated to the urban areas were increasingly incorporated into the informal sector, as the demand for industrial labor was much smaller than the numbers of people being expelled from the rural sector. This segment of the economy offered them enough to maintain a marginal existence, often supplemented by wages earned during the harvest. As Biderman observed, "even urban residents continued to rely on cotton harvest wages to supplement their earnings, and constituted nearly one-third of total cotton harvest labor."[14]

In some years the heavy labor demands of the harvest period were not met. For example, as cotton cultivation expanded there was a corresponding increase in the demand for harvest workers.[15] The agroexporters responded to this labor supply problem by dramatically increasing the level of mechanization in cotton production, thereby not only combating labor shortages but weakening the bargaining position of the harvest workers as well. However, by the late 1960s the use of harvesting machines was once again in decline, fostered in large part by an increasing reliance on imported labor, principally from El Salvador and Honduras.[16]

Following the 1969 war between El Salvador and Honduras, the exodus of laborers provided a needed safety valve for population pressures within these countries. In the case of El Salvador, this pressure had itself contributed to the causes of this war. For Nicaragua, this "bracero-type" program reduced the need for mechanical harvesters.[17] In addition, "this reserve army of labor helped keep wages low despite the high profits obtained in cotton cultivation."[18]

In sum, prerevolutionary Nicaragua was characterized by the seasonal variation in labor demands typical of agroexport production. These demands were met by employing large numbers of workers during the peak harvest period. These harvest workers were then sent back to their minifundios, to the urban informal sector, or to their native countries. This pattern of labor supply contributed on the one hand to the "growth" that accompanied the expansion of cotton production, that is, growth purely in terms of capital accumulation. On the other hand, the increase in underemployment that accompanied this growth contributed greatly to urban and, in particular, to rural poverty. One of the by-products of this process was the development of rural unrest. The extent to which this unrest had developed by the late 1970s was evidenced by the large number of rurally based people who fought or collaborated in the insurrection that overthrew Anastasio Somoza Debayle on July 19, 1979. The FSLN was able to gain the support of the campesinos not only because of their opposition to Somoza's tyranny; equally important to the rural poor was the FSLN's program for fundamental transformation of the agrarian sector. Thus, even before the victory celebrations were over, agrarian reform policies were being generated by the new government.

THE AGRARIAN POLICIES OF THE GOVERNMENT OF NATIONAL RECONSTRUCTION

The Revolution brought a new emphasis on addressing the needs of the majority of the population. This translated into a focus on Nicaragua's poor and, in particular, its rural poor. The Government of National Reconstruction (GNR) attempted to restructure Nicaraguan society in a way that promoted two objectives: economic development and income distribution.[19] Because agriculture played such an important role in the country's economy, and because the political support of the agrarian population was critical to the government's revolutionary program, the most profound changes implemented were in the agrarian sector.

The Agrarian Reform Program was designed to meet two basic objectives: to increase production, and to raise the standard of living of the rural population. For our present purposes we will focus on the policies of the Agrarian Reform Program and their impact on the agroexport portion of the agrarian sector, which was of increasing importance. As the country's economic situation continued to become more delicate, the foreign exchange earnings obtained from agroexport production became ever more critical. Within this context the Ministry of Agricultural Development and Agrarian Reform (MIDINRA) attempted to reorient the structure of the agrarian sector to meet the needs of Nicaragua's rural population.

Vice-Minister of Agrarian Reform Salvador Mayorga delineated the following general reform measures that were implemented in an effort to create an agrarian sector more oriented to the needs of the rural poor:[20]

- Greater access to land on the part of poor rural workers.
- Reduced rents.
- Weakening the control of intermediaries and access to better prices for the small farmers.
- An increase in the amount of credit extended to small farmers who produce basic grains. (The amount has been sixfold over that of the historic ceiling.)
- An increase in the salaries of agricultural workers.

All of these measures benefited the rural poor, including the harvest workers mentioned above. Perhaps the most fundamental assumption underlying them was: "What many rural poor want, above all, is year-round work."[21] But how could agroexport production be expanded at the same time that an attempt was being made to reorient the priorities of production in this sector toward the needs of the rural poor? More concretely: What was the relationship between agrarian reform and the harvest labor supply problems encountered in the agroexport sector? In order to understand this tension between agroexport production and agrarian reform we must begin with an analysis of the first several harvests following the FSLN Triumph. We will focus on coffee and cotton because together they brought in more than 50 percent of Nicaragua's foreign exchange earnings and generated 86 percent of the total harvest labor force.[22]

THE FIRST POST-TRIUMPH HARVEST

The 1980/81* crop cycle was the first "normal" one following the overthrow of Somoza. Agricultural production during the 1979/80 cycle had been significantly affected by the war and the dislocation that followed it. Cotton production was especially hard hit, with cotton acreage dropping from 248,200 manzanas[†] in the 1978/79 cycle to 54,600 manzanas in the 1979/80 cycle.[23] Coffee production was affected in other ways, although not as severely as cotton.

There was a big increase in the acreage cultivated with cotton in 1980/81 over that of 1979/80. By that time, much of the immediate dislocation caused by the war had been straightened out. Finally, this was also the first year in which the initial effects of the agrarian reform could be seen. This meant that the hints of an agrarian reform/agroexport dilemma experienced during the 1979/80 harvest became more apparent in the 1980/81 harvest. The clearest expression of this dilemma was found in the cotton harvest.

The large increase in cotton production between the 1979/80 and 1980/81 crop cycles created a corresponding increase in labor demands, particularly in the harvest period. Unfortunately, a number of factors combined to produce a serious labor shortage in the 1980/81 harvest; and, in turn, this labor shortage had a significant negative impact on the agroexport sector. The data cited below illustrate the severity of the problem during the 1980/81 crop cycle.

---

*Since the crop cycle runs from April to March, it overlaps two calendar years.
[†]One manzana is approximately 1.73 acres.

The cotton harvest usually takes place between December and March with January and February being the months of most intense work. Agrarian reform policymakers estimated that the 1980/81 harvest lasted until almost the beginning of May as a result of the labor shortage.[24] Cotton reaches a point where it must be harvested or it rapidly deteriorates; thus, extending the harvest over so many months can affect yields. Furthermore, while the expected ratio of workers to manzana was 0.7, the actual ratio was approximately 0.33. In other words, the deficit in the number of harvest workers was approximately 50 percent. This deficit was experienced at the same time that the demand for labor was half of what it traditionally had been as a result of the production decline during the insurrection. This represents a labor shortage of much greater significance than the deficit percentage alone suggests.

Various factors combined to produce this critical shortage. An examination of them will help in understanding what happened during the 1980/81 harvest and what measures could be taken to correct this problem before serious limitations in agroexport production might result.

SPECIFIC ASPECTS OF AGRARIAN REFORM POLICIES AFFECTING HARVEST LABOR SUPPLY

Several agrarian reform policies played a critical role in fostering the labor shortage experienced in the 1980/81 cotton harvest. These policies combined to produce what is commonly known in Latin America as *campesinización*. This catch-all term refers to the tendency among many workers to stay and work on their own small plots of land, as opposed to going to work on the agroexport estates as wage-laborers. The specific policies producing this campesinización include greater access to land, the government's new credit policies, rent reductions, and access to better prices for what the campesinos produced. Large numbers of workers who previously had no choice but to supplement their income by working in the harvest could now choose to stay at home.

The overthrow of Somoza was followed by the immediate confiscation of the Somoza family's property as well as that of their cronies. The governmental decree that authorized the confiscation "set in motion the nationalization of almost 2 million acres in approximately 2,000 farms and ranches. Overnight about 20 percent of Nicaragua's agricultural land became part of the 'People's Property.'"[25] This decree also legalized the FSLN-organized land takeovers that occurred in the last months of the war, primarily in the north Pacific region. This nationalization process constituted the first phase of agrarian reform. The second phase was not begun until mid-1981. Although the agrarian reform ministry decided it would be most productive to maintain intact the large estates, this first phase still provided more access to land for the small farmers:

> Approximately 500,000 acres of this land were designed to be distributed to small or landless peasants. Smaller farms owned by National Guardsmen, and unused land on the largest estates were pegged for redistribution, beginning the process of deconcentrating land ownership.[26]

Small farmers were organized into Sandinista Agricultural Cooperatives (CAS) in order to obtain the greatest benefit from the redistribution.

The second phase of agrarian reform, promulgated on August 21, 1981, authorized the confiscation of estates above specified size limitations (these vary by crop and region), and the land of those who had left the country. Underutilized and uncultivated farmland was also to be confiscated. Both of these phases resulted in a significant increase in the amount of land available to the rural poor, including the formerly landless and land-poor rural workers. This new access to a better standard of subsistence reduced the campesinos' need to offer their labor in the agroexport harvests.

Perhaps the most important of these policy changes were those related to the distribution of credits for agricultural production. Minister of Agricultural Development and Agrarian Reform Jaime Wheelock acknowledged the role of credit policies in fueling the labor shortages:

> We already know that in many areas, particularly in the western region [where most cotton production takes place], we've had productivity problems . . . now that the revolution has opened up credit possibilities for the small farmers, we've noticed that they want to stay on their own land and this has had sharp repercussions on the export-economy.[27]

An enormous amount of credit was made available during the 1980/81 crop cycle, which had an important impact on the campesino sector of the rural population. Credit offered to the rural poor was increased by 639 percent in the 1980/81 crop cycle, with 81 percent of the small producers receiving these benefits in 1980 as opposed to 18 percent in 1978.[28] The significant increase in credits reflected an attempt to increase basic grain production and to facilitate the structural changes that constituted the agrarian reform.[29] However, the unprecedented subsidization of the small farmer directly affected the needs of these workers to supplement their incomes with the wages earned from the harvest. Thus the credit policies diminished the number of campesinos who would leave their own plots to work on the agroexport estates during the harvest.

The redistribution of land was complemented by ceilings placed on rents for land in rural areas. These rents varied according to the type of crop grown and the region. The regulation of rent brought to an end years of control by the rural upper class over the subsistence of the tenant farmers and opened up even more land to the campesino sector. Furthermore, the rent reduction was thought to provide a stimulus for increasing food production. Collins states that "the new rents work[ed] out to be about 85 percent less than the previous going rates."[30] In addition to the previously mentioned policy reforms, lowered rents further reduced the need for the supplemental income usually earned in the harvest.

The government also became involved in purchasing and distributing the goods produced by these small farmers. Government planners reasoned that food production would be increased by offering these farmers higher guaranteed prices. In less than two years from the implementation of this policy, the price of corn was raised 25 percent and of beans 50 percent.[31] Exerting some control over the marketing and pricing of products for internal consumption facilitated the elimination of some of the middlemen who had reaped enormous profits over the years at the expense of the small farmer.

Regulations concerning the wages of the harvest workers were another factor contributing to the harvest labor shortage of 1980/81. Anastasio Somoza García (the first of the three Somozas to rule Nicaragua) had promulgated a series of labor regulations in the 1940s, designed to provide legitimacy to the regime. However, these laws, which included minimum wage regulations, were never enforced. When the Sandinistas came to power they undertook a series of reforms to protect the rights of the workers. As part of this new program, the Ministry of Labor (MITRAB) established minimum wages for the myriad of positions offered during both the preharvest period and the harvest itself. During the first year, due perhaps to inexperience as well as inadequate planning, the wage scale established for harvest workers was set too low. This reduced the incentive to work in the harvest. Given the arduous nature of harvest labor, the wage scale had to provide a significant incentive to attract these temporary workers, particularly where other traditional forms of economic and political coercion have been reduced or eliminated. The more secure position the campesinos attained through the four agrarian reform measures discussed above enabled them to reject a wage scale that was not commensurate with rising expectations and standards.

The reduced harvest wage scale also influenced Nicaragua's migrant labor force. Nicaragua traditionally offered better wages for harvest labor than had its neighbors. Consequently large numbers of Salvadoran and Honduran workers had worked in the Nicaraguan harvest since the early 1970s.[32] Their participation in the harvest helped keep harvest wages low since their numbers were abundant and the opportunities in their own countries limited.[33] However, in the 1980/81 harvest the pay scale set by MITRAB was, in real terms, 10 to 20 percent lower than the wages being offered in El Salvador and Honduras.[34] This contributed to the reduction in the number of workers migrating to Nicaragua for harvest labor.

In sum,

> these [more access to land, credit and better prices] and other measures and more fundamentally, the rupture in the bases which sustained the somocista model of development, have provoked a sudden consequence in the agricultural sector: a shortage of seasonal labor in the coffee and cotton harvests, as a result of the tendency towards campesinización of the semiproletariat.[35]

ADDITIONAL FACTORS NOT ORIGINATING IN GOVERNMENTAL POLICIES

Several other factors contributed to the reduced labor supply that were not directly related to the government's agrarian reform policies. These latter factors are more geopolitical and conjunctural in nature and while they must be taken into account to understand what happened in the 1980/81 harvest, they are less important in thinking about the more fundamental issue of tensions arising in the agroexport sector due to agrarian reform policies.

An important factor in reducing the number of foreign harvest workers was the regional turmoil that was escalating by the time of the 1980/81 harvest. The civil war in El Salvador was by this time seriously disrupting that country and sending many of its citizens into permanent exile. The Nicaraguan Revolution had also altered Nicaragua's relationship with the right-wing regimes ruling both Honduras and El Salvador, thus affecting the ease with which workers passed back and forth across its borders. The end result was a virtual elimination of foreign workers available to work the harvests in Nicaragua.

Two other factors contributed to the labor shortage, although they carried less weight than the conditions previously discussed. First, following the ouster of Somoza, the army was restructured to form the Sandinista Popular Army (EPS). The new army incorporated many campesinos or their teenage sons and daughters who would have otherwise joined the seasonal labor force. The EPS offered reasonable, stable wages as opposed to the insecurity characterizing seasonal labor. Furthermore, as the regional tension increased it became necessary for the Nicaraguan government to expand its military forces, thus taking away even more potential harvesters. The second factor was the dislocation that followed the civil war, which had not been completely stabilized by the time of the 1980/81 harvest, resulting in many workers not arriving for the harvest.

POST-1980/81 HARVEST

The difficulties encountered with labor shortages in the 1980/81 cotton harvest continued to affect the cotton and coffee harvests following that first crucial year. Each of the subsequent three harvests, including that of 1983/84, were plagued by this problem. Evidence of the shortages appeared in a number of forms, particularly in the extensive media coverage of the issue and the large number of volunteer pickers mobilized to fill the void caused by the lack of "professional" pickers.

The fundamental reasons for the continuing agroexport harvest labor shortages had not changed radically since the harvest of 1980/81. In the 1982/83 and 1983/84 harvests, campesinización and military mobilizations were the most commonly mentioned causes of this critical problem. The various factors leading to campesinización all contributed to the reduction in the size of the work force available for the cotton and coffee harvests. It had become more profitable for the rural poor to "become" campesinos than to become agricultural wage laborers. Land, credits, and better prices were readily available and were raising the standard of living of the campesino sector. At the same time, agricultural wages had not kept pace with inflation. Working one's own land, instead of participating in the agroexport harvests, had become economically advantageous.

While agrarian reform measures worked together to produce the campesinización that lay at the base of the harvest labor shortages, this trend was compounded in the 1982/83 and 1983/84 harvests by the mobilization of thousands of people into the various branches of the military to fight the counterrevolutionaries. These mobilizations affected all sectors of Nicaraguan society. Reserve battalions and militias composed of government functionaries, factory workers, agricultural workers, Sandinista youth, and so on, were sent to the "front."

The counterrevolution was likely to continue to keep people away from the agroexport harvests. That would be determined by whether or not the U.S. continued its financial and technical support for the contras. However, it appeared that even the cessation of the counterrevolution would not completely resolve the problem of harvest labor shortages. The continued advancement of the Agrarian Reform Program would further the process of campesinización begun in 1979. As one high-level agrarian reform official stated, the development of the various agrarian reform projects would increasingly absorb workers who had traditionally labored in the harvest.[36] These projects, which provide alternative sources of employment to the rural poor, range from the development of cooperative farming, to irrigation systems facilitating year-round production, to several agroindustrial programs such as milk processing plants and the huge sugar refinery, Malacatoya, being constructed at that time.

The structural reforms being carried out provided powerful incentives for small producers to increase their food production. While these reforms eliminated much of the need to work in the harvests, they were basic to the government's agrarian policies and had not been, nor were they likely to be, done away with in order to generate a harvest labor supply. This tension between agrarian reform and agroexport production led to the conclusion that effective long-term policies had to be developed that fostered the agroexport process while maintaining and advancing the Sandinista commitment to agrarian reform. The labor supply issue is but one example of the more general tensions the FSLN had to resolve if it was to pursue its dual goals of economic development combined with social equity.

CONCLUSION

The need to resolve the issue of labor shortages in the agroexport harvests can be understood when one takes into account the critical role played by agroexport production in the Nicaraguan economy. Given its heritage of dependent development, the revolutionary government began with a social/economic structure dominated by its agrarian sector. Agroexport production was the economic foundation of the society that the new government took charge of in 1979. The Sandinistas sought to overcome this legacy of dependency on agroexport production by developing other strong sectors of the economy and a more equitable distribution of the society's productive resources. But they recognized that this dependency and extreme inequality could not be overcome overnight.

As Nicaragua's economic situation became more critical, industrial development, or even the maintenance of the industrial sector, gave way to an increasing reliance on agroexport and agroindustrial production to keep the economy afloat. Agroexport production and agroindustry would thus remain the basis for Nicaragua's future development. One analysis in *Barricada*, the official organ of the FSLN, indicated: "The features of the 1983 economic program show that priority must be placed on agricultural activities. In addition to assuring articles of basic consumption, these activities are the principle generators of the foreign exchange earnings required by our economy."[37] In this context, labor supply problems could not be allowed to undermine the levels of production in this sector.

It was clear that reliance on using a voluntary work force could not serve as a long-term means of resolving the labor shortage problems. The revolutionary enthusiasm that typically characterizes the initial period of a transformation such as that being experienced by Nicaragua could not be expected to continue indefinitely. The undeclared war imposed on Nicaragua served to rekindle the nationalist sentiment of many of its citizens. This would probably translate into a continuing willingness to sacrifice, including participating in volunteer labor. However, a productive structure could not be based on the participation of volunteer workers over the long run.[38]

Another proposed solution to labor supply problems was increased mechanization. This also had severe limitations. As the economic blockade being waged by the United States continued, Nicaragua's ability to import the needed machinery decreased. Even with regard to the machinery Nicaragua already had in its possession, the country's deteriorating foreign exchange status and the U.S. blockade made it increasingly difficult to obtain spare parts needed to keep these machines running.

At the same time the government had to be conscious of the political need to meet the demands of the rural poor for agrarian reform. It could not use economic coercion to force the campesinos to work in the agroexport harvest. It was precisely the economic coercion and extreme inequality produced by Nicaragua's previous agrarian structure that fueled the struggle against Somoza. A platform of structural change in this sector that promised to bring about more equality fostered campesino support for the FSLN. The maintenance of this political support required fundamental structural changes to improve the lives of the rural poor.

An intriguing, although as yet unrealized, proposal addressing the issues of labor shortages was made by the Rural Workers' Association (ATC) in 1981. The ATC formulated a strategy to prevent labor shortages during the coffee, cotton, and sugar harvests. According to the proposal, a plan would be developed "whereby the beneficiaries of the land distribution will spend eight months of the year on their own plots, producing grain for domestic consumption, and the other four as paid labourers on the state-owned and private farms."[39] That is, they would enter into a contractual arrangement with the state as part of their receiving land and participating more generally in the Agrarian Reform Program.

Another proposal that merited consideration was that of promoting the cooperativism of the state-owned agroexport farms. The logic of this proposal was as follows: If the workers had more of a stake in guaranteeing that the harvest was completed on time, it would be done more effectively. Whereas if the workers were simply wage-laborers who were paid regardless of the manner in which the harvest proceeded, the task might very well not be completed. This logic had already led to some cooperativism in the coffee growing regions. However, it would require some time before the effectiveness of this method of addressing the harvest labor issue could be evaluated.

Both of these proposals were important in that they combined the benefits gained by the campesinos through the agrarian reform with an on-going responsibility to the Nicaraguan state and society. Thus receiving a land title was not just one of the fruits of victory. It also symbolized a responsibility to the revolutionary transformation of society. Both proposals represented an attempt to formalize this responsibility and the relationship between the state and the popular classes within the revolutionary policy process.

In conclusion, there was a need to find alternative solutions to meet the labor demands of the agroexport sector for both the short and long terms. As the acreage cultivated with agroexport crops increased, agrarian planners would have to come to terms with labor supply problems in a way that both increased the level of production in this sector and improved the lives of the rural workers who made this production possible. The Sandinista government had made the commitment to carry out these social reforms. The task remained for both policymakers and rural workers to find solutions that would pursue these reforms while maintaining a viable agroexport sector for the long-term development of the Nicaraguan revolution.

NOTES

1. Ministerio de Desarrollo Agropecuario y Reforma Agraria (MIDINRA), *Informe de Nicaragua a la FAO* (Managua: Centro de Investigación y Estudios de la Reforma Agraria (CIERA), July 1983), p. 51.

2. The agroexport sector is primarily composed of cotton, coffee, and sugar cane, although a variety of other commodities contribute to agroexport income.

3. Jaime Biderman, *Class Structure, the State and Capitalist Development in Nicaraguan Agriculture* (Berkeley: University of California, Ph.D. dissertation, 1982), p. 30.

4. The natural variation in labor demands in cotton production was heightened by the gradual mechanization of preharvest operations. The Nicaraguan state aided greatly in subsidizing the mechanization process. This process promoted the expansion of the area under cotton cultivation. In addition it increased labor productivity and "initiated a profound transformation in the use of labor, which became increasingly proletarian yet seasonal in nature." Ibid, p. 92.

5. David Kaimowitz and Joseph Thome, "Nicaragua's Agrarian Reform: The First Year (1979-80)," in *Nicaragua in Revolution*, edited by Thomas W. Walker (New York: Praeger, 1982), pp. 223-240.

6. Salvador Mayorga, "La Experiencia Agraria de la Revolución Nicaragüense," in *Reforma Agraria y Revolución Popular en América Latina*, Vol 2 (Managua: CIERA, July 1982), p. 96.

7. CIERA, "Nicaragua: Capitalismo y Agricultura 1950-80," unpublished manuscript (Managua: CIERA, 1982), p. 13.

8. Biderman, *Class Structure*, p. 94.

9. Mayorga, "La Experiencia Agraria," p. 96.

10. Campesinos in Latin America are generally small farmers, many of whom work as wage laborers during a portion of the year.

11. See Programa Centroamericano de Ciencias de la Salud, *Los Trabajadores en la*

Agricultura Centroamericana (Condiciones de Trabajo y de Vida) (San José: Universidad Nacional de Costa Rica, 1983).

12. CIERA, "Nicaragua: Capitalismo y Agricultura," p. 22.

13. The term "informal sector" represents all small businesses and industries with five or less employees. They range from market women with fruit and vegetable stalls to the tailor working out of his home and employing four assistants. This economic sector plays an extremely important role throughout Latin America as formal industry is insufficiently developed to keep this part of the population employed and provide the necessary range of goods and services. The nature and scope of the informal sector in Nicaragua are not well understood. It is currently the focus of a major research project being carried out at the Centro de Investigación y Asesoría Socio-Económica (CINASE) in Managua.

14. Biderman, *Class Structure*, p. 109.

15. Cotton production took its first big leap in the early 1950s, moving from 5 percent of Nicaragua's total exports in 1950 to 39 percent in 1955, at which point cotton displaced coffee as the country's top export product (Biderman, "Class Structure," p. 82). In the second half of the 1950s, cotton production took a downswing, but in the early 1960s Nicaragua repeated the pattern of expansion set a decade earlier. The net effect in terms of the demands for harvest labor that accompanied this growth were labor shortages during this peak demand period.

16. This is a common feature of agricultural production in developed countries as well. Even in areas such as the Southwest region of the United States where mechanization was well underway by the turn of the century, access to cheap imported labor instead of technological innovation and mechanization remained the dominant feature. See Carey McWilliams, *Factories in the Fields: The Story of Migratory Farm Labor in California*, (Santa Barbara, Calif.: Peregrine, 1971); Ernesto Galarza, *Merchants of Labor: A Study of the Managed Migration of Farm Workers in California, 1942–1960*, (Santa Barbara, Calif.: McNally and Loftin, 1964); Theo Majka, "Regulating Farmworkers: The State and the Agricultural Labor Supply in California," *Contemporary Crisis* 2, no. 2 (April 1978): 141–155.

17. The Bracero Program was the most developed in a series of U.S.-Mexico temporary workers agreements. The program was designed to "provide access to temporary workers from Mexico whenever labor shortages occurred." See Douglas L. Murray, "The Abolition of El Cortito, the Short-Handled Hoe: A Case Study in Social Conflict and State Policy in California Agriculture," *Social Problems* 30 (October 1982): 26–39. See also Galarza, *Merchants of Labor*, for an interesting account of the role of temporary workers in the struggle to organize California farm labor.

18. Biderman, *Class Structure*, p. 109.

19. Solon Barraclough, *A Preliminary Analysis of the Nicaraguan Food System* (Geneva: United Nations Research Institute for Social Development, 1982).

20. Mayorga, "La Experiencia Agraria," p. 102.

21. Joseph Collins, *What Difference Could a Revolution Make? Food and Farming in the New Nicaragua* (San Francisco: Institute for Food and Development Policy, 1982), p. 72.

22. For data on the harvest labor force see Instituto Centroamericano de Administración de Empresas (INCAE), "Nicaragua: Estudio de la Situación del Empleo, la Absorción de la Mano de Obra y otros Aspectos en Fincas y Productores de Café y Algodón," unpublished manuscript, IDRC Rural Employment Project (Managua, July 1982), p. 9.

23. *Latin American Commodities Report* (London, May 21, 1982).

24. The following information came from an interview with an agrarian reform official on May 12, 1983. Many of my informants, including this official, asked that I maintain their anonymity and that I not cite some of the internal ministerial documents that they provided me. Hereafter these sources will be cited by ministry and date.

25. Collins, *What Difference*, p. 31.

26. Rose J. Spalding, "New Directions in Nicaragua's Agricultural Economy (1979–1982)." Paper presented at the 30th Annual Meeting of the Southeastern Council of Latin American Studies (San Juan, Puerto Rico, April 7–9, 1983), p. 10.

27. Quoted in Peter Marchetti, "Reforma Agraria y la Conversión Difícil: Reubicación de Recursos, Redistribución de Poder, y los Explotados del Campo en Chile y en Nicaragua," *Estudios Rurales Latinoamericanos* 4 (January-April 1981):47–67.

28. Barraclough, *A Preliminary Analysis*.

29. The role of credits in the agrarian reform is the focus of my current research.

30. Collins, *What Difference*, p. 37.

31. Ibid., p. 112.

32. One official study found that only 2 percent of harvest labor was made up of Salvadoran and Honduran laborers. However, the validity of this study has been strongly questioned. Furthermore, numerous informants have cited the loss of Honduran and Salvadoran labor as being an important contributing factor to the labor shortage of 1980/81.

33. This is especially true of the Salvadorans in whose country the ratio of manzanas to inhabitants is low, 0.7, as compared to Nicaragua's ratio of 7.6, or that of Honduras, 4.7 (CIERA, "Nicaragua: Capitalismo y Agricultura," p. 22). The concentration of land ownership in El Salvador is also more extreme than that of Nicaragua. See also Carmen Diana Deere, "A Comparative Analysis of Agrarian Reform in El Salvador and Nicaragua 1979–81," *Development and Change* 13:1–41, (Beverly Hills: Sage Publishing).

34. MIDINRA, internal ministerial document, n.d.

35. Mayorga, "La Experiencia Agraria," p. 102.

36. Interview, March 15, 1984.

37. *Barricada*, September 12, 1983, p. 3.

38. The experience of the Cuban Revolution with volunteer labor is an interesting example of the difficulties encountered in the heavy reliance on this form of labor. See Terry Karl, "Work Incentives in Cuba," *Latin American Perspectives* 2, no. 4, Issue 7, Supplement (1975):21–41.

39. *Latin American Regional Reports* (London, August 14, 1981), p. 5.

Chapter 13
The Industrial Sector

JOHN WEEKS

After the fall of the Somoza dictatorship in July 1979, the new government of Nicaragua inherited an economy in ruins, ravaged by two years of warfare. As the state sought to take control and give direction to the reconstruction of the economy, the massive destruction of physical assets proved to be a serious but secondary problem. For a number of reasons, the economy of the late-Somoza period could not be successfully reconstructed, particularly with regard to manufacturing. While some success was achieved in reactivating production in the agro-export sector, attempts to generate a general recovery in manufacturing met with failure. In 1983, when the Nicaraguan economy was one of the few in Latin America to show a positive rate of growth, manufacturing output fell by 5 percent (the same rate at which GDP rose),[1] dropping back to the level of 1980.

The explanation for why reactivation of the manufacturing sector was so difficult is not obvious. During the 1960s, Nicaragua had the fastest rate of manufacturing growth in Central America, with quite diversified exports to the regional market. In the 1970s manufacturing growth declined but remained respectable. In 1960 Nicaragua's share of manufacturing in GDP was only 12 percent, roughly the same as for Guatemala and Honduras, and well below the proportions for Costa Rica and El Salvador. Ten years later the share had risen to 20 percent, the highest for any of the five Central American countries.[2]

A number of explanations have been offered for the persistent difficulties encountered with manufacturing reactivation since the Triumph, particularly arguments about the "dependent" nature of Nicaragua's industrialization and the alleged inefficiency of the plant and equipment installed under the Somozas' rule. The manufacturing sector had simply exhausted its growth possibilities by the end of the 1970s, and even without a successful war of national liberation and the destruction associated with that war, the manufacturing sector of the 1970s could not have provided the basis for further industrialization in the 1980s. Even less could the manufacturing sector of the 1970s provide the basis for industrialization in a context of new priorities for meeting basic needs and moving toward national self-sufficiency.

Thus, the Nicaraguan manufacturing sector was a striking success as late as the early 1970s and a collapsing disaster just ten years later. The dramatic transformation has both political and economic explanations. The political explanation lies in the noncooperation and outright sabotage by the private sector in the task of post-Triumph reconstruction.[3] The economic explanation derives from largely external forces set in motion in the mid-1970s, which culminated in the de facto dissolution of the Central American Common Market (CACM). To a great extent, the political and economic explanations are separable: that is, had Somoza not been overthrown, or, once overthrown, had the private sector cooperated in industrial reconstruction, the economic problems would still have generated a collapse of manufacturing in the late 1970s or early 1980s.

MANUFACTURING BEFORE THE TRIUMPH

During the three decades 1950–80, Nicaraguan society underwent rapid economic transformation and growth, a growth interrupted catastrophically by the war of national liberation from the Somoza dictatorship. However, from 1950 to 1977 the rate of growth of GDP was 5.5 percent per annum. This was above average for Latin America as a whole but not spectacular. The rate of growth during the 1960s was spectacular: from 1960 to 1967 GDP grew at an annual rate of over 8 percent. The growth of the manufacturing sector was even more impressive for these years—12.5 percent per annum in real terms. However, from 1967 to 1977 growth was dramatically slower, half the rate during 1960–67 in both agriculture and manufacturing.[4]

The decline in the growth of output after 1967 was reflected in a weaker export performance. In current prices, exports grew at similar rates before and after 1967, but in constant prices, export performance declined dramatically. Export volume grew at less than 5 percent per year after 1967, compared to almost 12 percent for 1960–67. In the case of manufactured exports (including agroindustrial exports), real growth was rapid until 1970, but subsequently it was not only slower but also showed extreme year-to-year fluctuations. The impressive development of manufactured exports from Nicaragua was due to the formation of the Central American Common Market. In 1960, exports to Central America were less than $1 million; they rose to $39 million in 1970, and in 1977–78 were over $100 million.

Though Nicaragua's regional trade expanded dramatically over two decades, the rate at which it grew dropped substantially in the 1970s. This was also the case for the regional trade of all of the CACM countries taken together. This stagnation of regional trade after 1970 has been used by some as the explanation for why the Nicaraguan economy experienced a slowdown in growth. It is commonly argued that the slower rates of growth reflect a "saturated" CACM.[5] This hypothesis, however, is incorrect as we have argued elsewhere.[6]

Two basic characteristics of the Nicaraguan economy, small size and openness, indicate the basic mistake of the market saturation hypothesis. It implicitly treats Nicaragua in terms of a Keynesian macroeconomic model and, therefore, as a closed economy for analytical purposes. The hypothesis that growth is constrained by the size of the market is based on the erroneous idea that there is something called the "domestic economy" that is separable from the export economy, and that the former provides the total system's dynamism. We argue that the growth of the Nicaraguan economy during the late Somoza period was in no meaningful sense constrained by aggregate demand, either from internal sources (personal expenditure, state expenditure, or investment by capitalists) or by external sources (exports). Rather, the growth of the economy reflected the interaction of relative prices and productivity.

In other words, the level of output in both agriculture and manufacturing tended to be a function of domestic costs of production; that is, given prices, output responded to the profit margin. The two most important determinants of production cost were the price of imported inputs and productivity. In the 1970s, imported inputs accounted for 40 percent of material costs for the manufacturing sector as a whole, more important than labor costs. Increases in productivity affected the profit margin by reducing unit labor costs. Productivity change itself was closely related to investment and the level of capacity utilization. Investment, in turn, was largely determined by the price of imported machinery, since virtually all fixed means of production came from overseas.

These theoretical points allow us to explain the stagnation of the Nicaraguan economy. From 1960 to 1967, both export prices and prices of imported inputs and fixed capital were relatively constant. Productivity, however, grew at about 7 percent per annum, with relatively constant money wages. As a consequence, profit margins rose rapidly, stimulating the growth of output, investment, and exports. It was such favorable conditions—stable product prices, which kept regional exports competitive, constant input prices, which kept costs low, and rapid productivity growth, which raised profits—that explain the success of the manufacturing sector from 1960 to 1967. However, the environment turned extremely unfavorable for the Nicaraguan economy and specifically for manufacturing.[7] After 1967, import prices rose rapidly. The cost of imported machinery increased substantially—by 100 percent from 1968 to

1976—which reduced the rate of investment. The lower rate of investment resulted in a slower rate of productivity growth, reducing the rate at which unit labor costs declined. At the same time, the price of imported inputs rose by over 150 percent from 1968 to 1976, so that unit total costs tended to rise. These factors resulted in a squeeze on profit margins, and the squeeze on profit margins reduced the rate at which output grew. At the same time, the increased input costs led manufacturing capitalists to use their market power to raise prices on the regional market in an attempt to maintain profit margins. However, the price increase reduced the competitiveness of Nicaraguan products vis-a-vis imports both from outside of the CACM and from producers in the other countries of the CACM.[8]

Thus, independent of the gathering social unrest in Nicaragua, the economy had entered a period of relative stagnation in the 1970s. Even had the CACM continued to function, new investments and perhaps even the closing of plants heavily dependent upon petrochemical imports would have been necessary to revitalize the participation of Nicaraguan manufacturing in the regional market. But by the end of the decade, the accords of the CACM began to break down. Because the collapse of the regional common market coincided with the wars of national liberation in Nicaragua and El Salvador, there is a temptation to attribute the disintegration to political causes. However, the collapse was basically economic in cause, with political conflict only accelerating the process.

Through the 1970s all five Central American countries suffered from balance-of-payments pressures created by relative price changes, a recession in the world economy, and a tighter international money market.[9] Facing these pressures, each government in effect decided to pursue a separate strategy to weather the crisis, rather than a collective one. The governments continued to profess commitment to regional cooperation even after political tensions reached explosive intensity between Nicaragua and its four neighbors.

This was, however, merely form. In practice all five governments violated the regional agreement repeatedly. The new Nicaraguan government suspended the free convertibility of the córdoba soon after taking power, a major step towards de facto withdrawal from the CACM.[10] One by one all of the other CACM members sought separate accords with the International Monetary Fund, arrangements that reduced the degree of regional coordination in trade policy.[11]

Nicaraguan manufacturing had been seriously weakened by relative price changes during the 1970s; the collapse of the CACM devastated it. High-cost and noncompetitive on the world market, it now lost its protected regional market. The seriousness of the situation was not at first obvious, because the collapse of the CACM coincided with the war of national liberation and the extensive destruction of plant and equipment in the last months of that war. However, had that destruction not occurred, the manufacturing power sector would still have been in extremely difficult circumstances. The manufacturing sector that the post-Triumph government inherited, even had it been intact, could not have provided the basis for industrialization in the 1980s.

WAR DAMAGE AND ABORTIVE RECOVERY

The war to overthrow the Somoza dictatorship proved catastrophically costly to the Nicaraguan people. Along with the tremendous loss of life went economic devastation.[12] National income fell slightly in 1978 as the fighting intensified, then dropped by 30 percent in real terms in 1979. The World Bank estimated that the loss of production alone during 1978–80 amounted to $2 billion, equal to national product in the peak year of 1977.[13] Table 13.1 gives sectoral output in 1980 prices for 1971 to 1980, and we see that despite a 10 percent recovery of gross domestic product in 1980, output barely reached the level of 1971.

TABLE 13.1
SECTORAL OUTPUT AT CONSTANT PRICES, 1971–80 (1977=100)

Years	GDP		Agri-culture	Manufac-turing	Construc-tion
	Per Capita	Total			
1971	93	76	77	68	48
1972	93	78	77	72	52
1973	94	82	82	74	60
1974	103	92	89	84	91*
1975	102	94	95	87	89
1976	103	99	96	91	102
1977	100	100	100	100	100
1978	90	93	109	102	60
1979	65	70	94	71	16
1980	70	76	86	83	30

Source: World Bank, 1981.
*Large increase due to the earthquake that destroyed Managua.

However, even the modest recovery in 1980 proved unsustainable. This came as a rude shock, for the first development plan had been extremely optimistic.[14] This optimism was not totally without basis. While the productive structure of the economy suffered major material destruction during the war,[15] the fall in current output in 1979 was much greater, leaving extensive unutilized capacity.

Putting this unutilized capacity back to work required foreign exchange for inputs, machinery, spare parts, and inventory accumulation. Immediately after the Triumph, it appeared that the foreign exchange problem would be alleviated by external borrowing. Multilateral agencies, particularly the World Bank and Inter-American Development Bank, quickly came forward with concessionary loans.[16] The generosity of multilateral and bilateral leaders was not unaffected by a hope to encourage the process along "moderate" lines. But whatever the motivation, the inflow of foreign exchange financed a huge balance-of-trade deficit that allowed for some recovery in 1980. Further, export earnings in 1979 had been only $90 million below 1978 despite the war, so it seemed reasonable to presume that on the basis of foreign loans and trade, recovery would continue. However, the recovery in 1980 did not indicate the future. On the contrary, it proved unsustainable, particularly in manufacturing.

As described above, manufacturing had lost its dynamism due to relative price changes and the collapse of the CACM. In addition, the consequence of the war on manufacturing was to make it substantially more import-using than before. This, in turn, meant that the expansion of manufacturing output placed an unsustainable burden on the balance of payments. As we noted, manufacturing had been dependent upon imported inputs before the Triumph, but this dependency increased dramatically. For example, during 1979 Nicaragua's cattle ranchers (and the Somoza family was the largest) decapitalized rapidly, slaughtering their herds or driving them across the border for sale. As a consequence, a number of inputs that had previously been supplied domestically had to be imported. The dairy sector virtually disappeared, so Nicaragua went from exporting powdered milk to importing it as an input for the domestic bottling plants, with a resultant annual loss of $10 million in foreign exchange. With the cattle herds reduced to a fraction of their former size, hides could no longer be exported; quite the reverse, quality hides for making shoes now had to be imported.

The destruction of domestic supply affected almost all sectors. Due to the sharp drop in cotton production, the supply of seed failed to meet the demand of the cooking oil factories. Again, Nicaragua switched from being an exporter to relying on imports to satisfy consumer demand. Even the chemical sector suffered. Prior to the war, extract of pine sap from forests on the Atlantic Coast represented an important input for both household and industrial chemicals. The struggle to overthrow Somoza itself disrupted communications, temporarily suspending supply. Subsequently, U.S.-funded counterrevolutionary activity turned the Atlantic Coast into a war zone, denying access to the forestry sector.

Relative price changes, loss of the regional market, and war destruction catastrophically transformed the import-export balance of the manufacturing sector. In 1974 the manufacturing sector as a whole had imported just $1 million in inputs over its exports, and if one subtracted out agroindustry the excess of import of inputs over exports was still only $16 million. In 1980, at the same level of output, the negative import-export balances had risen to perhaps as much as $30 and $80 million, respectively. The new situation was even more serious than these figures indicate. Prior to the war, manufactured exports had tended to increase faster than imports of inputs as the economy expanded, so that growth tended to *improve* the economy's trade balance. This, of course, is one of the reasons that the manufacturing sector had grown so rapidly. After the war, the reverse held: expansion of manufacturing worsened the balance of trade.

In part as a consequence of the recovery of the manufacturing sector, Nicaragua ran a trade deficit of $350 million in 1980, which represented over 15 percent of GDP. A modest expansion of the economy in 1981 increased the deficit to $400 million. By 1981 it was clear to even the casual observer that the situation called for extreme policy measures. As structured, the manufacturing sector could not be maintained at its 1980–81 level: Its import requirements were too great and its export prospects too few. Further, foreign exchange became scarcer with each succeeding month as the Reagan Administration sought to freeze the Nicaraguan government out of international financial markets.

STRUGGLE TO CONTROL

The difficulty of restructuring manufacturing was made all the more intractable for the new government because of the lack of state control over the sector. Shortly after the Triumph, the state confiscated the property of the fallen dictator and many thought that the seized property would provide the basis for rational planning. It emerged, however, that the Somoza family had controlled considerably less of the manufacturing sector than had been rumored. Pre-Triumph estimates ran as high as 50 percent of industrial plant, but once the first wave of confiscations ended, less than one-third of manufacturing production fell under state control, as Table 13.2 shows.

If one includes the petroleum subsector (100 percent private), majority state companies accounted for approximately 30 percent of manufacturing output in 1980 and 1981, and totally private companies 50 percent. In the remaining companies, the state held a minority of equity. These latter companies should be considered part of the private sector with regard to decisionmaking, for the limited manpower of the state allowed for little intervention in their day-to-day affairs. One could argue that the

TABLE 13.2
PROPORTIONAL DISTRIBUTION OF MANUFACTURING OUTPUT BY OWNERSHIP CATEGORIES, 1980 AND 1983 (IN PERCENTAGES)

Enterprises	All Manufacturing		Excluding Petroleum	
	1980	1981	1980	1981
Majority state owned	29	31	39	40
Minority state owned	20	18	22	24
100 percent private	51	51	39	36
	100	100	100	100

Source: Instituto Nicaragüese de Estadística y Censos, industrial surveys for 1980 and 1981, preliminary results.

petroleum subsector should be excluded from the calculation, since it had few links to the rest of manufacturing, and state regulation of crude oil imports effectively controlled the output level. In addition, the state controlled the price of the output. Indeed, it could be argued that the state had more effective control over petroleum refining than it did over many companies nominally in the public sector. If petroleum refining is excluded, state companies accounted for 40 percent of manufacturing output in 1980 and 1981.

However, the actual control that this allowed over the operation of the manufacturing sector should not be exaggerated. Ownership of assets is normally taken to be synonymous with effective control over production, but this is an ideological inference, not an analytical one. Control of production is a concept with different levels of meaning, and one must specify these analytically. At one level, ownership relates to a claim on the return on capital. At this level, the Nicaraguan manufacturing sector remained predominantly in private hands during the first five years after the Triumph. The majority claim on profit-yielding assets was in private hands, and, in addition, private companies were more nominally profitable than state companies. It is important to stress that we refer to "nominal" profitability, for losses by state companies in part reflected pricing decisions based upon criteria other than profitability at the enterprise level—for example, the decision to provide commodities at prices that made the products accessible to the poor.

At a second and more fundamental level, control of production refers to the capacity to direct and manage production consistent with pre-determined priorities. At this level, ownership of assets does not indicate control. The Nicaraguan economy five years after the Triumph remained overwhelmingly a market economy, the degree of state ownership not-withstanding. This was particularly the case in manufacturing, where even state enterprises bought their inputs and sold their output as any capitalist enterprise might do. In effect, the confiscation of assets brought the state a claim on a portion of the return on capital without allowing for effective control over the economy and particularly the manufacturing sector.

This lack of effective control is what justifies the use of the term "mixed economy." Ignoring for the moment the conflict between the state and private capital, one can characterize the Nicaraguan manufacturing sector as having a "mix" of state and private ownership, in an environment governed by market forces. The state's inability to assert its dominance over production in part derived from the basis upon which the confiscations were made. These were carried out as a punitive measure against the Somoza family and its court of associates. While the business empire of the Somoza family was no doubt rationally organized for the purpose of private profitability, it had a structure of little use for purposes of economic planning. In 1980 there were approximately 400 manufacturing enterprises hiring 20 or more workers, and in only 82 of these did the state have majority ownership.[17] Further, these 82 were scattered through the sector in a largely random manner. In few subsectors of any importance did state enterprises constitute the majority of companies or contribute the majority of production.

The typical case was the one in which a state enterprise produced and marketed in direct competition with private capital. In addition, state enterprises had little vertical integration so they constituted no coherent entity within the manufacturing sector. Given this irrational ownership pattern, the body responsible for state enterprises, COIP (Corporación Industrial del Pueblo) found itself in an untenable situation. Competition with private capital at the level of individual products made a coherent, centralized price policy virtually impossible, and the lack of input-output linkages among state enterprises left little basis for a centrally directed investment policy. In effect, COIP found itself in a role analogous to a capitalist holding company, with little choice but to let decisionmaking devolve to the enterprise level. This implied surrendering control of production to the logic and anarchy of the market.

This situation prevailed for the first four years following the Triumph. While hardly desirable, the means to remedy it were politically explosive. In the absence of political constraints, the solution to the chaotic ownership of manufacturing would have been for the state to nationalize or expropriate additional enterprises while divesting itself of others, according to some coherent strategy. Whatever that strategy might be, the existing ownership pattern had glaring anomalies: on the one hand, COIP accounted for less than 5 percent of output in the strategic basic chemicals industry; on the other hand, its ownership of a brewery had questionable relevance for economic planning.

Any move to rationalize ownership would have provoked a violent outcry from the private sector and been used by the government's opponents as evidence that "pluralism" and the "mixed economy" were being abandoned in favor of "dogmatic socialism."[18] Whether because it wished to avoid such a confrontation with private capital, or for other reasons such as internal divisions over economic strategy, the government took no major steps toward rationalizing the manufacturing sector until the pressure of war forced it to do so.

Certainly it was in the interest of private capital to perpetuate the chaotic situation in the manufacturing sector. Given that private capital had lost state power and had little prospect to remedy the loss, the economic disorganization served its goals. On the one hand, state ownership of 30 percent of manufacturing could provide superficial support to the argument that the Sandinista leadership intended to control the economy and build Soviet-style socialism. On the other hand, that ownership allowed for little effective control, and in practice the government repeatedly took steps to encourage the private sector.

The need to assert control over the manufacturing sector represented one aspect of an economic civil war that began in Nicaragua virtually from the moment Somoza fell from power. From the outset, the landlords and capitalists organized themselves to undermine the effort for economic reconstruction. In the political sphere this opposition would eventually result in support for counterrevolutionary insurgency.[19] In the economic sphere, the capitalists used their control over production to undermine the Sandinista-led coalition government.

In manufacturing the capitalists pursued a clandestine war against the state. Aware of the economic sabotage, the government enacted a law against decapitalization, with confiscation as a sanction for private producers who failed to maintain their plant and equipment or to utilize it sufficiently. However, the law proved virtually impossible to enforce. Given the shortage of foreign exchange, it was difficult in practice to distinguish between underutilization of capacity due to shortage of inputs and spare parts or due to willful reduction of output designed to create shortages.

But a number of actions by private capital provided plentiful *prima facia* evidence of calculated resistance. In 1980 and 1981 the Nicaraguan government had received loans from the World Bank intended for the replacement of equipment and inventories destroyed during the war of national liberation. The loans explicitly stipulated that part of the funds should go to the private sector.[20] The terms of the loans made the money virtually a free gift to private capital: They could be repaid in local currency and the interest rate was less than half the rate of domestic inflation. Yet, by the second half of 1981, few applications for use of these funds came forward from the private sector, and those applications submitted were subsequently withdrawn.

Two examples indicate the scope of private sector resistance. In early 1982 the local subsidiary of a multinational shoe company applied for several million dollars to reactivate a dormant assembly line. When the bureaucratic process was virtually complete, the local manager withdrew the request, explaining that the project had been vetoed by the head office in Canada. About the same time, the Nicaraguan owner of a small shoe company applied for money to replace a machine destroyed during the fighting, then abandoned his request. In private conversation he reported that he had come under extreme pressure from his fellow capitalists to drop the project.[21] Rumors of even more blatant techniques of economic resistance circulated in Managua.[22]

Thus the government was faced with a rapidly deteriorating situation in manufacturing. As a result of relative price changes during the 1970s and the collapse of the CACM, the manufacturing sector was in need of reorganization no matter what its ownership structure. At the same time, private capital owned 70 percent of the sector and was virtually on strike against the state. For the 30 percent of state-owned manufacturing, the enterprises were heterogeneous, managers were obsessed with day-to-day crises, and operating decisions were dictated by competitive pressure from private enterprise so that coherent and integrated planning proved virtually impossible. The situation in manufacturing through 1983 verified the comment of a sympathetic and frustrated foreign advisor to the Nicaraguan goverment: "In Nicaragua the state owns 25 percent of the economy and controls none of it."

RESOLUTION THROUGH ATTRITION

In late 1981 the Nicaraguan government arrested, tried, and sentenced to detention three prominent businessmen. The precise charges against the defendants were only of legal interest; in effect, the government issued a formal declaration, recognizing a state of economic insurrection that had been gathering strength for two years. The arrests provoked an international outcry, and even supporters of the Nicaraguan Revolution judged them as a political blunder in terms of both the foreign and domestic impact. The government's opponents advertised the detentions as proof that the Sandinista leadership intended to destroy the private sector. Moderate and social democratic supporters of the Revolution feared that this might prove a correct prediction.

Certainly it could be justified that the moment to move purposefully against the insurrection by private capital had come. Investment by private capital in manufacturing had been negative since the Triumph, and the longer the chaotic situation persisted, the more plant and equipment would deteriorate. The wider political context also had grown .more hostile: Agents of the U.S. government were funding an armed insurrection in the Atlantic Coast and an invasion force of ex-National Guardsmen was being prepared in Florida and Honduras.

Ironically, the celebrated detention of the businessmen presaged not a bold move to rationalize the economy under state direction, but a concerted and ultimately unsuccessful attempt to induce private sector economic cooperation. In January 1982 an export promotion scheme was initiated at the urging of Alfredo César, then President of the Central Bank. Prior to the measure, producers received their export revenue in córdobas at the official exchange rate (10 to the dollar). The new program allowed manufacturing firms to take 40 percent of their receipts in the form of an import certificate or convert the same portion to córdobas at the parallel exchange rate (28 to the dollar). The latter alternative in effect increased a firm's export revenue by over 70 percent. The advantage of the certificate was that it allowed a firm to bypass virtually all of the bureaucratic steps involved in securing an import license and the foreign exchange to go with the license.

When the scheme was being debated, considerable concern was expressed over the feasibility of issuing import certificates. Since manufacturing firms suffered from a severe shortage of foreign exchange and most private firms were making profits, it seemed reasonable to predict that there would be a robust demand for the certificates. But if capitalists opted for certificates to any great extent, the Central Bank might not have sufficient foreign exchange to honor them. At the very least, failure to honor the certificates would have been embarrassing to the Central Bank.

As matters developed, the concern proved unnecessary. During the first four months of the export promotion scheme's life, over $5 million in certificates could have been claimed, and only $10,000 in certificates were issued.[23] Virtually without exception capitalists took their córdobas at the parallel exchange rate rather than opting for certificates that would have allowed them to expand production. A sudden surge in the black market rate for the córdoba strongly suggested that private manufacturers were selling their windfall córdobas for dollars and sending the dollars abroad. This chain of events prompted the joke that César's scheme had indeed stimulated exports—of dollars. The Nicaraguan government had further evidence of where the loyalty of private capital lay.

During the rest of 1982 the government took a number of initiatives to encourage private sector cooperation, including a formal reopening of the dialogue with the opposition that had been suspended the previous year. In the Council of State a debate began on a number of laws to prepare for national elections. While these political questions did not seem directly related to issues of investment and production, in fact they represented the heart of the matter. Private capital's basic complaint lay not in the economic sphere, but over who would hold political power.

However, none of the conciliatory steps by the government stimulated any truce in the clandestine war being fought in the spheres of production and distribution. Decapitalization by private sector producers proceeded, forcing confiscations of several manufacturing plants. Due to lack of management personnel and broader political considerations, confiscations were made reluctantly. At one point it was intended that a list of companies to be confiscated would be announced at the third anniversary celebrations (July 1982). Partly with an eye to the foreign impact of this (President Luis Herrera Campíns of Venezuela was the guest of honor at the celebration), no expropriations were announced. But subsequent evidence of decapitalization made expropriations inevitable.

For four years the Nicaraguan government had pursued a policy based on concilation with the private sector. While relations between the government and private capital had been antagonistic and laced with fiery rhetoric from both sides, the fact remained that the state had had the power to eliminate private capital from the economy and had chosen not to do so. During 1979–83 private capital had been quite profitable, and the limits to its profits resulted not from state regulation but from a shortage of foreign exchange, a malady suffered by capitalists in the other countries of Central America.

The consequence of the conciliation policy was the progressive deterioration of the manufacturing sector. This probably would have occurred in any case. Had the state initiated a bold plan of expropriation in 1980 or 1981, it would have faced insurmountable difficulties. The state lacked the personnel to manage the 80 or more enterprises actually confiscated much less double that number. A clear move toward state control of manufacturing might well have resulted in the flight of agricultural capitalists, whom the government successfully induced to cooperate with it. Further expropriations soon after the Triumph would certainly have resulted in loss of multilateral sources of credit, and very likely many bilateral sources—France, the Federal Republic of Germany, and most of the Latin American governments. And, of course, isolation of Nicaragua diplomatically as a "communist" country would have been much easier. The consequence of early and bold action might well have been to leave the Nicaraguan government with a manufacturing sector it owned and controlled but could not manage or supply with inputs.

Insofar as the goal of manufacturing policy was to reactivate and restructure the sector to the basic needs of the population and the struggle against counterrevolution, the policy proved a failure, in contrast to agriculture, where the same goals met with relative success. Why agricultural policy was more successful lies beyond the scope of this chapter, but the answer lies in the structural and social characteristics of the two sectors, not in the relative merit of the policies followed.

As of 1984 the clandestine war raging in Nicaraguan manufacturing was resolving itself through the decline and partial collapse of the sector. From 1980 through 1983, the economy's external trade deficit averaged $350 million and significant reduction of this deficit would require a contraction of manufacturing production, as occurred in 1983 (when the economy as a whole grew by 5 percent). After 1981 the government allocated less and less foreign exchange to the manufacturing sector. As a result, dozens of factories fell idle and more would close their gates in the following years, probably not to open again. In the early 1980s this was common throughout Central America and South America, and it may be that the decline in Nicaragua was slower than elsewhere.

NOTES

1. *Central American Report* (Guatemala City) 11, no. 8 (February 24, 1984):58. The preliminary estimate of a 2 percent growth rate, announced at the end of 1983, was subsequently revised to 5 percent.

2. For a further discussion, see John Weeks, *The Economies of Central America* (New York: Holmes & Meier, 1985), Chapters 2 and 6.

3. We refer here only to the private sector's behavior in industry. The role of private capital in agriculture was considerably more cooperative.

4. For a comparison of growth rates among the Central American countries in the 1960s and 1970s, see Weeks, *The Economies*, Chapter 3.

5. World Bank, *Memorandum on Recent Economic Development and Prospects of Nicaragua* (Washington, D.C., 1978).

6. See Weeks, *The Economies*, Chapters 3 and 4.

7. The impact on agriculture was also strongly depressing, primarily due to increased costs of fertilizer and pesticides.

8. The effects we summarize here are presented in more detail in an unpublished paper in which the Nicaraguan manufacturing sector's behavior during 1960–77 is simulated in a six-equation simultaneous econometric model. Using that model, we conclude that changes in import and export prices reduced manufacturing output by 15 percent during 1967–77 below what it would have been had import and export prices remained constant at the 1968 levels. See John Weeks, "Impact of Relative Price Changes on Nicaraguan Manufacturing" (Washington, D.C., 1982).

9. The impact of changes in the terms of trade during 1960–80 on the balance of trade for the five CACM countries is calculated in Weeks, *The Economies*, Chapter 4.

10. A nonconvertible córdoba had serious implications for the settlement of trading accounts, since it required Nicaragua's external payments to be controlled by the Central Bank.

11. See Weeks, *The Economies*, Chapter 8.

12. Economic Commission for Latin America (ECLA) *Nicaragua: The Impact of Recent Political Changes* (Santiago, Chile: United Nations, 1981), pp. 17–18. this report assesses war damage and summarizes the program of the new Nicaraguan government.

13. The war ended in July 1979, but agricultural production was disrupted for the next year's harvest because of the timing of the agricultural cycle.

14. Ministerio de Planificación, *Programa de Reactivación Económica en Beneficio del Pueblo* (Managua: MIPLAN, 1980), Chapter 1.

15. See ECLA, *Nicaragua*, p. 36. Destruction of manufacturing plant and equipment, almost all caused by the National Guard, amounted to approximately 20 percent of capacity.

16. For the breakdown of foreign loans during the first two years after the Triumph, see Weeks, *The Economies*, Chapter 7. All multilateral lending amounted to 28 percent of the $1,100 million debt incurred during the two years, with Latin American governments the source of another 23 percent, and private banks 13 percent. East European governments contributed only 11 percent of the total.

17. These numbers are based on the manufacturing survey of 1980.

18. The leaders of the Revolution were frequently accused of this sin. See, for example, Arturo Cruz Sequiera, Jr., "Nicaragua: A Revolution in Crisis," *SAIS Review* (School of Advanced International Studies, Johns Hopkins University) 4, no. 1 (Winter-Spring 1984).

19. Alfonso Robelo, member of the first post-Triumph Junta and one of Nicaragua's largest capitalists, was a key figure in the planning of a counterrevolutionary band operating out of Costa Rica.

20. World Bank, *Staff Appraisal Report, Nicaragua: Industrial Rehabilitation Credit Project* (Washington, D.C. June 5, 1981).

21. This episode was revealed in a confidential interview granted to this author in May 1982.

22. A Nicaraguan capitalist mildly favorable to the government reported to this author that he had been offered dollars in a Miami bank account to compensate him for reducing production. Obviously, such arrangements are impossible to document.

23. Information supplied by the Central Bank of Nicaragua.

PART IV
SOCIAL POLICY

The real measure of a revolutionary government is whether or not it works effectively and quickly to implement changes that uplift the condition of the common citizen. The chapters in this section discuss Sandinista social programs in areas such as agrarian reform, popular education, health, social welfare, housing, food policy, and culture.

Given the overwhelming economic problems faced by the country in this period, one might have expected that the new government would have been able to accomplish very little in the social realm. In reality, however, the Revolution achieved more social reform in five years than most prerevolutionary Latin American countries had accomplished in decades. Part of this success can be attributed to the fact that such limited budgetary resources as did exist could now be spent honestly and with maximum impact. Then, too, in areas such as housing and land usage, the simple passage and enforcement of laws designed to ease the exploitation of the common citizen helped considerably.

The real key to the implementation of otherwise utopian projects, however, lay in the voluntary participation of hundreds of thousands of common citizens through the Sandinist grass-roots organizations. It was through this vehicle that the spectacular 1980 Literacy Crusade—which won Nicaragua international acclaim including a very prestigious UNESCO award—was made possible. And grass-roots participation also played a crucial role in the ongoing program in popular education as well as in preventive health care, neighborhood sanitation, low-income housing, food distribution, crime prevention, and so on.

Sadly, however, by 1984 many Sandinista social programs had to be curtailed somewhat as a result of the contra war. In spite of the crucial role played by grass-roots voluntarism, the exigencies of war had forced many scarce and precious human and material resources to be diverted out of social programs into defense. This condition was likely to continue as long as the aggression that occasioned it prevailed.

Chapter 14
Agrarian Reform

JOSEPH R. THOME
DAVID KAIMOWITZ

Even before the final overthrow of the Somoza dictatorship the Sandinista forces initiated the land reform long promised in their political programs. As new areas fell into their hands, the triumphant revolutionaries began the confiscation and redistribution of lands owned by Somoza and his followers. Within days after the final victory, the new government (JGRN) institutionalized this process and embarked upon an ambitious and long-range program of agrarian reform and agricultural development. The most immediate goal was political: to recover from the Somoza clan all the properties that its members had accumulated over 45 years of dictatorship. The government also hoped to dramatically transform the structure of resource distribution and power relationships in the countryside and increase agricultural production, within a context of a mixed economy and through a process that would be responsive to the needs and involve the participation of the small peasant farmer and landless rural worker.[1]

Given the length and bitterness of the revolutionary struggle, and the inequitable social, political, and economic structures that prevailed in Nicaragua prior to the Sandinista victory, these goals were hardly surprising. What may be surprising to some, in light of the cold-war rhetoric used by the Reagan Administration and most of the media to describe the Nicaraguan government and its actions, is the pragmatism and flexibility of this agrarian reform. Strict adherence to preconceived models was largely avoided in favor of eclectic, usually thought-out but sometimes improvised, policies and programs. Even more surprising perhaps, given the serious disruptions caused by the U.S. economic blockade and the U.S.-supported *contra* revolutionary activities and the usual problems generated by any process of drastic social change, was that the Nicaraguans were by and large progressing toward their stated agrarian reform goals.

THE FORMATIVE PHASE: 1979 TO JULY 1981

The first phase of the Nicaraguan agrarian reform was characterized by the swift and drastic reduction of privately owned *latifundia* and the concomitant formation of a strong state sector in agriculture (Area de Propiedad del Pueblo.).[2] During this period, the government concentrated most of its efforts on the management of this newly formed state sector and on a series of Keynesian credit and services measures aimed at reactivating an economy paralyzed by the war. The legal and institutional foundations necessary for a complete process of agrarian reform were also laid at this time.

Acting under Decrees No. 3 of July 20, 1979, and No. 38 of August 8, 1979, the Nicaraguan government had by December 1979 confiscated all of the rural properties owned by the Somoza family and its cronies: a total of 1,500 estates with an area of 800,000 hectares (2 million acres), representing 20 percent of Nicaragua's cultivatable land.* Mostly modern farms dedicated to export crops or cattle raising, these properties included many processing plants and stockyards and represented 17 to 20 percent of the gross agricultural production of the country and 43 percent of all the land held in properties larger than 500 manzanas.[3] The financial system, the export of agricultural goods, and natural resource industries were also nationalized.

The extent and nature of this confiscatory process was almost unique among agrarian reform processes. For one thing, it was virtually costless, in political as well as fiscal terms. Unlike Cuba, no multinational enterprises were affected; indeed, foreign investment in agriculture, even by individuals, was virtually nonexistent in Nicaragua. Moreover, as most commercial farmers in Nicaragua both despised the Somozas and operated farms smaller than 500 manzanas, they were neither alienated nor particularly threatened by these confiscations, at least at that time.[4]

While socialist ideology may have played a major role in the establishment of a state-farm tenure system over most of these confiscated estates, their large size and concentration on export production was also crucial in determining the type of tenure they were to have. The foreign exchange generated by the production from these large farms was crucial for the national economy. Distributing these farms and their agroindustrial components among the landless could have lowered or disrupted their production; this was a risk the government was simply not willing or able to take. Thus were born the state farms, or Unidades de Producción Estatal (UPE), which along with all other nationalized or state enterprises came to be known as the Area de Propiedad del Pueblo, or APP. These UPEs were organized into agricultural "complexes," which in turn formed part of financially autonomous "companies" (empresas). By 1984 there were 92

---

*1 manzana = 0.7 hectares = 1.75 acres

agricultural empresas, representing over 1,000 UPEs and employing 64,855 workers (the empresas included processing plants, stockyards, and the like).[5]

A product of a January 1980 fusion of the Institute of Agrarian Reform (INRA), a special agency created after the Revolution, and the old Ministry of Agriculture, the new Ministry of Agricultural Development and Agrarian Reform (MIDINRA) since that date administered the agrarian reform as well as all other state-run programs in the agricultural sector.[6] Aside from managing the large state-farm sector, MIDINRA in this initial phase also instituted or participated in other programs designed to increase production, help the small tenant and peasant farmer, promote cooperative organization, and ensure the participation of the rural worker and peasant farmer in the agrarian reform process.

By the end of 1980, for example, the total amount of agricultural credit had been increased from 2.3 billion córdobas (1978) to 5.2 billion, with the share of the small producer sector growing from 4 to 18 percent. Credit was given preferentially to those small farmers organized in credit and service cooperatives (CCS) or production cooperatives (CAS). These cooperatives were also charged lower rates of interest—10 and 8 percent respectively, as compared to 17 percent to individual farmers not associated in co-operatives.[7]

The increased credit was crucial for reactivating an agricultural sector devastated by the war. With the exception of corn, basic grain production rose rapidly to approximately prewar levels. In other products the recovery was not as substantial. But this improved access to credit was not achieved without problems. The recovery rates were fairly low, due in part to the indiscriminate nature of the program and inadequate means to store and transport any marketable surplus. (Most loan defaults were finally written off in 1983.)

Although emphasis in this first period was placed largely on economic recovery and the development of the new state sector, a number of other significant programs were also carried out. Workers participation was promoted through the Asociación de Trabajadores del Campo (ATC), the association or union that represented both rural labor and small peasant farmers. Though enjoying close ties with the Sandinist front, the ATC nevertheless displayed its independence on various occasions. It promoted a successful campaign to keep the government from returning lands that for various reasons had been confiscated from nonsomocistas in the first months after the Revolution. The ATC also frequently complained of poor conditions on state and private farms, demanding compliance with existing regulations.[8]

Encouraging the integration of the small producer into cooperatives was also one of MIDINRA's goals. Other agricultural policies designed to favor small peasants included a dramatic increase in the quantity (although not always the quality) of technical assistance, direct government purchase and sale of basic grains, and rent control for agricultural lands.[9]

Despite the government's confiscation of Somoza properties, the private sector continued to play a predominant role in the agricultural sector. By 1981, private, commercial farms concentrating on such export products as cotton, coffee, cattle, and sugar still accounted for approximately 60 percent of Nicaragua's cultivable land. The government used various mechanisms to maintain cordial relations with the larger private farmers. UPANIC (the Agricultural Producers Association), for instance, was assigned one seat in the State Council, Nicaragua's new legislative assembly, and also allowed to participate in various government technical commissions. There was also an attempt to provide economic incentives to these commercial farmers. Low-interest loans were made available, and the government assured access to the necessary inputs and set prices calculated to produce substantial margins of profit. Personal income and corporate profits were taxed at low rates in an attempt to stimulate private investment.

At the same time, new limits and controls were placed on the private sector. Private producers were denied direct access to foreign exchange. Social legislation regulating working conditions, wages, and the freedom of unionization was enforced, probably for the first time in Nicaragua's history.[10]

While most rural workers, small peasant farmers, and larger private producers adjusted to the new framework, certain problems and tensions began to develop during this period. In spite of economic incentives for production, many commercial producers pushed for concessions from the government in the political spheres and for guarantees against future confiscations. In addition, some large landowners were reluctant during 1979/80 to enter into sharecropping or rental agreements with small producers, and in certain cases even evicted tenants and sharecroppers. This created increased pressure for land from landless peasants and workers and resulted in some land invasions. As explained below, MIDINRA's responses to these problems did not placate either the landless or the landowners, both of whom clamored for clear and predictable rules of the game.[11]

THE CONSOLIDATION PHASE: JULY 1981 THROUGH MID-1984

If we summarize the two major concerns of agricultural policy in the first period as economic reactivation and the creation of a state-farm sector based on confiscated Somoza properties, the promulgation in August 1981 of the Agrarian Reform Law marked a new policy concern for the Nicaraguan government: A strategy had to be created for long-term economic growth in a form that benefited the impoverished majority and reacted to the increasing military difficulties created by the U.S. support of counterrevolutionary activities.

In this section we will examine a number of the more important policies and institutional mechanisms that were initiated in this second phase of the agrarian reform. Among these changes or adjustments were the enactment of an agrarian reform law aimed at converting inefficient latifundia into agricultural production cooperatives; a deemphasis on the state-farm model, with a corresponding emphasis on the small farm sector and on the production of basic grains; increased participation by the rural workers and small farmers in the agrarian reform process; more regional autonomy; and greater security for the private farmer, whether large or small.

The Agrarian Reform Law and Its Implementation

In August 1981 the Nicaraguan Council of State promulgated Decree No. 782, known as "The Agrarian Law."[12] The need for a land reform law that would deal directly with the problems of large inefficient farms and precapitalist tenure mechanisms had been apparent for over a year. The initial legal instrument for confiscating properties owned by Somoza or his allies had long exhausted its possibilities. Since then, the ATC as well as other campesino groups had been clamoring for more lands; some landless campesinos had gone beyond demands and had engaged in the invasion of idle lands, both private and public. MIDINRA responded with ad hoc measures. Its regional offices, for instance, often acted as extraofficial conflict resolution institutions, mediating disputes between landowners and the peasants, or even between peasants and the state. Some landowners agreed to lease the land to the land invaders, and some state lands were either rented or temporarily lent in "usufruct" to the campesinos. A few private properties were purchased from the landowners, and, in rare instances, campesinos were evicted from the occupied lands.

But these did not satisfy anyone. The landowners insisted that security of tenure was a prerequisite for raising productivity. ATC and other campesino groups kept pressuring the government to live up to its promises of making more land accessible. The government itself wanted a planned and controlled process of land redistribution that would promote rather than discourage productivity among both small and large farmers.

The result was a very moderate law. The first article, for example, proclaimed that "[the] present law guarantees the rights to private property over the land to all those who employ it productively and efficiently." Its second and third articles made subject to expropriation only those portions of properties in excess of 500 manzanas in the Pacific area and 1,000 manzanas in the rest of the country that also lay idle, or were underused or being rented out. Lower limits of 50 manzanas in Pacific provinces and 100 manzanas for the rest of the country existed only for properties owned by absentee landlords that were being worked through sharecropping or similar arrangements.

In expropriating properties, MIDINRA was to follow an administrative process established by the law, including judicial review by newly established agrarian tribunals. Compensation was based on the values declared by the owners for property tax purposes and was payable through bonds maturing in 15 to 25 years. Landless campesinos who worked in the expropriated estates as sharecroppers or in other precarious forms of tenancy were to be given priority in the subsequent redistribution. Beneficiaries were encouraged to form production cooperatives, but individual or family assignments were also permitted. In any case, the land was assigned gratuitously, together with property titles subject to conditions: The land could not be sold or otherwise transferred or subdivided, but it could pass in an indivisible form to the beneficiary's heirs.[13]

Through November 1983, 436 farms with an area of 421,000 manzanas were expropriated under the new law. Of these, 18 percent were expropriated because the farms were abandoned; 62.9 percent due to inefficient exploitation; and 18.1 percent for illegal rental and sharecropping arrangments. From this expropriated land, 1,418 titles covering 381,396 manzanas were distributed benefiting 26,000 families. Production cooperatives received titles to 79 percent of this land; campesinos received individual titles to the remaining 21 percent. Most of this expropriation and distribution occurred during 1983.[14]

Table 14.1 clearly indicates the significant change brought about in Nicaragua through the confiscation of Somoza lands and the application of the 1981 agrarian reform law. The latifundia, defined in Nicaragua as farms/estates larger than 500 manzanas,[15] and other farms larger than 200 manzanas had their control over cultivable land reduced from 55 to 22 percent, while family to medium-sized farms (10 to 199 manzanas) slightly increased their share of the land from 42.6 to 44 percent. Yet, private, individually operated farms continued to control 70 percent of the land. The reform sector (CAS and APP) went from 0 to 30 percent; interestingly enough, in 1983 there was a slight decline in the amount of land held by state farms, as some of it was distributed to CAS.

This decrease in the area in state farms was part of a more general tendency in Nicaragua to deemphasize the state farms in comparison with production and credit and service cooperatives. This new view could be seen in the long-term projections made by the MIDINRA minister,

TABLE 14.1
LAND TENURE FROM 1978 TO 1983 (PERCENTAGES OF CULTIVABLE LAND IN EACH CATEGORY)

Type and Size of Landholdings	1978	1982	1983
Private (individual)			
Over 500 manzanas	41.2	16.5	12.0
200 to 500	13.8	12.0	10.0
50 to 199	29.7	29.7	30.0
10 to 49	12.9	12.9	14.0
Less than 10	2.4	3.0	4.0
Production Cooperatives	0	1.9	7.0
State Farms	0	24.0	23.0
Total	100.0	100.0	100.0

Source: "Reforma Agraria: Esta es la Democracia," Barricada, Lunes Socio-Económicos No. 32 (December 19, 1983).

Comandante Jaime Wheelock, of a rural structure in which 20 percent of the agricultural land would be owned and operated by the state, 40–50 percent by cooperatives, and the remaining 30–40 percent by non-cooperative private producers.[10]

Investment Strategy: PAN and Agroindustrial Projects

By 1981 the Nicaraguan government began to take a hard look at its agricultural production needs and the means to meet them. The overall situation was very difficult. The country suffered from balance-of-payments deficits and its foreign indebtedness was increasing. At the same time, demand for foodstuffs was growing rapidly due to increased incomes and population growth. An increasing percentage of imports were devoted to basic grains, particularly corn.

MIDINRA officials concluded that self-sufficiency in food staples such as corn and beans was a necessary precondition for successful agrarian reform and agricultural development. For decades, however, the production of beans and corn had been relegated to small peasant farmers working marginal lands, while the best lands and most resources had been dedicated to export crops. The consequent stagnation in the yields constituted one of the basic causes of rural poverty and restricted the growth of the internal market, one of the key barriers to the country's national development.

For these and other reasons, in March 1981 the JRGN enacted as a priority program the Plan Alimentario Nacional—PAN (the National Food Program). The basic objectives of PAN were to guarantee self-sufficiency in food staples; to establish an efficient national distribution system for agricultural products; and to increase rural employment and the real wages and incomes of rural workers and small- to medium-sized farmers, primarily via the prices paid for basic products.

The PAN had a twofold plan for increasing basic grain production. On the one hand it coordinated a campaign to increase production in traditional areas by small and medium producers. This was to be accomplished through favorable prices for producers, land redistribution, and increased services. Basic infrastructure, such as access roads and inexpensive grain storage facilities, was also improved.

The second part of PAN's program was based on a "Basic Grains Contingency Plan," designed to increase grain production rapidly in the Northern Pacific region through irrigation and advanced technology. The Contingency Plan, although more expensive than peasant production, focused on areas less subject to military aggression than the traditional basic grains producing regions of the country.[17]

Although perhaps the largest, the PAN was not the only investment program designed to promote import substitution and export production, particularly of processed agricultural products. Nicaragua began in mid-1981 to promote a number of large investment projects, concentrated chiefly in the state sector and financed in large part with foreign loans and donations. The Tipitoya-Malacotoya sugar mill project, initiated in 1982, was designed to be the largest of its type in Central America. Other major investment projects were also initiated for the capital-intensive production of milk (Chiltepe), cigarette tobacco for export, cacao, African palm, coconut, processed vegetable and fruit products, and others.[18]

The realization of these projects was a calculated risk for Nicaragua; it remained to be seen whether or not they would pay off in the future. These new investments monopolized much of the administrative, technical, and capital resources in the country and increased its indebtedness. If successful, these projects would show profits and form the basis for future growth. If not, they threatened to create debt and production problems for the country.

The Formation of UNAG

Created on April 26, 1981, the Union Nacional de Agricultores y Ganaderos (UNAG), or National Union of Farmers and Cattle Ranchers, was a response both to new policy determinations as represented by PAN and to the complaints of the small- and medium-sized producers, who felt unrepresented in the worker-dominated ATC and were beginning to join UPANIC, the agricultural producers' union controlled by the larger commercial farmers. If the small and medium producers were really to represent one of the principal groups favored by government policies and be represented in the decisionmaking process, these producers needed their own organization.[19]

The UNAG functioned through both "producers base committees" (UPB) and the various cooperatives it helped to form. In every municipality (county) the UNAG had its own board of directors and professional organizers. In 1983 it claimed a dues-paying membership of some 46,000 affiliates. In fact, in one way or another the UNAG worked with most of the 200,000 or so small- and medium-sized farmers that existed in the country. As an organization UNAG involved itself in most of the issues affecting its membership, from problems with roads and credit to promoting land distribution. The UNAG, like the ATC, was represented in most government councils and decisionmaking bodies affecting agriculture.[20]

The Promotion of Service and Production Cooperatives

In 1984 approximately 75 percent of the registered agricultural producers in Nicaragua were small- and medium-sized farmers.[21] Of these, most owned tiny parcels or had no land of their own and worked as individual producers under rental sharecropping or other precarious tenancy arrangements. Some were squatters or settlers on public domain land and only recently had begun to receive title to their holdings.

The dispersal of these small producers throughout the territory of Nicaragua complicated their participation in the agrarian reform process, the implementation of coherent agricultural development plans, and the provision of credit and technical assistance or other services. MIDINRA thus actively promoted the formation of production and service cooperatives among both existing small producers and the beneficiaries of agrarian reform programs. The PAN program provided an additional stimulus in this direction.

Lower interest rates and other subsidized services were among the incentives utilized to encourage cooperative organization. Decree No. 826 of September 17, 1981, the Ley de Cooperativas Agropecuarias (Agricultural Cooperatives Law), provided the institutional framework and guidelines for organizing and operating such cooperatives while at the same time protecting the individual rights of the members, particularly crucial in cases where individual peasant farmers integrated their small parcels into production cooperatives.[22] By the end of 1982, 499 production co-ops with 7,081 members; 1,587 credit and service co-ops with 52,052 members; and 710 cooperatives of other types with 5,758 members had been organized in the country (not including the Departments of Zelaya and Rio San Juan).[23]

Most of the credit and service cooperatives limited their functions to applying jointly for credit and serving as forums to discuss different problems affecting the producers. In the CAS, on the other hand, production was carried out collectively, typically on lands given to the cooperative by the government. While the CCS often had as many as 40–60 members, most CAS were formed by groups of 10–20 heads of families, most of whom had no previous access to land.

Special Titling Programs

From the 1950s onward Nicaragua had experienced a movement of thousands of peasant families into the agricultural frontier. By and large, this frontier consisted of public-domain lands in the northern and eastern sections of the country. Reacting to pressures from the United States, particularly the Alliance for Progress, Nicaragua promulgated a land reform law in 1961 and established a land reform agency, the Instituto Agrario Nacional (IAN). IAN carried out little if any expropriation and redistribution of privately owned lands, but it did try to provide some assistance—through credit programs, the provision of some minimal infrastructure, and the promise of land titles—to the impoverished peasant farmers or *colonos* who were settling in these remote and often marginal lands. Very few titles were actually distributed, however, and even those were never registered nor had any legal validity. Thus the tenure rights of these settlers remained insecure throughout these years.

In late 1982 MIDINRA initiated an ambitious program to distribute secure land titles to these settlers. Working in collaboration with UNAG, priority areas were selected for titling programs, and promoters were sent out to collect the necessary information so that the farmers could receive title to their lands. The titles themselves had some limitations; though they could be passed on to the campesino's direct heirs they could not be transferred to a third party without MIDINRA's authorization. During 1983 some 300,000 manzanas of land were titled through this process. Plans for 1984 called for the distribution of an additional 300,000 to 400,000 manzanas.[24]

The PAN policy of providing more incentives to the small producer was not the only factor that determined the big push toward titling programs during 1983 and 1984. For one thing, since its inception UNAG had been pushing for more land to peasant or small farmer producers, including the distribution of titles to those occupying public-domain lands. Maintaining or increasing the political support of UNAG and the settlers became particularly crucial during 1983–84, given the elections scheduled for November 1984 and, even more important, the counterrevolutionary activities in northern Nicaragua.[25]

The process of titling lands in the agricultural frontier was not, perhaps, one of the basic policies affecting production or even land redistribution as such. Its key feature was its pragmatic and antidogmatic nature. In spite of the fact that as a general policy the Nicaraguan government sought to socialize the agricultural production process and limit the realm of individual isolated farms, the government showed itself willing in given circumstances to put aside its preferences and support an individual land titling program, such as the one described above.

Decentralization and Regional Autonomy

During the 45-year rule of the Somoza family, the Nicaraguan government tended to centralize all decisionmaking in the national capital, Managua. While there existed local governments in each of Nicaragua's 16 departments and all of its municipalities, these governments were weak and the little power they did have was concentrated in the local large landholders who used their positions to pressure the national government for services. This pattern was inherited by the Sandinista government in the first period of the agrarian reform. MIDINRA had regional offices in each of the country's 16 departments, but the key decisions on production, land tenure, credit, and other services were concentrated in Managua.

This centralization, however, turned out to be inefficient and cumbersome. Nicaragua's regions were extremely heterogenous and both the problems and the solutions for a region like the Pacific Coast, where agriculture was based on large capital-intensive enterprises producing cotton or sugar with wage laborers, were quite distinct from those in the Northern and Central regions of the country, where peasant production and extensive cattle ranches dominated. The latter in turn presented features completely different from Nicaragua's Atlantic Coast, with its tropical slash-and-burn agriculture. At the level of production, investment decisions and effective administration could not be carried from a central office in Managua, where information systems were weak and there was little knowledge of local conditions. Finally, as military difficulties mounted due to U.S.-supported military incursions into Nicaragua, it was increasingly important that each region have a certain degree of self-sufficiency and autonomous decisionmaking power to deal with sensitive or emergency situations.

All of these considerations led to the decision in mid-1982 to reorganize the politicoadministrative structure of the country, allowing for greater local control over decisions. Gradually, nine regional governments (six regions and three "special zones") came to replace the 16 departmental governments as basic administrative units.[26] This process of regionalization included not only MIDINRA but all of the other ministries, the FSLN, and the popular organizations, although its speed of implementation varied from one institution to the next. Most state-owned enterprises, for example, came to be managed by the regional governments and had more independence than previously in terms of financing, investment plans, and personnel policies.

The regional offices of MIDINRA came to control the redistribution of land, production plans, and other key variables (although these were ill-coordinated on a national level), and this allowed for agrarian reform strategies that varied greatly from region to region. In the Northern Region of "Las Segovias" (Estelí, Madriz, and Nueva Segovia), for example, the agrarian reform strategy tended to emphasize small and medium producers and production cooperatives. The role of the state sector was largely reduced to servicing these producers as well as a small number of employment-generating enterprises engaged in tobacco and coffee production. On the other extreme, perhaps, would be the special zone of "Rio San Juan," where over 50 percent of the land was in the hands of the state and the regional government proposed to resettle much of the population and transform them into wage laborers. In León, Chinandega, Matagalpa, and Jinotega, large private producers and state farms formed the basis for the region's development plan.[27]

PARTICULAR CHARACTERISTICS OF THE NICARAGUAN AGRARIAN REFORM PROCESS AND CONCLUSIONS

As noted by Baumeister, one of the most peculiar characteristics of the Sandinist agrarian reform was the persistence of a strong capitalist sector within a political and ideological context of socialist goals.[28] The concept of the "mixed economy under popular hegemony," the description given by the Sandinistas of their economic policies, found its theoretical roots in the view that in the development of capitalist agriculture, the actual process of production is subject to the constraints of credit, marketing, and other external sectors linked to it. Thus, as Minister of Agriculture Jaime Wheelock stated, "more than control of the means of production, we are interested in controlling the economic surplus in order to distribute justly the nation's wealth."[29]

According to Baumeister, this view of the problem of agrarian reform and agrarian transformations was rooted in the particular structural features of Nicaragua's agrarian sector. Various factors, including Nicaragua's low population density and pressure for land, the late and limited (compared with other Central American countries) development of capitalist agriculture, and the overall political weakness of the medium and large producers outside the Somoza group all led to the creation of a key sector of "medium-size producers" or "multifamily farms" (farms with an acreage between 50 and 500 manzanas employing 12 or less workers).[30]

These medium-size producers were traditionally oriented by the available facilities of credit, marketing possibilities, and political structures. As a social grouping under Somoza they were willing to maintain production under the existing ground rules, in exchange for a quota of profits. The Sandinistas hoped that this relationship could be maintained in a somewhat transformed fashion.

The banks, agroindustries, and marketing channels that in the past were dominated by the Somoza group and influenced by foreign loans and import and export firms were taken over by the revolutionary state. Due to the conflicts that existed between the medium-size producers and Somoza, the Nicaraguan government was somewhat successful in presenting its policies as a usable alternative for private producers. This was substantially distinct from the case of other Central American countries such as El Salvador or Guatemala, where the rural areas were polarized between large landowners, who largely controlled the government and its credit and marketing policies, and the mass of disenfranchised minifundistas and landless rural workers. These structural factors also help to explain the 1981 agrarian reform law, whose underlying premise was that the Nicaraguan reform could achieve a process of structural change wherein a strong state farm and cooperative sector could coexist with an important nucleus of small, medium, and even large individual farm and agro-industrial enterprises.[31]

Table 14.2 highlights the key role in agricultural production played by medium and small commercial farms, the principal subjects of Nicaragua's "mixed economy" policy. It also indicates a production structure that differed significantly from other socialist countries, such as Cuba, at a corresponding period of development.

TABLE 14.2
AGRICULTURAL PRODUCTION IN STATE AND PRIVATE SECTORS
(IN PERCENTAGES)

		Private Farms			
	State Farms	Large	Medium	Small	Totals
Export crops	24.0	37.3	21.7	17.0	100
Internal market crops	15.7	14.7	8.1	61.5	100
Cattle	24.7	11.0	30.4	33.0	100
Agro/industry	28.0	63.9	5.7	2.4	100

Source: "Poder Político y Economía Mixta," *Barricada*, Lunes Socio-Económico No. 29 (November 28, 1983).

In implementing these goals, the government and MIDINRA adapted their policies and problems to structural constraints and possibilities, as well as to shorter-term pressures, demonstrating a capacity to subsume ideological goals and values in favor of political pragmatism, economic reality, and result-oriented policies.[32] While this process created some tensions within the FSLN—particularly between those who favored centralized planning and controls as against those who supported a more decentralized and participatory process—and modifications of programs sometimes seemed more like hasty improvizations than carefully crafted adaptations to reality, Nicaragua's agrarian reform process nevertheless progressed toward its goal of maintaining agricultural productivity in the context of profound transformations in income and resource distributions.

If we look at what happened to agricultural production during the first three years we see a general pattern of progress from 1979–80 on, with varying rates of success (see Table 14.3).

TABLE 14.3
AGRICULTURAL PRODUCTION
(IN PERCENTAGES)

	1977–78 (index)	1979–80	1980–81	1981–82
Production for export markets				
Cotton	100	62	53	55
Coffee	100	103	109	112
Sugar-cane	100	98	119	106
Bananas	100	94	104	73
Cattle	100	88	49	70
Production for domestic markets				
Corn	100	101	110	104
Beans	100	70	145	119
Rice	100	134	189	182
Pigs	100	99	110	158
Chickens	100	162	180	268
Eggs	100	194	239	348

Source: MIDINRA, Informe de Nicaragua a la FAO (Managua, 1983), p. 55.

Three products stand out as lagging in production levels for reasons worth elaborating: cotton, corn, and cattle. In the case of cotton, whose production rose in 1982–83 and 1983–84 but was still under prerevolutionary levels, the constraints were both politics and prices. World prices were low in those years and producers tended to move into alternative crops such as sorghum, sesame, or sugar. On the political side, cotton had traditionally been grown by large capital-intensive commercial producers who demonstrated their lack of support or confidence in government policy by decapitalizing and lowering production. The increases in production of 1982–83 and 1983–84 were largely limited to the state farms, production cooperatives, and small private producers. Lands cultivated in cotton by small farmers, for instance, went up over 200 percent from the 1980–81 agricultural year to the 1983–84 year.[33]

Livestock production was and would be affected for some years by the indiscriminate depletion of the herd during the war. Nicaragua made major efforts during the first five years of its agrarian reform to reestablish its cattle sector, with only mixed results. The stagnation of corn production was also related to a complex set of factors, notably the low relative price of corn and the poor lands and productive techniques in most areas where corn was produced.[34]

The drops in cotton, cattle, and corn production were also responsible for problems in the production of cooking oil, soup, leather, and chickens fed with corn; all subproducts of these crops. On the other hand Nicaragua succeeded in elevating its coffee, rice, bean, and industrial poultry production to levels well above those of 1977–78.

Under prevailing circumstances, projecting the outlook of Nicaragua's agrarian reform and agricultural production in 1984 was extremely difficult. Electoral politics and the counterrevolutionary threat have already been mentioned as short-term factors influencing agrarian reform policies and programs. Another crucial factor was the balance-of-payments crisis that was already placing severe strains on the Nicaraguan economy, making difficult the importation of necessary raw materials, foodstuffs, and spare parts, and limiting access to new investment capital.

Nicaragua was also suffering from a shortage of both skilled and unskilled workers. The lack of skilled labor and trained professionals, which was made even worse by the levels of employee mobility within the Nicaraguan government, inhibited the optimum implementation of government policies. The lack of unskilled labor was particularly serious in the harvest periods, and was aggravated by the recruitment into the military or militias of many unskilled workers, by low relative wages, by fear of entering certain areas because of military problems, and by increased alternative employment perspectives.

Access to foodstuffs by the population was plagued with a number of problems, ranging from lagging production to problems in distribution or in obtaining materials to package the products.[35]

In spite of these and many other difficult problems, the Nicaraguan agrarian reform had achieved many of its goals during its first five years. The standard of living of much of the rural poor rose significantly, as did their access to land and services, and production levels were generally maintained or increased. As of July 1984, one had the distinct feeling that

Nicaragua, if left alone, could carry out one of the most successful and significant agrarian reform programs in this hemisphere. However, as long as the U.S. economic blockade and the military incursions into Nicaraguan territory by U.S.-supported counterrevolutionaries continued to sap Nicaragua's already weak economy, it would be difficult, if not impossible, for Nicaragua to make major economic advances in the coming years.

NOTES

1. Ministerio de Planificación, *Plan de Reactivación Económica en Beneficio del Pueblo* (Managua, 1980), pp. 11–15.

2. Ibid.

3. Eduardo Baumeister, "Notas Para la Discusíon de la Cuestíon Agraria Nicaragüense." Paper read at the III Congreso Nicaragüense de Ciencias Sociales, Managua, October 29–31, 1982, pp. 42–43.

4. Ibid., p. 45.

5. Centro de Investigaciones y Estudios de Reforma Agraria (CIERA), *Participatory Democracy in Nicaragua* (Managua, 1984), p. 98.

6. David Kaimowitz and Joseph R. Thome, "Nicaragua's Agrarian Reform: The First Year," in *Nicaragua in Revolution*, edited by Thomas W. Walker (New York: Praeger, 1982), p. 228.

7. MIDINRA, *Informe de Nicaragua a la FAO* (Managua, 1983), pp. 79–80.

8. Kaimowitz and Thome, "Nicaragua's Agrarian Reform," p. 232.

9. Ibid., pp. 233–234.

10. Ibid., pp. 235–236.

11. Ibid., p. 237.

12. *La Gaceta-Diario Oficial* (Managua), No. 188, August 21, 1981, p. 1737.

13. Decree 782 of 1981, Articles 8–11. See also Decreto 832, *La Gaceta* No. 233, October 15, 1981, p. 2201; and "Reglamento a la Ley de Reforma Agraria," *La Gaceta* No. 248, October 31, 1981, p. 3046.

14. "Reforma Agraria: Esta Es La Democracia," *Barricada*, Lunes Socio-Económicos No. 32, December 19, 1983.

15. Baumeister, "Notas para la Discusíon," p. 42.

16. "Sólo Queremos La Soberanía Para Trabajar Por Nuestro Pueblo," *Encuentros* (Managua), No. 1 (February 1982), p. 11.

17. CIERA-PAN-CIDA, *Informe del Primer Seminario Sobre Estrategia Alimentaria* (Managua, February 21–25, 1983) (CIERA, 1983, pp. 6–12).

18. Ibid., pp. 15–21.

19. Peter Marchetti, S.J., "Reforma Agraria y Consumo Básico," in *Encuentro*, Revista de la Universidad Centroamericana en Nicaragua, No. 19 (1983), pp. 13–14.

20. MIDINRA, "Informe FAO," pp. 66–67.

21. Ibid., p. 40.

22. *La Gaceta*, No. 222, February 10, 1981, p. 2081.

23. CIERA, *Censo de Cooperativas* (Managua, 1982).

24. Interviews at Legal Department, Agrarian Reform Directorate, MIDINRA, January 1984.

25. Interview with Peter Marchetti, S.J., January 1984.

26. See Chapter 2 of this volume.

27. CIERA, data and interviews, January–May 1984.

28. Baumeister, "Notas Para La Discusión," p. 1.

29. CERES, September–October 1981, p. 47.

30. Baumeister, "Notas Para La Discusión," p. 6.

31. Ibid., p. 46.

32. Xabier Gorostiaga, "Nicaragua: Los Dilemas de la Revolución Sandinista a los Tres Añõs Del Triunfo," in *Economía de América Latina: Perfiles y Contradicciones del Desarrollo Agrícola Reciente* (CIDE, Instituto de Estudios Económicos de América Latina, México) No. 9, (2d quarter 1982), p. 196.

33. "Poder Político y Economía Mixta," *Barricada*, Lunes Socio-Económico No. 29 (November 28, 1983).

34. CIERA PAN CIDA, "Informe del Primer Seminario," p. 30.

35. Ibid., pp. 31–38.

Chapter 15
Popular Education

DEBORAH BARNDT

"WE HAVE BLOWN APART THE MYTH"

One of the early militants of the FSLN, Commander Omar Cabezas, described the slow and steady process of working with the peasants during the important organizing years (1967–74), when the strategy was "to accumulate forces in silence":

> We would take hold of the hand of a peasant, their hands were big, strong, rough . . . and we would ask them: "and these callouses, where do they come from?" And they would respond that the callouses were from the machete, from working the land. And we would ask them that if they got callouses from working the land, why wasn't the land theirs, rather than the bosses? We tried to slowly awaken the peasants to the dream that they had. . . . [1]

Although this work was not part of a formal educational system, it was a critical aspect of an education process aimed at developing the political consciousness and popular organization necessary to overthrow the dictatorship. It was "popular education" in many senses: It acted in the interests of the popular classes (the poor, exploited majority), it started with the daily experience and economic reality of the peasant, it posed the key contradiction for the peasant: that he worked land he did not own. A growing political consciousness of this basic inequity motivated peasants to organize in order to change it. This educational and organizational work was built on relationships of respect: FSLN militants learned from the peasants, who in turn learned from the militants.

Cabezas's experience was not an isolated one, nor was that of the FSLN. The growing organization of dispossessed peasants and workers throughout Latin America was accompanied by a growing consciousness: Popular education emerged as a tool integral to these liberation efforts. It was also a key element in the development of new revolutionary societies. The Nicaraguan experience, in fact, shed new light on our understanding of the role of education in shaping ideology and consciousness, in reproducing any economic system:

> Popular education, and education in general, plays a determining role in the consolidation of any model of development, whatever it may be. Somocismo [for example] implanted not only a particular economic development model, but [also] a particular education that corresponded to that development model.... Somoza didn't have any interest in the people having access to wealth ... to welfare ... to democracy ... to any kind of participation, and because of this it ... created an economic model that required a work force with preferably the least possible consciousness, the easier to be exploited without any resistance....
>
> The Revolution does not merely propose a [new] economic model, but rather proposes the construction of a society where there are neither exploiters nor exploited. And to do so, the Revolution has to give to our people, through education, the instruments that the people need to be authentic participants in this new society.[2]

Popular participation was the base of this new society, and was both the cause and effect of popular education. Education was to prepare people for participation by developing the technical skills necessary for economic development, by transmitting revolutionary ideology, by providing practice in collective analysis leading to action. It was critical for the consolidation of the Revolution. But education could not be considered in isolation; its leaders stressed: "No single program of the Revolution can be understood without understanding the Revolution integrally, because the principal force of the Sandinista Revolution is integration."[3]

As integral to an unfolding revolutionary process, popular education took different roles at different moments. "Conscientization,"[4] or development of critical political consciousness, was part of the process that led the Nicaraguan people to take power; at the stage of consolidating that power, it had a different focus. Once isolated and clandestine, educational work came to take the form of massive national projects, not only through the formal education system, but through popular education programs of many other state institutions, mass organizations, and religious groups. "The formation of the new person [was] not the monopoly of the educational system."[5] This pervasiveness of education was striking:

> This is the hour of non-formal education in Nicaragua ... it is up to us to define the state apparatus, the ideological apparatus. The educa-

tional system is a gigantic upsurge, like a tidal wave, which shows itself in the mass media, the newspapers, in a CDS [neighborhood Sandinist Defense Committee] meeting, in every facet of the class struggle. The participation of the masses in the whole range of economic and other activities, through non-formal education outside the classroom, is building up revolutionary ideology in all sections of the population. We have blown apart the myth that education is something which only takes place in schools.[6]

"AND THE RICH STUDIED ABROAD"

Public education before the 1979 popular victory served the interests of the Somoza dictatorship. It reflected the material conditions of a dependent capitalist society, dominated by a national elite and the foreign interests of U.S. imperialism. Like most "banana republics" of the Central American isthmus, Nicaragua's agroexport economy needed an unskilled rural labor force, whose services were used primarily during the three- or four-month harvest season. Literacy and technical training were not necessary for this work, which required only brute force.

As in most Latin American colonial systems, formal education evolved to meet the needs of an urban elite, reproducing patterns of economic and cultural domination. That education was not a priority under Somoza is clear in this summary of his legacy (1976–77):

- 67 percent of all students were from urban areas.
- 68 percent of all primary-age children entered school, but half of those dropped out during the first year (only 5 percent of all rural children finished primary school).
- Secondary school was accessible to 18 percent of the eligible population; over half studied business, while less than 10 percent prepared for work in agriculture.
- A mere 0.3 percent of the population completed higher education.

Most of the urban and rural poor were effectively eliminated from the educational system before finishing primary school.

For those who did have the opportunity, education had limited offerings. Teaching standards were low, training was inadequate, there was favoritism in hiring. Classrooms were crowded, and most rural schools had only one teacher for six grades. The contents of the textbooks, most of them imported through USAID programs, "reflected experiences and values alien to the Nicaraguan peasant. And the rich studied abroad."[7]

There was no rationalization of the curriculum according to the real economic needs of the country. The several technical training centers established by Somoza were more like businesses for his friends; there were ten accounting or business schools in 1979, for example, while there was only one agricultural school with 200 students (in a country whose foreign exchange depends on agricultural export). "The figures reveal the aspirations of the Nicaraguan elite to continue to work in (and control) the professions, and their disregard for the productive sector from which their wealth derived."[8]

It was classically an education for the development of underdevelopment. It did not respond to the interests of the large poor majority; their illiteracy was a condition of underdevelopment, keeping them uninformed and passive. Ironically, Somoza initiated one of his only literacy projects in the north when some of the most exploited peasants in that region began to organize against the government. Plan Waslala, as it was called, was part of a counterinsurgency strategy: between 1977 and 1979, 108 "literacy teachers" were appointed to this region where there was a history of intense guerrilla activity. In fact, they were "security agents" who identified FSLN sympathizers, leading to some of the most brutal peasant massacres during the war of liberation. Nicaraguan poet and Minister of Culture Ernesto Cardenal etched Somoza's educational legacy clearly in our memory with these words: "[Now] everything is fine in Waslala, the capital of terror and death for the peasants of the north. The school in Waslala will have teachers and not security agents."[9]

"TO BE CLEAR ABOUT WHY WE WERE FIGHTING"

The textbooks used during the Somoza period, when they referred to Nicaraguan history, were devoid of stories of popular organization and struggle. If Sandino was mentioned, a picture was painted of him as a bandit who robbed the peasants and murdered their children. But the heroic tales of the "General of All Free Men" and his "Army-Defender of Sovereignty" remained alive, passed on orally by the thousands who in the 20s and 30s had participated in the successful efforts to oust the U.S. Marines.

Part of the legacy of Sandino was his commitment to literacy as a tool for liberation, exemplified by his teaching of reading and writing to General Altamirano, his second in command. This aspect along with others was incorporated into the original political platform of the FSLN. Carlos Fonseca, the chief leader of the Revolution, encouraged literacy teaching as a part of the training of new combatants: Tomás Borge recalls: "German Pomares and I were training a group of peasants, teaching them how to use a Garand, an M1 carbine, an M3 machinegun, and a 45 revolver, when

Carlos Fonseca came along and said 'and also teach them to read.' "[10] This casual comment became the inspirational slogan of the Literacy Crusade, the first national project initiated by the new Sandinista government in 1979.

Popular education became a more conscious part of the organizational strategy of the FSLN after the 1967 Battle of Pancasán. Reflecting on this military defeat but political victory, FSLN militants recognized that a broader educational process was necessary to build a popular base of support: "It was the work of ants . . . in the barrios, in the countryside, in the mountains that [eventually] created the immense network of collaborators, affiliates, and militants. Armed struggle was rooted in, and fed by, the work of political conscientization."[11]

This educational work took many forms; there were flyers and open letters, broadcasts of FSLN communiqués,[12] and use of the clandestine Radio Sandino. Strategic actions (such as the taking of Chema Castillo's home and, later, the palace) played an important conscientizing role. Popular culture, too, gave outlets for the expression of the oppressed and efforts to organize their liberation: clandestine peasant theater, poetry, and music. In the later stages of the insurrection, songs by the popular Mejía Godoy brothers actually gave instructions on the handling of weapons and the fabrication of home-made bombs.

Both students and teachers in Somoza's educational system became important participants in the growing opposition to his regime. Primary school teachers were the first to organize, though initial actions were strikes for their own economic interests. Carlos Fonseca helped organize COPEM (secondary school teachers) and APU (university professors), then encouraged them all to unite (which finally happened in 1979 when the Nicaraguan Teachers' Association was formed).

University students played a special role in building a popular base of support for the FSLN; founders of FSLN, in fact, first organized as students. Members of the Revolutionary Students Federation (FER) did political educational work in barrios[13] and work places; FER was also a recruiting ground for the FSLN. The National Autonomous University (UNAN), protected by international respect for its autonomy, was at the center of left-wing intellectual activity. Somoza once tried to repress it by not paying teachers for three months. When a nationwide protest gathered even more resources for UNAN, Somoza decided it was more economical to pay them. "Defense of the university became a mass political issue."[14] It was possible to organize opposition to Somoza with less risk within the university, because university authorities were also opposed to Somoza.

The church was another institution that offered a favorable climate for educating and organizing. Some of the most effective popular education work was done through biblical reflection in study circles and literacy classes organized by Christians committed to the revolutionary option.[15] This was the "option for the poor" encouraged by the Second Vatican Council and the Medellín Bishops Conference, which later made the "popular church" a major force in the development of ideological consciousness in Latin America through its "theology of liberation." The Jesuits in Nicaragua were instrumental in setting up programs like CEPA (Center for Agrarian Education and Promotion), which combined technical agricultural training, literacy, and conscientization. Delegates of the Word in the north and the Capuchin order in the Atlantic Coast region did important educational work. Church publications such as "The Peasant Christ" gave new interpretations to Nicaraguan history through a gospel of liberation. As one religious worker noted, even the Christian educators eventually came under the suspicion of the dictatorship: "These materials were as dangerous to the Somoza guard as a communiqué from the Frente."[16]

The popular education strategy of the FSLN—integral to the organizing of Christians, students, peasants, workers—paid off after years of this "work of ants." The final insurrection was its culmination, and perhaps the most intense educational experience to date. A young combatant recalls the systematic analysis that went on in the midst of the fighting: "I was responsible for political education in our battalion, to help develop the political clarity of the compañeros, to be clear about *why* we were fighting."[17] In the accelerated pace of the last months of fighting, people learned to organize themselves, to mobilize limited resources with great ingenuity. "The first great popular school was the war of national liberation."[18] It was this "insurrectional" spirit that came to characterize the new education so integral to the construction of the revolutionary society.

"TO BECOME PROTAGONISTS OF HISTORY RATHER THAN SPECTATORS"

If the insurrection was the most intense educational experience for the Nicaraguan people, it gave them the skills and spirit to organize the "greatest popular mobilization in the history of the country"[19]—the National Literacy Crusade. As the first national project of the new revolutionary government, it constituted an educational and political event without precedent in history. It laid the ground for all other reconstruction projects and became the midwife for all other popular educational programs to follow.

"The Literacy Crusade was a political project with pedagogical implications."[20] It offered the first opportunity to redress the centuries of exploitation of the poor, "the historical debt to the popular classes."[21] It was the first project based on the "logic of the majority," the basis for the new economic model. The focus, then, was on the poor, peasants, and workers, who were to become the driving force of the Revolution, who finally had the chance to "become protagonists of history rather than spectators."[22] Learning to read and write was just part of the process of preparing them "both politically and technically to become the genuine authors of development and the only legitimate owners of the Revolution."[23]

The Crusade was not an afterthought of the war of liberation; the FSLN who had always viewed it as a strategic project had proposed in their 1969 political program "a massive campaign to immediately wipe out illiteracy."[24] Literacy was one more tool of liberation and the Crusade was considered a "second war of liberation" to "conquer ignorance." By initiating it so early, the new leaders were able to grab the historical moment and channel the tremendous energy unleashed by the insurrection into the reconstruction of the new society.

Outsiders thought the Nicaraguans a bit unrealistic in undertaking such a project in a country ravaged by war, with a foreign debt of $1.6 billion, and with a dearth of skilled technical and material resources. But the revolutionary momentum, supported by the legitimacy of the leadership and organized popular participation, made possible what seemed impossible. The Nicaraguans applied the "poor man's formula," mobilizing the human resources and legendary "revolutionary spirit" to make up for lack in funds or experience.[25]

The Literacy Crusade had multiple objectives for the newborn revolutionary society. Teaching reading and writing was a necessary precedent to developing the technical skills required by the new economic model. At the same time, the political consciousness-raising integral to the literacy process prepared people for active participation in other projects. In fact, the Crusade helped build the massive network of "mass organizations" that would assure such participation. Where they already existed they took on logistical tasks, setting up classes in work places and communities, and recruiting volunteer teachers and potential students from their membership.

The Sandinistas Youth Organization (JS-19 de Julio) had a major role in recruiting and preparing the 60,000 high school students who became brigadistas in the Popular Literacy Army (EPA). The National Association of Nicaraguan Educators organized teachers in "red-and-black" brigades to train and supervise the brigadistas. The Sandinista Workers' Central (CST) organized classes in work places and formed a Workers' Literacy Militia, while the Rural Workers' Association (ATC) identified illiterates in their communities, arranged accommodations, set up classes, and recruited peasant volunteers. Urban residents, housewives, professionals, and students got involved through the women's association (AMNLAE), the neighborhood defense committees (CDSs), or special brigades organized by all the state institutions. Thus, all sectors of the population were engaged for an intense five-month period in this massive educational event; it inevitably strengthened their own organization and deepened their revolutionary consciousness and commitment. In areas where mass organizations had not existed, the literacy classes became a kind of community organization, encouraging the formation of these other entities as the basis for ongoing popular participation.

The political education of the youth was another critical objective of the Crusade. During the time of Somoza, it had been a crime to be young in Nicaragua; many youth were executed for their involvement in the liberation struggle. The Literacy Crusade offered these young warriors a chance to channel their energies in a more constructive form. They rallied to the opportunity, which was purely voluntary, as though it was the natural next step in their mission. One brigadista summarized this feeling: "How can you believe in the revolution and not join the literacy brigades? Last year I took up a gun; this year, it's an exercise book, but I don't see any real difference. It's all part of a war to liberate our country."[26]

After securing the permission of their parents, many teenagers joined the "cultural insurrection." It was to transform them personally while also transforming the country. "My daughter left as a girl of 14, and returned a woman of 15," observed one mother.[27] The experience involved much more than teaching what they knew to illiterate peasants; their rural students also became their teachers, introducing them to the hardships of the poor, teaching them the skills of surviving on the land. The experience deepened their consciousness of the conditions inherited from Somoza, and deepened their commitment to help change those conditions. The new leaders of the Revolution were being forged.

The meeting of the city and the country, exemplified in the deep bonds formed between young urban brigadistas and their campesino "families," was also another explicit objective of the Crusade. Like most dependent capitalist economies in the Third World, Nicaragua had experienced the mass migration to the cities that accompanied increased industrialization while further impoverishing the countryside. Sending 60,000 urbanites to the most remote corners of the country was the first of many conscious efforts to reverse that process, developing a new collective consciousness and sense of national unity.

A special literacy campaign for the Atlantic Coast region was another important attempt to reverse historical processes. Under Somoza, the indigenous and Caribbean (black) populations of the Coast had been geographically isolated and socially deprived. Thus a special literacy campaign in the latter part of 1980 that offered training in English, Miskitu, and Sumo languages initiated the extremely complex process of integrating the historically marginalized Atlantic with the Pacific region.

"YOU TEACH US TO READ AND WRITE, AND WE'LL TEACH YOU TO WORK THE LAND"

With so few resources, how did the Nicaraguan people and its new revolutionary leadership actually accomplish this pedagogical project? As an event that made international education history, earning the UNESCO Literacy Prize in 1980, it offers lessons for educators anywhere.

Apart from the obvious and most critical factor—that such a massive and intensive activity can only be born of a revolution—the undertaking required a complex administrative structure and logistical support:

> What did it imply to equip tens of thousand of volunteers? Where did you find 60 or 70 thousand boots, raincoats, lanterns or mosquito nets? How did you pay for them? How did you locate the vehicles to transport that many people all on the same weekend? How many water purifying tablets did 60,000 people consume in a five-month period? How many bandages?[28]

Although the Crusade's leadership had little or no experience in planning literacy programs, they did have the invaluable experience of the insurrection: The Nicaraguan people knew how to organize themselves, so they went about this next seemingly impossible task with the same discipline required in the war. The structure of the Crusade in fact borrowed from military structure; regions were divided into the same major "fronts" that carried out the insurrection, literacy volunteers were organized into "squadrons" and "brigades."

The military metaphor had not only structural but also spiritual implications. Units of the Popular Literacy Army were named after combatants fallen in the war of liberation. These compañeros, who were among the 50,000 who lost their lives in the war, became the inspiration for the "literacy warriors," who kept their memory alive by carrying on the struggle they had begun. The campaign was implemented in the name of the "heroes and martyrs of the Revolution" and paid special hommage to the fallen leader, Carlos Fonseca. His charge "and also teach them to read" became their challenge, and at the Crusade's end, they publicly pronounced: "Carlos, we have met the challenge. And now, what is our next task?"

One of the tasks preliminary to the Crusade was to test this "military" discipline and organization. A national census was required to identify both the illiterate and potential literacy volunteer teachers. Over 1.4 million people were canvassed, and in just one month the results were calculated by hand by 1,500 volunteers. UNESCO experts who evaluated the process were impressed by the accuracy of the peoples' research. The data revealed an illiteracy rate of 50.35 percent (over 90 percent in some rural departments); almost one-quarter of that number being youth between the ages of 10 and 14.

In order to finance this "immense school," support was sought from international sources: church organizations, development agencies, solidarity groups, and sympathetic governments.[29] Community groups and institutions in Nicaragua organized fund-raising events and many public and private sector workers offered a day's wages for each month of the campaign. The total cost of the Crusade was about $10 million (200 million córdobas); almost half of that took the form of material donations. The original budget had been cut in half and in the end no public funds were used. The Crusade was made possible by the same mixture of ingenuity and commitment of the Nicaraguan people along with critical international solidarity that had fueled the first war of liberation.

The development of a methodology and curriculum was the next major task. The Nicaraguans consulted the literacy experience of many other countries and drew theoretical inspiration from the approach developed by the Brazilian educator, Paulo Freire: They "learned from many sources and copied from none."[30] When Freire arrived in Nicaragua as one of many internationalists consulted, he supported the Nicaraguans' developing their own unique program to fit their own historical context and political objectives. The major differences between his literacy approach and the Nicaraguans' were two.[31] A national text, rather than regional or local materials, was the principal instrument of the Literacy Crusade; it was to help develop national unity as the war-torn country was setting out on the road to reconstruction. The other difference was that rather than use only one "generative" word to introduce a lesson, the Nicaraguans used phrases, or "slogans" that captured an entire thought or action.

There were three texts that accompanied the brigadistas as "arms" in their "battle against ignorance": a literacy primer, an arithmetic workbook, and a teacher's manual. The primer, entitled *The Dawn of the People*, allowed the new literates to discuss, read, and write, for the first time, the history of the Revolution, the social programs of the new government, and the civil defense necessary to defend them.

A photo introduced each lesson and was the starting point for a discussion of the theme as it related to the daily lives of the students. Called "the dialogue," this was often the most difficult part of the method. Discussion was to move naturally from description and analysis of the theme to planning for concrete collective action. "It has to be a conversation, not a lecture. And it has to come from the campesinos themselves, from their experiences."[32] Young brigadistas had to fight against their own training in a "banking approach" rather than a "problem-posing approach,"[33] and to gently challenge the centuries of passivity the peasant learners brought as their inheritance. Popular participation was being nurtured in these moments of the literacy process. The dialogue was followed by phonetic exercises; reading and writing practice also encouraged their participation: in the creation of words from newly learned syllables and in the composition of collective texts around the theme applied to their community.

Training was of utmost importance, as young teachers not only had to learn the methodology but also deepen their own understanding of the content themes. Participatory techniques such as role play, debate, simulation, and cultural expressions (drawing, drama, song) were used to encourage more active and collective forms of learning.

A core group of 80 teachers tested the materials and methods in pilot projects during December 1979 and January 1980; many adaptations resulted from that immersion in reality. The same "Group of 80" became the nucleus of trainers, who in February trained 600, who in turn trained 12,000, who in turn trained the tens of thousands of brigadistas. This multiplier process, the only solution to the challenge of preparing 100,000 for battle, was not without its defects, but it became a model for training in many social projects to follow.[34]

During the campaign, which began in March 1980, there emerged the need for ongoing training, so regular "Saturday workshops" were instituted. These brought together brigadistas in an area to undertake criticism and self-criticism of their work of the preceding week, and to prepare systematically for the lessons of the coming week. Problems were presented and analyzed; solutions were proposed. There was an ongoing methodological orientation. Other sources of support were offered through a daily radio program "Puño en Alto" (Fist on High). Cultural brigades and medical brigades traveled from one community to another, maintaining morale and tending to health problems.

The work of the brigadistas was not limited to teaching literacy. They administered pills as a part of a malaria-control program, undertook agricultural surveys, collected oral histories of combatants in the war of liberation, dug up archeological relics, and uncovered many forms of popular culture in legends and music. New songs were created, too; one peasant sang: "You teach us to read and write, and we'll teach you to work the land."[35] It was this new relationship between student and worker, between city and country, between young and not so young that was the base for the educational methodology revolutionized by the Crusade. On leaving for the countryside, brigadistas had been charged: "You will be a catalyst of the teaching-learning process. Your literacy students will be people who think, create, and express their ideas. Together, you will form a team of mutual learning and human development."[36] Yet none could imagine the deep human bonds that would develop as urban teenagers learned how to milk a cow and make tortillas, lived in a makeshift hut with peasants and experienced their poverty, "learned to read their book." Nor could they have anticipated the pride of the peasant, whose rough hands had plowed the earth for decades, when he finally mastered the pencil and wrote slowly and deliberately "l-i-b-e-r-a-t-i-o-n." These relationships— both personal and political—were the basis for the formation of the "new men" and "new women," for the construction of a new society.[37]

While progress of the Crusade at the community level was evaluated in weekly workshops, the national project was carefully and systematically examined. Again the approach was revolutionary. Literacy commissions in 16 departmental capitals involved citizens' groups, workers' associations, and public institutions in an ongoing monitoring of the process. To maximize involvement, two national planning and evaluation congresses were held in June and September. Over 100,000 people were involved in preliminary meetings leading up to the congresses, which involved over 1,000 people; achievements and weaknesses of the Crusade were assessed and suggestions for improvement made.[38]

On August 23, 1980, 200,000 Nicaraguans gathered in the 19th of July Plaza to declare their country "territory liberated from illiteracy." The results—in mere statistical terms—were impressive: In five short months, the illiteracy rate had been lowered from 50.35 percent to 12.96 percent. Over 100,000 volunteers (mainly young people) had taught over 400,000 (mainly adults) to read and write. The most important results could not be measured on graphs. One new literate peasant spoke for many: "Now I can hold my head up high." At the end of the Literacy Crusade, a whole nation held its head up high. This was just a base for the continuing process of transformation; neither the educational system nor the society would ever be the same.

"DEVELOPING THE NEW PERSON . . . TO CONTRIBUTE TO THE TRANSFORMATION OF THE NEW SOCIETY"

The Crusade was in many ways an "experiment" of new educational policies. The country's resources could not be mobilized indefinitely; besides, teachers and students had to return to "school." The longer-term process of transforming the overall educational system had just begun. Yet if the literacy and adult education program was "born without debts and in the heart of the people,"[39] formal education in Nicaragua was heavily indebted to the past, born in the apparatus of the Somoza regime. In one sense, it was easier to start from scratch in adult education, which had not existed before, than to tackle the elitist alienating conception of education that permeated the primary and secondary schools and more so the inarticulate higher education system.

The new government leaders knew that this change could not take place overnight; besides, human and material resources were sorely lacking. First the philosophy of education had to change, the new policy clearly defined in the context of the revolutionary project. Then the changes in programs, texts, and methodology could be introduced to the teachers; they were the ones to carry out the transformation.

As might be expected, the process of developing the principles of the new education became in itself another great exercise in popular participation. A few months after the Crusade officially ended, the National Education Consultation was initiated. This was the second major moment in the transformation of the educational system. In January and February 1981, over 50,000 people participated in community-level discussions around 55 questions, defining what they wanted the "new person" to be and what educational principles would nurture such qualities. It was a massive participatory research process for those thousands who spent seven hours one Sunday in January studying these issues.

Again it was the popular organizations that provided the infrastructure and the volunteer labor that made such a project possible. Representatives of over 30 mass organizations, political parties, and religious groups agreed to carry out the consultation within their own organization. They formed study circles with approximately 10 percent of their affiliates in each community and appointed regional and municipal instructors. As a team they synthesized the data gathered from municipal cells, at the departmental level, and finally at the national level. Results from participating organizations were analyzed by the National Educational Advisory Council, by the government Junta, and by the FSLN National Directorate.

The resulting document, "Goals, Objectives, and Principles of the New Education," was made public by Carlos Tunnermann, the Minister of Education in early 1983.[40] The overall goal was "the development of the 'new man' [and 'new woman'] . . . to contribute to the transformation of the new society." The characteristics sought were enumerated in political, social, and moral terms: among other things, the new person was to be patriotic, internationalist, disciplined, cooperative, modest, and able to understand that "individual interest should coincide with social and national interest."[41] Among the 12 objectives articulated were the value of productive work, a deepening of cultural roots, and participation in defense. The 12 principles maintained that education is a fundamental right, a function of the state, a priority social investment, and that it must contribute to solutions of the country's social and economic problems.

The educational planning that built on this philosophical foundation of course had to be congruent with the economic project of the Revolution. The new economic model, aimed at serving the interests of the 90 percent (poor majority) rather than the 10 percent, had three major goals: to meet basic needs, to achieve economic independence, and to develop a new model of accumulation. Each of these goals had educational implications. Meeting basic needs involved changing the forms of production and ownership; this required an educational process and political organization. Economic independence as well required a new labor force and new relations of production; it depended on developing the capacities of people to produce what before was imported. This goal implied education oriented toward work. The new model of accumulation was the key to economic transformation, changing both forms of ownership and relations of production; new attitudes, technical skills, and organizational capabilities needed to be developed through a coherent educational plan.[42]

A key factor that influenced the structure and process of economic development was the regionalization of the country that went into effect in 1982; it allowed for more direct participation in economic planning based on the productive capacity of a region. The Ministry of Education actually regionalized its structure in 1980 and 1981; regional employees reported to both the regional government and the national Ministry of Education. This structure assured a more integral relationship between educational and economic projects. It also encouraged better coordination between educational programs and the work of mass organizations.

The Revolution's economic and political goals reflected in the "goals, objectives, and principles of the new education" guided the three major areas of change in the educational system in the early 1980s: expansion, improvement, and transformation.

Expansion

The first goal was to make education accessible to all Nicaraguans by expanding the system. Figure 15.1 summarizes this growth.[43] One calculation is startling: in 1983, over 1 million Nicaraguans (almost half of the population) were studying. This is quadruple the number participating in Somoza's system in 1978. There was an equally dramatic rise in the number of teachers working in the postrevolutionary system: from 12,975 to 41,422, about half of this new figure being "popular teachers" of the Adult Education Program.

Another indicator of expansion was the increase in the number of classes and schools, and the construction of new educational facilities. While there were 2,681 centers in 1979, there were 5,377 in 1982. This material growth occurred within a context of extreme economic constraints. The war had destroyed or damaged much of the infrastructure. Following

FIGURE 15.1 EXPANSION OF NICARAGUAN EDUCATIONAL SYSTEM, 1978–83

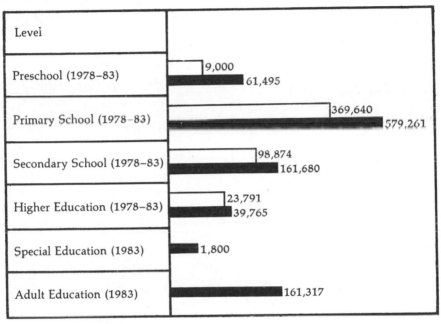

1979, funding was further affected by military aggressions, the economic blockade, and inadequate international support. Initially, there was a substantial loan from the World Bank and major contributions from UNESCO, while major material donations came from Sweden, the Soviet Union, the German Democratic Republic and Federal Republic of Germany.

The major support, however, was national, reflecting the new policy that "education is a social investment," and thus a priority in Nicaragua. The education budget almost quadrupled, from approximately $18 million to $50 million, representing an increase from 1.4 percent to 5 percent of the GNP. Between 1980 and 1983, capital costs dropped from 15 to 7.5 percent; program costs accounted for about 85 percent of the budget, half of that for primary education. While overall costs doubled between 1980 and 1983, salaries also increased by 84 percent.

The expansion of the educational system, however, cannot be conceived in pure numerical and material terms. Expansion in itself represented the "transformation" of the education population, for schools that once served the elite began to serve the masses. The major campaign for universal free education took the form of the "Battle for Grade Four," a concerted effort to assure that by 1990 everyone in Nicaragua would have at least the equivalent of a grade four education, considered the "basic popular education." The major factor pushing the new education model was political and historical: "the emergence of the overwhelming majority as protagonist of the development model."[44] Educationally, as in all other ways, their time had come.

Improvement

The second orientation was toward improving quality as well as quantity. Several new programs initiated by the ministry after 1980 reflected this goal. One involved the "nuclearization" of the educational system, a process parallel to the regionalization of the country. Twenty-three rural educational nuclei were established to coordinate the work of schools in an area; one school became a base center of each nucleus, with other schools being subbases and satellites. Nuclearization was a political-educational strategy to encourage rural integrated development by integrating the school and the community, the learners and the productive process. This was another indicator of the decentralization of education, promoting direct coordination with the local mass organizations and a curriculum adapted to a specific community's problems: "The soul of nuclearization is, without doubt, popular participation."[45]

The lack of relevant learning materials was one of the great challenges facing the Ministry of Education after the popular victory. As it was impossible to produce new revolutionary texts for all programs overnight, "transition programs" were developed, providing primary, middle, and technical teachers with a basic study plan, a program outline, objectives, and methodological orientation. "We didn't dominate the new methodology, nobody had experience in elaborating texts, we had to prepare ourselves slowly," explained one of the ministry staff.[46] Teachers also improvised in the face of this lack of materials. "The old textbooks, prepared by the CIA for use throughout Central America, have all been dumped. We are now making use of a lot of FSLN publications, particularly *Barricada*, its daily newspaper. In brief, anything which will best develop the childrens' consciousness of their own national reality."[47]

By 1982–83 the transformed study programs began to appear. They were gradually introduced, starting with the first grade materials—both for students and teachers. The first reader, *Los Carlitos*, was sold throughout the country, available to all Nicaraguans, not just the school population. An innovative materials production project (PERME) trained community teams in several key regions to produce simple learning materials related to the priority areas of production and health. Beginning in 1983, the ministry also adopted the "phonic-analytic-synthetic method," standardizing the learning of reading and writing for the first time. The approach encouraged active participation in the learning process, while developing the critical conceptual skills of analysis and synthesis.

No matter what new methods or materials were developed, the key to their success lay in their use; teachers had to learn them and apply them in their classrooms. Although most teachers were involved in the insurrection, their revolutionary commitment did not mean they had assimilated the new methodology, especially when they had been trained with the old concept of the teacher as an authority figure and the students as passive. The first priority, thus, was to train those teachers who would carry out the transformation. Educational Training, Program, and Evaluation Workshops (TEPCEs) brought together teachers and school directors every two months. They featured an evaluative analysis of work over the previous two months, the development of plans and programs for the weeks to come, and methodological orientation. In addition, the ministry also organized workshops on planning, research and evaluation, materials, methods, and techniques.

Another new focus was vocational training and occupational orientation. Work-study experiences, vocational visits, and school gardens were projects that encouraged children to become interested in careers, to match personal and social interests. These efforts reflected a key characteristic of the new education: "Work constitutes the most important education factor of men [women]. If before, work was usually the horizon that opened when the educational processes ended, now work is an integral and fundamental part of that process."[48]

Other programs deserve mention: the growth of a school library system to 300, a supplementary nutrition program in selected regions of the country. The latter incorporated interventions with the diagnosis of the nutritional state of Nicaraguans and the training of teachers in nutritional concepts. Research was also given new importance as the base for more conscious educational planning.

Transformation

Although these programs reflected a process of transformation of education in the new Nicaragua, certain programs implicated major structural changes, based on the newly defined revolutionary educational principles.

The Rural Work-Study Schools (ERETs) were born of the Revolution and represented efforts to integrate theory with practice, testing and developing scientific knowledge through productive activity. By 1983 there were 10 such "formation" centers, providing agricultural technical training to 1,500 students, with specialties determined according to the needs of the Revolution.

The Program of Communal Educational Development (PRODECO) combined courses in basic skills (sewing and carpentry) with community constructions of schools, latrines, parks, recreation centers, and school gardens. Peasant Agricultural Schools, or EACs, were another form of technical and political preparation for peasants, offering them, on completion of studies, a skilled worker diploma and the equivalent of a sixth grade education. Other technical specializations, again rationalized according to national economic needs, were built into the secondary school system, which included both a "basic production cycle" (three years) and a "diversified cycle" (two years). Graduates of the basic production cycles received a "qualified worker" diploma; those who completed a diversified cycle received high school diplomas.

All of these new programs reflected the new vision of an education that would respond to the economic needs of a society in transformation, whose driving force was to be the workers and peasants of Nicaragua.

"DAILY ASSEMBLIES WHERE THE PLANS AND PROBLEMS OF THE REVOLUTION ARE DISCUSSED"

No program more clearly represented this driving force than the Adult Education Program. After the Literacy Crusade ended, a Vice-Ministry of Adult Education was established to offer literacy training to those who had not participated in the campaign and to provide ongoing basic education for those who had. It continued to be a program of "strategic priority" within the Revolution.

When the brigadistas left the communities where they had taught reading and writing, they set up learning groups called Popular Education Collectives (CEPs) and selected outstanding new literates to coordinate them. The "popular teacher" was thus born. Once again the Nicaraguans drew on their most valuable resource, the people, to compensate for the lack of trained educators. And once again they revolutionized the concept of the teacher; because they were drawn from their own communities, popular teachers were more likely to share the interests of fellow classmates. Two hours daily, five nights a week, they joined neighbors in a collective learning process; the CEPs became "daily assemblies where the plans and problems of the Revolution are discussed."[49]

By 1983 there were 17,377 CEPs and 19,661 popular teachers, 2,790 of them serving as "promoters," whose responsibility was to help set up and supervise several CEPs in one geographic area. The program was concentrated in the north central mountain region (51 percent), with less activity in the Pacific region (37 percent) and even less (12 percent) in the Atlantic Coast region. It was geared primarily to a peasant population: 82 percent of the CEPs were in rural areas, with only 18 percent in the cities. A majority of popular teachers were women (51 percent), although that figure dropped in rural areas. The student population numbered 161,317 and one-quarter of them were under 14 years of age; especially in the agricultural economy, children took on the work of adults at an early age, joining their parents in the field during the day and in the CEPs at night.

By 1984 there were six levels (or semesters) of Popular Basic Education beyond the introductory literacy level. Studies in natural and social sciences were added to the basic training in language and math skills. Besides the national texts, supplementary materials were developed, such as CAMINEMOS, a magazine for new readers to carry along with them as they migrated during the harvest season. Some regional production teams were also trained to develop materials that would better respond to the specific needs of a region. "Libro Abierto," or "Open Book," was instituted in 1983 as a one-page weekly supplement to the newspaper Barricada; it was produced in large print specifically for use in the CEPs and incorporated both historical elements and present experiences of popular teachers.

Teacher training was a priority of this program; as the program developed more advanced levels of studies, popular teachers required orientation in both content and methodology. A three-step process formed the core of the methodology and curriculum; each lesson focused on a central social theme and moved students from observing that theme in their own community (step 1) to analyzing the issue in more depth (step 2) to organizing action that could be taken around it (step 3). This last step, linking education to organization, was the most critical and perhaps the most difficult one. It required close coordination with the mass organizations in each community, so that discussions about an issue such as defense could stimulate greater involvement in the Sandinista Defense Committees or an analysis of health care in Nicaragua before and after the Revolution might motivate participation in the Popular Health Campaigns.

Besides annual training seminars, applying the same multiplier effect used during the Crusade, weekly workshops continued to bring teachers together to evaluate and plan their work. "Puño en Alto," the radio program initiated during the Crusade, remained a daily form of motivation and ongoing training for teachers.

The continued effort to "professionalize" the popular teachers was one of several challenges still facing the program in 1984. Increasing aggressions—both military and economic—were taking their toll: economic boycotts accentuated the shortage in paper supplies, for example, and defense committees were regularly threatened by fighting in the north. All of these pressures made it difficult to anticipate the shape of the program needed to follow the six semesters of basic adult education: technical training specifically geared to economic needs defined by the new development model.

Nonetheless, this program "born of the Revolution" continued to be characterized by a flexibility that constantly had to adapt to the rhythm of the revolutionary process. There was some concern that, as it became more integral to the overall Ministry of Education program, it should also become more institutionalized, while other ministry programs, traditionally more formal, needed to become more flexible. It was hoped that this dialectic, between the formal and nonformal, between two programs with "two different mothers," would feed a creative process, each contributing to the transformation of education and of the society at the same time.

Two other programs of the Ministry of Education also responded to populations sorely neglected under the Somoza regime. Preschool education enrollment increased from 9,000 before the Revolution to 61,495 in 1983. The expansion took several forms: 17 preschool centers were established, preschool classrooms were added to 644 primary schools, and 45 Infant Development Centers (CDIs) were set up. The latter represented a joint effort of the Ministries of Social Welfare and Education, "offering facilities for the integral development of the full creative potential of the young child (0–6)," and "not seen as having a custodial function."[50]

A Department of Special Education was created in 1979; in the next four years, the number of centers grew from 6 to 25. Children with hearing and sensory deficiencies, mental retardation, and slow social development were attended in 1983 by 142 teachers and 49 community developers. These programs received special support from UNICEF and the Organization of American States.

"WHAT ONCE SERVED ONLY AN ELITE"

Another area of tremendous expansion following 1979 was the field of higher education. While only 0.3 percent of the population completed university studies under Somoza, enrollment almost doubled in the first five years of the Revolution. The student body was qualitatively different, too, as universities opened their doors to those who had never before had the chance for advanced studies. "What once served only an elite"[51] now welcomed peasants, workers, and combatants. For those who had finished only primary school, a three-year transition program prepared them for university study, offering scholarships to cover not only tuition costs but also basic needs such as housing and clothing.

In February 1980 the National Council of Higher Education (CNES) was founded to develop and administer postsecondary programs. University and advanced technical training was rationalized according to the careers needed in the development of the new society; study plans were developed for three priority areas: health, agriculture, and education. Those centers that did not have the capacity to offer training in those areas (primarily the many business schools set up by Somoza's friends) were closed. The remaining institutions—the National Autonomous University, the Catholic University, and the Polytechnical University—were reorganized to better meet the needs of the new economic model. Engineering programs were merged into a new National Engineering University in 1983 and there were plans to open an agricultural university.

There was an attempt to decentralize studies so that they were not all concentrated in Managua. Enrollment quotas were developed not only according to careers needed but also by region. Mass organizations, such as the National Association of Nicaraguan Teachers (ANDEN), CST, and ATC, shared the responsibility for identifying people in the regions for training in relevant fields (the Rural Workers' Association, for example, selecting members for agricultural study). This assured that people from all over the country had a chance for higher education and that they would return to meet the needs of their regions.

Perhaps more difficult than expanding the university system was the transformation of curriculum and methodology. The first step was to develop a "professional profile" for each field, which delineated the ideal characteristics of persons working in that field and what they should study. Related institutions were consulted and study plans developed for each field (the Ministry of the Agrarian Reform [MIDINRA], for example, helped develop the profile for an agronomist).

A critical part of the study plan was the work-study component, called "production practice." Incorporated into the program of any field, it required students to spend 200 hours per year (or 5 out of 30 weeks) working with a respective institution or business. This practical experience served multiple objectives: It helped the student learn manual skills, eliminate elitist attitudes, and integrate theory and practice, thus developing one's social, political, and technical capacity at the same time. After participating in a "familiarization practice" in the first years of study, students would be fully integrated as workers through a specialized production practice in the last two years. In the later stage they might undertake research that could contribute to the solution of problems encountered in the work process.

This more active orientation to research was another feature of the reformed university methodology, which had been underdeveloped before 1979. Special "science campaigns," similar to science fairs, annually encouraged collective research on real problems; projects ranged from the production of a high school chemistry manual to the study of separation and family disputes. Often these research projects were done in collaboration with institutions—medical research linked to work of the Health Ministry, for example.

The work-study and action research components both reflected an effort to change the traditional teaching methodology so imbedded in a university context. Pedagogical courses were developed for professors at the beginning of a school year, and ongoing weekly workshops offered training in specific skills, such as use of audiovisuals. School directors were also offered workshops in educational administration, leadership, and planning.

The problems confronted in transforming higher education were both similar to and different from those faced by public and adult education programs. A shortage of professors was the first major obstacle. Some had left the country in 1979; many others (particularly from the National Autonomous University) became leaders in the new government. One response to this lack of teachers was the formation of a Movement of Student Assistants. The best students were selected in their first year of study; after two years of working alongside professors in their fields of specialization, they became responsible for classes. Over 750 student assistants were teaching by the mid-1980s. Internationalist professors also helped to fill the need for qualified instruction.

Lack of material resources was a consistent obstacle to carrying out the new programs. Since 1980, when universities were overwhelmed with swelling enrollment, physical space was at a premium. Shifts of class schedules from 7 A.M. to 11 P.M. and use of high schools helped to accommodate the great numbers. Concomitantly, there was a serious shortage of textbooks. Although the shortage was even more acute during Somoza's regime, by 1983 there were still only three or four per student, and many of those were obsolete or from another cultural context. Some professors began writing new texts that would respond to real needs and better reflect the values of the new Nicaragua.

As counterrevolutionary activity demanded increased military response in the mid-1980s, more and more students were forced to leave their studies temporarily and join battalions in defense of the country. Special classes were set up to help returning combatants catch up with fellow students. This and other pressures contributed to a crisis of low academic achievement, which motivated widespread debate about its causes and solutions and a greater analysis of the process of educational transformation.

Although higher education was administered separately from the Ministry of Education, the president of the CNES sat on a National Education Council, along with the Minister of Education, the Vice-Minister of Adult Education, and the heads of ANDEN and the Sandinista Youth Association. The Council, headed by government Junta member Sergio Ramírez, allowed for a coordination of developments in the various levels of formal education programs and for a collective confrontation of problems shared by all member institutions.

"WHEREVER THESE QUESTIONS ARE ASKED, ANALYZED, AND ANSWERED, EDUCATION TAKES PLACE"

A review of the transformation of education in the Nicaraguan Revolution must include the role of education in the transformation of Nicaraguan society. And, in a revolutionary context, that role is never limited to formal state education programs. A key characteristic of popular education in Nicaragua, as argued from the outset, was its permeation of all activities of reconstruction. Most state institutions and mass organizations established popular education departments within their structures. These programs are alluded to in other chapters that focus on the different sectors, so they shall be described briefly here in terms of their contributions to a massive popular education process. The communications media and other forms of popular culture also fall into this broader definition of education:

> The starting point for education is two basic questions: What is happening? and What can we do? Wherever these questions are asked, analyzed, and answered, education takes place, whether in the media, in the official propaganda of the FSLN, or in local meetings of a revolutionary committee.[54]

The mass organization most directly immersed in educational questions was, of course, ANDEN. Having united the primary, secondary, and university teachers' unions by 1979, it became the major organizational base for teachers' involvement in the revolutionary process. Membership drives increased the number of affiliates to 16,000 by 1983 (all but 20 percent of elgible teachers). Though autonomous, ANDEN had a close relationship with the Sandinista Workers' Central and participated with other workers' associations in the Trade Union Coordinating Committee.

ANDEN's relationship to the Ministry of Education became one of collaboration rather than confrontation (as had been the case when teachers joined other popular organizations in opposing the Somoza dictatorship). It sat with the Ministry of Education (MED) on the National Educational Council and helped organize the National Consultation. The association's initiatives were complementary to those of the ministry: "Our role is related to the teachers, to their own adaptation to the revolutionary changes, to the formation of new values."[53] Training workshops with both political and pedagogical components were a key forum for teachers in clarifying and consolidating their role in educational transformation and in the development of the "new person." Weekend courses offered teachers who had no formal training the opportunity to "professionalize" what was often an "empirical" practice. But changing age-old approaches to teaching was seen as a long-term and gradual process "with more importance given to the revolutionary practice of teachers than to change through books and seminars."[54] Participation in the Literacy Crusade, in production batallions and reserve batallions, in the debate on "low academic achievement" were all examples of that practice.

The Sandinista Youth Organization complemented ANDEN's work with teachers by focusing on the mobilization of students, primarily in secondary schools. Its role in orienting the political education of Nicaraguan youth continued after the Literacy Crusade through various forms of popular communication (such as the magazine Los Muchachos) and through the organization of youth batallions for both production and defense tasks.

Training that integrated technical and organizational skill development with political conscientization was organized through the Sandinista Workers' Central and the Rural Workers' Association and, after its formation in 1982, the National Union of [Small] Farmers and Ranchers. The Sandinista Defense Committees collaborated with the Ministry of Housing in 1982 to train community leaders in popular education methodology. These skills were applied to various tasks, including education at the community level around the issues of shortages of basic goods and the development of new distribution systems. This educational task was also assumed by groups such as the Women's Association, which used the collection of empty tomato sauce bottles as a catalyst to get women talking about the origins of the economic boycotts and food shortages.

"Economic literacy" was a theme of popular education materials produced by the Ministry of Planning from 1980 on, when annual economic plans needed to be presented to the Nicaraguan people in a form that would enable them to understand somewhat complex concepts and participate in new measures and programs. The Ministry of Health perhaps made most immediate and extensive adaptation of popular education principles developed through the Literacy Crusade when they launched major health campaigns in 1981 and 1982. They trained health brigadistas using the "multiplier" approach and produced a wide range of popular cartoon booklets aimed at educating the population in a preventive rather than a curative approach to health care. The Ministry of Culture was another state institution that conceived of popular education as integral to its work; popular culture centers, for example, offered community-based training in the arts. Poetry workshops and popular theater training programs adopted popular education approaches. Many other institutions concerned themselves with the education of their employees, including the Ministry of the Interior, the Popular Sandinista Army, the Ministry of Labor, the Ministry of Transport, and so on.

The popular church, which had an historic role in the development of popular education in Nicaragua, continued to use participatory methods in their "Christian Schools" and in support of the education work of mass organizations. The Agrarian Education and Promotion Center (CEPA) established in the mid-1970s by the Jesuits continued to work closely with the ATC after the victory in 1979. CEPA began to take on a consultative role to other organizations and state institutions who requested assistance in setting up their own training programs. In 1983, in fact, CEPA along with MIDINRA invited other institutions to collaborate in setting up the first "Methodological School," which provided systematic training in popular education methodology for educational and training staff of over 20 Nicaraguan organizations. This more systematic and collaborative approach to methodological training was supported by ALFORJA, a regional network of popular education centers in Central America (to which CEPA belonged).

Another popular education effort initiated by Christians in Nicaragua was the publication of a newspaper, *Tayacán*. Since 1982, the 12-page weekly has tackled current issues of concern to all Nicaraguans through photo-stories, biblical reflections, and other popular forms. Of the three daily newspapers in Nicaragua, the FSLN publication *Barricada* made the most effort to develop a more popular education approach, not only with content reflecting the interests of the popular classes, but also with forms that animated readers to discuss and act: for example, an in-depth analysis of a key socioeconomic issue was given one page every Monday, another page was used as a forum of critique offered by readers; the National Fishing Company promoted the nutritional value of fish in cartoon form, while full-page spreads were used as educational tools on the walls of schools and workplaces.

Radio and TV also played an educative role. The fact that sexist advertising was prohibited was just one indication of change in content and use of the mass media. The Nicaraguan Film Institute (INCINE) made real advances in producing documentary material on the ongoing revolutionary process, reflecting it back to the people as well as in an international arena. The multiple cultural forms unleashed by the Revolution all served this function in a more direct and daily way. Popular theater organizations such as MECATE involved peasants in acting out and discussing issues that affect them at a community level. Masks and puppets accentuated points in larger festivals. And walls provided an endless forum for conscientization with slogans, murals, posters, and wall newspapers. Culture and education were really inseparable in the process of ideological formation in revolutionary Nicaragua.

"NOW THAT THE CONTRADICTIONS HAVE SHARPENED"

Education in Nicaragua, of course, faced all of the difficulties that other social programs did as counterrevolutionary activity increased. And yet, as in the case of other national projects, it was not cut back but rather redefined to meet the urgent tasks of defense of the Revolution. As the ideological struggle deepened, the role of popular education became all the clearer and more critical.

The impact of the aggressions on education programs took multiple forms. Economic boycotts made it all the more difficult to get the materials and supplies needed for new schools and increased enrollment. The channeling of 25 percent of the budget into defense left fewer financial resources for education. The destruction of key production centers and transport systems further diminished economic resources; schools were also damaged. More seriously, teachers (and especially adult educators) became targets of counterrevolutionary attacks, a dramatic warning to peasants in the north, in particular, not to participate in programs of the Revolution. In many instances, classes continued meeting, but clandestinely, the students burying their books between classes.

Such attempts to inhibit educational activity only confirmed its strategic importance. Education was "serving the development of a new economic model and transmitting a new ideological conception,"[55] both essential roles in the consolidation of the Revolution. And "now that the contradictions have sharpened,"[56] popular education had an even greater challenge of counteracting the ideological attacks, which increased at a par with military and economic aggressions. The press, the church, the family—all became new battlegrounds as misinformation and proselytizing fueled the fire. Charges of "totalitarianism," "aetheism," and "censorship" attempted to discredit the revolutionary process in forms now recognized as classical tactics of destabilization. Popular education had to become an element of defense in every mass organization; constant analysis of the volatile situation was necessary to understand the sacrifices it demanded and to mobilize people to continue the battle against tremendous forces both external and internal.

In the first five years of Revolution, there was little opportunity for sitting still in any educational undertaking. The "insurrectional" quality that characterized popular education in the Revolution from the time of the Literacy Crusade was maintained as Nicaraguans confronted the dual challenge of creating a new society while also having to defend that creation.

The contributions Nicaragua made to educational history in the first five years of the Revolution were innumerable: an intimate link between education and work, preparation of a poor majority for active participation in a new economic model and in social organizations representing their interests, and the dialectical development of new educational theory and methodology out of a practice that responded to the dynamic historical process that is the Revolution itself. "The education of the people begins with a recognition of itself as a people with a vocation and mission of freedom, of sovereignty, of development, of justice."[57] Popular education in Nicaragua began with the first struggles for national sovereignty over a century ago and was integral to its war of liberation. Since 1979, as the consciousness of the people deepened, popular education continued to take its rhythm from the revolutionary process, moving with it toward its historic mission.

NOTES

1. Omar Cabezas, *La Montaña es Algo Más Que Una Inmensa Estepa Verde* (Managua: Editorial Nueva Nicaragua, 1982), p. 240.

2. Ernesto Vallecillo, Vice-Minister of Adult Education, interview with the author, Managua, November 16, 1983.

3. Francisco Lacayo, Vice-Minister of Culture, former Vice-Minister of Adult Education, interview with the author, Managua, October 1983.

4. The term "conscientization" is a translation of the Portuguese *concientização*, the term that Brazilian educator Paulo Freire used to describe the education process implied in the literacy methodology he developed in the early 1960s; since that time, the practice and the term have spread in usage throughout the Third World.

5. Vallecillo, interview.

6. Miguel de Castilla, quoted in George Black and John Bevan, *The Loss of Fear: Education in Nicaragua Before and After the Revolution* (London: Nicaraguan Solidarity Campaign-World University Service, 1980), p. 36.

7. Ibid., p. 16.

8. Ibid., p. 20..

9. Ernesto Cardenal, Minister of Culture, quoted in ibid., p. 27.

10. Tomás Borge, Minister of Interior, quoted in ibid., p. 43.

11. Lacayo, interview.

12. In the taking of the Chema Castillo home, for example, the FSLN succeeded in

having a communiqué broadcast on national radio that incorporated a substantial and detailed analysis of the Nicaraguan reality; for full text, see Gabriel García Marquez, *Viva Sandino* (Managua: Editorial Nueva Nicaragua, 1982), pp. 102–113.

13. Julián Corrales Manguia, who was the Vice-Rector of UNAN in the mid-1970s, recalled the growing distrust of the community work initiated by students as research during the time of Somoza: "If students went into any neighborhood to do research, if they only asked 'How many men and how many women live in this barrio?' nothing more, they were considered suspect, detained, tortured," interview with the author, Managua, November 1983.

14. Black and Bevan, *The Loss of Fear*, p. 29.

15. See Penny Lernoux, *Cry of the People* (Middlesex, England: Penguin Books, 1980).

16. Roberto Saenz, Program Director of the Adult Education Program, Ministry of Education, interview with the author, Managua, October 1983.

17. Testimony of Jorge Luís in María Gravina Telechea, *Que Diga Quincho* (Managua: Editorial Nueva Nicargua, 1982), p. 81.

18. Lacayo, interview.

19. Ministry of Education, *La Educación en Cuatro Años de Revolución* (Managua: MED, 1983), p. 40.

20. Roberto Saenz, Program Director of Adult Education Program quoted in Sheryl Hirshon with Judy Butler, *And Also Teach Them to Read* (Westport, Conn.: Lawrence Hill, 1983), p. 7. This book, by a North American woman who joined the Crusade as a technical coordinator in a northern peasant region, is a rich and gripping personal chronicle of the five-month campaign—as it unfolded day to day—with all its joys and tribulations.

21. Adolfo López, Director of Planning, Adult Education Program, Ministry of Education, interview with the author, Managua, October 1983.

22. Fernando Cardenal, quoted in Valerie Miller, "The Nicaraguan Literacy Crusade" in *Nicaragua in Revolution*, edited by Thomas W. Walker (New York: Praeger, 1982). Cardenal, a Jesuit priest, was the Director of the National Literacy Crusade and in mid-1984 was named the Minister of Education, replacing Carlos Túnnerman, who was named Nicaraguan ambassador to the United States.

23. Sergio Ramírez, government Junta member, "La Crusade en Marcha," National Literacy Crusade Bulletin No. 4, (April 1980), p. 8.

24. Quoted in Hirshon, *And Also Teach*, p. 4.

25. Nicaraguans proudly point to the fact that no "developed society," with ample skilled technicians, financial and material support, has been able to pull off a similar undertaking to eradicate illiteracy.

26. Quoted in Black and Bevan, *The Loss of Fear*, p. 250.

27. Interview in Managua on August 24, 1980, the day after her daughter returned from the Crusade.

28. Miller, "Nicaraguan Literacy Crusade," p. 250.

29. International support was detailed by Roberto Saenz in a presentation he made to an International Seminar in Berlin in October 1983; his keynote address was entitled "Solidarity as an Alternate Form of International Cooperation: The Experience of the National Literacy Crusade in Nicaragua."

30. Black and Bevan, *The Loss of Fear*, p. 42.

31. This exchange with Paulo Freire was recounted by former Vice-Minister of Adult Education Francisco Lacayo, in a speech to a conference on popular education in Toronto, April 1981.

32. Hirshon, *And Also Teach*, p. 104.

33. Paulo Freire used the term "banking approach" to apply to the traditional methodology of teaching, in which the teacher "deposits" knowledge into the head of the

ignorant student; he advocated the "problem-posing approach," which involved students in collectively analyzing the problems of their daily lives.

34. Many recognized that the quality of training through the "multiplier process" diminished as it worked its way down through the four levels to the grass roots.

35. This song was recorded live with peasants who came to Managua to join the final celebration of the end of the Literacy Crusade, August 1980.

36. Carlos Carrión, FSLN representative to the Literacy Crusade, quoted in Hirshon, *And Also Teach*, p. 13.

37. I had the privilege of returning with a young brigadista to visit her "peasant family" a year after the Literacy Crusade was over. Such visits are still common, and they go both ways. It was very moving to witness the genuine affection in this relationship born of the Crusade.

38. Budd Hall, Secretary-General of the International Council for Adult Education, who was an invited guest at the final congress, expressed amazement at how "small groups" of 250 and plenary discussions of 1,000 achieved active criticism and self-criticism.

39. Francisco Lacayo, quoted in an interview with Carlos Tamez, Ministry of Education, Managua, October 1983.

40. Carlos Túnnerman was also one of the Group of Twelve, prominent professional and intellectual leaders who led opposition to Somoza and gave critical support to the FSLN as the vanguard.

41. *Fines, Objectivos, y Principios: La Nueva Educación* (Managua: DEPEP, March 1983).

42. This analysis was summarized from a discussion with Juan Arrien and Edgar Silva, Planning Division, Ministry of Education, Managua, October 1983.

43. Ministry of Education, *Educación en Cuatro Años*, p. 50.

44. Ibid., p. 15.

45. Ibid., p. 92.

46. Juan José Montenegro, Program Division, Ministry of Education, interview with the author, Managua, October 1983.

47. Miguel de Castilla, quoted in Black and Bevan, *The Loss of Fear*, p. 33.

48. Ministry of Education, *Educación en Cuatro Años*, pp. 118–119.

49. Vallecillo, interview.

50. Black and Bevan, *The Loss of Fear*, p. 34.

51. Julian Corrales Manguia, Nicaraguan Council of Higher Education, interview with the author, Managua, November 1983.

52. Black and Bevan, *The Loss of Fear*, p. 37.

53. Nathan Sevilla, Executive Secretary, ANDEN, interview with the author, Managua, October 1983.

54. Ibid.

55. Ernesto Vallecillo, "Popular Education: A Weapon in the Ideological Struggle." Presentation to the International Conference of Popular Education for Peace, Managua, September 1983.

56. Ibid.

57. Lacayo, interview.

Chapter 16
Health Policy: The Dilemma of Success

THOMAS JOHN BOSSERT

Taxi drivers always complain about national problems, so it was no surprise to find my Managua cabbie ranting on about shortages of meat, gas, and spare parts, which he blamed on the Sandinistas and the state bureaucracy, but then he suddenly turned to me and said, "But you know, the one thing this government has been able to do well is provide health care. We have more and better hospitals, more doctors, we are more aware of health and nutrition problems and we've had several good vaccination campaigns." As my research progressed it became obvious to me also that, while other sectors of Nicaraguan economic and social life were suffering major difficulties, the health sector had made significant, visible gains in five years of Revolution.

They had much to overcome. Health care conditions under Somoza were among the worst in Central America. The health system was one of the most inefficient and inequitable and most oriented toward curative, rather than preventive, services. Like the rest of the Somoza regime, the health system was a highly centralized patronage system, which at the same time was fragmented into many weak and competing institutions and programs. The Sandinistas were able quickly to unify the fragmented system and to make it more responsive to popular demands. They upgraded both hospital and preventive programs, in some cases with dramatic results. Hospital and clinic utilization mushroomed. Training programs to multiply the number of physicians and other health professionals were accelerated. Immunization and sanitation campaigns were particularly effective, and a broad network of oral rehydration centers appeared to have made marked inroads in reducing mortality from diarrhea—once the main killer of children under 5 years of age. Also

Research for this study was supported by a Post-doctoral Research Fellowship from the Tinker Foundation and an Andrew Mellon Faculty Development Grant from Sarah Lawrence College. Field research was conducted in Nicaragua in 1975, 1976, 1980, and 1983. I am indebted to Joyce Riegelhaupt, Thomas Walker, Richard Garfield, and Claudia Reeder for comments and suggestions.

important was the successful effort to produce genuine popular participation, which involved both voluntary efforts to implement programs and a means to make health officials more responsive to community demands and needs. All these achievements contributed to the legitimacy of the Sandinista government, gaining even grudging acknowledgement from opponents of the regime.

This very success, however, posed a classic dilemma of public health systems: the difficulty of achieving improved health status and growing political legitimacy while also maintaining an acceptable level of public spending for health services. This dilemma involves a choice of the appropriate balance between high-cost, hospital-based, physician-oriented, curative care and the more efficient, community-oriented preventive programs. In most health systems curative care is given overwhelming priority; however, curative care is often the most costly and least effective method of approaching the problem of providing health for a population. This is especially true in Third World countries where the most prevalent causes of death and illness are diseases we are now able to prevent in more developed countries: diarrhea and respiratory and infectious diseases. Furthermore, curative care is subject to ballooning cost increases that few nations have been able to contain. Physician-based curative care is also primarily available in urban areas—making it equally available to low-population areas is far too costly for Third World countries. Preventive programs are generally more equitably distributed.

Most international health experts now agree that programs designed to address preventable diseases with community-oriented, nonphysician health workers are a much more effective and efficient means of improving health in Third World countries.[1] These programs are part of an approach called primary health care, which emphasizes activities designed to organize the community to improve water supplies, build latrines, clean up the local environment, and to provide pre- and postnatal care, health and nutrition education and vigilance, continual first aid, and, when necessary, referral to higher levels of care. Considerable emphasis in this primary care approach is placed on participation of the community in health activities and in decisionmaking about health programs.[2]

It is not easy for a nation to shift its health policy to give greater emphasis on preventive primary care. To do so would mean having to attack the historical preeminence of curative medicine, sidestep the accelerating growth in curative technology, overcome the resistance of physicians and other health providers whose interests lies in the continued dominance of curative care, and address the problem of gaining legitimacy through preventive rather than curative achievements. This last problem is a particularly difficult one. It is a crucial characteristic of health care that most people perceive the need for services only when they are already sick, rather than being concerned with preventing the occurrence of disease.

Regime legitimacy, then, comes mainly from the provision of those curative services that serve sick people. This orientation makes it difficult to gain political legitimacy without providing improved curative services, even if these services are a less efficient means of improving health.

Nevertheless, the consequences of failing to shift health policy toward the preventive primary care approach are great. The curative care system is the most prone to growing popular demand for services, least amenable to equitable distribution and access, and most subject to accelerating cost increases. Its growth either means a trade-off within the health sector—making less resources available for the more efficient preventive programs—or it means a growing health budget—a trade-off with other social and economic goals and priorities. This last trade-off is probably the most important since it is likely that advances in social and economic well-being have a greater impact on health than do health services themselves.[3] Furthermore, as my cabbie's remarks suggested, gains in health may be made at the cost of resources that might have been applied to solving problems in other areas of the economy. This trade-off might gain legitimacy through health services at the cost of a loss of legitimacy through failures in other sectors.

The Sandinista Revolution made serious and impressive strides forward in both curative and preventive programs. Their achievements in both areas already matched or exceeded those of most other Central American countries. They were on a path that could shift the balance of health policy more securely into less costly preventive programs. However, they were still at an uncertain juncture along that path. They still had not squarely faced the dilemma of the trade-offs within the health sector and between health and other social and economic priorities. The curative sector continued to account for at least 85 percent of the national health budget—a figure comparable to that of other Central American countries. It is perhaps a more dangerous situation that, at a time of economic crisis and external invasion when conserving scarce resources for economic and military priorities was of prime importance, they had not controlled the accelerating costs of the health sector, which by most estimates grew much more rapidly than other sectors in the government budget.[4] The gains in primary care were made as part of a generally expanding health budget and not in terms of trade-offs within the health sector. This early failure to impose trade-offs by restricting the curative care system was likely in the future to make it increasingly difficult to impose a more equitable and preventive system and to restrict growth in health sector spending—the classic problems of most health care systems.

We should not be surprised that the Nicaraguan Revolution had not been able to ovecome the curative emphasis of its health system. Few nations had. The other Central American health systems had also made only tentative shifts in health policy toward primary care. The most effective Central American system, that of Costa Rica, made primary care gains the same way Nicaragua did—at the same time as advances in hospital care were accelerating and at the cost of resources that might have gone to other sectors.[5] Cuba, too, has a highly curative and very costly system.[6] However, as other chapters in this volume show, the Nicaraguans were more creative and more cost-conscious in their policies in other sectors of the economy and society. Their failure to achieve a more efficient and rational health system than their neighbors will be discussed in the context of their broader successes.

HEALTH AND HEALTH SERVICES UNDER SOMOZA

There is little doubt that the health conditions of Nicaraguans during the Somoza dictatorship were extremely poor, similar to other repressive Central American regimes, like those of Guatemala and Honduras. Life expectancy was 53 years, and infant mortality, often taken as an indicator of the general health status of the whole population, was estimated at an extremely high rate—between 120 and 146 per 1,000 live births.[7] Guatemala and Honduras had similar high rates, while by contrast wealthier and more progressive Costa Rica had a life expectancy of 70 years and infant mortality of 29 per 1,000. As in Guatemala and Honduras, preventable diseases were the principal causes of death: diarrhea and infectious diseases accounted for 31.4 percent of all deaths and over 50 percent of infant mortality. Measles, tetanus, and polio were major causes of illness and mortality. Malaria and tuberculosis were endemic and growing problems. Nutrition levels were also extremely low, contributing to mortality from other causes: 66 percent of children under 5 years of age were estimated to have some degree of malnutrition.

At first glance, the Somoza health system appears not to have been severely inadequate to the task of caring for the rather small population of 2.3 million. In 1977 there were 50 hospitals and clinics with a total of 4,675 beds, or 2 per 1,000 people. In 1975 it was estimated that there were 1,357 doctors in Nicaragua, a fairly high average of 6 per 10,000 peole. These figures compared very favorably with Guatemala and Honduras and were not far below those of Costa Rica. Nicaragua was spending between 15 and 20 percent of its national budget in health, or 2 to 4 percent of the GDP, compared to Costa Rica, which spent around 30 percent of its national budget, or 5 to 6 percent of the GDP.[8]

Nicaragua, however, had an extremely inequitable health system. Like most public health systems, the Nicaraguan system did not serve the upper class—those who could easily afford private medical care and who could go to the United States for specialized treatment. Nevertheless, the system tended to favor the better-off middle classes in urban areas. For instance, the Social Security Institute (INSS), which, like most Latin American social security agencies, provided a significant portion of the medical care in the country—an estimated 40 percent of the health sector expenditures—served no more than 10 percent of the population. This 10 percent was almost entirely urban employees in fairly secure jobs. While the public hospital system was officially responsible for both urban and rural areas, it overwhelmingly favored the former, a phenomenon not unusual in Central America but perhaps more extreme in Nicaragua. In 1973, over half of the hospital beds in the country were in the three major cities and only five health facilities with beds were in rural areas. Even the most simple facilities—the health centers without beds—were much more prevalent in urban than rural areas. Only 35 out of the 119 health centers were in rural areas and most were staffed with untrained auxiliary nurses. While Managua had only 25 percent of the population, 50 percent of the physicians and 70 percent of the professional nurses worked there. Urban areas had averages of more than 11 physicians per 10,000 population, while the countryside had 2.5 or fewer. Provision of potable water and sewage systems was also skewed toward urban areas.

Inefficiency of the hospital system, again, is not unusual for Central America but may have been even more extreme in Nicaragua. In stark contrast to what happened after the Revolution, the hospital services of Somoza were not being used. In spite of the large number of hospital beds in the country, there were only 4 reported hospital discharges per 1,000—compared to 26 discharges per 1,000 in Honduras. Most health facilities were in extremely poor condition, lacked necessary equipment and medicines, and had very low utilization rates.

A general problem of public health systems in Latin America is that usually two major institutions are responsible for health facilities—the Ministry of Health and the Social Security Institute. This dual system often leads to duplication of services and tremendous inefficiencies. The Nicaraguan system was unusual in that it not only had this dual character but was actually even more fragmented.[9] In addition to the Ministry of Health, which was primarily responsible for preventive medicine and small clinics, there were autonomous governing boards for each public hospital (19 Local Social Assistance Boards [JLAS]) and another national agency responsible for financing hospital construction through the national lottery (National Social Assistance Council [JNAPS]). This fragmentation added to the confusion in a sector that also had the Social Security Institute, an autonomous water and sewer agency, and military hospitals. Furthermore, even the Ministry of Health was fragmented internally with several vertically run programs that functioned with relative autonomy.

Preventively oriented, public health programs were also sporadic and poorly developed. Potable water systems served only 41.4 percent of the urban population and less than 10.9 percent in rural areas. Sewage systems reached only 29.4 percent of the urban population and latrine use in rural areas was extremely limited. Vaccination programs reached few in the target populations. Polio vaccinations in 1974 were administered to only 17 percent of the population at risk and vaccinations for diphtheria, pertussis, and tetanus reached only 5.7 percent of those at risk. Malaria control programs were increasingly ineffective, in part due to the growing resistance of mosquitos to the widely used pesticides in agriculture.

What really set Somoza's Nicaragua apart from other Central American countries was that there was no major attempt to improve the system and redress the inequalities. In the early 1970s, Guatemala, Honduras, and Costa Rica began significant new programs that emphasized primary care and preventive activities for their extremely underserved rural areas. These programs actually did shift the expenditure patterns of the governments, demonstrating much more of a commitment to public-health programs for rural areas than was apparent in Somoza's Nicaragua, where only a few small, foreign-funded primary care programs were initiated in the late 1970s.

FIRST STEPS IN REVOLUTIONARY HEALTH POLICY

One of the first declarations of the new Sandinista government was a clear commitment to improving the health of Nicaraguans. The government's program stated that the new regime would "stimulate and organize popular participation to solve the major national problems: hunger, unemployment, malnutrition, illness, illiteracy, and housing—the despicable results of 50 years of Somocismo." The new government moved quickly to unite the fragmented health organizations of the Somoza period into a single system under the authority of the Ministry of Health. This gave the ministry direct control over not only the hospitals in the two Social Assistance systems (JLAS and JNAPS), but also all of the Social Security hospitals, ending the duplication of facilities and the preferential medical care for the small percentage of the population covered by Social Security. Furthermore, the new reorganization of the ministry did away with the variety of semiautonomous vertical programs, all of which were to be fully integrated into the administrative structure of the ministry.

While unifying the fragmented system, the ministry also moved to decentralize Somoza's inefficient and unresponsive decisionmaking process in a variety of ways. They began to create regional offices with greater responsibility and flexibility. While strengthening the national health planning information system, they enhanced the planning role of health officials at all levels.

Perhaps the most significant feature of the new health system was the open commitment to the participation of the community in health programs. The neighborhood Sandinista Defense Committees and other mass organizations like the Association of Farm Workers, the Nicaraguan

Women's Association, and the local Councils of Reconstruction supported the activities of the Ministry of Health. At the local level and at higher administrative levels these organizations participated in ministry decision-making in Popular Health Councils. From all reports, this participation was enthusiastic and effective.[10] Through these popular organizations the Ministry implemented its immunization campaigns, promoted the installation of latrines, distributed food supplements, and completed a census of children at risk. These organizations began their own initiatives in providing materials, labor, and equipment for construction of health posts and for preventive programs. They also took responsibility for assuring that the price controls for some food items were respected. While it is clear that popular participation was more prevalent in some areas than others— rural areas were still weakly organized—and that the ministry was often unable to respond to popular organization requests for supplies, equipment, and manpower, the government clearly made a significant commitment to achieving massive popular participation at a level rarely reached in other countries. Although participation primarily involved organizing people for vaccination campaigns, latrine building, and educational programs, there were efforts to involve the community in decisionmaking, so as to make the health system more responsive to local needs and demands. These efforts were made at all administrative levels of the ministry. They included weekly meetings between the minister and representatives of mass organizations as well as periodic requirements for local officials to "Face the People" in large community meetings, in which they were expected to explain health programs and respond to criticism and demands of the local community.

The new government also initiated several major programs in preventive medicine. In the early months it began a widespread vaccination campaign against polio, measles, and other infectious diseases, reaching an estimated 85 percent of the target population. In the first six months, a sanitation campaign distributed 4,200 latrines—twice the number the Somoza regime distributed in all of 1978.[11] Using materials supplied by UNICEF, the ministry established 250 centers for oral rehydration treatment for diarrhea. These centers, located in health facilities all over the country, provided an easily administered solution of salts and sugar, which is perhaps the most effective and inexpensive means of reducing mortality from diarrhea. By 1981 these centers had treated 92,000 children, most of whom were under one year old. Only 2.6 percent needed further treatment and only 17 children died. Nutrition programs involving complementary feeding were also rapidly expanded, reaching over 100,000 children a year by 1981. Population control measures, while not emphasized by the government, were nevertheless made available and by 1982 over 80,000 women, out of an estimated 670,000 fertile-aged women, were in the family planning program. In association with the Ministry of Education, a program was also developed to add a health education component to the massive Literacy Crusade in 1980—one out of ten brigadistas was especially trained to promote health activities. In another new effort, occupational health and safety problems were addressed by the formation of promotion and inspection teams in coordination with the Ministry of Labor. In 1982, 6,488 inspections of work areas were made.

Consistent with these early reforms, it was in the first year of the Revolution that the Sandinistas had the clearest opportunity to place major emphasis on a new primary health care system. Unfortunately, they did not grasp this opportunity.[12] They made many valiant efforts to improve the deteriorating Somoza health system but in the process strengthened the curative hospital and clinic structure, ultimately at the expense of preventive primary care programs.

The central effort of the new government during the first year was to reconstruct the services and economy that had been destroyed by several years of civil war. In the health sector, this emphasis was interpreted as a mandate to restore the hospitals and clinics that had been destroyed during 1979 by the National Guard bombings. The new government, however, soon also committed itself to a major new program of hospital construction. Largely with foreign funding, from Western Europe and the Inter-American Development Bank, five new hospitals were under construction or completed by 1984. This was a popular move that symbolized Sandinista commitment to health. However, restoring hospitals also assured that the high cost of maintaining these services would continue to be the dominant expense in the national health budget.

A second crucial choice involved training of new health professionals. Although all types of health workers were to be increased and to receive more adequate training, it was the curative professionals—doctors and their hospital-based assistants—who received the greatest attention. Existing medical school facilities were expanded at the university in León, an additional medical school was created in Managua, and the entering class of medical students jumped from 100 to 500. While on the surface it might appear that more physicians would improve a health system, physicians are trained primarily to cure sick people and only add to pressures for curative and high-cost services rather than the more effective and more mundane preventive programs. Furthermore, physician salaries are considerably higher than those of nonphysician health workers, even in more equalized salary systems like Nicaragua's. In 1983, physicians received three to four times the salary of auxiliary nurses, and they could more than double this salary in private practice.

These two choices—expanding both hospital construction and physician training—were to set the basis for a long-term structural necessity to give priority to the curative sector. Both hospitals and physicians require continual high levels of funding to be effective in delivery of care. A poorly supplied, equipped, and maintained hospital or clinic generates demands for improvements from both staff and users—demands that few political systems successfully resist for long periods. Once health care—especially the availability of curative care—is made a cornerstone of a regime's legitimacy, as it has in Nicaragua, it is all the more difficult to resist demands to maintain and upgrade an established curative system.

Why, then, when the Sandinistas were initiating broad reforms in the health sector did they miss the opportunity to place stronger emphasis on primary care and avoid the pitfalls of an expanding curative system? The most immediate reason was that physicians with little or no public health or preventive medicine training dominated decisionmaking in the ministry during the first year of the regime. Evidence around the world suggests that physicians in policymaking positions in health ministries seldom grant sufficient priority to preventive programs.[13] Physicians were chosen apparently because the Sandinistas felt it necessary, in their broader interests of creating an enduring alliance of classes, to assure the continuing support of physicians and their middle-class clients.[14] Furthermore, taking their ideological inspiration from Cuban and Soviet models—which emphasize curative care—the Sandinistas incorrectly viewed primary care as "second-class" care since it did not emphasize the use of fully trained physicians.[15] They were also encouraged by initial foreign donations from Sweden and West Germany, which provided funds for the construction of two hospitals, and by the brigades of international physicians who came to provide curative care in previously inaccessible rural areas. Perhaps most importantly, the Ministry had to respond to an immediate and rapid growth in popular demand for curative services. This general policy appeared to respond to the immediate demands from the crucial urban and semiurban areas from which the Revolution had drawn its initial and most important political support. In the health sector, it was this population that appeared to be flooding the hospitals that they had avoided under Somoza but now considered to be rightly theirs, and it was in these areas that the most widespread spontaneous creation of popular clinics occurred. In order to consolidate its base of support in the early period of the regime, the Nicaraguan revolutionary government emphasized an immediate response to this demand.

INITIATING PRIMARY HEALTH CARE PROGRAMS

By 1981 a variety of converging forces managed to initiate changes in ministry policy that finally brought a greater emphasis on preventive programs. While not a major shift away from the curative orientation, nevertheless these efforts successfully fostered a new and important commitment to primary care activities. Crucial to these changes was the appointment of a nonphysician as Minister of Health. Replacing Dr. César Amador Kuhl, a highly specialized neurosurgeon, Lea Guido built on her previous experience as Minister of Social Welfare to encourage the Health Ministry to place less emphasis on the expensive curative system and more on outreach community programs. In addition, as an important FSLN militant, Guido had a base of political support from which to modify the physician dominance in the ministry. She was aided in this effort by many public health officials in the ministry, including the large Departments of Health Education and Preventive Medicine. Furthermore, the Pan American Health Organization—committed to promotion of primary care strategies in Latin America—increased its primary care advisors and stepped up efforts and funding for primary health care activities. UNICEF also expanded its successful oral rehydration program.

The results of these changes in the ministry were twofold. First, a systematic program of large-scale public health activities was organized as massive weekend vaccination and sanitation campaigns called "Popular Health Days." These programs involved periodic nationwide efforts in which the ministry coordinated and supplied volunteers from the mass organizations and neighborhood CDSs, to immunize against polio, tetanus, diphtheria, and measles, and to become involved in sanitation projects and assist in malaria control. Five Popular Health Days involved over 30,000 volunteers and gave over 1 million doses in three separate phases in 1982.[16] These campaigns appear to have been largely responsible for the rapid decline in incidence of transmissable diseases: polio dropped from 101 cases in 1979 to none in 1982, diphtheria from 11 to 2, and measles from 1,270 to 226. In 1981 an unusual massive three-day campaign distributed antimalaria pills to an estimated 75 percent of the population in an attempt to break the disease chain and facilitate subsequent control efforts. These immunization campaigns also contributed to health education and popular participation in general health programs. For all their success, however, these efforts are best seen as temporary approaches to disease control. The mobilizing efforts can be quite costly compared to permanent multipurpose community services—although not nearly as costly in the long run as curative efforts. Furthermore, continual vigilance and control efforts necessary after large-scale campaigns are best achieved through a permanent network of primary care health posts and outreach activities of nonphysician health workers. Massive campaigns can have dramatic effects on disease patterns but a more permanent system is necessary to continue maintaining low levels of disease.

The second initiative was an attempt to address the need for this permanent network by creating a department of primary health care in the ministry. This department was responsible for the construction and rehabilitation of 363 health posts and the special training, equipping, and supervising of auxiliary nurses to work in these health posts and in outreach programs in the local communities. This program represented the first major nationwide, institutionalized effort in primary care ever achieved in Nicaragua. A program similar to the efforts initiated in the mid-1970s in the rest of Central America, it represented a significant beginning but by no means a full-scale commitment to primary care. As in the other Central American countries, the portion of the national health budget committed to this program was low—no more than 15 percent— and the number of health posts and auxiliaries was sorely insufficient to meet goals of broad coverage and easy access. Despite the construction of 300 new health posts, in 1984 there were still only 1.5 posts per 10,000 people and many in rural areas were still denied any real access to continuous health services.

FUTURE TRENDS

One of the hallmarks of an equitably oriented socialist state is a strong planning institution. Planning is a potential means of promoting a more efficient and rational allocation of resources, especially if it is capable of overcoming the structural political power of established service bureaucracies and interests. Effective planning can be responsive to local needs and correct for inefficiencies if adequate participation, responsibility, and information systems are developed.[17] In the health sector, health planning efforts around the world have given rise to greater awareness of inequalities and inefficiencies and have been an important tool for increasing equity and efficiency in some countries. Coordination between health planning activities of ministries of health and strong national planning ministries have been particularly conducive to sponsoring and maintaining greater efforts in primary care and constraining growth in the urban-oriented curative sector.

In Nicaragua, health planning had steadily improved from its very weak stature—almost nonexistent—under Somoza and during the first year of the Revolution. Planning activities during the Somoza period were initiated by the Pan American Health Organization and USAID and received little support from the ministry. In the first year of the Revolution, there was no operating planning office and the health information system was in frantic disarray. Incremental efforts since then established a functioning planning office with trained health planners, an increasingly sophisticated health information system, and greater participation at all levels in the ministry in health planning activities.

These efforts established the basis for a more powerful role of planning but they were not yet sufficient to constrain the growth of the curative sector. Indeed some health planning efforts led in the opposite direction. One major planning document, the Prospective Plan, projected a capacity to fund a considerable growth in the hospital sector as well as replace auxiliaries in the primary care system with fully trained physicians and larger staffs.[18] This plan was based on wildly optimistic economic assumptions and although it was soon recognized as an unrealistic guide for yearly planning, it was still seen as a goal toward which the health system should be oriented.

There were several reasons for the failure of health planning to make significant changes in the health system. First, planning officials themselves were not committed to reducing the cost of health care. The chief of planning was trained in a more curative-oriented system and was suspicious of the "second class" appearance of primary care. Futhermore, within the ministry, health planning was still not given the high priority necessary for it to guide the hard distribution choices. But perhaps more important was the general weakness of planning in the rest of the national government in Nicaragua. The Ministry of Planning was underfunded and dependent on other ministries for planning and financial data. Only one official at the Ministry of Planning was responsible for the health sector and she had to rely entirely on the Ministry of Health planning office for statistical information and analysis. This structure meant that there was little pressure from the national level to encourage the Ministry of Health to restructure its priorities and contain the high-cost, curative sector. While the yearly budgeting process provided some clear constraint, it tended only to establish a budget ceiling (which nevertheless continually expanded as extraordinary funding was made available to the ministry) and paid little attention to internal distribution of ministry funds. Futhermore, since health budgets after 1980 were a growing proportion of the national budget, there was little structural incentive to reduce long-term ministry expectations of continued growth in the health budget. Current financial constraints were seen as temporary obstacles that did not force a significant reordering of priorities.

Two other conditions suggest that needed trade-offs in the health sector would be increasingly difficult to achieve. First, the health system had one of the two most powerful unions in Nicaragua, with a long history of militancy even during the Somoza period. During the late 1970s this union, FETSALUD, led courageous strikes that helped mobilize opposition to the Somoza regime. Since then it had successfully maintained its autonomy of direct Sandinista control, while at the same time not joining the opposition.[19] It was also one of the few successful unions to gain wage concessions prior to the government's wage freeze. The wage structure under Somoza was so low, inequitable, and inconsistent that the initial wage restructuring appeared clearly justified. However, since FETSALUD primarily represented hospital workers, one damaging consequence of its successful wage struggles was to add to the cost of maintaining the hospital sector and reduce the resources available for primary care programs.

Physicians also mobilized successfully to press for their particular interests in curative care. The medical association, FESOMENIC, created after the triumph of the Revolution, joined a larger interest group of professionals, CONAPRO, with direct representation on the Council of State. While tensions between conservative and progressive physicians led to splits within FESOMENIC, both groups tended to pressure the government effectively for physician dominance in the health sector and limit government regulation of private practice.

A second, and perhaps more complex, impetus toward curative care was popular demand. As noted above, popular demand for hospital and clinic care grew rapidly immediately after the fall of Somoza. With increases in popular participation and incentives for health officials to be more responsive to demands of mass organizations and of local communities in the "Face the People" meetings, demand for curative care was increasingly hard to resist. The wrenching dilemma of popular participation is the difficulty of achieving broad popular awareness of needed trade-offs and of the significant benefits of preventive-oriented primary care. Popular participation contributes to growth in popular awareness of health issues, popular willingness to join effective programs, and responsiveness of health officials to local needs, but it also clearly increases the demand for more costly, curatively oriented care. This demand is particularly critical when the health sector has assumed a crucial role in legitimitizing the regime.

What could have been done to reverse these trends? Especially in a period of economic decline and external invasion, resources devoted to the least efficient high-cost social service needed to be reallocated to more pressing economic and military needs. The community-based, low-cost, preventively oriented and more effective primary health care system needed to be granted much higher priority. However, the government had achieved a considerable amount of popular legitimacy precisely because it had devoted much of its resources to hospital and clinic doctor-oriented care. Having missed the chance early in the Revolution, the Sandinista government could not significantly withdraw from the high-cost sector without risking some deterioration of popular support. Future commitment to primary care depended on the ability to resist pressures for new hospital construction and increasingly to reduce physician training while at the same time increase spending for water and sanitation projects, auxiliary nurse training, and community-based health posts.

There would be no easy way to achieve this long-term incremental shift.[20] It was likely that a strengthening of the coalition of forces that allowed the introduction of primary care could continue to lead the way. Nonphysician social service officials like Lea Guido, with an independent base of political support within the FSLN, could play a greater role in ministry decisionmaking. Personnel decisions based on public health credentials rather than physician training could be emphasized within the ministry. International agencies that promote primary care, like the Pan American Health Organization and UNICEF, could continue to exert pressure, while at the same time international funding sources for hospital construction could be strenuously resisted.

Perhaps most importantly, the Sandinista government probably needed to establish a much stronger planning ministry, with independent sources of information, adequate, well-trained staff, and control over the budget. This agency not only would have to establish ceilings but also make decisions about distribution of services.

Finally, building on the growth of active popular participation, the effective health education campaigns, the "Popular Health Day" activities, and the "Face the People" meetings could place increasing emphasis on the need to make rational trade-offs and place greater priority on primary care programs. In 1984 there was some evidence that popular pressure for preventive health programs was growing, although it did not yet seem to be couched in terms of trade-offs with curative programs. Government programs in other areas suggest that such efforts could be effective if given proper priority. For instance, in the Farm Workers' Association widespread recognition of the need for workers to increase production while restricting demand for wage increases was achieved early in the Revolution. Other efforts to develop popular recognition of the need for austerity were also somewhat successful. Such an effort in health might increase recognition of the more important role preventive programs play in bringing health to the population and in the process gain legitimacy for the regime that was promoting such activities.

By 1984 the Nicaraguan Revolution had produced a successful health system of which they were rightly proud. It had achieved significant reductions in major diseases, had apparently reduced infant mortality, and had begun to make changes in living and working conditions that were likely to improve health. It had also made available a complex health care delivery system that made easy access a reality for most of the Nicaraguan people. The combination of health improvements and access to services made a major contribution to the legitimacy of the regime. I have suggested here that this success produced a dilemma because the health system was not as preventively oriented or as egalitarian as it could have been and because it was likely to become increasingly costly to maintain its overwhelmingly curative institutions. This argument was not to take away from the achievements, but rather to note continuing inequalities, to warn against the future drain on the increasingly scarce resources of the country, and to suggest lessons for future revolutionary regimes in other countries. Early choices might have been made radically to enhance the primary care sector and limit growth in curative care without necessarily weakening the legitimizing capacity of the health system. Later choices would have to be more incremental and would involve restraining very powerful, structurally induced pressures for growth in curative care. All governments currently face these choices. Revolutionary regimes, however, should have greater structural and moral capacity to rationalize the health sector and reduce its costs.

THE COUNTERREVOLUTION

The U.S.-funded invasions of Nicaragua by the contras (counterrevolutionaries based in Honduras and Costa Rica) had special consequences in the health sector. They, of course, destroyed lives and productive capacity in target areas, adding casualties that needed to be attended by health services and weakening economic and social conditions necessary for health improvements. By one estimate, over 1,000 people were killed and 56,000 forced to flee to refugee areas by early 1984. Accompanying this disruption were upsurges in infectious and contagious diseases, like malaria and diarrhea, which reached epidemic proportions in some areas near the Honduran and Costa Rican borders.[21]

The health system itself had also become a special target. Health workers, including foreign physicians and local volunteers, were threatened, tortured, and killed. Rural health posts and clinics, as well as medical supply lines, became special targets for destruction. In the Miskitu area of the North East near Honduras, where the contras were initially most active, one of the most successful primary care systems was all but destroyed by mid-1983.

These special direct attacks on the health system appear to have been motivated by the very success of the system in gaining popular legitimacy for the regime. The contras were targeting the health workers, posts, and medicines, disrupting these important services in order to reduce the capacity of the regime to respond to popular demands for health services. Up to mid-1984, however, the consequences of these attacks appear to have seriously reduced services only in extremely low-density areas like the North East and did not appear to have reduced the legitimacy of the regime. On the contrary, as one health official asserted to me, there appears some truth to the saying: "The Revolution is like a stake. When struck, it sure hurts . . . but it also becomes more deeply implanted."

NOTES

1. Stephen C. Joseph and Sharon Stanton Russell, "Is Primary Care the Wave of the Future?" *Social Science and Medicine*, 14C (1980):137–144; Davidson Gwatkin, Janet R. Wilcox, and Joe D. Wray, *Can Health and Nutrition Interventions Make a Difference?* (Washington, D.C.: Overseas Development Council, 1980); Julia A. Walsh and Kenneth S. Warren, "Interim Strategy for Disease Control in Developing Countries," *The New England Journal of Medicine* 301, no. 18 (November 1, 1979):967–974; Oscar Gish, "The Political Economy of Primary Care and 'Health by the People': An Historical Exploration," *Social Science and Medicine* 13C (1979):203–211.

2. World Health Organization and United Nations Children's Fund, *Primary Health Care* (Geneva: World Health Organization, 1978); World Bank, *Health Sector Policy Paper* (Washington, D.C.: World Bank, 1980).

3. See Thomas McKeown, *The Role of Medicine: Dream, Mirage, or Nemesis?* (Oxford: Basil Blackwell, 1979).

4. Budget data were increasingly difficult to obtain in Nicaragua in 1983. These estimates are from unpublished balance sheets of the actual yearly expenditures calculated by the Division of Finance of the Ministry of Health, *Ejecución Presupuestaria* for 1980, 1981, and 1982. Other estimates can be found in Richard Garfield and Eujenio Taboada, "Health Service Reform in Revolutionary Nicaragua," *American Journal of Public Health*, October 1984.

5. See Thomas John Bossert, "Can We Return to the Regime for Comparative Policy Analysis, or The State and Health Policy in Central America," *Comparative Politics* 15, no. 4 (July 1983):419–441.

6. See Ross Danielson, *Cuban Medicine* (New Brunswick, N.J.: Transaction Books, 1979); Vincente Navarro, "Health, Health Services, and Health Planning in Cuba," *International Journal of Health Service* 2, no. 3 (1972):397–432; and Milton Roemer, "Health Development and Political Policy: The Lesson of Cuba," *Journal of Health Politics, Policy and Law* 4, no. 4 (Winter 1980):570–580.

7. Nicaraguan health figures for the Somoza period are from: República de Nicaragua, Ministerio de Salud Pública, *Proyecto de mejoramiento de servicios rurales de salud* and *Informe sobre el estado de salud en Nicaragua 1974–1977* (Managua, 1977); Junta Nacional de Asistencia y Previsión Social, *Anuario Estadístico 1974* (Managua, 1974); Office of International Health, United States Department of Health, Education and Welfare, *Syncresis: The Dynamics of Health, An Analytical Series on the Interactions of Health and Socio-economic Development: Nicaragua* (Washington, D.C.: U.S. Government Printing Office, 1974); Dirección de Educación y Communicación Popular en Salud, Ministerio de Salud, *Aportes para el análisis histórico de la educación y la participación popular en salud* (Managua, 1980).

8. Comparative budgetary figures from Thomas John Bossert, *The State and International Agencies in Central America: Comparative Health Policy-Making* (in progress).

9. See Bossert, "Can We Return to the Regime"; and John M. Donahue, "The Politics of Health Care in Nicaragua Before and After the Revolution in 1979," *Human Organization* 42, no. 3 (Fall 1983):265–6.

10. Report by Fritz Müller, External Consultant for Pan American Health Organization, in Pan American Health Organization, *Nicaragua: Atención primaria en salud 1981–1983: Documentos* (Managua: unpublished documents, 1981–83). See also Donahue, "Politics of Health Care."

11. Figures for the revolutionary period are from: Ministerio de Salud, *La Salud en Nicaragua antes y despúes del triúnfo de la revolución* (Managua, 1980); *El Sistema Nacional Unico de Salud: Tres años de Revolución 1979–1982 (Managua, 1982); Plan de Salud 1981, 1982, 1983* (Managua); División de Estadística e Informática, Ministerio de Salud, *Anuario Estadístico 1982* (Managua, 1983); Instituto Histórico Centroamericano, "Un pueblo más

sano," *Envío* (Managua) 23 (May 1983):1c–11c; Garfield and Taboada, "Health Service Reform"; and interviews with various health officials in February 1980 and June 1983.

12. For a more detailed analysis of this period, see Thomas John Bossert, "Health Care in Revolutionary Nicaragua," in *Nicaragua in Revolution*, edited by Thomas W. Walker (New York: Praeger, 1982), pp. 264–271. See also José Carlos Escudero, "Starting from Year One: The Politics of Health in Nicaragua," *International Journal of Health Services* 10, no. 4 (1980):647–657.

13. On the issue, see Antonio Ugalde, "The Role of the Medical Profession in Public Health Policy-Making: The Case of Colombia," *Social Science and Medicine* 13C (June 1979):109–119.

14. Interview with Paulino Castillón, Director of International Relations, Ministry of Health, in Managua, July 1983.

15. For analysis of high-cost Cuban system, see especially Roemer, "The Lesson of Cuba."

16. Material on this period is from: Ministerio de Salud, *Las Jornadas Populares de Salud* (Managua, 1982); *Estrategias de Atención Primaria de la República de Nicargua* (Managua, 1981); Pan American Health Organization, *Nicaragua*; interviews with Lea Guido, Minister of Health; Manuel Martínez, subdirector of Popular Health Days Program; Carlos Jarquín G., Director of Primary Care Division; and Roberto Capote Mir, Pan American Health Organization Primary Care Advisor, in Managua, July 1983.

17. See Brian Abel-Smith, *Poverty, Development, and Health Policy* (Geneva: World Health Organization, 1978); and Naomi Caiden and Aaron Wildavsky, *Planning and Budgeting in Poor Countries* (New York: John Wiley, 1974).

18. Ministerio de Salud, *Plan Perspectivo de Desarrollo de los Servicios de Atención Primaria y Secundaria* (Managua, 1982) and *Programa de Extención de Cobertura* (Managua, 1980); interviews with Julio Zapata, Director of Health Planning; René Darce, Vice-Minister of Health; and Milton Valdés, Director of Preventive Medicine, in Managua, June 1983.

19. Garfield and Taboada, "Health Service Reform"; interviews with Santo López, Secretary General of FETSALUD, in Managua, June 1983; FETSALUD, *Boletín Informativo*, No. 1–5 (1982.)

20. For a broader analysis of the political processes involved in promoting primary care, see Thomas John Bossert and David Parker, "Political and Administrative Context of Primary Health Care in the Third World," *Social Science and Medicine* 18, no. 8 (1984):693–702.

21. Richard Garfield, "Nicaraguan's Health," *New York Times*, February 2, 1984; Mary Elsberg, "Trail Blazing on the Atlantic Coast: A Report on Nicaragua's Health Care Brigadistas," *Science for the People* 15, no. 6 (November/December 1983):14–19.

Chapter 17
Social Welfare

REINALDO ANTONIO TÉFEL
HUMBERTO MENDOZA LÓPEZ
JORGE FLORES CASTILLO

INTRODUCTION

From 1979 onward, social security legislation underwent profound changes as expressed particularly in the 1982 social security law. The point of departure for the administrative work of the Nicaraguan Social Security and Welfare Institute (INSSBI) at the time of the overthrow of Somoza was an institution that, as a result of the pillage and the 680 million córdoba debt owed by Somoza's central government to the old Social Security Institute, was totally bankrupt. The debt owed by the central government under Somoza was never paid despite the fact that deductions continued to be taken out of the salaries of state employees. Furthermore, the value of economic benefits distributed up to 1979 had to be raised since that aid was extremely small and was not even enough to provide minimally for a socially acceptable standard of living for the pensioner and his family.

There were profound changes in the orientation of social security in Nicaragua. The new guidelines of INSSBI were oriented to extending benefits to all sectors of the country's economy, in both urban and rural areas, thereby applying the principle of universality. INSSBI's programs covered not only economically active sectors, but also those sectors that had particular needs. The latter could receive benefits even though they had not paid into the social security system. Also covered were those sectors of the population who had dedicated much of their lives to production but who, because of the unjust conditions in which they worked, were not covered by social security. It was in this context that the revolutionary government passed laws protecting miners, as well as persons such as circus artists, whose contribution to Nicaraguan culture was recognized by the revolutionary government and who were now covered with old-age pensions so long as they had worked in Nicaragua for at least five years. Other programs that were promoted along these same lines included protection for those who suffered losses in the War of Liberation and for members of the Popular Militia and Revolutionary Vigilance in recognition of their participation in the defense of the homeland. These achievements were just some of the benefits the

365

Government of National Reconstruction promoted in the area of social security, making it possible for every Nicaraguan to be covered by this system.

SOCIAL SECURITY UNDER SOMOZA

The social security system was in a state of complete bankruptcy at the moment of the Triumph, with the Somoza state owing it more than 680 million córdobas. The pensions were so small that they did not even cover the minimal needs of the pensioners, whose standard of living was below that called for by basic human dignity. The administration of the Social Security Institute was characterized by bureaucracy, administrative corruption, and delays in providing services. There was even a constantly applied law designed to prevent those covered by social security from claiming their benefits. The most important aspect of the Institute as far as the Somoza government was concerned was that it served as an instrument through which to collect funds with which to sustain the state bureaucracy that legitimized the perpetuation of the dictatorial regime. The Social Security Law had a series of restrictions in application, medical attention, and economic benefits. The amount of the pensions was calculated according to different criteria for each situation (old age, disabilities, death). There were no minimal pensions to cover those who, having experienced a problem, needed aid before having filled the required number of quotas during their qualifying period. Thus relatives or dependents of those suffering a disability or accidental death before having completed their quotas were helpless.

In short, the administration and application of the services of the Social Security Institute were oriented to benefit a small number of people who worked for the Somoza regime or were close relatives of the Somozas. The working class and peasantry received minimal social protection, while being exploited to the benefit of the dominant classes. Nicaragua's first Social Security Law dated from December 1955. It provided protection for dependent workers against the contingencies of illness, maternity, disability, old age, death, and professional risks. Beginning in 1966, a new set of pensions was applied covering disability, old age, and death for all public servants; but even this brought coverage to only 10 percent of the country's population.

POST-TRIUMPH LEGISLATION CONCERNING
SOCIAL SECURITY

In August 1979 the Junta of the Government of National Reconstruction proclaimed the Statute on the Rights and Guarantees of Nicaraguans. Article 33 established the following:

All persons have the right to Social Security; to obtain the satisfaction of rights that are indispensable to their dignity and to the development of their personality; to an adequate standard of living, which guarantees them, as well as their family, health and well-being, especially food, clothing, housing, medical assistance and necessary social services; to social security in case of unemployment, illness, maternity, disability, widowhood, old age, death, orphanhood, professional risks or other cases of loss of the means of subsistence.

The new social security system was established on this basis, thereby necessitating the restructuring of the laws that existed at the moment of the Triumph. Through Decree No. 35, the Junta abolished the National Board of Aid and Social Security and the Local Social Aid Boards, which had been established by the previous Organic Law of Social Security. It also made fundamental transformations in the social security system, among which the Unified National Health System and the Ministry of Social Welfare stand out.

THE UNIFIED NATIONAL HEALTH SYSTEM

The Unified National Health System was created under the jurisdiction of the Ministry of Health. That ministry thus assumed direct administrative responsibility for all the medical installations and services of both the Nicaraguan Social Security Institute and the local boards so as to offer the best possible medical attention guaranteeing the same technical quality for the entire population regardless of one's occupational status.

The Ministry of Health was made responsible for everything related to illness and maternity, including caring for the insured, who before were part of the social security program. The Law for the Creation of the Unified National Health System determined that INSSBI would continue to grant illness and maternity subsidies in the name of the Unified National Health System. Health was seen as a generic right without conditions for all Nicaraguans. Nonetheless, it was a duty of those who were healthy, active, and had economic possibilities to contribute to the sustenance of the system. Based on this principle, active workers paid a "solidary contribution" to the Unified Health System.

Workers and employers participated in sustaining the Unified National System with their solidary contribution that INSSBI then transferred to the Ministry of Health after deducting the amount paid to insured workers in the form of subsidies for temporary incapacity due to illness, maternity, or professional risks. This arrangement was unique among Latin American social security institutions. In conclusion, it was not a matter of paying into the system in order to recover one's own health. Rather, one contributed in solidarity when one was healthy to the benefit of all who were ill.

The Ministry of Social Welfare

The Ministry of Social Welfare was created as part of the revolutionary government. Its strategy for action and its principal goal was to solve social problems, strengthening the organizational structures that would allow for community participation in the implementation and development of services in accordance with their needs.

The part of the population affected by begging, abandonment of minors, alcoholism, and other similar problems had developed a passive attitude to the paternalistic methods of attention that Somocismo had promoted in the state institutions responsible for attending to these sectors. INSSBI, which saw a need to avoid programs that would strengthen these attitudes, proposed that the problems should be solved with the participation of the organized population.

This led to the introduction of a tendency aimed at breaking with the reformism and paternalistic welfare with which social problems had been treated, in order to develop instead a new approach to welfare services such as pensions, economic aid for funeral services, the handing out of crutches, eyeglasses, wheelchairs, food, and so on. The new approach was also to be implemented in the centers that attended to children, the elderly, and the disabled.

The actions were developed with a revolutionary content, which allowed for the social, economic, and political integration of all those people who for one reason or another were covered by the government's social security system.

SPECIAL SOCIAL SECURITY PROGRAMS

Parallel to the study, analysis, and process of discussions concerning the New Social Security Law and its General Statute, new measures were formulated in order to resolve situations that required immediate attention, whereby social security benefits were granted as if the recipients had previously been paying into the social security system. Under these guidelines the Nicaraguan Institute of Social Security and Welfare developed a number of programs (which are listed here in chronological order).

The Program to Aid Those Who Suffered Losses in the War of Liberation

On the basis of a law decreed August 28, 1979, economic benefits were granted to those who had suffered losses in the war, either directly or to the relatives of those who had been killed. The subsidies or pensions granted under this provision were considered to fall under the category of Occupational Hazards, given that these persons had suffered damages for the liberation of the homeland.

The First Revaluation of Pensions Already Being Paid

In December 1979 the first revaluation of the unduly low pensions was carried out. Such pensions had been conceded on the basis of wages prevailing 20 years earlier. Of course, the wage structure, and in particular the minimum wage, had changed considerably since then. Recalculating them on the basis of the current minimum wage was considered an absolute necessity for all types of workers. The revaluation represented an average increase of 84 percent and benefited 1,837 insured pensioners of a total of 7,918 pensions granted, representing a total monthly increase of 240,774.74 córdobas.

The Second Revaluation of the Pensions

Beginning in February 1980, a second revaluation of a general character was implemented, covering all valid pensions, that is, including those that had already been revalued. This general revaluation was carried out on the basis of a 10–30 percent increase, in accordance with a scale based on the amount of the pension, with higher percentage increases for the lowest pensions. The total monthly increase in payments brought about by this policy was 749,062 córdobas.

The Mineworkers Program

A law decreed February 29, 1980, extended protection to all the uninsured mineworkers who for many years had sold their services to multinational companies yet lacked protection. This covered the miners as well as their families. This group now received the whole gamut of pensions, that is, for disability, old age, or for survivors in case of death (widows, orphans, and other dependents).

The Program for the Protection of Literacy Teachers

A law decreed July 28, 1980, granted social security benefits to literacy teachers who participated in the National Literacy Crusade that took place from March 23 to August 23, 1980. It offered economic benefits in the form of subsidies and pensions for the insured for damages suffered because of occupational hazards.

The Program for the Protection of Members of the People's Militia

By a law decreed December 12, 1980, similar social security benefits were offered to members of the People's Militia, organized to safeguard national security, for damages suffered during their period of mobilization or in acts of service to the homeland.

The Special Law for Public Servant Pensions

A law decreed on May 2, 1981, repealed all orders and regulations concerning pensions existing in the various branches of public administration, leaving INSSBI as the only managing body of the system of pensions. Also, the law recognized pensions for disability, old age, or survivors, for all the years of civil service, even if they had not been paid in totality or in conformity with the norms laid out in the Social Security Law.

Protection for Those who Carry Out Revolutionary Vigilance

By a law decreed on September 24, 1982, INSSBI recognized benefits for occupational hazards for all members of the Sandinista Defense Committees carrying out revolutionary vigilance in the streets of the country's cities whenever they suffered damages in defending and promoting the revolutionary process.

Pensions of Good Grace and in Recognition of Services to the Homeland

By a law decreed November 22, 1982, pensions of good grace were authorized for persons over 60 years old, and for disabled of any age, who were not protected, did not have a right to tributary social security, nor have relatives who could assume economic responsibility for them. Based on this same law, the government Junta could bestow pensions of recognition to people who stood out for their assistance or services rendered the homeland.

THE NEW SOCIAL SECURITY LAW

The purpose of the Social Security Law of 1982 was to make the protective coverage of social security universal and integral. The field of the law's coverage was broadened, as was the coverage included in the benefits. Also, new services were created to dignify and promote the new citizens being forged through the revolutionary process. The law was based in the conceptual and revolutionary breadth of the term "social security," extending protection to the entire population, within the tributary regime of Obligatory Social Security as well as the nontributary welfare regime, which covered that part of the population in a state of social need. Within the context of the nation's economic realities and possibilities, it offered the necessary protection to guarantee the complete and integral human welfare of the entire working population and their families with neither conditions nor privileges. Each individual contributed according to his or her income and received benefits according to his or her needs with the same quality of treatment, as deserved by any human being, guaranteed to all.

The recommendations and agreements of the International Labor Organization and other international organizations were taken very much into account in the drafting of this law. Particularly helpful were the advances made in similar legislation in Mexico, Cuba, Costa Rica, Panama, and other countries. All of the above made it possible for us to include the best elements that would be viable within the Nicaraguan context, and within the economic possibilities of the country, so as to satisfy the country's needs. The draft of the new law was submitted to the Council of State at the end of 1981 and after extensive analysis and debate, approved by the government Junta, entering into effect March 1, 1982.

Principles

The new law upholds the following principles and criteria:

Unity. Above all else, the fundamental criterion was that of unity; to have a single social security institution responsible for granting economic benefits to the insured. In many countries there are several institutions, each protecting distinct sectors with separate benefits, with some institutions giving more and others less. That is, there are differences in coverage and rights, and worst of all, many of these institutions lack the means to keep track of the relationship with the insured. Thus serious problems arise when one switches from one institution to another.

Universality. Social security originally protected only the weak, economically dependent workers. Nonetheless the 1982 law applied to the entire economically active population, with no limits based on wages or income, according to the principle that everyone should participate in accordance with their means within the broadest possible concept of fraternity and social solidarity. That is, he who knows more, he who can do more, and he who has more, owes more to the society in which he lives. Naturally, that is a profound reality of great social and human content.

When we say the law applied to the entire economically active population this is because it protected not only workers dependent on wages but also all those working with the Agrarian Reform programs, all members of production cooperatives, and members of associations of trades that did not have employers but, nevertheless, were true workers promoting and struggling for the development of their area of production. Social security was obliged to seek out the mechanism for the incorporation of these nonwage workers. Finally, the law embraced self-employed persons in general, that is, all those persons making a living through economic activity and part of the economically active population of the country. In sum, in the new Nicaragua, all those who performed any service of any nature were eligible for social security. It was expected that the agrarian reform process, the cooperative movement, and the coming together of the professional associations in the National Council of Professionals would prove to be extraordinarily helpful in applying this criterion.

Completeness.   Another fundamental criterion was that of completeness: the notion of social security should be widened and deepened to the point where it almost becomes confused with the very purpose of the state. The International Labor Organization has determined that social security, within its classic definition, refers to the most probable contingencies that one might encounter in the course of life and work. That is, individuals should be protected against misfortunes caused by occupational hazards, common accidents, illness, disability brought about by illness, maternity, and (though they do not constitute a mishap) children, as they can cause economic problems and thus can be considered social contingencies.

The specific contingencies now covered by INSSBI were disability, old age, and the consequences of death and work, as well as family subsidies and social services. The latter benefit applied not only to the active working member of the insured family but also to the nonworking members, the disabled, elderly, orphans, and so on, for whom there were special centers and services. Finally, the intention was to apply the program of family subsidies as a new benefit of social security that still did not exist in the region.

It was felt that wages should be sufficient to provide for the needs of the workers and their families, that is, applying the principle of equal work, equal pay. Nonetheless, this principle is not always fair—for example, paying the same wage to a single man as to a man with a wife and children. This situation needed to be regulated through an institution that could take up this concern and seek a solution. A variety of systems were tried, but it was decided that the most appropriate arrangement was to pay a percentage of the wage for each dependent.

In the 1982 law the program of family subsidies covered only those persons with modest wages, because those earning above a certain level could take care of their family responsibilities directly. But the worker earning near the minimum wage undoubtedly needed protection in this regard.

The 1982 law embodied conceptual changes in the definition of contingencies resulting from disability, as well as the commitment to rehabilitate the worker medically or psychologically and train him or her for another job. In this respect there was a need for the support of businessmen; a need to make employers aware that workers could not just be left in the street when they become incapacitated or partially disabled through illness or an occupational or other type of accident. The employer was obliged to relocate the worker in another job based on his residual capacities. INSSBI had guidelines concerning, and kept a close watch on, the implementation of this policy of job relocation. At the same time it coordinated efforts with other state institutions that also participated in readaptation and training in new skills. The 1982 law also committed INSSBI to supply, maintain, and renew all ambulatory and orthopedic equipment as needed for disabled persons to live with their disability in a human and dignified way. Finally the law established a new benefit for disabled or incapacitated persons in need of the constant help of another person in order to move about. In such cases the pension would be increased by 20 percent.

In the field of old age, changes were also made. Retirement ages were redefined to address the reality of Nicaragua in the 1980s. The 1982 law employed the definition of old-age pensions laid out in the old law, but the new pensions were truly retirement pensions, appropriate to the workers' needs when their aptitude for work was diminished by old age and they deserved a rest. The law also recognized that there were cases in which an individual's health suffers a general decline, or one undergoes illness leading to disability at an early age. Under the new law, a healthy person on turning 60 was given the option to retire. In most countries the retirement age is 65. Nicaragua lowered it to 60, not with the idea that at that age one can no longer work, for in special cases the worker would be encouraged to postpone his retirement by a promise of greater benefits. In such cases, however, the worker could not live off the pension and continue working for a wage beyond the work necessary to make up the difference between the pension and the wage as of the time of retirement. The retirement age for teachers was dropped to 55. This was done in consideration of the fact that teachers, in working with so many children with such a range of characters—including hyperactive and anxious ones—are subjected to all sorts of pressures and, ultimately, mental fatigue. Individuals performing physical labor causing premature physical aging could also retire at age 55. This applied, for example, to miners and dockworkers. If there were medically verified signs of serious physical degeneration after 15 years of work, such workers could retire or draw a pension upon turning 55.

In widowhood special situations were to be considered. In general the objective of the widowhood pension was to ensure the continuity of the means of subsistence for the family nucleus at the same level as it was at the time of death of the head of the family. It was not just a matter of widowhood nor of children, but rather of the family nucleus. The only ones with a right to receive the pension were those relatives who, because of age or disability, were unable to work. A widow younger than 45 was considered able to work and thus should be employed. Nonetheless, if she had not been working or even if she had and the impact of losing the spouse had damaged the household income, a two-year pension was to be granted. But if the widow was 45 or more years old and considered, therefore, to have passed her sexual prime and thus to have little likelihood of reconstituting a full family unit, a lifetime annuity was to be granted unless she remarried. Under Somoza, children's pensions were granted for dependents under age 14 at the time of the death of the insured parent. In the new law the age was raised to 15 and could be extended to 21 if the children were in school. The family nucleus could be made up of parents, brothers and sisters, aunts and uncles, and so on, but they were eligible for pensions only if they were over 60 or if they were disabled and lived from the earnings of the insured deceased relative.

Occupational Hazards

Occupational hazards were traditionally covered by social security as part of the overall program of protection for the worker. The new law, interestingly, included in this category not only disabilities resulting from a work accident but also those incurred through common accident or illness. It recognized that one left disabled because of an accident suffered while traveling in a vehicle for a work-related mission or even in a private capacity had the same material needs calling for the same protection. But in most legislation dealing with these matters a distinction is made for work-related accidents. Pensions are greater in these cases than in the case of a common accident, as there is an employer who can be obliged to pay. The intention of the 1982 law was to offer a uniform pension based on a minimum percentage of the average wage with increments earned for additional years of work.

Under the new law there were three categories for any type of pension (disability, old age, surviving a spouse, or for professional risks): minimum, basic, and maximum. Minimal pensions were equivalent to 40 or 45 percent for the first three years, determined on the basis of the basic wage according to whether it was above or below double the general minimum wage. Basic pensions were those that came with additional increments (of 1.6 or 1.35 percent) for each additional year of work, coming to 56 or 64 percent, respectively, for one who had paid the quota for 15 years. Maximum pensions were equivalent to 80 percent of the salary earned by the worker. As can be observed, the differentiation was meant to favor those persons with lower wages, so that after 15 years they reach 64 percent, whereas those with higher wages reach 56 percent. The idea was to have the average equal 60 percent of the base wage. What is described above was the situation for an insured worker without any family to support. Where there were family members to support, these appropriate increments were paid: 15 percent for the wife and 10 percent for each child or dependent over 60 years old or disabled persons of any age who were part of the family nucleus.

The Hierarchical Status of the Nicaraguan Institute of Social Security and Welfare

The organization, operation, and administration of social security was the responsibility of INSSBI, a decentralized institution of the central government having its own assets and legal personality (*personería jurídica*) and, therefore, the authority to acquire rights and contract obligations. The Executive President, named by the government Junta and carrying the rank of Minister, had maximum responsibility for INSSBI. Therefore the institution was essentially a Ministry of Social Security, with regard to its area of responsibility—that is, economic benefits and the development of social services.

Though fundamentally autonomous, INSSBI was, nevertheless, a specialized state institution charged with solving problems of a socioeconomic nature. Accordingly, its programs were carried out in coordination with other ministries and entities in charge of overall economic and social policy. It also participated in socioeconomic research projects necessary for planning programs for the country's welfare, productivity, and economic development. INSSBI worked in close coordination with the Ministry of Planning in matters concerning the investment of INSSBI's funds or technical resources. The Ministry of Planning provided guidelines for the use of these funds in a manner consistent with the development plans formulated by the various parts of the government. To this end, the Executive President also participated periodically in meetings of the social sector of the cabinet closely linked to the government Junta.

THE NEW NICARAGUAN INSTITUTE OF SOCIAL SECURITY AND WELFARE

By Decree No. 976 of the government Junta, effective March 5, 1982 (four days after the New Social Security Law took effect), all of the functions, programs, allocations, and other aspects of the Ministry of Social Welfare were annexed onto the Nicaraguan Social Security Institute, thereby transforming the INSS into the new body known as INSSBI. This broadened the field of activities of social security to include welfare-related social protection measures as well. With the integration of the social programs included under the welfare area, INSSBI developed an integral response in accordance with the revolutionary conception of "social security," which not only included the economic benefits of traditional social security programs but also covered that part of the population that had not paid quotas within an obligatory regime. It is within this broad concept that the INSSBI came to promote a series of programs for the purpose of protecting children who, because of historical circumstances, were in a state of abandon, social danger, or in peril of suffering irregularities in social-psychological development. Attention was also offered to all of that part of the population that, because of its social and economic situation, was not involved in production because of age or disability. Thus the new coverage offered by INSSBI represented a qualitative leap in the attention traditionally offered by social security systems.

The programs comprising the social welfare area were the following:

Tutelary Programs for Children

The Tutelary Programs for children were aimed specifically at minors in need of a variety of care and protection. There were Child Development Centers in the cities and Rural Children's Services in the countryside that offered day care assistance for working mothers. The Rural Children's Services, which operated primarily in the cotton and coffee agroexport regions of the west and center-north, also offered community training services in nutrition, child care, preventive health, and so on. There were also Rural and Urban Children's Soup Kitchens designed to prevent malnutrition among poor children. Finally, there were Preventive Centers for Minors at Risk, Centers for Protection and Prevention, and Reeducation Centers. These provided a variety of training, motivational, or educational services to children in a socially precarious position or minors who were either delinquent or in danger of becoming so.

The Integral Rehabilitation Program

This program arose from the need to provide handicapped persons with adequate means through which to develop their residual capabilities, be they mental or physical, so as to incorporate them into the production of goods and services. The attention offered through this program fell into two areas: occupational rehabilitation, for the treatment of the blind, deaf, mentally retarded, paraplegics, and so on, through centers that attend the handicapped; and social-psychological rehabilitation, offering reeducational attention for individuals who, despite being in full possession of their capabilities, had not made productive use of themselves (prostitutes, alcoholics, and drug addicts). The centers where this population was assisted were provided with the equipment necessary for productive activities (agricultural, small-scale production, semiindustrial, technical, and so on). Thus they helped promote the learning of a number of skills that could give an income to the handicapped, making it possible within a short period of time for the latter to support his or her family.

The Program of Protection for the Elderly

At the time of the Triumph there was no state protection at all for the elderly. There were only two private nursing homes, with inadequate food, no medical attention, and substandard hygienic conditions. Here the elderly waited to die. Therefore, the creation of Nursing Homes administered by INSSBI was an important achievement. These homes offered recreational, cultural, and productive activities; room and board; psychological and psychiatric attention; clothing; and other services. In addition, by 1983 six Nuclei for the Social Integration of the Elderly (houses open during the day) were being developed. The same services would be offered, with the exception of lodging. Free pensions would also be provided to those elderly people in a state of extreme necessity having no relatives

The Family Orientation and Protection Program

This program was responsible for interpreting and resolving the question of food subsidies that parents and/or descendants should provide for their dependents. The Law to Regulate Mother-Father-Child relations provided a conceptual framework concerning the values to be upheld by the Nicaraguan family, thereby allowing the program to offer more integral family counseling. People working in the program were to keep abreast of actions and events related to family law, including legal documents of recognition of children, official documents recognizing numerous offspring, and suspension of migratory rights for those evading their family responsibilities. Existing on a nationwide basis, this program offered its services from offices throughout the country's provinces.

The Welfare Aid Program

This program was to protect that part of the population whose basic needs were not assured, guaranteeing economic and social support when, for a number of reasons, their income fell or ceased. Welfare Aid was initiated after the popular Triumph of July 19, distributing the donations of friendly countries that had been sent as an immediate response to the problems of thousands of homeless or wounded persons, orphaned children, widows, and so on. In practice the Welfare Aid program reflected a growing dynamic that allowed for the satisfaction or attenuation of the needs of growing sectors of the population temporarily or structurally marginalized from the production of goods and services. The program was based on the concept that the services provided were temporary and would disappear to the degree that the level of production allowed for greater socioeconomic development.

The Refugee Program

Services for refugees were initiated in Nicaragua in the first months of 1980, as many fellow Central Americans fleeing the repression of unpopular regimes sought the solidarity the Sandinista Revolution offered to peoples fighting for their liberation. In February the revolutionary government ratified the Convention Relating to the Status of Refugees signed in Geneva in 1951 and the U.N. Protocol Relating to the Status of Refugees signed in 1967.

In order to fulfill effectively the main objective of the revolutionary government—to integrate the refugees into the country's economic life without having a negative effect on employment for Nicaraguans—the National Refugee Office was created as part of INSSBI by Decree No. 1096. In order to help it meet its objectives, the office received firm support from the Ministry of Agricultural Development and Agrarian Reform, the National Union of Farmers and Ranchers, the Ministry of Industry, the National Development Bank, and other institutions of the revolutionary state. Furthermore, the National Refugee Office received aid from United Nations High Commissioner for Refugees (UNHCR), Oxfam-Belgium, French Relief Service (Socorro Popular Frances), and other international organizations.

Social Services

Article No. 86 of the Social Security Law provided for the following social programs promoted by the Institute:

The Vacation System. This program was initiated with the confiscation of numerous rural and summer homes that had been the property of the Somocistas and developed into an effective response to the historic challenge of creating the conditions necessary for workers and their families to enjoy their well-deserved vacations in an adequate setting. The main vacation centers developed were the spas at the Pacific Ocean beaches of El Velero and El Tránsito. The program also created a program for youth, the "Xilonem Country Outing." Within this context several activities were developed in conjunction with the Sandinista Children's Association to the benefit of children from urban neighborhoods and schools.

The "Juan Carlos Herrera Cuarezma" People's Optical Industry. In cooperation with one of the country's best private optical businesses, the Institute also set up an optical industry to provide the insured and their families low-cost eyeglasses, taking advantage of the high-level technology of the private company. By 1983 an average of some 100 pairs of eyeglasses were being manufactured every day. The sale price of each unit was about one-third that charged by private optical companies. It also offered the services of an optometry clinic.

The Labor and Cultural Center for Retired Persons. This center was founded in September 1982 with the purpose of helping those with old-age pensions to fully adapt to new conditions that arise with retirement. It was open to all retired persons pensioned by the Institute. The latter could spend the day, were provided food and a number of services appropriate to their physical condition, and could develop recreational activities to their liking, which could be shared with their visitors. The Institute provided free transportation in its own buses.

Financing

Social security was financed through the contributions of workers, employers, and the state, based on percentages derived from the total salary or income of the insured. Special programs decreed by the government Junta in order to resolve special situations, which INSSBI was put in charge of, were financed by the general funds of the central government. To complement financing from sources within the country, finances in the area of welfare benefited greatly from international solidarity, especially from European nongovernmental foundations.

Financing for social welfare was based on three sources of income. Some funds derived from the payments of taxes specifically for social welfare as dictated in the taxation plans of the respective municipalities. In addition, profits generated by the People's Lottery were used to finance both health and social welfare programs. Finally, there was income from the Zacarías Guerra Foundation, which was originally created by the philanthropist Zacarías Guerra, who left all his possessions to found a home for Nicaraguan orphans. These assets were administered by INSSBI and the income was used to contribute to programs to protect children in a state of need.

THE EXTENT OF SOCIAL SECURITY COVERAGE

With the creation of the National Unified Health system at the time of the Triumph, medical benefits were granted to the entire population. All workers making solidary contributions to finance the system were guaranteed the right to receive subsidies for temporary disabilities in case of illness, maternity, or professional liabilities, as spelled out in the Social Security Law. Thus the right to health care was a universal right recognized for all Nicaraguans by the Sandinista Revolution and granted with no preestablished conditions.

INSSBI was the only governing body of the system of economic benefits accorded to those insured in the tributary area of social security (pensions for disability, old age, and survivors, including those derived from professional liabilities, based on the average salary, years of service, and family responsibilities) and in the nontributary area for benefits as spelled out in the special programs that were the responsibility of the central government. Accordingly, INSSBI experienced an important qualitative and quantitative leap, as its benefits improved considerably and were extended to cover the whole country, with both tributary and nontributary programs. During the period from May to October 1982, social security services were extended to the provinces of Managua, Masaya, León, Chinandega, Granada, Carazo, and Rivas, covering all workers in urban areas who had not been incorporated into the social security system, also including industrial businesses or workplaces, mines, commercial outlets, and service and agroindustrial workplaces located outside of the urban areas. From February to October 1983, social security was extended to the rest of the provinces, that is, Estelí, Nueva Segovia, Madriz, Zelaya Norte, Río San Juan, Zelaya Sur, Matagalpa, Jinotega, Boaco, Chontales. These programs incorporated 54,800 new workers into the social security system.

It is interesting to compare statistics regarding social security coverage and benefits after the Triumph with those existing under the Somozas. Table 17.1 provides detailed information. However, in global terms, we note that twice as many pensions at five times the cost were granted in the first four years of the Revolution as in the previous 25 years of the Somoza dictatorship. Whereas a total of 7,918 pensions were granted before July 19, 1979, 16,473 were authorized through September 1983. And, whereas 2.5 million córdobas were paid out before, 12.8 million were expended in the first four years of the system.

TABLE 17.1
SOCIAL SECURITY ACHIEVEMENTS BEFORE AND AFTER THE REVOLUTION

Field of Application	Through July 19, 1979	Through September 1983	Percent Increase
Insured contributing workers	122,597	246,807	101.3
Protected population	202,548	366,787	81.1
Geographic extension of INSSBI	Managua, Tipitapa, León Chinandega, Chichigalpa, El Viejo, Port of Corinto, Mining area by Prinzapolka, and as regards disability, old age, and death for public bank employees in the entire country	Managua, León, Chinandega, Carazo, Masaya, Granada, Rivas, Nueva Segovia Madriz, Estelí, Zelaya, Río San Juan, Matagalpa	

Ordinary Pensions Already Being Paid	Number	Amount (in thousands of córdobas)	Number	Amount (in thousands of córdobas)
Ordinary	7,918	2,554	16,473	12,833.9
Special				
Killed combatants and relatives			4,750	1,712.2
Literacy teachers			65	22.9
Miners			3,852	6,123.1
Public servants			1,085	3,389.0
Militia and relatives			271	195.5
Grace			1,029	578.9
For services rendered for the homeland			40	64.8
Circus workers			13	19.5
Revolutionary watchpersons			6	7.5
Total pensions being paid	7,918	2,554	27,584	24,947.3

CONCLUSION

Profound changes took place in Nicaragua's social security system in the first five years of the Sandinista Revolution, greatly benefiting the

Nicaraguan worker and his or her family. The new government had inherited a bankrupt, class-biased institution, in a clear state of crisis. This required the urgent implementation of policies that in the short term would make it possible to generate the trust of both workers and employers. The policy of developing a comprehensive social security system led to the annexation of the Ministry of Social Welfare to the Nicaraguan Social Security Institute, which had already begun its revolutionary transformation. This created a more dynamic, advanced, and technified social policy instrument. In this way, the Nicaraguan social security system became one of the most advanced in the Western Hemisphere.

Chapter 18
Housing Policy

HARVEY WILLIAMS

Throughout the Third World, rapid demographic growth and urbanization have put considerable strain on the economic and political organizations responsible for the provision of basic necessities. Housing, requiring extensive capital investment and frequently providing little direct or immediate return, has presented a particularly difficult challenge. Turner has asked: "Who shall do what about housing?"[1] The answer usually involves some combination of actions of the public sector (the state), the formal private sector (the market), and the informal private sector (the community). In the typical laissez-faire response, common throughout Latin America, the state limits itself to regulatory actions and enough public sector housing to quiet social unrest and maintain "good face."[2] Public housing projects may also be initiated in response to private sector pressure to keep down the labor cost or, in the case of most slum clearance projects, to gain access to valuable land. The result is that the private sector reaps the direct profits from the construction of private housing and much of the subcontracted public housing, as well as from the reduced labor costs and the increases in land value that are generated by the public sector investments in infrastructure.[3] The informal private sector, primarily the poor, is left to its own devices.

This pattern was evident in Nicaragua under the Somoza regime. Government housing policies favored the upper class and proved inadequate for the vast majority of the citizens. The policies developed and carried out by the Government of National Reconstruction during the first five years after the overthrow of the dictatorship were clearly different. They provide an interesting alternative for analysis.

Research for the preparation of this chapter was supported in part by a professional development grant from the University of the Pacific. The author acknowledges the kind and extensive cooperation of the government and the people of Nicaragua.

GENERAL BACKGROUND

The housing situation in Nicaragua had been a concern for many years before the Revolution.[4] Nicaragua had an extremely high population growth rate. The development of nonlabor-intensive agriculture encouraged migration to urban centers, even though there was little industry to provide employment. An already serious housing situation was made critical by the earthquake of 1972, which destroyed the core of the capital city, Managua, and some 40,000 housing units.

Following the earthquake, and impelled by large amounts of foreign aid, the Somoza government supported considerable housing construction. The pattern of support was similar to the traditional laissez-faire approach. Of the estimated 85,000 housing units that were constructed between 1973 and 1979, approximately 55 percent were built by the informal private sector and consisted primarily of low-income owner-constructed and -occupied units with limited services. The formal private sector constructed about 11,000 units of middle- and upper-class housing units in fully serviced housing developments. Although this represented only about 15 percent of the total number of units, it constituted more than half of the total funds invested in housing. The remaining approximately 24,000 units were provided by the public sector. Of these, some 11,000 units were temporary wooden structures financed by USAID. The remaining units were low-cost units in fully serviced developments.

The policies of the Somoza regime greatly benefited Somoza and other capitalists. By refusing to rebuild the central core and by severely limiting squatter settlements, they created a demand that led to the illegal subdivision of large tracts of marginal land on the outskirts of the city. The movement of the population toward the outskirts, and the subsequent extension of infrastructure to those areas, led to large increases in the value of undeveloped land closer to the center of the city that was held by speculators. The Somoza family itself profited at several levels: through their interests in banking, through their investments in the construction industry, and through their extensive land holdings. One crony realized a quick profit when he purchased a large plot of land that was (unbeknownst to the original owner) to be used for public housing and then resold it to the government for more than 100 times the price he had paid the week before.

The plight of the urban poor was less favorable. The majority of the urban population lived in substandard housing with limited services. Tenure was insecure, since most of the plots that had been sold in the illegal subdivisions did not carry valid titles. Profiteering was rife, both in the sale and rental of housing. In the smaller cities and in the rural areas the situation was worse. Services and infrastructure were less common and of lower quality. Agricultural laborers lived in extremely precarious circumstances, particularly those who migrated from one harvest to the other. Added to these conditions were the destruction caused by the War of National Liberation (over 4,000 houses in urban areas severely damaged or destroyed) and by a tropical storm that left nearly 30,000 persons homeless in late 1979. This was the deteriorating housing situation that faced the Sandinistas and the JGRN when they came to power.

HOUSING POLICY UNDER THE GOVERNMENT OF NATIONAL RECONSTRUCTION

On July 18, 1979, the day before the Triumph of the popular forces, the new Junta proclaimed its Program of Government for Nicaragua.[5] Within the social area it announced a four-point program for housing that included urban reform, national planning, a program of rural housing, and an emergency program for marginal urban neighborhoods. The JGRN formed a Ministry of Housing and Human Settlements (MINVAH), which would have the responsibility to develop and administer the new national programs pertaining to housing. In the Program for Economic Reactivation, the major objectives for MINVAH were defined as follows:

(a) Initiation of a territorial ordering of human settlements with the goal of reinforcing production, improving the life conditions of the population centers in the interior of the country. . . .
(b) Planning and massive construction of popular housing in the city of Managua in order to attend in part to the deficit inherited from the Somoza dictatorship. . . .
(c) Impelling an Urban Reform that permits the distribution of the benefits of urbanization to all social sectors. . . . [6]

From the very beginning the policies of the JGRN deviated from the laissez-faire approach. Housing policies were carefully integrated into a broader program of national development. The national development objectives stressed the recognition of agriculture as the base of the Nicaraguan economy and the responsibility of the JGRN to plan and coordinate its development. They emphasized a more just distribution of social benefits, not only for the urban poor but also for the traditionally neglected rural population. While Nicaragua did not yet have a centrally planned economy, this model was much closer to the socialist than to the capitalist model.

During the first five years of the revolutionary process MINVAH pursued the objectives defined for it by the JGRN. In cooperation with other governmental units, and responding to the social, political, and economic constraints that were encountered, MINVAH developed and modified programs in three major areas: national development, urban reform, and housing construction.

NATIONAL DEVELOPMENT

The program for national development was directed toward the reactivation and strengthening of the economy, particularly the agricultural and agroindustrial sectors. The role of MINVAH was to cooperate with several other ministries in the planning of programs and to assume the major responsibility for the actual housing developments and their supportive infrastructure. National planning during the first years was gradually replaced by more localized planning, especially following the regional reorganization of 1982. MINVAH programs in support of national development were the construction of housing for workers and the establishment of new settlements.

Housing for Workers

Although MINVAH constructed general housing for workers in urban settings, many of its projects were specifically developed for workers in nonurban areas as part of the national effort to revitalize the rural sector. For example, during the first year housing projects were constructed for miners and sugar refinery workers, and during 1983 six of the nine housing projects initiated were for the benefit of cotton, tobacco, and sugar workers in rural areas.[7]

New Settlements

The establishment of new settlements in rural areas was an early priority for MINVAH. Having committed itself to a program of redistribution of social benefits to all, the JGRN recognized that it would be necessary to encourage concentration of the rural population. It was deemed not to be economically feasible to extend "the benefits of urbanization" to people who were so widely dispersed. Community services, utilities, and production cooperatives could not be developed without critical masses. The early policy of the JGRN was to have MINVAH develop new settlements gradually, beginning first with land that had been expropriated by the state and was suitable for cooperative agricultural development. However, the unstable and dangerous situation caused by the aggression of the counterrevolutionary forces along the international frontiers changed the priorities of MINVAH. It was necessary to provide safe and defensible communities for those who were threatened or who had been driven from their scattered and remote locations.

Many of these settlements were developed during the first five years of the revolutionary process. The most notable was the group of settlements known collectively as Tasba Pri. These were built in Zelaya for the resettlement of Miskitu natives who were evacuated from the frontier zone. By 1984 more than 1,800 housing units had been constructed. Schools, health centers, and other community facilities had also been built, and utilities were being installed. Other smaller settlements were being initiated along the frontier area, particularly in the north.

URBAN REFORM

From the beginning, the JGRN and MINVAH identified urban reform (together with agrarian reform) as fundamental elements in the new government's program.[8] Urban reform was described as a national effort to formulate a rational response to the problems created by uncontrolled urban growth. There were two key elements to urban reform: the regulation of urban and suburban land use, and the resolution of the housing problems of the urban popular sectors.

Regulation of Urban and Suburban Land

MINVAH identified the free-market system of property ownership and exchange as the basic factor responsible for irrational urban development, particularly in Managua. It declared that urban land represents a social need to which everyone has a right, and which should not be a commodity subject to the vagaries of the marketplace. For that reason, MINVAH was to develop policies that would strengthen the government's control over urban land use, tenure, and transfer, and would eliminate private profit generated from increases in market value.

The first target for MINVAH was the central core of Managua. Most of the core remained undeveloped following its destruction from the 1972 earthquake, even though the Somoza regime had spent considerable time and money in planning its reconstruction.[9] At the time of the Triumph the government already owned a significant portion of the core. The JGRN decreed a law in 1980 to encourage the donation of privately held properties within the core. This was followed in 1981 by another law that gave the government the right to expropriate for public use any unoccupied lands within the core. As a result of these laws, the government gained control of more than 90 percent of the central area. This eliminated the impact of speculators and greatly facilitated planning of this important area.

Another law was passed in 1980 giving the government the right to control the development and use of land within new settlements and other public properties. In 1982 an important new law gave the government the right to expropriate any unused urban land for social use. This law was used to allow the development of the progressive urbanizations, described below.

The development of city plans was a priority for MINVAH. Much effort and expense were directed toward their completion. The plans were produced somewhat slowly, the first not being completed until 1982. This was due both to the limited technical workers available, and to the thorough job done. Not only were extensive technical studies carried out, but there was also considerable social input from the community. By the end of the first five years, most of the cities had finished their plans or were in the process of doing so.

The Managua City Plan[10] was one of the first to be completed. Although it was the largest and most detailed, it was completed early because of the priority of the capital city, and because much of the technical work had already been done. It contained clear guidelines for the future development of Managua, particularly emphasizing the gradual "densification" (filling in) of the areas closer to the center. It described the zoning regulations and those regulations concerning construction of all types of commercial and residential projects. Careful attention was paid to provisions for social and community services, and for protection of the environment.

Even after five years, no definitive policies had been established for limiting the ownership of housing. There was no limit to the number of houses or property an individual could own. As long as one paid one's taxes and did not violate the provisions of the rental law, the government did not intervene. The council of state was still debating laws that had been proposed by the JGRN that would limit the number of houses that a person could own to three (one for residence, one for business, and one for recreation) and that would eliminate private rentals. It was proposed that all excess houses would be sold to the tenants, or to the government. The latter would be resold or would be added to the more than 3,000 houses whose rental MINVAH administered.

Resolution of Housing Problems

The JGRN early acknowledged the precarious state of housing of the majority of the urban poor, particularly in Managua. MINVAH set a high priority on responding to what Turner has identified as the three general objectives of marginal urban dwellers: to resist eviction and secure tenure, to improve their property, or to seek a better location.[11] Most of the residents of Managua lived in illegal subdivisions. Even though many of the houses were well constructed and had some services, the occupants had no legal title to their property. Many others lived in squatter settlements in unhealthful or dangerous areas. One of the very first laws announced by the JGRN was that of illegal subdivisions, which decreed the government's intervention in these neighborhoods and assigned to MINVAH the responsibility to administer and develop them.

In total there were more than 400 illegal subdivisions with over 50,000 houses. The first in a series of laws dealing with the illegal subdivisions relieved the private subdividers of their control over the land. The residents were required to continue to make their assigned payments to MINVAH instead of to the previous owner. These payments were deposited in accounts for each subdivision, the funds to be used for community improvement and infrastructure. The law declared that if there was any money remaining after the completion of the necessary projects, that sum would be returned to the subdivider. However, if the payments were not sufficient to pay for the projects, the subdivider would be held responsible for the deficit. While the impact of the law was positive in that it gave the residents a feeling of increased security, the burden of payment was too great for many.

In response to petitions from the residents, presented through the Sandinist Defense Committees, payments were reduced in 1980. The following year, on the anniversary of the Triumph, a proclamation was issued ending all payments and promising all residents titles to their property. Later that same year a law was passed that described more completely MINVAH's responsibilities in this and other areas of government controlled housing. MINVAH was to oversee the administration of the subdivisions and squatter settlements, facilitating the process of entitlement. Each family could apply for title to one plot that it controlled. The title could be passed on to one's heirs but could not be sold without the permission of MINVAH. By 1984 some 12,900 titles had been issued to residents, and over 7,000 more titles were awarded to nonresidents for vacant plots within the subdivisions.[12]

A key factor in the development of the subdivisions was the close coordination between MINVAH and the local CDS. National and regional boards were established to administer the subdivision projects, and local residents were participants on all of these. The CDS were part of a two-way communication system for the planning and execution of projects. Within MINVAH there was a division for community development education for the training of local leaders. Working with the local CDS, MINVAH completed projects for the installation of community services and infrastructure that, by mid-1984, benefited some 250,000 persons.

The control of rental and mortgage payments was another area that early attracted the attention of the JGRN. In early 1980 the first rental law was issued. Very similar to the first rental law of the Cuban Revolution, it reduced rentals for most tenants by 40 to 50 percent and set the maximum annual rent at 5 percent of the total assessed value of the dwelling.[13] The law also provided protection for the tenants against eviction and set standards for the quality of rental housing. Over the next four years there were several suspensions and revisions of the rental law, as MINVAH attempted to administer it in a way that would be fair to both the tenants and the owners. In most cases the problem was to decide whether the owner had a legitimate motive for evicting the tenant. The original law had strongly favored the tenant. Modifications in late 1981 spelled out the conditions under which a tenant could be evicted: nonpayment of rent, abuse of the dwelling, unauthorized subletting, use for illegal activities, and when the owner wished to use it for his or his family's residence. They also created regional and municipal delegations of local citizens to resolve complaints. It was hoped that the proposed law eliminating private rentals would greatly reduce the number of cases to be adjudicated.

Following the Triumph, MINVAH took over the responsibility for administering the public housing projects and the housing that had been sponsored by the savings and loan banks (which had been nationalized). There were nearly 30,000 houses in various stages of mortgage. In 1980 a decree was issued that regularized and extended the mortgage payments and forgave some past nonpayment.

While the programs to intervene in the illegal subdivisions and to control rental and mortgage payments did much to encourage feelings of security among those who had adequate housing, the problem of providing housing for those without was yet to be resolved. Not only were there many families who lived in dangerous or unhealthful conditions, but there continued to be a flow of rural-to-urban migrants in need of housing. MINVAH had hoped to be able to construct sufficient new housing to accommodate these families, but it soon became evident that the resources of the government were too limited. Pressure increased for a rational response, especially after severe flooding forced the evacuation of several thousand families in 1982.

The most appropriate response appeared to be some form of sites and services program, frequently suggested as one of the most reasonable and efficient methods of developing low-income housing.[14] In the sites and services approach the government acquires and subdivides land, installs community infrastructure, and provides a plot of land with minimum service connections (and sometimes a basic shelter) for each family. The residents are responsible for expansion and improvements. MINVAH was initially very hesitant about undertaking such programs. The example provided by the postearthquake, USAID-sponsored projects was not encouraging, and the inherent potential of such programs to promote individualism and discourage community participation[15] ran counter to the government's general policies of social development and community cooperation. But the need overcame the initial reluctance, and MINVAH initiated the program of "progressive urbanizations."

The progressive urbanizations program was begun in 1981. At that time MINVAH, using the law that allowed expropriation of vacant urban land for social uses, began several small projects to promote densification in areas of Managua that had been partially destroyed by the earthquake and not yet rebuilt. Most of these were less than a block in size. It was relatively easy to provide services and infrastructure, since they were already in place or close at hand. Families were assigned plots of land and were promised titles. Each progressive urbanization organized its own CDS, which was responsible for organizing the future development of the project.

Following the floods of 1982 the progressive urbanization projects were greatly increased, especially in Managua. There were more than ten times the number of lots conditioned in 1982 as there were in 1981 (see Table 18.1). Several very large progressive urbanizations that contained hundreds of parcels were initiated in Managua. These required extensive clearing and grading, the laying out of streets, and the introduction of electrical and water lines to the periphery of the projects. Communal areas were designated, including sites for educational, recreational, and health centers. Materials for housing were not provided by the government, although MINVAH facilitated the transfer of salvageable materials from the residents' former sites. As in other neighborhoods, the CDSs served as the main communication link between the people and the government, facilitating a two-way flow of information. The CDSs in these larger projects were organized with individual blocks forming their own groups, each with representation on the larger project CDS. The heavy dependence on the CDSs was essential in maintaining the social goals of the government: reducing individualism and alienation.

HOUSING CONSTRUCTION

When one speaks of housing policy, one usually thinks of housing construction. In Nicaragua under the revolutionary government, housing policy was seen as an integral part of a broader national program of social and economic reforms, of which housing construction was only one aspect. The housing programs of MINVAH reflected two principles: integrated planning and the maximization of limited resources. Housing programs that addressed the needs of the workers in the productive sectors were

TABLE 18.1
TYPES OF HOUSING ACTIVITY BY THE MINISTRY OF HOUSING, 1980–83

Type of Activity	1980	1981	1982	1983	Totals
War damage repairs (number of houses repaired)	4,676	—	—	—	4,676
Housing projects (number of units completed)	1,146	1,906	3,215	3,895	10,162
Materials Bank (number of units completed)	—	202	349	1,322	1,873
Progressive urbanizations (number of parcels distributed)	—	854	8,810	5,814	15,478

Source: MINVAH, 1983 Informe Anual (Managua, n.d.).

emphasized, as were programs that integrated urban marginal populations and reinforced the development of the mass organizations. In housing construction, MINVAH concentrated its efforts in two areas: the actual construction of housing projects, and the development, production, and distribution of housing materials.

Housing Projects

Initial housing policy declarations by the JGRN may have led some to expect that the government would undertake the construction of massive public housing projects, such as those that were built by the revolutionary governments of Cuba and Chile.[16] However, although MINVAH completed several projects, it was soon obvious that the limited resources of the government were not sufficient to build housing for all. Over time MINVAH shifted its priorities from urban mass construction to rural settlements, and from housing projects to other activities (see Tables 18.1 and 18.2).

Early statements by MINVAH[17] stressed the development of housing that would promote progressive social development. As in Cuba,[18] projects that reinforced community support and interaction, such as apartment units and individual units with communal social and recreational areas, were to be given preference over those that followed the traditional patterns of separation and individuality of residences. An examination of early housing projects illustrated how these policies were put into action and how some of the lessons learned influenced their modification.

MINVAH proposed to respect and maintain the sense of community in dealing with the slum housing. New housing projects were to be rebuilt

TABLE 18.2

HOUSING PRODUCTION BY THE MINISTRY OF HOUSING, 1980–1983; NUMBER OF HOUSING UNITS, WITH PERCENTAGES

Area	Estimated Percent of National Population in Area	1980		1981		1982		1983		Totals	
		Number	Percent	Number	Percent	Number	Percent	Number	Percent	Number	Percent
Managua	30.0	697	60.8	1,421	7.6	1,348	41.9	679	17.4	4,145	40.8
Other Pacific	32.0	423	36.9	414	2.7	704	21.9	1,378	35.4	2,919	28.7
Central Zone	29.0	0	0.0	0	.0	89	2.7	1,365	35.0	1,454	14.3
East Coast	7.0	26	2.3	71	.7	1,074	33.4	473	12.1	1,644	16.2
Totals		1,146		1,906		3,215		3,895		10,162	

Source: MINVAH, 1983 Informe Anual (Managua, n.d.).

on the original sites for the original residents where possible. In those cases where the sites were dangerous or unhealthful, the whole community or neighborhood was to be moved to a new housing project. One of the first housing projects undertaken by MINVAH in Managua provided a model for the upgrading of a squatter settlement. With the financial assistance of the Venezuelan government and with the active cooperation of the residents, the old and unhealthy slum was demolished and replaced with 463 new houses. These were constructed in an open pattern with minimal space on the sides and front, and with an open common area in the rear. Although there were some residents who complained about the new housing, the majority seemed delighted. However, two problems soon surfaced. First, many of the residents would not tolerate the open pattern. Although they were discouraged from doing so, they constructed fences to separate themselves from their neighbors, to create privacy, and to protect their property and gardens. Second, it was soon discovered that most of the families had very low incomes, and many of the residents were true lumpen proletariats, marginally integrated into society and not productively employed. These conditions made it difficult to organize the CDSs for the development of the neighborhood, and housing payments that MINVAH assessed as reasonable were greater than many could afford.

Another Managua housing project was designed by MINVAH with the intention of relocating squatters from precarious areas. The idea was to relocate them en masse. In addition to the now-anticipated problem of insufficient income to make payments, MINVAH was confronted with the reluctance of many of the residents to relocate. Many preferred their current site because they had become accustomed to it, because of its relationship to their place of employment, or because they disliked the proposed site.

In order to deal with these problems, MINVAH made several modifications in its housing project policies. First, it reduced the investments in the projects for the upgrading of slums, so that the replacement housing would be within the means of the residents. Second, it made relocation more of a voluntary process, allowing residents the option of applying for housing in projects, or for plots in progressive urbanizations. Persons who wished to apply for project housing needed to have a regular family income great enough that the required monthly payments would not exceed 15 percent of it. They also had to be recommended by their union or mass organization. And third, MINVAH relaxed the emphasis on communal living areas, respecting the traditional desire to enclose plots.

Original plans called for MINVAH to built 550 low-rise apartment units in the central core area, for the resettlement of low-income families. During the first three years, only one complex of 64 apartments was completed. The expense of construction far exceeded early estimates. Because of the cost, and because they were close to the government buildings of the central area, they were redesignated for middle-level government workers. In 1983 MINVAH shifted to the construction of two-story duplex units, also for government workers. Although MINVAH continued to view multistory building as necessary to accommodate the future projected growth, the cost severely restricted construction. By mid-1984 there were fewer than 100 of the duplex units completed.

In order to manage more efficiently the construction of housing projects, the JGRN created the Housing Construction Corporation (COVIN) in 1981. COVIN was a public corporation under the administration of MINVAH. The creation of COVIN greatly increased MINVAH's ability to plan and manage the construction of housing projects by limiting the influence of the private sector. By 1984 there were close to 3,000 workers employed by COVIN in various projects.[19]

Housing Materials

From the beginning, one of the principal goals of MINVAH was to promote the development of inexpensive construction materials, relying on local sources and appropriate technologies as much as possible. As the demand for housing rose, and as financial and political constraints made the importation of materials (particularly steel and zinc-coated roofing) increasingly difficult, MINVAH directed more attention to this area.

Initial efforts were consolidated in 1981 with the formal creation of the Materials Bank. After a relatively slow start, this program began to increase significantly the production of basic prefabricated units, using wood and fiber-cement panels. These units were particularly popular in the progressive urbanizations, where they replaced the initial makeshift dwellings. MINVAH made the materials available at low cost, with long-term, low-interest loans. In addition, technical assistance and tools for construction were provided. The acceptability of these units was demonstrated by the fact that demand consistently exceeded supply.

As with the purchase of public housing, the selection process for purchases from the Materials Bank utilized the participation of the CDSs and other mass organizations. Within the guidelines established by MINVAH, the local groups were assigned the responsibility for selecting those who were most deserving of the benefits of the program. This local control was viewed as a key element in the cooperative relationship between the government and the people.

CONCLUSIONS

In 1979 the revolutionary government inherited a housing situation that had deteriorated under the Somoza regime despite considerable expenditures and international assistance. The circumstances of the low-income population, largely neglected by the dictatorship, was particularly problematic. During the first five years, the JGRN and MINVAH developed a set of national policies to deal with national development, urban reform, and housing construction. These policies were seen as integral parts of the government's plan for economic recovery and were described as having the long-range goal of bringing the benefits of urbanization and modernization to the masses. The new policies stressed governmental control, particularly in the area of urban development, and emphasized redistributive programs that utilized strong mass organization support and involvement.

In developing its policies the government rejected the traditional laissez-faire approach in favor of a socialist model. Initially the JGRN relied heavily upon the Cuban experience for general guidelines and for specific policy statements (such as the rental law), but over the first five years many modifications were made. MINVAH learned from the problems encountered in Cuba and Chile, and it responded to the social, political, and economic realities of revolutionary Nicaragua. While the policies stressed government control, they avoided a heavily centralized, authoritarian approach. Decisionmaking was diffused through the regional and municipal boards, and the people were integrated into the process through the CDSs and other mass organizations. Extensive capital investment in mass housing was abandoned in favor of facilitating low-cost, owner-constructed housing. The provision of secure title was emphasized over the provision of physical structures. In addition, the priority shifted from providing housing to the urban marginal residents to reinforcing agricultural production by developing rural resettlement projects.

At the end of five years MINVAH had made much progress. Early problems of organization and popular support had been largely overcome.[20] But the critical economic situation and the U.S.-sponsored aggression still severely restricted MINVAH's ability to realize its goals, particularly in the rural frontier areas. Also the chronic shortage of technicians made it difficult to keep up with the demand for construction, conditioning of new progressive urbanizations, and the verification of claims for titles. Yet in spite of these problems, and the tremendous pressures created by urban migration and a very high population growth rate, MINVAH's efforts produced more than had been produced under the Somoza regime.[21] Thus the Nicaraguan experience suggested that a socialist model for housing policy might be a successful alternative for other Latin American countries.

NOTES

1. John Turner, "Who Shall Do What About Housing?," in *Urbanization in Contemporary Latin America*, edited by A. Gilbert (New York: John Wiley, 1982), pp. 191–204.

2. Turner, ibid.; and Lisa Peattie, "Housing Policy in Developing Countries: Two Puzzles," *World Development* 7 (1979), pp. 1017–22.

3. World Bank, *Housing: Sector Policy Paper* (Washington, D.C.: World Bank, 1975); and Peattie, "Housing Policy."

4. For more complete discussion of the prerevolutionary period, see Harvey Williams, "Housing Policy in Revolutionary Nicaragua," in *Nicaragua in Revolution*, edited by Thomas W. Walker (New York: Praeger, 1982), pp. 273–90.

5. Junta de Gobierno de Reconstrucción Nacional, "Programa de Gobierno," *Encuentro* 17 (1979), pp. 31–47.

6. Ministerio de Planificación, *Plan de Reactivación Económico en el Beneficio del Pueblo* (Managua: Secretaría Nacional de Propaganda y Educación Política del FSLN, 1980), pp. 109–110.

7. Ministerio de Vivienda y Asentamientos Humanos (MINVAH), *1983 Informe Anual* (Managua: MINVAH, n.d.).

8. MINVAH, "Conclusiones del Seminario sobre Políticas, Funciones y Alcances del Ministerio de Vivienda y Asentamientos Humanos " (Managua: MINVAH, 1980).

9. William Gelman and Jesús H. Hinajosa, "Managua: Un Resumen del Programa de Reconstrucción Post-Terremoto," *Revista Interamericana de Planificación* 10 (1976), pp 40–62.

10. MINVAH, *Plan Regulador de Managua* (Managua: MINVAH, 1982).

11. Turner, "Who Shall Do What About Housing?"

12. MINVAH, "EL MINVAH: Organización y Gestión" (Managua: MINVAH, 1984).

13. Douglas S. Butterworth, *The People of Buena Ventura* (Urbana: University of Illinois Press, 1980)

14. D. J. Dwyer, *People and Housing in Third World Cities: Perspectives on the Problem of Spontaneous Settlements* (London: Longman, 1975).

15. John D. Herbert, *Urban Development in the Third World: Policy Guidelines* (New York: Praeger, 1979); and John Lea, "Self-Help and Autonomy in Housing: Theoretical Critics and Empirical Investigators," in *Housing in Third World Countries*, edited by Hamish S. Murison and John Lea (New York: St. Martin's Press, 1980), pp. 49–53.

16. Peattie, "Housing Policy"; Butterworth, *The People of Buena Ventura*; and Susan Eckstein, "The Debourgeoisement of Cuban Cities," in *Cuban Communism*, 3d ed, edited by Irving Louis Horowitz (New Brunswick, N.J.: Transaction Books, 1976), pp. 443–74.

17. MINVAH, "Conclusiones."

18. Hugh Stretton, *Urban Planning in Rich and Poor Countries* (Oxford: Oxford University Press, 1978).

19. MINVAH, *1983 Informe Anual*.

20. Williams, "Housing Policy."

21. Fanny Acevedo Correa, "La Política Social en Nicaragua." Paper presented at the XI International Congress of the Latin American Studies Association, Mexico City, 1983.

Chapter 19
Food Policy

JAMES E. AUSTIN
JONATHAN FOX

The food problem is acute, and whatever path the Revolution takes, from the point of view of its own development, it has to resolve first the problem of the basic consumption needs of the population; that is the priority which we have given to the Revolution.

Comandante Jaime Wheelock, 1983[1]

To feed the people, that has been the Sandinistas' self-imposed social priority, and food policy has been a cornerstone of the Revolution's social policy. The government confronted the problem of hunger by creating a strategy to ensure consumer access to food and to increase food supply. It made significant progress in its first five years, but many challenges remained.

THE INHERITED HUNGER PROBLEM

In 1970 half of all Nicaraguans consumed a daily average of 1,767 calories per capita, about 70 percent of the recommended allowance.[2] Over 56 percent of children under five years of age were estimated to be malnourished and over one-fourth of these were suffering from severe second or third degree malnutrition.[3] Malnutrition was undoubtedly a significant factor contributing to the very high infant mortality rate of 120 per 1,000 live births.[4]

Hunger in Somoza's Nicaragua reflected the prevailing poverty and skewed income distribution. The richest 20 percent of the population consumed almost twice the calories and protein as the bottom 50 percent.[5] The large and medium landowners constituted only 3.5 percent of the economically active rural population but received 63 percent of all rural income. The small producers were 46 percent of that population but received only 29 percent of the income. The 51 percent of the rural population who were landless laborers earned only 8 percent of the income.[6] Of the 170,000 rural laborers in 1978, only 18 percent were estimated to have stable employment.[7]

This economic structure was, in part, a result of the agroexport strategy of the 1950s and 1960s. Large-scale cotton production displaced small-scale food production from the fertile Pacific Coast provinces. Maize and bean output there fell 50 percent between 1952 and 1964.[8] At times the government used armed force to evict small landholders, renters, or sharecroppers.[9] Thus the Sandinistas inherited a hunger problem rooted in the economic structure of the old Nicaragua.[10]

ENSURING FOOD ACCESS

The new government began to address these structural economic problems in the consumption and production sides simultaneously. The strategy for consumption was to find mechanisms to ensure the population's access to adequate food supplies, and these fell into two related areas dealing with economic and physical access.

Economic Access

Three economic instruments were deployed to improve the consumers' purchasing power: price controls, consumption subsidies, and employment. The Ministry of Interior Commerce (MICOIN) concentrated its price control efforts on basic staples: rice, beans, maize, beef, pork, poultry, eggs, milk, cheese, sugar, salt, cooking oil, and coffee. MICOIN inspectors were primarily concerned about maintaining these official prices. They alone, however, could not monitor price controls effectively; communities themselves had to organize volunteer inspectors to ensure compliance of the public and private distributors. An additional 50 products had officially set prices, and the supervision of these rested primarily with the volunteer inspectors from the neighborhood CDSs. This reliance on the mass organizations had the double benefit of relieving the government of an administratively burdensome task and of empowering the people to make the food system more responsive to their needs and legal rights.

The government's approach to dealing with those who violated the price controls, hoarded, and speculated changed over time. Initially the violators were fined, but evasion remained widespread. The speculation that occurred after the May 1982 floods, however, evoked such a public outcry that some of the major violators were jailed; hoarding of essentials having already been declared a crime. By 1984 MICOIN was considering a new approach: to confiscate the merchandise and pay the official price for it, thereby causing the speculator to forego the illegal gain and absorb the loss. Prices in the Mercado Oriental, the traditional wholesale/retail market in Managua, remained largely unregulated. This created an island of available supplies for those consumers who wished to acquire larger quantities and had the money to pay the higher-than-official prices. In one sense this constituted a semicontrolled black market.

Consumption subsidies, the second policy instrument, aimed to keep food prices lower and more stable than they otherwise would have been. The subsidy was the result of MICOIN selling basic foods at far below the purchase and logistics costs. Between 1980 and 1982 the subsidy tripled, with 59 percent going for basic grains, 34 percent for sugar, and 7 percent for milk.[11] The total consumption subsidies accounted for approximately 6 percent of the national budget and over 30 percent of the fiscal deficit.

The subsidies were used to resolve the basic food policy dilemma of trying to preserve low prices for consumers and high prices for producers. They did provide purchasing power protection to consumers at a time when real incomes were stagnant or falling, and they did enable food producers to receive higher prices in real terms. By 1984, however, the fiscal burden was becoming increasingly difficult to bear, given the dire straits of the economy. In 1984 the subsidies were reduced, but selling prices for rice, maize, beans, sugar, and milk remained below the government's purchase prices and handling costs.

Increasing employment was the third strategy to ensure access to food. In the first two years of the Revolution the government became the major generator of jobs. Payrolls swelled in the administrative apparatus and the state productive enterprises. Efficiency considerations took a secondary place to the social and political exigencies of providing income sources through employment in the first two years. This was probably a reasonable short-term measure, given the major social dislocations from the 1979 war. Although it was a helpful safety net, it was fiscally unsustainable. Furthermore, it accelerated the release of heightened consumption expectations that grew out of the Revolution, putting even greater strain on food supplies. Prices for Nicaragua's exports plunged and the international debt servicing costs rose, leading in 1981 to the "Year of Austerity and Efficiency." There was a concerted move to eliminate redundant jobs in the public sector. With this source of income protection being removed, the burden on the price controls and consumption subsidies instruments became even greater.

Physical Access

In order for its economic regulatory instruments to be effective, the state felt it necessary to manage the commodity flows more directly. It did this primarily at four points in the food distribution channels: importing, domestic procurement, wholesaling, and retailing. The main institutional vehicle for these activities was the state-owned food marketing enterprise (ENABAS).

Imports were used heavily in the first years to meet the accelerating demand while the domestic production apparatus recuperated from the dislocations of the war. Bean imports were 33 percent of consumption in 1980 and fell to 4 percent in 1982; rice imports dropped from 67 percent to 0; maize imports varied but remained around 25 percent because of production problems. Imports were essential to price stabilization, but the country's extreme foreign exchange shortage made continued import dependence very costly.[12]

On the domestic side, ENABAS began a program to buy basic grains from producers at the established official purchase prices. Its initial efforts were fraught with problems. The inherited storage, drying, and transport infrastructure was largely defective or inappropriately located. Many farmers were not accessible and at least 20 percent of the grain purchased was lost because of poor facilities. The government mounted a major storage construction program and promoted the building of small on-farm storage units. ENABAS also found it very difficult to collect efficiently the grain from the tens of thousands of peasants scattered in remote areas. Recognizing the limits of the state, ENABAS pragmatically altered its strategy: instead of continuing to compete with the traditional inter-mediaries, it began working with those whom the peasant organizations designated as honest. These moves resulted in ENABAS's share of basic grains growing from nothing to 45 percent in 1982 and 62 percent of total supply in 1983. Beans remained a problem since private buyers paid higher prices for the quality beans and then resold them at up to double the official price in the parallel market. ENABAS was left with the lower quality beans that even many low-income consumers rejected.[13]

At the wholesale level, the government sought to replace the traditional wholesale market, Mercado Oriental, with a large new facility. Not surprisingly, this effort had little effect. Such markets are tightly woven socioeconomic units with an extraordinary tenacity for survival. The government chose not to force its will on the Mercado Oriental, which continued to be the source of employment for thousands of low-income traders, mostly women. Increased speculation did, however, prompt the state in 1982 to take over the wholesaling of sugar, cooking oil, and flour.

At the retailing level, ENABAS began by creating a network of medium-sized People's Stores, which numbered over 100 by 1984. Most of these were located in towns and areas outside of Managua. Their purpose was to ensure physical access by low-income consumers to basic foods at official prices. Although the stores had a narrow product line, limited hours, and were not well integrated into the community, they appeared to have held down prices and were requested frequently by low-income communities. To offset some of these deficiencies, MICOIN planned to open 30 new stores to be operated by local governments or merchants approved by the CDSs.[14]

The principal retail outlets used by ENABAS were existing private shopkeepers selected by a community organization to become a distributor of ENABAS commodities. As of the end of 1983 there were 3,747 of these People's Stores nationally. They accounted for over 40 percent of ENABAS's basic grain sales in Managua and were the principal supplier of maize and rice to the capital's low-income consumers. This approach, in effect, took advantage of the private entrepreneurs' superior capacity to operate on the small-scale retail level and also helped fuse a bond between the small shopkeeper and low-income consumers in the same community.

Contrasting with these small neighborhood stores were seven wholly and partially owned state supermarkets. Prior to the Revolution, these supermarkets served only middle- and upper-income consumers; now they were patronized by all economic classes. Foreign exchange shortages dramatically reduced the traditionally high portion of imported goods these stores offered.

A fourth type of outlet ENABAS supplied was Workplace Commissaries. The unions organized 520 of them by 1983, mostly in Managua. Their potential coverage was limited because only about 40 percent of the workforce in the capital were permanent wage earners. The subsidized food constituted an important part of the "social wage" workers received instead of cash wage increases.

In rural areas the government's food distribution efforts were greatly hampered by physical inaccessibility, personnel limitations, and organizational structure. As of 1982 there were 45 Rural Outlets and 260 Rural Supply Centers.[15] Efforts were further complicated by counterrevolutionary attacks. ENABAS was making several steps in 1984 to strengthen the rural distribution system, including the use of local mass organizations as direct grain distribution channels to cooperatives and farmworkers. In addition, a decentralized and regionalized organizational structure was increasing the institution's flexibility. An effort was launched in 1984 to create Intermediate Assembly Centers, which would bring the ENABAS buying station and retail store together with offices of the National Development Bank, the Ministry of Agriculture, and a health clinic. By mid-1984 the Ministry of Internal Commerce had reorganized its activities so that ENABAS dealt only with the procurement side and a new entity handled distribution.

In addition to these commercial distribution activities, the government also donated food directly to groups of nutritionally vulnerable preschoolers and pregnant and nursing mothers in low-income families, reaching an estimated 60,000 people.[16]

Since early 1982, the government's food distribution encountered the increasingly difficult problem of intermittent scarcities of certain foodstuffs. There were five main causes of these shortages. The first was seasonality, resulting from the agricultural cycle or unexpected adverse weather conditions. Second, problems arose from government policy decisions or administrative actions. For example, in 1982 sugar exports were excessive and led to domestic shortages; in 1983 bureaucratic red tape kept the lids to vegetable oil containers on the docks, causing a cooking oil shortage. A third cause was chronic production problems such as in cotton (the seed of which is used to make cooking oil) and beef, both of which had suffered serious declines during and immediately after the war and had not yet recuperated. Fourth, there were logistical obstacles to serving remote areas, as in the case of the Atlantic Coast, where transportation difficulties were compounded by terrorist attacks. Finally, high, uncontrolled prices for some products—for example, beef, cheese, and some vegetables— created scarcity for the lowest income consumers.[17] According to a MICOIN study, in 1982 ten basic products experienced shortages due to one or more of these causes, indicating "serious weaknesses in the commercialization systems, including the secure [government] channels."[18] An underlying factor contributing to scarcities was increased effective demand for food. Additionally, the political environment encouraged rumors of shortages that sparked runs on normal supplies, thereby causing temporary shortages.

To help manage these scarcities the government introduced a rationing system to handle the sugar shortage in 1982. In cooperation with the CDS's, ENABAS issued Guarantee Cards entitling each family to five pounds per month. The government also launched a massive educational campaign to lessen the political costs of instituting rationing. Furthermore, it tolerated a black market for those who needed more. This initial experience led to the creation in 1983 of local People's Supply Committees that attempted to assess the communities' food needs and find solutions to them. Local people's organizations handled most of the administration of the ration cards, thereby relieving ENABAS of this burden. The ration system was expanded in 1983 to include rice, maize, beans, cooking oil, laundry soap, and toilet paper. In July 1984 rice was removed from the ration list because there were abundant supplies.

Although using local CDS's had administrative advantages, there were instances of favoritism and other abuses, as is common in administrative rationing systems. These included requiring political support in exchange for the cards. The Sandinista leadership spoke out publicly against such abuses.[19] As one MICOIN Vice-Minister said: "Food should never be used as a political weapon."[20]

Over the first four years, policy emphasis shifted from state-run stores to People's Outlets and from trying to replace the market to regulating and integrating the numerous small private channels. This helped preempt the growth of a significant urban counterrevolutionary social base. Food policymakers recognized the structural limits to state economic power and administrative capacity, but they were also unwilling to let the market freely determine food allocation. Their vision of the future stressed popular participation as the answer, especially for products whose supply was particularly unstable.

The Popular Mobilization for Self-Supply was launched in 1983 in an effort to improve diets by converting food consumers into producers. Urban lots were plowed, the ministries and armed forces planted gardens, and family plots were encouraged. The effort was aimed at encouraging the people to take their own initiative rather than rely on the state alone.

INCREASING FOOD PRODUCTION

The effort to raise output involved a new National Food Program, changes in the production structure, and pricing and credit policies.

National Food Program

The National Food Program, PAN, began as a crisis response to the cutoff by the United States of wheat shipments in March 1981. Over the next two years it evolved into a medium- and long-term vision of how to meet the food needs of the people while maintaining a mixed economy. This constituted a strategy aimed at "achieving food security for the Nicaraguan people through self-sufficiency in basic grains and the creation of a distribution and commercialization system based on the interests and participation of the masses."[21] Many of the measures discussed above to improve food access were guided in part by the PAN strategy.

Having prioritized the production of basic grains, the government was faced with an apparent conflict: to produce staples to meet domestic consumption needs or produce crops for export to earn badly needed foreign exchange. The government opted to do both, with a long-run goal of exporting surplus grain. Moreover, many of the export crops were also consumed locally (sugar, coffee, beef) and many had by-products that were key inputs into the domestic food system (cottonseed for cooking oil, hides for leather processing, and protein sources for animal feed). To the extent that conflict existed regarding land use alternatives or foreign exchange or credit allocation, the trade-offs were viewed as manageable and the alternatives as generally not mutually exclusive.

Production Structure

The government became directly involved in production through the nationalization of the Somoza agricultural and agroindustrial properties. This land had largely produced sugar, cotton, and beef for export. The state farms also grew rice, but the rest of the basic grains were in the hands of private producers. In 1982 the peasantry produced an estimated 90 percent of the maize and 94 percent of the beans. Large and medium-sized farms produced 50 percent of the rice and sorghum. The government's state farms accounted for 32 percent of the rice and 14 percent of the sorghum, with the peasantry growing 38 percent of the sorghum and 18 percent of the rice.[22]

In conjunction with PAN, the government began to change the pattern of who was producing basic grains and under what conditions. These moves were prompted by the unsatisfactory production response and weather problems of 1982. The transformation of the foodgrain production process was required because the relatively low productivity of traditional producers made large and rapid increases in output difficult. The quality of most land devoted to basic grains was low; it was nonirrigated and generally not fertilized. The planned response was to shift basic grain cultivation to more fertile land, increase the area under irrigation, and stimulate the use of modern inputs.

The first move was to have the state sector make significant investments in irrigation to "weather-proof" part of the grain harvest. A $10 million modern production operation was jointly established with the Mexican government to produce rice for the domestic market as well as for export to Mexico. As of 1984 progress had been made on this project but administrative difficulties hampered its development. For maize, the state farms planted, in rotation with cotton, 10,500 acres under irrigation in 1983 with 24,500 scheduled for 1984.[23]

Second, the 1983 acceleration of the agrarian reform began to transform the quality and quantity of land available to basic grains producers. The combination of economic austerity and counterrevolutionary terrorism reduced the state's ability to extend social and economic services into the remote areas. Consequently, it was more feasible to redistribute wealth, in the form of land, than income. By the end of 1983, 7 percent of all arable land was titled to production cooperatives, mostly in the fertile Pacific region. The land recipients were mainly former landless members of the small producers association (UNAG) who produced basic grains for the domestic market.[24] With over half of the peasant producers organized into cooperatives, the government and UNAG chose 554 of them to receive special attention for grain production.[25]

Larger private commercial farmers continued to be important producers of rice, sorghum, and cottonseed for the domestic food economy. Nonetheless, their diminished political influence with the government created a perceived negative investment climate. However, their economic importance led the government to offer considerable economic incentives to them. The small and medium farmers in UNAG saw their political influence increase relative to prerevolution days when they had little, if any, voice in the political arena. This led to a more positive view of the investment climate by the more numerous small and medium farmers. In effect, the government's strategy regarding the structure of production was to preserve a mixed economy while altering the prerevolutionary role of the state and the relative positions of the various private producer groups.[26]

Prices and Credit

Support prices and credit were the government's principal policy instruments to stimulate production. Official prices administered through ENABAS were increased significantly for the 1981–82 crop year: maize up 66 percent, beans 13 percent, and rice 77 percent.[27] The producers proved responsive to these increases, thus corroborating the effectiveness of price policy as an incentive mechanism.[28] Support prices continued to increase through 1983–84, indicating improved terms of rural trade. The greatest increases were for maize, which had been least responsive.

Nationalizing the banks gave the government complete control of the formal credit channels, so production loans were the principal instrument used initially to stimulate production. In 1980 the government flooded the countryside with credit: a sevenfold increase over 1978 levels. It quickly became apparent that the credit was distributed far beyond the reach of the state procurement network. Because of limited access to other inputs, production did not increase proportionately, and much of what did increase stayed in the peasant households, partly because of the low prices offered by the state at the time. Resulting repayment problems were compounded by flood and drought in 1982. UNAG successfully campaigned for massive debt forgiveness in 1983.[29]

This experience and the economic pressure of austerity led to a retrenchment in credit. The area financed was reduced by about one-fourth in 1981–82, but it was still almost two-thirds greater than the 1977–78 levels. The share of the financed area planted for domestic consumption rather than export had risen to 47 percent compared to 33 percent in 1977. Small and medium farmers received 44 percent of the financing, large producers 36 percent, and state farms 20 percent.[30] The efficiency and effectiveness of credit delivery increased, partly because of providing the credit in the form of agricultural inputs and partly because of increased skills of bank personnel.

As of 1984, productivity of maize remained a significant problem. More modern production technology had not yet been widely adopted: about half of the credit recipients still employed the traditional methods, while another 40 percent used parts of a semitechnified package.[31] Lack of improved seed varieties and technical extension were serious constraints on output. According to the PAN strategy, food security would be achieved only in the medium run by increasing yields and extending basic grain area to higher quality lands, a process directly linked to the agrarian reform.

PRODUCTION AND CONSUMPTION RESULTS

How effective were the government's strategies and actions to increase food production and consumption? On the production side, the greatest success was in rice output, which in 1981–82 was 66 percent above the 1973–78 trend; the following year it reached record levels at 74 percent above trend. Nicaragua basically achieved self-sufficiency in rice. Bean production was 32 percent above the average in 1981–82 and remained 5 percent over trend in 1982–83. Maize remained the problem crop. It was 5 percent above trend in 1981–82, but the floods of 1982 caused output to fall to 87 percent of the prewar trend. However, the 1983–84 harvest recovered to a level 10 percent over the trend. Sorghum production grew rapidly initially, responding to the demand of the booming poultry industry for feedgrains. Output in 1981–82 was 51 percent above the trend, but subsequent problems caused shortfalls and the need to import 115,850 tons of feedgrains in 1983. However, the 1983–84 harvest was once again at record levels. In terms of livestock, poultry and pork were up 85% from 1977 and egg production had quadrupled. Beef and milk production experienced sharp declines, falling in 1983 to 65 percent and 45 percent of 1977 levels, respectively. On the export side, sugar and coffee output hit record levels in 1982–83, but poor weather caused drops in 1983–84. Cotton production continued to increase but was still only 62 percent of the 1977–78 level.[32]

On the consumption side, precise estimates were not possible because consumption data disaggregated by income class did not exist; nor were any national surveys of nutritional status available. Nonetheless, based on the supplies available from domestic production and imports, it appeared that per capita consumption increased, not a small feat given Nicaragua's annual population growth rate of 3.3 percent. The consumption pattern varied considerably by product. Per capita rice intake was more than 60 percent above 1977 levels, the best economic year under Somoza. In contrast, maize consumption was no better than 1977 and beans improved only slightly. Poultry was up 80 percent, cooking oil 30 percent, eggs 21 percent, while beef was down 10 percent and milk 4 percent.[33] Consumption of nonbasic goods was reduced to about 35 percent of the 1977 levels. Imports were hardest hit, disrupting the traditional consumption patterns of middle- and upper-income families.[34]

The two-thirds of the rural population with access to land probably experienced the greatest relative improvement in consumption. By 1983, peasant producers consumed more from their increased production and received higher prices for that portion that they sold. The landless laborers and urban poor were under a major consumption squeeze as a result of economic crisis with its high unemployment and inflation. The economic crisis was throughout Central America, however, and the price controls, subsidies, and production gains allowed Nicaragua to hold down the 1982 inflation rate for a basic goods market basket to 11.1 percent, while, for example, El Salvador experienced a 24 percent increase and Costa Rica a 102 percent rise.

PROGRESS AND CHALLENGES

After its first four years, the Revolution had not yet eradicated hunger, but it was moving in the right direction. Its actions on the food distribution side were important steps toward enfranchising the low-income consumers. Similarly, its efforts on the production side brought about structural change while preserving output growth of both domestic foodstuffs and export crops. This also revealed that a flexible approach to a mixed economy can effectively balance the sometimes competing interests of state, private, peasant, and cooperative producers. The recovery of both export and domestic crops, albeit uneven, indicates that what may appear to be an inherent conflict may instead be a series of trade-offs that can be managed. The basic grains did not compete significantly with the export crops for scarce foreign exchange, because the former used few imported inputs. As basic grains production was modernized, however, this potential conflict would increasingly materialize. Making better use of underutilized land also lessened the competition for common land, but this would also likely change in the future.

Just as the apparent food and export crop dichotomy was manageable, so too was the contradiction between food distribution by the free market and according to need. Any transition to a new system of food distribution would be disruptive; the issue was how different groups would be affected.

The government tried to regulate the market without replacing it. Both producers and consumers were subsidized, and price controls were enforced with popular participation. The state created parallel channels throughout the distribution system as well as state monopolies at certain points for basic goods particularly vulnerable to disruption.

Despite this progress, however, many problems remained. Administrative and infrastructure weaknesses continued to hamper the food distribution efforts. Many poor consumers still did not have adequate economic or physical access to food. Low productivity in maize continued to be a major constraint on the domestic grain supply. Correcting problems in both of these areas constituted a continuing challenge, and promising actions were under way. Another major challenge was to continue the pragmatic approach of finding productive and socially desirable ways of using the private sector's skills to carry out selected economic functions rather than creating an inefficient and unresponsive governmental bureaucracy. Sandinista pragmatism generally prevailed over ideological dogmatism. The state increasingly turned to popular participation rather than bureaucracy to deal with the market.

These tasks would be extremely difficult for any government, but Nicaragua also faced the added burden of having to contend with the economic and military aggression from the United States and the counterrevolutionaries, necessitating the diversion of scarce food and other resources toward the armed forces and away from the development process. As attacks increased in 1984, forcing the organization of a war economy, Nicaragua's food policy faced the increasingly central challenge of finding ways to bear equitably the growing burdens of defending the Revolution's hard won freedom.

NOTES

1. Jaime Wheelock, *El Gran Desafío* (Managua: Editorial Nueva Nicaragua, 1983).

2. FAO-SIECA, "Perspectivas para el desarrollo y la integración de la agricultura en Centroamérica" (Guatemala, May 1974).

3. U.S. Agency for International Development, "Nutrition Sector Assessment for Nicaragua" (Washington, D.C.; USAID, 1976).

4. Thomas John Bossert, "Health Care in Revolutionary Nicaragua," in *Nicaragua in Revolution*, edited by Thomas W. Walker (New York: Praeger, 1982); David C. Halperin and Richard Garfield, "Developments in Health Care in Nicaragua," *New England Journal of Medicine* 307 (August 5, 1982).

5. FAO-SIECA, "Perspectives."

6. Joseph Collins, *What Difference Could a Revolution Make?* (San Francisco: Institute for Food and Development Policy, 1982).

7. Jaime Biderman, *Class Structure, The State and Capitalist Development in Nicaraguan Agriculture* (Berkeley: University of California, 1982). Ph.D. dissertation, (Ann Arbor: University Microfilms International—8312757, 1982).

8. Pedro Belli, *An Inquiry Concerning the Growth of Cotton Farming in Nicaragua*. (Berkeley: University of California, Ph.D. dissertation, 1968); Orlando Núñez, "El Somocismo y el Modelo Capitalista Agro-Exportadora" (Managua: UNAN, 1980).

9. FIDA, *Informe de la Misión Especial de Programación a Nicaragua* (Rome: FIDA, 1980).

10. The health system under Somoza was also skewed to the wealthier classes. Consequently, the negative synergism between infection and malnutrition exacerbated the consequences of inadequate food intake. See Bossert, "Health Care," as well as Chapter 16 in this book.

11. MICOIN, *Sistemas de Comercialización: Productos Básicos de Consumo Popular* (Managua: División de Planificación, March 1983).

12. CIERA, PAN, CIDA, *Informe del Primer Seminario Sobre Estrategia Alimentaria* (Managua: CIERA, June 1983).

13. Collins, *What Difference*.

14. ENABAS, "ENABAS en la Revolución" (Managua: MICOIN, January 3, 1984); *El Nuevo Diario*, September 9, 1983; CIERA, *Informe*.

15. CIERA, *Informe*.

16. CIERA, *Distribución y Consumo de Alimentos Populares en Managua* (Managua: CIERA, February 1983).

17. CIERA, *La Situación del Abastecimiento* (Managua: MIDINRA, June 1983).

18. MICOIN, *Sistemas de Comercialización*.

19. See Commander Arce's letter to the CDS's in "A Revolution That Is Self-Critical," *Envío*, No. 17 (November 1982).

20. Interview with Luis Miranda, March 1984.

21. PAN, "Programa Prioritario de la Revolución: Programa Alimentario Nacional," May 1981.

22. *Barricada*, October 10, 1983.

23. PAN, "Plan Contingente de Granos Básicos," 1983; interview with Vice-Minister Pedro Antonio Blandón, March 1984.

24. *Barricada*, December 19, 1983.

25. Comité Nacional de Pequeña y Mediana Producción, "Resúmen de Políticas de Producción y Servicos para Granos Básicos," April 3, 1984.

26. For a detailed analysis of this subject, see James E. Austin, Jonathan Fox, and Walter Kruger, "The Role of the Revolutionary State in the Nicaraguan Food System," *World Development*, February 1985.

27. CIERA, *Informe de Nicaragua a la FAO* (Managua: MIDINRA, July 1983).

28. Collins, *What Difference*.

29. *Barricada*, July 7, 27, 1983.

30. CIERA, *Tres Años de Reforma Agraria* (Managua: MIDINRA, August 1982).

31. Carmen Diana Deere, Peter Marchetti, and Nola Reinhardt, "Agrarian Reform and the Transition in Nicaragua, 1979-83," November 1983, University of Massachusetts.

32. Data from PAN, MIDINRA, and JGRN, "Informe de la Junta de Gobierno de Reconstrucción Nacional de Nicaragua Presentado al Consejo del Estado," May 4, 1983.

33. MICOIN, *Sistemas de Comercialización*.

34. *Barricada*, November 21, 1983.

Chapter 20
Culture

ELIZABETH DORE

From the time of the insurrection through the first five years of the new revolutionary government, Nicaragua's leaders, many of whom were also writers and poets, stressed the Revolution's nationalist character. Ernesto Cardenal, Minister of Culture, priest, and poet, declared that "the basic objective [of the Revolution] is the conquest of our national identity."[1] Sergio Ramírez, member of the governing Junta and novelist, said:

> [T]he struggle of the Sandinistas was in its essence a process of the creation of a culture: a culture that derives from a nationalist and an anti-imperialist position. It is this nationalism and anti-imperialism which gives the struggle its mass base; because in Nicaragua the defense of the nation has been a class question.[2]

The nature of the liberation struggle and of the Revolution responded to the historical reality of the U.S. domination of Nicaragua. While the political and economic development of all of the countries of Latin America was strongly influenced by their relationship to the United States, this influence was qualitatively more profound in Central America and the Caribbean than in South America. This was due to the region's particular historical development. For more than a century the governments of the United States have directly intervened politically, economically, and militarily in Central America and the Caribbean.

The history of Nicaragua was, in many respects, the prototype of this relationship. The country, in essence, had become a neo-colony of the United States.[3] In the 1850s a U.S. citizen, William Walker, briefly established himself dictator of Nicaragua and legalized slavery. His government was officially recognized by the Pierce Administration. In 1909 the U.S. government supported a successful revolt against President José Santos Zelaya of Nicaragua because he refused to concede complete sovereignty over a portion of national territory to the United States for the construction of a canal. Zelaya's successor, chosen with the participation of a special U.S. envoy, formally accepted U.S. protectorate status. This

413

stimulated such dissent that the new president requested troops from Washington to quell the opposition. Thus began almost 20 years of occupation by the U.S. Marines. The U.S. government accomplished its earlier objective in 1916 when the United States and Nicaragua signed the Bryan-Chamorro Treaty, which conceded perpetual rights to a canal route through Nicaragua.

Resistance to the U.S. occupation was led by Augusto César Sandino. His small peasant army forced the Marines to withdraw from Nicaragua in 1933. Subsequently, Sandino and many of his followers were murdered, apparently at the personal order of Anastasio Somoza Garcia, whom the U.S. government had chosen to lead the newly created National Guard. With the defeat of the first Sandinista movement Anastasio Somoza ingratiated himself with the U.S. ambassador. Subsequently (and not coincidentally) he had himself elected President in 1936. This marked the beginning of a family dynasty that ruled for more than 40 years. The Somoza family always recognized that it governed at the pleasure of the U.S. administration and, accordingly, regarded Washington as its most important constituency. The result of this relationship was not only that Washington maintained political control over the government in Managua, but also that U.S. economic interests received favored treatment. North American influence was equally strong in the social and cultural life of the Nicaraguan people.

The imperialist domination and oppression of Nicaraguan culture was promoted consciously and actively as well as passively. Traditionally, popular culture in all of Latin America has incorporated themes of oppression and resistance. Festivals, songs, and dramas reenacting the Spanish conquest, the subsequent oppression of the Indian population, and the resistance to the oppressors have been performed for generations among the peasantry. In Nicaragua the most famous of such dramas is "El Güegüense," the story of a "superman" who resists (although in relatively mild ways) the oppression of the Spanish. During the Somoza dynasty the history of Sandino was completely suppressed, with references to him limited to those in which he was depicted as a bandit and a butcher of peasants. However, knowledge of Sandino's nationalist struggle was kept alive for Nicaraguan workers and peasants through the many popular peasant songs that recounted the stories of the battles that Sandino led against the Marines. These songs, dramas, and other forms of popular culture were threatening to the Somoza dynasty, since they dealt with (if not explicitly promoted) resistance to oppression. As a result they were either officially suppressed or ignored, depending upon the current political climate as well as on the nuances of their political content.

The suppression of Nicaragua's cultural heritage was not confined only to manifestations of popular culture. While it was neither possible nor desirable to ignore the cultural contributions of Rubén Darío (1867–1916), the world-renown Nicaraguan poet, information about his life and works was cleansed to eliminate any references to his political views. In his homeland he was officially portrayed as interested only in literary and artistic questions. It was not until after the triumph of the Sandinista Revolution that his political essays were published in Nicaragua. These are the writings of a nationalist and antiimperialist who was extremely critical of U.S. intervention in Central America.

Even those artistic forms that merely reproduced Nicaragua's cultural identity, in the absence of a political content, were viewed with disfavor by the Somoza regime. It was perceived that these forms of popular culture might contribute to the development of a nationalist consciousness that would be opposed to the domination of U.S. imperialism in Nicaragua and to its ally: the Somoza regime. Although these cultural forms were not overtly suppressed by the dictatorship, they were discouraged through an active campaign to denigrate their worth.

While for the past century there has been an on-going and active debate among Marxists as to the meaning and role of culture,[4] there exists a basic agreement that the concept of culture expresses the development of consciousness through the historical interaction between the world of ideas and the reproduction of knowledge, on the one hand, and the material reproduction of society, on the other.[5] There is also a certain accord that neither conceptually nor in practice can one divorce culture from the class divisions in society. Each class has its own historical traditions, consciousness, artistic forms, struggles, aspirations, and limitations; and these are represented by and reflected in that particular class's culture. Likewise each national group has its own distinct cultural identity and traditions. In light of this, in Nicaragua there is not one national culture, rather there coexist several different cultures: the working class, peasant, and bourgeois cultures of the Spanish-speaking population; the indigenous cultures of Monimbó and Subtiava, as well as the cultures of the Indians (Miskitu, Sumu, Rama); and of the English-speaking blacks of the Atlantic coast.

During the Somoza regime the culture of the bourgeoisie dominated Nicaraguan society. The ruling class denigrated popular or mass culture not only because it was frequently nationalist but also precisely because it was popular. It emerged from the working class and the peasantry and reflected their life-styles, their interests, and sometimes their low level of formal education. The official policy was one of neglect of the country's varied cultural traditions. Because Nicaragua's popular cultures were not considered by the ruling class to be "cultured," there was no encouragement of performances nor efforts to record, study, or to preserve the country's artistic heritage. As a result of the combined policies of the suppression of threatening cultural traditions and the neglect of others, forms of indigenous cultural expression were rapidly becoming extinct in the 1950s and 1960s.

The history of Nicaragua could be used as a textbook case to demonstrate that culture is an expression of the interaction among political, economic, and social processes. The hegemony of U.S. political and economic interests in Nicaragua was accompanied by the dominance of U.S. culture. The Somoza family and the ruling class fervently embraced the mass culture of the United States. Miami became the cultural capital of Nicaragua and the cultural values and cultural expressions of middle-class North Americans were upheld as the zenith of artistic achievement. The indigenous cultures of Nicaragua were replaced by the more homogenous foreign culture of the United States.

In the 1960s there began to emerge nationalist cultural movements that opposed the denigration and suppression of the autochthonous cultures of Nicaragua. These movements sought to rediscover and revitalize local forms of cultural expression. Ventana (Window), one of the first of these movements, was composed of writers and poets who incorporated into their writings native cultural values, themes, and aspirations. This was part of a larger cultural movement originating in León that was highly critical of what passed for cultural events, such as the visits of the U.S. Marine Band. In order to provide an alternative to officially sponsored entertainment, a group of students from the university formed a theater group that presented productions in the poor neighborhoods of León. These plays interpreted themes reflecting the history and experience of the workers and peasants of Nicaragua.

Later these and other groups such as Praxis and Grada (Step) became more developed theoretically and more militant in their activities. The artists involved in these movements were conscious that the cultural domination of Nicaragua was only one aspect of the generalized imperialist control of the Nicaraguan economy and society, and that the elimination of U.S. domination of Nicaragua was the first step in a process of the valorization of the indigenous cultures. Many of these artists joined the FSLN and fought for the national liberation of Nicaragua.

Cultural forms became important propaganda tools in the armed struggle. During this period, a beloved and brilliant fighter on the cultural front was the composer and singer, Carlos Mejía Godoy, who wrote songs that were based upon the collective consciousness as well as the musical and cultural traditions of the peasantry. During the intense days of the war against Somoza, Mejía and other composers wrote songs that directly served the armed struggle. A significant problem during the insurrection was that the mass of the population had no training in how to handle arms. Mejía wrote a series of songs about how to load, fire, unload, and clean different types of rifles, with each stanza comprising a short lesson. These songs, which were sung throughout Nicaragua, served as the only military training that some of the supporters of the FSLN received.

The development of the national liberation struggle contributed to a growing sense of national identity that itself resulted in the strengthening of the struggle against Somoza. Ideas and consciousness not only are reflections of the material world but are also part of material reality and effect the transformation of that reality. As the population supported and participated in the struggle against the neocolonial domination of Nicaragua it developed pride in its own heritage and culture. This new awareness of and estimation for its cultural traditions turned into a material force as this consciousness contributed to people's determination to support or join the struggle against the dictatorship.

As the liberation struggle grew stronger, and as the petty bourgeoisie and significant fractions of the bourgeoisie entered into alliances with the FSLN beginning in 1977, a national cultural identity began to emerge. This was based on the common struggle to eliminate the Somoza dynasty. However, this nationalist consciousness was as fragile as were the class alliances that gave birth to it. There was agreement only on the necessity of overthrowing the Somoza dictatorship. There was no unity on the more fundamental issue of the essential nature of the future society, whether it should be capitalist or socialist, nor even on the nature of the relations that the new government would strive to establish with the United States.

The Triumph of the Revolution unleashed a tremendous surge of creativity that had been repressed for generations. The initiative of the masses was applied to solving the problems inherent in the material as well as the social and cultural reconstruction of society. But the more basic challenge was not so much the "reconstruction" or resurrection of the old economic forms and units of production, with their corresponding social relations of production, but the struggle to develop new, revolutionary forms of social organization. This struggle was explicitly rejected by some fractions of the petty bourgeoisie and virtually all of the bourgeoisie that had collaborated with the Sandinista Front in overthrowing the Somoza dynasty. After the Triumph these differences gradually began to emerge, accompanied by an intensification of the class antagonisms that had traditionally characterized Nicaraguan society.

Throughout the liberation struggle the Sandinistas very effectively utilized cultural forms and tools to mobilize the population in the fight against Somoza. After the Triumph they continued to place great emphasis on the importance of cultural work. The day following the Triumph the new government announced the formation of a Ministry of Culture. In one of his first speeches as Minister of Culture, Ernesto Cardenal, referring to Marx's statement that the role of theory is to change reality, said that the role of culture is also to transform reality.

All people engage in the practice of interpreting the world, usually in an unsystematic and uncritical form, based on their individual perception and experience. Marxist-Leninist theorists abstract from these concrete experiences to reveal the underlying laws of motion and class relations in society. Revolutionary theory is the scientific analysis of how society functions and of how to transform that society. This analysis, or theory, itself becomes a material force as the basis for educating the masses about the specific nature of their exploitation and oppression. This knowledge then allows people to participate more effectively in the struggle to change society.

Forms of artistic expression are powerful tools with which to present the conclusions of theoretical analysis to the masses of people. Songs, paintings, and plays are not mere reflections of reality but are interpretations of selected aspects of individual experience. This is especially true of politically motivated art, whose primary objective is to convey specific ideas, to increase the sensitivity of the audience to a particular vision of the world, and to move people to participate in the struggle to transform their society.

After the Triumph, the political theory of the Sandinistas remained nationalist and antiimperialist. This responded to U.S. aggression against Nicaragua: the undeclared war carried out by mercenary troops composed primarily of former members of Somoza's National Guard, who enjoyed major support and assistance from the Honduran army and the CIA; the mining of Nicaraguan ports by the CIA; and the economic blockade orchestrated from Washington. In essence the struggle after the Triumph represented the direct continuation of the war against Somoza. Both could be seen as struggles to liberate Nicaragua from U.S. domination. In this context the role of culture remained the same: to develop a strong nationalist and antiimperialist sentiment, to forge a sense of national unity, and to instill a willingness to participate in the defense of the sovereignity of Nicaragua.

The first major national campaign after the Triumph was the Literacy Crusade. This was not only an educational effort, but also a cultural and political task. To actively participate in the transformation of society the population had to be literate. The campaign was not only successful in the narrow perspective of teaching the population to read and write; more importantly, it contributed to the development of a sense of nationhood. Urban youth went to the countryside as educators, and through their work they became familiar with how the peasantry lived. Just as the songs of Carlos Mejía contributed to the success of the insurrection, the songs of his brother Luis Mejía Godoy were tools in the battle against illiteracy.

Culture became a weapon in the revolutionary struggle in various ways. For one, artists, artisans, writers, and performers in Nicaragua were organized in the Sandinista Association of Cultural Workers (ASTC). The director of the association was the poet and long-time political activist Rosario Murillo. The organization not only supported cultural work and the rights of cultural workers but also developed a political analysis of the role of cultural work in transforming society. The cultural workers affiliated to the association were active in the preservation and presentation of indigenous forms of artistic expression, and they also played a central role in transmitting the theory, ideology, and aspirations of the Revolution. Composers and musicians continued to write and popularize songs that reaffirmed the staunch resolve of the masses of people to prevent the Somocista armies from returning, and to defend the recently conquered national independence of Nicaragua.

Second, the painters of Nicaragua developed a flourishing school of primitive art, with its initial roots on the Island of Solentiname. These paintings depict the everyday lives of common men and women. After the Triumph, Julie Aguirre and other artists interpreted more overtly political subjects such as battles in the war against Somoza, demonstrations, and meetings of the Sandinista Defense Committees. These paintings captured the intensity of political events and the struggle against imperialism, incorporating the popular political themes and slogans of the moment in creative ways.

From the time of Rubén Darío, Nicaraguans have considered themselves to be a nation of poets. This myth became a reality after the Triumph when the Ministry of Culture promoted the activities of poetry workshops throughout the country. In rural villages, in poor urban neighborhoods, in the state bureaucracy, in the army, the militia, and the police, groups of people met once a week to study the principles of poetry, to read and write poems, and to criticize each other's writings. The participants frequently wrote excellent poems that came to play an important role in forging and preserving a collective memory of the struggle against Somoza and of the early years of the Revolution. Personal experiences, usually the themes of these poems, provided a unique insight into how the lives of ordinary men and women were affected by the Revolution. The workshops also provided an opportunity for the poets to analyze how their lives and feelings reflected the larger struggle that engulfed the entire society.

In a revolutionary society, a major purpose of plays, and of other forms of cultural expression, is the development of political understanding. Their creation is based on a methodology similar to that employed in the development of revolutionary political theory. This methodology was adopted by the Nixtayolero Theater Collective of Matagalpa, under the direction of Alan Bolt. The members of the theater collective spent several months living in different peasant communities in order to become more familiar with popular traditions, customs, language, and myths, and to discover the primary concerns of the population at the moment. The actors then returned to the workshop and analyzed the essence of the major political and social issues and the nature of the social relations that give rise to these conditions. They attempted to distill this reality to its essence, which then became the central theme of a play. Their audiences saw an analytical presentation of the collectivity of individual experiences, with the underlying causes and social relations that produced these experiences revealed through the medium of the drama.

When the Nixtayolero Theater Collective performed in Cuba it was criticized for tending to concentrate on the problems that emerged in the course of the struggle to transform society. In fact, however, this was the strength of the theater group, not its weakness. Bolt and the members of the collective stressed that there inevitably develop tremendous problems in the construction of a revolutionary society. The theater collective attempted to make a critical analysis of the process of transforming social and economic relations, and of the effects of this on the lives of peasants and workers. They felt that this analytical and critical process was essential in order to learn from and correct the mistakes that had been made, and to build upon the successes.[6]

In the area of theater, the Sandinistas masterfully employed humor and satire in developing the consciousness and political understanding of the masses. Through humorous skits and songs, political analyses were presented in forms that were very accessible to a mass audience. "El tren de las seis" (The Six O'Clock Train), a brilliantly humorous daily radio program, took whatever issue was uppermost in people's minds and presented a political analysis of it in a short satirical skit. Through the use of humor, the show's writers, Chuno Blandón and Otto de la Rocha, were able to characterize the speeches and activities of many of the leading figures in the opposition in order to reveal the essential nature of their political positions. This radio show achieved such popularity that the fictional characters in the program became public figures to be reckoned with in the political arena, as real to Nicaraguans as Archie Bunker is to North Americans.

No aspect of Nicaraguan society lay beyond the bounds of the class struggle, least of all its cultural life. After the Triumph the three national daily newspapers—Barricada (the official newspaper of the Sandinista Front), El Nuevo Diario (a newspaper that supports the government), and La Prensa (the voice of the opposition)—each published a weekly cultural magazine. The pages of these supplements served as one of the major battlefields in the class struggle over cultural values. Barricada and El Nuevo Diario published poems written by peasants or workers, many of whom fought in the war against Somoza. These writings reflected upon the brutality and oppression of life under the dictatorship and upon the advances of the revolutionary society. The stories and poems published in *La Prensa*, written mostly by members of Nicaragua's bourgeoisie and petty bourgeoisie, were either apparently apolitical or appeals for a return to the "true heritage" of Nicaragua. This represented a thinly disguised form of calling for the elimination of the social and economic transformations of the Revolution and for the reinstitution of the cultural values of the United States. The development of national pride in Nicaragua's indigenous traditions placed constraints on the forms of cultural expression used by the bourgeoisie. The masses would no longer accept the denigration of Nicaragua's autochthonous cultures. Even the bourgeois opposition, as represented by *La Prensa*, recognized that in order for its cultural presentations to be accepted and to appeal to a mass audience, they had to appear to be consistent with, if not emulate, the newly emerging nationalistic cultural values.

As long as society is characterized by classes, classes will retain their distinct cultural traditions. Only through the elimination of classes is it possible to develop truly national cultures. These will be based on the specific history and traditions of different groups, be they defined by their common ancestors, their regional customs, or their history of oppression and of struggle. By the end of the first five years of the Sandinista government it was clear that as long as there was an impending threat of a massive direct U.S. military intervention in Nicaragua and in Central America, the Nicaraguan Revolution would remain primarily an anti-imperialist struggle. It might be possible to suppress some of the class-based cultural differences in Nicaraguan society in the context of this nationalist struggle. However, if the Nicaraguan Revolution developed into a struggle for socialism, the class struggle would surely intensify in all areas of life, especially on the cultural and ideological fronts.

NOTES

1. Ernesto Cardenal, "La Cultura de la Nueva Nicaragua: Un Cambio de Todo," in *Hacia una política cultural de la Revolución Popular Sandinista* (Managua: Ministerio de Cultura, 1982), p. 272.

2. Sergio Ramírez Mercado, "La Revolución: El Hecho Cultural Más Importante de Nuestra Historia," in idid., pp. 148–149.

3. John Weeks, *The Economies of Central America* (New York: Holmes and Meier, 1985).

4. V. I. Lenin, "On Proletarian Culture," in *Collected Works* (Moscow: Progress Publishers, 1974), pp. 316–317; Georg Lukács, *History and Class Consciousness* (Cambridge, Mass.: MIT Press, 1971); Herbert Marcuse, *One-Dimensional Man* (Boston: Beacon, 1968); Herbert Marcuse, *Negations: Essays in Critical Theory* (Boston: Beacon, 1968); Antonio Gramsci, *Selections from the Prison Notebooks*, edited by Quintin Hoare and Geoffrey Nowell Smith (New York: International Publishers, 1971).

5. Marcuse, *One-Dimensional Man*, p. 94.

6. Judith Doyle, "Theatre of Extraordinary Reality: Interview with Alan Bolt," *Impulse* (Toronto) 11, no. 1 (Summer 1984): 56–57.

PART V
THE INTERNATIONAL DIMENSION

Another important aspect of the Nicaraguan Revolution was its international dimension. Taking a lesson from the Cuban experience, the Sandinistas were determined to avoid, if possible, the type of international isolation that ultimately forced that earlier revolutionary system to become overwhelmingly dependent on the Soviet bloc. Instead, they sought to maintain or establish normal relations with as many states as possible, regardless of ideology. The chapters in this section examine Nicaragua's relations with the United States, the Communist states, the Nonaligned movement, Western Europe (and the Socialist International), and Latin America. William LeoGrande details the growing conflict between the United States and Nicaragua, as the Carter Administration, which had grudgingly decided to coexist with Sandinista Nicaragua, was replaced by a reactionary administration openly determined to reverse history in that respect. Theodore Schwab and Harold Sims discuss Nicaragua's growing ties with the Communist states that, they claim, "flourished in direct proportion to the deterioration of U.S.-Nicaragua relations." Waltraud Queiser Morales and Harry Vanden examine Nicaragua's role in the Nonaligned movement, which they argue was crucially important in preventing the country's international isolation and in mustering world support in organizations such as the United Nations. Nadia Malley then examines the history of the more tenuous, though still very important, relationship between Nicaragua and Western Europe. Finally, Max Azicri explores the diverse and, in some cases, surprisingly fruitful set of relationships that Nicaragua maintained with various other Latin American governments. Over all, these chapters show that, though harassed by the United States, Nicaragua had been quite successful in developing and maintaining good relations with a wide variety of nations.

Chapter 21
The United States and Nicaragua

WILLIAM M. LEOGRANDE

As the insurrection against Somoza gathered momentum in 1978 and early 1979, the clear objective of U.S. policy was to prevent the FSLN from gaining a predominant position in a post-Somoza regime. Washington bent every effort to this end, with the sole exception of restoring large-scale military assistance to the National Guard—an option so at odds with the human rights emphasis of the Carter Administration's foreign policy that it was ruled out.[1]

When the dynasty collapsed on July 17, 1979, U.S. policy shifted 180 degrees from an attitude of outright hostility toward the FSLN to one of cautious cordiality. The change was no less stark for having been forced by circumstances, since it carried with it the implication that even radical social and political change in Nicaragua did not necessarily endanger the vital interests of the United States.

Nevertheless, considerable tension born of mistrust lay below the surface of this peculiar friendship. The long history of U.S. support for the Somozas could not be wholly forgiven or forgotten by Nicaragua's new leaders, nor could they shake the fear and suspicion that Washington might yet concoct a counterrevolutionary scheme to rob them of their victory. In Washington, policymakers could not ignore the Marxist origin of many of the Sandinista leaders, even though Somoza's defeat had been engineered by a politically heterogeneous multiclass coalition. There was always the possibility that the guerrillas, having won power, would shed their moderate garb, dump their middle class allies, and steer the Revolution sharply to the left down the road of Cuban-style Marxism-Leninism.

Yet the interests of both Nicaragua and the United States lay in maintaining cordial relations if at all possible. Nicaragua was in desperate need of foreign assistance to rebuild an economy shattered by war. The United States had pledged to help in the recovery effort as part of the arrangements for Somoza's departure, but the maintenance of cordial relations was obviously a necessary condition for the fulfillment of that promise. Moreover, international assistance from Latin America, Western

Europe, and the international financial community would tend to follow the lead of the United States. A deterioration of U.S.-Nicaraguan relations would therefore have economic ramifications far beyond the aid dollars from Washington alone.

For the United States, maintaining cordial relations was a means of salvaging something from the failure to keep the FSLN out of power. Although, from Washington's perspective, the insurrection had been "lost," perhaps Nicaragua itself need not be. Policymakers in the United States set out quite consciously to avoid repeating the errors of 1959–60 when U.S. hostility drove the Cuban Revolution into alliance with the Soviet Union.

The Carter Administration's objectives were realistically suited to circumstances in which the United States had limited leverage. Washington recognized that the revolutionary coalition was inherently unstable. Once the overriding objective of defeating Somoza had been accomplished, the coalition was bound to deteriorate as it confronted the issue of what postrevolutionary Nicaragua should look like. The Sandinistas' "logic of the majority" could be pursued only at the expense of their upper and middle class allies, and that would inevitably produce conflict. Washington's objective was not to prevent such conflict, but rather to keep it within reasonable bounds, preventing a radicalization of the Revolution that would eliminate the private sector and any vestige of political pluralism.

In foreign policy, it was clear that Nicaragua would have a strong and friendly relationship with Cuba, the only country that had consistently supported the FSLN in its struggle against Somoza. Washington had no illusion that it could block a close relationship between Cuba and Nicaragua, but it hoped to minimize it, particularly in the military field. There was little doubt that the Sandinistas would support the Salvadoran guerrillas, since they had supported the Sandinistas during the insurrection against Somoza. But Washington hoped to restrain Nicaraguan involvement so that it would not constitute a major factor in the Salvadoran war.

During the first year of revolutionary government in Nicaragua, none of the worst fears of either side was realized. Despite conflicts between the FSLN and the private sector, capitalism was not abolished and pluralism, though not robust, survived. On occasion, U.S. Ambassador Lawrence Pezzullo acted as mediator between the government and opposition to prevent their disputes from escalating into apocalyptic confrontation.

Nicaragua's relationship with Cuba blossomed quickly as Cuba sent several thousand teachers, hundreds of medical experts, and scores of technical advisors (including some military personnel) to help Nicaragua reconstruct. The Sandinistas preferred Cuban military advisors to Panamanians, but their numbers remained relatively small.[2]

Finally, though there was evidence of arms flows from Nicaragua to El Salvador in early 1980, the amounts were not substantial. President Carter chose to interpret the intelligence findings generously, accepting the Nicaraguan government's assurances that any arms smuggling was being undertaken contrary to its policy. In September he certified to Congress, as required by law, that Nicaragua was not exporting violence to its neighbors and was therefore eligible to receive $75 million in economic assistance.[3]

As the 1980 U.S. presidential election approached, the Carter Administration's efforts to moderate the Nicaraguan Revolution seemed reasonably successful. The Sandinistas understood the implicit "rules of the game" and generally abided by them. Nicaragua, Ambassador Pezzullo declared, was "an acceptable model" of revolution.[4]

THE REAGAN TRANSITION

The architecture of Carter's whole Central America policy began to collapse as soon as Ronald Reagan was elected president. Throughout the region, political forces on both the right and left began acting in anticipation of what Reagan's policy would be. The Republican Party platform called for halting U.S. aid to "Marxist" Nicaragua and helping the Nicaraguan people "restore democracy." Key Reagan advisors were on record attacking the Carter Administration for "losing" Nicaragua to communism and urging less reticence in the use of military force abroad to resist Cuban-Soviet expansion.[5] In December the report of Reagan's State Department transition team was leaked to the press; at the top of a "hit list" of ambassadors slated for immediate replacement were Robert White in El Salvador and Lawrence Pezzullo in Nicaragua.[6]

In both Washington and Managua, virtually everyone expected the new administration to adopt a policy of hostility toward Nicaragua and to vastly increase U.S. miltiary aid to El Salvador. The Salvadoran revolutionary movement sought to preempt Reagan by mounting a "final offensive" to depose the Salvadoran regime on the eve of Reagan's inauguration, thereby confronting him with a fait accompli.

For the arms to mount such an offensive the Salvadoran guerrillas turned to Cuba, Nicaragua, and the Eastern bloc. For Managua, the request posed a difficult dilemma. The Sandinistas had faced a similar supply problem prior to the final offensive against Somoza, and Cuba had helped fill the breach. Yet the issue of Nicaraguan aid to the Salvadoran insurgency was the most sensitive issue in Managua's relations with Washington. Though the Sandinistas had turned a blind eye to the Salvadorans' use of Nicaragua as a way station in their own arms smuggling operations, the Nicaraguans had refrained from making a major commitment to the guerrillas in order to maintain their relationship with the United States.

The expectation that Reagan's policy toward Nicaragua would be a hostile one regardless of how the Sandinistas behaved diminished the incentive for moderation so carefully crafted by the Carter Administration. In November and December 1980, U.S. intelligence detected a major increase in the flow of arms into El Salvador from Cuba and Nicaragua.[7]

In its last few weeks in office, the Carter Administration was forced to respond to the unraveling of its Nicaragua policy, even though events had slipped beyond control through no fault of its own. The September certification that Nicaragua was not exporting revolution had been the subject of intense controversy within the administration, partly because the intelligence community had evidence of some arms flows even then, and partly because conservatives in the administration had hoped to block the certification until after the November election. In December 1980 and January 1981, as evidence of Nicaragua's complicity in the arms smuggling became unequivocal, the pressure to "decertify" became intense.[8] In January the Carter Administration announced that it was suspending the $15 million in economic aid not yet disbursed from the $75 million aid package on the grounds that Nicaragua was shipping arms to the revolutionaries in El Salvador. By suspending the aid rather than canceling it, Washington held out the prospect that it might be restored if Nicaragua changed its behavior. That, however, would be a determination that would fall to President Reagan.

The Reagan Administration immediately seized upon Central America as a perfect issue with which to assert its new hard line foreign policy. Secretary of State Alexander Haig, anxious to establish himself as the "vicar" of foreign policy, declared the region to be a "test case" in the struggle with international communism.[9] Haig's major concern was the defeat of the guerrilla insurgency in El Salvador; his metaphor of "drawing the line" against communism was apt, for Haig's policy was vintage containment.

The lesson Haig learned from Vietnam was that you must "go to the source" to defeat a guerrilla insurgency—that is, cut off external logistical support for the insurgents. But during the early weeks of the new administration, Haig was not irrevocably convinced that "going to the source" required military action; if external support for the Salvadoran Revolution could be ended by diplomatic means, that would do just as well.

Pezzullo was able to convince Haig that it was possible to reestablish the understanding between Nicaragua and the United States that had prevailed during the Carter Administration. With the proper mix of economic incentives and the specter of U.S. hostility, the Sandinistas could be persuaded to halt their material assistance to the Salvadoran guerrillas. Pezzullo was so convincing that in February he was able almost single-handedly to defeat an effort by administration hard-liners to make the suspension of economic aid to Nicaragua permanent. Instead, the administration set a 30-day deadline for Nicaragua to end the arms flow into El Salvador.[10]

From Managua's perspective, the Reagan Administration was not acting quite as anticipated. Pezzullo had not been fired; on the contrary, he was insisting that the old rules of the game, if reestablished, could still form the basis of a workable relationship. The Salvadorans' final offensive had failed so dismally it was clear that there would be no victory there in the foreseeable future, and the Sandinistas' irritation at having been misled by the Salvadorans about their strength made Nicaragua amenable to Pezzullo's proposal. Nicaragua assured Washington that it would refrain from further aid to the Salvadorans, closed a clandestine Salvadoran radio station operating on the outskirts of Managua, and began to curtail the flow of weapons. By mid-March, U.S. intelligence indicated that the flow was much reduced, and the administration's 30-day deadline was extended because of Nicaragua's efforts to comply.[11]

At this point Pezzullo's efforts were derailed by administrative hard-liners whose objective was not simply to contain the insurgency in El Salvador but also to roll back "communism" in Nicaragua. In late March they launched a second effort to cut off economic aid. Pezzullo was not informed until the decision had already been made, and it was leaked to the press before he had an opportunity to notify the Nicaraguans. The announcement of the aid cutoff was made, appropriately enough, on April Fool's Day. A few months later Pezzullo resigned his ambassadorship and retired from the Foreign Service.

Relations between Nicaragua and the United States stagnated for the next few months, but Central America returned to the top of the Reagan Administration's agenda in June when the Salvadoran guerrillas launched a surprisingly strong offensive that destroyed Washington's hopes for a quick military victory there. Once again, Haig was intent upon "going to the source," initiating the first of several attempts to convince Reagan of the need to blockade Cuba.[12]

With regard to Nicaragua, Thomas Enders, the newly installed Assistant Secretary of State for Inter-American Affairs, was prepared, like Pezzullo had been, to try to close the Nicaraguan arms channel by diplomatic means. He convinced a reluctant Haig to let him make the effort.[13]

In August 1981 Enders traveled secretly to Managua to open discussions with the Sandinistas. He set forth two basic conditions for an improvement in bilateral relations: Nicaragua must halt its support for the

Salvadoran guerrillas, which intelligence sources indicated was continuing, albeit at a level well below that of late 1980; and it must curtail its own military buildup, which had accelerated after the collapse of the Pezzullo initiative. In exchange, the administration would sign a nonaggression pact with Nicaragua under the terms of the Rio Treaty, make an effort to close exile paramilitary training camps in the United States, and ask Congress to restore economic aid to Nicaragua.[14]

The Sandinistas, deeply skeptical of Washington's intentions after the fiasco of February–March, did not respond positively to Enders's proposals. They denied supplying arms to the Salvadoran guerrillas and rejected any constraint on their own military posture as a violation of their sovereignty. They also regarded Washington's promises as hollow. The Rio Treaty already obligated the United States to refrain from the threat or use of force against Nicaragua, and the U.S. Neutrality Act prohibited training camps of the sort operating in Florida and California. If the Reagan Administration was unwilling to comply with domestic and international laws already on the books, of what value would any additional pledge be? The idea that Congress would restore economic aid was particularly farfetched, since only the most strenuous efforts of the Carter Administration had managed to get congressional approval of the $75 million aid package in 1980.

Between August and October 1981, Nicaragua and the United States exchanged a number of communications on these issues. Within the Reagan Administration, the hardliners were able to insist that Washington's proposals be phrased in imperial language certain to irritate the nationalism of the Sandinista leadership. The only agreement that was reached was that each side would refrain from using incendiary public rhetoric against the other.

Even this thin thread was broken in October when the United States conducted an amphibious assault exercise with the Honduran Armed Forces as part of the Halcon Vista joint manuevers. At the United Nations, Daniel Ortega denounced the exercises as a rehearsal for an attack on Nicaragua. Washington interpreted this as a violation of the agreement to suspend the war of words and on that basis broke off the diplomatic dialogue.[15]

Two years later, with the wisdom of hindsight, the Sandinistas wished they had been more receptive to the Enders proposal since, despite the language in which it was posed, it was close to Pezzullo's offer. By allowing their distrust of Washington and their offense at the proposal's style to divert them from its substance, they allowed the hard-liners in the Reagan Administration to defeat those who sought a diplomatic concordat. With the failure of the Enders initiative, Washington turned to the more traditional means of dealing with renegade Latins—brute force.

THE NOT-SO-SECRET WAR

In early October 1981 the Salvadoran guerrillas launched a major offensive against the government, scoring successes far beyond anything anticipated in Washington. While their June offensive had produced serious concern within the administration, their fall offensive set off a panic. A full-scale review of U.S. policy in Central America was undertaken; some, including Secretary Haig, warned ominously of the collapse of El Salvador unless the United States acted decisively. True to form, Haig still looked to the source, recommending direct military action against both Cuba and Nicaragua, if not El Salvador itself.[16]

Haig's call to war was opposed within the administration by the Joint Chiefs of Staff. The Joint Chiefs recommended against Haig's proposal to blockade Cuba on the grounds that it risked confrontation with the Soviet Union, would divert naval forces from more critical theaters around the globe, and would probably not achieve its professed objective of halting arms shipments to Central America. They also opposed direct involvement in El Salvador or Nicaragua, not wishing to enlist in a potentially unwinnable and politically unpopular ground war that could demolish the recently reconstituted congressional majority for a major strategic buildup.

In a series of National Security Council meetings in November, President Reagan approved a ten-point policy plan for Central America. Haig's proposals for direct military action were rejected; instead the United States would increase military aid to El Salvador and Honduras, expand the U.S. military presence throughout the Caribbean Basin by mounting large military exercises, expand the CIA's intelligence-gathering capacity in Central America, develop military contingency plans for the region, and initiate covert paramilitary operations against Nicaragua. In part, approval of covert operations against Nicaragua was a consolation prize for Haig, to ease the pain of his failure to convince Reagan of the need for direct military action.[17]

During the November National Security Council meetings, the CIA proposed a variety of covert operations. The least controversial was to continue a program of financial aid to internal opponents of the Sandinistas begun by the Carter Administration and expanded when Reagan first came to office. Recipients of this largesse reportedly included opposition labor organizations, political parties, press, and the private sector. A second program, also approved without opposition, was to expand U.S. intelligence-gathering capabilities in Central America as a whole.[18]

Among the paramilitary operations proposed, the most ambitious called for the CIA to assemble, train, and arm a commando force of 500

Latin Americans, mostly Cuban exiles, to conduct military operations against Nicaragua from base camps in Honduras. The primary mission of this force would be to attack Nicaragua's economic infrastructure in the hope that the resulting economic hardship would produce political destabilization. It was also suggested that such a force would enable the United States to take "paramilitary action against special Cuban targets" in Central America. The initial budget for this option was reportedly $19.95 million.[19]

A second paramilitary option, proposed as a complement of rather than an alternative to the first, called for the United States to provide financial and logistical support for an Argentine effort, already underway, to train 1,000 Nicaraguan exiles for the purpose of overthrowing the Nicaraguan government.[20]

A third more limited option involved funneling military aid, particularly small arms, through the Honduran Armed Forces to Nicaraguan exiles already operating along the Nicaraguan-Honduran border. This may have been simply an extension of a paramilitary operation approved in March 1981 to interdict arms flows from Nicaragua to guerrillas in El Salvador and Guatemala.[21]

The CIA's paramilitary plans touched off a heated debate within the Reagan Administration over the goals of U.S. policy toward Nicaragua. Some officials argued that the program of covert operations should be aimed at overthrowing the Sandinista government. Others, including some officials from the State Department, the Defense Department, and even the CIA itself, argued that the objective of U.S. policy should be the more limited one of interdicting the flow of arms from Nicaragua to the Salvadoran guerrillas. This second group argued that efforts to overthrow the Sandinistas would inevitably entangle the United States in a partnership with the remnants of Somoza's National Guard—an association that would allow the Sandinistas to rally popular opinion in their favor. They also warned that efforts to depose the Sandinistas could spark a wider regional war, drawing the United States into direct military involvement.[22]

After an extended debate within the administration, President Reagan signed National Security Decision Directive 17 as well as a December 2, 1981, Presidential Finding that granted the CIA broad authority to conduct covert political and paramilitary operations against Cuba and Cuban supply lines in Nicaragua and elsewhere in Central America, and to cooperate with other governments to accomplish this.

The CIA was authorized to proceed with the creation of the 500-man commando force, to assist Argentina in the creation of a larger army of Nicaraguan exiles, to establish direct liaison with exile groups based in Honduras, and to work toward the creation of a broad political opposition front to the Sandinistas. Those in the administration who sought to overthrow the Sandinistas won a victory; all the operations initially proposed were approved. Those who thought a program to overthrow the Sandinistas would be counterproductive managed to salvage something, though. The objective of the paramilitary programs approved by the president was defined as the limited one of interdicting arms flows, and it was to be implemented without giving direct assistance to the former National Guardsmen.[23]

When the CIA's program of covert operations was presented to the Intelligence Committees of Congress, many members voiced concerns similar to those that had been debated within the administration. There was strong bipartisan opposition to creating the 500-man commando force to attack "special Cuban targets." As a result, this aspect of the operation was apparently dropped. In addition, the intelligence committees approved guidelines restricting the objective of the paramilitary operations to arms interdiction.[24]

Like most policies that are arrived at through a process of bureaucratic bargaining and compromise, the elements of the CIA's covert operation against Nicaragua were not entirely consistent with one another. In order for the United States to avoid involvement with Somoza's Guardsmen, Argentina was slated to supervise the creation and operation of the exile army, and to act along with Honduras as a conduit for military supplies.[25] It made little substantive difference, however, whether U.S. aid to the contras was provided directly or laundered through Honduras and Argentina. Moreover, while the United States was supposedly limited to interdicting arms, Argentina was explicitly creating an exile army in order to overthrow the Sandinistas, and the exiles themselves were, of course, dedicated to that same end.[26] Finally, within the Reagan Administration itself, operational control over the covert war fell to people who had, from the outset, advocated getting rid of the Sandinistas rather than simply containing them.

The Falklands/Malvinas war brought these inherent problems to the surface. When Washington sided with Great Britain, Argentina began to withdraw from Central America. As Argentina withdrew, the United States gradually assumed control over the operations that Argentina had begun— providing arms, money, and training to the expanding exile army in Honduras. To stay within the original guidelines of the policy (which prohibited direct U.S. aid to the exiles) an elaborate system was constructed so that U.S. efforts could be handled through the Honduran Armed Forces. But this arrangement could not conceal the fact that the United States had assumed the central role in the covert war in the wake of Argentina's withdrawl.[27]

The covert war was the most important element in the administration's policy of hostility toward the Sandinistas, but it was by no means the only one. As the exile army was being assembled, the administration mounted a campaign to cripple the Nicaraguan economy by cutting off external sources of financing. The Sandinistas inherited an economy devastated by war and bankrupted by Somoza's larceny. They faced a Herculean task of reconstruction at a time of global recession that, under the best of circumstances, would have meant hardship for an underdeveloped export economy like Nicaragua's. During the first two years of revolutionary government, the Sandinistas received crucial financial aid from international financial institutions, Latin America, Western Europe, and the United States.

The Reagan Administration halted bilateral aid to Nicaragua almost immediately. As the policy of hostility unfolded in late 1981 and early 1982, the administration moved to cut off other sources of bilateral and multilateral assistance as well. To discourage private businesses in the United States from investing in Nicaragua or trading with the Sandinista government, Nicaragua was excluded from the programs of the Export-Import Bank (which provides short-term credits to facilitate trade) and the Overseas Private Investment Corporation (which offers insurance for U.S. companies investing abroad). To discourage private banks from loaning to Nicaragua, the U.S. government's Inter-Agency Exposure Review Committee, which rates underdeveloped nations' creditworthiness, downgraded Nicaragua's rating in early 1983 from "substandard" to "doubtful"— despite the fact that Nicaragua was at that time on schedule with its repayment of the massive external debt inherited from Somoza.[28]

From November 1981 onward, the United States voted against all loans to Nicaragua in both the World Bank and the Inter-American Development Bank on the dubious grounds that the macroeconomic situation in Nicaragua was so bad that development loans could not be used effectively. In general, the United States was outvoted when loans came up for review, but when serious objections to a loan are raised in these banks, the normal procedure is to defer consideration of it. The size of the U.S. contribution to the banks gives the U.S. representative considerable political leverage. The exercise of that leverage to block loans to Nicaragua caused sharp controversy within the banks, but the fact remains that loans to Nicaragua virtually ceased. In 1979 Nicaragua received $179 million from the Inter-American Development Bank and the World Bank; in 1983 it received only $30 million.[29]

Following the model established by the CIA's successful destabilization of the Allende government in Chile, the Reagan Administration's credit blockade was combined with a program of economic sabotage. Beginning in mid-1982, the exile raids from Honduras targeted economic resources—farms, bridges, warehouses, and so on. In 1983 the CIA took direct control of major sabotage operations, carrying out the successful attack on the oil storage facilities at Corinto on October 11, and a series of speedboat attacks on shipping in Nicaraguan harbors. In January 1984 the CIA escalated its campaign to disrupt shipping by mining Nicaragua's major ports, but the mining operation brought forth such a firestorm of criticism from Latin America, Western Europe, the U.S. Congress, and the World Court that it was subsequently halted.[30]

In addition to the covert war and the effort to strangle the Nicaraguan economy, the Reagan Administration's policy of hostility also included a major political offensive with several distinct elements: explicit threats of military action designed to intimidate the Sandinistas; vociferous denunciations of the Nicaraguan regime designed to build domestic political support for the administration's overall Central American policy; and diplomatic efforts to isolate Nicaragua from both its neighbors and potential friends in Western Europe.

In the last week of November 1981, both Haig and Presidential Counselor Edwin Meese warned that although Reagan had ruled out the use of U.S. troops in Central America, other military actions, including a naval blockade of Nicaragua, were still being considered. The rhetoric grew so intense that Mexican president José López-Portillo was moved to describe it as "verbal terrorism" and to warn that a U.S. attack on Nicaragua would be "a gigantic historical error."[31]

At the Organization of American States (OAS) meeting in St. Lucia in December, Haig invoking the Rio Treaty, called for joint hemispheric action to block Nicaraguan and Cuba subversion. He also repeated the warning that the United States would do whatever was "prudent and necessary" to prevent any nation in Central America from becoming a "platform for terror and war."[32]

At home, the Reagan Administration launched a public relations campaign to portray Nicaragua as a Marxist-Leninist dictatorship guilty of gross human rights abuses, a pawn of Cuba and the Soviet Union, and the primary source of external support for the Salvadoran insurgency. United Nations Ambassador Jeane Kirkpatrick led the assault on Nicaragua's human rights record, characterizing the regime as a totalitarian dictatorship "even more repressive . . . than was the dictatorship of Somoza." Secretary Haig focused on Nicaragua's alleged assistance to the Salvadoran guerrillas. In March he charged that the Salvadoran insurgency was being run out of Managua.[33]

By far the most impressive element of the administration's public relations campaign against the Sandinistas was a press briefing conducted jointly by the CIA and the Defense Intelligence Agency. The briefing was organized to convey the drama of the Cuban Missile Crisis. It was conducted by the same analyst, replete with aerial reconnaissance photographs labeled in the same way as the famous missile sites two decades earlier. The thrust of the briefing was that Nicaragua had undertaken a major military buildup with Cuban and Soviet assistance, a buildup so far beyond normal defense requirements that it must be intended for aggressive use against Nicaragua's neighbors.[34]

The substance of the briefing was not very compelling. The most ubiquitous photographic evidence was "Cuban-style obstacle courses" at various Sandinista military bases. Absent from the briefing was any evidence that the Nicaraguans had introduced major new weapons systems or that they were systematically channeling arms to the Salvadoran guerrillas. As the Nicaraguans were quick to point out, they had never denied that they were strengthening their military or that they were receiving military aid from the socialist bloc; what did the United States expect, Sergio Ramírez asked, when Washington was fomenting counter-revolution?[35]

The aerial briefing, for all its theatrics, was fundamentally disingenuous. The administration was fully aware that the Sandinistas had neither the capability nor the intention of invading their neighbors, and that their military buildup was, as they claimed, defensive. Administration spokesmen, in a classified version of the aerial briefing given to the House Intelligence Committee, admitted as much.[36]

The administration's public relations campaign collapsed a few days later when the State Department arranged a press briefing to display a Nicaraguan soldier allegedly sent to command guerrilla forces in El Salvador. The young Nicaraguan, captured the previous year in El Salvador, recanted his story as soon as briefing began. He claimed that he had gone to fight in El Salvador on his own accord, and that the story of his being ordered there after training in Ethiopia was entirely fabricated—a product of torture at the hands of the Salvadoran armed forces. The debacle produced an immediate suspension of the administration's campaign to rally domestic opinion.[37]

On the diplomatic front, the administration sought to isolate Nicaragua from its Central American neighbors and to reduce West European support for the Sandinistas. In early 1982, France announced that it had agreed to sell $16 million of military equipment to Nicaragua. The administration was outraged. Under U.S. pressure, France delayed shipment of the military supplies and agreed not to make any additional sales.[38] Similar pressures were brought to bear on other West European countries, not only to prevent arms shipments to Nicaragua but to reduce economic support for the Sandinistas as well. This effort was only partially successful. No further military equipment went to Nicaragua from Europe, but significant amounts of economic assistance continued to flow.

In Central America, the United States organized the Central American Democratic Community, composed of Costa Rica, Honduras, and El Salvador. The explicit objective of the new organization was to seek joint measures to counter Nicaragua, but the whole enterprise was so transparently a creation of the United States that it faded quickly into oblivion after its initial meetings.

The administration combined these diplomatic moves with military actions designed to intimidate the Sandinistas. In addition to the constant drumbeat of rhetoric about Nicaraguan subversion and the willingness of the United States to counter it with force, the administration undertook a massive military buildup in Honduras. From fiscal year (FY) 1980 to FY 1984, U.S. military aid to Honduras rose from $3.9 million to $78.5; the number of U.S. military personnel stationed there (apart from troops participating in exercises) rose from 26 to 346; and the United States built or planned to build 11 military installations at a total cost of $87.85 million.[39] All of this was justified to Congress as necessary to counter the threat of aggression from Nicaragua.

But the most dramatic efforts at intimidation were the U.S. military exercises mounted in Honduras and off Nicaragua's coasts. Beginning with the relatively small Halcon Vista joint manuevers with Honduras in October 1981, the implicit or in some cases the explicit purpose of all the exercises was to "pressure" Nicaragua by demonstrating the ability of the United States to project military force into Central America. The exercises grew larger and longer in duration; by 1984 they had become virtually continuous, leading some congressional critics to conclude that the exercises were a facade for the permanent stationing of U.S. forces in the region.

THE SEARCH FOR PEACE

As the U.S. policy of hostility toward Nicaragua unfolded, Mexico became increasingly fearful that the conflict in Central America might spiral out of control, leading to direct U.S. intervention. To avert such a catastrophe, President López-Portillo on several occasions offered Mexico's good offices as an intermediary between Nicaragua and the United States. In December 1981 Haig traveled to Mexico City to confer with López-Portillo, and the Mexicans agreed to convey the Reagan Administration's concerns to Nicaragua.

Mexico's mediation led to a meeting between Haig and Nicaraguan Foreign Minister Miguel D'Escoto in St. Lucía just prior to the OAS General Assembly. Haig raised the two issues that had been discussed by Enders in the August-October exchanges—Nicaragua's arms buildup and its aid to the Salvadoran guerrillas—but he also added a new issue: U.S. concern over the decline of political freedom inside Nicaragua. D'Escoto repeated earlier Nicaraguan denials that it was aiding the Salvadorans or that it had any intention of acquiring MIG fighter aircraft—a charge that had been made repeatedly by administration spokesmen. Little more than a restatement of positions on both sides, the meeting had no salutary effect.[40]

The Mexicans, however, were not prepared to give up. Having failed in their attempt at quiet diplomacy, they launched a more public effort. Speaking in Managua in late February, López-Portillo warned of the "three knots of tension" in Central America: the conflict in El Salvador, the hostility between the United States and Nicaragua, and the hostility between the United States and Cuba. He offered Mexico as mediator to help launch negotiations around each of these issues.

Nicaragua, Cuba, and the Salvadoran opposition quickly accepted the López-Portillo initiative. The United States was less interested. President Reagan, in a major address to the OAS given the week after López-Portillo's proposal, made no reference to the Mexican plan. Administration spokesmen told the press that no improvement in relations with Nicaragua were possible until the Sandinistas stopped aiding the Salvadoran guerrillas.[41]

Congress, however, responded positively to the Mexican initiative; 106 members of the House of Representatives signed a letter to Reagan urging him to accept the Mexican plan. The administration was forced at least to pronounce its receptivity to the initiative, lest it appear to be the major obstacle to peace in the region. After a series of meetings between U.S. and Mexican officials, the administration finally agreed to allow Mexico to convey the U.S. position to Nicaragua. The agenda of U.S. concerns was essentially the same as what Haig had presented to D'Escoto in December. Nicaragua responded immediately that it was willing to discuss all the issues raised by the United States and set forth an agenda of its own as well. The United States, however, was not prepared to begin discussions until after the Salvadoran election in late March.

The Salvadoran election was a benchmark for U.S. policy in Central America. With the war in El Salvador going badly, the administration had wagered a great deal on the outcome of the elections. They would, it was hoped, convince the Congress to continue its support of administration policy. In that regard at least, the election proved to be a great success. In their wake, the administration's attitude toward Nicaragua hardened perceptibly. U.S. officials told reporters that the administration would not open direct discussions with Nicaragua until it halted its aid to the Salvadoran guerrillas, regardless of the Mexican proposals. Yet even this position was something of a façade. One official explained the administration's attitude toward the López-Portillo initiative: "We were cool to the initiative from the beginning, but we were effectively ambushed by Congress and public opinion. We had to agree to negotiate or appear unreasonable."[42]

In fact, the administration had no interest in negotiating with Nicaragua. The text of a National Security Council planning document written during this period summarizes U.S. policy as stepping up pressure on Nicaragua, isolating Mexico, and "coopt[ing] the negotiations issue." No mention is even made of the López-Portillo initiative.[43]

Contacts between Nicaragua and the United States under the auspices of the López-Portillo plan limped along until August 1982, with Nicaragua constantly urging that negotiations be started and the United States refusing. Finally, in August the administration abandoned even this pretext; Nicaragua's diplomatic note of August never recieved a reply.

During July and August 1982, Nicaraguan exiles launched a series of major attacks against Nicaragua from their base camps in Honduras. As rumors of war between Nicaragua and Honduras swept the region, President Herrera Campins of Venezuela and López-Portillo appealed to Nicaragua, Honduras, and the United States to take swift diplomatic action to avert the outbreak of war. It was the first joint Mexican-Venezuelan initiative on Central America and marked a change from Venezuela's previous support of U.S. policy.

The Mexican-Venezuelan letter proposed measures to reduce the border tensions between Nicaragua and Honduras and urged the United States to upgrade its diplomatic contacts with Nicaragua. Once again, congressional support for the initiative was strong. President Reagan's response, however, was noncommital. In his reply to Herrera Campins and López-Portillo, he reiterated U.S. policy and the proposals made a few weeks earlier at a meeting of the Central American Forum for Peace and Democracy—a successor to the Central American Democratic Community and, like its predecessor, a creation of U.S. diplomatic efforts to isolate Nicaragua. Without the support of the United States, nothing came of the Mexican-Venezuelan initiative.

CONGRESS AND THE COVERT WAR

The covert war against Nicaragua changed in several important ways during the summer and fall of 1982, and these changes produced a growing concern in Congress about the ultimate intent of U.S. policy. As Argentina gradually withdrew from the region in the wake of the Falklands/Malvinas war, the CIA assumed control over the exile army that Argentina had been constructing. The military assistance provided by the United States transformed the exile forces from a ragtag collection of small, independent groups numbering fewer than 1,000 men in total into a well-equipped and professionally trained army of some 4,500 by July 1982. Calling itself the Nicaraguan Democratic Force (FDN), it increased the size and frequency of its forays into Nicaragua during the summer of 1982.[44]

Most of the attacks came across the eastern and central portions of the Nicaraguan-Honduran border, far from the purported arms-smuggling routes in the west. This, combined with the contras' disclaimer that they were trying to interdict arms, made it difficult for the Reagan Administration to keep up the fiction that the purpose of the covert war was to interdict arms flowing from Nicaragua to the Salvadoran guerrillas. In the fall of 1982 the administration changed the basic rationale for the covert war, at least as it was presented to Congress. Direct arms interdiction was replaced by the stated objective of harassing and punishing Nicaragua in order to convince the Sandinistas to end their support for the Salvadoran insurgency. As one administration official explained, "it became clear that cutting the roads from Nicaragua was not enough. It was necessary to raise the cost to the Sandinistas and the Cubans of meddling in El Salvador."[45]

In practice, harassment meant exile attacks on border towns, economic targets, and Nicaraguan army posts—exactly the sorts of operations originally proposed by the CIA in November 1981 to overthrow the Nicaraguan government, and rejected for that reason. With this change in U.S. strategy, the line between harassing Nicaragua to get the Sandinistas to behave and trying to overthrow them became difficult to discern since the operations being mounted served either purpose equally well. In practice, the line disappeared completely since both the U.S. officials running the operations and the contra commanders carrying them out were dedicated to deposing the Nicaraguan regime. By the fall of 1982, the contra army in Honduras was already three times the size of the CIA invasion force at the Bay of Pigs. By mid-1984 it would be almost ten times as large.

As the covert war widened, both the House and Senate Intelligence Committees began to worry that the operation was spiraling out of control. In an effort to hold the CIA to its original objective of arms interdiction, the committees added language to the Classified Annex of the 1983 Intelligence Authorization Act prohibiting U.S. aid to paramilitary groups "for the purpose of overthrowing the Government of Nicaragua or provoking a military exchange between Nicaragua and Honduras."[46]

This language, signed into law in August 1982, was not designed to bring the covert operation to a halt. On the contrary, it was intentionally crafted to register the Intelligence Committees' unease while at the same time allowing the covert war to continue. The Reagan Administration was able to interpret it as allowing support for the contras so long as the purpose of the United States was not among those proscribed by the law. The administration continued to assert that its purpose was merely to halt the flow of arms, so even though the recipients of the CIA's largesse were trying to overthrow the Sandinistas, the law did not make them ineligible for assistance.

This mild restriction remained a secret until December when Representative Tom Harkin (D-Iowa) offered an amendment to the Defense Appropriations Bill (which included appropriations for intelligence activities) to prohibit U.S. assistance to any group involved in paramilitary actions against Nicaragua. Representative Edward Boland (D-Massachusetts), Chairman of the House Intelligence Committee, offered as a substitute for Harkin's amendment the language that had earlier been included in the Intelligence Authorization Act. The Republican leadership, seeking to avoid a vote on the Harkin amendment, supported Boland's substitute, which passed 411-0 and was eventually signed into law.[47]

The administration continued to expand the covert war during the early months of 1983, and the issue returned to the top of the congressional agenda as the war escalated. In March, 1,500 exile troops invaded Nicaragua. Though they were thrown back to Honduras, the new attacks prompted a series of stories in the U.S. press documenting the continued U.S. involvement in training, financing, arming, and advising the exiles.[48]

The new revelations convinced several members of Congress that the administration's real intention was to overthrow the Sandinistas, in violation of the Boland amendment. Daniel Patrick Moynihan (D-New York), Vice-Chairman of the Senate Intelligence Committee, reported that a number of his colleagues on the Committee shared that suspicion. Senator Patrick Leahy (D-Vermont) traveled to Central America on behalf of the Intelligence Committee to investigate U.S. operations and upon his return said that it appeared to him the administration was ignoring the intent of Congress. Representative Wyche Fowler (D-Georgia) conducted a similar investigation for the House Intelligence Committee and returned with the same conclusion. Finally, Boland himself declared that the evidence was "very strong" that the administration was violating the amendment bearing his name.[49]

The pervasive and growing congressional suspicion of the administration's conduct of the covert war led the House Intelligence and Foreign Affairs Committees to propose the Boland-Zablocki amendment to the 1984 Intelligence Authorization Act, an amendment that effectively cut off all funds for the covert war against Nicaragua. On July 28, after several days of bitter debate, the House of Representatives passed the Boland-Zablocki amendment by a vote of 228-195.[50]

The Republican majority in the Senate, however, was not prepared to halt the war. Eventually, the House and Senate reached a compromise whereby the administration received $24 million (about half its initial request) to keep the covert war going from October 1983 to June 1984. In June the administration returned to Congress seeking an additional $21 million, which the Senate again approved. The House, however, was willing to compromise no further; the administration was unable to secure additional funds for the war during 1984. A final congressional review of the issue was slated for March 1985.

The congressional rebellion against the covert war was rooted in a variety of issues: the ineffectiveness of the operation in achieving its stated goals, its counterproductive effects, its tenuous legality, and, perhaps most important, the apparent contempt in which the administration held congressional prerogatives.

The ineffectiveness of the covert war in actually interdicting arms shipments from Nicaragua to El Salvador was apparent early on—no significant amount of arms was ever captured. Virtually no one even within the administration was willing to argue that the operation could actually overthrow the Sandinistas. Moreover, the operation seemed counterproductive in a number of ways. It tended to polarize the internal political situation in Nicaragua, contributing to a reduction of political freedom for the opposition while at the same time rallying the population in support of the Sandinistas. Internal economic difficulties could be, and were, rationalized as the fault of the United States and its Somocista allies. In effect, all the warnings articulated by people within the Reagan Administration who had initially opposed a major commitment to the covert war came true.

Internationally, the covert war angered U.S. allies in Latin America and Europe, and raised the danger of open warfare between Nicaragua and Honduras—a war the Honduran economy was in no shape to sustain. Moreover, the covert war was such an obvious violation of U.S. treaty obligations under the OAS Charter, the Rio Treaty, and the United Nations Charter that the standing of the United States in the international community as a whole suffered considerably as the war intensified.

But the issue that ultimately led the House of Representatives to repudiate the war was one of institutional prerogatives. The quality of the administration's reporting to the Intelligence Committees was so poor that members simply stopped believing what they were told. Their efforts to restrain the operation were ignored or circumvented by convoluted interpretations of the law, until they felt there was no alternative but to bring the whole operation to a halt.

PREPARING FOR WAR

By early 1983, the Reagan Administration's Central American policy was in crisis. The war in El Salvador was slowly but surely being lost to the guerrillas, the contras had made no military progress against the Sandinistas, and the U.S. Congress was growing restive at the ever-escalating cost of a policy that had yet to show any signs of success. This crisis produced a showdown inside the administration between the relative moderates in the State Department, led by Enders, and the hard-liners in the White House, led by National Security Advisor William Clark and U.N. Ambassador Jeane Kirkpatrick. Various tactical and strategic policy differences divided the two factions, but perhaps the most fundamental issue was whether the United States could prevail in Central America through a strategy of containment (that is, winning the war in El Salvador and containing Nicaragua), or whether the United States would have to roll back "communism" in Nicaragua by removing the Sandinista regime. The hard-liners won, Enders was fired, and the State Department lost control over policy in Central America to the National Security Council, the CIA, and the Department of Defense.

The practical effect of the hard-liners' victory was quickly apparent. In August, just after the House of Representatives voted to halt the covert war, the United States launched Big Pine II, the largest and longest military exercise in Central American history. It lasted seven months and at its height, two carrier battle groups stood off the shores of Nicaragua. The Pentagon also announced a series of further exercises that, taken together, meant virtually continuous manuevers through 1988. Displaying a sardonic sense of humor, the administration dubbed the exercises after Big Pine II as Granadaro I, no doubt to remind the Sandinistas that the invasion of Grenada began as a naval "exercise."[51]

The newly ascendant hard-liners moved to step up the covert war as well. The CIA was authorized to expand the contra forces to 15,000 men—an army larger than the National Guard the Sandinistas defeated in 1979. It was also at this point that CIA operatives took direct control of sabotage operations against Nicaraguan ports and oil storage facilities.[52]

The intensification of the war was accompanied by an intensification by other countries of the search for peace. In January 1983, Mexico and Venezuela joined with Panama and Colombia to form the Contadora group (named for the Panamanian island where it first met). Fearful that the United States was moving inexorably toward direct military intervention, the four nations hoped their joint efforts might succeed at finding a diplomatic solution for the Central American crisis. In a number of meetings with the foreign ministers of the five Central American nations, the Contadora states made some modest progress. In September the Central American nations, meeting under the auspices of Contadora, reached agreement on 21 objectives in the areas of security, economic cooperation, and politics. In January 1984 these principles were spelled out in greater detail, and working groups were formed to draw up formal accords for implementing them.

In the area of security, where agreement was most difficult to achieve, the basic objectives of Contadora were to remove Central America as much as possible from the East-West rivalry, and to begin to demilitarize the area. The 21 points called for a prohibition on foreign military bases and troops, a reduction of foreign military advisors, a halt to the regional arms race, and an end to external support for insurgencies.

Despite verbal support for the process, the posture of the Reagan administration was a major obstacle for Contadora. In the first place, the United States continued its military buildup in Honduras and El Salvador, as well as its support for the contras, despite the fact that these actions ran counter to the objectives espoused by Contadora. Moreover, the United States consistently held that any diplomatic agreement would have to be both multilateral and comprehensive—that is, all the Central American nations would have to agree on all issues before any agreement on any issue could be concluded.

Although the United States had no direct participation in Contadora, its influence in Honduras and El Salvador gave it the ability to effectively block any agreement that did not suit its policy. The Reagan Administration insisted that a necessary part of any agreement would be a verifiable pledge by the Sandinistas to hold free and fair elections that met Washington's definition of pluralism.[53]

Until June 1984, the administration consistently refused to reply to Nicaraguan diplomatic initiatives, characterizing them as Sandinista efforts to subvert Contadora. In June, however, the United States suddenly reversed itself and agreed to begin bilateral talks with Nicaragua. Those talks lasted until early 1985, when they were abruptly terminated by the United States.

As the United States entered its own 1984 election campaign, the policy of the Reagan Administration toward Nicaragua seemed to be consolidated and well-defined: to depose the Sandinista government. Indeed, administration spokesmen, including the President himself, had come close to saying so explicitly on several occasions. Deputy Secretary of Defense Fred Ikle called repeatedly for "military victory" for the "forces of democracy" in Central America, and he warned that the continued existence of the Sandinistas would require a partitioning of Central America analogous to the partitioning of Europe.[54] President Reagan referred to the contras as "freedom fighters" at every opportunity and announced his doubt that peace could be restored to the region as long as the Sandinista government survived.[55] Finally, the Kissinger Commission, which offered the most complete rationale for Reagan's Central American policy, concluded that a policy of "static containment" toward Nicaragua was unacceptable, that the Sandinistas would remain a permanent threat to peace in the region unless the character of the Nicaraguan regime were changed. The Commission held out the vague hope that the Sandinistas might somehow agree in negotiations to remove themselves from power but, failing that, it noted that force would remain the "ultimate recourse" for achieving U.S. objectives.[56]

The Reagan Administration's dilemma, however, was how to implement this policy. The covert war, under growing attack in the Congress, had not succeeded in posing any serious military threat to the Sandinistas. The economic embargo had damaged the Nicaraguan economy but had not brought it to collapse. The other nations of Central America showed little interest in reviving the Central American Defense Council as an instrument for use against the Sandinistas. In short, Reagan's policy of hostility seemed incapable of achieving its goal. By late 1984 it seemed clear that the second Reagan Administration would have to face the choice of tolerating the Nicaraguan Revolution or intervening directly and massively to exterminate it.

NOTES

1. For a detailed discussion of U.S. policy toward Nicaragua during the insurrection, see William M. LeoGrande, "The United States and the Nicaraguan Revolution," in *Nicaragua in Revolution*, edited by Thomas W. Walker (New York: Praeger, 1982), pp. 63–77.

2. For a more detailed discussion of Cuban relations with Nicaragua during the first year after Somoza's fall, see William M. LeoGrande, "Cuba and Nicaragua: From the Somozas to the Sandinistas," in *The New Cuban Presence in the Caribbean*, edited by Barry B. Levine (Boulder, Colo.: Westview, 1983), pp. 43–58.

3. *Review of the Presidential Certification of Nicaragua's Connection to Terrorism*, Hearings before the Subcommittee on Inter-American Affairs of the Committee on Foreign Affairs, House of Representatives, 96th Cong., 2d sess., September 30, 1980 (Washington, D.C.: U.S. Government Printing Office, 1980).

4. *Newsweek*, July 20, 1980.

5. See, for example, Jeane Kirkpatrick, "Dictatorships and Double Standards," *Commentary*, November 1979, pp. 34–35; and the Committee of Santa Fe, *A New Inter-American Policy for the Eighties* (Washington, D.C.: The Council, 1980).

6. New York *Times*, December 11, 1980.

7. The administration made its case public with the release of U.S. Department of State, *Communist Interference in El Salvador*, Special Report No. 80, February 24, 1980. This report so exaggerated the available evidence that it was severely criticized in the press. The two major critiques appeared in the *Wall Street Journal*, June 8, 1981, and the Washington *Post*, June 9, 1981.

8. New York *Times*, September 13, 1980.

9. Washington *Post* and New York *Times*, February 29, 1981.

10. Washington *Post*, March 3, 1981.

11. Washington *Post*, March 13, 1981.

12. Washington *Post*, April 29, 1984.

13. Ibid.

14. Washington *Post*, March 4 and 16, 1982.

15. Ibid., and New York *Times*, December 3, 1981.

16. Haig's recommendations are discussed in the New York *Times*, November 11, 1981. The objections to them from the military are discussed in the Washington *Post*, March 4, 1982.

17. Washington *Post*, March 4, 1982.

18. For details of the programs approved in early 1981, see *Newsweek*, November 2, 1982, and the New York *Times*, April 8, 1983. Regarding the less-controversial elements of the program approved in December 1981, see the New York *Times*, March 14, 1982, and March 11, 1983.

19. New York *Times*, March 14, 1982. The *Times* obtained copies of both the option papers developed by the CIA for the National Security Council meetings in November and the Presidential Finding signed by Reagan in early December. See also New York *Times*, March 17, 1982, and Washington *Post*, March 10, 1982.

20. Ibid.

21. Washington *Post*, February 14, 1982; New York *Times*, November 2, 1982; Philadelphia *Inquirer*, February 16, 1983.

22. The elements of this debate are recounted in the New York *Times*, December 4 and 19, 1982.

23. New York *Times*, March 14, 1982, and April 8, 1983; Washington *Post*, March 10, 1982; and *Newsweek*, November 2, 1982.

24. Philadelphia *Inquirer*, February 16, 1983.

25. *Newsweek*, November 2, 1982.

26. New York *Times*, March 14, 1982, and April 8, 1983.

27. Ibid.; and *Newsweek*, November 2, 1982.

28. Washington *Post*, March 25, 1984.

29. Ibid.

30. *Wall Street Journal*, April 6, 1984; *Christian Science Monitor*, May 4, 1984.

31. For examples of rhetoric from Haig and Meese, see the New York *Times*, November 23, 1981. López-Portillo's reaction is reported in the Washington *Post*, November 25, 1981.

32. The text of Haig's OAS address is reprinted in the New York *Times*, December 5, 1981.

33. New York *Times*, February 21, 1982, and March 5, 1982.

34. The text of the briefing is included in the New York *Times*, March 10, 1982.

35. Ibid.

36. *U.S. Intelligence Performance on Central America*, Permanent Select Committee on Intelligence, House of Representatives (Washington, D.C.: U.S. Government Printing Office, 1982).

37. Washington *Post*, March 13, 1982.

38. Washington *Post*, January 8, 1982.

39. *United States–Honduras Relations* (Washington, D.C.: Central American Historical Institute, 1984).

40. New York *Times*, December 3, 1981.

41. Washington *Post*, February 24, 1982.

42. New York *Times*, May 10, 1982.

43. The text of the document is printed in the New York *Times*, April 7, 1983.

44. *Newsweek*, November 2, 1982.

45. Ibid.

46. *Congressional Record*, August 11, 1982, p. H9156.

47. Ibid., pp. H9148–H9159.

48. See, for example, the stories in the New York *Times*, April 3, 1983, and the Washington *Post*, April 3, 4, and 5, 1983.

49. Senator Moynihan's views were reported in the New York *Times*, April 1, 1983; Senator Leahy's in the Washington *Post*, April 8, 1983; and Congressman Boland's in the New York *Times*, April 14, 1983.

50. Ibid., July 29, 1983.

51. *United States–Honduras Relations*.

52. *Wall Street Journal*, April 6, 1984; *Christian Science Monitor*, May 4, 1984.

53. William Jesse Biddle, *U.S.–Nicaragua Talks: Going Through the Motions* (Washington, D.C.: Center for International Policy, 1983).

54. Remarks by Fred C. Ikle, September 12, 1983, News Release, Department of Defense.

55. New York *Times*, April 12, 1984.

56. *Report of the National Bipartisan Commission on Central America* (Washington, D.C.: U.S. Government Printing Office, 1984).

Chapter 22
Relations with the Communist States

THEODORE SCHWAB

HAROLD SIMS

In the first half decade following the Sandinista victory Nicaragua developed close ties with many of the Communist states. Tracing the development of these relations will enable us to speculate why such ties advanced. It is our contention that these relations developed in response to challenges and in a timely fashion.

THE KEY REGIONAL RELATIONSHIP: CUBA AND NICARAGUA

The Communist state with which Nicaragua developed the closest ties was Cuba. Their relations may be divided into three areas: economic, military, and international, but perhaps of greatest importance were economic relations. During the period from July 1979 through 1982 Cuban economic assistance came to total $286 million.[1] This aid was in two forms: emergency assistance and economic and technical aid.

Cuba provided large-scale emergency assistance on two occasions. The first occurred immediately after the FSLN victory of July 1979. By means of daily shipments, by Air Brittania, Cuba delivered both material aid and personnel. The material assistance included food, medical supplies, and equipment for emergency hospitals. Cuban volunteers departing for Nicaragua included doctors, nurses, medical technicians, and health administrators. Within weeks, several hundred Cuban health workers had arrived.[2] Cuba also rushed emergency assistance in June 1982 in response to the worst floods of the twentieth century. Again Cuban aid came in the form of both material and human assistance. On this occasion Cuban volunteers were more important and more numerous. The stature of the delegation members who arrived to survey the damage and design relief

The authors wish to thank George Reid Andrews, William Chase, Eldon Kenworthy, David Scott Palmer, and Thomas W. Walker for their criticisms of an earlier draft of this chapter.

programs testified to the importance of the Cuban initiative. Led by Vice-President and Defense Minister Raúl Castro, the first contingent of volunteers included representatives from Cuba's Ministries of Transportation, Education, Construction, Communications, and the Revolutionary Armed Forces. In addition, on this occasion 2,000 Cuban workers were dispatched to Nicaragua.[3]

Just as Cuba's human assistance was far greater in the wake of the May 1982 floods, so was its material aid. Once all relief programs were in place, Cuban assistance was valued at $80 million, an amount unsurpassed by any other international donor. Cuban-sponsored programs provided the materials, equipment, and manpower necessary to reconstruct bridges, a hospital, housing, and roads.

Cuba consistently provided development aid as well. Economic and technical assistance came in several areas, most notably education and health. Cuba helped design and implement the educational system by providing scholarships for Nicaraguans to study in Cuba, supplying Cuban professors and primary school teachers, and providing advice in the design of programs.

By July 1980 Nicaragua and Cuba had signed an educational cooperation agreement providing for the services of 1,000 Cuban primary school teachers, 40 university professors, and scholarships for 3,000 Nicaraguans to study in Cuba. As a result, the Minister of Education, Carlos Tunnerman, could announce that Nicaragua would develop educational programs based upon the Cuban model. The Sandinistas soon made good Tunnerman's promise by bringing in Cuban administrators to reorganize the national university.[4] The Cubans made fundamental academic and administrative changes, especially in curriculum planning. When some 17 Nicaraguan professors dissented from the Cuban reorganizational scheme, the university administration simply dismissed them.[5]

The Literacy Crusade was another important program that, at least partially, followed the Cuban model. Four Cubans helped administer the campaign from Managua, and 1,000 Cuban primary school teachers served as instructors.[6] By 1983, 1,000 more Cubans were teaching in Nicaragua and scholarships for study in Cuba had grown to 12,000.[7] While the number of Cuban teachers was still increasing in early 1983, by the end of the year their numbers had temporarily diminished. At the urging of the Sandinistas, Cuba began removing some of its personnel (teachers, as it turned out) in November 1983, partly on rotation, possibly in an effort to forestall a U.S. invasion similar to the one in Grenada. In mid-March 1984, 1,500 additional Cuban teachers began arriving, to work in rural areas unaffected by contra attacks. This followed the return in February of 1,600 young Nicaraguans, trained in Cuba, to begin literacy work among campesino children.[8]

Another crucial aspect of Cuban aid was medical assistance. Moving beyond the task of emergency relief, Cuban medical aid took on a development role. Through the donation of human, material, and technical assistance, Cuba helped Nicaragua develop and implement its public health programs. Cuban human assistance grew rapidly during the months immediately following the victory: By the end of 1979, some 400 Cuban doctors, nurses, medical technicians, and health administrators served in Nicaragua. The number continued to grow, reaching 500 in 1981, 600 in 1982, and 900 in 1983.[9] Cuba also denoted material medical aid, building a 150-bed hospital in Managua during 1982, for example.[10] Nicaraguan doctors received training in Cuba, and by July 1980 many were already returning to serve in the public health system, while others continued to study in Cuba.[11]

By January 1982, according to Bayardo Arce, the *comandante* in charge of creating the FSLN party, in four and one-half years, "Cuba ha[d] sent 2,000 teachers each year and a total of 1,500 doctors who ha[d] provided five million medical consultations, performed 65,000 operations and delivered 30,000 babies."[12]

Cuba contributed economic and technical assistance in areas other than education and health. According to Arce, these include the "mining, fishing, forestry and sugar industries, road construction, food production, and other areas, including military affairs."[13] In 1980 Cuba provided assistance to Nicaragua's state bureaucracy and industries. The government statistics center was one such bureaucracy that by April 1980 was receiving Cuban aid. In addition, Cuba contributed logistical support to the Ministries of Education and Health by ferrying supplies and equipment to the education and health workers serving in the Nicaraguan hinterlands.[14]

Cuban industrial development assistance also arrived in two forms: technical assistance for industries and training in Cuba for Nicaraguan technicians. The poultry industry, for example, was receiving Cuban aid by March 1980. Meanwhile, Nicaraguan technicians were training in a Cuban civil aviation center as well as on the Isle of Youth.[15]

In 1981, Cuban construction workers began building a 426-kilometer coast-to-coast highway from Puerto Cabezas to western Nicaragua. In addition, aid to the sugar industry included the construction of a sugar mill, the loan of Cuban canecutters, donations of equipment, and the provision of sugar credits.[16]

During 1982–83, established Cuban assistance programs were augmented and efforts developed in new areas. Examples of the former were the construction of an additional sugar mill plus assistance in constructing another highway, originating in Nueva Guinea. Examples of the latter included the participation of Cuban advisors in the Nicaraguan dairy and fishing industries, the media, the Ministry of Planning, and the Foreign Ministry.[17]

In 1983, the Cubans built yet another highway, extending from Managua to northeastern Nicaragua. In addition, the two countries launched a joint effort in the shipping industry. Cuba sent an additional 1,500 technicians, some of whom worked in Nicaragua's new hydroelectric and telecommunications facilities, recently constructed by the Soviets and the Bulgarians.[18]

Nicaragua's military ties with Cuba became vital to the relationship. Increasing military collaboration included the provision of advisors, arms, and training for Nicaraguan military personnel, the coordination of Nicaraguan and Cuban efforts in the training and apparently the arming of El Salvador's FMLN (Farabundo Martí National Liberation Front) and the construction of extensive military facilities.[19]

From its founding in 1961 until 1979, the FSLN had received both arms and training while in exile in Cuba. In the months immediately following the July 1979 victory, Cuban training of FSLN cadres continued, both in Cuba and in Nicaragua. In October 1979 the FSLN acknowledged that Cubans advised the Popular Sandinist Army. By December, 120 Nicaraguans were receiving military training in Cuba. Upon completing their courses, these cadres would return to Nicaragua to train and lead the militias.[20]

In addition to increasing to 700 the number of advisors serving the Nicaraguan military, in 1981 Cuba sent arms including tanks, attack helicopters, and ground-to-air missiles. The Sandinistas also approached Cuba to acquire MIG fighters, but aircraft were not sent, possibly because of U.S. warnings.[21] These developments may have tipped the balance in Washington in favor of authorization for U.S. support for a contra army, a decision that was reached in November 1981.

During 1982, Cuban collaboration began in an even more controversial area: the arming and training of El Salvador's FMLN. Nicaraguan and Cuban officers instructed the FMLN in Nicaragua, and Cuban war material was apparently channeled through Nicaragua to guerrillas in El Salvador.[22]

Cuban military assistance escalated dramatically in 1983. In addition to constructing dozens of military bases, Cuba greatly increased its arms shipments. The importance attributed to the relationship was signaled by the arrival in June of Cuba's top combat commander, General Armando Ochoa Sánchez, on the first of several such visits. It also merits mention that the thousands of Cuban workers in Nicaragua pledged to defend the country against a U.S. invasion as their comrades did in Grenada.[23]

Cuba and Nicaragua also drew closer in their international relations. Cuba was calling for national and international solidarity with the FSLN long before the rebel victory. In June and early July 1979, Fidel Castro made numerous appeals for Cubans and people around the world to support the Sandinista Revolution. A show of Cuban solidarity came soon after the July 1979 victory when representatives of the Government of National Reconstruction (GRN) and the FSLN leadership were guests of honor at Cuba's annual July 26 ceremony. In 1980 Fidel Castro promised Cuba's "unswerving" support and Nicaragua responded by giving Castro a prominent role in the first anniversary celebration of the FSLN victory.[24]

The two countries also established intergovernmental ties. The first links between the GRN and its Cuban counterpart were formalized on July 23, only four days after the FSLN victory. During the first year members of the GRN made numerous trips to Cuba for discussions with Castro and other leaders.[25] This may have contributed to the convergence of the foreign policies of Cuba and Nicaragua. On July 29, 1979, the GRN requested admission to the Nonaligned Movement then led by Cuba, and in April 1980 Nicaragua refused to accept antigovernment Cuban refugees.[26]

Close ties with Cuba were made all the more likely by the Reagan Administration's selective economic boycott launched in 1981 and, especially, by its patronage of military efforts beginning in January 1982 to punish the Sandinista regime for its ideology and foreign policy. Cuba and Nicaragua eliminated visa requirements in October 1981.[27] The most important development of 1981 may have been Humberto Ortega's declaration in August that "Marxism is the scientific doctrine that guides our revolution . . . our doctrine is Marxism-Leninism." The Sandinista military chief may have signaled the first Marxist state in Central America.[28] While Daniel and Humberto Ortega, Bayardo Arce, Henry Ruiz, and other Sandinist leaders were espousing Marxist principles, they were allowing Cubans to occupy key positions in the regime. There was a sizable Cuban presence in the Ministry of the Interior, the Armed Forces, and the Foreign Ministry, to cite only the most important cases. Nicaraguan and Cuban officials asserted that by cooperating in the running of their Foreign Ministries, for example, the two states could benefit from each other's experience.[29]

While the foreign policies of Nicaragua and Cuba had been in harmony on most issues since 1979, the two nations were clearly coordinating many aspects of their foreign policies by 1982. Their votes were often identical in the United Nations and other international forums and they jointly supported and served as spokesmen for El Salvador's FMLN in its efforts to gain recognition through negotiations.

By 1983 the Sandinistas were publicly declaring the permanence of Nicaragua's relations with Cuba. Both Daniel Ortega and Bayardo Arce articulated this long-range commitment, stating that their government's Cuban relations were "nonnegotiable."[30] We should not be surprised by this, for as Tomás Borge asserted more than once, Cuban assistance was free.

SOVIET-NICARAGUAN RELATIONS

Nicaragua's Soviet ties, like those with Cuba, can be considered under three categories: economic, military, and international. Economic relations consist of three components: emergency aid, economic and technical assistance, and trade.

Nicaraguan-USSR relations were most highly developed in economic and technical assistance. On October 18, 1979, the day diplomatic relations were formalized, the Soviet ambassador proposed several long-term economic agreements. Interestingly, while these pacts were offered in 1979, they would not be signed until 1981, awaiting, perhaps, the launching of the U.S. economic "boycott."[31] Long before the agreements were promulgated, however, Soviet economic and technical cooperation had begun. In 1980, for example, Nicaraguan technicians were already training in the USSR, and Soviet research vessels were surveying ocean resources, as geologists explored Nicaragua's mineral resources. Also, TASS (the Soviet News Agency) technicians had begun to advise the Nicaraguan government's media organs.[32]

In April 1981, seemingly in response to the Reagan Administration's punitive economic policies, the first economic-technical pacts were formalized. Among the first to be signed was a fishing and ocean resources agreement that called for the training of Nicaraguan technicians as well as the establishment of research and repair facilities. By the end of 1981 several other pacts had been signed, including one to enhance the development of radio and television services. A second aspect of Soviet economic assistance commenced in September 1981: The USSR provided $50 million in concessionary trade credits to finance the importation of Soviet heavy machinery.[33]

During 1982, following the Reagan Administration's unleashing of CIA-supported contras, Soviet assistance increased dramatically. A large component of the increase came in May when Daniel Ortega led a sizable delegation of government and FSLN officials to Moscow and signed several pacts worth an estimated $166.8 million. While no balance-of-payments assistance was forthcoming, these agreements called for the construction of two hydroelectric plants and a 400-bed hospital, an additional $100 million in trade credits, and the installation of radio transmitters and a ground-based telecommunications receiver (similar to one just installed in Cuba) that would link Nicaragua with the Soviet Inter-Sputnik system. An important part of the new agreements was a joint Soviet-Bulgarian project to develop a deep-water port at El Bluff and an inland waterway system utilizing the Río Escondido to Rama. In addition, the USSR provided a grant of $31 million to help develop small industry. To carry out these projects, the Soviets sent numerous scientists and technicians.[34] A major new project was the construction in 1983 of a drydock in San Juan del Sur to be used by the Soviet tuna fleet.[35]

USSR donations, which began arriving shortly after the FSLN victory, were of three kinds: educational, health, and food assistance. During 1980 the Soviets assisted Nicaragua in its educational endeavors by providing scholarships and material assistance to the Literacy Crusade. Donations to the latter included 10,000 pairs of shoes, boots, and glasses; 20,000 notebooks; 1,000 radios; and the loan of two helicopters and crews that were used to ferry supplies to the instructors serving in the hinterlands of Nicaragua.[36] By 1981 USSR donations to Nicaragua's education programs were considerable: The Soviets built vocational schools in León, Matagalpa, and Managua, and the total of scholarships reached 300.[37] Scholarships increased to 1,000 in 1982, 30 of which were utilized for the training of math professors.[38] By 1983, Soviet educational aid included a direct contribution to the Nicaraguan educational fund.[39]

Unlike USSR educational aid, Soviet medical assistance remained small, growing only in response to the floods of May 1982. The first Soviet medical donations arrived in October 1979. On that occasion and again in May and September 1981, the USSR donated millions of vaccinations.[40] In response to the flood disaster, the Soviets sent $30 million in emergency relief, including both medical equipment and personnel. Thirty medical professionals, a field hospital, medicines, and other equipment arrived on a Soviet airlift early in June. The USSR also donated emergency assistance to the Red Cross.[41]

The Soviet Union contributed large quantities of food as well. Beginning in spring 1981, when the Reagan Administration halted U.S. government financing of wheat sales to Nicaragua, the USSR began shipping wheat. By June 1984 the total of these shipments had reached 50,000 tons.[42]

Nicaragua and the Soviets also established trade relations. From 1980 to 1984 trade increased dramatically. While both Nicaraguan exports to the USSR and Soviet exports to Nicaragua grew, the latter exceeded the former by a wide margin. In fact, Nicaragua's trading position with the USSR and Eastern Europe deteriorated from a $23 million surplus in 1980 to a $28 million deficit in 1982.[43] And this increased in January 1984 when the Soviets delivered 10,000 barrels of aviation fuel and 15,000 barrels of kerosene to Corinto, while 240,000 barrels of Soviet crude were expected at Puerto Sandino.[44]

Nicaragua's exports to the Soviet Union began in January 1980 with the initiation of coffee sales. Later that year and again in 1981 Nicaraguan trade delegations visited the USSR to promote increased exchange. By fall 1981 their efforts were rewarded when Nicaragua began importing large quantities of Soviet machinery, a trend that continued in 1982.[45]

Much of Soviet imports were financed by concessionary trade credits. Between 1979 and December 1983, these credits amounted to $215.9 million. Soviet terms of trade for the credits were concessionary, ranging between 2.5 and 5 percent interest, with a repayment period of from 10 to 25 years. Some credit arrangements included grace periods of up to five years.[46]

By fall 1983 the Soviets claimed to have placed a hold on concessionary credits to Nicaragua. In fact, the trade credit projected for the three-year period 1983–85, $100 million, was less than half of the amount extended during the four-year period 1979–82. Perhaps this reflects the difficulty Nicaragua would have in repaying larger sums, as evidenced in its debt payment suspension with its neighbors and Mexico and Venezuela. A Soviet decision to cut back would have caused dismay among the Sandinists who had repeatedly requested more credits.[47]

The USSR and Nicaragua also developed extensive military relations. During 1981–82, with the advent of the hostile Reagan Administration, USSR military involvement expanded considerably. Defense Minister Humberto Ortega met with Marshall Ustinov in Moscow in December 1981.[48] According to the U.S. State Department, Soviet vessels brought 10,000 tons of armaments each year, including tanks, antiaircraft guns, armored cars, artillery, and other ordnance. It is important to note that these arms were not altogether gratis, as payment was sometimes made in hard currency.[49] Shipments sent between 1979 and 1982 have been valued at $125 million by U.S. intelligence sources.[50] During 1983, Soviet military aid increased dramatically, as arms shipments doubled, reaching 20,000 tons for the year.

Nicaragua's international relations with the USSR grew as well. By October 1979 the Soviet ambassador was urging the FSLN to establish ties as rapidly as possible with the USSR and the Sandinistas responded with calls of their own for closer relations. The Union of Journalists of Nicaragua was admitted to the communist International Organization of Journalists (along with their Ethiopian and Kampuchean [Cambodian] counterparts) in November 1979.[51] Three Sandinist decisions in 1980 reflected the rapprochement. First, in the United Nations and other international forums, the Sandinistas abstained on the question of the Soviet invasion of Afghanistan. Second, the GRN refused to admit Polish Solidarity spokespersons and took the Soviet-Cuban line in its press treatment of the Polish labor movement. Finally, there was an agreement between the USSR and Nicaragua to institute regular flights by Aeroflot.[52]

During 1981 the FSLN made direct political contacts for the first time with the Soviet Communist Party (CPSU). Bayardo Arce, for example, met with CPSU chief Konstantin Chernenko in October 1981.[53] In March 1981 a delegation from the FSLN participated (as a "front") in the twenty-sixth annual congress of the CPSU, an occurrence that Ambassador Shliapnikov declared (incorrectly) to be unprecedented in Soviet history. Later in October, Bayardo Arce, in charge of creating the Sandinista political party, returned to the Soviet Union for additional talks with the CPSU.[54] As such party-to-party ties developed, some FSLN leaders openly claimed that the Sandinista Revolution was based on Marxist-Leninist principles.

The political committee of the FSLN held additional meetings during 1982 with the CPSU, and other Sandinista leaders proclaimed their commitment to Marxism-Leninism. It is worth noting that Hugo Torres, Head of the Political Leadership of the Popular Sandinista Army, made such claims most vigorously on the eve of the major trek to Moscow of May 1982, during which the Soviets granted Nicaragua sizable aid. Moreover, the official slogan launched for May Day 1982 declared that Nicaragua favored "the construction of socialism." Consider, for example, the $50 million of trade credits of September 1981 that followed the August 1981 proclamation, and, also, the $166.8 million pact of May 1982 that followed a similar proclamation in April. This pattern suggests that Soviet aid may have been facilitated by the Sandinista commitment to socialism.[55]

There were other signs in 1982–83 of growing relations between Nicaragua and the USSR. In March 1982 the two nations signed an agreement to establish additional Soviet consulates and to facilitate the acquisition of travel visas. Moreover, prior to the May 1982 Moscow visit, the FSLN affiliated its mass youth, women's, and labor organizations with their respective Soviet-sponsored international bodies. And the Sandinista press supported the Soviets in the incident involving the shooting down of a Korean airliner, while Nicaragua abstained on the UN vote.[56] There can be little doubt that the FSLN party saw itself as "fraternally" linked to the CPSU, as well as to its Cuban counterpart.

NICARAGUA'S RELATIONS WITH EAST EUROPEAN STATES

Next in importance were relations with Bulgaria, though they did not develop until 1980. It appeared, in fact, that Bulgaria would play a major role in Nicaragua, in harmony with the USSR, just as it had in Cuba.[57] Nicaragua's Bulgarian relations developed much like those with Cuba and the USSR, including economic, military, and international aspects. Economic relations may be subdivided into three elements: donations, economic-technical cooperation, and trade.

During the summer of 1980, Bulgaria sent medical donations worth $500,000. Later that year a protocol was signed establishing a framework for future donations and other assistance. Bulgarian donations grew to $20 million in 1981.

Economic-technical cooperation also commenced in 1980, and two major cooperation pacts were signed. The first provided for the construction and maintenance of a dam on the Yeye River, while the other established joint Nicaraguan-Bulgarian enterprises in the canning and leather industries, raised the number of scholarships, and increased the level of trade credits.[58] By 1981 another agreement was reached providing technical assistance to the food-processing industry. Bulgaria sent wheat in response to the U.S. credit freeze. The two states signed cooperation pacts in April, May, June, and July 1982, alloting technical assistance to agriculture, the fishing, forestry, and mining industries, providing for equipment deliveries, a $10 million loan to the telecommunications industry, and the financing of the joint Bulgarian-Soviet construction project to develop a deep-water port and inland waterway from El Bluff to Rama. Then, during 1983, yet another cooperation agreement was signed substantially increasing assistance, including a trade credit of $140 million to be spread over 1983–85.[59]

Nicaragua and Bulgaria also established trade relations in 1980. By January, Nicaragua had begun exporting coffee to Bulgaria and in 1981–82 the latter reciprocated with canned goods. These and other commodities were financed by trade credits that by the end of 1982 had reached $37 million. In March 1983 the two countries signed a new trade agreement.[60]

Bulgaria also launched military training programs. During 1982 the Reagan Administration became preoccupied by reports of Nicaraguan pilots training in Bulgaria. In 1983 military assistance included the training of additional pilots and the transport of arms from Communist countries.[61]

Nicaraguan-Bulgarian international relations included direct contacts between the Bulgarian Communist Party (BCP) and the FSLN, as well as intergovernmental discussions.[62] Bayardo Arce met with representatives of the BCP in 1980 and 1981. In December 1980 a BCP delegation met in Nicaragua with the Political Committee of the FSLN and members of the GRN. In October 1981 Arce visited with representatives of the BCP in Bulgaria. Then in late 1981 yet another BCP delegation met with the FSLN in Nicaragua.[63] Just as the Sandinistas established firm ties with the Cuban and Soviet ruling parties, they met just as frequently with the Bulgarian Party.[64] These frequent party-to-party contacts tended to cast doubt on the possibility of the FSLN pursuing the "Mexican path" in the future.

Soon after the victory of 1979, Nicaragua established relations with the German Democratic Republic (GDR). Though the GDR provided immediate medical aid for seriously wounded Sandinistas, Nicaragua's relations with that country were primarily economic and intergovernmental. Economic relations with the GDR, like those with the USSR, may be divided into three categories: donations, economic-technical cooperation, and trade.

East German donations began arriving in August 1979, with a shipment of medical supplies valued at 1 million marks. By 1981, GDR donations had reached $100 million, part of which came in the form of wheat shipments begun in 1981 in response to the U.S. credit freeze. Another portion of the total represented educational aid. The GDR contributed $1 million in June 1982, following the floods. In 1983, GDR donations included the installation of an electronics workshop and a Christmas gift of 40,000 tons of toys.[65]

The GDR began its economic and technical cooperation with Nicaragua soon after the first donations arrived. In early September 1979 the GDR pledged to construct textile factories in Nicaragua. During 1981, economic-technical cooperation increased with the signing of three more cooperation pacts in three areas: public health, transportation, and education.[66] Trade relations with the GDR commenced in 1980, when Nicaragua began importing trucks and exporting coffee.[67] In addition, Nicaragua held intergovernmental discussions with GDR Communist Party chief Honecker and other officials on several occasions.[68]

Nicaragua developed relations with Hungary in 1980, though these were limited to economic ties and intergovernmental discussions. Hungarian economic aid to Nicaragua was of two types: donations and economic-technical cooperation. In September 1980 Hungary provided a number of scholarships. By 1981, $5 million in donations had arrived, some destined for the mining industry.[69] Economic and technical cooperation began when a team of public health and regional planning experts arrived.[70] Intergovernmental discussions also commenced in 1981 and were held annually thereafter.[71]

Relations with Poland and Romania were initiated during 1980. As of 1983, these were limited to trade, with coffee exports beginning in 1980.[72] Romania was supplying police cars to Nicaragua by 1983.[73]

Relations with Czechoslovakia (CSSR) began in 1981 with economic, military, and international assistance. Economic relations involved donations, economic and technical cooperation, and trade. The CSSR made several contributions amounting to $35 million in 1981, and donations continued in 1983.[74] Czech economic-technical assistance also began in 1981. As of 1982, two major economic-technical pacts had been signed, one in May 1981 and another in January 1982.[75] Nicaraguan-CSSR trade also began during 1981. By December the Czechs had financed $40 million in exports, including heavy production equipment, trucks, and textile plants. During 1982–83 additional exports were financed, with the terms formalized in agreements of January 1982 and July 1983.[76]

Czech military relations encompassed both the arming and training of the Popular Sandinista Army. The program began in 1981 when 35 Nicaraguans received flight training in the CSSR. In 1983 the Czechs sent several SL 39 pilot "trainers."[77] Arms shipments also commenced in 1983 when the Nicaraguan army received new Czech rifles.[78] International relations had progressed by December 1981 to the point where a consular agreement eliminated the need for travel visas.[79] In both 1982 and 1983 the two states held intergovernmental talks as well.[80]

RELATIONS OUTSIDE THE SOVIET BLOC

Nicaragua's contacts with Yugoslavia were limited to economic and intergovernmental relations. Yugoslavia provided economic assistance by offering a $40 million loan, to help the struggling state through its debt crisis, and by assisting in the development of Nicaragua's agriculture, especially its corn production. Intergovernmental discussions with Yugoslavia occurred in 1979, 1980, and 1982.[81]

Relations with Vietnam were limited to intergovernmental discussions and military assistance. Early talks occurred with Premier Pham Van Dong, on the occasion of his visit in September 1979. Military support was evident from the use of Vietnamese-style defenses in the north at Ocotal. In response to a call of March 13, 1984, by the GRN for arms and military supplies, Vietnam responded affirmatively, pledging "its indestructible solidarity."[82]

The People's Republic of China (PRC) commenced relations with Nicaragua in 1980, after ties were established with most of the East European states. Contacts with the PRC were linked to trade and intergovernmental relations. A traditional supplier of cotton to China, Nicaragua continued to trade with the PRC in 1980. In fact, in that year the Chinese offered to buy all of Nicaragua's cotton exports. Intergovernmental talks began in 1980 as well, and discussions continued in 1981.[83] Chinese ties were not publicized in Nicaragua since then. Aid was never contemplated but in 1984 China still purchased one-third of Nicaragua's cotton crop.[84]

North Korea was the final Communist state to develop relations with Nicaragua in 1981. The ties were limited to intergovernmental discussions and trade, which grew considerably after 1981. North Korean exports amounted to just $1 million in 1981, but by 1983 trade had reached $30 million, financed by the Koreans.[85] Intergovernmental discussions began in summer 1980, and new talks were held in spring 1982.[86]

While the GRN recognized the People's Republic of Kampuchea in summer 1979, there is no evidence of trade or aid, in either direction. The same may be said in the cases of Mongolia and Albania.

THE QUANTITATIVE DIMENSION SUMMARIZED

The GRN reported that by July 1982, 18 percent of its loans had come from the Soviet bloc, while by December 1982, 11.9 percent of imports and 7.7 percent of exports were tied to bloc states.[87] These totals appear low in light of the extensive projects and programs noted in this chapter. One explanation would be that Cuban aid and trade, as well as all military and security training and supplies, were excluded from these figures. Moreover, donations, technical assistance, and aid other than loans were excluded as well.

Our survey of promised economic assistance to Nicaragua by 11 Communist states during 1979–83 resulted in a surprising total value of $1,216,450,000. Broken down into categories, the figures (in millions) were $451 in economic aid, $423.9 in concessionary trade credits, $193.75 in donations, $81 in nontrade-related loans, and $66.8 in technical assistance.[88] These are often long-term projects and programs extending at least through 1985, and we suspect that much of the funding had not yet been expended by 1984. The absence of hard currency to assist in meeting Nicaragua's balance-of-payments problem with the West is also notable.

Economic assistance totals for 1979–83 resulting from our survey for each of the 11 Communist states were (in millions), in rank order: USSR $443.7, Cuba $286, Bulgaria $232.5, the GDR $103.25, Czechoslovakia $75, Yugoslavia $40, North Korea $31, and Hungary $5. In the cases of Poland, Romania, and the People's Republic of China no actual values were reported. The total for the seven states traditionally defined as the Soviet bloc was $859.45 million.

THE MODUS OPERANDI OF NICARAGUAN-COMMUNIST STATE RELATIONS

Nicaragua's ties to Communist states evolved as the result of a combination of internal and external forces. Among the internal forces were challenges to the Revolution—for example, the destruction that occurred in Nicaragua in the course of the 1978–79 insurrection, plus the May 1982 floods. Recovery was an immediate necessity. In both of these cases, the FSLN turned to the Communist states, among others, for emergency relief. Once the immediate crisis passed, the FSLN was faced with the challenge of developing social programs. Communist states' assistance to the Nicaraguan educational and public health systems helped the Sandinistas meet the former, while economic and technical assistance from these sources helped the FSLN face the latter challenge. The Sandinistas claimed that by helping to make Nicaragua less dependent on international supplies of oil and high-priced imported finished goods, economic and technical assistance from the Communist states helped Nicaragua to achieve real economic growth during 1983.[89]

Another challenge was the ideological and pragmatic imperative to develop and equip a revolutionary armed forces. To do this the FSLN needed to reorganize and professionalize its military and deploy standardized weapons. Through the training of personnel and the provision of arms, the Communist states helped the new authorities in Managua achieve this goal.

Yet another challenge, the urge to develop enduring revolutionary institutions and a strong centralized state, led the FSLN to establish close ties with Communist states. Advice in these matters, especially concerning the creation of mass organizations, state-controlled labor unions, and a revolutionary party, helped the FSLN to assure its continuation in power.

While the need to develop revolutionary institutions explains why Nicaragua would look to other national models for guidance, it does not explain why the FSLN chose, in particular, the Communist states to serve as revolutionary models. One factor that helps explain the decision is the commitment of certain key Sandinista leaders—including some still-active ex-Insurrectional Tendency leaders—to Marxist-Leninist principles. Given this commitment, it was only natural for such leaders to choose institutional models based on these ideological principles, though the result proved to be a variation on previous revolutionary models.

It is evident, then, that the development of Nicaragua's economic, military, and international ties were motivated by internal challenges to the Revolution. However, to understand why these challenges led the Sandinistas to deepen their relations with the Communist states, rather than limit their ties to within the Western alliance and especially the United States, one must note the external factors constraining decisions made by the FSLN Directorate. Of greatest importance were the foreign policies of the United States and the USSR. Quite simply, since the Sandinist victory in July 1979, an increasingly hostile U.S. policy led to a deterioration of U.S.-Nicaraguan relations, while supportive Communist state policies contributed to the growth of Nicaraguan-Communist state ties.[90]

Nicaragua's economic relations with the latter developed following this pattern. While the Carter and Reagan Administrations were attempting to alter the course of the Revolution by making the delivery of U.S. aid contingent upon U.S.-dictated changes, Communist Party states gave

Nicaragua "untied" aid tailored to its needs (and to the economic plans of the Sandinista leaders). This encouraged the FSLN to act in a manner calculated to maximize benefits to be derived from Communist state relations (and to rely increasingly upon the West European and Third World states, as treated elsewhere in this volume). The result was a serious diminution of Nicaraguan-U.S. economic relations and the steady growth of such relations with the Communist states.[91]

Nicaragua's military ties to the Communist countries also developed according to this pattern. Immediately following the victory, the FSLN petitioned the United States to provide arms and training for the armed forces.[92] The Carter Administration declined and encouraged its European allies to do likewise. When all but the French complied with the U.S. request, the Sandinistas were left with virtually no weapons sources and were thus pushed into a dependence on Soviet bloc arms. The Reagan Administration's behavior, in turn, forced the Sandinistas to increase the magnitude of bloc arms shipments. By launching and escalating paramilitary campaigns against the Sandinistas in early 1982, and building up the arsenals of Honduras, the United States compelled an already security-conscious FSLN to prepare to defend its Revolution. Most military aid consisted of training and material involved in these defense preparations.

Nicaragua's international ties with the Communist states flourished in direct proportion to the deterioration of U.S.-Nicaraguan relations. While the Carter Administration implicitly denied the legitimacy of the FSLN regime, as is reflected by the attempts to alter its complexion, the Reagan Administration explicitly denied the legitimacy of the Sandinista government, portraying it as a totalitarian, Soviet-imposed dictatorship. Given these hostile views on the part of U.S. policymakers, it was impossible for Nicaragua to foster cordial ties with the United States. Hence, ironically, it would have been unwise for the FSLN to turn solely to the West in search of political and social institutional models.

Communist state policies, on the other hand, fostered cordial relations with the Sandinistas and Nicaragua. By encouraging and supporting the FSLN, both rhetorically and materially, they curried Nicaragua's favor. In the resulting environment, in fact, support by the Communist states became vital. As a result, the Sandinistas were encouraged to study Communist institutional models and to return the favor in the form of frequent support for Cuba and the USSR in international forums.

As of 1984 Nicaragua had little reason to expect direct Cuban and Soviet military support in case of a U.S. invasion—both Communist states had made that clear.[93] How much credit and economic assistance the Communist states could provide remained to be seen. Nicaragua's growing external indebtedness (up from $1.6 billion in 1979 to over $3.4 billion in 1984) could result in repayment postponements, as occurred in the Cuban case. According to our figures, at least $524.9 million was owed to the Communist states by 1984. The Council of Mutual Economic Assistance (COMECON) appeared ready in spring 1984 to embark upon programs and projects in Nicaragua whose cost could rise substantially in the future.[94] By spring 1984, then, all indications were that the limits of Communist state support for Nicaragua had by no means been reached.

NOTES

1. Managua, Radio Sandino (RS), March 27, 1981, in *United States Foreign Broadcast Information Service, Latin American Report (FBIS/LA)*, March 27, 1981; *La Prensa (LP)* (Managua), August 1, 1982.

2. Madrid EFE, August 11, 1979; Havana Domestic Service (HDS), August 13, 1979; Havana International Service (HIS), August 22, 1979, in *FBIS/LA*, August 13–14, 1979 (*FBIS* cited hereafter by dates only, in parentheses).

3. *Barricada Interacional (BI)* (Managua), June 7, 1982; *La Nación Internacional (LNI)* (San José), June 4, 1982.

4. HDS, August 24, 1979 (August 27, 1979), and William LeoGrande, "Cuba and Nicaragua," *Caribbean Review*, Winter 1980, p. 48.

5. Managua Domestic Service (MDS), October 3, 1979 (October 9, 1979); HDS, October 25, 26, 27, 1979 (October 29, 1979).

6. *Barricada* (Managua), October 14, 1979 (October 23, 1979); LeoGrande, "Cuba and Nicaragua," p. 48, and Valerie Miller, "The Nicaraguan Literacy Campaign," in *Nicaragua in Revolution*, edited by Thomas W. Walker (New York: Praeger, 1982), pp. 241–58.

7. HDS, April 6, 1982; MDS, April 6, 1982 (April 7, 1982).

8. *This Week: Central America and Panama* (Guatemala City), March 19, 1984; *BI*, February 20, 1984.

9. HIS, July 25, 1979 (July 26, 1979); HDS, August 13, 1979 (August 14, 1979); HIS, August 22, 1979 (August 23, 1979); HDS, September 8, 1979 (September 10, 1979); MDS, April 16, 1982 (April 21, 1982); HIS, September 4, 1982 (September 6, 1983).

10. *LP*, August 1, 1982; *Miami Herald (MH)*, June 24, 1983.

11. *El Nuevo Diario (END)* (Managua), July 10, 1980 (July 30, 1980); HDS, January 26, 1981 (January 27, 1981).

12. *BI*, January 16, 1984.

13. Ibid.

14. *END*, October 23, 1980; *Barricada*, March 27, 1980 (April 4, 1980).

15. MDS, September 1, 1979 (September 7, 1979); *LP*, September 23, 1979 (October 2, 1979); HDS, March 17, 1980 (March 18, 1980).

16. HDS, September 30, 1980 (October 14, 1980); HDS, February 5, 1981 (February 5, 1981); RS, March 24, 1981 (March 26, 1981); HDS, April 4, 1981 (April 8, 1981); RS, June 14, 1981 (June 16, 1981); RS, March 27, 1981 (March 30, 1981).

17. HIS, December 23, 1981 (December 24, 1981); MDS, April 7, 1982 (April 16, 1982).

18. *END*, June 30, 1983 (July 8, 1983); New York *Times (NYT)*, June 19, 1983.

19. Paris, Agence Français de Presse (AFP), July 25, 1979 (July 26, 1979); LeoGrande, "Cuba and Nicaragua," p. 44. A guerrilla leader in El Salvador told the San Diego *Union* (March 1, 1981) that "the Salvadoran guerrillas have a permanent commission in Nicaragua overseeing the smuggling of weapons from that country to here." In March 1982 the Reagan Administration provided "hard evidence" of a gun-running operation from Nicaragua to

Salvadoran guerrillas for a "blue ribbon group, including 26 prominent officials of past Republican and Democrat administrations" (MH, March 12, 1982). The sophisticated means whereby evidence is electronically captured is described in "Radio Link for Latin Leftists." *NYT*, April 22, 1984, confirming information we obtained from outgoing ambassador Anthony Quainton, Pittsburgh, April 10, 1984. U.S. charges are backed by "Western European and Latin American diplomats" interviewed by Stephen Kinzer, *NYT*, April 11, 1984. The United States is not intercepting such shipments; rather it is simply recording air and sea traffic.

[The editor of this volume would like to go on record as disputing the charges made by Washington. He argues that (1) Quick, closed-door presentations to one blue ribbon group and to the House Intelligence Committee ought not to be seen as definitive proof of anything. Even the discredited "White Paper" of 1981 would likely have "held water" if presented in a similar way to the same carefully selected audiences rather than being exposed to public scrutiny. (2) There is no common border between Nicaragua and El Salvador. War material would have to cross the Gulf of Fonseca (where the United States stationed electronically equipped naval vessels throughout the period) or be transported by air (in full "sight" of an ultramodern U.S. radar blanket that sees literally all takeoffs and landings throughout the Isthmus), or be carried overland across Honduras (the base of operations for the multimillion dollar, CIA-coordinated contra activities designed explicitly to "interdict" such arms flows). Had a significant amount of arms been moving from Nicaragua to El Salvador, numerous interceptions would surely have taken place. Virtually all evidence from such seizures could easily have been made public without endangering U.S. intelligence operations. However, from late winter of 1981 through the summer of 1984, no evidence of this sort was presented. The most logical conclusion, therefore, is that the arms flow, if it existed *at all*, was trivial. This conclusion was corroborated in mid-1984 when David C. MacMichael until a few months previously, a CIA employee involved in Central American planning—made a series of public statements to the effect that the CIA itself had no evidence of such an arms flow in the previous three years. From an interview of MacMichael on CNN, June 11, 1984.]

20. Panama City, Agencia Centro Americana de Noticias, (ACAN), October 23, 1979 (October 25, 1979); Paris AFP, January 8, 1980 (January 11, 1980).

21. Buenos Aires Latín, (news agency), December 2, 1981; RS, December 2, 1981 (December 3, 1982); *La Nación (LN)* (San José), November 30, 1981; Washington *Post (WP)*, November 19, 1982.

22. The admission by Tomás Borge and others in November 1983 that some 2,000 Salvadorans connected with the FMLN were present gave credence to the U.S. claim that an FMLN "command and control center" existed in Managua. The state-financed Mario Carrillo "fishing cooperative," according to its own members, had been used as a base for arms shipments (WP, September 29, 1983).

23. MDS, October 25, 1983 (October 27, 1983); *NYT*, June 19, 1983.

24. HDS, June 22–23, 1979 (June 25, 1979); HDS, July 23, 1979 (July 24, 1979); Paris AFP, June 3, 1980 (June 4, 1980).

25. HDS, July 23, 1979 (July 24, 1979); MDS, August 28, 1979 (August 29, 1979); HDS, February 29, 1980 (March 3, 1980).

26. Belgrade Domestic Service, July 27, 1979 (July 30, 1979); RS, April 16, 1980 (April 17, 1980).

27. MIS, October 25, 1981 (October 27, 1981).

28. See, for example, quotes from the speech of Humberto Ortega in August 1981 to a group of military officers, cited in *La Nación* (San José) and *Est et Ouest* (Paris), August 25, 1981, and in *O Estado de São Paulo* (Brazil) October 10, 1981: "Marxism-Leninism is the scientific doctrine that guides our revolution. Our Vanguard's analytic tool for . . . carrying out the revolution . . . We cannot be Marxist-Leninist without Sandinism. Without Marxism-Leninism Sandinism cannot be revolutionary. Thus they are indissolubly linked. . . . Our

political strength is Sandinism and our doctrine is Marxism-Leninism." Hugo Torres, speaking before the Society for Friendship with Socialist States (and the Soviet ambassador) in April 1982, stated that "the principles of Marxism-Leninism wisely applied to the reality of our society guided the revolutionary actions of the FSLN." (MDS, April 23, 1982) [April 28, 1982]. See also RS, February 26, 1983 (February 28, 1983). On the ideological content of various FSLN speeches, see MH, November 26, 1981. On the May Day speeches of 1982, see WP, May 5, 1982. In Spring 1984 FSLN leaders insisted to Secretary of State George Schultz's emissary, Ambassador Otto Reich, that they h ad never made such statements. (Interview, Ambassador Reich, Washington, D.C., April 4, 1984.)

29. HIS, December 3, 1981 (December 24, 1981); Paris AFP, November 15, 1981.

30. HIS, September 4, 1983 (September 6, 1983); BI, January 16, 1984.

31. HDS, October 19, 1979 (October 23, 1979); RS, July 13, 1981 (July 14, 1981); Managua: Sistema Sandinista de Televisión (MSSTV), September 9, 1981 (September 10, 1981); RS, September 7, 1981 (September 11, 1981).

32. MSSTV, July 31, 1980 (August 1, 1980); MDS, August 5, 1980, Barricada, July 30, 1980 (August 6, 1980); RS, September 19, 1980 (September 23, 1980).

33. BI, May 10, 1982; RS, July 13, 1981 (July 14, 1981); MSSTV, September 9, 1981 (September 10, 1981); RS, September 7, 1981 (September 11, 1981). Cole Blasier has argued that Soviet credits are not aid but "inducements to buy Soviet goods, similar to Export-Import Bank credits." See his The Giant's Rival: The USSR and Latin America (Pittsburgh: University of Pittsburgh Press, 1983), p. 66.

34. Barricada, September 2, 1982; BI, May 16 and 31, 1983; RS, December 20, 1982 (December 21, 1982); Latin America Weekly Report (LAWR) (London), May 14, 1982; MH, May 11, 1982; Pittsburgh Post Gazette (PPG), May 11, 1982; Wall Street Journal (WSJ), May 11, 1982.

35. PPG, June 1, 1983.

36. RS, September 19, 1980 (September 23, 1980); Managua Radio Corporación, October 30, 1980 (October 31, 1980).

37. RS, October 15, 1981 (October 15, 1981).

38. Barricada, September 2, 1982.

39. FBIS/LA, April 24, 1983.

40. MDS, October 19, 1979 (October 23, 1979); END, April 26, 1981 (May 5, 1981); Paris AFP, September 29, 1981 (September 30, 1981).

41. MDS, June 3, 1982 (June 7, 1982); MIS, September 15, 1982 (September 16, 1982).

42. LNI, November 24, 1983; La Voz de Nicaragua (LVN) (Kansas City, Mo), June 4, 1984.

43. Baltimore Sun, August 28, 1983.

44. PPG, January 27, 1984. By April 1984 the Soviets were supplying 25 percent of Nicaragua's oil needs and the U.S.-owned Esso refinery was processing Soviet crude. (Interview, Ambassador Quainton, Pittsburgh, April 10, 1984.)

45. MIS, August 9 and 15, 1981; LP, August 14, 1981 (August 17 and 18, 1981); La Prensa (San Pedro Sula), August 23, 1982 (August 24, 1982); MDS, December 17, 1982 (December 19, 1982).

46. Barricada, September 2, 1982; RS, August 28, 1983 (August 29, 1983); END, November 14, 1982; Deputy Planning Minister Vázquez, quoted in La Prensa (San Pedro Sula), August 23, 1982 (August 24, 1982). Ambassador Quainton asserted that Soviet terms are not so concessionary: down payment is sometimes required in hard currency and repayment commences immediately. (Interview, Pittsburgh, April 10, 1984.) This is similar to public statements by the Soviet trade representatives but differs from official comments in the Sandinista press.

47. RS, August 28, 1983 (September 1, 1983); END, November 14, 1982. In late 1982

sources in the Soviet Union told Cole Blasier that "the total package" of export credits extended to Nicaragua consisted of just $150 million (see Los Angeles *Times*, December 16, 1982). Our total is $215.9 million through 1982. According to Stephen Kinzer (*NYT*, March 28, 1984), Soviet-Nicaraguan aid early in 1984 was actually up 25 percent over 1983: The trend may be the reverse of what was indicated by Soviet spokespersons, therefore (see Baltimore *Sun*, July 28, 1983).

48. RS, December 1, 1981 (December 2, 1981).

49. Interview, Ambassador Quainton, Pittsburgh, April 10, 1984.

50. U.S. Department of State, *Current Policy Statement 476* (Washington, D.C., April 12, 1983); *WP*, July 2, 1983.

51. HDS, October 19, 1979 (October 23, 1979). On International Organization of Journalists admission, see the *Daily World* (New York: U.S. Communist Party), November 24, 1979.

52. Panama City ACAN, January 20, 1980 (January 23, 1980); MDS, February 8, 1980 (February 11, 1980); RS, April 7, 1980 (April 8, 1980); *LP*, July 6, 1980 (July 12, 1980); *END*, July 5, 1980 (July 14, 1980). On the Solidarity incident, see "Is Nicaragua Independent?," *The Nation* (New York), March 13, 1982.

53. RS, October 29, 1981 (November 3, 1981).

54. *Barricada*, February 23, 1981 (February 27, 1981); RS, October 17, 1981 (October 19, 1981). Historian William Chase contends that Schliapnikov is in error concerning this "precedent."

55. MDS, April 23, 1982 (April 28, 1982); MDS, June 7, 1982 (June 8, 1982). See *WP*, May 5, 1982 on the May Day rallies.

56. RS, March 2, 1982 (March 3, 1982); *NYT*, May 30, 1982; *The Times of the Americas* (*TA*) (Washington, D.C.), October 14, 1983.

57. MSSTV, July 11, 1980 (July 30, 1980); *LP*, August 15, 1980 (September 28, 1980); *Barricada*, December 21, 1980 (December 31, 1980); RS, January 28, 1981 (January 29, 1981); MDS, April 7, 1982 (April 9, 1982); HIS, October 12, 1981 (October 12, 1981).

58. *LP*, August 15, 1980 (August 28, 1980); *Barricada*, December 21, 1980 (December 31, 1980).

59. RS, January 4, 1982 (January 7, 1982); Managua Radio Mundial (MRM), July 15, 1982 (July 16, 1982); *Financial Times* (*FT*) (London), March 17, 1983; MDS, April 7, 1982 (April 7, 1982); *LNI*, June 4, 1982; *PPG*, June 1, 1983.

60. RS, January 28, 1981 (January 29, 1981); MDS, April 7, 1982 (April 9, 1982); Panama City Televisora Nacional, March 12, 1983 (March 16, 1983); RS, January 26, 1980, *LNI*, July 22, 1982.

61. *NYT*, March 27, 1983; *PPG*, March 6, 1983.

62. RS, October 29, 1981 (November 3, 1981).

63. RS, September 30, 1980 (October 2, 1980); RS, December 23, 25, 1980 (December 30, 1980); *FBIS/Eastern Europe*, April 3, 1981; RS, October 29, 1981 (November 3, 1981); RS, December 3, 1981 (December 7, 1981); *END*, September 20, 1982 (October 1, 1982); *FBIS/Eastern Europe*, November 24, 1982; HIS, December 24, 1982 (December 28, 1982).

64. RS, July 8, 1983 (July 9, 1983).

65. *Daily World*, November 10, 1979; East Berlin International Service, July 31, 1979 (August 1, 1979); RS, June 29, 1981 (July 1, 1981); *LP*, October 16, 1981 (October 28, 1981); MDS, June 14, 1982, RS, June 11, 1983 (June 17, 1983); *LVN*, December 5, 1983.

66. MDS, September 6, 1979 (September 7, 1979); RS, May 15, 1981 (May 21, 1981); *Barricada*, December 4, 1981 (December 11, 1981); *END*, December 24, 1981 (December 30, 1981).

67. HIS, June 17, 1980 (June 19, 1980); RS, June 26, 1980. For a summary of Nicaraguan-GDR exports, see *FBIS/LA*, January 19, 1982.

68. *FBIS/Eastern Europe*, April 7, 1980 and June 16, 1982; MSSTV October 13, 1981

(October 16, 1981); RS, October 29, 1981 (November 3, 1981); RS, February 12, 1983 (February 16, 1983).

69. RS, September 19, 1980 (September 23, 1980); RS, December 7, 1981 (December 10, 1981); HIS, October 12, 1981 (October 16, 1981).

70. MIS, February 6, 1981 (February 6, 1981).

71. RS, November 13, 1981 (November 17, 1981).

72. RS, January 26, 1980 (January 29, 1980).

73. RS, January 26, 1980 (January 29, 1980); San José Radio Reloj, March 14, 1983 (March 18, 1983).

74. RS, July 24, 1981 (July 29, 1981); RS, November 12, 1981 (November 13, 1981); RS, August 25, 1983 (August 26, 1983); HIS, October 12, 1981; RS, August 26, 1983.

75. Barricada, April 23, 1981 (May 5, 1981); RS, January 6, 1982 (January 7, 1982).

76. END, November 24 and December 19, 1981 (December 28, 1981); LP, October 24, 1981 (November 4, 1981); RS, January 6, 1982 (January 7, 1982); MSSTV, July 7, 1983 (July 12, 1983); LP, October 24, 1981 (November 4, 1981).

77. HIS, June 20, 1983 (June 21, 1983).

78. Panama City ACAN, October 20, 1983.

79. END, December 19, 1981 (December 24, 1981).

80. RS, October 6–7, 1982 (October 8, 1982); MDS, November 30, 1982 (December 1, 1982); HIS, January 23, 1983 (January 25, 1983).

81. Panama City ACAN, March 19, 1980 (March 20, 1980); RS, June 22, 1982 (June 23, 1982).

82. MDS, September 14, 1979 (September 14, 1979); Intercontinental Press (New York: Socialist Workers' Party), October 1, 1979; LNI, March 29, 1984.

83. RS, September 10, 1980 (September 11, 1980).

84. Interview, Ambassador Quainton, Pittsburgh, April 10, 1984.

85. FBIS/Asia and Pacific, March 17, 1982, MDS, March 17, 1982 (March 18, 1982).

86. RS, June 10, 1980 (June 12, 1980); MDS, April 12, 1982 (April 15, 1982).

87. This estimate is from Envío, 13 (Managua: Instituto Histórico Centroamericano, July 1982).

88. The Cuban data are for 1979–82. Many projects and programs were publicly assigned no monetary value and could not be added to our totals. The value of technical assistance is clearly understated. We utilized only the statements of offical spokespersons and the official media in Nicaragua, Cuba, and the USSR for our numbers.

89. MDS, September 6, 1979 (September 7, 1979); Klaes Brundenius, University of Pittsburgh, January 19, 1984.

90. Richard Ullman, "At War with Nicaragua," Foreign Affairs (Fall 1982), pp. 39–58.

91. Central American Historical Institute, A Chronology of Nicaraguan-U.S. Relations (Washington, D.C., 1983).

92. Harold Sims, "Revolutionary Nicaragua. Dilemmas Confronting Sandinistas and North Americans," in Confrontation in the Caribbean Basin: International Perspectives on Security, Sovereignty and Survival, edited by Alan Adelman and Reid Reading (Pittsburgh: Center for Latin American Studies, 1984), pp. 51–78.

93. Interview, Ambassador Quainton, Pittsburgh, April 10, 1984.

94. Nicaragua signed an agreement with COMECON in September 1983, obtaining "observer" status, and attended the 37th session of COMECON, held in Berlin, in October 1983. COMECON Vice-Minister Angel Chauchev led a delegation to Nicaragua in February 1984 "to organize scientific, technical and cultural cooperation." Nicaragua thus became one of "over 90" states receiving such aid. See BI, February 20, 1984; LVN, March 9, 1984.

Chapter 23
Relations with the Nonaligned Movement

WALTRAUD QUEISER MORALES

HARRY E. VANDEN

I will not abandon my struggle while my people have one right yet to win. My cause is the cause of my people, the cause of America, the cause of all oppressed peoples.

Augusto César Sandino

We have, from the very outset, been consistently opposed to bloc politics and foreign domination, to all forms of political and economic hegemony.

Josip Broz Tito
Sixth Summit, Nonaligned Movement

The nonaligned movement was born in the postcolonial period as increasing numbers of Third World nations sought to establish a direction in their foreign policy that would allow them to ensure their political—if not economic—independence in a world that was increasingly dominated by the two great powers. The roots of the movement extend back to 1955 when a group of Afro-Asian states met as a group to denounce colonialism, promote economic development, and call for a relaxation in world tensions. Josip Broz Tito, one of the early founders of the movement, aligned Yugoslavia with the new group, attacking the division of the world into two hostile camps. In the first formal meeting of the Nonaligned, 25 nations gathered in Belgrade in 1961 and focused on the need for world peace. Subsequent Nonaligned summit conferences (Cairo in 1964, Lusaka in 1970, Algiers in 1973, Colombo in 1976, Havana in 1979, and New Delhi in 1983) continued to mention the importance of an independent foreign policy and nonparticipation in Cold War military pacts (despite

The authors wish to thank Mary K. Meyer for assisting with initial research for this chapter. Harry E. Vanden gratefully acknowledges previous field research support from the Division of Sponsored Research of the University of South Florida.

Pakistan's alignment with the United States, and Cuba's eventual ties with the Soviet Union).

Yugoslavia and a growing number of Third World nations used the new grouping as a mechanism to chart their own course in foreign policy and development. The evolution of the movement witnessed increasing concern over political hegemony and economic domination, particularly from Western powers. Thus as the focus shifted from world peace and a scrupulous equidistance from East and West, the new emphasis became solidarity with anticolonial struggles, the political economy of the New International Economic Order, and open criticism of perceived Western domination in political or economic areas.[1] Support for liberation movements gradually became the primary focus of the movement with some nations like Yugoslavia and Algeria warning of U.S. and Soviet imperialism (the two-imperialisms thesis) and others like Cuba arguing that the socialist countries were natural allies. "By the 1970's the movement itself had become so radicalized that Cuba's views were widely shared," thus challenging the scrupulous neutralism of the earlier years.[2]

THE INTER-AMERICAN SYSTEM

If conditions were changing rapidly in Africa and Asia, traditional aspects of the Inter-American system made nonalignment quite a different story in the Western Hemisphere. From the 1823 Monroe Doctrine onward, the United States reserved an hegemonic position for itself. It was the first among equals and as such enjoyed certain rights and responsibilities that did not accrue to lesser states. The development and subsequent expansion of the North American economy coincided with a series of State Department initiatives that culminated in the creation of a Pan American system that helped to legitimize the special status of the largest member of the Inter-American family. As the industrial growth in the North outstripped the rural agrarianism of the South, the Latin American nations witnessed a variety of policy instruments: the big stick, gun boat and dollar diplomacy, and finally the good neighbor policy. Though the methods might vary, the end result was always the same: Convince the Latin American states to follow the U.S. lead. When more subtle methods failed, American presidents often sent in the Marines to secure the North American position. Such was the case in Nicaragua where Marines intervened from 1912 to 1925 and from 1926 to 1933. The last occupation was in response to Augusto César Sandino's Army in Defense of Nicaraguan National Sovereignty.

Sandino and his guerrilla fighters tried to establish a nationalist regime that could pursue independent domestic and external policies. The modest achievements of the first six years of the Sandinista struggle, however, were soon undermined by the treachery of the U.S.-organized National Guard. The resulting Somoza family dictatorship remained in power until July 1979 and was characterized by almost total subservience to North American policy interests. A Somoza could always deliver the Nicaraguan vote in crucial meetings of the United Nations or the Organization of American States. Nicaragua, like most of her sister republics, remained closely allied to the United States from the 1930s through the 1960s. Direct intervention did, however, cause increasing uneasiness among some Latin American states. Although much of the rest of the Third World remained under direct colonial rule, the Inter-American system began a restructuring process that culminated in the formation of the OAS. In International Law, and increasingly in Inter-American public opinion, nonintervention in the internal affairs of any member state became the indicated norm.[3]

Led by the postrevolutionary independence in Mexican foreign policy, the Latin American states pushed to enlarge the parameters of action in foreign affairs. Argentina under Perón remained neutral during most of World War II and pursued an independent course in the postwar period. Buenos Aires asserted its independence by recognizing the Soviet Union in 1946 and extending trade relations with both East and West. Years before the Colombo Conference, Peronist foreign policy was calling for a Third Force that was not aligned with either of the emerging power blocs. Argentina openly expressed reservations about the traditional North American hegemony in the new hemispheric system developing after World War II, and it waited several years before ratifying the 1947 Rio Pact and the OAS Charter.[4] Perón's ouster by the military in 1955, however, returned Argentina to the Pan American fold, abruptly terminating the first hemispheric flirtation with nonalignment.

If Peronism's fascist origins saved Argentina from the Cold War hysteria that the United States increasingly was interjecting into its relations with Latin neighbors, other nations were less fortunate. Guatemalan attempts at structural change and foreign policy realignment through the most minimal relations with Eastern Europe became the basis for a vicious U.S. campaign that characterized the revolutionary regime as a beachhead for international communism. The CIA-sponsored coup of 1954 terminated Guatemala's experiment with a more independent foreign policy. After the 1952 revolution, Bolivia's faltering steps in this path were tolerated only for the few years needed to moderate the course of the revolution through economic pressure.

The interjection of the Cold War into the hemispheric system allowed for even less maneuverability on the part of the Latin American nations, since it was assumed that common cultural, historic, economic, and political ties inextricably bound them to the West in the North American war with Eastern Communism. As suggested by the Cuban case, the United States tended to overreact to nationalist programs to change internal or external economic and political relationships. Deviation from Western policies was perceived as an unwarranted, active movement toward the communist camp. Foreign policy initiatives that were part and parcel of India's relations with both camps in Asia were prohibited for neighboring Latin American nations. Cuba's radical nationalism soon conflicted with the constraints imposed by the newly defined Pan Americanism. Meanwhile, 25 nations gathered in Belgrade in 1961 to conduct the first conference of the Nonaligned nations. Cuba sent a delegation. "Havana's presence signalled that Cuba's international perspective was undergoing change; the hemispheric parameters that historically had defined its sphere of concern were being replaced with a vision of itself operating in concert with kindred Afro-Asian states on the larger world stage."[5] The United States reacted negatively to this and other alterations in Cuban diplomatic behavior. As Cuba sought new external alignments, U.S. displeasure increased and was ultimately expressed in the CIA-sponsored Bay of Pigs invasion. On North American initiatives, Cuba eventually was excluded from full participation in the Inter-American system in 1962. Not only did this action strain the system itself, but it caused Cuba to offset this diplomatic isolation through a more committed integration into the Nonaligned Movement and (at different times) stronger ties with the Soviet Union and China. Nonalignment and socialist ties offset the geopolitical constraints imposed by the island's location.

The economic and political realities of the 1960s, the example of Cuba, and a general increase in Third World independence and assertiveness combined to encourage other Latin American nations to reevaluate their foreign policy options. Somoza followed the anti-Cuban line, often embellishing on the communist threat to garner even more aid from Nicaragua's large neighbor to the North. Mexico, in contrast, continued to pursue a more independent course, refusing to break diplomatic relations with Cuba when most other Latin American nations had yielded to U.S. pressure to do so. Argentina reasserted its independence and would not vote for the U.S.-sponsored resolution in the OAS to expel Cuba from the organization. The reemergence of Peronist leadership in 1973 prompted the new civilian government to announce its interest in joining the Nonaligned Movement.[6] Under the short-lived Quadros-Goulart regime in the early 1960s, Brazil pursued an increasingly independent foreign policy, and eventually declared its intention to become one of the Nonaligned nations. The United States was disturbed by this latest manifestation of Brazilian nationalism; a military coup soon reoriented Brazilian foreign policy back to traditional lines. Although military regimes often replaced movements that had attempted a change in foreign and domestic policy (Chile), the example of Peru (1968–75) equally demonstrated that even the Latin American military was not completely isolated from the new nationalist currents that propelled more and more Latin American countries to take a nonaligned posture.

By the late 1970s there were increasing numbers of Latin Americans who experienced a growing affinity with the assertive Third World nationalism that emanated from the meetings of the Nonaligned Movement. In the years that followed, the movement came to include several Latin American nations—not only Cuba, Nicaragua, and Peru—but Argentina, Colombia, Bolivia, Ecuador, and Panama. Venezuela, Brazil, Costa Rica, and Mexico attended the frequent conferences as observers. The once small group of 25 had expanded to nearly 100 nations by the time the FSLN had defeated Somoza's forces in July 1979.

NICARAGUA AND THE HISTORIC ROOTS OF NONALIGNMENT

In *Beyond Cuba: Latin America Takes Charge of Its Future*, Luigi Einaudi notes that "Latin American nationalism remains opposed to any form of dependence on Capitalist or Communist powers . . . most Latin American radicals envisage a form of neutralism in world politics, hoping . . . the sardines can find room between the sharks to swim safely."[7] The revolutionary leaders who emerged in Nicaragua were both radical and nationalistic and essentially wanted to chart an independent course as their nation underwent its second revolution for national sovereignty. Indeed, it would appear that the Cubans had warned them of the dangers inherent in unnecessarily alienating one shark only to be forced to swim in the wake of another. As the revolutionary regime in Managua established its independence and sought to maximize flexibility in its foreign relations, it seemed natural that it would be drawn to the principles and goals of the Nonaligned Movement.

Less than two months after the new government established itself in Managua, the Sandinistas decided to make their country a member of the Nonaligned Movement. Nicaragua sent a delegation to the Sixth Nonaligned Summit when it convened in Havana in early September 1979. Declaring that the Sandinistas favored the restructuring of their international relations on the basis of justice and desired a New International Economic Order, Junta member Daniel Ortega explained that the Nicaraguans were joining the Nonaligned Movement because in it they saw "the broadest organization of the Third World States that play an important role and exercise increasing influence in the international arena and in the people's struggle against imperialism, colonialism, neocolonialism . . . "[8] Nicaragua had clearly taken a different tack from the days when Somoza declared he was the best friend the United States ever had.

To understand the reasons for such a drastic shift in Nicaraguan foreign policy one needs to examine the evolution of the Sandinista movement. The very essence of the nationalist experience of Sandino himself was the affirmation of the principle of national sovereignty and independence. He saw his struggle as that of an oppressed people and believed that all people who suffered such oppression should unite in the common struggle.[9] His nationalism implied the liberation of Nicaragua from direct military intervention and the political and economic dominance of the United States. Sandino's message of sovereignty was fundamentally antihegemonic. Although predating the founding of the Nonaligned Movement, Sandino's appeals to continental and global opinion demonstrated the very principles of popular solidarity and national self-determination that would become the hallmarks of the Third World movement in Asia and Africa. Characteristically anticolonial, his manifestos were addressed universally to struggling peoples everywhere: to the Nicaraguan people, the people of America, the Indo-Latin American continent, and the progressive forces of the world. This anticolonial sentiment was an outgrowth of the Nicaraguan historical experience and was further developed by the FSLN to become the very cradle of contemporary Sandinista foreign policy. This made the Nonaligned Movement the most "natural" and "friendly" forum for the expression of the new and revolutionary foreign policy goals. The September 1979 Sixth Summit of the Nonaligned Countries in Havana was an ideal international forum for the declaration of the new Nicaraguan foreign policy.[10] Nicaragua began to seek support outside the U.S.-dominated Inter-American system.

As was the case in other Third World countries, the historical roots of Sandinista nonalignment were also socioeconomic. The new foreign policy that emerged in 1979 was an external reflection of an internal realignment of class and economic forces, a revolution both in domestic and foreign policies. The Somocista system of economic and political domination was broken and, with it, its external expression—a "captive" foreign policy. Dependent internal and external controls on prerevolutionary society, politics, and economics were being challenged. The new Nicaraguan Foreign Minister, Miguel D'Escoto, explained several years after the Revolution that "when the Sandinista Revolution triumphed, Nicaragua did not have what would normally be understood as a Chancery. Evidently it was not necessary . . . since all the fundamental decisions . . . were made by the State Department or in the United States Embassy in Managua."[11] The new Nicaraguan policy fully intended to expand its foreign policy parameters.

Nonalignment, therefore, was truly the expression of a newfound independence. From an artificial foreign policy that had been a faithful "echo" of the position of the United States in international and regional forums like the United Nations and the Organization of American States (and that endorsed the intervention of Guatemala in 1954, and permitted the use of Puerto Cabezas for the 1961 Bay of Pigs invasion of Cuba), Nicaraguan foreign policy elevated nonalignment to be one of the three main pillars of the FSLN government. This nonalignment might well mean criticism of the North American position in Latin America and the Third World. However, this did not mean that Nicaraguan foreign policy was categorically hostile to that of the United States. It did mean that the new regime reserved the right to judge other nations' actions according to its own criteria. Nicaraguan nonalignment must, therefore, be understood within the context of the country's revolutionary experience.

The revolutionary struggle from Sandino onward imposed a psychological, moral, and even political commitment to liberation struggles. One of the basic conditions for membership in the Nonaligned Movement was support for anticolonial liberation movements. Clearly there was a natural convergence in the goals of the movement itself and the historical and philosophical base upon which Nicaraguan foreign policy rested. Thus it would be unreasonable and irrational if Nicaraguan foreign policy were to scrupulously ignore other revolutionary struggles whether in Central America or other regions of the Third World in order to prove its nonalignment as defined by the United States. Because of the anticolonial and revolutionary philosophy and historical experience, the "natural" foreign policy direction of Nicaragua sometimes found expression in anti-American positions, but did so as much because of how the United States defined its foreign policy as how the Nicaraguans conceptualized theirs. And, given the historical and political context, it may have been categorically impossible for Nicaragua to define nonalignment to the satisfaction of the United States, since this would suggest the continuation of a dependent foreign policy and indeed even the "Finlandization" of Nicaragua's external aspirations.

THE BIRTH OF A NONALIGNED POLICY: THE SIXTH SUMMIT

The Nicaraguan people have earned the right to be here today with their own blood. In this way they have broken with their past history of servility to imperialist politics.

Daniel Ortega, Sixth Summit of
the Nonaligned Movement[12]

One of the first foreign policy statements of the new Sandinista government was the recognition of the People's Republic of Kampuchea. At the Sixth Summit of the Nonaligned Countries, held in Havana September 3–9, 1979, Daniel Ortega explained to the assembled Third World nations that this action did not mean that Nicaragua had allied itself with the Soviet bloc as was being speculated in the press, but that it represented Nicaragua's active stand against imperialism.[13] Not only did entry into the Nonaligned group of nations symbolize an antiimperial policy, but it sought to amplify the important role of Third World countries in world affairs and, by extension perhaps, a foreign policy activism on the part of Nicaragua. This statement was also the first foreign policy pronouncement of Nicaragua in an international forum. Daniel Ortega elaborated the rationale for membership specifically in terms of the struggle of peoples against imperialism, colonialism, neocolonialism, apartheid, racism, Zionism, and all other forms of oppression. He established Nicaraguan support for the principles of an active peaceful coexistence, the absence of blocs and military alliance systems, the reestablishment of international relations upon just foundations and a new international economic order.[14]

In his rationale for Nicaragua's membership Ortega argued that "in the Sandinista revolution there is not any alignment; but an absolute and consistent support for the aspirations of peoples who have achieved independence or are struggling to do so. That is why we are nonaligned."[15] Based on this explanation one can understand Nicaragua's subsequent support for the Southwest African People's Organization in Namibia, the Palestine Liberation Organization, the Polisario Front in the Western Sahara, East Timor's independence, Cuba, and Puerto Rican nationalism during the meeting. By taking this stand Nicaragua assumed a position consistent with the Nonaligned Movement. Nonaligned meetings from the Foreign Ministers Conference in Georgetown during August 1972 to the 1979 Havana meeting had passed resolutions extending solidarity and support to these groups. Nicaragua's reciprocal support was not, therefore, unusual but mainstream for the movement. The Nicaraguans had previously been backed in their liberation struggle; now they would support similar struggles elsewhere. At the foreign ministers' meeting in New York on October 2, 1978, the Nonaligned Movement expressed support for the Revolution in Nicaragua in a resolution criticizing the actions of the Somoza government.[16] In subsequent ministerial meetings (New Delhi, February 9–13, 1981; Havana, May 31–June 5, 1982; and October 4–9, 1982) the Nonaligned countries continued to maintain interest in the postrevolutionary developments in Nicaragua, often focusing global attention on the instability in Central America, the growing political and economic pressure on Nicaragua, and the interventionist role of the United States in El Salvador.[17] For example, in the ministerial meeting at New Delhi the organization "condemned the political and economic aggression, both direct or through certain international financial organizations, which was being exercised or attempted against Nicaragua in order to interfere with the revolutionary process."[18] The Nonaligned Movement was becoming the principal forum where Nicaragua's foreign policy position could be heard and understood. As it supported liberation movements, so would others support the Nicaraguan Revolution. It was becoming a matter of diplomatic survival for the Revolution. That was why the Extraordinary Ministerial Meeting of the Coordinating Bureau of the Nonaligned Countries on Latin America and the Caribbean, in Managua January 10–14, 1983, was so important.

NONALIGNMENT AND DEFENSE OF THE REVOLUTION

The special ministerial meeting in Managua served as a diplomatic "coup" for the revolutionary government of Nicaragua. The attendance of some 89 countries, liberation movements, and international organizations as members and observers and the resulting "Managua Communiqué" turned attention to Nicaragua. The meeting itself was important for the diplomatic, and also the economic and political, survival of the Sandinista Revolution. Alan Riding in the New York Times wrote that "by acting as host at the meeting, however, Nicaragua appeared to have succeeded in focusing on the growing number of attacks by Honduras-based anti-Sandinist rebels into northern Nicaragua."[19] The Reagan Administration had to moderate the ultimate language of the meeting to soften the condemnation of U.S. policy in the region.

Attendance at the Managua ministerial meeting may also have been high because the State Department prodded more moderate members to participate in order to offset attempts by Cuba and Nicaragua to denounce U.S. activity in Central America. Initially, the draft of the final declaration, prepared by Nicaragua and Cuba, "called specifically for condemnation of U.S. support for anti-Sandinist groups based in Honduras."[20] Movement moderates, such as Jamaica, Egypt, and Singapore, who were sympathetic to the United States, were able, however, to "soften" the final declaration.[21] Despite the general wording of the final draft, which ultimately called for peaceful solutions between the warring groups in El Salvador and negotiations between the United States and Nicaragua, the meeting had concentrated largely on the situation in Central America. This alone was an important precedent for the Nonaligned Movement, which in the past rarely focused attention on a particular region of the world. For the first time the nonaligned focused on a Latin American problem and the specific regional conflict in Central America.[22] Latin America was no longer the exclusive preserve of the U.S.-dominated OAS. Nicaragua would not be isolated from the world movement it had helped to shape.

The Managua meeting also established the necessary conditions to continue discussion of the Central American crisis in the upcoming New Delhi summit of March 7–12, 1983. Managua further served as a dress rehearsal for the "diplomatic defeat" the United States suffered at the United Nations later that month. Nicaragua, in partial testimony to the success of its foreign policy, was elected as one of the nonpermanent members of the Security Council on October 19, 1982. The U.S. delegation had lobbied with determination on behalf of the Dominican Republic in an attempt to block Nicaragua, but on the second ballot, Nicaragua mustered the 104 countries needed for the two-thirds majority. Nicaragua's election to the Security Council, therefore, was seen as a major defeat for the United States.[23] Managua's successful election further bolstered its position as the Nonaligned ministers convened in New Delhi in early March. This was also an important Nicaraguan success for another reason. Now Nicaragua had immediate access to the Security Council in the event of a threat to its national security.[24] On March 23 Nicaragua brought such a charge before the council.

The U.N. Security Council considered Nicaragua's complaints about the acts of aggression against it on March 23, 24, 25, 28, and 29, 1983. In the debate Nicaragua denounced the increase of U.S. aggression and counterrevolutionary attacks from Honduras, suggesting they were the most recent examples of the Reagan Administration's CIA-orchestrated secret war.[25] As it had been in the New Delhi meeting, Nicaragua's position was reaffirmed in the United Nations.[26] "After four days of occasionally heated debate on the fighting in Nicaragua, the U.S. [became] virtually isolated in the Security Council in its attempts to portray the conflict as an internal Nicaraguan affair."[27]

Countries that had often allied with the United States were skeptical or openly critical of U.S. policy in Central America and specifically toward Nicaragua. Among them were Mexico, Venezuela, Spain, Pakistan, India, the Netherlands, Panama, and France. Nicaraguan support was even stronger among sympathetic Nonaligned nations like Tanzania, Zaire, and Algeria. Jeane Kirkpatrick appeared so annoyed with the attitude that she was quoted as having decried the "systematic bias, systematic lies, systematic redefinition of key political values and distortion of key political processes."[28] This development was certainly a coup for Nicaragua's policy of nonalignment, which had intended to use the Third World movement, not only as a source and forum for "objective," "sympathetic" information on the Nicaraguan Revolution, but as a medium of diplomatic defense and initiative. Tellingly, only Honduras and El Salvador sided strongly with the United States in the UN debates. The Nonaligned Movement and, through it, the nonaligned Third World countries in the United Nations came to the defense of the Nicaraguan Revolution. Unlike Guatemala in 1954, Nicaragua was not isolated and overthrown by a CIA-backed invasion.

Nicaraguan diplomacy had guaranteed access to Third World countries and extrahemispheric organizations that were not subordinated to policy constraints imposed by regional U.S. hegemony.

THE CONSOLIDATION OF THE REVOLUTION: THE SEVENTH SUMMIT AND AFTER

Nicaragua insists on attentive international opinion in order to slow the ongoing interventionist escalation in Central America. It is thankful for the concern and solidarity that it has always found in the bosom of the Movement.

Daniel Ortega, Seventh Summit of
the Nonaligned Movement[29]

At the very first meeting of the Nonaligned countries that Nicaragua attended in 1979, Daniel Ortega had linked the consolidation of the Nicaraguan Revolution to the strengthening of the struggle of the underdeveloped nations. At the Seventh Summit he made it clear that the liberation struggle in Nicaragua continued and that Nicaragua "needed the disinterested assistance of the nonaligned nations" more than ever.[30] These words and subsequent declarations indicated two important positions in Nicaraguan foreign policy and its relations with the Third World. Like Guatemala and Cuba earlier, Nicaragua was preoccupied with the security threat posed by the United States and feared for the consolidation of its Revolution. However, unlike Cuba between 1959 and 1962, Nicaragua had decided to create the appropriate international climate for revolutionary consolidation by showing close solidarity with the Third World rather than the Soviet Union.[31] Internationalism—but of a somewhat different variety than the revolutionary internationalism of Cuba—was seen as a major platform for national self-defense. Through a type of "diversified dependence" on many different nations (but with special ties to the Nonaligned countries) Nicaragua hoped to offset aggressive designs by the United States.[32] Unlike Cuba, Nicaragua had avoided the hemispheric diplomatic isolation imposed by the United States. As more and more Latin American countries joined the Nonaligned Movement—at New Delhi the membership had increased to 101 countries, which included ten Latin American and Caribbean members—it became more difficult to isolate Nicaragua as had been done with Cuba. The arena was much broader and the national actors were much more independent.

Nicaragua attempted to bridge the positions of the more radical members of the Nonaligned Movement and the more pro-Western countries. It had accepted neither the "natural ally" thesis of Cuba, which saw in the socialist countries, especially the Soviet Union, a natural alliance for dependent, developing countries; nor had Nicaragua espoused the "two imperialisms" thesis of Algeria, which feared both domination of advanced capitalist and advanced socialist systems over dependent countries.[33] Nicaragua's preferred position in the movement appeared to be with the "pivotal" states (like Tanzania) in previous summits. They were "not so radical as the Cubans but more radical than the Yugoslavs"—they were in the "middle group" of nonaligned.[34] This "middle group" truly practiced "flexible nonalignment," at times siding with the radicals and at others with the moderates, depending upon the issue and circumstances. Nicaragua, confronting the military and economic opposition of the United States, and the extensive needs of revolutionary reconstruction, could not afford ideological or any other form of exclusivity. Moreover, its policy in action, as well as in philosophy, was genuinely "more" nonaligned than that of Cuba.

A major issue—the Soviet invasion of Afghanistan—confronted Nicaragua shortly after its Revolution as its delegation was seated in the United Nations. The Nicaraguan vote on Afghanistan was cited repeatedly as an example of Nicaragua's "support" of the Soviet Union and of "its incorporation into the Soviet bloc," to paraphrase U.S. Ambassador Jeane Kirkpatrick.[35] Examination of the vote demonstrated, instead, the non-alignment of Nicaragua with either the Soviet Union or the United States. On January 14, 1980, in the Sixth Emergency Special Session of the United Nations under the "uniting for peace resolution," the members voted 104 in favor, 18 opposed, with 18 abstentions on a resolution calling for the immediate withdrawal of Soviet troops from Afghanistan. Nicaragua, unlike the countries aligned with the socialist bloc, abstained, as did India, Algeria, Cyprus, and Finland. The countries that abstained seemed to prefer a studiously "neutral" position, which did not specifically "criticize" Soviet actions. Nevertheless, in the debate Nicaragua listed among events that threatened world peace "the presence of Soviet forces" in Afghanistan. The countries that opposed the UN resolution included Soviet-bloc nations and countries sympathetic to the Soviet position like Cuba, Angola, Grenada, Ethiopia, and Mozambique.[36] Similarly, in the September 1983 Security Council resolution criticizing the Soviet downing of the Korean airliner in which 269 died, Nicaragua abstained as did China, Guyana, and Zimbabwe. Nicaragua argued that doubts as to the facts existed.[37]

On the other hand, Nicaragua's interpretation of nonalignment was not intended necessarily to be synonymous with neutrality on all issues— for that could indicate the lack of foreign policy direction. An example was the Nicaraguan position on the U.S. invasion of Grenada. In contrast to

Afghanistan, Nicaragua initiated a request on October 25, 1983, in the Security Council to end armed intervention and to begin immediate withdrawal of troops, deploring the flagrant U.S. violation of international law. Nicaragua, with two other Security Council members (Guyana and Zimbabwe), sponsored this critical draft resolution. Because the resolution was vetoed by the United States, Nicaragua brought it before the General Assembly in November where, in a vote of 108 for, 9 against, with 27 abstentions, the U.S. action was deplored. Nicaragua had not only supported the resolution but had been its author and major promoter. In the debate Nicaragua described the U.S. intervention as "naked armed aggression."[38] The Grenada vote was immediately interpreted as proof of Nicaragua's anti-American (and by implication pro-Soviet) "alignment." A more realistic explanation flowed from the geographical proximity of Grenada and the obvious comparisons that had been made between Grenada and Nicaragua by the Reagan Administration, and by the Nicaraguans themselves. The Grenadan intervention had been widely interpreted as a "dry run" for Nicaragua. Faced with this clear security threat, the precedent of the Grenadan intervention had to be forcefully condemned not only to uphold the principles of nonintervention but also to protect the Nicaraguan Revolution itself.

If the United States—ignoring the meaning of nonalignment—interpreted the Nicaraguan votes on Afghanistan and Grenada in terms of "he who is not with us is against us," the Nonaligned nations did not.[39] Nicaragua's easy election to the Security Council, in contrast to the failure of Cuba earlier, was an indication of Nicaragua's acceptance by the Nonaligned as one of them. In 1980, Cuba's bid for a Security Council seat was blocked by India and Nigeria, and the election was deadlocked after 156 ballots. Although Cuba was chairman of the Nonaligned Movement at the time, it was viewed by many in the movement as too radical and not truly "nonaligned."[40] The majority support of Nicaragua's charges of U.S. aggression in the United Nations in March, May, and September of 1983, and at the New Delhi Seventh Summit of Nonaligned Nations was further evidence of Nicaragua's support and growing acceptance among the Nonaligned and in the world community at large. At the 38th General Assembly Daniel Ortega emphasized this broad support: "There is agreement among very different ideological positions throughout the world in condemning the aggressive and bellicose escalation occurring in the Central American region and in demanding that dialogue be the means for resolving these problems."[41]

In the Nonaligned Movement as in UN voting in the General Assembly and Security Council, Nicaragua avoided siding with either the most radical or the most conservative blocs. Unless national interests or foreign policy goals were directly involved, Nicaragua's position in the movement was flexible and conciliatory, strongly affirming the principles of nonalignment, but especially emphasizing opposition to imperialism and support of liberation struggles. Nicaragua perceived solidarity and unity as the movement's greatest strength and leverage in the international forum, especially in the reform of the international economic system, a major Nicaraguan goal. In Nicaragua's first U.N. session, Daniel Ortega employed the term "the unity of the weak," and at the 1983 Managua ministerial meeting of the Nonaligned he explained the Nicaraguan position:

> It is true that ours are countries with their own characteristics and even with diverse ideological and political positions, but they are also countries with shared problems and objectives. Ours are poor, dependent countries in an unfair economic order that are exposed to political, military and economic attacks and pressures; countries that cannot win the battle for justice and freedom individually; countries that need large-scale solidarity in order to stand up against the oppression that the colonial, industrial, and technological metropolises have institution-alized, bringing pain and poverty to our peoples.
>
> Therefore, the most important thing to preserve is the unity of this Movement. Our enemy knows of our differences and will try to play on them in order to divide, fragment and destroy us.[42]

The Seventh Summit of the Nonaligned Movement demonstrated the natural convergence of Third World interests and goals and those of Nicaraguan foreign policy. Defense of the Nicaraguan Revolution and its consolidation through Third World solidarity would obviously benefit Nicaragua and the Nonaligned, Nicaragua argued. Daniel Ortega even termed Nicaragua the "strategic reserve of the Nonaligned Countries Movement."[43] The summit also issued the strongest denunciation to date of contra and U.S. "acts of aggression against Nicaragua," which were described as "a deliberate plan to harass and destabilize that country."[44]

Continued attacks on Nicaraguan territory, the mining of its harbors, and several naval attacks prompted the Nicaraguan foreign ministry to intensify its diplomatic activities in the United Nations, the Organization of American States, the Contadora Group, the International Court of Justice, and especially in the Nonaligned Movement so as to ease the critical situation in Central America. In March 1984 Nicaragua denounced the external attacks in the UN Security Council and succeeded in convening an emergency session of the Coordinating Bureau of the Nonaligned Movement.[45] The diplomatic offensive was particularly urgent because of the U.S. Senate's approval of $21 million to fund covert CIA operations in the region, extensive U.S. military aid to Honduras, and escalating U.S. troop and naval maneuvers in the region. Nicaragua countered diplomatically and denounced the U.S. attempt to "create the political, propagandistic, and international psychological conditions for the acceptance of the presence of permanent North American combat troops in Central America."[46] Another diplomatic coup was achieved in May 1984 when, on a Nicaraguan complaint, the International Court of Justice unanimously condemned the U.S.-sponsored mining of Nicaraguan ports. Other initiatives and successes included the decision by the Geneva-based General Agreement on Tariffs and Trade that the U.S. reduction of the sugar quota from 58,000 short tons to 6,000 had been discriminatory and politically motivated.[47]

CONCLUSION

Pluralism in internal relations and pluralism in international relations is the foundation of nonalignment.[48]

Nicaragua's active and successful participation in the Nonaligned Movement demonstrated the close affinity between its historical experience and philosophical foundations and those of other anticolonial, developing nations. Nicaragua's stature in the movement was largely the consequence of a foreign policy of greater diversity and flexibility than that of Cuba— that is, a truly nonaligned foreign policy. Despite repeated assertions by the Reagan Administration, the world was not so clearly divided into East and West; and this reality had given Nicaragua many more alternatives than were open to Cuba earlier. Nicaragua had broken the hemispheric mold without limiting its foreign policy options. Diversity in foreign policy was expressed in broad relations with West European countries, the Nonaligned nations, Latin America, and the socialist bloc. Receipt of international assistance, patterns of international trade, and voting records in international organizations demonstrated diversity and nonalignment.[49] As Junta member Sergio Ramírez once said, "If all of that diversified support disappeared, hypothetically, we might be left with the support of only the Eastern European countries. But we don't think that moment will come."[50]

After 1979 the Sandinista regime charted a new, highly independent foreign policy course. In so doing it not only placed itself squarely within the Nonaligned Movement, but brought the Movement's perspectives and politics to bear on Nicaragua's position as an independent state in a region that traditionally had been dominated by U.S. hegemony. It maximized decisionmaking latitude for the Nicaraguans and made nonalignment much more possible for other Latin American states. If the Reagan regime proved unsympathetic to Nicaraguan initiatives at Nonaligned summit meetings and in the United Nations, the revolutionary government met with a series of diplomatic successes and foreign policy firsts, and on at least one occasion even managed virtually to isolate the United States in the United Nations because of its aggressive actions toward Nicaragua.

Nicaragua's carefully cultivated relations with the Nonaligned Movement were used to solicit support at a crucial time in the development of the Revolution. Thus as the United States was increasing external pressure on Nicaragua in early 1983, the revolutionary government was able to host a special meeting of Nonaligned ministers. The resulting "Managua Communiqué" supported the Nicaraguan position and criticised U.S. policy in the region.[51] This type of attention forced the United States and Honduras to proceed much more carefully and thus minimized the possibility of a direct invasion of Nicaraguan territory.

The Nonaligned Movement had maximized decision autonomy; it provided a true "third alternative" for a small dependent nation like Nicaragua to exert influence and achieve foreign policy goals. As a forum to disseminate information to the peoples of the world the movement had served as a natural "instrument of denunciation" for U.S. actions against the Nicaraguan government. Membership in the Nonaligned Movement had permitted Nicaragua to marshal extracontinental support for its policies and the necessary votes to overcome U.S. influence in the OAS and the United Nations. From the Nicaraguan perspective the Movement was central to its foreign policy priorities of self-defense, internationalism, and autonomy.

The revolutionary government had carefully cultivated good relations with all segments of the Nonaligned Movement (and other nations that could respect nonalignment) and had successfully employed these ties to achieve its policy objectives. By doing so, Nicaragua had controlled the type of CIA-organized, externally based aggression that had overthrown the Arbenz government in Guatemala in 1954. Likewise, it prevented the type of diplomatic and economic isolation that had forced Cuba to rely even more heavily on the Soviet Union. The small Central American state had shown that there were indeed many schools of fish in the oceans of the world and that one need not swim in the wake of any one large fish for fear of being eaten by another.[52]

NOTES

1. William M. LeoGrande, "Evolution of the Nonaligned Movement," *Problems of Communism*, January-February 1980, pp. 38–39.

2. Ibid., p. 43.

3. See Article 15 of the Charter of the Organization of American States.

4. John J. Finan, "Argentina," in Harold Eugene Davis, Larman C. Wilson et al., *Latin America Foreign Policies* (Baltimore: Johns Hopkins University Press, 1975), p. 268.

5. H. Michael Erisman, "Cuba and the Third World: The Nonaligned Nations Movement," in *The New Cuban Presence in the Caribbean*, edited by Barry Levine (Boulder: Westview Press, 1983), p. 150.

6. Finan, "Argentina," pp. 268–69.

7. Luigi Einaudi, ed., *Beyond Cuba: Latin America Takes Charges of Its Future* (New York: Crane, Russak, 1974), p. 32.

8. Speech delivered by Daniel Ortega to the Havana Nonaligned Conference, cited by Alejandro Bendaña, "The Foreign Policy of the Nicaraguan Revolution," in *Nicaragua in Revolution*, edited by Thomas W. Walker (New York: Praeger, 1982), p. 320.

9. *Barricada International* (Managua), February 20, 1984, p. 2.

10. Interview with Victor Hugo Tinoco, Deputy Foreign Minister, Managua, March 14, 1984.

11. "Nicaragua's Foreign Policy: Nonalignment," *Envío*, January 1983, p. 7.

12. "Discurso ante el plenario de la Sexta Cumbre del Movimiento de Países No Alineados, La Habana, 6 de septiembre de 1979," in Daniel Ortega, *El acero de guerra o el olivo de paz* (Managua: Editorial Nueva Nicaragua, 1983), p. 14.

13. Ibid., p. 16.

14. Ibid., p. 17.

15. Ibid.; translation that of the authors.

16. "Pronunciamientos Referentes a América Latina Extraidos de Documentos de Conferencias y Reuniones Ministeriales Habidas desde 1961 a 1982," no date or source; working papers from the Ministerio de Relaciones Exteriores, Managua.

17. Ibid., pages unnumbered.

18. Ibid.

19. Alan Riding, "Nonaligned Bloc backs Nicaragua; 'Systematic Attacks' Against Sandinistas are Denounced," New York *Times*, January 15, 1983, I, p. 8.

20. Alan Riding, "U.S. is Target at Nicaragua Talks," New York *Times*, January 11, 1983, I, p. 4.

21. Egypt had been critical of the Cuban position in the Movement since the 1978 foreign ministers' meeting in Belgrade and had challenged Cuba's credentials as a nonaligned nation.

22. Interview with Victor Hugo Tinoco.

23. *Keesings Contemporary Archives* 29:1 (January 1983):31933. Nicaragua was also elected as one of 54 members of the Economic and Social Council until January 1984. For further interpretation of the UN events, also see "Third World Nations Expected to Assail U.S.," New York *Times*, January 9, 1983, I, p. 3; and "Complaints by Chad and Nicaragua Debated Extensively," in *UN Chronicle* 20:5 (May 1983):3–22. The Nicaraguan address and charges of U.S. aggression were extensively considered and debated on March 23, 24, 25, 28, and 29, 1983.

24. As an historical note, it should be pointed out that Guatemala was denied access to the UN Security Council in 1954, when the U.S. representative (serving as president for that month) refused to place the Guatemalan charges on the agenda, referring the issue to the U.S.-dominated OAS. See, *inter alia*, Richard H. Immerman, *The C.I.A. in Guatemala: The Foreign Policy of Intervention* (Austin: University of Texas Press, 1982).

25. *UN Chronicle* 20:5 (May 1983):3–22.

26. Panama, for example, interpreted the Nicaraguan action in the United Nations as confirmation of the assessment made of the situation in Central America by the New Delhi summit meeting of Nonaligned countries. Ibid., p. 16.

27. Bernard D. Nossiter, "U.S. Finds Itself Virtually Isolated in U.N. Over Nicaraguan Crisis," New York *Times*, March 29, 1983, I, p. 1.

28. *UN Chronicle* 20:5 (May 1983):18. Algeria, for example, was outspoken in its support.

29. Ortega, *El acero de guerra*, p. 111, "Discurso pronunciado en la Séptima Cumbre del Movimiento de Países No Alineados."

30. Ibid., p. 25.

31. To compare with Cuba, see Erisman, "Cuba and the Third World," p. 150.

32. Term used in "Nicaragua's Foreign Policy," *Envío*, p. 12.

33. Erisman, "Cuba and the Third World," pp. 157–164; and *Envío*, p. 10.

34. LeoGrande ("Evolution") used these phrases and concepts, although not in reference to Nicaragua, see p. 50.

35. *UN Chronicle* 20:5 (May 1983):14.

36. *UN Chronicle* 17:2 (February 1980):5–7. In subsequent votes on Afghanistan Nicaragua continued to abstain, see the vote on Res. 38/29 of November 23, 1983, *UN Chronicle* 21:1 (January 1984):22.

37. *UN Chronicle*, 20:11 (November 1983):19.

38. *UN Chronicle*, 20:11 (November 1983):15; and 21:1 (January 1984):4.

39. Term used by Jordan in support of Nicaragua in the UN debate of March 1983, see *UN Chronicle* 20:5 (May 1983):19.

40. LeoGrande, "Evolution," p. 50.

41. *UN Chronicle*, Special Supplement, "The Nations Speak," March 1984, p. 12.

42. "Extraordinary Ministerial Meeting of the Coordinating Bureau of the Nonaligned Countries on Latin America and the Caribbean, Final Communiqué," Managua, January 10–14, 1983, pp. 37–38.

43. Ibid., p. 42.

44. "7 Cumbre de los NOAL, New Delhi 1983, Recomendaciones y Conclusiones Sobre Asuntos Latinoamericanos y del Caribe," Center for International Communications, Nicaragua, 1983, p.15.

45. "Nicaragua denuncia en la ONU y NOAL," *Barricada*, March 14, 1984, p. 5.

46. "Comité pro Reconstrucción de Nicaragua, reunido aquí," *El Nuevo Diario*, March 16, 1984, p. 9; statement by Victor Hugo Tinoco to the group.

47. "Ante boicot azucareño de EU, GATT respalda a Nicaragua," *Barricada*, March 14, 1984, p. 2; "Consejo del Gatt aprueba condena a Estados Unidos," *El Nuevo Diario*, March 14, 1984, pp. 1 and 10; and "Condenan a EE.UU." March 13, 1984, pp. 1 and 10.

48. Xabier Gorostiaga, "Geopolítica de la crisis regional," *Cuadernos de pensamiento proprio, INIES y CRIES* (Managua, 1984), p. 47.

49. Aid and trade figures vary. An *Envío* study, based on the work of Gorostiaga and others, noted international loans to Nicaragua in these percentages: 49.4 percent from Third World countries; 32 percent from capitalist countries, and 18.5 percent from socialist bloc countries (including Cuba). From 1979 to 1982, Western Europe provided 33 percent of Nicaraguan loans. See *Envío*, January 1983, p. 12–13; the chapters in this volume by Nadia Malley (Chapter 24) and Theodore Schwab and Harold Sims (Chapter 22); *Archives Barricada Internacional*, December 1983, p. 3; and supplement to *Barricada Internacional*, December 26, 1983.

50. Sergio Ramírez, "Playboy Interview: The Sandinistas," *Playboy*, September 1983, p. 190.

51. *Keesings Contemporary Archives* 29:8 (August 1983), pp. 32349-55.

52. See Juan José Arévalo, *Fábula del tiburón y las sardinas* (*The Shark and the Sardines*) (New York: L. Stuart, 1961).

Chapter 24

Relations with Western Europe and the Socialist International

NADIA MALLEY

Nicaragua's relations with Western Europe and the Socialist International (SI) following the Sandinista Revolution constituted an important new international development. The relationship reflected the emergence of Western Europe as an active, independent political actor in the traditional "backyard" of the United States during the late 1970s and early 1980s. The political, moral, and economic support that the Sandinistas received from Western Europe, most notably from socialist and social democratic forces, was remarkable given the revolutionary—not merely social democratic—character of the Nicaraguan regime. It was all the more significant in light of the SI's basically reformist orientation in Western Europe. Despite these advances, however, the relationship underwent a marked deterioration after the first year and a half of the Revolution.

CONTEXT

Western Europe's involvement in Nicaragua must be placed within the broader context of Western Europe's interest in Latin America in general and Central America specifically. Given the growing economic links between Western Europe and Latin America, one could explain European—in particular social democratic—political activities in Latin America as an effort to contain revolutionary upheavals in the region in order to pave the way for European business interests. However, the direct economic motives behind Western Europe's presence in Central America should not be exaggerated, as Europe's investments in the area were relatively insignificant.[1] Alternatively, one could argue that the progressive

The author would like to thank Cathryn Thorup, Richard E. Feinberg, Terry Karl, Stanley Hoffmann, Rita Cauli, and Emile Benson for their valuable assistance.

485

positions on Central America adopted by European social democratic governments were intended for "domestic consumption," in that such policies constituted a convenient means to "placate" their more left-wing supporters. It is true that important sectors of opinion in Western Europe have been extremely sympathetic to the Sandinista Revolution, but, although domestic political considerations cannot be completely dismissed, such an explanation is overly simplistic since it minimizes other genuine preoccupations of the West European governments.

The main impetus for Western Europe's political involvement in Central America stemmed from Europe's concern for both East-West and North-South relations. The clear preference of most Europeans for flexibility and negotiated solutions in the region was rooted in the fear that belligerent policies on the part of the United States would polarize the international environment, thereby endangering East-West relations and driving the region's liberation movements closer to the Soviet bloc. No doubt, some European Christian Democrats were inclined to blame external "communist" forces for the Central American turmoil. However, most Europeans emphasized the internal socioeconomic and political causes of the conflict and felt that attempts to block revolutionary change in Central America were likely to entail high political costs for Western Europe and the United States in terms of their relations with the Third World.[2] Rather than pursuing counterproductive policies, Europe's Social Democrats sought to provide these liberation movements with an alternative source of support.

By the same token, Sandinista Nicaragua needed to maintain and develop its links with the West for both structural and ideological reasons. Indeed, as a poor developing nation extremely dependent on foreign credits, Nicaragua had to remain integrated with the international economic market. As a result of the shortage of foreign exchange, the only means for Nicaragua to service its huge foreign debt and purchase foodstuffs and raw materials was through international economic assistance. Nicaragua's relations with Western Europe also followed logically from the ideological principles guiding the Revolution: a mixed economy required the development of new markets; political pluralism implied a dialogue with political movements such as the SI; and nonalignment entailed an opening toward Western Europe, Latin America, and the socialist countries.

Western Europe's attempt to provide an alternative for the Third World thus coincided with Nicaragua's need to diversify its relations through a wide range of international linkages in order to secure its national independence. This convergence of interests led Nicaragua and Western Europe to develop important political and economic ties at various levels.

NATURE OF THE RELATIONSHIP

Europe at the Regional Level

On an average, from 1979 to 1982, Western Europe accounted for 14 percent of Nicaragua's imports and 28 percent of its exports.[3] In addition, between 1979 and 1981, European donations (in cash and in kind) amounted to over $61 million, or 32.5 percent of total donations to Nicaragua. The European Economic Community (EEC) alone donated $16 million. During the same period, Western Europe granted Nicaragua $93 million in bilateral loans, which corresponded to 18 percent of total bilateral loans to Nicaragua.[4] Western Europe's political support for Nicaragua, through the EEC, was no less important than its economic assistance. At a summit in Stuttgart in July 1983, for example, the ten leaders of the EEC indirectly criticized the Reagan Administration's policies in Central America. They asserted that the region's problems could not "be solved by military means but only by a solution springing from the region itself," urged respect for the "principles of non-interference and inviolability of frontiers," and endorsed the Contadora peace initiative.[5]

The EEC constituted a valuable asset for the Sandinistas by counteracting the Reagan Administration's efforts to asphyxiate Nicaragua economically and to isolate it politically. However, it is difficult to pinpoint a specific "European policy," since the emergence of a coherent positive stance toward Nicaragua was hampered by the divisions within the EEC. For example, objections by Margaret Thatcher's government in Great Britain were sufficient to exclude Nicaragua from the EEC's proposed Central American Cooperative Program in 1982.

National Level: France, West Germany, Spain

Following the election in May 1981 of socialist leader François Mitterrand, France distinguished itself in Central America through its strongly worded criticism of U.S. policies and various diplomatic initiatives in the region. In late 1981 the French government signed a declaration with Mexico recognizing the FDR/FMLN in El Salvador as a representative political force. The French socialist regime also extended political and economic support to Nicaragua. The economic assistance, in particular, helped to finance several industrial projects and ease Nicaragua's balance-of-payments problems. Most significantly, Mitterrand's government was the only one in Western Europe to provide military aid to the Sandinistas. In December 1981, France signed a contract with Nicaragua to send "nonoffensive" weapons valued at 90 million francs and consisting of two patrol boats, two helicopters, a dozen trucks, as well as arms and munitions to supply them. The French government also agreed to train ten Nicaraguan naval officers and ten pilots. Furthermore, in the spring of 1984 the Mitterrand government criticized the U.S. mining of Nicaragua's ports, claiming that it represented a "blockade undertaken in peacetime against a small country, which presents serious problems of political ethics." France offered to help Nicaragua clear its ports if one or more European countries were willing to cooperate.

In concrete terms, however, France's economic and military assistance remained relatively modest in comparison to Nicaragua's needs and in light of what might have been expected from a socialist government. Clearly, France had other foreign policy priorities, particularly with regard to its former African colonies. Nonetheless, symbolically, France's support was significant.

This progressive role served, in part, as a means for Mitterrand to placate his more radical supporters (the Communists and important sectors of his own Socialist Party) who felt uncomfortable with the government's austerity measures and its anti-Soviet positions. Yet, above all, the motivation for Mitterrand's policies in Central America derived from the French Socialists' conviction that the causes of the crisis were internal and that it was the responsibility of the West in general to prevent revolutionary Third World movements from turning to the Soviet camp. It is within this framework of an "enlightened" Western power that the Mitterrand regime's economic and military aid to Nicarâgua must be viewed. France did not establish an important economic position in Latin America; its main goal was to develop a political, moral, and cultural presence in the region. Hence, the French Socialists were interested in averting an escalation of the conflict in Central America and in maintaining good relations with Nicaragua.[6] In this endeavor to keep open its channels of influence, the Mitterrand government both adhered to and drew upon the French Gaullist tradition of relative independence toward the two superpowers.

West Germany's stance regarding Nicaragua—even when the Social Democrats were in power—was rather cautious. Although economic aid to Nicaragua surpassed that of France until 1982, Bonn adopted a generally low profile and avoided public criticism of the United States.[7] The main reason for this difference in approach lay in the broader context of West Germany's relations with Washington. U.S. leverage and pressure on West Germany was potentially stronger than on France because of the greater political and strategic dependence of the Federal Republic on the United States. In contrast to France, which was not part of NATO's military command and had its own independent nuclear strike force, West Germany relied completely on the U.S. military umbrella for its protection.

As a consequence, the Social Democratic (SPD) government pursued a difficult balancing act in the conduct of its foreign policy. On the one hand, Helmut Schmidt's government believed that German and Western interests in general were being jeopardized by the Reagan Administration's policies in Central America. In order to promote long-term stability in the region and to protect Germany's growing political and economic interests in Latin America, the SPD government favored a negotiated settlement in El Salvador and support for the Sandinistas. On the other hand, West Germany felt compelled to minimize its differences with the United States. Bonn's specific approach to Central America hence was a form of "quiet diplomacy": The government was prudent at the official level, preferring to push its initiatives through multilateral or party channels.

West Germany's cautious posture toward the United States was accentuated in late 1982 by the new Christian Democratic government, headed by Helmut Kohl. The government decided to wind down aid to Nicaragua and, despite Kohl's support for the Contadora peace initiative, shared Thatcher's conviction that Europe should not interfere in matters where U.S. vital interests seemed to be at stake.

Spain's Socialist government was caught in a predicament similar to that of the German SPD government. The election of a Socialist regime headed by Felipe González in October 1982 held out promise for a radical departure in Spanish foreign policy, particularly with regard to Central America. The potential for an active Spanish policy in Central America did not reside in economic aid—which, given Spain's precarious economy, could only be limited—but in the new political role assumed by González. This idea was spurred by González's high-profile diplomatic initiatives and his interest in Latin America as a whole, and Central America in particular. The new Socialist (PSOE) government criticized the Reagan Administration's attempt to destabilize Nicaragua and affirmed its support for a negotiated solution in El Salvador and for the Contadora process. Nevertheless, González's overall posture constituted a significant retreat from the PSOE's electoral platform, and González frequently took pains to downplay his differences with Washington.[8]

Important constraints on Spanish foreign policy accounted for this relative moderation. The PSOE government confronted other more pressing concerns such as consolidating the new regime and entering the EEC (which would help Spain's ailing economy). The government also had to resolve the NATO question without alienating either the United States or Spanish public opinion—which in its majority remained opposed to Spain's joining NATO.[9] All these issues were interrelated because if Spain refused to enter NATO or followed other policies inimical to the United States, Washington could make life difficult for the new regime by, for example, pressuring its British and German allies to oppose Spanish entry into the EEC. At the same time, the PSOE had an interest in preventing an escalation of U.S. involvement in Central America that by engulfing the region in a generalized war, could exacerbate the anti-U.S. sentiments of the Spanish public and thereby make entry into NATO even more problematic.

Hence, although its relationship with the United States was central to the Spanish government's thinking on Central America, the implications were contradictory. González found himself on a tightrope: While he could not afford to antagonize Washington, U.S. policies in the region risked undermining Spain's broader foreign policy goals. The strategy adopted by the PSOE government was dictated by pragmatism: Spanish disagreements with the United States regarding Central America were not denied, but they took a back seat to other aspects of U.S.-Spanish relations with the result that González left the initiative on Central America to the Contadora countries.

The Party Level: The Socialist International

Although the emergence of a forceful policy of support for the Sandinistas in France, West Germany, and Spain was hampered to varying degrees by the interaction of internal and external constraints, another important political force was pulling in the opposite direction: the Socialist International. The SI's relations with Nicaragua were significant because the SI commanded wide influence in Western Europe and Latin America and constituted, in several instances, the main impetus behind the most dynamic initiatives of European governments in Central America. In addition, the SI's positions reflected the views of large sectors of European public opinion, even if many European governments were unable or unwilling to put them into practice.[10]

Initial contacts between the FSLN and the SI in 1977-78 epitomized the SI's recent "Latin-Americanization" and its opening toward radical liberation movements in the Third World in general. These contacts also fit into one of the FSLN's objectives at the time, which was to obtain widespread domestic and international support in the struggle against Somoza. The relationship remained informal until the SI reached a consensus in late 1978 to grant open support to the Sandinistas.[11] It should be pointed out, however, that the FSLN never was a member of the SI, although it participated in SI meetings as an observer from the Vancouver Congress of November 1978 onward.

Although West European governments did not break diplomatic relations with Somoza's regime, as the Vancouver Congress had urged them, they did implement the SI's recommendations not to renew military, economic, or technical aid agreements. Moreover, the FSLN received financial support from the Swedish, West German, and Austrian social democratic parties, while the Venezuelan Acción Democrática (AD) government supplied the Sandinistas with arms and flew planes over Costa Rica in a gesture of solidarity when Costa Rica was under threat by Somoza for its assistance to the FSLN. When the Sandinistas triumphed in July 1979, the SI declared its total support for the goals of the Revolution and urged its member parties and organizations to give concrete substance to their backing.[12] This support was reiterated at the first conference of the SI's Regional Committee for Latin America and the Caribbean in March 1980, and at the SI's Madrid Congress in November 1980. The Congress also created the Committee in Defense of the Nicaraguan Revolution, which was headed by González and sought to stimulate international solidarity and aid, disseminate information, prevent foreign intervention, and guarantee respect for Nicaragua's right to self-determination. Finally, during the Albufeira Congress in April 1983 the SI condemned U.S. policies in Central America and renewed its support for the "democratic aims" of the Revolution. Although this latter formulation is sometimes interpreted as a form of veiled criticism, the resolutions endorsed by the Congress were considered very positive by the Sandinistas.[13]

It should be noted, however, that the SI's positions on Nicaragua did not represent the unanimous position of all member parties. In reality, the differences within the SI were quite important and, although there was agreement concerning the negative impact of the Reagan Administration's policies on Nicaragua's evolution, SI member parties disagreed on the extent of responsibility that should be assigned to the Sandinistas themselves. In late 1981 the SI faced serious internal dissension regarding its supportive stance toward the FSLN. The fourth reunion of the Regional Committee for Latin America and the Caribbean, scheduled for early 1982 in Caracas, Venezuela, was canceled because the host party (AD) protested the presence of the FSLN. Another source of opposition to the SI's position on Nicaragua stemmed from Costa Rica's member party, the Partido de Liberación Nacional (PLN), under the leadership of President Monge.

In fact, many SI members seemed closer to Edén Pastora's group (the Democratic Revolutionary Alliance) than to the FSLN.[14] Nevertheless, although Pastora was received by a number of SI parties (in particular, by Soares's Portugese party) during his European tour in 1983, he was unable to obtain public support from them against the FSLN. Regardless of the sympathy several SI members showed toward Pastora, the SI as a whole would not abandon its support for the Sandinista government—considered as legitimate—in favor of opposition groups that were either ideologically tainted or unrepresentative of the Nicaraguan people.

Three interrelated goals underlay the SI's support for the FSLN. First, the SI's commitment to prevent an extended war in Central America and to mitigate the Reagan Administration's aggressive policies implied a constructive relationship with the FSLN. A second aim was to provide the Sandinista Revolution with international political and economic space in an attempt to circumvent East-West polarization. Finally, the SI sought to contribute to the positive development of the Revolution's "original project" of political pluralism, mixed economy, and nonalignment. According to SI leaders, the most effective way to maintain leverage over Nicaragua was not through public criticism but through friendly, private pressure.[15]

It is difficult to assess the impact of the SI upon either Nicaragua's evolution or U.S. policies. No doubt, the loosening of internal political controls announced by the Sandinista leadership in late 1983 was partly the result of pressures by European and Latin American Social Democrats; but the Sandinistas were also influenced by the Contadora group and by the fear of a U.S. intervention in the aftermath of Reagan's invasion of Grenada. Regarding the United States, while the SI could exert some degree of influence over the Carter Administration, the Reagan Administration was quite unreceptive—if not overtly hostile—to the SI's criticisms. Nonetheless, through its positive stance toward Nicaragua, the SI enabled the Sandinistas to avoid total isolation and encouraged some European governments to extend political and economic support for the Revolution.[16]

In its attempt to influence both the United States and Nicaragua, the SI found itself in a difficult dilemma: On the one hand, the SI believed U.S. policies to be fundamentally flawed, yet, on the other hand, it did not want to alienate the Reagan Administration. Similarly, to preserve its credibility with Western public opinion, the SI could not condone what it perceived as antidemocratic trends in Nicaragua, yet it avoided public criticism for fear of losing its leverage with the Sandinistas. Moreover, the SI did not have any real binding power over its members parties and had only limited financial resources. Given these problems, the main role of the SI was to formulate and disseminate ideas that received wide support in Europe and Latin America. The SI facilitated contacts and influenced world public opinion, thus affecting governmental decisions.

EVOLUTION OF THE RELATIONSHIP

Nicaragua's relations with Western Europe and the SI thus provided the Sandinistas with valuable support but were fraught with contradictions and limitations. The relationship actually deteriorated following the first year and a half of the Revolution. Most visible was the growing disillusionment of many of Nicaragua's European friends. A loss of enthusiasm and increasing skepticism regarding Nicaragua was apparent in West European governments, political parties, and public opinion in general.

Nicaragua's Evolution

At face value it would appear that the causes for the growing estrangement between Nicaragua and much of Western Europe were rooted in Nicaragua's own revolutionary dynamic and retreat from the original goals of nonalignment, mixed economy, and political pluralism. More specifically, West European critics of the Sandinistas became disullusioned by what they perceived as Nicaragua's alignment with the socialist bloc, encroachments on the private sector, and limitations on political democracy. Concerning the latter issue, in addition to press censorship and similar restrictive measures, there were two incidents that received wide coverage in Western Europe: the alleged organization of hostile demonstrations by the FSLN against the Pope during his visit to Nicaragua in March 1983, and "mistreatment" of the Miskitu population.

In response to such charges, Sandinista leaders have claimed that it was the Pope's own misreading of Nicaragua's situation that provoked the anger of the crowd, and they have openly acknowledged that errors were committed at the beginning of the Revolution with regard to the Miskitus.[17] In general, the Sandinistas conceded that they had adopted restrictive internal measures and turned to the socialist countries for support, but they argued that such policies represented necessary defensive actions in the face of Reagan's interventionism. While these responses seem largely justified, Nicaragua was also partly responsible for the deterioration of its relations with Western Europe.

The Sandinistas have often handled their "public relations" campaign awkwardly vis-a-vis Western Europe. For example, Nicaragua presented only a few development projects to the international credit institutions and did not press for them effectively. In recognition of this problem, the government decided to establish an economic office in Europe to handle loan applications and to represent Nicaragua in various countries.[18] Moreover, Nicaragua failed to convince most Europeans of its need to adopt "defensive" policies. Even Fidel Castro urged the Sandinista leadership to implement structural changes slowly and to retain good relations with the church, Western Europe, and the Third World, as Nicaragua's primary goal—in the face of its internal and external enemies—was to consolidate the Revolution.[19]

The Sandinistas themselves contributed to the reluctance of many European Social Democrats to grant unconditional support to the Revolution. Undoubtedly, "Marxist-Leninst" terminology put some

Europeans ill at ease. More fundamentally, it seems that the Sandinistas did not take seriously enough the pervasive anticommunism, the deeply rooted religious sentiments, and the strong attachment to the principles of political pluralism that characterize Western Europe and the SI. Even while the Sandinistas' policies seemed largely warranted, their failure to persuade many Western Europeans cost them important political and economic support. It is clear that the willingness of Western Europe to continue or increase its level of support to Nicaragua often depended upon perceptions as much as upon reality.

Western European Responsibilities

Western Europe itself, however, was also at fault for the worsening of its relations with Nicaragua. In general, most European governments lacked a coherent strategy. Since Western Europe potentially had more leverage over Nicaragua's international orientation than over its domestic policies, a constructive approach would have meant providing the Sandinistas with the means to adopt genuine nonalignment—in particular, by increasing economic assistance.[20] Instead, Europe's attention seemed to focus upon Nicaragua's internal restrictions on political democracy.

In fact, much of Europe's "disillusionment" with Nicaragua's internal evolution arose from unrealistic expectations regarding the application of Western prescriptions for political democracy. Many European Social Democrats hoped that, through the influence of Nicaragua's "moderate" bourgeois sectors, the Revolution would evolve in a social democratic direction. Lacking was the recognition that Nicaragua's revolutionary path did not need to follow Western conceptions of democracy to qualify as authentic, popular, and autonomous. Moreover, despite their professed understanding of the need for Third World revolutions to avoid the fate of the Popular Unity government in Chile by taking defensive measures, many European Social Democrats balked at their practical application. What is noteworthy in the case of Nicaragua is less the adoption of restrictive policies than the surprising degree of political pluralism that remained, given the internal and external counterrevolutionary threats.

Furthermore, Western Europe failed to offer Nicaragua sufficient economic aid to make it possible for the Sandinistas to choose not to turn toward Cuba or the Soviet bloc for help. Although Europe's economic assistance was valuable, it fell short of Nicaragua's needs. No doubt, the differences among European governments hindered the emergence of a consistent and forceful policy of economic aid to Nicaragua. The governments of Thatcher in Great Britain and Kohl in West Germany were hardly inclined to lend a willing ear to the Sandinistas' call. It is true that Western Europe was confronting a difficult economic situation in the early 1980s, but the role of the French Socialist government in Africa—most notably in Chad—shows that some European countries did manage to find the resources to come to the aid of their friends. The crux of the problem was that Nicaragua was not a high priority for most European governments. It was even less likely that these governments would augment their economic aid to the Sandinistas in the face of U.S. opposition, given that Western Europe considered its relations with Washington to be of crucial importance.

The Role of U.S. Policies under the Reagan Administration

Although it would be overly simplistic to ascribe all of Nicaragua's problems to the United States, it is undeniable that the Reagan Administration's policies made it more difficult for Nicaragua to retain the same level of international support that it enjoyed in 1979 and 1980. In the first place, the Reagan Administration pursued a deliberate policy of isolating the Sandinista regime, through direct pressures on Nicaragua's friends in Western Europe and the SI. Even though the results of this policy were not entirely satisfactory for Washington, there is reason to believe that U.S. pressures contributed to the growing reluctance of some European governments and SI parties to support Nicaragua.

The effects of U.S. bilateral pressures on West European governments were uneven. On the one hand, the United States could not hope to apply effective pressures on a country like Sweden, which was not a member of the Atlantic Alliance and, in the words of a Swedish diplomat, was "a hopeless case" for the Reagan Administration.[21] On the other hand, with a close ally such as West Germany, Washington did not need to exert much effort to persuade the Christian Democratic government to restrict aid to Nicaragua. More ambiguous is the case of France, a close U.S. ally but highly critical of Washington's Central American policy. During President Mitterrand's visit to Washington in March 1982, the Reagan Administration purportedly achieved its "most notable success," obtaining a delay in the arms shipment to Nicaragua and a relative cooling down of France's relations with the Sandinistas.[22] It is true that following Mitterrand's visit the French government announced that the shipments "would take time." However, although direct U.S. political pressures were no doubt felt, it remained unclear whether the shipments were deliberately delayed. In any case, the United States did not always need to apply direct political pressure on the French government: Economic leverage was often sufficient to make many moderate French Socialists wary of irritating the United States by adopting a pro-Sandinista stance.

The main incident that lent credence to the idea of effective U.S. pressures on SI member parties was the cancellation of the Caracas SI meeting, scheduled for February 1982. Many SI parties (such as the Dutch Labor Party and the French Socialist Party) suggested that the U.S. State Department influenced the Venezuelan host party, AD, and the Dominican Revolutionary Party (PRD) to oppose the SI's support for the Sandinistas, and encouraged AD to protest the FSLN's presence at the conference.[23]

In addition to direct pressures, the U.S. indirectly increased Western Europe's disenchantment with the Sandinista Revolution by pushing Nicaragua in a more "radical" direction. In effect, the Sandinistas' well-grounded fear of a U.S. military intervention in Central America prompted them to restrict political pluralism and to look to other countries for protection, in particular Cuba. Similarly, the Reagan Administration's cutoff of economic assistance, combined with Western Europe's un-willingness to increase its level of aid, forced the Sandinistas to rely more heavily on the East European countries and Cuba. Overall, the Reagan Administration's strategy of destabilizing Nicaragua induced the Sandinistas to resort to defensive measures that, in turn, were publicized and often misrepresented in the international media, thus making it more problematic for Nicaragua to enlist West European support.

In fact, the Reagan Administration's policies toward Nicaragua had a double effect on the perceptions of many West European governments and SI members. On the one hand, by pushing the Sandinistas to harden their policies Washington exacerbated the tensions between Nicaragua and Europe's Social Democrats. On the other hand, these strains were superseded by Europe's opposition to Reagan's interventionism. Even those West European Social Democrats who refused to exonerate the Sandinistas from their responsibilities could not fail to see that U.S. policies were contributing to those developments in Nicaragua they most deplored. And as one SI member exclaimed, "you can't expect the SI to criticize Nicaragua if it is invaded!"[24]

CONCLUSION

The deterioration of Nicaragua's relations with Western Europe and the SI underscored the difficulties involved in sustaining a constructive dialogue in the face of polarization. As of 1984, the overriding concern of most Europeans and SI members to prevent U.S. policies from further "radi-calizing" the Sandinista Revolution and leading to a generalized war in Central America had forestalled an open break with the Sandinistas. It was possible, however, that a point would come when West European governments and the SI would feel compelled to voice their growing disillusionment publicly and reverse their supportive stance toward the Revolution. The threshold might be reached were Nicaragua to become a "second Cuba"—or be perceived as such by most West European and Latin American Social Democrats.

No doubt, the future evolution of the Sandinista regime lay largely beyond the control of Western Europe, since much would be determined by the impact of U.S. policies and Nicaragua's own internal dynamics. Nevertheless, Western Europe was not devoid of influence. Depending on its level of support for the Sandinistas, Western Europe could either curtail or enhance Nicaragua's margin of maneuver in its internal and external policies. Clearly, it was not sufficient for Western Europe simply to tolerate revolutionary developments: Concrete support for established revolutionary regimes was imperative in order to provide them with the means for independence.

Through its economic and political presence in Nicaragua, Western Europe could aspire to an active and independent role in Central America, becoming the catalyst for a negotiated solution in the area in conjunction with regional powers such as Mexico and Venezuela. The conditions for such a role, however, had not been met by mid-1984: Sustained pressure on the U.S. government to dampen its belligerent policies, combined with a more forceful policy of economic and political support for Nicaragua, would constitute the basic elements of a positive West European strategy in Central America. In this light, the development of Western Europe's relations with the Sandinista regime would test Western Europe's potential to adapt effectively to revolution situations and, more generally, to play an independent and constructive role in the Third World.

NOTES

1. In fact, the investments of the European Economic Community countries in Central America represented merely 0.3 percent of all their overseas investments in 1978 and only 0.5 percent of their total trade in 1979. See Erik-Jan Hertogs, "Western European Responses to Revolutionary Developments in the Caribbean Region." Discussion paper prepared for the policy workshop on "An Alternative Policy for Central America and the Caribbean," sponsored by the Institute of Social Studies in cooperation with the Instituto de Investigaciones Económicas y Sociales, The Hague June 6–23, 1983, p. 3.

2. See Wolf Grabendorff, "Western European Perceptions of the Central American Turmoil," in *Central America: International Dimensions of the Crisis*, edited by Richard E. Feinberg (New York: Holmes and Meier, 1982), p. 203.

3. Calculated from "Comercio Nicaragua-Europa Occidental," 1979-1982, Estadísticas de Comercio Exterior, Banco Central de Nicaragua.

4. The figures in this chapter concerning Western Europe's donations and bilateral loans to Nicaragua were calculated from the United Nations General Assembly, *Assistance to Nicaragua: Report of the Secretary-General*, A/36/280 (New York: November 5, 1981), pp. 4–5, as cited in Hertog's "Western European Responses," pp. 16–17.

5. The Contadora initiative was a regional peace effort lauched in January 1983 that included Mexico, Venezuela, Colombia, and Panama.

6. Interview with a member of the Latin American section of the French Socialist Party, Paris, August 2, 1983. Anonymity was requested. All following unnamed sources indicate a request for anonymity.

7. From 1979 to 1981, West Germany offered Nicaragua almost $4 million in donations and $28.8 million in bilateral loans while the conservative Giscard government in France donated about $1 million and granted $12.2 million in loans during the same period. The following section on West Germany draws from the analysis of Hertogs, "Western European Responses," and of Wolf Grabendorff, "The Role of Western Europe in the Caribbean Basin" (Ebenhausen, Federal Republic of Germany: Research Institute for International Affairs, 1983).

8. Washington *Post*, June 22, 1983 p. A16.

9. For an analysis of the constraints facing González's government, see Eusebio Mujal-Léon, "Rei(g)ning in Spain," *Foreign Policy*, No. 51 (Summer 1983).

10. The French Socialist Party, the German SPD, and the Spanish PSOE are members of the SI. The SI represents about 77 parties and organizations with 20 million members and 210 million voters.

11. Interview with the FSLN official in charge of Western Europe in the Department for International Relations, Managua, July 5, 1983.

12. See Gregorio Selser, "Presencia de la Internacional Socialista en América Latina y el Caribe," in *Centro América: Crisis y Política Internacional* (Mexico: CECADE, CIDE, 1982).

13. *Envío* (Managua), No. 23 (May 1983), p. 6a.

14. According to a U.S. State Department official, the Portuguese Socialist leader, Mario Soares, was "the patron of Pastora within European Socialist circles" and was Pastora's main supporter at the SI's Albufeira Congress, along with the Italian member parties and the Spanish PSOE (interview in Washington, D.C., July 19, 1983).

15. Interview with a member of the SI's permanent staff, London, July 22, 1983.

16. Additionally, as one analyst pointed out, "the SI's support for Nicaragua was joined by that of the Contadora group. The latter played a key role in keeping the alternative of a negotiated solution to the crisis in Central America as a viable option in the eyes of the U.S. public and the U.S. Congress." Interview with Cathryn Thorup, Director of the U.S.-Mexico Project at the Overseas Development Council, Washington, D.C., January 31, 1984.

17. Interview with the FSLN official in charge of Western Europe in the Department for International Relations, op. cit.

18. Interview with Jorge Sol of the Institute for Policy Studies, Washington, D.C., June 15, 1983.

19. Interview with a delegate to the Seventh Summit Meeting of the Nonaligned Movement, Paris, August 19, 1983.

20. Interview with Richard E. Feinberg, Vice-President, Overseas Development Council, Washington, D.C., June 1983.

21. Interview with a high-level Swedish diplomat, Washington, D.C., June 15, 1983.

22. Interview with Larry Birns, Director of the Council on Hemispheric Affairs, Washington, D.C., June 17, 1983.

23. According to a vice-president of the SI from AD, however, the cancellation of the Caracas meeting was due to an internal conflict between the AD leadership and its labor union base, which threatened to organize a huge demonstration against the Sandinistas if the FSLN was invited. (Interview with Beatrice Randel, March 16, 1984, Boston.)

24. Interview with a member of the SI's permanent staff, London, July 22, 1983.

Chapter 25
Relations with Latin America

Max Azicri

INTRODUCTION

The foreign policy of Nicaragua after July 19, 1979, was studiously crafted like that of a major country. A sensible balance and a coherence between internal and external policies were maintained by carefully choosing the operational principles of Sandinista foreign policy reflecting the social and political reality of the new Nicaragua as it was emerging under the revolutionary leadership of the FSLN. Nonalignment included such principles as antiimperialism, anticolonialism, and pro-Third World(ism). Foreign policy decisions based on these principles usually drew a positive broadly based international response. Nicaragua's international policy was instrumental in generating diverse international support for the Revolution and its ambitious national development programs. These programs were rather costly and, therefore, many times beyond the financial capacity of the nation's budget, which was heavily burdened by national defense expenditures.[1]

Nonetheless, in Latin America, the home of the Sandinista Revolution, Managua achieved more positive and lasting political results in South America than in Central America and the Caribbean area—with the exceptions of Mexico and Cuba, two pillars of regional support for Nicaragua, and Grenada until the U.S.-led invasion on October 27, 1983. In Central America the real issue was not how skillful and well planned a foreign policy could be, but the existence of the Nicaraguan Revolution itself. Its very presence worked as a catalyst for the forces both supporting and opposing social change in the Central American and Caribbean area and elsewhere.

Given the political characteristics of Latin American countries, and the strength and weaknesses of their political systems, the existence of a new revolutionary regime in the vicinity caused inevitable and far-reaching repercussions in the Western Hemisphere. Regional conservatives, and particularly the military, always readily available to oppose genuine social change and progress in their own countries or in neighboring ones, found an enthusiastic supporter and champion for their ideologically laden cause in U.S. President Ronald Reagan.

Central America became an arena for covert-overt counterrevolutionary war, endless U.S.-sponsored military exercises, and a growing and menacing American military presence. The result was a growing possibility of an imminent military intervention by the United States in Nicaragua and El Salvador (where approximately one-fourth of the country was under the control of the FDR-FMLN guerrilla forces). It was in this charged and volatile context that Nicaragua's relations with neighboring countries were pursued. Obscuring the reality of Nicaragua's national and international politics, and of other regional countries' legitimate concerns, the ongoing conflict made Central America synonymous with revolutionary and counterrevolutionary warfare. At the center of this quagmire, and largely responsible for it, stood Reagan's anti-Sandinista, anti-FDR-FMLN Central American policy, with its contra war and unlawful CIA support and complicity.

EXAMINING FOUR AREAS OF HEMISPHERIC RELATIONS

Nicaragua's Latin American relations are discussed here under four categories of diplomatic exchange and concern: Central America and the Caribbean, South America, Mexico and Cuba, and the Contadora process. The distinction between Central and South America as the foci of Nicaraguan diplomatic attention is significant in a political situation in which geographic proximity to (or distance from) Nicaragua makes a difference. It relates to whether the Sandinista Revolution was a primary or secondary political and military issue for the ruling elite and the level and intensity of U.S. pressure exerted on a given Latin American country.

CENTRAL AMERICA AND THE CARIBBEAN

The Downtrend of Regional Economies

All Central American countries, not only Nicaragua, came to learn that war is bad for business, both nationally and internationally. In 1982 and 1983 the Central American Common Market (CACM) suffered its sharpest decline in 20 years of existence. Intraregional commerce declined for three consecutive years so that by 1983 it reached barely two-thirds of its 1980 volume. International trade agreements were progressively eroded by political and military conditions in the area that came to be characterized by generalized and "accepted unlawfulness." Regional trade meetings continued to be held, and some initiatives to reactivate the Common Market were agreed upon, but no real trust was left among Central American producers for the immediate viability of the CACM, thus practically no new credits were being extended under its provisions. (An exception to this general situation, however, was Nicaraguan and Guatemalan bilateral commerce, mostly due to the suspicion by the latter that if their trade would come to a halt it could be even more difficult to collect Nicaraguan debts.) Regional producers were divided further by the ongoing crisis, losing confidence in the viability of regional business. While Nicaragua's exports to Central America in 1970 represented 26 percent of its total trade, it had declined to 13.2 percent by 1982.[2]

This malaise was to some extent a reflection of the growing hostility between Managua and Washington and the behavior of U.S. allies in the region. The main trade partner of prerevolutionary Nicaragua was the United States, which in 1970 bought 70 percent of its exports. By 1982 it had declined to 22.6 percent, due largely to Reagan's anti-Sandinista trade and financial policies. On the other hand, by the same year, Nicaraguan exports had become diversified following an increment in trade partners and volume but not a total trade income gain: Western Europe, 22.9 percent; socialist (COMECON) countries, 7.3 percent; and others, 34 percent (this included countries in Africa and Asia, like Lybia and Japan).

A similar trend was followed regarding Nicaraguan imports. From 1981 to 1982 there were descending and ascending import rates paralleling the export curve. Decreasing imports for the years 1981 and 1982 involved the United States, from 26.3 percent to 19 percent; and the CACM, from 21.1 to 15.1 percent. Increasing imports for the same period involved Mexico, from 12 to 21.1 percent; France, from 0.9 to 4.2 percent; Spain, from 1.2 to 2.8 percent; socialist countries, from 3.3 to 11.5 percent.[3]

Opposition to Managua's Policies

The harsh reality of international commercial and political relations for most developing nations gives some credence to the policy rationale behind Managua's determination to diversify its external relations away from its traditional dependence on the United States. Not that diversified dependence should be a goal in itself, but at least it could be a means eventually to overcome all forms of dependence. The exercise by the revolutionary regime of its newly gained sovereignty and national independence made possible this kind of policy thinking and policy implementation. Its political effects, however, were conflictive in a region traditionally and still dominated by conservative, pro-Washington regimes. For them, Sandinistas external relations were as objectionable as

Managua's internal policies—that is, the national defense and military preparedness program. External relations with such countries as Cuba, the Soviet Union, and other socialist states (particularly the military assistance Nicaragua received from them) and support for the Salvadoran FDR-FMLN guerrillas, even if in actuality limited mostly to moral and political help, were used as handy arguments against Managua by the Revolution's external foes. Central American politics turned increasingly into politics of mutual, directed hostility.

The net political effect of these events was that hard-liners, mainly military leaders and their supporting cliques, came to eclipse civilian leadership in Northern Central America, even where there were civilian governments as in Honduras. Costa Rica's long-standing democracy—which had eliminated its regular army in 1948—was subjected to additional, severe strains. President Luis Alberto Monge was pressured by conservatives inside and outside his administration and by the United States to take a more direct and militant stand against Nicaragua, even to the extent of violating the nation's commitment to a policy of neutrality.[4] (In the fall of 1983 Costa Rica had issued a constitutional declaration of neutrality that applied to the Central American conflict, and particularly to Nicaragua.)

Honduras and Costa Rica came to allow their territory to be used by U.S.-sponsored counterrevolutionary forces fighting the Sandinistas. The Honduran military cooperated directly with the Somocista Nicaraguan Democratic Force (FDN) in such attacks, and the Costa Rican Rural Guard was accused of helping Edén Pastora's Democratic Revolutionary Alliance (ARDE) in military actions against Nicaragua's southern border. The pressure exerted by the U.S. Central Intelligence Agency to have ARDE join forces with the Honduran-based FDN led to the terroristic attack on May 30, 1984, in which Pastora was wounded and two journalists and several of Pastora's men were killed. Significantly, Pastora accused the CIA of the attack—after having initially accused Managua of masterminding it—in response to his adamant refusal to merge his forces with the FDN military command dominated by former Somoza officers.[5]

Under different circumstances, with a less hostile administration in Washington, relations between Nicaragua and her closest neighbors, though still difficult, might have been manageable. This might have been particularly true for Honduras and Costa Rica. In fact, however, regional politics came to be dominated by General Paul F. Gorman, Chief of the U.S. Southern Command in Panama, of whom it was said: "He couldn't speak a word of Spanish—but that didn't really matter. He spoke Ronald Reagan's language."[6] The militarization of the region carried out under his leadership after 1983 had devastating political and economic effects for countries like Honduras and Costa Rica. As expected, it increased the level of anti-Nicaraguan rhetoric in isthmian politics and augmented the possibility of regional war. Under Gorman's leadership an effort was made in October 1983 to revive the infamous Central American Defense Council (CONDECA)—originally organized in the 1960s by the late Anastasio Somoza—which comprised Guatemala, El Salvador, Honduras, and Panama. Costa Rica stayed out of this organization on the basis that it had no army. Nicaragua was not invited.[7]

Nicaraguan relations with neighboring countries during this period mostly continued already established links and new ill-fated measures aimed primarily at neutralizing the impact of hostile, anti-Managua policies. Reinforcing Nicaragua's diplomatic effort was the Contadora process, a peace-keeping effort initiated by Colombia, Mexico, Panama, and Venezuela at a meeting on the Panamanian Island of Contadora in January 1983. Although Managua was not always in agreement with the Contadora countries in every matter, both had a vested interest in preserving peace in Central America.

In the Caribbean, as well as in Central America, the memory of the swift and militarily massive invasion of Grenada by the United States, acting upon a "request" issued by the Organization of Eastern (English-speaking) Caribbean States, lingered in everybody's mind. The open display of readily available American force continued in the Caribbean in 1984, with military exercises paralleling the Central American war games. One of the largest maneuvers ever held in the Caribbean, Ocean Venture '84, involved 30,000 U.S. military personnel from all service branches and 350 ships. It lasted from April 20 to May 6 at a cost of $25 million, and included the evacuation of 300 people from the U.S. naval base at Guantanamo, Cuba. After the U.S. invasion of Grenada, Cuba was the only active supporter the Sandinistas had in the Caribbean.

The Hardening and Softening of Positions

Throughout almost five years of Revolution, Nicaragua was able to preserve diplomatic relations with all Central American countries. Its contacts with Honduras, however, were so strained that they came close to collapsing entirely with the expulsion on May 11, 1984, of the Nicaraguan ambassador in Tegucigalpa, Ewin Zeblah. The expulsion was the Honduran response to the "May 8 downing [by Nicaragua] of a military helicopter with U.S. insignia and a Honduran crew" that had penetrated Nicaraguan territory. Tegucigalpa acted in spite of Managua's assurances reiterating "its unbreakable decision to never take the first step in a military confrontation with Honduras." For the Sandinistas the incident "conceal[ed] ulterior motives of aggression" and was the "product of the deterioration of relations in the region brought about 'at the instigation of the United States administration.' "[8] Examined from afar, the episode was further evidence that political actors in the area needed to undertake bolder diplomatic initiatives if they wished to influence the course of events, rather than simply be used by a manipulative outside power.

Relations with Costa Rica followed a similar path. Although ARDE's military actions in the southern border were not initially as frequent, costly, and deadly as the FDN's in the north, they had escalated dangerously by 1984—as Pastora's temporary occupation of the isolated and abandoned port of San Juan del Norte in April seemed to indicate. However, this demonstration of audacity by Pastora ultimately proved to have more negative political implications for ARDE in that it was a source of embarrassment for the Monge Administration. The May 3 Peñas Blancas affair demonstrated clearly to San José and Managua that a diplomatic way out was urgently needed. On that day the Costa Rican radio announced that the country was being invaded by 2,000 Sandinistas. Colonel Oscar Videla, head of the Costa Rican police force, denied the report but acknowledged that "rifle and artillery fire had been exchanged in the border area."[9] According to Managua's version of the incident, "counterrevolutionaries began firing mortars into Costa Rican territory" with the intention of making it appear as if the attack was coming from Nicaragua. Also, Managua denied responding to the fire, which was seen as a clear provocation engineered by ARDE and its Costa Rican allies.[10]

It was precisely at the border post of Peñas Blancas that the Nicaraguan-Costa Rican Commission for Supervision and Prevention (of border incidents) was summarily inaugurated on May 26. Proposed by Costa Rica at a Nicaraguan-requested meeting after ARDE's May 3 border provocation, the border commission was expected to prevent future attacks such as those that were increasingly occurring along their 320-kilometer border. The six-point declaration creating the border commission had been agreed upon by both parties only 11 days earlier—at a meeting held in Panama between the foreign ministers of Nicaragua and Costa Rica, Miguel D'Escoto and Carlos José Gutiérrez, respectively. Also in attendance were the deputy foreign ministers of the Contadora countries, who provided the support of their group for the important peace initiative.

According to D'Escoto, the bilateral agreement was "one of the most significant achievements since the Latin American (Contadora) peace initiatives began a year and a half ago." For Nicaragua's deputy foreign minister, José León Talavera, "it prove[d] that escalated tensions in the area can be eased through bilateral means." The Costa Rican ambassador in Managua, Jesús Fernández, stated that the bilateral agreement confirmed Costa Rica's "neutrality and determination to prevent any actions from taking place against the Nicaraguan government." This reflected his government's current position, as well as a significant sector of Costa Rican public opinion. On May 15 a peace demonstration led by former presidents José Figueres and Daniel Oduber was held in San José with 50,000 marchers shouting "Peace, yes. War, no."[11]

In a region increasingly dominated by bellicose statements and actions, the bilateral agreement was a historical landmark for Central American diplomacy. Nonetheless, it remained to be seen what the future had in store for the border commission. In the spring the Costa Rican chamber of commerce had demanded that "the government break diplomatic relations [with Nicaragua], arm the country, and get out of Contadora." Also, former foreign minister Gonzalo Facio had stated: "There can be no peace in the region as long as there is a government of Communist extraction. . . . We cannot accept an accommodation with a totalitarian regime in Nicaragua. We have to act accordingly." Conservative leaders calling for confrontation and war were neither quieted nor discouraged by Monge's neutrality policy.[12]

The Monge Administration was walking a fine line alternating between conciliatory and hostile gestures toward Nicaragua. His administration resisted American pressure for the U.S.-assisted construction of roads and settlements of tactical military value on its northern (Nicaraguan) border, a move that would have taken Costa Rica decisively toward its final "Hondurization." An important part of the overall policy goal pursued by Washington to isolate Nicaragua effectively in the region, this scheme had been communicated to San José by U.S. Ambassador Curtin Winsor and by Undersecretary of Defense Fred S. Ikle and General Gorman in visits they made to Costa Rica in fall 1983 and spring 1984, respectively.[13] In 1984 Costa Rica received $2.5 million in U.S. military aid, with $10 million more expected in 1985. Also, San José requested and was readily granted $7.85 million in defensive military equipment in 1984. Nevertheless, a presidential spokesman in San José was quoted in Managua's *Barricada Internacional* as saying: "The Monge administration's alliance with the United States government should not be interpreted as a willingness to do whatever the United States wants." He recognized, however, that "Costa Rica [was] under great pressure to abandon its principle of neutrality."[14]

Moreover, according to the Washington *Post*, a "secret [U.S.] State Department report" recognized the importance of turning the present Sandinista-ARDE confrontation into a Nicaraguan-Costa Rican conflict. In the words of the State Department report: "To the extent Nicaragua succeeds in protraying its activities as a response to armed provocation by anti-Sandinista guerrillas, our gains will be limited and potential political backing *for our response* will not materialize. . . . For public relations, it is important to neutralize 'the ARDE factor.' . . . The story should be Nicaragua-vs.-Costa Rica, not [Nicaragua]-vs.-armed opposition."[15]

Nicaragua's Honduran Crucible

Reflecting on his country's predicament, an unidentified Honduran politician commented: "Under General [Walter] López Reyes. . . . the United States will 'still have a friend in the Honduran military—what they won't have is a slave as they had in Alvarez.' "[16] The latter, General Gustavo Alvarez Martínez, had been ousted as military chief-strongman by disaffected officers on March 31, 1984. Under Alvarez, Honduras, the central piece in Reagan's Central American policy, had become an American pawn, losing prestige through its role as surrogate. Led by General Alvarez and American Ambassador John D. Negroponte, Honduras had changed almost overnight into a huge U.S. military base.[17] In a symbiotic relationship that extended from Tegucigalpa to Washington, Alvarez was always readily disposed to please Negroponte, and the latter was equally disposed to please Reagan. Paradoxically neither stayed in complete control for long. The Honduran military, though conservative and anti-Sandinista like Alvarez, could not accept seeing the country used so blatantly by the United States for the sake of Reagan's regional policy interests; so Alvarez was sent handcuffed into exile. Similarly, Negroponte finally had to yield his inordinate power to General Gorman, the individual who really came to exercise American control in Central America. Negroponte did, however, remain as ambassador. In doing so he was unique in surviving a major shakeup in 1983 and early 1984 which cost the jobs of ambassadors Dean Hinton in El Salvador, Anthony Quainton in Nicaragua, and Frederic Chapin in Guatemala, all of whom had run afoul of Gorman in one way or another.[18]

But had there been real changes in Honduran political and military policy under General López, other than publicized statements that the days in which American commands and wishes were followed in the way Alvarez did were over? As before, President Roberto Suazo Córdova followed the military leadership, having to acquiesce to the ousting of General Alvarez when faced with the ultimatum of either to endorse "the move or leave the country too."[19] The extent of the nation's militarization was described by Jorge Arturo Reina, Secretary General of the Liberal Party's progressive wing (ALIPO), as follows: "Here in Honduras we have four armies: our own, that of El Salvador, that of the United States, and the anti-Sandinista counterrevolutionary forces."[20]

After the completion of the latest in a continuous series of joint U.S.-Honduran military exercises, Granadero I in June 1984, there were approximately 2,500 U.S. military left behind, waiting for the next round of maneuvers to start again. The anti-Sandinista counterrevolutionaries continued using Honduras as a staging area and sanctuary in their war against Managua, although they were keeping a "low profile" as requested by the new military leadership. Nevertheless, some noteworthy issues were raised by General López and his associates, including: (1) the need to renegotiate the U.S.-Honduran agreement on the Regional Military Training Center at Puerto Castilla so that in the future more Hondurans and fewer Salvadorans would be trained; (2) questioning the advisability of continuing to use Honduras as a rear base and command headquarters for anti-Sandinista guerrillas and their CIA advisers (although the FDN forces continue to operate under General López as before); and (3) recognizing their fears that if the United States were to change its Nicaraguan policy (finding some possible accommodation with Managua) it would "leave Honduras exposed on its own." Also, there were serious economic complaints and reservations. Honduras had to raise taxes in spite of its highly troubled economy so it could pay $10 million in fuel as its contribution to the joint maneuvers with the United States. Its poor economic performance was being aggravated by what General López called " 'dangerous social-economic imbalance' caused by the country's declining export income and rising imports costs—an imbalance aggravated by soaring military spending."[21] In short, General López wanted more economic and military aid in payment for Honduras's role as the center for the U.S. military presence and control of the region, especially if, as was reported, the U.S. Southern Command were to be moved in the future from Panama to Honduras.[22]

Political protests against the Suazo Córdova Administration for "placing the interests of the U.S. above the needs of the Honduran people" became more vocal and frequent. In the 1984 May Day parade approximately 60,000 people in Tegucigalpa protested "U.S. intervention in Honduras . . . demanding the withdrawal of foreign troops. . . ." This theme was the main rallying point for the opposition. In a full-page ad published in a major newspaper six weeks earlier, 126 prominent citizens rejected the use of force by Honduras, indicated their support for the Contadora process, and pleaded for the "withdrawal of foreign troops from Honduras and Central America and for removal of U.S. bases from Honduras."[23] Congressional leaders expressed their frustration over the overwhelmingly American presence in their country. Mario Rivera López, leader of the opposition National Party, characterized Honduras as a "country semi-occupied by U.S. soldiers and without congressional authorization."[24]

It appears that the U.S. militarization of Honduras had compromised the nation's sovereignty and political independence, imperiled the fragile return to civilian authority, and shifted the balance of power again to the military. Political unrest had resurfaced, with signs of more to come. Given these conditions, the worsening of relations between Managua and Tegucigalpa in mid-1984 was almost inevitable. The future was not promising. The Pentagon reportedly had "plans to continue military maneuvers in Honduras until the year 2,000, bolstering the military infrastructure along the way."[25] In this light, the U.S. drive for the "Hondurization" of Costa Rica discussed earlier becomes clearer. The U.S. goal was to have Managua contend with a "Honduras" on both borders.

For Nicaraguan diplomacy the ongoing Central American conflict was a challenge of endurance, and of having to pursue diplomatic avenues and probe initiatives to defuse one crisis after another in what seemed an endless series of provocations. To talk peace in the face of hostility and war involved much self-constraint. The Contadora process in spite of shortcomings and vacillations was increasingly recognized by Managua in 1983 and 1984 as the only alternative for peace in the region. The international support and prestige enjoyed by Contadora provided Nicaragua with access to neighboring countries that otherwise it would not have had under existing conditions.

El Salvador, Guatemala, and Panama

The American support for the contras operating from Honduras and Costa Rica was rationalized in Washington as the evenhanded retribution based on "symmetry": What Nicaragua was doing to El Salvador—allegedly supporting leftist guerrillas fighting that government—was being done to Managua by the United States and its allies in retribution.[26] However, David MacMichael, a former CIA estimates officer specializing in Central America, denied that there was any evidence supporting Washington's charges against Nicaragua. He claimed that "intelligence reports of crossborder shipments 'fell to nothing' after the failure of the Salvadoran guerrillas' 'final offensive' in the spring of 1981." Moreover, he charged that the Reagan Administration had "systematically misrepresented Nicaraguan involvement in the supply of arms to Salvadoran guerrillas to justify its efforts to overthrow the Nicaraguan government."[27]

In a broader sense, the real question was: Would Nicaraguan relations with El Salvador or any other Central American country be free of U.S. meddling if there were no civil war in El Salvador? Managua was dubious,[28] claiming that Washington under Reagan would be anti-Sandinista with or without a Salvadoran problem. Thus there was almost no possibility for Nicaraguan regional relations to be a legitimate reflection of real indigenous problems free from those artificially created by hostile parties. Accordingly, diplomatic relations between Managua and San Salvador were correct but tense. Newly elected President José Napoleón Duarte failed to visit Nicaragua in his tour of Central American nations on his way to Washington in 1984. And, in public statements he stressed how difficult it would be to coexist with a regime like that in Nicaragua. Salvadoran participation in maneuvers such as Granadero I drew the country even closer to U.S.-sponsored regional military preparedness program. It was reported that the Salvadoran military, under CIA supervision and direction had participated in the mining of Nicaraguan waters early in 1984.[29]

On August 8, 1983, General Oscar Mejía Victores overthrew General Efrain Ríos Montt in what seemed a Guatemalan palace revolt closely coordinated with the United States.[30] Mejía Victores was expected to be more supportive of regional anti-Sandinista policy than Ríos Montt. As expected, two months later Guatemala hosted the regional military summit in which CONDECA was brought back to play an active role. Seemingly, all the different pieces of the Central American puzzle were falling in place. It appeared that if only Guatemala would adopt a confrontational policy toward Nicaragua similar to that of Honduras, Washington's anti-Sandinista policy for Managua's regional isolation might succeed.

Surprisingly, Guatemala did not behave as planned. Mejía Victores was not significantly more anti-Sandinista than Ríos Montt. Guatemala was integrated further into the overall Central American military program, as evidenced by Granadero I. However, as before, domestic problems seemed to prevail: its level of integration into a regional military structure appeared motivated mainly by internal pressures and its need to receive more U.S. economic and military aid.[31] In all, Guatemala was less of a worry for the Sandinistas than the other Central American republics.

Panama's Central American policy in 1984 was a contradictory composite made of two opposed elements: first, it was a founding member of the Contadora group (which was seeking regional peaceful solutions based on diplomacy); second, however, it was one of the four area countries that agreed on the reactivation of CONDECA (which was seeking regional military solutions based on force). Furthermore, Panama had joined the United States and three Central American republics in the Granadero I maneuvers and was expected to continue participating in future regional military planning and exercises.

Panama's ambivalent regional role was played against a history of political instability and, more recently, electoral politics: The 1984 presidential elections were the first in 16 years. The resignation of President Ricardo de la Espriella on February 13, 1984, and his replacement by Jorge Illueca were attributed to political pressure exerted by the armed forces—not unlike what happened to President Arístides Arroyo in 1982, who was replaced then by de la Espriella. Two top-ranking military officers were mentioned as the real power holders in early 1984: General Manuel Antonio Noriega (who attended the 1983 CONDECA meeting as Panama's representative) and Colonel Roberto Díaz Herrera.[32] The close electoral victory of Nicolás Ardito Barletta on May 6, 1984, signaled the beginning of a new constitutional period. Barletta was the candidate of the official six-party alliance known as the National Democratic Union (UNADE).

Regarded as a no-nonsense technocrat, he had been an economic advisor in the administration of the late Brigadier General Omar Torrijos and had served as Minister of Planning and Economic Policy from 1973 to 1978. As a member of both Contadora and CONDECA, Panama could reinforce its peaceful role under Barletta. Furthermore, it could also exert a meaningful moderating influence upon hard-liners gathered under the CONDECA banner. In this sense, Panama's diplomatic role had importance for Managua. Panama's geographic position on the isthmus linking Central and South America served to dramatize its diplomatic regional role.

MANAGUA'S SOUTH AMERICAN RELATIONS

For Nicaraguan foreign policy, Central and South America were quite distinct. As indicated above, there was little room under prevailing conditions for close relations between Managua and her Central American neighbors. The ruling elites of Central America had responded to the Revolution in Nicaragua out of fear, deeply threatened by the notion that someday their own societies could undergo similar social changes. Active interference by the United States in most aspects of Central American political and military life had aggravated an already difficult situation, providing additional obstacles to peaceful solutions for existent problems. However, in South America the Sandinistas could pursue diplomatic goals in a more constructive international environment. As a result, though not always successful, Nicaraguan diplomacy faced relatively fewer obstacles south of the Isthmus.

Nicaragua's South American relations were conducted with a set of countries of diverse internal political conditions. The southern hemisphere includes larger, more developed countries. Their governments are not as susceptible to control or manipulation by the United States. Also, Central American political upheavals appear to have less threatening and direct impact on the ruling elites of South America than on their counterparts to the north. Therefore, with the lone exceptions of Cuba and Mexico, the Sandinistas enjoyed considerably better relations with South American countries than with their Central American and Caribbean neighbors.

Nicaragua's South American relations underwent important changes in the first five years of Sandinistas rule. Most notable are the cases of Argentina, Colombia, Bolivia, and Paraguay. As a general rule, South American countries that initially had diplomatic difficulties with Managua improved their relations over the years. In the case of Paraguay, however, the opposite was true: after an initial period of diplomatic relations they were later terminated.

In the first years of the Reagan Administration the Argentine military regime actually provided military training and support for Nicaraguan exiles in Honduras. Buenos Aires, Tegucigalpa, and Washington had agreed on a common policy aimed at destabilizing the Sandinista Revolution. However, the 1982 Malvinas/Falklands Islands war changed this situation. Washington's support for England and Nicaragua's verbal defense of Argentina in such international forums as the Organization of American States, the United Nations, and the Nonaligned Movement were decisive. Nonetheless, it was not until after the inauguration of civilian President Raúl Alfonsín in 1983 that Argentine support for the contras was entirely terminated (January 1984). Subsequently, relations between both countries improved to the point of being close and mutually supportive. In spite of open U.S. opposition to any type of help for the Sandinistas, and in spite of Argentina's troubles with its staggering external debt, Buenos Aires came to advocate a peaceful solution to the Central American conflict and even granted Managua $45 million in credit and food aid.[33]

After an initial territorial dispute between Colombia and Nicaragua over who had sovereignty rights over the San Andrés and Providencia Islands—which chilled but did not interrupt diplomatic relations—the political rapport between both countries improved noticeably, especially with the inauguration of President Belisario Betancur in 1982. Colombia's central role as one of the four Contadora countries reinforced a commonly shared interest by Managua and Bogotá in a peaceful solution of the Central American conflict.

Bolivia and Paraguay followed opposite directions in their relations with Nicaragua. Bolivia had broken diplomatic relations with Nicaragua in 1980 after Managua's condemnation before the OAS of the military coup carried out by General Luis García Mesa. However, once the constitutional process was reestablished with the inauguration of President Hernán Siles Suazo on October 10, 1982, relations were rapidly resumed. Subsequently, La Paz provided significant political support for the Sandinistas in hemispheric and other diplomatic circles. On the other hand, Paraguay had extended diplomatic recognition to the Sandinista regime in 1979, but ended diplomatic relations with Managua after Anastasio Somoza was killed in Asunción in 1980 under circumstances that remain unclear. Relations were not reestablished.

Chile was a difficult case, handled better than Paraguay by Nicaragua. Although they did not exchange ambassadors—their diplomatic business was conducted at first through their ambassadors at the United Nations and later through a Chilean chargé d'affairs in Managua—Chile and Nicaragua were able to sustain a reasonable level of diplomatic exchange. Though it seems surprising given the nature of the Pinochet regime, Santiago was not interested in alienating itself entirely from Managua. This was part of Chile's campaign to muster the widest possible range of diplomatic contacts and potential support to use in its territorial dispute with Argentina over the ownership of three islands in the Beagle Channel. From Managua's perspective, while still keeping considerable political distance from Santiago, it was applying here its general policy of conducting diplomatic relations with countries representing a wide range of political systems. This was also true even in this case when their internal and external policies were very much opposite.

Even though relations with Venezuela did not undergo major diplomatic changes, they nevertheless improved over the years. Political relations with Caracas were initially marred by President Luis Herrera Campín's support for the then Salvadoran civilian-military junta headed by José Napoleón Duarte—a fellow Christian Democrat. During this period Venezuela was an important trading partner for Managua as one of its oil suppliers. Political relations improved but oil sales diminished. The inauguration of President Jaime Lusinchi in early 1984 provided Commander Daniel Ortega, head of the Sandinista governing Junta, with an invaluable political and diplomatic opportunity for holding direct talks with heads of state and political leaders. Former President Carlos Andrés Pérez, always influential in the ruling Democratic Action Party and in the Socialist International, was one of the forces behind Venezuela's improved Central American policy and the key role it played in the Contadora process. As a middle-size regional power, Venezuela added considerable weight to the Latin American diplomatic effort seeking peaceful solutions to regional disputes.

Managua's good relations with Perú and Ecuador, established in 1979, remained positive. This was demonstrated not only in their bilateral exchanges, but in Lima's and Quito's manifestations of support for Managua in different international organizations. Their exchanges were not limited to diplomatic and political contacts, but included cultural and commercial relations.

Nicaragua also had good relations with Brazil. Immediately after the Sandinista victory, the two countries exchanged commercial attachés and, throughout the period, Rio extended credits and technical assistance to Managua. In early 1984 the diplomatic relationship was elevated to an exchange of ambassadors. Although Brazil sometimes exhibited caution in its relations with Nicaragua—an apparent bow to the wishes of the United States—President Figuereido came to support strongly a nonmilitary solution for Central America, siding openly with the Contadora group. Mexico's critical role in this process reinforced Brazil's position on this issue.

Quantitatively, Nicaragua's diplomatic relations with South America showed one minus (Paraguay), while in Central America they were all positive. As mentioned earlier, however, qualitatively, relations with the former were superior by all standards. This was no mean diplomatic achievement given the magnitude and determination of the forces bent on undoing the Nicaraguan Revolution.

MEXICAN AND CUBAN RELATIONS

The two countries in the Western Hemisphere with which Nicaragua had the best relations were Mexico and Cuba. Their unswerving support was invaluable for the Sandinistas. Geographic proximity and a common historical and cultural tradition may at least partly explain this phenomenon. And yet, the same common features are present among other Latin American countries that did not share such affinity for the Nicaraguan Revolution. Cuban-Nicaraguan affinity may be explained as an expression of similar (though not identical) social reality and revolutionary processes that provided the policymaking context as well as the major values and goals for internal and external policies. The friendly relationship with Mexico, on the other hand, flowed less from similarities in contemporary social policy (the Mexican Revolution had died in the 1940s for all practical purposes) than from Mexican historical experience and revolutionary myth and a long tradition of Mexican reluctance to be dominated by the United States.

There was a lack of understanding in the United States and other countries as to why Mexico supported the Sandinistas economically and diplomatically, and, moreover, why this support should also be a major component of its broader Central American policy. Contrary to Washington's belief, Mexico was not carrying out an arbitrary or self-defeating policy blindly agreed upon by a misguided ruling elite, supposedly acting as it did because it could not understand that it was bringing about its own demise. To the contrary, Mexico's Central American policy, and its special relationship with Nicaragua, were the result of a careful evaluation of the Central American problematic from a "South" perspective, acknowledging the built-in conflict and inequities present in North-South relations. Also, it reflected and incorporated Mexico's internal and external political concerns.[34] Managua's foreign policy in this regard was a pragmatic recognition of these political facts. It acknowledged that, even if equally supportive, Mexico's and Cuba's Nicaraguan and Central American policies, representing different political systems and interests, were decided by different policymaking structures. The Sandinistas' realistic understanding of the nature and practice of this historically unique relationship, which allowed them to maintain close and profitable relations with both countries, was a credit to them.

In opposition to Mexico's (and Cuba's) Nicaraguan policy, the United

States viewed Nicaragua, and the Central American conflict in general, as part of the East-West conflict: thus Managua and Havana were no more than surrogates for Soviet hemispheric subversion. This approach was consistent with American anti-East rhetoric and posturing. Also, it took place at a time when North-South asymmetrical relations and their inimical impact upon developing countries was downplayed by Washington. The contradictory nature of the Central American policy of Mexico and United States was evidenced again during President Miguel de la Madrid's official visit to the United States in mid-May 1984. Discussing Mexico's perspective before a joint session of Congress, de la Madrid stated: "We are convinced that the Central American conflict is a result of the economic deficiencies, political backwardness, and social injustice that have afflicted the countries of the area."[35] A State Department official admitted that "some within the Administration are 'dissatisfied with Mexico's attitude on Central America and would have us try to modify that'."[36]

The goals of Mexico's pro-Sandinista policy were to keep the economy afloat and to keep Nicaragua out of the East-West conflict. By pursuing these goals it hoped to prevent a direct U.S. military intervention in Nicaragua and a situation in which the Sandinistas would be forced for their own survival to move into the Soviet orbit. In a broader regional sense, Mexico perceived itself as performing the role of mediator: among the Central American republics through the Contadora process, and directly with the United States in bilateral contacts. Mexico's oil supply to Managua amounted in 1981 to over $93 million for a total of over $105 million in exports to Nicaragua; its imports from Managua amounted to over $7 million in the same year—a significant increment in both directions.[37] There was more than supportive rhetoric in Mexico's policy; Nicaragua's moderation in internal and external politics already had the imprint of Mexico's (and Cuba's) moderating influence.

Cuba's main foreign policy principle—proletarian internationalism—took on a special meaning when it came to Nicaragua: solidarity with a triumphant revolution in a country so close to home in every regard sharing so many common features. Just a few days after the 1979 victory, an official Sandinista delegation attended Cuba's celebration of its main revolutionary holiday on July 26. A year later, July 19, 1980, President Fidel Castro went to Managua for the celebration of the first anniversary of the Sandinista victory.

From the outset, Cuba helped lavishly in the reconstruction of Nicaragua after its devastating war of 1978 and 1979. The literacy campaign, launched in 1979 immediately after the ousting of the Somoza dictatorship, provided an ideal opportunity for Cuban-Nicaraguan cooperation. Cuba sent 1,200 literacy volunteers, the largest among many international delegations, to teach thousands of Nicaraguans. Technical assistance in other civilian fields and military matters soon followed, including agriculture, industry, public works, education, culture, public health, economic planning, and national defense and military preparedness. Resisting pressure from within and abroad to sever its close ties with Cuba, especially after the invasion of Grenada, Managua announced early in 1984, on the occasion of Cuba's 25th revolutionary anniversary, that Nicaraguan-Cuban friendship was a nonnegotiable issue, that the bonds uniting both revolutions were permanent. Nonetheless, in a pragmatic gesture aimed at defusing the mounting pressure against Nicaragua by the counterrevolution and other actions, the Sandinistas announced in late 1983 and early 1984 that Cuban personnel, including teachers, would start leaving the country soon. The United States complained in mid-1984, however, that Cuban military advisors and personnel were still stationed in Nicaragua. The announced Cuban withdrawal was not enough for Washington.

The emphasis Washington put on the Havana-Managua military connection obscured and mystified the real nature of the mutually supportive relationship between these two genuine Latin American revolutions. As discussed above, the United States also misunderstood the motivations and goals of Mexico's politically progressive but nonrevolutionary pro-Sandinista policy. Although Mexico and Cuba had a history of mutual cooperation and long-standing relations, the Nicaraguan Revolution provided additional grounds for agreement on Central America: their regional policies converging on supporting the Sandinistas—as well as the Salvadoran FDR-FMLN.

MANAGUA AND THE CONTADORA PROCESS

The founding of the Contadora group early in 1983 by Mexico, Venezuela, Colombia, and Panama constituted an act of Latin American assertiveness. A new awakening and solidarity seemed to prevail among Latin American countries in the aftermath of the Malvinas/Falklands war in the spring of 1982. The growing Central American conflict, the ensuing U.S. militarization of the region, the threat of the revolutionary war in El Salvador, and the counterrevolutionary war launched against Nicaragua from Honduras (and later from Costa Rica) created a sense of urgency. The region was running out of time, and something had to be done. Latin Americans had to undertake diplomatic action if a peaceful resolution of the conflict responding to legitimate Latin American interests and aspirations and not to those promoted by the United States were to be attained.

The results were mixed. Nonetheless, the very fact that a diplomatic conflict-resolution structure became readily available was instrumental in keeping countless dangerous confrontations, kidnappings, sabotage, border skirmishes, and other incidents from escalating into uncontrollable warfare for several years. Nicaragua had been under attack from Washington and its surrogates, not only militarily but also diplomatically, financially, economically, and particularly through a mass media disinformation campaign. Naturally, Managua profited the most from Contadora. Contadora was hardly partial to the Sandinistas, but Nicaragua, more than any other Central American republic, needed a medium for diplomatic exchange and negotiation; a forum for open discussion of the mounting problems—even if many of the meetings did not lead to positive results.

Contadora was also a challenge to creative individual diplomacy. The opportunity was not lost to the Sandinistas. In addition to its active participation in the Contadora process itself—notably the signing with the other Central American republics of the 21-point Contadora peace proposal in January 1984—Managua undertook several peace initiatives of its own. On July 19, 1983, Commander Ortega presented a six-point plan dealing with such Nicaraguan and regional issues as ending the counter-revolutionary war, withdrawing foreign troops, terminating military exercises with foreign troops, and dismantling foreign bases. On October 15, 1983, Nicaragua presented an elaborate peace proposal in the form of four draft treaties dealing with the United States, Honduras, El Salvador, and with all regional countries. In a characteristic anti-Sandinista stance, Washington, San Salvador, and Tegucigalpa ignored and/or rejected the Nicaraguan proposal. Also, Managua modified its earlier position of asking for bilateral negotiations with each one of the parties involved to an acceptance of multilateral negotiations as the diplomatic procedure to follow. This concilatory step did not move Managua's adversaries closer to the negotiating table either.

The United States had its own agenda. American support for Contadora was ambivalent at best. Publicly Washington endorsed the diplomatic process while privately continuing policies that ran against Contadora's peaceful quest. The overwhelming international support for Contadora left no room for a public disregard of this Latin American initiative—especially when it included the United Nations, OAS, U.S. allies in Western Europe and elsewhere, nonaligned and Third World countries, and socialist nations. However, none of Nicaragua's peace initiatives seemed to mollify Washington's hard-line stance and active pursuit of a military solution. Nonetheless, by mid-1984 there were signs that the Reagan Administration was running out of opportunities to further its war policy at least via the contras. The CIA had used up the $24 million allocated for 1983 and Congress, including finally the Senate, rejected the administration's request for an additional $21 million. This left Reagan with two alternatives (other than giving up): requesting funds later in 1984 and/or supporting the contras's quest for funds elsewhere.[38]

On the positive side, the June 1984 visit by Secretary of State George Schultz to Managua was followed by new meetings in Mexico City between Harry Schlaudeman (who replaced Reagan's first Special Envoy to Central America) and Nicaraguan deputy Foreign Minister Victor Hugo Tinoco. Also, Edén Pastora made the rounds in Washington early in the summer in pursuit of his new nonmilitary strategy (which he devised after splitting with the ARDE forces that joined the Honduras-based FDN). This included seeking participation in the electoral process by "forcing" the Sandinistas to open further the political participation leading to the November 4, 1984, elections.[39] At the time when Nicaragua was approaching its fifth revolutionary anniversary, U.S. anti-Sandinista policies, including those related to the contras, were in disarray.

Meanwhile, the Nicaraguan electoral process aimed at the institutionalization of the Revolution, and the military effectiveness of the Sandinista armed forces (which had not allowed a single town or city to fall to the contras), had reinforced Managua's stance in its complex diplomatic relations with Latin America. In all, diplomatic and other kinds of difficulties seemed a greater challenge to Nicaragua than military self-defense.

NOTES

1. See other chapters in this volume discussing Nicaragua's international relations. For a general discussion of Nicaragua's international relations with emphasis on Latin America, see Max Azicri, "Nicaragua's Foreign Relations: The Struggle for Survival," in *The Dynamics of Latin American Foreign Policies: Challenges for the 1980s*, edited by Jennie K. Lincoln and Elizabeth G. Ferris (Boulder, Colo.: Westview, 1984), pp. 229–250.

2. This analysis draws on *Centro América 1983, Análisis Económicos y Políticos Sobre la Región* (Ciudad de Guatemala: Inforpress Centroamericana, 1983), pp. 1–42.

3. Ibid., pp. 16–17.

4. Joanne Omang, "Are We Trying to Nudge Costa Rica Out of Neutrality? State Dept. Envisions More Pressure on Nicaragua," Washington *Post* National Weekly Edition, May 21, 1984, p. 17. The polarization within Costa Rica over what the country's standing in the regional dispute should be was dramatized by these opposing views: "We are in the Western camp," said Fernando Volio, the former foreign minister who had resigned in fall 1983 in opposition to Costa Rica's neutrality, "The Nicaraguans, who have expansionist pretensions, simply interpret neutrality as weakness." *Newsweek*, May 28, 1984, p. 44. Opposing him, former president José Figueres, current president of the ruling National Liberation Party, stated that "he was against any type of U.S. military aggression on Nicaragua," adding that "the Sandinistas are a tough nut to crack." *Granma Weekly Review*, December 23, 1983, p. 10.

5. William Robinson, "Crisis for the Contras," *The Guardian*, June 13, 1984, pp. 1, 14; Jesús Cebeiro, "Pastora Había Anunciado la Ruptura con la Rama Política de ARDE Minutos Antes de la Explosión," *El País*, June 4, 1984, pp. 2–3; "Atentado Contra Pastora Acelera Unión ARDE-FDN," *La Nación Internacional*, May 31–June 6, 1984, pp. 6–7.

6. "Reagan's Commander," *Newsweek*, March 19, 1984, p. 38; Stephen Kinzer, "The Tough U.S. General On Duty in Latin Lands," New York *Times*, May 19, 1984, p. 5; and

Loren Jenkins, "A General Outflanks the Diplomats in Central America," Washington *Post* National Weekly Edition, January 16, 1984, p. 15.

7. Speaking frankly about what was in store for Nicaragua behind the movement reactivating CONDECA, the U.S. ambassador in Costa Rica, Curtin Winsor, stated publicly: "An invasion of Nicaragua is not an impossibility," adding that CONDECA is "part of a pattern of persuasion and pressure against Nicaragua." *La Nación Internacional*, November 17–23, 1983, pp. 4–5. Also, see "Reactivan al Condeca para Agredir a Nicaragua: Ortega; Reunión Secreta en Guatemala," *Excelsior*, October 2, 1983, pp. 1, 18. For the U.S. military buildup in Central America, see Philip Taubman, "U.S. to Spend Millions on Latin Bases," New York *Times*, May 16, 1984, p. 3; and Fred Hiatt, "Central America—The U.S. Military Buildup Continues," Washington *Post* National Weekly Edition, April 30, 1984, pp. 16–17.

8. "Airspace Violations: An Ongoing Policy," *Barricada Internacional*, May 14, 1984, pp. 2, 1, 4; "Honduras: A Virtual Rupture of Relations with Nicaragua," *Boletín Semanal*, *Agencia Nueva Nicaragua*, May 12, 1984, p. 9.

9. "Chronicle of an Invasion Foretold," *Barricada Internacional*, May 14, 1984, p. 3.

10. Ibid.

11. *Barricada Internacional*, May 21, 1984, pp. 6–7; June 4, 1984, p. 4; "Joint Costa Rican-Nicaraguan Commission: A Blow for the United States' Aggressive Policy," *Boletín Semanal*, *Agencia Nueva Nicaragua*, May 19, 1984, pp. 1–3.

12. "Hawks and Doves Go At It," *Central America Report*, May 25, 1984, pp. 155–156.

13. William Robinson and Kent Norsworthy, " 'Hondurizing' Costa Rica," *The Guardian*, May 16, 1984, pp. 1, 15; *Time*, May 28, 1984, p. 44; Christopher Dickey, "Central America: From Quagmire to Cauldron?" *Foreign Affairs* 62, no. 3 (1984):683–684.

14. "U.S. Plans: 'Portray Nicaragua as Aggressor'," *Barricada Internacional*, May 21, 1984, pp. 6–7.

15. Omang, "Are We Trying," p. 17. (Emphasis added.)

16. Richard J. Meislin, "Honduras Hints at a Softer Line," New York *Times*, June 10, 1984, p. 4E.

17. Ronier Lovier, "Americans Turning Honduras into Occupied Nation," Atlanta *Journal*, April 1, 1984, pp. 14B–15B; New York *Times*, February 24, 1984, p. A4, April 23, 1984, pp. A1, A8. In addition to the joint U.S.-Honduran Ahuas Tara, or Big Pine I and II military exercises, and Granadero I including Salvadoran, Guatemalan, and Panamanian troops, held almost consecutively in 1983 and 1984, the military buildup by the Pentagon in Honduras included: expanding airstrips in Comayagua, La Ceiba, San Pedro Sula, and others, at a cost of $21 million; a $150 million air and naval base; a radar station 40 kilometers southeast of Tegucigalpa monitoring aircraft movements throughout the region as far as 370 kilometers built at a cost of $5 million and manned by 50 U.S. military personnel; and the Regional Military and Security Training Center (CREMS) at Puerto Castilla, where 2,400 Salvadoran military were trained. In addition, the American Embassy was reported as being the "headquarters for coordinating CIA and counterrevolutionary activity against Nicaragua, which has included numerous violations of Nicaraguan air space." *Central America Alert* 2, no. 1 (February 1984); and "Honduras: Un Gobierno Civil Cada Vez Mas Militarizado," *Centro América 1983, Análisis Económicos y Políticos*, p. 39.

18. "Reagan's Commander," p. 38 (Quainton also had problems with Henry Kissinger, Chairman of the U.S. Presidential Bipartisan Commission on Central America appointed by Reagan).

19. Beth Stephens, "U.S. Role in Barracks Coup Unclear," *The Guardian*, April 18–24, 1984, pp. 1–2.

20. "Military Have Last Word in Honduran Democracy," *Latinamerica Press*, February 16, 1984, p. 1–2.

21. Meislin, "Honduras Hints at a Softer Line," p. 4E.

22. Gregorio Selser, "Honduras: Entretelones de un Relevo," *Pensamiento Propio* 1, no. 13 (April 1984):25–26, and his *Honduras, República Alquilada* (México: Mex-Sur Editorial 1983).

23. David A. Mintz, "In Honduras, Incipient Anti-Americanism," New York *Times*, June 17, 1984, p. 22EY.

24. "Blocking Diplomatic Channels to Nicaragua," *Central America Report*," May 18, 1984, p. 149.

25. Ibid.

26. Dickey, "Central America: From Quagmire to Cauldron?" pp. 668–671.

27. "Challenging the CIA's Evidence," *Time*, June 25, 1984, p. 19; and the NBC's "Today" show, in which MacMichael was interviewed on June 12, 1984.

28. Interviews conducted by this writer with Nicaraguan officials at the Nicaraguan Foreign Ministry, Managua, in July 1983.

29. Jack Colhoun, "Will CIA's Mines Sink Reagan's Policy?," *The Guardian*, April 18, 1984.

30. Fred Murphy, "U.S. Aids Ouster of Rios Montt," *Intercontinental Press*, September 5, 1983.

31. After the cutoff of military aid by the Carter Administration due to its horrible human rights record, Guatemala established its own sources of military assistance, that is, Israel: "Israel Doing U.S. Dirty Work," *The Guardian*, October 19, 1983.

32. "Centroamérica Se Puso el Quepis," *La Nación Internacional*, December 1983-January 1984.

33. Marlise Simons, "Argentines, Long Aloof, Seeking Latin Ties," New York *Times*, April 6, 1984, p. A10.

34. Gabriel Rosenzweig, "La Cooperación Económica de México con Centroamérica. Perspectivas para los Próximos Años," in *La Política Exterior de México: Desafíos en los Ochenta*, edited by Olga Pellicer, (México:Centro de Investigación y Docencia Económica, 1983); James Lee Ray and Fred R. Harris, "The U.S.-Mexican-Nicaraguan Connection: Past and Present." Paper presented at the annual meeting of the International Studies Association, Atlanta, March 1984; Marlene Dixon, Susanne Jonas, and Ed McCaughan, "Revolution in Central America: Its Impact on Mexico and the United States" (San Francisco: ISLEC, 1984); and Mario Ojeda, "Some Basic Misconceptions About the Present Mexican Crisis," *LASA Forum* 14, no. 2 (Summer 1983):8–10.

35. Francis X. Clines, "Mexican Continues to Differ with Reagan on Latin Issue," New York *Times*, May 17, 1984, p. 6.

36. Stephen Engelberg, "Mexican Leader to Meet Reagan Today," New York *Times*, May 15, 1984, p. A3.

37. Ojeda, "Some Misconceptions," p. 10; Rosenzweig, "La Cooperación Económica," pp. 260–261.

38. "United States support for Nicaraguan [contras] has been supplemented in the last year by shipments of medicine, food and military uniforms provided by American political and religious organizations. . . . The supplies reaching the [contras] . . . were part of more than $17 million in relief aid sent to help civilian refugees and pro-American military forces in Central America by politically conservative organizations. . . . Some shipments of medicine and food were transported free of charge to Central America by the Air Force and the Navy after being stored at military bases in Maryland, Michigan, Virginia, and Mississippi. . . . *[T]he aid, Administration officials said, has permitted the C.I.A. to spend more of its money on arms and ammunition for the [contras] and could help sustain the insurgents over the [1984] summer as United States assistance is reduced.* . . . Senator Jim Sasser, Democrat of Tennessee, said . . . that he was concerned. *It's just part of a pattern of conducting as much of*

our policy in Central America as possible undercover. " New York *Times*, July 15, 1984, pp. 1, 4. (Emphasis added.)

39. "Cutting Off Nicaragua's *Contras*," *Time*, July 9, 1984, p. 18.

PART VI

EPILOGUE: THE 1984 ELECTIONS

On November 4, 1984, Nicaraguan citizens went to 3,892 conveniently located voting places to elect a President, Vice-President, and National Assembly. With about a 75 percent turnout of eligible voters, the FSLN won 67 percent of the valid votes in a field of seven parties, of which three each were to their left or their right. The FSLN took 61 of the 96 seats in the Assembly and Sandinista candidates Daniel Ortega and Sergio Ramírez were elected President and Vice-President, respectively. All elected officials were to hold office for six years unless the Assembly—which was also charged with writing a constitution—decided otherwise.

This landslide victory for the FSLN was surprising to almost no one who had observed Nicaraguan politics for any length of time. Whereas none of the opposition parties—including those that chose to abstain—had any significant organizational infrastructure, the FSLN had mobilized around half of the entire eligible population into Sandinista grass-roots organizations. Further, the Sandinistas enjoyed the advantages of incumbency and of having a patriotic image associated with their role in both the War of Liberation and the ongoing struggle against the U.S.-sponsored contras.

Given the fact that a Sandinista victory in 1984 was a forgone conclusion, the election strategy adopted by the foreign and domestic enemies of the Revolution was not particularly surprising. Clearly, it was felt in some circles that, if the Sandinistas could be deprived of a participating opposition, the elections could be written off as meaningless. Therefore, while the Reagan Administration publicly predicted a "Soviet-style farce," it worked feverishly behind the scenes to cajole, council, pressure, and, reportedly, bribe as wide a segment of the opposition as possible to abstain from the election. In the long run the United States was only partially successful. The Coordinadora Democrática and its internationally hyped "candidate," Arturo Cruz, played a series of cat-and-mouse games while refusing to register for the election. Last-minute splits in both the Liberal Independent and Democratic Conservative parties weakened the participation of those two center-right groupings. Even so, by all objective measurements, the Nicaraguan elections were far cleaner, fairer, and more meaningful in terms of range of options than were, for instance, the U.S.-sponsored elections in El Salvador earlier that year.

Indeed, as John Oakes, a former Senior Editor of the New York *Times*, quipped in a November 15 op-ed piece to that publication, "The most fraudulent thing about the Nicaraguan Election was the part the Reagan Administration played in it."

The short chapter that follows is a part of the report of a delegation of the Latin American Studies Association (LASA) that was sent to Nicaragua to observe the 1984 election. LASA is the major professional organization of the thousands of scholars (primarily based in the United States) who study and teach about Latin America. The full report—which is too long to be published here—can be purchased as indicated in the note at the bottom of the next page.

Chapter 26

A Summary of The Report of The Latin American Studies Association Delegation to Observe the Nicaraguan General Election of November 4, 1984

THE LATIN AMERICAN STUDIES ASSOCIATION

PREFACE

On August 15, 1984, an invitation was extended to the Latin American Studies Association by the Supreme Electoral Council of Nicaragua, the fourth branch of the Government of National Reconstruction, to observe the electoral campaign and the general election to be held in Nicaragua on November 4, 1984. In mid-September the LASA Executive Council considered and accepted this invitation, and asked Professors Thomas W. Walker and Richard R. Fagen, Co-Chairs of the LASA Task Force on Scholarly Relations with Nicaragua, to make preparations and assemble a delegation. During the week of October 22, the LASA Executive Council reconsidered its earlier decision to send the delegation, in light of the October 21 decision of a key Nicaraguan opposition party, the Independent Liberal Party (PLI), to withdraw from the election. Once again, by majority vote, the Executive Council approved the sending of a delegation to Nicargua.

This was the first time in LASA's history that an official LASA delegation was sent to observe an election in Latin America. The Executive Council believed that in light of the unusual international circumstances surrounding this particular election, and the paucity of information from academic (rather than journalistic and governmental) sources concerning these matters that was available to LASA members and to the general public in the United States, a LASA-sponsored fact-finding mission could perform a valuable service. Accordingly, the delegation was charged with

This chapter is drawn from the summary and introductory sections of LASA, *The Electoral Process in Nicaragua: Domestic and International Influences* (Austin, Texas: The Latin American Studies Association, 1984). It is reprinted here with the permission of LASA. Readers are urged to obtain the full report by purchasing it at $3.00 per copy from The LASA Secretariat, S.W. Richardson Hall, Unit 1, University of Texas, Austin, TX 78712, or by referring to *LASA Forum* 15, no. 4 (Winter 1985):9–43.

conducting a wide-ranging investigation of the Nicaraguan electoral process and the various political and economic forces—both domestic and international—that impinged upon it.

The delegation included the LASA President-elect and one former President, several members of the LASA Executive Council, several members of the LASA Task Force on Scholarly Relations with Nicaragua, and other members of the Association with special expertise on Central America. Half of the delegation members had had substantial field research experience in Nicaragua. In forming the delegation, special care was also taken to insure that a wide range of views regarding the Nicaraguan Revolution would be represented, which was, in fact, the case. Although four women members of the Association were invited, only one was able to participate. The delegation members were as follows:

Wayne A. Cornelius (Political Science, University of California-San Diego), President-elect of LASA. (Head of the delegation)

Michael E. Conroy (Economics, University of Texas-Austin; Co-Director, Central America Resource Center), member of LASA Task Force on Nicaragua. (Co-Coordinator of the delegation)

Thomas W. Walker (Political Science, Ohio University, Athens), Co-Chair, LASA Task Force on Nicaragua. (Co-Coordinator of the delegation)

Laura Enriquez (Sociology, University of California-Santa Cruz, in residence in Nicaragua), member of LASA. (Local Arrangements Coordinator of the delegation)

Max Azicri (Political Science, Edinboro University of Pennsylvania), member of LASA.

John A. Booth (Political Science, North Texas State University), member of LASA.

Thomas J. Bossert (Political Science, Sarah Lawrence College), member of LASA.

Michael Dodson (Political Science, Texas Christian University, Forth Worth), member of LASA.

Paul Doughty (Anthropology, University of Florida), former President of LASA.

James Malloy (Political Science, University of Pittsburgh), member of LASA Executive Council.

Lars Schoultz (Political Science, University of North Carolina), Co-Chair of LASA Task Force on Human Rights and Academic Freedom.

Richard Sinkin (History, University of Texas-Austin), Executive Director of LASA.

Charles Stansifer (Latin American Studies, University of Kansas), member of LASA Task Force on Nicaragua.

John Weeks (Economics, American University), member of LASA Task Force on Nicaragua.

Norman Whitten, Jr. (Anthropology, University of Illinois-Urbana), member of LASA Executive Council.

The delegation was accompanied by Professors Howard Frederick and John Higgins (Telecommunications, Ohio University, Athens), who produced a documentary videotape on the Nicaraguan election, including interviews with many of the individuals who were interviewed by our delegation. This one-hour videotape is available for purchase from: Department of Telecommunications, Ohio University, Athens, Ohio 45701.

The members of the LASA delegation received credentials from the Supreme Electoral Council of Nicaragua as official international election observers, but we were not guests of the Nicaraguan government. All expenses incurred by delegation members were covered by themselves personally, their home institutions, or by LASA. This was deemed essential to maintain the delegation's independence and neutrality. While a few of the delegation's interviews were arranged with the assistance of the Supreme Electoral Council, the vast majority of contacts were made directly by delegation's Co-Coordinator, Michael Conroy, its Executive Secretary, Laura Enriquez, or other members of the delegation. Some logistical assistance was provided by the Nicaraguan Federation of Professional Associations (CONAPRO) with which LASA has had a cooperative agreement since 1983.

THE CONDUCT OF THE INQUIRY

Most members of the LASA delegation arrived in Managua on October 28 and departed on November 5. Throughout this period, there were no restrictions on the members' mobility, except in the Atlantic Coast region. The delegation rented a 20-person microbus for use during its entire stay in Nicaragua. We determined our own itinerary and spoke with anyone whom we chose to approach (as well as numerous people who spontaneously approached us). During the last days of the electoral campaign and on election day, we traveled throughout the city of Managua and to provincial cities (Masaya, Matagalpa, Granada) and smaller localities (for example, an agricultural cooperative near Matagalpa). We visited two war zones (Matagalpa, Puerto Cabezas) where counterrevolutionary forces (the contras) are active.

The delegation sought information from representatives of all of the key political and economic actors in Nicaragua today, as well as "grass-roots" organizers and development practitioners. We conducted detailed (one- or two-hour) interviews with a total of 45 "key informants," including national and regional leaders of all of the political parties participating in the November 4 elections and two of the parties that boycotted or withdrew from the election. The list of interviewees is as follows:

Political Party Leaders

Virgilio Godoy, Presidential candidate of the Independent Liberal Party (PLI).

Sergio Ramírez, member of the Nicaraguan Junta de Gobierno and Vice Presidential Candidate of the Sandinista National Liberation Front (FSLN).

Adán Fletes, President of the Social Christian Party (PSC) and Vice Presidential candidate of the Democratic Coordinating Committee ("La Coordinadora").

Clemente Guido, Presidential candidate of the Democratic Conservative Party (PCD). [tape-recorded interview provided to the LASA delegation by Professor Martin Diskin of M.I.T.]

Guillermo Mejía, Vice Presidential candidate of the Popular Social Christian Party (PPSC).

Luis Humberto Guzmán, Head of International Relations and candidate for the National Assembly from Managua, Popular Social Christian Party (PPSC).

Carlos Zamora, regional director of the Sandinista National Liberation Front (FSLN), Matagalpa region.

Celestino Gutiérrez González, regional coordinator of the Independent Liberal Party (PLI), Matagalpa.

Eli Altamirano Pérez, Secretary-General of the Central Committee, Communist Party of Nicaragua (PCdeN), Managua.

Santo Amado, candidate for National Assembly from Puerto Cabezas, Popular Social Christian Party (PPSC).

Electoral Officials

Mariano Fiallos, President, Supreme Electoral Council (CSE), and Rector, National University of Nicaragua, León (on leave).

Rosa Marina Zelaya, Executive Secretary, Supreme Electoral Council.

Sadros Zeledón, Director, Regional Electoral Council (CRE), Matagalpa.

Francisco Gutiérrez, Secretary, Regional Electoral Council, Matagalpa.

Danilo Taylor, representative, Regional Electoral Council, Zelaya Norte region.

Myrna Taylor, representative, Regional Electoral Council, Zelaya Norte.

William Rivera, representative, Regional Electoral Council, Zelaya Norte.

FSLN Government Officials

Jaime Wheelock, Comandante de la Revolución; Minister of Agrarian Reform, Nicaraguan Government of National Reconstruction.

Nora Astorga, Vice Minister of Foreign Relations, Nicaraguan Government.

Alejandro Bendaña, Director of International Organizations, Nicaraguan Foreign Ministry.

A senior official, Nicaraguan Foreign Ministry (no more specific identification permitted).

Carlos Túnnermann Bernheim, Nicaraguan Ambassador to the United States.

Francisco Campbell, Counselor for Political Affairs, Embassy of Nicaragua, Washington, D.C.

Comandante Julio Ramos, head of military intelligence, Nicaraguan Government.

Paulino Castillón, Director of International Relations, Nicaraguan Ministry of Health.

Nicolás Quirós, Regional Director, Ministry of Health, Zelaya Norte region.

Dr. Montoya, Regional Director, Ministry of Health, Matagalpa region.

Freddy Cruz, President, Nicaraguan Federation of Professional Associations.

Silvia Narváez, Vice President, Nicaraguan Federation of Professional Associations.

E.V.K. Fitzgerald, senior economic advisor to the Nicaraguan Junta de Gobierno.

U.S. Government Official

A senior U.S. diplomat in Central America (no more specific identification permitted under the ground rules established by the U.S. Embassy for this interview).

Nicaraguan Scholars

Xabier Gorostiaga, S.J., Director, Institute of Economic and Social Research (INIES).

Carlos Vilas, advisor to the Center for Research and Documentation on the Atlantic Coast (CIDCA).

Juan Hernández Pico, S.J., researcher, Institute of Central American History, Universidad Centro-Americana (UCA).

Church Leader

Bishop Pablo Antonio Vega, President, Nicaraguan Council of Bishops.

Development Practitioners

Sister Beatriz Zaragoza, Maryknoll Order, community development worker, Managua.

Rev. James Goff, Presbyterian missionary, Centro Valdivieso.

Margaret Goff, Presbyterian missionary, Centro Valdivieso.

Douglas Murray, health and occupational safety consultant to CARE, Inc., in Nicaragua.

Local Community Leaders

Unidentified community leader, officer of a Sandinista Defense Committee (CDS), Ciudad Sandino, Managua.

Three unidentified rural cooperative leaders, Cooperative "Valdivia," Matagalpa region.

Private Business Owner

Gladys Bolt, large private farm owner (coffee producer), Matagalpa region.

U.S. Journalist

Stephen Kinzer, Correspondent, the New York *Times*, Managua.

In addition to these key interviews, the delegation had conversations with dozens of individual citizens whom we encountered on the streets or in other public places.

The delegation was not able to interview anyone in a position of authority at *La Prensa*, the principal conservative opposition newspaper in Nicaragua. Both its editor, Pedro J. Chamorro, and its co-director, Pablo Antonio Cuadra, were reportedly out of the country during the entire period of our visit. Also, despite more than ten telephone requests, we were not able to secure an interview with an officer of the principal association of private business owners in Nicaragua, the Superior Council of Private

Enterprise (COSEP). However, the views of COSEP are strongly reflected in most articles appearing in *La Prensa* (which was read daily by the delegation), as well as by the "Coordinadora," whose vice-presidential candidate, Adán Fletes, we interviewed.

The delegation was given unrestricted access to all records of the Supreme Electoral Council concerning complaints of campaign abuses filed by all of the political parties participating in the November 4 elections. Three members of the delegation spent several hours examining these files, taking extensive notes, and photocopying a large number of documents, which we selected. The results of this documentary research are summarized in the section of [the full report] entitled "Issues Raised by the Electoral Process."

SUMMARY OF FINDINGS

In August 1980, the Sandinista (FSLN) government in Nicaragua pledged that elections would take place within five years (that is, sometime in 1985). That timetable was accelerated, primarily due to external pressures. The date of November 4, 1984, was selected so that Nicaragua would have a legitimate, elected government in place before the anticipated reelection of Ronald Reagan in the United States on November 6. The Sandinistas hoped that a competitive election with heavy turnout would help to deter a U.S. military intervention in Nicaragua.

The electoral process was marked by a high degree of "open-endedness," taking the form of continuous bargaining between the FSLN and opposition groups over electoral rules and structures, as well as more general aspects of the political system and public policies. The record shows that both before and during the campaign, the Sandinistas made major concessions to opposition forces on nearly all points of contention.

The national voter registration effort was remarkably successful, especially considering that it was conducted under wartime conditions. In just four days, 93.7 percent of the estimated voting-age population was registered.

The Nicaraguan electoral law of 1984 provided a broad array of protections to assure fair access, procedural honesty, and an accurate vote count. The actual voting process was meticulously designed to minimize the potential for abuses. The vote was truly a secret ballot, and was generally perceived as such by voters. We observed no evidence of irregularities in the voting or vote-counting process.

Despite efforts by U.S.-backed counterrevolutionary groups and several nonparticipating political groups to encourage voter abstention, 75 percent of the registered voters cast ballots. Most voters interviewed by our delegation and by foreign journalists did not feel coerced into going to the polls.

The FSLN won 63 percent of the total votes cast and 67 percent of the valid votes (see Table 26.1). Invalid ballots comprised only 6.1 percent of the total votes cast. Twenty-nine percent of the valid votes went to three parties ideologically and programmatically to the Right of the FSLN; and another 3.8 percent was divided among three parties distinctly to the left of the FSLN. The opposition parties together took 36.5 percent of the seats in the 96-member National Assembly elected on November 4, including six seats that will be held by their defeated presidential candidates. The Sandinista government deliberately chose a West European-style proportional representation system that would maximize representation of opposition parties in the national legislature, rather than a U.S.-style single-member district system.

TABLE 26.1
ELECTION RESULTS

Party	Number of Votes (Presidential)	Percent of Valid Votes Cast	Seats Won In Assembly
Sandinist Front for National Liberation	735,967	67.0	61
Democratic Conservative Party	154,327	14.0	14
Independent Liberal Party	105,560	9.6	9
Popular Social Christian Party	61,199	5.6	6
Communist Party of Nicaragua	16,034	1.5	2
Nicaraguan Socialist Party	14,494	1.3	2
Marxist-Leninist Popular Action Movement	11,352	1.0	2
(null)	71,209	—	
TOTAL	1,170,142	100.0	96

The range of options available to the Nicaraguan voter on most issues was broad, but it would have been even broader if the U.S. government had not succeeded in persuading or pressuring key opposition leaders to boycott or withdraw from the election. We found that the behavior of U.S. officials during the six months preceding the elections was clearly interventionist, apparently designed to delegitimize the Nicaraguan electoral process by making sure that the FSLN had no externally credible opposition to run against.

External critics of the Nicaraguan process have argued that, because legitimate opposition groups (especially Arturo Cruz and his Coordinadora coalition) were "excluded" from the process, the elections were illegitimate and uncompetitive. The facts do not support this notion of exclusion. No major political tendency in Nicaragua was denied access to the electoral process in 1984. The only parties that did not appear on the ballot were absent by their own choice, not because of government exclusion. The weight of the available evidence suggests that the Coordinadora group made a policy decision to pursue its political goals in 1984 outside of the electoral process.

While all the opposition parties that chose to run candidates had some valid complaints about the government's management of the electoral campaign, no party was prevented from carrying out an active campaign. Opposition parties received their legal allotments of campaign funds and had regular and substantial access to radio and television. The legally registered opposition parties were able to hold the vast majority of their rallies unimpeded by pro-FSLN demonstrators or by other kinds of government interference. Most of the restrictions on political activity imposed in March 1982 in response to an upsurge in counterrevolutionary activities were lifted at the beginning of the electoral campaign, and government censorship of the press was notably relaxed (though not eliminated).

The FSLN took substantial advantage of its incumbent position and, in some ways, abused it. However, the abuses of incumbency do not appear to have been systematic; and neither the nature of the abuses (for example, use of neighborhood-level Sandinista Defense Committees to distribute FSLN campaign propaganda and to mobilize people to attend FSLN rallies) nor their frequency was such as to cripple the opposition parties' campaigns or to cast doubt on the fundamental validity of the electoral process. Generally speaking, in this campaign the FSLN did little more to take advantage of its incumbency than incumbent parties everywhere (including the United States) routinely do, and considerably *less* than ruling parties in other Latin American countries traditionally have done.

Neither did the FSLN use its control of mass organizations, the food rationing system, or police to create a generalized climate of fear and intimidation. Our delegation interviewed some individuals who clearly *felt* intimidated by the Sandinista government, but we also observed that many people in Nicaragua are not reluctant to criticize the government, in public, and often in the harshest possible terms. In this election year the government made little effort to stifle the vigorous criticism of its policies and performance that the electoral campaign generated.

The 1984 elections brought about significant changes in the Nicaraguan political process. In addition to an unprecedented relaxation of political controls, a "National Dialogue" involving all of the country's political and economic power groups (including those that chose to boycott the November 4 elections) was launched. This ongoing process of negotiations between the FSLN and opposition forces will determine many of the rules of the political game to be followed in the postelection period. Newly elected opposition party members of the National Assembly have vowed to use their enhanced role in the political system to challenge FSLN positions on major issues like the military draft and to shape the constitution that will be drafted by the National Assembly beginning in January. The Sandinista government has committed itself to holding regular elections in the future.

These developments augur well for the future of political pluralism in Nicaragua. However, the political opening process could be truncated, or even reversed, by an intensification of U.S.-financed counterrevolutionary activities or by continuation of the three-year-old undeclared economic blockade of Nicaragua by the United States. If the pressures of a war economy and war psychology are relieved, there is a good chance that political liberalization will proceed. Despite U.S. interference, the elections of November 4, 1984, were an impressive beginning.

Index
and
The Editor
and the Contributors

Index

The Editor and the Contributors

The Contributing Editor

THOMAS W. WALKER is Associate Professor of Political Science at Ohio University, Athens, Ohio, and a former Director of Latin American Studies at the same institution. He holds a B.A. in political science from Brown University, an M.A. in Latin American studies from the University of New Mexico, and a Ph.D. in political science, also from New Mexico.

Professor Walker is the author of *The Christian Democratic Movement in Nicaragua*, *Nicaragua: The Land of Sandino*, and a number of articles, chapters, and so forth on Latin America in general and Nicaraguan politics in particular. He is also the editor/coauthor of *Nicaragua in Revolution* (Praeger, 1982) and from 1983 to 1984 served as a founding Co-chair of the Latin American Studies Association's Task Force on Scholarly Relations with Nicaragua.

The Chapter Authors

JAMES E. AUSTIN is a professor at the Harvard University Graduate School of Business Administration. He has authored or coauthored 12 books and many articles on the subjects of food policy and management in developing countries. His recent books include: *Agroindustrial Project Analysis*, *Nutrition Programs in the Third World: Cases and Readings*, and *Confronting Urban Malnutrition*.

Professor Austin holds a B.A. from the University of Michigan and MBA and DBA degrees from the Harvard University Graduate School of Business Administration.

MAX AZICRI is a Professor of Political Science at Edinboro University of Pennsylvania. He holds M.A. and Ph.D. degrees from the University of Southern California, a Doctorate of Law from the University of Havana, and a Manuel Márquez Sterling professional journalist degree from the Havana School of Journalism.

Professor Azicri conducted field research in Nicaragua in 1983 and 1984 studying its foreign policy and the institutionalization of the Revolution, as well as its electoral process, from a political, legal, and judicial perspective. In addition to Nicaragua's institutionalization, his current work in progress includes a book-length manuscript, *Cuba: Politics, Economics, and Society*, to be published in England and the United States in late 1985.

DEBORAH BARNDT is a part-time instructor of Adult Education at the Ontario Institute for Studies in Education of the University of Toronto. She has also taught at Brookdale Community College in New Jersey and Concordia University in Montreal. Since 1977 she has worked as an affiliate of the Participatory Research Group in Toronto and, in 1981 and 1983, as a consultant for the International Council for Adult Education on projects with the Adult Education Program of the Nicaraguan Ministry of Education.

Professor Barndt holds M.A. and Ph.D. degrees in Sociology from Michigan State University. Her doctoral thesis on literacy programs in Peru was published as *Education and Social Change: A Photographic Study of Peru*. She has also published various articles and books on adult education methodology, participatory research, photographic methods of education and research, and popular education in Nicaragua.

JOHN A. BOOTH is Associate Professor of Political Science at North Texas State University.

Professor Booth has published *The End and the Beginning: The Nicaraguan Revolution* (1982, 1985) and coedited *Political Participation in Latin America, Vols. I and II* (1978, 1979). His articles on political participation in Latin America and on Nicaragua, Colombia, Guatemala, and Costa Rica have appeared in *Comparative Political Studies*, *Latin American Research Review*, *Western Political Quarterly*, and *Journal of Inter-American Studies and World Affairs*. Professor Booth holds a B.A. from Rice University, and an M.A. and a Ph.D. from the University of Texas at Austin.

THOMAS JOHN BOSSERT is a member of the faculty of Political Science at Sarah Lawrence College. Previously he was Assistant Professor of Government/Political Science at Dartmouth College, McGill University, and Swarthmore College. He is also Visiting Lecturer in Health Policy and Management at the Harvard School of Public Health.

Professor Bossert has published in the area of political science, Latin American Studies, and public health. His articles, chapters, and reviews have appeared in *Latin American Research Review*, *Comparative Politics*, *Political Science Quarterly*, *Social Science and Medicine*, *Latin American Perspectives*, and *Nicaragua in Revolution*.

He holds an A.B. from the Woodrow Wilson School at Princeton University and an M.A. and a Ph.D. from the University of Wisconsin at Madison.

PHILIPPE BOURGOIS is a doctoral candidate in anthropology at Stanford University, where he is completing a dissertation on the role of ethnicity in the United Fruit Company's operations in Costa Rica and Panama.

In 1980 Mr. Bourgois worked for the Nicaraguan Agrarian Reform Institute, among the Miskitu Amerindians. His chapters and articles have appeared in *Latin American Perspectives, Nicaragua in Revolution, Monthly Review, Diálogo Social, La Mosquitia en la Revolución*, and elsewhere.

He holds a B.A. from Harvard College and M.A.s from both the Food Research Institute and the Anthropology Department of Stanford University.

MICHAEL E. CONROY is Associate Professor of Economics at the University of Texas at Austin and is Co-Director of the Central America Resource Center, a private, nonprofit organization located in Austin. Professor Conroy has published in numerous journals, including *Third World Quarterly, The Journal of Regional Science, Southern Economic Journal*, and *Latin American Research Review*. His present research focuses on the "survival strategies" of the urban poor in Honduras.

Professor Conroy earned a B.A. in Economics and Latin American Studies from Tulane University and an M.S. and a Ph.D. in Economics from the University of Illinois at Urbana. In 1985 he was named Chair of LASA's Task Force on Scholarly Relations with Nicaragua.

MICHAEL DODSON is Associate Professor of Political Science at Texas Christian University.

Professor Dodson has published extensively in the area of religion and social change in Latin America. His research articles and chapters have appeared in *Polity, Journal of Latin American Studies, Journal of Inter-American Studies and World Affairs, Latin American Perspectives, Nicaráuac*, and *Nicaragua in Revolution*.

Professor Dodson holds a B.A. from the University of South Dakota, an M.A. from the University of New Mexico, and a Ph.D. from Indiana University.

ELIZABETH W. DORE is a Washington, D.C.-based economist. She worked in the Planning Ministry and in the Ministry of Internal Commerce in Nicaragua from 1981 to 1983. In 1983 she received a grant from the Social Science Research Council to write a book on the production, distribution, and consumption of basic foodstuffs in Nicaragua.

Dr. Dore has published widely in the area of economic development. Her articles have appeared in *Latin American Perspectives, Nova Americana*, and *Estudios Andinos*, as well as in other journals and books. She holds a Ph.D. from Columbia University.

CHARLES DOWNS is Assistant Professor of City Planning at Columbia University. During 1981–83 he worked as advisor to the Nicaraguan Ministry of Local Government, Ministry of Housing and Human Settlements, and the Regional Government of the Third Special Zone. He has also taught and consulted in Portugal.

Professor Downs has published in the *International Journal of Urban and Regional Research*, has contributed chapters to books, and is the co-author of *Os Moradores a Conquista da Cidade*.

Professor Downs holds an MCP and a Ph.D. in City and Regional Planning from the University of California (Berkeley) and a BA in Social Change from the University of Michigan.

LAURA J. ENRIQUEZ is a Ph.D. candidate in sociology at the University of California, Santa Cruz.

From 1982 to the end of 1984 she was a Research Associate at the Center for Socioeconomic Investigation and Analysis (Centro de Investigación y Asesoría Socio-Económica, CINASE) in Managua, while conducting dissertation research on policymaking in the agrarian sector of the economy.

Ms. Enriquez holds a B.A. from the University of California, Santa Barbara, and an M.A. from the University of California, Santa Cruz.

JORGE FLORES CASTILLO, a Licenciate in Social Work, is a professor of Social Movements at the National Autonomous University of Nicaragua. His publications touch on themes such as "Prostitution in Nicaragua," "Child Labor," "The Social Norms of Marriage," and "The Family in the Revolution."

JONATHAN FOX is a Ph.D. candidate in political science at the Massachusetts Institute of Technology. He also worked for two years on the research staff of the Harvard Business School. His work focuses on the political economy of the state in the Latin American countryside. Mr. Fox holds a B.A. from Princeton University, and he has lived and worked in Nicaragua and Mexico.

DENNIS GILBERT is Associate Professor of Sociology at Hamilton College, Clinton, New York.

Professor Gilbert is the author of *Tres Familias: La Oligarquía en el Perú* and coauthor of *The American Class Structure*. His articles on Latin American society have appeared in *Journal of Inter-American Studies*, *Studies in Comparative International Development*, and *American Ethnologist*. He holds a B.A. from the University of California, Berkeley, and a Ph.D. from Cornell University.

STEPHEN M. GORMAN, until his untimely death in 1983, was Associate Professor of Political Science at North Texas State University. He received his Ph.D. in Political Science from the University of California at Riverside in 1977, and had previously taught at Dickinson College and Purdue University.

Professor Gorman was contributing editor of *Post-Revolutionary Peru* and *Leftist Opposition in Contemporary Political System*. He was also coauthor of *The Roots of Failure: U.S. Policy in the Third World* and *The Yom Kippur War*. His other publications include articles in *Journal of Latin American Studies, Government and Opposition, Journal of Inter-American Studies and World Affairs, Inter-American Economic Affairs,* and *Orbis*. He also served as occasional translator for *Latin American Perspectives*.

DAVID KAIMOWITZ is a doctoral candidate in agricultural economics at the University of Wisconsin, Madison. He has followed the Nicaraguan agrarian reform closely since its inception as part of a broader interest in noncapitalist agricultural models in Third World countries.

Mr. Kaimowitz received his B.A. at the University of California, Berkeley, in 1979.

WILLIAM M. LEOGRANDE is Associate Professor at American University, Washington, D.C. Until 1978 he was Assistant Professor at Hamilton College in Clinton, New York. Professor LeoGrande has published widely in the field of Latin American politics. His articles have appeared in *Foreign Affairs, Foreign Policy, American Political Science Review,* and *Latin American Research Review*.

Professor LeoGrande holds B.A., M.A., and Ph.D. degrees from Syracuse University in Syracuse, New York.

NADIA MALLEY is a doctoral candidate in government at Harvard University, specializing in Latin American Studies and International Relations. She holds a B.A. in Government from Cornell University.

SYLVIA MAXFIELD is a doctoral candidate in government and an Associate of the Center for International Affairs at Harvard. Her research and writing is on the political economy of debt in Latin America. She has studied and carried out research in Argentina, Spain, Nicaragua, and Mexico.

HUMBERTO MENDOZA LÓPEZ, a graduate of the National Autonomous University of Nicaragua (UNAN), later earned a Doctorate of Law from the Central University of Madrid under a scholarship from the

Iberoamerican Organization of Social Security in Spain. With specialists from the International Labor Organization, he was involved in designing the Organic Law of Social Security of Nicaragua. He was the first Director of the School of Social Work at UNAN. At The Nicaraguan Institute of Social Security and Welfare he became Social, Legal, and International Relations Advisor with the responsibility of designing social security laws in general.

MAXINE D. MOLYNEUX teaches sociology of Latin America at the University of Essex in Britain and specializes in social revolutions in the periphery. She is the author of *Women Under Socialism, State Policies and the Position of Women in Democratic Yemen*, and coauthor (with Fred Halliday) of *The Ethiopian Revolution*. Her articles have appeared in *World Development, Monthly Review, New Left Review, Desarrollo y Sociedad, Feminist Review*, and elsewhere.

Dr. Molyneux holds a Ph.D. in sociology from Essex University and is currently writing a comparative study of the policies of peripheral socialist states with respect to women and the family.

WALTRAUD QUEISER MORALES is Assistant Professor of Political Science at the University of Central Florida in Orlando. She received her B.A. in International Studies from Catholic University, and an M.A. and a Ph.D. in International and Comparative Studies from the Graduate School of International Studies of the University of Denver. Her special interests are the Latin American region and revolutionary change, especially Bolivian affairs.

Professor Morales is the author of *Social Revolution: Theory and Historical Application* and *Bolivia: Land of Struggle*. Other publications include articles and contributions in *Current History, International Philosophical Quarterly, Journalism Quarterly, Revista/Review Interamericana, Encyclopedia of Political Systems*, and *Television Coverage of International Affairs*.

JOHN SPICER NICHOLS is Associate Professor of Journalism at the Pennsylvania State University and a specialist in international communication and comparative foreign journalism.

His articles and a chapter on the Nicaraguan media have appeared in *Nicaragua in Revolution, World Press Encyclopedia, The Quill*, and *World Media Report*.

He holds B.A., M.A., and Ph.D. degrees in journalism and mass communication from the University of Minnesota.

LAURA NUZZI O'SHAUGHNESSY is Associate Professor of Government at Saint Lawrence University, Canton, New York. She is the author of articles and a chapter on Mexico, El Salvador, Honduras, and Nicaragua and the coauthor (with Luis Héctor Serra) of *The Church and Revolution in Nicaragua.*

Professor O'Shaughnessy received her B.A. from Queens College of the City University of New York and her M.A. and Ph.D. degrees from Indiana University. She was a member of Mutuality in Mission, an interdenominational lay mission team that traveled to Central America in 1981 to observe the role of the churches in that region. Since then she has returned to Nicaragua on several research trips.

THEODORE SCHWAB is an honors student of politics, philosophy, and economics at the University of Pittsburgh. In addition to conducting anthropological field studies in the Mediterranean region, the Middle East, and South and East Asia in 1982, he lived in the Dominican Republic and researched the history of its labor movement in 1983.

LUIS HÉCTOR SERRA, an Argentine, is a Professor of Sociology at the Central American University in Managua. Since 1979 he has resided in Nicaragua where he has worked in the Literacy Crusade, with the Christian revolutionary movement, and with peasant popular education. In that respect, he presently works as an accessor to the National Union of Farmers and Cattlemen (UNAG), the popular organization of small and medium landholders.

Professor Serra is a graduate in law and history from the National University of Buenos Aires. He also holds masters' degrees in international affairs and political science from Ohio University. His recent works include "Educación Popular y Revolución en América Latina," and the coauthorship (with Laura O'Shaughnessy) of *The Church and Revolution in Nicaragua.*

RICHARD STAHLER-SHOLK is a Ph.D. candidate in Political Science at the University of California, Berkeley. He worked as a research intern at the Latin American Program of the Wilson Center in 1981–82, and has previously written on the subject of the bourgeoisie in postrevolutionary Nicaragua.

Mr. Stahler-Sholk holds a B.A. from Brandeis University and an M.A. from the University of California, Berkeley.

HAROLD SIMS is Professor of History at the University of Pittsburgh, where he has taught since 1966. Professor Sims has published primarily in the field of history. His three books on early nineteenth-century Mexico were published by Fondo de Cultura Económica in Mexico City and

Madrid. His articles have appeared in *Historia Mexicana, Historical Methods, International Migration Review, Iju Kenkyu* (Tokyo), *Americas, Peasant Studies, Cuban Studies/Estudios Cubanos, Latin American Indian Literatures, Ibero-Americana* (Stockholm), and *Occasional Papers in Social Change.*

Professor Sims holds a B.A. from Stetson University, Deland, Florida, and an M.A. and a Ph.D. from the University of Florida, Gainesville.

REINALDO ANTONIO TÉFEL is President/Minister of the Nicaraguan Institute of Social Security and Welfare. Educated at Fordham University (New York), and universities in Managua and Madrid, he later taught sociology at the Central American University in Managua.

Professor Téfel struggled much of his life against the Somoza dictatorship. He was an important leader of the Nicaraguan Christian Democratic Movement; he founded and directed the Institute for Human Promotion (INPRHU); and, in 1977, just prior to the insurrection, he joined the "Group of Twelve" (los Doce) of the FSLN. His books include *Socialización en la Libertad, El Infierno de los Pobres,* and *La Revolución Sandinista.* He was elected to the National Assembly in the November 1984 general election.

JOSEPH R. THOME is Professor of Law at the University of Wisconsin, Madison, and a Research Associate of the Land Tenure Center of the same university.

Professor Thome has published widely on land tenure and agrarian reform in Latin America and was the coordinator for a collaborative research program between MIDINRA and the Land Tenure Center.

Professor Thome holds a B.A. from the University of California at Los Angeles and an LL.B. from Harvard Law School.

HARRY E. VANDEN is Associate Professor of Political Science at the University of South Florida, Tampa. A former Fulbright Scholar, he has extensive field experience in Latin America.

His articles have appeared in *Latin American Research Review, Latin American Perspectives,* and *Journal of Interamerican Studies and World Affairs.* His books include *José Carlos Mariátegui: Influencias en su formación ideológica.* Currently he is completing a bibliography of Latin American Marxism and conducting research for a book on Nicaragua.

JOHN F. WEEKS is Professor of Economics at the American University, Washington, D.C. He formerly taught at the University of Sussex and the University of London and has worked in Nigeria, Jamaica, Peru, and Nicaragua.

Professor Weeks has published widely on the problems of economic development and is the author of *Capital and Exploitation*, a book on Marxian crisis theory. He is also the author of *The Economics of Central America*.

Professor Weeks holds a B.A. from the University of Texas at Austin, and an M.A. and a Ph.D. in economics from the University of Michigan, Ann Arbor.

HARVEY WILLIAMS is Associate Professor of Sociology at the University of the Pacific in Stockton, California. From 1973 through 1976 he was a Fulbright Latin American Teaching Fellow at the Universidad Centroamericana in Managua. He has served as a consultant for research and social program planning and development, and has prepared several articles and professional papers on the development of social programs since the Revolution. During academic year 1984–85, he held a Senior Fulbright appointment at the Center for Latin American Social and Political Studies in Mérida, Venezuela.

Professor Williams holds a B.A. from the University of California, Berkeley, and M.A. and Ph.D. degrees from Vanderbilt University.